Hermann Brendel
Axel Grießmann

Großes Wörterbuch der Wirtschaftsinformatik

IWT Verlag GmbH

CIP-Titelaufnahme der Deutschen Bibliothek

Brendel, Hermann:
Grosses Wörterbuch der Wirtschaftsinformatik : Englisch–Deutsch, Deutsch–Englisch ; über 40 000 Begriffe aus der Praxis / H. Brendel ; A. Griessmann. – 3., überarb. Aufl. – Vaterstetten : IWT-Verl., 1992
Bis 2. Aufl. u.d.T.: Brendel, Hermann: Grosses IWT-Wörterbuch der Computer-Technik und Wirtschaftsinformatik
ISBN 3-88322-384-0
NE: Griessmann, Axel:; HST

ISBN 3-88322-384-0
3., überarbeitete Auflage 1992

Alle Rechte, auch die der Übersetzung, vorbehalten. Kein Teil des Werkes darf in irgendeiner Form (Druck, Fotokopie, Mikrofilm oder einem anderen Verfahren) ohne schriftliche Genehmigung des Verlages reproduziert oder unter Verwendung elektronischer Systeme verarbeitet, vervielfältigt oder verbreitet werden.
Der Verlag übernimmt keine Gewähr für die Funktion einzelner Programme oder von Teilen derselben. Insbesondere übernimmt er keinerlei Haftung für eventuelle aus dem Gebrauch resultierende Folgeschäden.

Die Wiedergabe von Gebrauchsnamen, Handelsnamen, Warenbezeichnungen usw. in diesem Werk berechtigt auch ohne besondere Kennzeichnung nicht zu der Annahme, daß solche Namen im Sinne der Warenzeichen- und Markenschutz-Gesetzgebung als frei zu betrachten wären und daher von jedermann benutzt werden dürften.

Printed in Germany
© Copyright 1987 by IWT Verlag GmbH
Vaterstetten bei München

Herstellung: Freiburger Graphische Betriebe, Freiburg
Umschlaggestaltung: CommunAction, München
Satz: Satzwerkstatt, München

ABKÜRZUNGEN

1D	one dimensional	AEGIS	agricultural ecological and geographical information system
1NF	first normal form		
2D	double density	AFC	automatic frequency control
2D	two dimensional	AFDSC	air force data services center
2NF	second normal form	AFTN	aeronautical fixed telecommunications network
2W	2-wire		
2W	two wire	AG	address generator
3D	three dimensional	AGT₁	arithmetic greater than
3NF	third normal form	AIDS	automated installation and diagnostic services
4NF	fourth normal form		
4W	4-wire	AIDS	automatic interactive debugging system
4W	four wire		
		AIET	average instruction execution time
AAGR	average annual growth rate	AK	acknowledge
AAME	american association of microprocessor engineers	AKO	a kind of
		AL	assembler language
AAU	address arithmetic unit	ALLOC	allocation
AB	address bus	ALU	arithmetic logical unit
ABEND	abnormal end	AM	amplitude modulation
ABS	absolute	AM	associative memory
AC	acoustic coupler	AM	asynchronous modem
AC	address counter	AME	average magnitude of error
AC	alternating current	AN	alphanumeric
ACA	asynchronous communications adapter	ANSI	american national standardization institute
ACC	account	AOL	application oriented language
ACC	accumulator	AP	accounts payable
ACCNT	accounting	AP	application program
ACG	automatic code generator	AP	arithmetic processor
ACIA	asynchronous communications interface adapter	AP	automatic pagination
		APC	assembled program count
ACK	acknowledge	APG	automatic program generator
ACK	acknowledgement	APIS	array processing instruction set
ACR	access control register	APL	A Programming Language
ACU	availability control unit	APPR	approximation
ACW	access control word	APU	analog processing unit
AD	abbreviation document	APU	arithmetic processing unit
AD	address	AR	accounts receivable
ADAC	analog to digital/digital to analog convertor	AR	address register
		AR	arithmetic register
ADC	analog to digital convertor	ARG	argument
ADD	addition	ARM	asynchronous response mode
ADDR	address	ARO	after receipt of order
ADDR	addressing	ARP	activity request packet
ADDR	address register	ARQ	automatic repeat request
ADH	arbitrary device handler	ART	average run time
ADM	asynchronous disconnected mode	ARTS	advanced radar traffic control system
ADMIN	administrator		
ADP	automatic data processing	AS	address space
ADR	address	ASCII	american standard code for information interchange
ADR	addressing		
ADRS	address	ASF	automatic sheet feeder
ADT	application design tool		

3

ABKÜRZUNGEN

ASIC	application specific integrated circuit	BERM	bit error rate monitor
		BERT	bit error rate tester
ASK	amplitude shift keying	BEX	broadband exchange
ASS	assembler	BG	background
ASSM	assembler	BI	batch input
AST	alternate sector table	BI	bus interface
ASYNC	asynchronous	BIOS	basic input output system
AT	address translator	BIPS	billions of instructions per second
ATC	air traffic controller	BISYNC	binary synchronous communications
ATCC	air traffic control center	BIT	binary digit
ATDM	asynchronous time division multiplexor	BJF	batch job foreground
		BKER	block error rate
ATM	automated teller machine	BKGRD	background
ATR	attribute	BKSP	backspace
ATT	address translation table	BL	block length
ATT	attribute	BLERT	block error rate test
ATT	average total time	BLINK	backward linkage
ATTR	attribute	BLK	block
AU	adder unit	BMC	bubble memory controller
AUX	auxiliary	BN	block number
AV	attribute value	BOE	beginning of extent
AV	average	BOF	beginning of file
AVA	absolute virtual address	BOG	beginning of group
AVE	average	BOP	bit oriented protocol
AVG	average	BOT	beginning of tape
AVR	automatic volume recognition	BP	batch processing
AWS	active work space	BPI	bits per inch
A/N	alphanumeric	BPS	bits per second
		BR	break
B	base	BR	bus request
B	bit	BS	backspace
B	bus	BSA	bit synchronous adapter
B	byte	BSC	binary synchronous communications
BA	base address	BSC	bit synchronous communications
BA	bus available	BSCA	bit synchronous adapter
BAK	backup	BSF	backward space file
BAM	block access method	BUF	buffer
BAS	business accounting system		
BASIC	beginner's all-purpose symbolic instruction code	C	carry
		C	clock
BAT	bad address table	C	constant
BAT	batch	C	counter
BB	broadband	CA	communications adapter
BBC	broadband coaxial cable	CA	control area
BBU	battery backup	CAA	computer aided administration
BCA	bitsynchronous communications adapter	CAC	computer aided crime
		CACH	communications adapter channel
BCD	binary coded decimal	CAD	computer aided design
BCO	binary coded octal	CAE	computer aided engineering
BCR	badge card reader	CAF	computer assisted fraud
BCSR	boot control and status register	CALC	calculate
BCTS	byte channel transfer switch	CAM	computer aided manufacturing
BER	bit error rate	CAM	computer assisted management

ABKÜRZUNGEN

CAM	correlatable access memory	CMA	control memory access
CAN	cancel	CMC	communication multiplexer controller
CAP	capacity		
CAP	computer aided planning	CMD	command
CAPP	computer aided process planning	CMND	command
CAQ	computer aided quality (control)	CMOS	C-metal oxide silicon
CAQ	computer aided quality assurance	CNC	communications network controller
CARR	carrier	CNC	computerized numeric control
CASE	computer aided software engineering	CNT	count
		COAX	coaxial
CATV	cable television	COAX	coaxial cable
CAW	channel address word	COL	column
CB	computer backup	COND	condition
CBL	computer based learning	CONST	constant
CC	computer center	CONV	conversion
CC	cursor control	COP	communication output printer
CCA	communication control area	COR	correction
CCB	command control block	CP	card punch
CCC	central computer complex	CP	central processor
CCITT	Comité Consultatif International Télégrafique et Téléfonique	CPH	character per hour
		CPI	character per inch
CCR	channel control routine	CPI	characters per inch
CCR	communication control record	CPM	cards per minute
CCW	channel command word	CPM	central processor module
CCW	counterclockwise	CPM	critical path method
CD	card	CPR	cursor position report
CD	carrier detect	CPS	cards per second
CD	chain data	CPS	central processing system
CDA	continuity data area	CPS	characters per second
CDI	common data interface	CPS	cycles per second
CDMA	code division multiple access	CPU	central processing unit
CDR	card reader	CPW	chain pointer word
CDT	channel descriptor table	CP/M	control program for microprocessors
CE	customer engineer	CR	card reader
CEO	chief executive officer	CR	carriage return
CERT	character error rate tester	CR	carry register
CG	color graphics	CRC	cyclic redundancy check
CGA	color graphics adapter	CRS	central repair service
CH	channel	CRT	cathode ray tube
CHAN	channel	CSC	control storage code
CHR	character	CSR	channel select register
CIM	computer integrated manufacturing	CSR	control status register
CIS	commercial instruction set	CSRA	control status register address
CK	clock	CSU	customer set up
CKSM	checksum	CT	connection timeout
CL	control line	CT	counter
CLA	communications line adapter	CTL	control
CLK	clock	CTMC	communication terminal module controller
CLR	clear		
CLS	clear screen	CTR	control
CLT	communications line terminal	CTRL	control
CM	control memory	CTS	clear to send
CM	core memory	CTS	conversational time sharing

ABKÜRZUNGEN

CU	control unit		DDE	distributed data entry
CUB	cursor backward		DDL	data description language
CUBA	control unit bit array		DDN	digital data network
CUD	cursor down		DDP	distributed data processing
CUE	control unit end		DDPL	data definition language processor
CUF	cursor forward		DDU	disk drive unit
CUP	communication user program		DEC	decimal
CUU	cursor up		DEC	decoder
CW	clockwise		DEC	decrement
CYL	cylinder		DECR	decrement
			DEF	definition
D	data		DEG	degree
D	decimal		DEL	delete
DA	destination address		DEMUX	demultiplexer
DA	device attributes		DES	data encryption standard
DA	display adapter		DEV	device
DAC	digital to analog converter		DEX	data exchange
DAM	direct access method		DF	data field
DAR	destination address register		DFC	data flow control
DAS	data access security		DFD	data flow diagram
DAS	directory allocation sector		DG	datagram
DAT	digital audio tape		DH	device handler
DB	data base		DI	data input
DB	decibel		DI	double integer
DBD	data base description		DIC	data interchange code
DBD	data base design		DID	device identifier
DBDL	data base description language		DIF	data interchange format
DBG	data base generator		DIL	dual in line
DBI	double byte interleaved		DIO	data input/output
DBL	double		DIP	dual in line pin
DBM	data base management		DIR	directory
DBM	data base machine		DISC	disconnect
DBMS	database management system		DISP	displacement
DBR	database recovery		DISP	display
DBS	data base system		DLST	dialog specification language translator
DC	data channel			
DC	data communications		DMA	direct memory access
DC	device controller		DMAC	direct memory access channel
DC	device control		DMCL	device media control language
DC	direct current		DML	data manipulation language
DC	disk controller		DMM	digital multimeter
DCB	data and control bus		DMP	data manipulation processor
DCB	data control block		DMS	data management system
DCE	data communications equipment		DN	destination node
DCM	data circuit module		DNC	distributed numeric control
DCR	data communication ready		DO	data output
DCU	disc control unit		DOA	dead on arrival
DCW	data control word		DOF	degrees of freedom
DCX	digital branch exchange		DOS	diskette operating system
DD	disk drive		DOS	disk operating system
DD	double density		DP	data processing
DDD	direct distance dialing		DP	double precision
DDE	decentralized data entry		DPD	disk partition data

ABKÜRZUNGEN

DPU	data processing unit		EFTP	ethernet file transfer protocol
DRAW	direct read after write		EGA	enhanced graphics adapter
DRC	direct robotic control		EI	external interrupt
DRE	digital radar extractor		EIA	Electric Industries of America
DRS	disk resident system		EIS	extended instruction set
DRV	drive		EL	end of line
DSL	dialog specification language		ELSI	extremely large scale integration
DSN	data set name		EM	electronic mail
DSR	device status report		EM	E-Mail
DSW	data status word		EMF	electromotoric force
DT	dial tone		EMF	evaluate memory fit
DTDR	digital time domain reflectometry		EMI	electromagnetical interference
DTE	data terminal equipment		EMP	electromagnetic pulse
DTE	digital target extractor		EMS	electronic message service
DTR	data terminal ready		EMS	electronic message system
DU	disk unit		EMS	electronic mail system
DUC	data unit control		ENQ	enquiry
DUP	diagnostic utilities protocol		EOA	end of address
DUP	duplicate		EOB	end of block
DUST	deferred user service tasks		EOC	end of character
DUV	data under voice		EOD	end of data
			EOD	end of deck
E	error		EOF	end of file
EA	effective address		EOJ	end of job
EAM	electronic accounting machine		EOL	end of line
EAN	european article numbering		EOM	end of message
EAPROM	electrically alterable programmable read only memory		EOP	end of page
			EOR	end of reel
EAR	extended address register		EOR	exclusive or
EAROM	electrically alterable read only memory		EOT	end of tape
			EOT	end of text
EBCD	extended binary coded decimal		EOT	end of transmission
EBCDIC	extended binary coded decimal interchange code		EOV	end of volume
			EOW	end of word
EBU	european broadcasting union		EPBX	electronic private branch exchange
EC	error correcting		EPROM	erasable programmable read only memory
ECC	error checking and correction			
ECC	error correction code		ERP	effective radiated power
ECO	engineering change order		ESI	externally specified index
ED	editor		ESS	event scheduling system
EDI	editor		ET	end of text
EDIT	editor		ETB	end of transmission block
EDP	electronic data processing		ETR	expected time of response
EDT	editor		ETX	end of text
EE	electrical engineer		EXOR	exclusive or
E-E	end to end		EXP	exponent
EEA	electronic engineering association			
EEPROM	electrically erasable programmable read only memory		F	false
			FA	field address
EEROM	electrically erasable read only memory		FAC	file access channel
			FAM	fast auxiliary memory
EFA	external function acknowledgement		FAP	failure analysis program
EFR	external function request		FAR	file address register

7

ABKÜRZUNGEN

FAX	facsimile		FR	file register
FB	file block		FRD	firmware resident diagnostics
FB	fixed block		FREQ	frequency
FB	foreground/background		FRU	field replaceable unit
FC	flow control		FS	facility status
FC	front end computer		FS	field select
FCB	file control block		FS	field seperator
FCC	federal communications commssion		FSF	forward space file
FCC	feed control character		FSP	flight strip printer
FCG	file control group		FT	feet
FCL	format control language		FTC	fault tolerant computer
FCO	field change order		FTF	file to file
FCP	file control program		FTP	file transfer protocol
FCS	frame check sequence		FTP	file transfer program
FD	file definition		FWD	forward
FD	file description		FY	fiscal year
FD	full duplex			
FDC	field description card		GASP	gas plasma display
FDC	floppy disk controller		GB	gigabyte
FDD	floppy disk drive		GCD	greatest common divisor
FDMA	frequency division multiple access		GCR	group coded recording
FDS	fexible disk system		GCR	group encoded recording
FDS	floppy disk system		GE	greater than or equal
FDS	forms description language		GIGO	garbage in garbage out
FDX	full duplex		GL	general ledger
FE	framing error		GND	ground
FE	front end		GOS	graphics operating system
FEC	front end computer		GP	general purpose
FEM	finite element modeling		GPIB	general purpose interface bus
FEP	front end procesor		GPSS	general purpose system simulator
FES	forms entry system		GRND	ground
FET	field effect transistor		GRS	general register stack
FF	flip flop		GRT	greater than
FF	form feed		GT	greater than
FIB	file information block		GUI	graphic user interface
FLAP	flow analysis program		GUST	global user service task
FLD	field		GW	gather write
FLINK	forward linkage			
FLOP	floating point operation		HA	half adder
FLP	floating point		HAL	hash algorithm library
FM	file management		HC	host computer
FM	format management		HCP	hard copy printer
FM	frequency modulation		HD	half duplex
FMR	failure and malfunction report		HD	high density
FMS	flexible manufacturing system		HDLC	high level data link control
FMS	forms management system		HDR	header
FNF	first normal form		HDX	half duplex
FNP	front end network processor		HERS	hardware error recovery system
FP	floating point		HEX	hexadecimal
FPO	federal post office		HF	high frequency
FPP	floating point processor		HI	high
FPS	frames per second		HIFT	hardware implemented fault tolerance
FPU	floating point unit			

ABKÜRZUNGEN

HIR	hierarchy	IM	index marker
HLL	high level language	IM	integrated modem
HLT	halt	IM	interrupt mask
HMBT	hardware master bit table	IMA	input message area
HP	host processor	IMM	immediate
HPCS	high performance control storage	IMM	intelligent memory manager
HPF	high pass filter	IMS	information management system
HR	hit ratio	IN	inch
HS	half subtractor	IN	internal node
HSB	high speed buffer	INC	increment
HSM	high speed memory	INCL	inclusive
HSP	high speed printer	INCR	increment
HT	horizontal tab	INP	input
HW	hardware	INP	integrated network processor
Hz	hertz	INP	intelligent network processor
		INT	integer
I	instruction	INT	interrupt
I	interrupt	INTA	interrupt acknowledge
IA	instruction address	INTACK	interrupt acknowledge
IADR	instruction address	INTL	international
IAR	instruction address register	INTR	interrupt register
IAR	interrupt address register	INTR	interrupt request
IATA	international airline telecommunications association	INTREQ	interrupt request
		INTRO	introduction
IB	identifier block	IO	input/output
IB	instruction bus	IOA	input/output adapter
IB	interface bus	IOB	input/output bus
IB	internal bus	IOB	input/output buffer
IB	is between	IOB	input/output block
IBF	input buffer full	IOC	input/output controller
IBG	interblock gap	IOC	input/output channel
IC	instruction counter	IOC	input/output control
IC	integrated circuit	IOC	input/output controller
ICAM	integrated communication access method	IOCS	input/output control system modules
		IOD	input/output device
ICG	interactive computer graphics	IOIH	input/output interrupt handler
ICI	intelligent communications interface	IOM	input/output microprocessor
ICR	integrated control register	IOM	input/output module
ID	identification	IOP	input/output processor
ID	input data	IOQ	input/output queue
IDA	input data acknowledge	IOR	input/output register
IDA	interactive debugging aid	IORB	input/output request block
IDE	interacitve data entry	IOS	input/output supervisor
IDL	idle	IOS	input/output system
IDP	information display planner	IOSYS	input/output system
IF	instruction field	IOT	input/output trap
IFI	interfault interval	IOU	input/output unit
IFR	interface register	IP	impact printer
IH	interrupt handler	IP	initialize polling
IHCS	interactive health care system	IP	instruction pointer
IJF	image journal file	IPC	interprocess communication
IKB	intelligent keyboard	IPG	interactive program generator
IL	instruction list	IPL	initial program load

ABKÜRZUNGEN

IPS	inches per second	LDX	long distance xerox
IPS	information processing system	LE	leading edge
IR	index register	LE	less or equal
IR	infrared	LED	light emitting diode
IR	instruction register	LEM	logical end of media
IR	interrupt request	LEV	level
IRAF	indexed random access file	LF	line feed
IRAM	indexed random access method	LFD	logical file definition
IRQ	interrupt request	LHS	left hand side
IS	international standard	LIBR	librarian
ISAF	indexed sequential access file	LINED	line editor
ISAM	indexed sequential access method	LL	local line
ISDN	integrated services digital network	LL	local loopback
ISO	international standardization organization	LN	line
		LO	low
ISR	information storage and retrieval	LOC	local
ISR	interrupt service routine	LOC	location
ITB	intermediate transmission block	LOE	loop on error
ITC	invitation to clear	LOGFED	log file editor
ITS	invitation to send	LOP	line oriented protocol
I/F	interface	LP	light pen
I/O	input/output	LP	linear programming
I/P	input	LP	line printer
		LPH	line protocol handler
JAF	job accounting facility	LPI	lines per inch
JAR	jump address register	LPM	lines per minute
JCL	job control language	LPN	logical page number
JJ	josephson junction	LPS	lines per second
JMP	jump	LPT	line printer
		LR	last record indicator
KB	kilobyte	LR	left to right
KBD	keyboard	LR	logical record
KDS	keyboard data station	LRA	logical record access
KEYBD	keyboard	LRL	logical record length
KF	key field	LS	low speed
KILOPAC	kilopackets	LSB	least significant bit
KMON	keyboard monitor	LSD	least significant digit
KW	kilowords	LSI	large scale integration
		LT	less than
LA	local address	LT	line terminator
LA	logical address	LTC	line time clock
LAN	local area network	LTC	local terminal controller
LAP	link access procedure	LUN	logical unit number
LAP-A	byte-oriented link access procedure	LVA	local virtual address
LAP-B	bit-oriented link access procedure	LWB	lower bound
LB	line buffer		
LB	logical block	M	memory
LBR	librarian	M	mode
LCD	liquid crystal display	M	modem
LCH	logical channel	M	multiplexer
LD	library document	MA	memory address
LD	log document	MAC	machine aided cognition
LD	long distance	MAC	macroassembler

ABKÜRZUNGEN

MAC	memory access controller	MIPS	megainstructions per second
MACLIB	macrolibrary	MIRAM	multiple indexed random access method
MACRO	macroassembler		
MAE	memory address extension	MIS	management information system
MAINT	maintenance	MIT	Massachusetts Institute of Technology
MAL	memory access logic		
MAP	macroassembly program	MITI	Ministry of International Trade and Industry (Japan)
MAP	main storage partition		
MAP	manufacturing automation protocol	MK	mask
MAR	memory address register	ML	machine language
MAS	macroassembler	MLD	machine language debugger
MASM	macroassembler	MLD	memory lockout register
MASM	meta assembler	MLP	machine language program
MAU	memory access unit	MM	main memory
MB	megabyte	MM	mass memory
MB	memory bus	MM	memory modul
MB	move backward	MMM	man/machine model
MBC	memory bus controller	MMR	main memory register
MBM	magnetic bubble memory	MMS	memory management system
MBR	member	MMU	memory management unit
MBR	memory base register	MN	message number
MBT	master bit table	MOD	model
MC	magnetic card	MON	monitor
MC	memory controller	MOS	memory oriented system
MCC	multichip carrier	MOS	metal oxide silicon
MCLA	microcoded line adapter	MP	macroprocessor
MCLK	master clock	MP	microprocessor
MCP	message control program	MP	microprogram
MCR	magnetic card reader	MP	multiprocessor
MCT	master configuration table	MPCB	main printed circuit board
MCT	message control table	MPE	memory parity error
MCU	memory control unit	MPLX	multiplexer
MDD	magnetic disk drive	MPLXR	multiplexer
ME	manchester encoding	MPMI	multiport memory interface
MEB	modem evaluation board	MPROM	mask programmed read only memory
MEG	megabyte		
MEM	memory	MPT	multipoint
MEMR	memory read	MPX	multiplexer
MEMW	memory write	MR	mask register
MESG	message	MRC	memory request controller
MF	master file	MRC	monthly rental charge
MF	move forward	MRD	memory read
MFD	master file directory	MRT	mean repair time
MFM	modified frequency modulation	MS	main storage
MGMT	management	MS	mass storage
MHS	message handling system	MS	measurement systems
MI	machine independent	MSA	multi-subsystem adapter
MI	maskable interrupt	MSB	most significant bit
MI	memory interface	MSD	most significant digit
MIL	military	MSG	message
MIN	minimum	MSP	main storage processor
MIN	minute	MSP	main storage partition
MINI	minicomputer	MSR	memory select register

11

ABKÜRZUNGEN

MSS	mass storage systems	NCP	network control program
MST	master station	NCS	network control system
MST	mean service time	NDR	non destructive read
MSU	main storage unit	NDRO	non destructive readout only
MSU	mass storage unit	NDT	network description language
MT	magnetic tape	NE	not equal
MT	master terminal	NEG	negative
MTBE	mean time between errors	NET	network
MTBF	mean time between failures	NETGEN	network generation
MTBM	mean time between maintenance	NF	normal form
MTC	magnetic tape controller	NFAM	network file access method
MTCU	magnetic tape control unit	NFAP	network file access protocol
MTD	month to date	NFE	network front end
MTH	magnetic tape handler	NFG	no fucking good
MTR	monitor	NFT	network file transfer
MTT	message transfer time	NIP	non impact printer
MTTF	mean time to failure	NIS	network information services
MTTR	mean time to repair	NIT	network interface task
MTTRT	mean time to restore	NL	new line
MTU	magnetic tape unit	NM	network manager
MU	multiuser	NMI	nonmaskable interrupt
MUL	multiplexer	NO	normally open
MUT	mean up-time	NOR	not OR
MUX	multiplexer	NP	negative-positive
MW	man week	NP	new page
MWD	megaword	NP	no parity
		NSA	National Security Agency
N	negative	NSC	network security center
N	node	NSC	network switching center
N	numeric	NSC	nodal switching center
NAC	network access contoller	NTC	National Telecommunications Conference
NACK	negative acknowledgement		
NAK	negative acknowledgement	NTSC	National Television Standard Code
NAM	network access method	NU	numeral
NAM	network access machine	NUM	number
NAND	not AND	NVM	nonvolatile memory
NAP	network access protocol	NYSE	New York Stock Exchange
NB	narrow band	N/A	not available
NBR	number		
NC	network contol	O	output
NC	no charge	OA	output acknowledge
NC	no connection	OB	output buffer
NC	normally closed	OBJ	object
NC	not connected	OBR	optical bar code reader
NC	numerical control	OCR	optical character recognition
NC	numerical controlled	OCR-A	optical character recognition-ANSI standard
NC	numeric control		
NCB	network control block	OCR-B	optical character recognition-international standard
NCC	network control center		
NCL	network control language	OCT	octal
NCM	network control module	OD	output data
NCN	network control node	ODA	output data acknowledge
NCP	network control process	ODE	ordinary differential equation

ABKÜRZUNGEN

ODR	output data request	PC	programmable controller
ODT	octal debugging technique	PC	project control
ODT	online debugging tool	PCA	partition control area
ODT	online debugging technique	PCB	page control block
OEM	original equipment manufacturer	PCB	printed circuit board
OF	overflow	PCB	process control block
OFL	overflow	PCB	program control block
OLRT	online realtime	PCI	program controlled interrupt
OLTP	online transaction processing	PCIOS	processor common input output system
OM	operations manager		
OMA	output message area	PCL	print control language
OP	operand	PCL	recall
OP	operator	PCM	plug compatible memory
OPR	operator request	PCM	plug compatible mainframe
OPS	operations	PCM	plug compatible manufacturer
OPT	optional	PCM	pulse code modulation
OR	or	PCR	page control register
OR	over run	PCS	production control system
OS	operating system	PCT	program control table
OSC	online scenario controller	PDN	public data network
OT	output terminal	PDP	procedure definition processor
OTS	orbital test satellite	PDS	program development system
OVF	overflow	PDU	plasma display unit
OVL	overflow	PE	parity error
		PERF	performance
P	pair	PEU	port expansion unit
P	parallel	PFEP	programmable front end processor
P	pointer	PFR	power fail restart
P	power	PG	page
P	procedure	PG	pagination
P	process	PG	program generator
P	processor	PGT	page table
PA	program address	PH	phase
PABX	private automatic branch exchange	PHP	PAD-Host protocol
PAD	packet assembly disassembly facility	PI	program interrupt
PAF	page address field	PIB	program information block
PAL	programmable array logic	PIC	position independent code
PAM	pulse amplitude modulation	PID	personal identification device
PAN	personal account number	PIN	personal identification number
PAR	page address register	PIO	parallel input/output
PAR	program address register	PIP	peripheral interchange program
PARM	parameter	PIPO	partition input partition output
PAS	partition alternate sector	PK	public key
PB	page buffer	PKA	public key algorithm
PB	proportional band	PL	plus
PB	push button	PL	program library
PBN	physical block number	PLA	programmable logic array
PBX	private branch exchange	PLF	page length field
PC	per cent	PLIB	program library
PC	peripheral controller	PLL	phase locked loop
PC	personal computer	PM	permanent magnet
PC	printed circuit	PM	preventive maintenance
PC	program counter	PMA	protected memory address

13

ABKÜRZUNGEN

PMG	processor mastership grant	PSW	processor status word
PMUX	programmable multiplexer	PSW	program status word
PN	page number	PT	paper tape
PN	processor number	PT	point
PNR	passenger name record	PT	processing time
PO	parity odd	PTP	paper tape punch
PO	power on	PTR	paper tape reader
POS	point of sale	PTR	pointer
POS	position	PTR	printer
POS	positive	PTT	postal telephone and telegraph
POST	power on self test	PVC	permanent virtual circuit
PP	parallel progessor	PW	password
PP	purge and poll	PW	pulse with
PPC	personal programmable calculator	P/R	payroll
PPS	production planning system		
PPS	pulses per second	Q	queue
PPX	private packet exchange	QA	quality assurance
PR	physical record	QC	quality control
PR	program register	QCB	queue control block
PRI	priority	QF	queue full
PRIO	priority	QIL	quad in line
PRM	programmer reference manual	QIO	queued input/output
PRN	printer	QL	query language
PROC	procedure	QLP	query language processor
PROC	proceedings	QUEL	query language
PROC	processor	QUIP	quad in line package
PROD	production		
PROG	program	R	read
PROG	programmer	R	reader
PROGR	programmer	R	real
PROJ	project	R	relation
PROM	programmable read only memory	R	reset
PROT	protected	R	right
PRT	printer	RA	return address
PRTR	printer	RAD	radiation absorbed dosis
PS	physical sequential	RAD	random access device
PS	power supply	RAM	random access memory
PS	programming system	RAM	relative address method
PSA	partial starting address	RAR	return address register
PSD	program status doubleword	RAW	read after write
PSDN	packet switching data network	RB	request block
PSDN	public switched data network	RBP	remote batch processor
PSECT	program section	RBT	remote batch terminal
PSK	phase shift keying	RCA	Radio Corporation of America
PSL	program status longword	RCD	record
PSLB	program status longword	RCI	remote control interface
PSM	power supply module	RCU	remote control unit
PSN	packet switching network	RCV	receive
PSN	public switched network	RCV	remote controlled vehicle
PSP	packet switching processor	RD	read
PSS	packet switching services	RD	receive data
PSS	packet switchstream	RD	research and development
PSTN	public switched telephone network	RD	restricted distribution

ABKÜRZUNGEN

RDB	relational data base		RQ	repeat request
RDE	radar data extractors		RR	receive ready
RDF	record definition field		RRN	relative record number
RDH	remote device handler		RS	Recommended Standard
RDR	reader		RSI	remote symbiont interface
RDS	remote data station		RSP	remote spoolout processor
RDW	record descriptor word		RST	remote station
RDY	ready		RST	reset
REC	receive		RT	realtime
REC	record		RT	receive timing
RECNUM	record number		RTC	realtime clock
REF	reference		RTD	realtime device
REG	register		RTI	remote terminal interface
REJ	reject		RTIO	realtime input/output
REL	relative		RTIO	remote transaction I/O
REL	relocatable		RTJ	return jump
REM	roentgen equivalent man		RTL	realtime language
REP	reply		RTL	realtime library
REPR	representation		RTL	runtime library
REQ	request		RTN	routine
REQD	required		RTP	remote terminal processor
REQS	requires		RTP	runtime package
RES	reset		RTS	request to send
RET	return		RVA	relative virtual address
RF	radio frequency		RVI	reverse interrupt
RFI	radio frequency interference		RW	read/write
RGB	red green blue		RWX	read/write/execute
RHS	right hand side		R&D	research and development
RID	remote identifier			
RIL	release interrupt lockout		S	scalar
RISC	reduced instruction set computer		S	second
RJE	remote job entry		S	sign
RJET	remote job entry terminal		S	stack
RJEX	remote job entry executive		S	synchronous
RJF	remote job entry facility		SA	source address
RJI	remote job initiation		SA	system administartor
RJO	remote job output		SA	system analyst
RJP	remote job processor		SAB	stack access block
RL	record length		SABM	set asynchronous balanced mode
RL	remote loop		SAC	storage access control
RMS	record management services		SAC	storage access channel
RMT	remote		SAM	scientific accelerator module
RNR	receive not ready		SAM	sequential access method
RO	receive only		SAR	segment address register
ROM	read only memory		SAR	source address register
RP	receive processor		SAR	storage address register
RPI	rows per inch		SARM	set asynchronous response mode
RPN	reverse polish notation		SATNET	satellite network
RPOSB	reposition backward		SAU	shared access unit
RPOSF	reposition forward		SAU	subsystem availability unit
RPS	records per sector		SAV	save
RPT	records per track		SB	standby
RPT	repeat		SBC	single board computer

ABKÜRZUNGEN

SBI	single byte interleaved	SO	shift out
SC	semiconductor	SOB	start of block
SC	session control	SOF	start of frame
SC	subcommittee	SOH	start of header
SCB	stack control block	SOM	start of message
SCC	system control center	SOT	start of text
SCCS	source code control system	SOUT	swap out
SCE	standard card enclosure	SP	scratch pad
SCN	scanner	SP	space
SCPD	scratch pad	SP	stack pointer
SCR	scatter read	SPA	scratch pad area
SCS	secondary clear to send	SPEC	specification
SCS	small computer system	SPI	shared peripheral interface
SCT	special character table	SPM	set program mask
SD	send data	SPR	software problem report
SD	single density	SPSS	statistical package for social sciences
SDB	segment descriptor block		
SDMA	shared direct memory access	SPT	sectors per track
SDT	segment descriptor table	SPX	simplex
SE	stack empty	SQ	square
SE	system extension	SR	send/receive
SEC	second	SR	senior
SEC	Securities and Exchange Commission	SR	speech recognition
		SR	status register
SEG	segment	SRM	short range modem
SER	serial	SRQ	service request
SF	short format	SS	system supervisor
SF	stack full	SSB	single sideband
SFA	short form address	SSR	secondary surveillance radar
SFC	screen format coordinator	SSR	solid state relay
SFG	screen format generator	SSR	system status report
SG	signal ground	ST	status
SG	system gain	ST	system test
SH	sample and hold	STA	status
SHF	shift	STAT	status
SHR	share	STD	standard
SI	shift in	STDM	statistical time division multiplexer
SIC	special interest committee	STK	stack
SIG	signal	STMT	statement
SIM	simulator	STN	switched telecommunications network
SIO	serial input/output		
SK	skip	STND	standard
SL	statement list	STOR	storage
SLM	synchronous line module	STOR	store
SLU	serial line unit	STR	status register
SM	set mode	STRAP	sensor receiver and processor
SMD	surface mounted device	STRT	start
SMI	shared memory interface	STRUC	structure
SML	small	STS	status
SMS	shared mass storage	STT	single transitition time
SN	sequence number	STX	start of text
SNF	second normal form	STX	start of transmission
SNR	sector number register	SUB	subroutine

ABKÜRZUNGEN

SUT	system under test	TEX	telex
SV	single value	THD	total harmonic distortion
SVC	switched virtual call	TI	terminal interface
SW	software	TIO	test input/output
SW	switch	TK	track
SWI	software interrupt	TM	tape mark
SWP	swapper	TM	test mode
SWU	switching unit	TM	turing machine
SX	simplex	TMO	timeout
SY	system	TMS	table management system
SYM	symbol	TN	transport network
SYM	system	TNF	third normal form
SYN	synchronous	TO	timeout
SYNC	synchronous	TOD	time of day
SYS	system	TOS	top of stack
SYSGEN	system generation	TOT	total
SYST	system	TP	transaction processing
		TPA	transient program area
T	temperature	TPH	telephone
T	terminal	TPI	tracks per inch
T	test	TR	throughput ratio
T	track	TR	track
T	transaction	TR	translation register
T	transmit	TR	trouble report
T	transmitter	TRA	transfer
T	true	TRAN	transaction
TAC	terminal access controller	TRAN	transmit
TAR	track address register	TRK	track
TC	technical committee	TRP	trap
TC	transmission control	TRR	tape read register
TCM	telecommunications monitor	TRX	transaction
TCP	transmitter clock pulse	TSB	terminal status block
TCS	telecommunications system	TSK	task
TD	tape drive	TSS	time sharing service
TD	test document	TST	test
TD	top down	TSV	turnkey system vendor
TD	transmit data	TT	teletype
TDD	top down development	TTW	teletypewriter
TDI	two wire direct interface	TU	transport unit
TDM	time division multiplexer	TV	television
TDMA	time division multiple access	TWP	twisted wire pair
TDR	time domain reflectometry	TWR	tape write register
TE	text editor	TWT	travelling wave tube
TE	trailing edge	TWX	teletypewriter exchange
TECH	technical	TXD	transmit data
TED	text editor	TXT	text
TELE-COM	telecommunications	TYP	type
		TYP	typewriter
TELEX	teletypewriter exchange	TYP	typically
TELEX	telex	TYP-WRTR	typewriter
TEMP	temperature		
TEMP	temporary	T/R	transmit and receive
TERM	terminal		

ABKÜRZUNGEN

U	unit	VCF	voltage controlled filter
U	update	VCG	voltage controlled gain
U	user	VCO	voltage controlled oscillator
UA	unnumbered acknowledge	VCS	video communications system
UAF	user authorization file	VD	virtual data
UART	universal asynchronous receiver/transmitter	VDB	vector data buffer
		VDC	video display controller
UB	upper bound	VDG	video display generator
UC	upper case	VDT	video data terminal
UCB	unit control block	VDU	video display unit
UCLA	University of California at Los Angeles	VFB	vertical format buffer
		VFU	vertical format unit
UCP	uninterruptable computer power	VG	vector generator
UCS	universal character set	VIA	versatile interface adapter
UCSD	University of California at San Diego	VID	video
		VL	vector length
UCW	unit control word	VM	virual memory
UE	user equipment	VMA	valid memory address
UHW	upper half word	VP	vector processor
UIC	user identification code	VP	virtual processor
UIO	universal input/output	VPN	virtual page number
UL	Underwriters Laboatories Inc.	VRAM	video random access memory
UL	upper limit	VS	virtual storage
ULC	upper/lower case	VSN	volume serial number
UNDEF	undefined	VT	video terminal
UPB	upper bound	VTOC	volume table of contents
UPC	universal peripheral controller	VTX	videotext
UPS	uninterruptable power system	W	watt
UPS	uninterruptable power supply	W	west
UR	unit register	W	width
UR	utility register	W	word
USART	universal synchronous/asynchronous receiver/transmitter	W	write
		WACK	wait acknowledge
UT	user terminal	WAK	wait acknowledge
U/L	upper/lower	WARC	World Administrative Radio Conference
V	vector		
V	virtual	WATS	Wide Area Telephone Service
V	volt	WBS	work breakdown structure
V	voltage	WC	word count
VA	virtual address	WD	word
VA	volt ampere	WDT	watch dog timer
VAC	volt alternating current	WE	write enable
VAL	value	WF	write fault
VAN	value added network	WG	working group
VANS	value added network service	WID	width
VAR	variable	WO	write only
VAR	variation	WP	word processing
VAS	value added service	WP	word processor
VAT	value added tax	WP	write protect
VAT	virtual address translator	WPM	words per minute
VB	voice band	WPRT	write protect
VC	virtual computer	WPS	word processing system

ABKÜRZUNGEN

WRE	write enable
WRT	write
WRU	who are you?
WS	work space
WTD	week to date
WTS	word terminal synchronous
WW	wire wrap
X	transmission
XEC	execute
XEQ	execute
XFER	transfer
XM	expanded memory
XM	extended memory monitor
XMIT	transmit
XMT	transmit
XOFF	transmitter off
XON	transmitter on
XOR	exclusive or
XR	external reset
XR	index register
XREF	cross reference
XS3	Excess Three
XTC	external transmit clock
XY	cartesian coordinate system
YACC	yet annother compiler-compiler
YR	year
YTD	year to date
Z	impedance
Z	zero

000-key 000-Taste
10 seconds cycle 10 Sekundentakt
15-pin female D-connector 15-Pin D-Stecker weiblich
16-bit processor 16-Bit-Rechner
1 block 1-Block
1 character block 1-Zeichen-Block
20mA option 20mA-Option
20mA switch 20mA-Schalter
2-step 2stufig
2-wire Zweidraht
3-phase wiring Dreiphasen-Anschluß
4-20mA input Eingang 4-20mA
4-20mA instrument wiring 4-20 mA Verdrahtung
4-bit-display 4-Bit-Anzeige
4 byte long 4 Byte lang
4-pin 4polig
4-pin coiled cord 4poliges Spiralkabel
4-wire Vierdraht
4-wire cable 4adriges Kabel
50-conductor cable Kabel mit 50 Adern
50-pin connector 50-Pin-Anschluß
760m tape 760m-Band
80 byte long 80 Byte lang
80-column punched card 80spaltige Lochkarte
8-board mit acht Karten

A

abandon abbrechen, beenden ohne Sichern
abbreviated address call Kurzaufruf, Kurzwahl
abbreviated addressing Kurzaddressierung, abgekürzte Adressierung
abbreviated dial code Kurzwahlzeichen
abbreviated keyboard command abgekürztes Tastaturkommando
abbreviated voucher journal Kompaktbelegjournal
abbreviation Abkürzung
abbreviation document Kurzrufdokument
AB-key AB-Taste
abnormal abnormal
abnormal end abnormales Ende
abnormal termination außerplanmäßige Beendigung, vorzeitige Beendigung
abnormal test Abnormalitätsprüfung
abort Abbruch, Blockabbruch, Programmabbruch, abbrechen, kontrolliert abbrechen, zurücknehmen
abort a program Programm abbrechen
abort code Abbruchcode
aborting Abbrechen
abort macro Abbruchmakro
abort transfer Übertragung abbrechen
abort without change abbrechen ohne Änderungen
about circa
above oben
above mentioned obengenannt
above-table position Übertischposition
abscissa Abszisse
absolute absolut, unbedingt
absolute address Absolutadresse, absolute Adresse
absolute address area Absolutadreßbereich
absolute addressing absolute Adressierung
absolute control block Absolutsteuerblock
absolute element ausführbares Element
absolute entry Absoluteintragung
absolute file Absolutdatei
absolute file reference Absolutaktenzeichen
absolute loader Absolutlader
absolute name Absolutname
absolute number Absolutnummer, Gesamtanzahl, Gesamtzahl
absolute program element Maschinenprogramm-Element
absolute programming absolute Programmierung
absolute selection Absolutauswahl
absolute shutdown Systemende
absolute text Absoluttext
absolute virtual address absolute virtuelle Adresse
abstract syntax abstrakte Syntax
acceleration control Beschleunigungsregelung
acceleration time Beschleunigungszeit
accentuated contrast Kontrastentscheidung
accept abnehmen, akzeptieren, annehmen
acceptance Abnahme, Akzeptanz, Annahme, Zulassung
acceptance terms Abnahmebedingungen
acceptance test Zulassungsprüfung
accept input eingabebereit sein
access Ansprung, Zugang, Zugriff, anspringen, zugreifen
access aid Zugriffshilfe
access authorization Zugangsberechtigung, Zugriffsberechtigung
access authorization check Zugangsberechtigungs-Prüfung
access authorized zugriffsberechtigt
access channel circuit modules Zugriffskanal-Schaltmodule
access charge Zugangsgebühr
access check Zugangsprüfung
access control Zugangssteuerung, Zugriffskontrolle
access control list Zugriffskontroll-Liste, Zugriffsteuerliste
access control register Steuerregister für Ein-/Ausgabekanal
access control word Zugriffssteuerwort
access cover Abdeckung, Deckel, Schutzabdeckung
access distribution module Anschaltverteilungsmodul
accessible register zugängliches Register
access information Zugangsinformation
access key Zugriffsschlüssel
access macro Zugriffsmakro
access matrix Zugriffsmatrix
access method Zugangsart, Zugriffsart, Zugriffsmethode
access method name Zugriffsmethoden-Name
access mode Zugangsart, Zugriffsmodus
access module Anschaltmodul, Zugriffsmodul
access network Anschaltnetz
access operation code Zugriffsoperationscode
accessories Zubehör

accessory Zubehörteil
accessory equipment Anbaugerät
access program Zugriffsprogramm
access protection Zugriffsschutz
access routine Zugriffsroutine
access standby switch Ausschalter
access time Zugriffszeit
access to index sequential files Zugriff auf indexsequentielle Dateien
access unit Zugriffseinheit
accommodation Aufnahme
accompanying list Begleitliste
accompanying message Begleitmeldung
AC component Wechselstromanteil
according to entsprechend, gemäß, laut
according to amount betragsmäßig
according to form formulargerecht
according to tax law steuerrechtlich
according to the rules ordnungsgemäß
account Benutzerkonto, Konto
accountant Buchhalter
account association Kontenzuordnung
account authorization Kontenberechtigung
account balance Kontosaldo
account category Kontenklasse
account classification Kontogliederung, Kontoklassifikation
account code Kontoschlüssel
account composition Kontenzusammenstellung
account consolidation Kontenzusammenführung
account control Kontensteuerung
account designation Kontobezeichnung
account display Kontoanzeige
account duration Kontolaufzeit
account formation Kontenbildung
account group Kontogruppe
account header Kontoüberschrift
accounting Abrechnung, Buchführung, Buchhaltung
accounting area Buchungskreis
accounting area authorization Buchungskreisberechtigung
accounting area code Buchungskreisschlüssel
accounting area consolidation Buchungskreiskonsolidierung
accounting area data Buchungskreisdaten
accounting area database Buchungskreisdatenbank
accounting area entry Buchungskreiseintrag
accounting area group Buchungskreisgruppe
accounting area level Buchungskreisebene

accounting area management Buchungskreisverwaltung
accounting area management record Buchungskreisverwaltungssatz
accounting area number Buchungskreisnummer
accounting area specification Buchungskreisangabe
accounting area table Buchungskreistabelle
accounting area text Buchungskreistext
accounting data Buchhaltungsdaten
accounting field Buchhaltungsbereich, Buchhaltungsfeld, Buchungsbereich
accounting file Abrechnungsdatei
accounting log file Abrechnungsprotokolldatei
accounting machine Buchungsmaschine
accounting method Kontenführung
accounting period Abrechnungsperiode, Abrechnungszeitraum, Buchungsperiode
accounting schedule Buchungsschema
accounting segment Buchhaltungssegment
accounting structure Buchhaltungsstruktur
accounting system Buchhaltungssystem
accounting transaction Buchhaltungstransaktion
accounting voucher Buchhaltungsbeleg
account inventory tape Kontenbestandsband
account level Kontenebene
account locating Kontofindung
account maintenance Kontenpflege
account master Kontenstamm
account master record Kontenstammsatz
account name Benutzerkonto-Name, Kontenbezeichnung
account number Kontonummer
account number position Kontonummernstelle
account number setup Kontonummernaufbau
account number supplement Kontonummernergänzung
account payable Kreditorenkonto
account plain text Kontoklartext
account posting Kontenbuchung
account processing Kontenbearbeitung, Kontoführung
account register Kontenverzeichnis
accounts clerk Buchhaltungssachbearbeiter
accounts closing Buchhaltungsabschluß
accounts display Kontenanzeige
account selection Kontenauswahl
accounts maintenance Kontenpflege
accounts management Kontenverwaltung
accounts master record Kontenstammsatz

accounts payable Kreditorenbuchhaltung, Kreditorenkonten, Verbindlichkeiten, Verbindlichkeiten aus Lieferungen und Leistungen
accounts payable accounting Kreditorenbuchhaltung
accounts payable analysis Kreditorenauswertung
accounts payable area Kreditorenbereich
accounts payable item Kreditorenzeile
accounts payable master Kreditorenstamm
accounts payable master record Kreditorenstammsatz
accounts payable number Kreditorennummer
accounts payable payment Kreditorenzahlung
accounts payable posting Kreditorenbuchung
accounts payable screen Kreditorenbild
accounts payable section Kreditorenteil
accounts payable settlement Kreditorenverrechnung
accounts payable voucher Kreditorenbeleg
account specific kontenspezifisch
accounts posting Kontenschreibung
accounts posting tape Kontenschreibungsband
accounts receivable Außenstände, Forderungen
accounts receivable accounting Debitorenbuchhaltung
accounts receivable analysis Debitorenauswertungen
accounts receivable area Debitorenbereich
accounts receivable master Debitorenstamm
accounts receivable master record Debitorenstammsatz
accounts receivable number Debitorennummer
accounts receivable section Debitorenteil
accounts register Kontoverzeichnis
account supplement Kontoergänzung
account table Kontentabelle
account totalling Kontenabsummierung
account type Kontoart, Kontotyp
account withdrawal transport Kontoauszugstransport
accrue anfallen, fällig werden
accumulate addieren, akkumulieren, auflaufen, kumulieren, sammeln
accumulation field Akkumulierungsfeld, Summenfeld
accumulation of value Wertbildung
accumulation speed Addiergeschwindigkeit
accumulator Akkumulator
accumulator computer Akkumulator-Rechner
accuracy Fehlerfreiheit, Genauigkeit
AC dump Netzausfall
achieve erreichen, leisten

achievement Leistung
ack Bestätigung
acknowledge Bestätigung, Quittung, bestätigen, quittieren
acknowledgement Bestätigung, Quittierung, Quittung
acknowledgement key Bestätigungs-Taste, Quittungs-Taste
acknowledgement mask Bestätigungs-Maske, Quittungs-Maske
acknowledgement message Bestätigungsmeldung, Quittungs-Meldung
acknowledgement mode Quittungsbetrieb
acknowledge the error Bestätigen des Fehlers
acoustic coupler Akustikkoppler
acoustic variable control akustische Steuerung
acoustic warning Warnton
acoustoelectric device elektroakustisches Gerät
AC power Wechselstrom
AC power cord Netzkabel
AC power transmission Wechselstromübertragung
acquire anschaffen, erfassen
acquisition Anschaffung, Erfassung, Warenzugang, Zugang
acquisition block Erfassungsblock
acquisition check Erfassungs-Nachweis
acquisition costs Einstandskosten
acquisition data Bezugsdaten
acquisition date Zugangsdatum
acquisition effort Erfassungsaufwand
acquisition expense Erfassungsaufwand
acquisition field Erfassungs-Feld
acquisition form Erfassungs-Form
acquisition format Erfassungs-Format
acquisition list Erfassungsliste, Zugangsliste
acquisition management Erfassungsabwicklung
acquisition marker Zugangskennzeichen
acquisition of information Informationsgewinnung
acquisition option Erfassungs-Möglichkeit
acquisition period Bezugsperiode, Erfassungszeitraum
acquisition posting Zugangsbuchung
acquisition price Einstandspreis, Lagereinstandspreis
acquisition process Erfassungsvorgang
acquisition program Erfassungs-Programm
acquisition screen Erfassungs-Bild
acquisition task Erfassungsaufgabe
acquisition technique Erfassungstechnik
acquisition type Bezugsart

23

acquisition value Anschaffungswert, Bezugswert, Einstandswert, Zugangswert
acronym Akronym
act Akt, Vorgang
action Aktion, Maßnahme
action designator Funktionsbezeichnung
action program Aktionsprogramm
activatable aktivierungsfähig
activate aktivieren, ansteuern, starten
activate facility Anschalteinrichtung, Einschalteinrichtung
activation Aktivierung, Ansteuerung, Inbetriebnahme, Start
activation marker Aktivierungskennzeichen
activation number Aktivierungsnummer
activation switch Aktivierungsschalter
activation voucher Aktivierungsbeleg
active aktiv, tätig
active cell aktuelles Feld
active data link channel Arbeitszustand des Übertragungskanals
active drive aktives Laufwerk, aktuelles Laufwerk
active field aktuelles Feld
active filter aktiver Filter
active folder aktueller Ordner, vorhandener Ordner
active light Kontrollampe
active program ablauffähiges Programm, aktuelles Programm
active task aktuelles Programm
active window aktuelles Fenster
active work space aktiver Arbeitsbereich
activity Aktivität, Tätigkeit
activity chain Aktivitätskette
activity chaining field Aktivitätskettenfeld
activity control Aktivitätensteuerung
activity file Kurzzeitdatei
activity request packet Aktivitätensteuerteil
actual augenblicklich, derzeitig, eigentlich, tatsächlich
actual amount Ist-Betrag
actual availability time Ist-Eindeckungszeit
actual balance Ist-Saldo
actual coordinate Ist-Koordinate
actual count Ist-Stand, aktueller Zählerstand
actual data Ist-Daten, aktuelle Daten
actual keyboard failure Tastatur nicht funktionsfähig
actual line Ist-Zeile, aktuelle Zeile
actually eigentlich, tatsächlich
actual quantity Ist-Menge
actual result Ist-Bestand

actual stock Ist-Bestand, tatsächlicher Bestand
actual stock on hand Ist-Lagerbestand
actual value Augenblickswert, Ist-Wert
actuator Stellglied
actuator circuitry (printer) Druckkammer-Schaltkreis
adapt adaptieren, anpassen, zuschneiden
adaptability Anpassungsmöglichkeit
adaptation Anpassung
adaptation charge Anpassungsgebühr
adaptation generation Anpassung der Software bei Systemgeneration
adapter Anschluß
adapter equipment housing unit Datenübertragungsanschlußeinheit
adapter memory Speicheradapter, Zusatzspeicher
adaptive anpassungsfähig
adaptive control anpassungsfähige Regelung, anpassungsfähige Steuerung
add addieren, hinzufügen, zurechnen
add carry Additionsübertrag
addend Additionswert
addend register Addendenregister
addendum Anhang
adder Addiereinrichtung, Addierer, Addierglied
adder unit Addierwerk
adding machine Addiermaschine
adding register Additionsregister
add instruction Additionsbefehl
addition Addition, Nachtrag, Zusatz
additional zusätzlich
additional address Zusatzadresse
additional agreement Zusatzvereinbarung
additional amount Zusatzbetrag
additional applications weitere Anwendungen
additional balance Nachtragsbilanz
additional charge Nachbelastung
additional charge order Nachbelastungs-Auftrag
additional delivery Nachlieferung
additional delivery costs Bezugsnebenkosten
additional device Zusatzeinrichtung
additional expenses Nebenkosten
additional hardware Hardwarezusätze
additional help weiterführende Hilfe, weiterführende Unterstützung, zusätzliche Hilfe
additional information Zusatzangaben, Zusatzinformationen
additional memory Speichererweiterung
additional name Zusatzname
additional option Zusatzfunktion, zusätzliche Aktion, zusätzliche Option

additional options key Zusatzfunktionstasten
additional posting Zusatzkontierung
additional posting check Zusatzkontierungsverprobung
additional search Zusatzsuche
additional segment Zusatzsegment
additional segment processing Zusatzsegmentbearbeitung
additional selection Nachselektion
additional stock Nebenbestand
additional text Zusatztext
additional text entry Zusatztexteingabe
additional text mask Zusatztextmaske
additional title Zusatztitel
additional total Zusatzsumme
additions and improvements Wertveränderung
additions to assets Anlagenzugänge
add mode Addiermodus, Hinzufügemodus
address Adresse, Anschrift, adressieren, ansprechen
addressability Adressierbarkeit
addressable adressierbar, ansprechbar
address arithmetic Adreßrechnung
address arithmetic unit Adreßarithmetik-Einheit
address assignment Adreßzuordnung
address bit Adreßbit
address blank Adressen-Leerstelle
address book statistic Adreßbuchstatistik
address bus Adreßbus
address calculating Adressenbearbeitung
address code Adreßschlüssel, Anredeschlüssel
address counter Adreßzähler, Befehlszähler
address data Adreßdaten
address data processing Adreßdatenverarbeitung
address decode logic Adreßdekodierung
address definition Adressendefinition
addressee number Adressatennummer
address enable Adreßanhängung
address error Adreßfehler
address field Adreßfeld, Anschriftsfeld
address for dispatch Versandadresse
address generator Adreßgenerator
address identification Adreßkennzeichen, Anschriftenkennzeichen
addressing Adressierung
addressing authority Adressierungsverwaltung
addressing domain Adressierungsdomäne
addressing mode Adressierungsart
addressing space Adreßraum
address input Adreßeingabe
address latch enable Adreßverriegelung

address list Adreßliste
address mark Adressenmarke
address modification Adressenänderung
address overflow Adreßüberschreitung
address part Adreßteil, Anschriftsteil
address printing Adressenschreibung
address register Adreßregister
address repertoire Adreßauswahl, Adreßrepertoire
address selecting system Adressen-Ansteuerungssystem
address space Adreßbereich, Adreßraum
address strobe input Adreßimpulseingang
address structure Adreßaufbau
address text Anredetext
address translation Adreßumsetzung
address translation table Tabelle zur Adreßübersetzung
address translator Adreßübersetzer
add up addieren, zusammenzählen
adhere einhalten, haften
adhesive selbstklebend
adhesive tape Trockenklebeband
adjacent darauffolgend, folgend, nachfolgend, neben
adjacent cell nachfolgendes Feld
adjacent segment Folgesegment
adjust abstimmen, einstellen, nachstellen
adjustable einstellbar
adjustable feedback einstellbare Rückkopplung
adjusted amount Verrechnungswert
adjusting lever Verstellhebel
adjustment Abgleich, Abschlag, Abstimmung, Anpassung, Anschluß, Einstellung
adjustment account Wertberichtigungskonto
adjustment routine Einrichtroutine
adjustment unit Justiereinheit
adjust mode Fließtextverfahren
adjust settings Einstellungen ändern
administer administrieren, verwalten
administration Administration, Verwaltung
administration command Administrations-Befehl, Administrations-Kommando
administration effort Verwaltungsaufwand
administration place Administrationsplatz
administrative component Administrationskomponente
administrative program Administrationsprogramm
administrator Administrator, Systemverwalter, Verwalter
admit zugeben, zulassen
advance beschleunigen, verschieben, voraus

advanced BASIC erweitertes BASIC
advanced procedures fortgeschrittenes Arbeiten
advanced radar traffic control system fortschrittliches Radarziel-Verfolgungssystem
advanced user backup options weitere Sicherungsaktionen
advanced user data weitere Benutzerdaten
advance filing of turnover tax Umsatzsteuervoranmeldung
advance notification Voranmeldung
advance one word nächstes Wort
advance payment Anzahlung, Vorschuß
advance print/punch Vorsetzen der Druck-/Stanzdatei
advantage Nutzen, Vorteil
advantageous nützlich, vorteilhaft
advice Avis, Avishinweis, Hinweis, Hinweisgabe
advice texts Avistexte
aerate belüften
aeronautical fixed telecommunications network festes Flugfernmeldenetzwerk
affordable bezahlbar
affricate Affrikat
afore mentioned obengenannt
after nach
after image nachfolgende Abbildung
after looks Protokollieren der Daten nach einer Veränderung
after receipt of order nach Auftragseingang
again nochmals
against gegen
age Alter, altern
age limit Altersgrenze
aggregate Aggregat
aggregate number Aggregatnummer
aging Altern, Ermüden, Verblassen der Anzeige
agree beistimmen, einverstanden sein, übereinstimmen
agreed abgesprochen, einig, vereinbart
agreement Absprache, Vereinbarung, Vertrag
agree upon vereinbaren
agricultural ecological and geographical information system Informationssystem für Agrikultur Ökologie und Geographie
aid Hilfe, Hilfsmittel
Aiken-Code Aiken-Code
aimed gezielt
air belüften
air blast circuit breaker Druckluft-Stromkreisunterbrecher

air break switch Druckluftschalter
air core transformer Lufttransformator, eisenkernloser Transformator
aircraft navigation Flugzeug-Navigation
air force data services center Rechenzentrum der amerikanischen Luftwaffe
air gap Luftspalt
air traffic control center Flugsicherungszentrale
air traffic controller Fluglotse
airway crossing Flugkurs-Kreuzung
a kind of eine Art von
alarming alarmierend
alarm message akustisches Signal
alert Warnton
algorithm Algorithmus
alias Alias, Deckname, Zweitname, weiterer Name, zusätzlicher Name
alias phase name symbolischer Abschnittsname
align ausrichten
align at the left margin linksbündig ausrichten
align at the right margin rechtsbündig ausrichten
aligned ausgerichtet
alignment Anschlag, Ausrichtung, Führung
alignment mark Vorschub-Zeichen
align paper Papier ausrichten
alkaline batterie Alkali-Mangan-Batterie
Allen screw Innensechskantschraube
allocatable vergebbar, zuordnungsfähig
allocate einrichten, reservieren, vergeben, zuordnen, zuteilen
allocated space vorgesehener Platz
allocate system resources zuordnen von Systemresourcen
allocation Reservierung
allocation data Zuordnungsdaten
allocation error Zuordnungsfehler
allocation map Zuordnungsliste
allocation method Zuordnungsmethode
allocation of numbers Nummernvergabe
allocation table Zuordnungstabelle
allow erlauben, gestatten, zulassen
allowance Erlaubnis, Gewährung
alone alleine
alpha Alphazeichen
alphabet Alphabet
alphabetic character Alphazeichen, Buchstabe
alphabetic collating device Alphabet-Mischeinrichtung
alphabetic interpreting Lochschrift-Übersetzung

alphabetic translation Lochschrift-Übersetzung
alpha character Alphazeichen
alpha code Buchstabencode
alpha input Alpha-Eingabe, Buchstabeneingabe
alphanumeric alphanumerisch
alphanumeric area alphanumerischer Tastenbereich
alphanumeric character set alphanumerischer Zeichensatz
alphanumeric display architecture alphanumerische Anzeigearchitektur
alpha symbol Buchstabensymbol
already bereits
also managed mitverwaltet
alter ändern
alterable änderbar
alteration Änderung
alteration code Änderungscode
alteration date Änderungsdatum
alteration line Änderungszeile
alteration rate Änderungsrate
alteration time Änderungszeit
alteration type Änderungsart
alternate zusätzlich
alternate collation sequence abweichende Sortierfolge, alternative Sortierfolge, andere Zeichenfolge
alternate key Sekundärschlüssel
alternate keypad Funktionstastenblock
alternate keypad mode mögliche Belegung des numerischen Tastenblocks
alternate key stroke Tastenwechselbetätigung
alternate program path alternativer Programmpfad
alternate ROM character sets zusätzliche ROM-Zeichensätze
alternate routing Umwegsteuerung
alternate sector Ersatzsektor
alternate sector assignment Zuweisung der Ersatzsektoren
alternate sector table AST-Tabelle, Ersatzsektorentabelle
alternate stacker zweites Ausgabefach
alternate track Ersatzspur
alternate track administration Ersatzspurverwaltung
alternating current Wechselstrom
alternating current generator Wechselstromgenerator
alternating current machine Wechselstrommaschine
alternating current motor Wechselstrommotor

alternating current transformer Wechselstromtransformator
alternating data pair Datenpaar im Wechselformat
alternative Alternative
alternative language Alternativsprache
alternative mode Alternativmodus
alternative offer Alternativangebot
alternative path Ausweichpfad
alternative program path alternativer Programmpfad
alternative to alternativ zu
aluminium Aluminium
aluminium capacitor Aluminiumkondensator
alveolar alveolar
always prinzipiell
always batched chargenpflichtig
always bundled gebindepflichtig
ambient condition Umgebungsbedingung
ambient temperature Umgebungstemperatur
ambiguous command mehrdeutiges Kommando
ambiguous letter Platzhalter
ambiguous verb mehrdeutiges Kommando
amendment cog Änderungsprotokoll
amendment date Änderungsdatum
amendment index Änderungsindex
American Association of Microprocessor Engineers Amerikanische Vereinigung der Mikroprozessor-Ingenieure
American National Standardization Institute amerikanische Normbehörde
American Standard Code Amerikanischer Standard-Code
American Standard Code for Information Interchange amerikanischer Standardcode für Informationsaustausch
amortization Abschreibung, Abschreibungslauf, Amortisation
amortization adjustment Abschreibungskorrektur
amortization amount Abschreibungsbetrag
amortization calculation Abschreibungsrechnung
amortization cancellation Abschreibungsstornierung
amortization code Abschreibungsschlüssel
amortization configuration Abschreibungskonstellation
amortization control Amortisationsüberwachung

amortization control field Abschreibungssteuerungsfeld
amortization costs Abschreibungskosten
amortization field Abschreibungsfeld
amortization forecast Abschreibungsprognose
amortization list Abschreibungsliste
amortization method Abschreibungsmethode
amortization mode Abschreibungsmodalität
amortization parameter Abschreibungsparameter
amortization period Abschreibungsdauer
amortization posting Abschreibungsbuchung
amortization rate Abschreibungsprozent, Abschreibungsprozentsatz, Amortisationsprozentsatz
amortization record Abschreibungssatz
amortization rule Abschreibungsregel
amortization type Abschreibungsart
amortization value Abschreibungswert
amortize abschreiben
amount Betrag, Wert, Zahl
amount adjustment Betragsberichtigung
amount allocation Betragszuordnung
amount authorization Betragsberechtigung
amount calculation Betragsausrechnung
amount cancelled Stornobetrag
amount carried forward Übertrag
amount correction Betragskorrektur
amount deviation Betragsabweichung
amount editing Betragsaufbereitung
amount for payment Zahlungsbetrag
amount input Betragseingabe
amount invoiced Rechnungsbetrag
amount of compensation Entgeltbetrag
amount of delivery costs Bezugskostenbetrag
amount of depreciation Abschreibungsbetrag
amount of inspection Prüfumfang
amount of memory Speicherkapazität
amount of space Platz
amount of the amortization Abschreibungshöhe
amount of the discrepancy Abweichungsmenge
amount of the order Bestellbetrag
amount of variables Variablen-Anzahl
amount posted Buchungsbetrag
amount posting Betragskontierung
amount transferred Umbuchungsbetrag
ampacity zulässige Stromstärke
amplidyne Amplidyne
amplifier Verstärker
amplify verstärken

amplitude-modulated signal amplitudenmoduliertes Signal
amplitude modulation Amplitudenmodulation
amplitude shift keying Amplitudenmodulation
analog analog
analog alarm Analogalarm
analog circuit Analogschaltung
analog computer Analogrechner
analog digital converter Analog-Digital-Umsetzer, Analog-Digital-Wandler
analog failure Analogausfall
analog gain Analogverstärkung
analog integrated circuit integrierte Analogschaltung
analogous analog
analog phase locked loop analoge Phasenverriegelungsschleife
analog processing unit Analogrechenwerk
analog supply Analogquelle
analog to digital convertor Analog-Digital-Wandler
analog to digital/digital to analog convertor Analog-Digital-/Digital-Analog-Wandler
analogy Analogie
analysation program Analyseprogramm
analyse analysieren, auswerten
analysis Analyse, Auswertung
analysis file Analysedatei
analysis function Analysefunktion
analysis program Analyseprogramm, Auswertungsprogramm
analysis purpose Auswertungszweck
analyst Analytiker
analyzer Analysator
A/N color mode alphanumerischer Farbmodus
AND circuit UND-Schaltung
AND gate UND-Gatter
angle Winkel
angle selector Winkelgeber
angular distance Winkelabstand
angular positioning Positionsbestimmung über Drehwinkel
anisochronous an-isochron
annotate kommentieren
annotated kommentiert
annotation Kommentar
announce ankündigen
annual jährlich
annual account posting Jahreskontenschreibung
annual amortization Jahresabschreibung
annual cut-off Jahresabgrenzung
annual depreciation Jahresabschreibung

annual details Jahresangaben
annual development Jahresentwicklung
annually jährlich
annual purchase order value Jahresbestellwert
annual roll-over Jahresverschiebung
annual statistics Jahresstatistik
annual tax certificate Jahresbescheinigung
annual turnover Jahresumsatz
annunciator akustisches Meldegerät, optisches Anzeigegerät
anode Anode
anode dissipation Anodenverlustleistung
anode loss Anodenverlustleistung
anode modulation Anodenmodulation
answer Antwort, Rückantwort, antworten, beantworten, rückmelden
answerback Kennung, Kennungsgeber, Rückmeldung
answerback device Kennungsgeber
answering Anrufbeantwortung, Beantwortung
anticipate vorwegnehmen
anticipated payment Abschlag
any beliebig
any desired beliebig
apart from ausgenommen
aperture card Filmlochkarte
aperture distortion Aperturverzerrung
apostrophe Apostroph, Hochkomma
apparent erscheinend
apparent profit calculation Scheingewinnermittlung
appear auftreten, erscheinen
appearance Auftritt, Aussehen, Erscheinung
append anfügen, anhängen, hinzufügen
append area Anhangbereich
appendix Anhang, Anhangbereich
appliance Gerät, Vorrichtung
applicability Anwendbarkeit
applicable anwendbar, einsetzbar, geltend, zutreffend
applicate anwenden
application Anwendung, Applikation, Einsatz
application context Anwendungskontext
application data Anwendungsdaten
application dependent anwenderabhängig
application design tool Erstellungshilfe für Anwendungen
application diskette Anwendungsdiskette
application documentation Anwendungsdokumentation, Anwendungsentwicklungssystem
application engineering Einsatzvorbereitung
application engineering function Einsatzvorbereitungsfunktion

application error Anwendungsfehler
application file Anwendungsdatei
application for approval Zulassungsantrag
application function Anwendungsfunktion
application information Anwendungsinformation
application interface Anwendungsschnittstelle
application keypad Funktionstastenblock
application keypad mode anwendungsbezogene Funktionstastenbelegung
application kit Anwendungspaket
application layer Anwendungsschicht, Verarbeitungsschicht
application log Anwendungsprotokoll
application oriented language anwendungsorientierte Sprache
application processing Anwendungsverarbeitung
application program Anwenderprogramm, Anwendungsprogramm
application program diskette Diskette mit Anwendungsprogramm
application program interface Anwendungsprogramm-Schnittstelle
application programmer Anwendungsprogrammierer
application program type Anwendungsprogrammtyp
application service element Anwendungsdienstelement
application software Anwendungssoftware
application statistics Mengengerüst
application system Anwendungssystem
applied function angewandte Funktion
applied instruction angewandter Befehl
apply anwenden, einsetzen, gelten, zutreffen
appointed date Vormerktermin
appointment text Verabredungstext
apportion bemessen
apportionment Betragserteilung
apportionment of freight charges Frachtkostenverteilung
approach annähern, zugehen
appropriate angebracht, entsprechend, gemessen
appropriate to the period periodengerecht
appropriate to the procedure prozedurgemäß
approval Zulassung
approval for specific use Einzelzulassung
approximate angleichen
approximately annähernd, circa, ungefähr
approximation Annäherung
arabic character arabisches Zeichen

arbitrary willkürlich
arbitrary analysis Schiedsanalyse
arbitrary device Nicht-Standardgerät
arbitrary device handler Exec-Schnittstelle für Papierperipherie-Gerätesteuerung
arc Bogen
arc control device Funkensteuergerät
arc cosine Arcuscosinus
arc discharge tube Bogenentladungsröhre
architecture Architektur
archive Archiv, archivieren
archive number comparison Archivnummern-Vergleich
archive tape Archivband
arc sine Arcussinus
arc suppression coil Petersenspule
arc tangent Arcustangens
area Bereich, Bezirk, Gebiet, Kreis, Sachgebiet
area allocation Bereichszuweisung
area code Vorwahl
area deallocation Bereichsauflösung
area flag Bereichskennzeichen
area level Kreisebene
areas of application Anwendungsgebiet
area start Bereichsanfang
area thinking Technik des kreativen Denkens
argument Argument
argument section Argumententeil
argument table Argumenttabelle
arithmetic arithmetisch
arithmetical instruction arithmetischer Befehl
arithmetic block arithmetischer Block
arithmetic expression arithmetische Gleichung
arithmetic function arithmetische Funktion
arithmetic greater than größer als
arithmetic instruction arithmetischer Befehl
arithmetic logical function Rechenwerk
arithmetic logic unit Rechenwerk, arithmetisch-logische Einheit
arithmetic operation arithmetische Operation
arithmetic overflow arithmetischer Überlauf
arithmetic procedure Rechenvorgang
arithmetic processing unit Arithmetikrechenwerk
arithmetic processor Arithmetikprozessor
arithmetic register Arithmetikregister, Rechenwerksregister
arithmetic shift Stellenverschiebung
arithmetic technique Berechnungsverfahren
arithmetic unit Arithmetik-Einheit, Rechenwerk
arm Arm
armature Anker, Läufer

armature winding Ankerwicklung
arm movement Positionierzeit
arranged data Verabredungsdaten
arrangement Anlage, Anordnung, Einteilung
array Datenfeld, Feld, Feldgruppe, Matrix, Matrize, Tabelle
array processing instruction set Befehlssatz zur Arrayverarbeitung
array variable Matrix-Variable
arrears Rückstand
ar register AR-Register
arrival Ankunft
arrive ankommen, eintreffen
arrow Pfeil
arrow key Pfeiltaste
article Artikel
article account Artikelkonto
article account number Artikelkontonummer
article catalog Artikelkatalog
article character Artikelcharakter
article code Sachnummer
article description Artikelbezeichnung
article group Artikelgruppe
article history file Artikelkontodatei
article immobilisation Artikelsperre
article master conversion Artikelstammkonvertierung
article master data Artikelstammdaten
article master extension Artikelstammerweiterung
article master field Artikelstammfeld
article master file Artikelstammdatei
article master maintenance Artikelstammwartung
article number criterion Artikelnummerkriterium
article report Artikelübersicht
article statistics Artikelstatistik
article type Artikelart
as a backup ersatzhalber
as a basic principle grundsätzlich
as a matter of principle prinzipiell
as a replacement ersatzhalber
as a result demzufolge
as a rule im Regelfall
as a substitute ersatzhalber
ascending aufsteigend, steigend
ascending order aufsteigende Reihenfolge
ascertaining the value Wertfeststellung
ascii file ASCII-Datei
ask fragen
ask for anfragen
aspect Aspekt, Form, Gesichtspunkt, Gestalt

aspect ratio Bildformat, Bildseitenverhältnis, Längenverhältnis, Seitenverhältnis
assemble assemblieren, montieren
assembled program count assemblierte Programmstelle
assembler Assembler, Assemblierer
assembler convention Assembler-Konvention
assembler definition Assembler-Definition
assembler directive Assemblerdirektive
assembler format Assemblerformat
assembler language Assembler, Assemblersprache
assembler language programmer Assembler-Programmierer
assembler module Assemblermodul
assembler primary program Assembler-Primärprogramm
assembler program Assemblerprogramm
assembler program link Assembler-Programmverknüpfung
assembler programmer Assembler-Programmierer
assembly Assemblierung
assembly procedure Assemblierungsprozedur
assembly program Assemblerprogramm
assertion Erklärung
assessment of wealth tax Vermögenssteuerwertermittlung
asset Anlage, Anlagengegenstand
asset advice Anlageanweisung
asset category Anlageklasse
asset completion Anlagenfertigstellung
asset development Anlagenentwicklung
asset disposal Anlagenabgang
asset disposal posting Anlagenabgangsbuchung
asset field size Anlagenfeldgröße
asset file Anlagendatei
asset investment Anlagenbestand
asset investment account Anlagenbestandskonto
asset investments Anlagenbestände
asset key Anlagenschlüssel
asset ledger Anlagenbuch
asset master Anlagenstamm
asset master data Anlagenstammdaten
asset master data transfer Anlagenstammdatenübernahme
asset master record Anlagenstammsatz
asset number Anlagennummer
asset posting Anlagenbuchung
asset posting lines Anlagenbuchungszeilen
asset re-postings Anlagenumbuchungen
assets Aktiva, Bilanzaktiva, Wirtschaftsgüter

assets account Anlagenkonto
assets accounting Anlagenbuchhaltung
assets accounting system Anlagenbuchhaltungssystem
assets accounting voucher Anlagenbuchhaltungsbeleg
assets analysis Anlagenspiegel
assets area Anlagenbereich
assets authorization Anlagenberechtigung
assets authorization group Anlagenberechtigungsgruppe
assets card Anlagenkarte
assets code Anlagenschlüssel
assets daily ledger Anlagenjournal
assets general ledger account Anlagenhauptbuchkonto
assets management Anlagenverwaltung, Anlagenwertführung
assets master record Anlagenstammsatz
assets record Anlagensatz
asset summary Anlagenkurztext
asset text Anlagentext
asset transaction record Anlagenbewegungssatz
asset transactions Anlagenbewegungen
asset transfer Anlagenumsetzung
asset voucher Anlagenbeleg
assign zuordnen, zuweisen
assignment Abtretung, Zuordnung, Zuweisung
assignment statement Zuordnungsanweisung, Zuweisungskommando
assistant suffix Mitarbeitersuffix
associate angehören, zugehörig, zuordnen
associated operation zugehörige Operation
associated record identification data Satzbeschreibungsarten
association Assoziation
association control service element Assoziationskontrolldienstelement
association number Zuordnungsnummer
association number table Zuordnungsnummerntabelle
association term Zuordnungsbegriff
associative memory Assoziativspeicher
associative relation Assoziativ-Relation
associative storage Assoziativ-Speicher, Assoziativspeicher
assume annehmen, unterstellen
assumed value Annahmewert
asterisk Sternchen
asterisked mit Sternchen versehen
asterisked accounts Sternchenkonten

asterisk indicator Wiederholungszeichen für Bezugszahlen
asymmetric asymmetrisch
asymmetric full duplex asymmetrisch Vollduplex
asynchronous asynchron
asynchronous application program Asynchronanwendungsprogramm
asynchronous balanced mode gleichberechtigter Spontanbetrieb
asynchronous communications adapter asynchroner Kommunikationsanschluß, asynchroner Übertragungsadapter
asynchronous communications interface adapter asynchroner Schnittstellenbaustein
asynchronous disconnected mode unabhängiger Wartezustand
asynchronous machine Asynchronmaschine
asynchronous modem asynchrones Modem
asynchronous motor Asynchronmotor
asynchronous multiplexer Asynchronmultiplexer
asynchronous operation Start-/Stopbetrieb, asynchrone Arbeitsweise
asynchronous program Asynchronprogramm
asynchronous response mode Spontanbetrieb
asynchronous start stop interface asynchrone Start/Stop-Verbindung
asynchronous system trap asynchroner Systemsprung
asynchronous time division multiplexor asynchroner Zeitmultiplexer
asynchronous transmission asynchrone Übertragung
at all überhaupt
at all times jederzeit
at any one time zu irgendeiner Zeit
at any time zu jeder Zeit
at first zunächst
at least mindestens
at no charge gratis
at optimal costs kostenoptimal
at present augenblicklich, gegenwärtig
at run time während der Laufzeit
at sign Klammeraffe (@)
at start time zur Startzeit
attach anfügen, hinzufügen, zuordnen
attachment plug Anschlußstecker
attachment-plug receptacle Steckerhülse
attain erlangen, erreichen, erzielen
attempt Versuch, versuchen
attempt to read Leseversuch

attempt to switch on remotely Ferneinschaltversuch
attendance sheet Anwesenheitsbeleg
attention Aufmerksamkeit
attention interrupt Bereitschaftssignal
attention request Anrufanforderung
attenuation Dämpfung
attenuator Dämpfungsglied
at the head of the file dateiführend
attitude Haltung
attracted angezogen
attribute Attribut, zurückführen
attribute byte Attributbyte
attribute identifier Attributkennzeichen
attribute modification Attributmodifikation
attribute sign Attributzeichen
attribute update Attributaktualisierung
attribute use Attributverwendung
attribute value Attribut/Wert
audible indicator akustisches Signal
audio amplifier Audioverstärker
audio communication equipment Audiokommunikationssysteme
audiofrequency signal Niederfrequenzsignal
audio output jack Phonoausgangsbuchse
audit file Auditdatei, Dialogprotokolldatei, Nachhaltedatei, Prüfdatei
audit trail Buchungskontrolle, Prüfpfad
authentication Beglaubigung
author Autor, Ersteller, Verfasser
authorization Anwendungsberechtigung, Authorisation, Berechtigung
authorization category Berechtigungsklasse
authorization check Berechtigungsprüfung
authorization flag Berechtigungskennzeichen
authorization group Berechtigungsgruppe
authorization identification Berechtigungskennzeichen
authorization mask Berechtigungsmaske
authorize berechtigen
auto Auto...
auto answer automatische Anrufbeantwortung
auto answerback automatisches Answerback
auto answerback enable automatisches Answerback einschalten
auto answer mode Auto-Antwortbetrieb
auto boot Autostart
auto create automatisches Erstellen
auto dialled selbst gewählt
auto dialler automatische Wählvorrichtung
auto feed automatische Zufuhr
auto job startup automatischer Jobstart

auto key repeat automatische Wiederholung des Tastendrucks
automated installation and diagnostic service System zur Installation und Wartung von Software
automated teller machine Geldausgabeautomat, Geldautomat, automatische Kassiermaschine
automatic automatisch, maschinell
automatic answer automatische Antwort
automatic answer disconnect automatische Anschaltleitungstrennung
automatic answer hang up automatische Anschaltleitungstrennung
automatic answering automatische Antwort
automatic calling and/or answering equipment automatische Einheit für ankommende und/oder abgehende Rufe
automatic cash dispenser Geldausgabeautomat
automatic changeover Datenumschaltsignal
automatic code generator automatischer Programmgenerator
automatic constant Konstanthaltung
automatic control system automatisches Steuerungssystem
automatic data processing automatische Datenverarbeitung
automatic dialling automatische Wahl
automatic feed automatische Papierzuführung
automatic frequency control automatische Frequenzregelung
automatic function automatische Funktion
automatic gain control automatische Verstärkungsregelung
automatic interactive debugging system automatisches Sytem zur Fehlersuche
automatic pagination automatischer Seitenumbruch
automatic program generator automatischer Programmgenerator
automatic repeat request Wiederholung nach Aufforderung
automatic sheet feeder automatischer Einzelblatteinzug
automatic switching center Telefonzentrale
automatic text processing machine Text-Automat
automatic transfer mode automatische Übertragung
automatic volume recognition automatische Datenträgererkennung
automatic word wrap automatischer Zeilenumbruch

automation Automatisierung
automatism Automatik
auto offset automatische Schirmbildverschiebung
auto print automatisches Drucken
autorecovery automatische Wiederherstellung
autorecovery bootstrap automatische Wiederherstellung der Systemsteuerung
autorepeat Autowiederholung
auto report facility automatische Quellprogrammgenerierung
autorestart Selbstanlauf, Selbstanlauf
auto screen blank automatische Bildschirmabschaltung
auto select automatische Wahl
autotransformer Autotransformator, Spartrafo, Spartransformator
auto turnaround automatische Umkehr
auto wrap automatischer Zeilenumbruch
auto XON XOFF automatisches XON/XOFF-Protokoll
auxiliary Hilfs-, Zusatz-, zusätzliche, zusätzlicher, zusätzliches
auxiliary analog input Analog-Hilfseingang
auxiliary cell Hilfszelle
auxiliary channel Zweitkanal
auxiliary contactor Hilfskontakt
auxiliary control process Hilfssteuerprozeß
auxiliary CRT for maintenance support Kontrollbildschirm
auxiliary device Zusatzeinrichtung
auxiliary duplication Hilfsduplizieren
auxiliary equipment Hilfsausrüstung
auxiliary field Hilfsfeld
auxiliary file Hilfsdatei
auxiliary function Hilfsfunktion
auxiliary interface Parallelschnittstelle
auxiliary label Hilfsmerker
auxiliary memory Seitenwechselspeicher
auxiliary order materials submission Beistellung
auxiliary program Hilfsprogramm
auxiliary register Hilfsregister
auxiliary routine Hilfsprogramm
auxiliary speaker Zusatzlautsprecher
auxiliary storage Hilfsspeicher, externer Speicher
auxiliary store Hilfsspeicher
auxiliary supplies Hilfstoffe
availability Mengenverfügbarkeit, Verfügbarkeit
availability calculation Verfügbarkeitsrechnung
availability check Mengenverfügbarkeitskontrolle, Verfügbarkeitskontrolle

availability control unit Systemkonfigurierungseinheit
availability date Verfügbarkeitsdatum
availability display Verfügbarkeitsanzeige
availability store Verfügbarkeitsspeicher
availability summary Verfügbarkeitsübersicht
availability time Eindeckungszeit, Verfügbarkeitszeit
available verfügbar, vorhanden
available command line forms mögliche Kommandoformen
available segment vorhandenes Segment
avalance diode Avalance-Diode
average Durchschnitt, Mittelwert, durchschnittlich
average acquisition price Lagereinstands-Durchschnittspreis
average annual growth rate durchschnittliche jährliche Wachstumsrate
average exchange rate Mittelkurs
average instruction execution time durchschnittliche Zeit zur Befehlsabarbeitung
average magnitude of error durchschnittliche Fehlergröße
average price Durchschnittspreis
average run time durchschnittliche Laufzeit
average total time durchschnittliche Gesamtzeit
average transfer rate mittlere Übertragungsgeschwindigkeit
average value Mittelwert
average value line Durchschnittswertzeile
average voltmeter Mittelwertspannungsmesser, Mittelwertvoltmeter
avoid umgehen, verhindern, vermeiden
aware aufmerksam

B

back zurück
back EMF Gegen-EMK
background Bildschirmhintergrund, Hintergrund
background color Hintergrundfarbe
background processing Hintergrundverarbeitung
background screen Hintergrund-Bildschirm
backing store Seitenwechselspeicher
backlink Rückverweis, Rückwärtsverkettung
backlog Bestand nicht eröffneter Jobs, Bestandsmenge, Rückstand
backlog investigation Rückstandsverfolgung
backlog of jobs Bestand nicht eröffneter Jobs
backlog posting Rückstandsbuchung
back orders Auftragsrückstand
backplane Steckrahmen
back post rückbuchen, zurückbuchen
back posting Rückbuchung, Zurückbuchung
back posting month Rückbuchungsmonat, Zurückbuchungsmonat
back posting period Rückbuchungsperiode, Rückbuchungszeitraum, Zurückbuchungsperiode, Zurückbuchungszeitraum
back pressure flow control Rückstauflußkontrolle
backslash Rückstrich, umgekehrter Schrägstrich
backspace Bandrücksetzen, Rückschritt, Rücktaste, Rückwärtsschritt
backspace key Rückschrittaste, Rücktaste, Zurück-Taste
backspace mechanism Rückschritteinrichtung
backspace positioning Rückwärtspositionierung
backspacing time Rückschaltzeit
backup Ersatz, Sicherung, Sicherungs-, sichern
backup bit Sicherungsbit
backup copy Reservekopie, Sicherungskopie
backup copy of diskette Sicherungskopie einer Diskette erstellen
backup directory Sicherungs-Dateiverzeichnis
backup diskette Sicherungsdiskette
backup diskette date Datum der Sicherungsdiskette
backup diskette menu Diskettensicherungsmenü
backup diskette name Name der Sicherungsdiskette
backup diskette time Uhrzeit der Sicherungsdiskette
backup exclusion file specifier Dateispezifikation der nicht zu sichernden Datei
backup file Sicherungsdatei
backup file specifier Dateispezifikation der zu sichernden Datei
backup file type Dateityp der Sicherungsdatei
backup master workstation Ersatz-Hauptarbeitsplatz, Ersatzmasterplatz
backup operation Sicherungsaktion
backup procedure Sicherungsverfahren
backup service Sicherungsprogramm
backup system Bereitschaftssystem
backup value Sicherungswert
backward rückwärts
backward chaining Rückwärtskettung
backward channel Hilfskanal
backward link Rückverweis, Rückwärtsverkettung
backward linkage Rückverweis, Rückwärtsverkettung
backward space file Dateirücksetzen
backward supervision Rückwärtssteuerung
backward wave tube Rückwärtswellen-Röhre
bad defekt, fehlerhaft, ungültig
bad address table BAT-Tabelle, Fehleradreßtabelle
bad block fehlerhafter Block
bad data ungültige Daten
badge card reader Ausweisleser
bad sector fehlerhafter Sektor
bad status negative Zustandsmeldung
bad syntax Syntaxfehler
bad track fehlerhafte Spur
bail bar Papierhalter
balance Ausgleich, Ausgleichssaldo, Berichtssaldo, Saldenbilanz, Saldenregister, Saldo, ausgleichen, ausziffern, saldieren
balance account Bilanzkonto
balance carried forward Bilanzvortrag, Saldenvortrag, Saldovortrag
balance check Bilanzprüfung, Saldenprüfung, Saldoprüfung
balance checking Ausgleichsprüfung
balance confirmation Saldenbestätigung
balance control Bilanzsteuerung
balance control code Bilanzsteuerschlüssel
balanced data link Übermittlungsabschnitt mit gleichberechtigter Steuerung
balance display Ausgleichsanzeige, Saldenanzeige

balance posting Ausgleichsbuchung
balance process Saldenverlauf
balance sheet Bilanz
balance sheet date Bilanzstichtag
balance sheet item Bilanzposition
balance sheet valuation Bilanzbewertung
balance table Ausziffertabelle
balance total Ausgleichssumme
balance transfer Saldenübernahme
balancing amount Ausgleichsbetrag
balancing code Ausgleichsschlüssel, Ausgleichsziffer
balancing data Ausgleichsdaten, Ausgleichsstoff
balancing date Ausgleichsdatum
balancing info Ausgleichsinformation, Auszifferinformation
balancing of accounts Kontenausgleich
balancing period Ausgleichsperiode
balancing procedure Ausgleichsvorgang
balancing process Ausgleichsvorgang
balancing value Ausgleichswert
balancing volume Ausgleichsvolumen
ball point pen Kugelschreiber
band Band, Frequenzband
band deflector Banddeflektor
band generator divisor latch Teiler-Speicher für Bandgenerator
band matrix Bandmatrix, Bandmatrize
bandpass amplifier Bandpaßverstärker
band selector Bandschalter
bandstop filter Bandsperre
band suppressor Bandsperre
bandwidth compression Brandbreitenkompression
bandwith Bandbreite
bank Bank, Gruppe, Reihe, Speicher, Speicherbank
bank account Bankkonto
bank account code Bankkontoschlüssel
bank address Bankadresse, Bankanschrift
bank charges Bankspesen
bank code Banknummer, Bankschlüssel
bank country code Bankländerschlüssel
bank credit transfer Banküberweisung
bank cycle time Reihen-Zykluszeit
bank data Bankdaten, Bankverbindungen
bank debit entry Banklastschrift
bank details Bankangaben, Bankverbindung
banking client Bankkunde
banknote Geldschein
banknote combination Scheinzusammenstellung

banknote feed Geldscheinabzug
banknote withdrawal Scheinabzug
bank number Bankleitzahl
bank posting Bankbuchung
bank posting amount Bankbuchungsbetrag
bank receipt Bankquittung, Bankquittungsverfahren
bar Balken
bar chart Balkendiagramm
bar code Strichcode
Baritt diode Baritt-Diode
bar pattern display Balkenmusteranzeige
barrier Sperre
base Basis, Grundplatte, Montageplatte, basieren, beruhen
base address Basisadresse
baseband Basisband
baseband transmission equipment Basisband-Übertragungseinrichtung
base date Basisdatum, Stichtag
base date for payment deadlines Zahlungsfristenbasisdatum
base date inventory Stichtagsbestand
base date value Stichtagswert
based on experience Erfahrungswert
base enclosure Montageplatten-Gehäuse
base limit Basisgrenzwert
base memory serienmäßiger Speicher
base number Basiszahl
base parameter file Basis-Parameterdatei
base plate Bodenplatte, Grundplatte
base price Basispreis
base register Basisadreßregister
base value Ausgangswert, Basiswert
base value for amortization Abschreibungs-Basiswert
base year Basisjahr
basic grundlegend, grundsätzlich
basically prinzipiell
basic amount Basisbetrag
basic bank cycle time Speicherverarbeitungsgeschwindigkeit der Standard-Reihen-Zykluszeit
basic charge Grundgebühr
basic colour Grundfarbe
basic constant Basiskonstante
basic control key Grundsteuertaste
basic control unit Haupt-Steuereinheit
basic costs Grundkosten
basic data Basisdaten, Grunddaten
basic discount Basisrabatt
basic discount table Basisrabattabelle
basic element Grundbestandteil
basic format list Basisformatliste

basic format name Basisformatname
basic function Basisfunktion, Grundfunktion
basic generation Grundgenerierung
basic information unit Informationsgrundeinheit
basic input/output system grundlegendes Ein-/Ausgabesystem
basic listing Grundübersicht
basic mode Hauptbetriebsart
basic module BASIC-Modul, Grundmodul
basic part format Basisteilformat
basic price calculation Basispreisermittlung
basic price table Basispreistabelle
basic printing Druckfunktionen
basic program step grundlegender Programmschritt
basic rule Grundregel
basics Grundfunktionen, Grundlagen
basic sheet Basisblatt
basic software Grundsoftware
basic system Basissystem, Grundsystem
basic system operation Bedienungsgrundlagen
basic table Grundtabelle
basic time state Basiszyklus
basic transport capability Grundtransportfähigkeit
basic troubleshooting Hauptfehlersuche und -behebung
basic unit Grundeinheit
basic value Grundwert, Stützwert
basic version Basisversion, Grundversion
basis Basis, Grundlage
basis for costing Kalkulationsbasis
batch Batch, Charge, Stapel-
batch bypass indicator Stapelüberspringkennzeichen
batch command Batchkommando, Stapelbefehl, Stapelkommando
batch command extension Erweiterung des Stapelkommandos
batch component Stapelkomponente
batch entry Batcherfassung
batch evaluation monitoring Batchauswertungsübersicht
batch file Batchdatei, Stapeldatei
batch file processing Batch-Dateiverarbeitung, Dateiverarbeitung im Stapelbetrieb
batch generation Batcherstellung, Batchgenerierung, Stapelerstellung
batching Zusammenfassen von Bewegungsdaten zu Stapeln
batch input Batchinput, Stapeleingabe
batch job Batchjob, Stapeljob

batch job foreground Vordergrund-Stapelverarbeitung
batch mode Batchmodus, Batchrahmen, Stapelmodus
batch multiprogramming Stapel- u. Mehrprogrammverarbeitungseigenschaften
batch number Chargennummer
batch of data Erfassungsabschnitt
batch operating Batchbetrieb, Stapelbetrieb
batch oriented batchorientiert, stapelorientiert
batch part Batchteil, Stapelteil
batch posting Batchbuchen, Stapelbuchen
batch posting flag Batchbuchungsflag, Stapelbuchungskennzeichen
batch print output Batchdruckausgabe
batch procedure Batchprozedur
batch processing Batchbearbeitung, Stapelbetrieb, Stapelverarbeitung
batch processing command Kommando für Stapelverarbeitung
batch program Batchprogramm, Stapelprogramm
batch qualifier Batchmerkmal, Stapelmerkmal
batch queue Stapelwarteschlange
batch record Chargensatz
batch relay option internes Durcharbeiten einer Datei
batch run Batchlauf
batch slot Hintergrundtask, Hintergrundverarbeitungsabschnitt
batch splitting Batchaufteilung, Chargensplitting, Stapelaufteilung
batch terminal Stapel-Datenstation
bathtub curve Badewannenkurve
battery Batterie
battery backup Batterienotversorgung, Sicherung Energieversorgung durch Batterien, Sicherung der Energieversorgung durch Batterien, Sicherungsbatterie, Stromausfallsicherung
battery buffered batteriegepuffert
battery charger Batterieladegerät
battery plate Akkumulator-Platte
battery powered device batteriebetriebenes Gerät
baud Baud
baud rate Baudrate, Übertragungsgeschwindigkeit, Übertragungsrate
BCD arithmetic function BCD-Arithmetikfunktion
beacon Bake, Funkfeuer, Sekundärradar
beam Balken, Strahl
beam-lead device Beam-Lead-Gerät
bear tragen

37

bearing seal Lagerdichtung
beep Pieps, Tastatursignal, Warnton, akustisches Signal, akustisches Zeichen, piepsen
beforehand vorher
before image vorhergehende Abbildung
begin Anfang, Start, anfangen, beginnen
begin field Feldanfang
beginning Anfang, Beginn
beginning mark Anfangskennzeichnung
beginning of a chain Kettenanfang
beginning of extent Bereichsanfang
beginning of file Dateianfang
beginning of group Gruppenanfang
beginning of line Zeilenanfang
beginning of page Blattanfang
beginning of tape Bandanfang, Bandanfangsmarke
beginning of text Textanfang
beginning of the page Seitenanfang
beginning of the text Textbeginn
behavior Verhalten, Verlauf
bell Glocke, Klingelzeichen, Signalton, Tonsignal
bell shaped insulator Glockenisolator
bell tone Tastatursignal
belong gehören
belong to gehören zu
belong together zusammengehören
below-table position Untertischposition
benchmark program Bewertungsprogramm
be present anstehen, vorliegen
bers type connector Bers-Anschluß
beside neben
best am besten
better besser
between zwischen
between key words zwischen Schlagworten
bezel Frontplatte
bidirectional bidirektional
bidirectional field Variablenfeld mit Ein- und Ausgaberichtung
bidirectional lookahead bidirektional mit Vorwärts-/Rückwärtssuche
bi-directional optical link in beide Richtungen betriebene optische Verbindung
bidirectional printing Druckvorgang in Vorwärts- und Rückwärtsrichtung, bidirektionales Drucken
big ausgedehnt, groß, mächtig, umfangreich
bill Rechnung, berechnen, verrechnen
billing Berechnung
billions of instructions per second Milliarden Befehle pro Sekunde

bill of exchange Ausgangswechsel, Wechsel
bill of exchange data Wechseldaten
bill of exchange discount Wechseldiskont
bill of exchange due date Wechselfälligkeit
bill of exchange duty Wechselsteuer
bill of exchange liability Wechselverbindlichkeit
bill of exchange payment Wechselzahlung
bill of exchange period Wechsellaufzeit
bill of exchange posting Wechselbuchung
bill of exchange request Wechselanforderung
bill of lading Verladeliste
bill of materials Stückliste
bill of materials dispersal Stücklistenauflösung
bill of materials dispersal flag Stücklistenauflösungs-Kennzeichen
bill of materials marker Verwendungskennzeichen
bills due Wechselforderung
bills due posting Wechselforderungsbuchung
bills of exchange charges marker Wechselspesenkennzeichen
bills payable Wechselobligo
binary binär
binary arithmetic function binäre Arithmetikfunktion
binary cell binäre Speicherzelle
binary code Binärcode, Binärschlüssel
binary coded decimal binär kodiertes Dezimalsystem, binär kodierte Dezimalzahl
binary coded octal binär kodierte Oktalzahl
binary conversion Binärumwandlung
binary counter Binärzähler
binary decimal conversion Binär-/Dezimal-Umwandlung
binary digit Binäreinheit, Binärstelle, Binärziffer, Bit
binary error correcting code binärer Fehlerkorrekturcode
binary error detecting code binärer Fehlererkennungscode
binary file Binärdatei
binary notation Binärdarstellung
binary number Binärzahl
binary operator Binäroperator
binary point Binärkomma
binary relation Binärrelation
binary semaphor binäres Semaphor
binary synchronous communications binärsynchrone Übertragung, bitsynchrone Kommunikation
binary synchronous communications protocol binärsynchrones Übertragungsprotokoll

binary text Binärtext
binary to decimal conversion Binär-/Dezimal-Umwandlung, Binär-Dezimal-Umsetzung
binary total Binärsumme
binary tree Binärbaum
bin cover Schachtverschluß
bin number Schachtnummer
bipolar bipolar
bipolar modulation Bipolar-Tastung
bipolar transistor bipolarer Transistor
bi-processor Biprozeßrechner
biquinary code Biquinärkode
bisect halbieren
bistable bistabil
bistable trigger unit Flip-Flop, bistabiler Multivibrator, bistabiles Kippglied
bit Bit
bit assignment Bitzuordnung
bit cell time Bitzellenzeit
bit check Bit prüfen
bit clear Bit löschen
bit density Bitdichte
bit envelope Bit-Vollgruppe
bit error rate Bitfehlerrate
bit error rate monitor Bitfehlerratenmonitor
bit error rate tester Bitfehlerratentester
bit image mode Bitabbildmodus
bit map Bit-Map, Bitbelegungsplan, Bittabelle
bit map access Bit-Map-Zugriff
bit map graphics Bitmustergrafik
bit map sector Bit-Map-Sektor
bit mask Bitmaske
bit order of transmission Bitfolge an der Übergabestelle
bit oriented protocol bitorientiertes Protokoll
bit-parallel bitparallel
bit pattern Bitmuster
bit per inch Bit pro Zoll
bit pick Bit prüfen
bit position Bitposition
bit rate Bitfrequenz, Bitgeschwindigkeit, Datenübertragungsgeschwindigkeit, Übertragungsrate
bit set Bit setzen
bit shift register Bit-Schieberegister
bit slice microprocessor Bit-Slice-Mikroprozessor
bits per character Bit pro Zeichen
bits per inch Bit pro Zoll
bits per second Bit pro Sekunde, Bit pro Sekunde
bit synchronous adapter bitsynchrone Schnittstelle

bit synchronous communications bitsynchrone Kommunikation
bitsynchronous communications adapter bitsynchrone Schnittstelle
bit test Bit prüfen
bit total error Bitsummenfehler
bit value Bit-Wert
black box Blackbox, Vierpol, schwarzer Kasten
blackout Netzausfall
blank Leerzeichen, auf Leerzeichen setzen, leer, löschen, radieren
blank card Leerkarte
blank column detector Leerspaltensucher
blank entry Leereintrag
blank field Leerfeld
blank format Leerformat
blank indicator Leerstellen-Bezugszahl
blanking Zeichenunterdrückung
blanking signal Dunkelsteuerimpuls
blank line Leerzeile
blank out auf Leerzeichen setzen, ausblenden, auslöschen, wegblenden
blank page Leerseite
blink blinken
blink protect Zeichenschutz für blinkende Zeichen
block Abschnitt, Baustein, Block, Satz, aufteilen, blocken, blockieren, einteilen, unterteilen
block access method Blockzugriffsmethode
block acknowledgement Block-Empfangsbestätigung
block address Satzadresse
block characters Blockzeichen
block check Blockprüfung
block check character Blockprüfzeichen
block check sequence Blockprüfzeichenfolge
block cursor Blockcursor, Blockschreibmarke
block descriptor word Blockbeschreibungswort
blocked blockiert
blocked process blockierter Prozeß
blocked-unblocked geblockt-ungeblockt, gesperrt-ungesperrt
block error rate Blockfehlerrate
block error rate test Blockfehlerratenprüfung
block format Blockformat
block gap Blocklücke
block header Blockkopf
block identification Blockkennung
blocking Blocken, Blockieren, Blockierung
blocking note Sperrvermerk
block length Blocklänge
block level Blockebene
block marker track Blockmarkierspur

39

block number Blocknummer
block screen Blockbild
block securing Blocksicherungsverfahren
block selection Blockansteuerung
blocks of contiguous space zusammenhängende Blöcke
block sort Blocksortierung
block statement Blockanweisung
block structured blockstrukturiert
block-to-block speed Blockgeschwindigkeit
block/unblock sperren/entsperren
blown up aufgebläht
board Karte, Leiterplatte, Platine
bobbin Spule
bobbin insulator Spulenisolator
bold Fettdruck, fett, fettgedruckt
bold attribute Attribut »fettgedruckt«
bold face character fettgedrucktes Zeichen, hervorgehobenes Zeichen
bolding Fettdruck
bold print Fettdruck
bold protect Zeichenschutz für fettgedruckte Zeichen
bold protected Fettdruck geschützt
bonding conductor Masseleiter
bonus Bonus
bonus calculation Bonusermittlung
bonus credit note Bonusgutschrift
bonus flag Bonuskennzeichen, Bonusmerkmal
bonus monitoring Bonusüberwachung
bonus scale Bonusstaffel
bonus settlement Bonusabrechnung
book Buch, buchen
book inventory Buchbestand
bookkeeping Buchführung, Buchhaltung
booklet Broschüre
book profit Buchgewinn
book value Buchwert
boolean Bool'sch
boolean algebra Schaltalgebra, boolesche Algebra
boolean operation boolesche Operation, boolesche Verknüpfung
boom Tragearm
boost verstärken
booster Verstärker
booster transformer Zusatztransformator
boot booten, laden, urladen
bootable medium Datenträger mit Bootblock, bootbarer Datenträger, urladbarer Datenträger
boot block Urladeblock
boot block record Selbstladeblock, Selbstladeprogramm
booth Stand
boot image ladefähiges Programm
boot menu Urlademenü
boot program Ladeprogramm
boot ROM Boot-ROM, Lade-ROM
bootstrap Urlader, spezielle rückgekoppelte Schaltung, urladen
bootstrap area Urlader-Bereich
bootstrap command procedure Urladekommandoprozedur
bootstrap loader Urlader
bootstrap loading urladen
bootstrap load program Selbstladeprogramm
border Grenze
border color Grenzfarbe, Rahmenfarbe
borrow Übertrag
borrower Darlehensnehmer
both way communication Vollduplex
both way communiction beidseitige Datenübermittlung
bottleneck Engpaß
bottom Ende
bottom address pointer unterer Adressenhinweis
bottom line Fußzeile, letzte Zeile, unterste Zeile
bottom margin Seitenfuß, unterer Rand
bottom of document Ende des Dokuments
bought in Fremdbezug, fremdbezogen
bought in order Fremdbestellung
bounce prellen
bouncing Prellen
bound gebunden
boundary Grenze, Rand
boundary alignment Ausrichtung auf Speichergrenze
boundary error Grenzwertfehler
boundary position Grenzposition
boundary value Randwert
box Box, Kasten, Kiste, Schachtel
box enable condition Box-Einschaltzustand
box function Boxfunktion
box position Kastenposition
brace geschweifte Klammer
bracket Klammer, eckige Klammer, runde Klammer
braided conductor geflochtener Leiter
brake Bremse, bremsen
branch Filiale, Verzweigung, Zweig, verzweigen
branch account Filialkonto
branch address Sprungadresse
branch and link Unterprogrammverzweigung

40

branch back zurückspringen
branch destination Verzweigungsziel
branch function Funktionsverzweigung
branch information system Zweiginformationssystem
branching Verzweigung
branching condition Sprungbefehl
branching module Programmverteiler
branch order Niederlassungsauftrag
branch prediction Verzweigungsvorhersage
branch symbol Verzweigungssymbol
branch to anspringen
braze hartlöten
break Unterbrechung, unterbrechen
breakage Bruch
break character Unterbrechungszeichen
break down Aufgliederung, aufgliedern, aufschlüsseln
breakfield Programmstop-Feld
breaking capacity Schaltleistung
breaking hyphen Trennstrich
break key Stoptaste
breakpoint Abbruchstelle, Haltemarkierung, Haltepunkt, Programmstop, Unterbrechungspunkt, Unterbrechungsstelle, programmierter Halt
breakpointed file Symbiontendatei
breakpoint register Stopregister, Unterbrechungspunkt, Wiederaufsetzpunkt
break scan code Unterbrechungscode
break signal Unterbrechungssignal
break time Länge des Signals
breakup Sprengung
bridge Brücke
bridge circuit Brückenschaltung
brief abgekürzt, kurz
brief content Kurzinhalt
brief description Kurzbeschreibung
brief initialization Kurzinitialisierung
brief letter content Brief-Kurzinhalt
brief list Kurzliste
bright hell
brightness Bildschirmhelligkeit, Helligkeit, Helligkeitsgrad
brightness adjustment Helligkeitsregulierung
brightness control Helligkeitsregler
brilliance Brillianz, Helligkeitsanzeige
bring up dynamically dynamisch aktivieren
broadband Breitband-
broadband coaxial cable Breitband-Koaxialkabel
broadband exchange Breitbandvermittlung
broadcast Rundfunk, Rundspruch, rundsenden

broadcast call equipment Konferenzeinrichtung
broadcast equipment Sendeeinrichtung
broadcast videotext Fernseh-Videotext
brought in eingebracht
brownout Schwankung in der Netzspannung, Spannungsabfall, Teilstromausfall
browse blättern
browse function Blätterfunktion
brush Bürste
brush compare check Bürstenvergleichsprüfung
brush rocker Bürstenhalter
bubble memory Magnetblasenspeicher
bubble memory controller Magnetblasenspeicher-Steuerung
bucket Plattenbereich, Speicherbereich
budget Budget, Finanzplan, Plan, planen
budget accounting Finanzplankontierung
budget balance sheet Planbilanz
budget category Finanzplankategorie
budget code Finanzplanschlüssel
budget control Budgetkontrolle
budget date Plandatum
budgeted amount Planungsbetrag
budgeted asset Planbetrag
budgeted assets Plananlagen
budget-effective finanzplanwirksam
budgeting type Planungsart
budget item Finanzplanposition
budget list Budgetliste
budget master Finanzplanstamm
budget master file Finanzplanstammdatei
budget master record Finanzplanstammsätze
budget month Planungsmonat
budget nature Planungscharakter
budget number Budgetnummer
budget period Finanzplanperiode
budget posted finanzplankontiert
budget posting voucher Planbuchungsbeleg
budget record Plannungssatz, Plansatz
budget re-distribution Budgetumverteilung
budget transaction Planbewegungen
budget type Planungsart
budget value Planwert
budget year Planjahr, Planungsjahr
buffer Puffer, Speicher, Zwischenspeicher, puffern, zwischenspeichern
buffer area Pufferbereich, Zwischenspeicherbereich
buffer end Pufferende
buffer file Pufferdatei, Zwischendatei
buffering system Puffersystem

buffer memory Pufferspeicher
buffer mode Puffermodus
buffer number Puffernummer
buffer occupancy Pufferbelegung
buffer offset Puffervorspann
buffer offset field Puffervorsatzfeld
buffer overflow Pufferüberlauf
buffer pointer position Pufferzeigerstand
buffer pool size Pufferbereichsgröße
buffer position Pufferposition
buffer size Puffergröße
buffer start address Pufferanfangsadresse
buffer storage Pufferspeicher
buffer store Pufferspeicher
buffer termination Beenden einer Pufferoperation
bug Fehler, Programmfehler
bugcheck Fehlerprüfung
build aufbauen, bauen, erstellen, zusammenbauen, zusammensetzen
builder segment Verknüpfungsprogramm
building block Baustein
build program Erstellungsprogramm
build up aufbauen, erstellen, zusammenbauen, zusammensetzen
built in eingebaut
built in portion eingebauter Teil
built in speaker eingebauter Lautsprecher
built up aufgebaut
bulb Lampe
bulk Groß-, Massen-, Sammel-, en gros
bulk acquisition Massenerfassung
bulk order Großbestellung, Massenbestellung, Sammelbestellung
bundle Bündel, Gebinde
bundled conductor Leiterbündel
buoyancy Auftrieb
burst Bündel
burst mode Burstmodus, Stoßbetrieb
burst transmission Bitbündel-Übertragung
bus Bus, Busschiene, Vielfachleitung
bus arbitrator Bus-Arbitrator
bus available Bus verfügbar
bus bar Sammelschiene
bus driver Bustreiber
bus error trap Sprung aufgrund eines Busfehlers
bus grant Busquittierungsleitung
bushing Durchführung, Einführungstülle, Lager
business Betrieb, Geschäft, Geschäfts-, betrieblich, betriebswirtschaftlich, geschäftlich, kommerziell

business accounting system Buchhaltungssystem
business computer Bürocomputer
business consultancy Beratungsfirma, Rationalisierungsgesellschaft
business data processing kommerzielle Datenverarbeitung
business division Geschäftsbereich
business division level Geschäftsbereichsebene
business graphics Geschäftsgrafik
business order Betriebsauftrag
business partner Geschäftspartner
business print set kommerzielle Schriftart
business transaction Geschäftsvorfall
bus interface Busschnittstelle
bus interrupt acknowledge signal Unterbrechungsantwort
bus load Busbelastung
busout Ausgabeteil des Systemdatenpfades
bus request Busanforderung
bus system Bussystem
busy condition Belegtzustand, Besetztfall
busy response Besetztmeldung
busy to other channel aktiv für anderen Kanal
button Druckknopf, Drucktaste, Knopf, Taste
button position Tastenposition
buy Einkauf, Kauf, einkaufen, kaufen
buyer Einkäufer, Käufer
buying rate Geldkurs
buyout aufkaufen, Übernahme
buzzer Signalton, Summer
by chance zufällig
bye Übertragung abbrechen
bypass Ausweichpfad, Umleitung, Umweg, ausweichen, übergehen, überspringen
bypass line Ausweichleitung
by row spaltenweise
byte Byte
byte channel transfer switch Bytekanalumschalter
byte count Byteanzahl
byte handling Bytebearbeitung
byte length Bytelänge

C

cabinet Ablage, Einbauschrank, Gehäuse, Gestellschrank, Schrank
cabinet file name Ablagename
cabinet size and extension Erstellungs- und Erweiterungsgröße des Speichers
cable Kabel
cable connector Kabelstecker
cable connector latch Steckerverriegelung
cable cover Kabelmantel
cable guide Kabelführung
cable junction Kabelverbindung
cable shield Kabelabdeckung, Kabelabschirmung
cable television Kabelfernsehen
cable text Kabeltext
cable tie Kabelbinder
cache Puffer, Pufferspeicher, puffern
cache disk processor Plattenspeicherrechner
cache memory Cache-Speicher, Pufferspeicher
cache mode Puffermodus
caching mode Puffermodus
calculate berechnen, disponieren, errechnen, rechnen
calculating control module-identification Rechensteuerbaustein-Kennung
calculating module Rechenbaustein, Rechenmodul
calculating module processing Rechenbausteinverarbeitung, Rechenmodulverarbeitung
calculating speed Rechengeschwindigkeit
calculation Berechnung, Ermittlung, Errechnung, Findung, Rechenoperation
calculation error Rechenfehler
calculation factor Rechenfaktor
calculation method Rechenart
calculation of amortization Abschreibungsberechnung
calculation of charges Gebührenberechnung
calculation of depreciation Abschreibungsberechnung
calculation of insurance value Versicherungswertermittlung
calculation procedure Rechenverfahren
calculation specification Rechenvorschrift
calculator Rechenmaschine, Rechner, Taschenrechner, Tischrechner
calendar date Kalenderdatum, Kalendertag
calendar month Kalendermonat
calendar week Kalenderwoche
calibrate eichen, kalibrieren
calibration position Kalibrierstellung
call Abruf, Aufruf, abrufen, anrufen, ansteuern, anwählen, aufrufen, benennen, rufen
call acceptance Rufannahme
call accepted Rufannahme
call attempt Verbindungsversuch
call clearing Verbindungsabbau
call collision Rufzusammenstoß, Zusammenstoß von Verbindungswünschen
call confirmation Anrufbestätigung
call-connected signal Verbunden-Signal
call control procedure Verbindungssteuerungsverfahren
call criterion Abrufkriterium
call duration Verbindungsdauer
called address Adresse der gerufenen Station, gerufene Adresse
called line identification Anschlußkennung gerufene Station
called off abgerufen
called station gerufene Station
called up abgerufen, aufgerufen
call for anfragen
call for application program Anwendungsprogramm-Aufruf
calling address Adresse der rufenden Station, Aufrufadresse, rufende Adresse
calling command Abrufkommando
calling DTE address Quelladresse
calling identifier Aufrufkennzeichen
calling line identification Anschlußkennung der rufenden Station
calling mechanism Aufrufmechanismus
calling sequence Aufruf-Reihenfolge
calling signal Anrufsignal
calling station rufende Station
call length Aufruflänge
call not accepted Ruf abgewiesen, Rufabweisung
call number Rufnummer
call-off Abrufauftrag, Bestellabruf
call-off date Abrufdatum
call-off documentation Abrufdokumentation
call-off number Abrufnummer
call-off values Abrufwerte
call progress signal Dienstsignal
call rejected Ruf abgewiesen
call rejection Rufabweisung
call set up Verbindungsaufbau
call up aufrufen
call user data Benutzerangaben, Benutzerdaten

43

camera tube Bildaufnahmeröhre
cam switch Nockenschalter
cancel Abbruch, Operation zurücknehmen, abbrechen, absagen, annullieren, löschen, stornieren, zurücknehmen
cancel a program Programm abbrechen
cancellation Absage, Rückgängigmachung, Storno, Widerruf
cancellation credit note Stornorechnungsgutschrift
cancellation flag Rücknahmekennzeichen
cancellation notice Absageschreiben, Absageschreibung
cancel line Zeile löschen
cancel mode Zurücknahme-Modus
cancel symbol Rücknahmezeichen
cancel the operation Operation zurücknehmen
cancel transmission Übertragung abbrechen
canned messages aufrufbare Nachrichten
canned test message abgespeicherte Testmeldung
can variable Kannvariable
capabilities Leistung
capability Fähigkeit
capable fähig
capable of an emergency run notlauffähig
capacitor Kondensator
capacitor bank Kondensatorblock
capacitor charger Kondensatorladegerät
capacitor paper Kondensatorpapier
capacity Auslastung, Fassungsvermögen, Kapazität, Speicherkapazität
capacity calculation Kapazitätsberechnung
capacity parameter Kapazitätsparameter
cap-and-pin insulator mehrteiliger Hängeisolator
capital freeze Kapitalbindung
capitalization Großschreibung
capital letter Großbuchstabe
capitals lock Dauerumschaltung auf Großbuchstaben
caps lock Dauerumschaltung auf Großbuchstaben
capstan Antriebswelle
captive eingeschränkt
captive account eingeschränktes Benutzerkonto
captive screw Sicherungsschraube
carbon Kohle
carbon copy Durchschlag
carbon resistor Kohlewiderstand
carcinotron Rückwärtswellenröhre
card Karte, Transportsicherung
cardboard Karton, Pappe, Transportsicherung

cardboard retainer Transportsicherung
cardboard slip case Transportsicherungskarton
card cage Kartenbehälter, Kartenmagazin
card cage door Klappe des Kartenmagazins
card case Kartenmagazin
card case door Klappe des Kartenmagazins
card controlled vorlaufkartengesteuert
card edge socket Kartensockel, Kartenstecker
card file Lochkartendatei
card format Kartenformat
card holder Kartenhalter
card input Karteneingabe
cardioid Herzkurve
card jam Kartensalat, Kartenstau
card output Kartenausgabe
card pattern Kartenaufbau
card punch Kartenlocher, Kartenstanzer
card puncher Lochkartenstanzer
card reader Kartenleser, Lochkartenleser
cards per minute Karten pro Minute
cards per second Karten pro Sekunde
card start address Kartenstartadresse
card support bracket Kartenführung
card type Kartenart
care Betreuung, betreuen, kümmern
caret letter Auslassungszeichen, Einschaltzeichen
C-arm C-Bogen, Fahrbogen
carriage Druckwagen, Kopfträger, Spedition
carriage control Vorschubsteuerung
carriage release lever Wagenlöser
carriage restraint card Transportsicherungskarte
carriage return Schreibkopfrücklauf, Wagenrücklauf
carriage return command Wagenrücklaufkommando
carriage return key CR-Taste, Returntaste, Wagenrücklauftaste
carrier Empfangssignalpegel, Frachtlieferant, Netzbetreiber, Netzwerkbetreiber, Spediteur, Träger, Trägersignal
carrier number Spediteurslieferantennummer
carrier's invoice Spediteursrechnung
carrier's note Spediteurnotiz
carry Übertrag
carry bit Übertragsbit
carry forward vortragen
carry forward account Vortragskonto
carry forward month Vortragsmonat
carry forward posting Vortragsbuchung
carrying handle Tragegriff

carry out durchführen, erfolgen, unternehmen, vollziehen, vornehmen
carry register Übertragsregister
cartesian coordinate system karthesisches Koordinatensystem
carton Karton, Kiste
cartridge Farbband, Kassette
cartridge disk unit Plattenkassetteneinheit
cartridge drive assembly Cartridge-Laufwerk
cartridge file Cartridge-Datei
cartridge fuse-link Sicherungspatrone
cascading Kaskadieren
cascading timer mehrstufiges Zeitglied
case Fall, Groß-/Kleinschreibung, Schachtel
case of error Fehlerfall
case of optimization Optimierungsfall
case of system crash Systemabsturzfall
cash Finanzmittel, Geld
cash dispensing Geldauszahlung
cash dividends declared beschlossene Bardividende auf Stammaktien
cash flow Geldfluß
cashless unbar
cash register Registrierkasse
cash sale Barverkauf
cash sorter Geldvereinzeler
cash totals field Kassensummen-Feld
cash transaction Geldbewegung
cash voucher Kassenbeleg
cassette Kassette, Kompaktkassette
cassette deck Kassettenlaufwerk
cassette magnetic tape Magnetbandkassette
cassette tape Bandkassette
cassette tape recorder Kassettenrecorder
cassette tape unit Bandkassetteneinheit
cast into integer umwandeln in Ganzzahl
catalog Katalog, Verzeichnis, katalogisieren, verzeichnen
catalog content Kataloginhalt, Verzeichnisinhalt
cataloged file katalogisierte Datei, permanente Datei, verzeichnete Datei
catalog effective katalogwirksam, verzeichniswirksam
catalog entry Katalogeintrag, Verzeichniseintrag
catalog facility Katalogisierungsfunktion, Verzeichnisfunktion
catalog indicator Kataloganzeige, Verzeichnisanzeige
catalog manipulation program Katalogbearbeitungsprogramm, Verzeichnisbearbeitungsprogramm
catalog manipulation routine Katalogbearbeitungsroutine, Verzeichnisbearbeitungsroutine
catalog manipulation utility Katalogbearbeitungsprogramm
catalog selection Katalogauswahl, Verzeichnisauswahl
categorization Klasseneinteilung
categorize aufteilen, auseinandergesteuert, einteilen, in Klassen einteilen
category Kategorie, Klasse
category number Klassennummer
category text Klassentext
cathedral window segmentiertes Fenster
cathode Kathode
cathode follower Kathodenverstärker
cathode ray tube Bildröhre, Bildschirm, Braunsche Röhre, Kathodenstrahlröhre
cathode ray unit display Bildschirm
caught up eingeholt
cause Anlaß, Ursache, bewirken, hervorrufen, veranlassen, verursachen, wirken
caution Achtung, Warnung
caution label Warnaufkleber
cell Feld, Zelle
cell cursor Feldcursor, Feldzeiger, Zellencursor
cell pointer Feldcursor, Feldzeiger, Zellencursor
celsius Celsius
center Zentrum, zentrieren
centering mark Zentriermarke
central zentral
central cabinet Zentralschrank
central computer complex zentraler Computerkomplex
central contract Zentralkontrakt
central group Zentralkomplex
centralized control Zentralsteuerung
centralized data processing zentralisierte Datenverarbeitung
central memory Hauptspeicher
central peripheral Zentralperipherie
central processing element Prozessorelement
central processing system Zentralsystem
central processing unit CPU, Prozessor, Zentraleinheit
central processor Hauptrechner, Verarbeitungsprozessor, Zentralprozessor
central processor features Leistungsmerkmale des Zentralrechners
central processor module Rechenprozessor
central repair facility zentraler Reparaturstützpunkt

central repair service

central repair service zentraler Reparaturdienst
central site Zentralsystem
ceramic keramisch
ceramic capacitor Keramikkondensator
certain sicher, bestimmt
certificate of origin Herkunftszertifikat, Herkunftszeugnis
chad Stanzabfall
chad chute Stanzabfallschacht
chain Kette, ketten
chain data verkettete Daten
chain duplicate field Formatwechsel-Duplizierfeld
chained file gekettete Datei
chain error Kettfehler
chain field Kettfeld
chain header Kettanker
chaining Verkettung, verketten
chaining address Verkettungs-Adresse
chaining error Verkettungsfehler
chaining field Kettungsfeld
chaining field indicator Kettungsfeld-Bezugszahl
chaining file kettende Datei
chaining indicator Kettungsanzeige, Kettungsbezugszahl
chaining structure Verweisstruktur
chain mode startup Kettenmodus-Jobstart
chain of errors Fehlerkette
chain pointer word Verkettungsadreßwort
chain printer Kettendrucker
challenge fordern, herausfordern
chance Wahrscheinlichkeit, Zufall
change Veränderung, auswechseln, umstellen, verändern, wechseln, ändern
change acknowledgement Änderungsbestätigung
change back Rückänderung
change bar Änderungskennzeichen
change characteristics Einstellungen ändern
change keyboard Ändern der Tastatur
change marker Änderungshinweise
change message Änderungsmitteilung
change mode Zeichenmodus
change note Änderungsvormerkung
change of accounting area Buchungskreiswechsel
change of date Datumsänderung, Terminänderung
change of demand Nachfrageschwankung
change of sign Zeichenwechsel
change of status Statusänderung
change of year Jahreswechsel

changeover Umstellung
changeover date Umstellungsdatum, Übergangsdatum
changeover terminal Wechselklemme
changeover year Umstellungsjahr
change posting Änderungsschreibung
change sign Vorzeichenwechsel
change storage diode Speicher-Schaltdiode
change string Änderungsfolge
change voucher Änderungsbeleg
change voucher number Änderungsbelegnummer
changing record key length Satzlänge verändern, Schlüssellänge verändern
channel Kanal, Übertragungskanal
channel address word Kanaladreßwort
channel command word Kanalbefehlswort
channel connection Kanalverbindung
channel control routine Kanalsteuerroutine
channel descriptor table Kanalbeschreibungstabelle
channel device identifier physische Geräteadresse
channel divider Kanalteiler
channel loading Kanalbelegung
channel module Kanalmodul
channel number Kanalnummer
channel numbering scheme Kanalnummernraum
channel select register Kanalauswahlregister
channel spacing Kanalabstand
channel splitter Kanalteiler
channel status word Kanalstatuswort, Kanalzustandswort
channel switch Kanalschalter
channel to channel Kanal zu Kanal
chapter Kapitel
character Stelle, Zeichen
character advance key Taste »Zeichen vorwärts«
character alignment Zeichenausrichtung
character attribute Zeichenattribut
character attribute byte Zeichenattributbyte
character backspace key Taste »Zeichen rückwärts«
character based zeichenorientiert
character bit Zeichenbit
character buffer Zeichenpuffer
character by character zeichenweise
character code Zeichencode, Zeichensatz
character coding Zeichenverschlüsselung
character dualing code Zeichenaustauschcode
character duration Zeichendauer

character editing Editieren im Zeichenmodus
character error rate tester Zeichenfehlerratentester
character expand Sperrschrifteinsteller
character feature Zeichenformat
character field Zeichenfeld
character fill Speicherauffüllung
character generator Zeichengenerator
character indication Textanzeige
characteristic charakteristisch, typisch
characteristics Kenndaten
characterize charakterisieren
character lines Zeichenreihen, Zeichenzeilen
character memory Zeichenspeicher
character mismatch Codeungleichheit, Druckzeichenungleichheit, abweichende Zeichen
character mode Zeichenmodus, zeichenorientiert
character output Zeichenausgabe
character output field Zeichenausgabefeld
character pitch Schreibdichte, Zeichenabstand
character position Zeichenposition
character printer Zeichendrucker
character rate Zeichengeschwindigkeit
character reader Klarschriftleser
character recognition Schriftenerkennung, Schrifterkennung, Zeichenerkennung
character recognition equipment Einrichtung zur Zeichenerkennung
character repertoire Zeichenvorrat
character representation Zeichendarstellung
character row Zeichenspalte
character scope Zeichenumfang
character sequence Zeichenfolge
character set Zeichensatz, Zeichenvorrat
character set utilities diskette Zeichensatzdienstdiskette
character signal Zeichensignal
character size Zeichengröße
characters per hour Zeichen pro Stunde
characters per inch Zeichen pro Zoll
characters per line Zeichen pro Zeile
characters per second Zeichen pro Sekunde
character stop key Zeichenstoptaste
character string Zeichenfolge, Zeichenkette
character subset Zeichenuntergruppe
character template Zeichenschablone
character transfer mode Zeichenübertragung
character transmission Übertragung von Zeichen
character value Zeichenwert
chararcter oriented zeichenorientiert

charge Gebühr, berechnen, buchen, zuschreiben
charge pattern Ladungsbild
charger Ladegerät
charge request Belastungsanforderung
charges Belastungen
charging information Gebührenzuschrift
chart Bild, Diagramm, Grafik
chart design Bildgestaltung
chart group Bildgruppe
chart of accounts Kontenplan
chassis Chassis, Grundplatte, Grundrahmen, Rahmen
check Kontrolle, Prüfung, Test, kontrollieren, nachprüfen, prüfen, testen, verifizieren, überprüfen, Überprüfung
check bit Bit prüfen, Prüfbit
checkbox program Basisprogramm
checkbox programming Basisprogrammierung
check control card Steuerkarte für Folgekontrolle
check digit Prüfzeichen, Prüfziffer
check for completeness Vollständigkeitsprüfung
checking routine Prüfprogramm
checking rule Prüfvorschrift
check instruction Prüfungsanweisung
check interval Kontrollintervall
check interval level Kontrollintervallebene
check list Kontrolliste
check mode Kontrollmodus, Prüfmodus
check module Kontrollmodul, Prüfmodul
check number Kontrollziffer, Prüfziffer
check off counter Abstimmzähler
check off table Prüftabelle
check of the segment type Segmenttypprüfung
checkout Abfertigung am Kassenplatz, Austesten, Überprüfung
checkout procedure Selbstdiagnose
check parity Paritätsprüfung
checkpoint Prüfpunkt, auslagern
checkpoint file Prüfpunktdatei
checkpointing Kontrollpunktverfahren
check purpose Kontrollzweck
check routine Prüfroutine
check state Status abfragen
checksum Kontrollsumme, Prüfsumme
checksum error Kontrollsummenfehler
checksum organization Kontrollsummenverwaltung
checksum register Prüfsummenregister, Quersummenregister
check text Prüftext
check total Prüfsumme

check total error Prüfsummenfehler
check total formation Prüfsummenbildung
chemical chemisch
chemical laser chemischer Laser
chemical variable control chemische Steuerung
chemics Chemie
cheque Scheck
cheque front side Scheckvorderseite
cheque payment Scheckzahlung
chief accountant Buchhaltungsleiter
chief executive officer Vorstandsvorsitzender
chip Chip, Halbleiterkristall
chipboard Spanplatte
chip enable Chip-Freigabe
chip select Chip-Auswahl
choice Auswahlmöglichkeit, Wahl
choose auswählen, selektieren, wählen
choosing the function Wahl der Funktion
chopper Zerhacker
chopper circuit Zerhackerschaltung
chosen line gewählte Zeile
chronological chronologisch, zeitgleich, zeitlich
chute Einzug
chute cover Schachtverschluß
chute number Schachtnummer
circle Kreis
circle of people Personenkreis
circuit Schaltkreis
circuit block Schaltungsblock
circuit board Leiterplatte, Platine, Schaltkreisplatine
circuit branch Schaltungsverzweigung
circuit breaker Auslösemechanismus, Leitungsschalter, Leitungsschutzschalter, Sicherungsautomat, Unterbrecher
circuit breaker component Teil eines Leistungsschalters
circuit card gedruckte Schaltung
circuit element Schaltungselement
circuit network Schaltungsnetzwerk
circuit property Eigenschaft der Schaltung
circuit switched network Netz mit Leitungsvermittlung, leitungsvermitteltes Netz
circuit switched service Datex-L
circuit switched sevice Leitungsvermittlung
circuit switching Leitungsvermittlung, Wählbetrieb
circuit theory Schaltungstheorie
circular kreisförmig, zyklisch
circular file cabinet Rundablage
circular interpolation Kreisinterpolation

circulating memory Umlaufspeicher
circumvent umgehen
cite anführen, zitieren
claim Anspruch, Beanstandung, Forderung, beanspruchen, behaupten
clamp Klemme, Schelle
clarification Klärung
clarify klären, verdeutlichen
class Klasse
classical klassisch
classification Einteilung, Gliederung, Klassenkennzeichnung, Klassifikation, Klassifizierung
classification keyboard Fachwählertastenfeld
classification point Gliederungspunkt, Klassifizierungspunkt
classification principle Gliederungsprinzip
classification scheme Gliederungsschema
classification table Tabellenwert
classifier Gliederungsschlüssel, Klassifikationsmerkmal, Klassifizierungsmerkmal
classify einreihen, klassifizieren
classifying scheme Klassifizierungsschema
class of data signaling rates Geschwindigkeitsklasse
clause Klausel, Satzglied, Satzteil
clean sauber
cleaner Reinigungsmittel
cleaning up measures Bereinigungsmaßnahmen
clean up bereinigen, säubern
cleanup routine Löschroutine
clear auslösen, durchsichtig, klar, klären, löschen, rein
clear all alles löschen
clearance Berechtigung, Sicherheitsüberprüfung
clearance level Berechtigungsstufe
clear bit Bit löschen
clear confirmation Auslösebestätigung
clear entry Eingabe löschen
clear entry key Eingabelöschtaste
clear indication Auslösemeldung
clear indicator Ausräumzeiger, Löschkennzeichen
clearing Auslösung
clearing account Verrechnungskonto
clearing breakpoints Programmstops entfernen
clearing items Verrechnungspositionen
clearing payment Zahlungsausgleich
clearing phase and quiescent states Freischalten (bei Leitungsvermittlung)
clear input key Eingabelöschtaste
clear instruction Löschbefehl
clear key Lösch-Taste, Tabulator-Gesamtlöschtaste

clear memory Löschen des Speichers
clear out löschen, räumen
clear out logic Räumlogik
clear out period Räumperiode
clear plastic cover durchsichtiger Plastikdeckel
clear request Auslöseanforderung
clear screen Bildschirm löschen, Rücksetzfunktion
clear storage key Speicherlöschtaste
clear switch Grundstellungsschalter
clear tab Tabulator löschen
clear text Klartext
clear to send Sendebereitschaft, sendebereit
clear to send indicator Anzeige »Bereit zum Übertragen«
clear to x überschreiben mit x
clear without memory löschen ohne Speicher
click Klick, klicken
clicking sound klickendes Geräusch
client Abnehmer, Auftraggeber, Kunde
client slot Kundenfach
clip Clip
clipboard Zwischenspeicher
clobber zerstören
clock Takt, Takt, Taktgeber, Uhr, Zeitgeber
clock accuracy Taktgenauigkeit
clock calendar Uhr und Kalender
clock chip trimmer Trimmer des Taktgenerators
clock frequency Taktfrequenz
clock generator Taktgenerator
clock rate Takt, Taktgeberrate
clockwise im Uhrzeigersinn
clockwise rotation Drehung im Uhrzeigersinn
close abschließen, auflösen, schließen
closed shop (operation) Auftragsbetrieb
closed user group Teilnehmerbetriebsklasse, geschlossene Benutzergruppe, geschlossene Teilnehmerbetriebsklasse
close error Fehler beim Schließen einer Datei
closely defined work area Arbeitsbereichssegment
close off item Abschlußposten
close of posting Buchungsschluß
closing Abschluß, Auflösung
closing an account Kontoauflösung
closing date Abschlußtermin
closing entry Abschlußbuchung
closing text Abschlußtext
clue Hinweis
cluster Cluster, Funktionseinheitengruppe, Gruppe
cluster computer Verbundrechner

cluster controller Stationsrechner
clutter Stördaten
coarse grob
coarse control Grobeinsteller
coaxial koaxial
coaxial cable Koaxialkabel
coaxial filter Koaxialfilter
coaxial line Koaxialkabel
COBOL program Cobol-Programm
co-channel Zweitkanal
code Chiffre, Code, Leitzahl, Schlüssel, chiffrieren, codieren, verschlüsseln
code block Codebereich
codec Codec
code conversion Codeumwandlung
code converter Codeumsetzer, Codeumwandler
code creation Codeerzeugung
coded character set kodierter Zeichensatz
code digit Kennziffer
coded plug kodierter Stecker
coded representation kodierte Darstellung
code edit listing Zielcodeliste
code extension Codeerweiterung
code extension character Codesteuerzeichen, Zeichen zur Codeerweiterung
code for system start-up System-Anlaufschlüssel
code independent data communication codeunabhängige Datenübermittlung
code independent transmission codeunabhängige Übertragung
code intensive codeaufwendig
code number Kennzahl
code output error Codeausgabefehler
code output field Codeausgabefeld
code segment Codesegment
code sharing operation Codesharing-Bearbeitung
code specification Codeangabe
code transparent data communication codetransparente Datenübermittlung
coding Kodierung, Verschlüsselung
coding diagram Kodierdiagramm
coding error Kodierfehler
coding example Kodierbeispiel
coding line handling Kodierzeilen-Bearbeitung
coding possibility Kodiermöglichkeit
coding programming Kodeprogrammierung
coding sheet Kodierformular
coding table Kodiertabelle
coil Spirale, Spule
coiled cord Spiralkabel
coincide zusammenfallen

49

coincidence Zufall
coincidence circuit UND-Schaltung
coincidental zufällig
coincident current memory Koinzidenzspeicher
coincident current selection Koinzidenzprinzip
cold kalt
cold cathode Kaltkathode
cold cathode tube Kaltkathodenröhre
cold start Initialisierungsstart
collapse zusammenbrechen
collate mischen mit gleichzeitigem Trennen
collation pass Mischlauf
collation sequence Sortierfolge
collection Inkasso, Sammlung
collection fee Inkassogebühr
collective bank remittance Banksammler
collective posting Sammelbuchen
collision protection Kollisionsschutz
collosion switch Kollisionsschalter
color Farbe
color burst signal Farberkennungssignal
color code Farbcode
color graphics Farbgrafik, Farbgrafik
color graphics adapter Farbgrafikkarte
color graphics monitor adapter Farbgrafik-Bildschirmadapter
color map mode Farbstufenmodus
color mode Farbmodus
color monitor Farbbildschirm
color select register Farbauswahlregister
color set Farbsatz
column Kolonne, Spalte
column binary card data format Binärkartencode
column content Spalteninhalt
column cut out contact Spaltenausschaltkontakt
column heading Spaltenüberschrift, Überschriftspalte
column indicating device Spaltenanzeigeeinrichtung
column mode Spaltenmodus
column number Spaltennummer
column of numbers Zahlenreihe
column selection Spaltenwahl
column skip key Spaltenüberspringtaste
column spacing Schreibstellenabstand
columns per inch Spalten pro Zoll
column splitting Spaltenaufteilung
column width Spaltenbreite, Spaltenstand
columnwise spaltenweise
combination Kombination, Zusammenspiel

combinational circuit Kombinationsschaltung
combinational logic kombinatorische Logikschaltung
combination of key words Schlagwortkombination
combine kombinieren, zusammenlaufen
combined file kombinierte Datei
combined station Hybridstation
combining invoices Fakturazusammenführung
come in eingehend
come up anfallen
coming into force Inkrafttreten
comm Kommunikation
comma Komma
command Befehl, Kommando
command communication Befehlsverkehr
command complement Befehlsergänzung, Kommandoergänzung
command control block Befehlssteuerblock
command execution Befehlsausführung, Kommandoausführung
command extension Befehlserweiterung, Kommandoerweiterung
command field Befehlsfeld, Kommandofeld
command file Befehlsdatei, Kommandodatei
command input Befehlseingabe, Kommandoeingabe
command interpreter Befehlsinterpreter, Kommandointerpreter
command key Befehlstaste, Kommandotaste
command keyword Befehlsschlüsselwort, Kommandoschlüsselwort
command language Befehlssprache, Kommandosprache
command language interpreter Befehlsinterpreter, Kommandointerpreter
command level Befehlsebene, Kommandoebene
command line Befehlszeile, Kommandozeile
command line form Befehlszeilenform, Kommandozeilenform
command mode Kommandomodus
command modifier Befehlsergänzung, Kommandoergänzung
command option Befehlsoption, Befehlszusatz, Kommandooption, Kommandozusatz
command parameter Kommandoergänzung, Kommandozusatz
command procedure Befehlsprozedur, Kommandoprozedur
command processing Befehlsbehandlung, Kommandobehandlung
command processor Befehlsprozessor, Kommandoprozessor

command qualifier Befehlsqualifizierer, Kommandoqualifizierer
command record Befehlssatz, Kommandosatz
command reject Befehlsrückweisung, Kommandorückweisung
command search path Kommandosuchpfad, Suchpfad für Kommandointerpreter
command sequence Befehlsfolge, Kommandofolge
command set Befehlssatz
command tail Kommandozusatz
command word Befehlswort, Kommandowort
comment Anmerkung, Erläuterung, Kommentar, kommentieren
commentary Kommentar
comment card Kommentarkarte
comment control command Kommentarsteuerkommando
commented kommentiert
comment field Kommentarfeld
comment line Kommentarzeile
comments Kommentar, Kommentarkennzeichnung
commerce Handel
commercial at Klammeraffe (@), je, à
commercial balance sheet Handelsbilanz
commercial instruction set kommerzieller Befehlssatz
commercial law Handelsrecht, handelsrechtlich
commercial system konventionelle Computersysteme
commission Provision, Provisionsabrechnung
commissioned goods index Kommissionierindex
commissioned goods list Kommissionierliste
commissioning Kommissionierung
commissioning documents Kommissionierunterlagen
commodities Handelswaren
common gemeinsam, gemeinsam benutzbar, gemeinsamer Bereich
common carrier öffentlicher Nachrichtenübermittler, öffentlicher Netzbetreiber
common carrier switch Telefonschalter
common code element gemeinsames Datenmanagement-Code-Element
common collector connection gemeinsamer Kollektor
common cross-reference table allgemeine Querverweistabelle
common data dictionary gemeinsames Datenverzeichnis

common data interface gemeinsame Datenschnittstelle
common event flag cluster Gruppe gemeinsamer Ereignismarkierung
common field gemeinsam benutzbares Feld
common lock gemeinsame Sperre
common process gemeinsamer Prozeß
common processing gemeinsame Bearbeitung
common return Nulleiter, Rückleiter
common storage Zentralspeicher
common voltage gemeinsame Spannung
common wire Nulleiter
communicate kommunizieren, verkehren
communication Datenübertragung, Kommunikation
communication adapter Datenübertragungsanschlußeinheit
communication area Kommunikationsbereich
communication cable Fernmeldekabel
communication computer Kommunikationsrechner
communication control Übertragungssicherungs-Verfahren
communication control area Datenübertragungssteuerbereich
communication controller Übertragungsablauf-Steuerung
communication control procedure Datenübertragungssteuerverfahren
communication control record Programm zur Steuerung von Datenübertragungsgeräten
communication control unit Fernbetriebseinheit
communication file Mitteilungsdatei
communication function Kommunikationsfunktion
communication interface Nachrichtenschnittstelle
communication line Fernmeldeleitung, Kommunikationsverbindung
communication line speed Übertragungsgeschwindigkeit
communication link Fernmeldeverbindung, Übertragungsstrecke
communication mode Kommunikationsmodus
communication multiplexer controller Datenübertragungssteuereinheit
communication output printer Kopiendrucker
communication paragraph Kommunikationsabschnitt
communication partner Kommunikationspartner

communication port Datenübertragungsanschluß, Kommunikationsanschluß
communication procedure Kommunikationsverfahren
communication process Kommunikationsprozeß
communication rate Datenübertragungsgeschwindigkeit
communication relation Kommunikationsbeziehung
communications adapter Kommunikationsschnittstelle
communications adapter cable Übertragungsadapterkabel
communications adapter channel Datenübertragungsanschlußkanal
communications area Verständigungsgebiet
communications connector Kommunikationsanschluß
communications control Übertragungsablauf-Steuerung
communications input/output control system physikalisches Ein-/Ausgabesteuersystem für Datenübertragung
communications intelligence channel Datenübertragungskanal
communications line adapter Datenübertragungssteuerteil
communications line interface Datenübertragungsleitung, Datenübertragungsschnittstelle
communications line terminal Datenübertragungssteuerteil
communications load module Datenübertragungslademodul
communications multiplexer subsystem Multiplexer für Datenübertragung
communications network controller Datenübertragungsnetzwerksteuerung
communication software Kommunikationssoftware
communications physical interface Kanalroutinenschnittstelle
communications port Datenübertragungsanschluß, Datenübertragungsschnittstelle
communications protocol Datenübertragungssteuerungsverfahren, Kommunikationsprotokoll
communications region Verständigungsbereich
communications setting menu Einstellung der Kommunikationsparameter
communications subsystem Untersystem für die Datenübertragung
communication state Kommunikationsstatus

communications terminal module Leitungsendgerät
communication terminal module controller Datenübertragungssteuereinheit
communication user program Datenübertragungsbenutzerprogramm
communication wiring Fernmeldeverdrahtung
community Gemeinde, Gesellschaft
commutator Stromwender, Umschalter
commutator motor Kollektormotor
commutator riser Kollektorfahne
compact gedrungen, kompakt
compact packaging große Packungsdichte
company Betrieb, Firma, Gesellschaft
company account Firmenkonto, Geschäftskonto, Gesellschafterkonto
company accounting Konzernbuchhaltung
company authorization Firmenberechtigung
company dependent firmenabhängig
company independent firmenunabhängig
company marker Firmenkennzeichen
company name Firmenbezeichnung, Firmenname
company specific firmenindividuell, firmenspezifisch
comparand Vergleichswert
comparator Komparator, Vergleicher
comparator check Prüfung durch Vergleich
compare gegenüberstellen, vergleichen
compare diskette drive Diskettenlaufwerk verifizieren
compare function Vergleichsfunktion
compare instruction Vergleichsbefehl
comparision greater than or equal Vergleichsoperator größer oder gleich
comparision less than or equal Vergleichsoperator kleiner oder gleich
comparision not equal Vergleichsoperator ungleich
comparison balance Vergleichssaldo
comparison check Prüfung durch Vergleich
comparison criterion Vergleichskriterium
comparison disagreement ungleiches Vergleichsergebnis
comparison equal Vergleichsoperator gleich
comparison figures Vergleichswerte
comparison greater than Vergleichsoperator größer als
comparison less than Vergleichsoperator kleiner als
comparison month Vergleichsmonat
comparison operator Vergleichsoperator

comparison period Vergleichsperiode, Vergleichszeitraum
comparison type Vergleichstyp
comparison value Vergleichsgröße, Vergleichswert
comparison year Vergleichsjahr
compartmentation Abgeschlossenheit
compass Kompaß
compass adjustment Kompaßeinstellung
compatibility Kompatibilität, Verträglichkeit
compatible kompatibel, vereinbar, verträglich
compatible with data processing datenverarbeitungsgerecht
compensation amount mask Entgeltbetrag-Maske
compete konkurrieren
competition Konkurrenz
competitor Konkurrent
compilation Kompilierung, Übersetzung
compilation mode Kompilierungsmodus
compilation time table Kompilierungszeittabelle
compile kompilieren, umwandeln, übersetzen
compiler Compiler, Kompilierer, Übersetzer
compiler advantages Vorteile von Kompilierern
compiler-assembler Vergleich: Compiler-Assembler
compiler directing statement Übersetzungsanweisung
compiler level languages Compilersprachen
compile time table Kompilierungszeittabelle
compiling program Compiler, Übersetzungsprogramm
compiling the source code kompilieren des Quellcodes
complement Komplement
complementing Komplementbildung
complete ergänzen, erledigen, komplett, vervollständigen, voll, vollständig
complete base quantity Gesamtbasismenge
complete delivery note Gesamtlieferschein
complete display Gesamtanzeige
complete freight Gesamtfracht
complete inventory Gesamtbestand
complete letter Ganzbrief
completeness field Vollständigkeitsfeld
complete operation vollständige Operation
complete order value Gesamtauftragswert
complete read/write cycle vollständiger Lese-/Schreibzyklus
complete run Gesamtlauf
complete sales order Gesamtauftrag
complete text Gesamttext

complete voucher Gesamtbeleg
completion Abschluß, Ergänzung, Erledigung, Fertigstellung
completion date Endtermin
completion flag Erledigungskennzeichen, Erledigungsmerkmal
completion notice Vollzugsmeldung
completion status Abschlußstatus
completion time Beendigungszeit, Endezeit
complex Komplex, komplex
complicated kompliziert
component Bauelement, Baugruppe, Baustein, Bauteil, Bestandteil, Funktionseinheit, Komponente, Teil
component acquisition Komponentenerfassung
component counter Kettsatzzähler
component item number Materialkomponente
component of a parts list Stücklistenkomponente
component record Komponentensatz
component selection character Gerätesteuerzeichen
component sequence number Stücklistenposition
compose kombinieren, zusammensetzen
compose character Kombizeichen, Sonderzeichen, zusammengesetztes Zeichen
compose character facility Funktion »Kombizeichen«
compose sequence Kombizeichensequenz
composite characters Zeichenkombinationen
composite color generator Generator für zusammengesetztes Farbsignal
composite electric machine elektrische Verbundmaschine
composite video Farbmischanzeige, Videoverbundsignal
composition Zusammenstellung
composition resistor Massewiderstand
compound Verbund
compound asset Sammelanlage
compound condition verknüpfte Bedingung
compound growth Aufzinsung
compound layers Ebenenverbund
compound letter Koppelbrief
compound range zusammengesetzter Bereich
compound sealing Dichtungsmasse
compress komprimieren, verdichten
compressed card mode Binärmodus
compressed font schmale Zeichenbreite
compression Komprimierung
compression code Verdichtungsschlüssel
compression/expansion Verdichtung/Entzerrung

53

compression group Verdichtungsgruppe
compression of information Informationsverdichtung
comprise umfassen
compulsory zwangsweise, zwingend
compulsory posting kontierungspflichtig
computational accuracy Rechengenauigkeit
computational error Rechenfehler
computation plan Rechenschema
computer Computer, DV-Anlage, Rechenanlage, Rechner
computer aided administration rechnergestützte Verwaltung
computer aided crime Computerstraftat
computer aided design computerunterstützter Entwurf, rechnergestützter Entwurf
computer aided engineering rechnergestützter Maschinenbau
computer aided manufacturing rechnergestützte Fertigung
computer aided process planning rechnergestützte Fertigungsplanung
computer aided quality control rechnergestützte Qualitätskontrolle
computer application Rechneranwendung
computer assisted fraud Betrug mit Computerunterstützung
computer assisted learning computerunterstütztes Lernen
computer assisted management computergestütztes Management (CAM)
computer backup Computer-Ausweicheinrichtung
computer based files Dateien
computer based instruction computergesteuertes Lernprogramm
computer based learning computergestütztes Lernen, rechnergestütztes Lernen
computer center Rechenzentrum
computer circuit Rechnerschaltung
computer code Computercode
computer compatibility Rechnerkompatibilität
computer component Computerbauteil, Computerbestandteil
computer computer communication Intercomputer-Kommunikation
computer control Rechnersteuerung
computer control unit Leitwerk
computer criminality Computerkriminalität
computer dependent rechnerabhängig
computer editing Editieren mit dem Computer
computer family Rechnerfamilie
computer file Computerdatei

computer hardware Computerhardware, Hardware
computer hierarchy Rechnerhierarchie
computer integrated manufacturing rechnerintegrierte Fertigung
computer interface Rechnerschnittstelle
computerized control Rechnersteuerung
computerized navigation Rechnernavigation
computerized numerical control numerische Maschinensteuerung
computerized stock control Lagerverwaltung mittels Computer
computer mode Computermodus
computer network Computernetz, Computernetzwerk, Rechnernetzwerk
computer network protocol Protokoll für Rechnernetzwerk, Rechnerverbundprotokoll
computer network system Computernetz, Rechnernetz, Rechnerverbundsystem
computer operating system Betriebssystem, Computerbetriebssystem
computer operation Verarbeitungsart
computer oriented computerorientiert, rechnerorientiert
computer oriented language computerorientierte Sprache
computer output microfilm Computerausgabe auf Mikrofilm
computer peripheral equipment Computerperipherie
computer printer Computerdrucker, Drucker
computer program Computerprogramm
computer run Computerlauf
computer software Computersoftware
computer statement Rechenanweisung
computer storage device Computerspeichereinheit
computer system Computersystem, Rechnersystem
computer system configuration Computersystemkonfiguration
computer technology Computertechnik, Computertechnologie, Rechnertechnik
computer terminal Computerterminal
computer voice advisories Computer-Sprachauskünfte
computer word Computerwort
computing centre Rechenzentrum
computing method Rechenmethode
computing power Rechenleistung
computing procedure Rechenverfahren
computing speed Rechengeschwindigkeit
concatenate verketten

concatenate files   Dateien koppeln, Dateien verketten
concatenation   Verkettung
concatenation operator   Verkettungsoperator
conceal   verbergen
concentrate   konzentrieren
concentration of information   Informationsschwerpunkt
concentrator   Konzentrator, Zentralschrank
concentric winding   Röhrenwicklung, Zylinderwicklung
concept   Konzept
conceptual allocation   Begriffszuordnung
conceptual variant   Begriffsvariante
concern   betreffen
concerning   betreffend, hinsichtlich
conclude   abschließen, daraus schließen, folgern
conclusion of an insurance   Versicherungsabschluß
concrement   Konkrement
concrete   konkret
concrete syntax   konkrete Syntax
concurrent   parallel
concurrent development   Parallelentwicklung
concurrent inquiry system condition   Abfragesystem mit Parallelzugriff
condense   kondensieren
condensed   kompakt
condition   Bedingung, Beschaffenheit, Kondition, Voraussetzung, Zustand
conditional   bedingt, konditionell
conditional end   bedingtes Ende
conditional execution of commands   bedingte Befehlsausführung
conditional jump   bedingter Sprung
condition code   Bedingungsschlüssel, Konditionenschlüssel, Konditionsschlüssel
condition no operation   Bedingung: keine Operation
condition text   Bedingungstext
condition type   Bedingungstyp
conductor   Leiter
conduit   Kanal, Rohrtülle, Schutzrohr
conduit bushing   Rohrtülle
conference   makeln
conference call equipment   Konferenzeinrichtung
confidence test   Funktionstest
configurable   einstellbar, konfigurierbar
configurable alarm   einstellbarer Alarm
configurable batch file   konfigurierbare Stapelverarbeitungsdatei

configuration   Einstellung, Konfiguration, Konstellation
configuration dependent   konfigurationsabhängig
configuration display   Konfigurationsanzeige
configuration file   Konfigurationsdatei
configuration option   Konfigurationsmöglichkeit
configuration oriented   konfigurationsorientiert
configuration program   Einstllungsprogramm, Konfigurationsprogramm
configuration specific   konfigurationsspezifisch
configuration template   Konfigurationsschablone
configuration verification program   Konfigurationsprüfprogramm
configuration worksheet   Konfigurationsblatt
configure   einrichten, konfigurieren
confirm   bestätigen
confirmation   Bestätigung
confirmation list   Bestätigungsliste
confirmation message   Bestätigungsmeldung
confirmation of services   Leistungsbestätigung
confirmation requirement   Bestätigungspflicht
conflict avoidance   Konfliktverhinderung
conflict situation   Konfliktsituation
congestion   Stauung
conjunction   Konjunktion, Zusammenhang
connect   anschließen, verbinden, verknüpfen
connect accross   parallel schalten
connected arrangement   Verbindungsanlage
connected DELNI LAN   angeschlossenes DELNI-Netz
connected operation   angeschlossene Operation, nachfolgende Operation, zugehörige Operation
connecting cable   Anschlußkabel, Kabel, Verbindungskabel
connect in parallel   parallel schalten
connection   Anschluß, Verbindung, Verknüpfung
connection clearing   Verbindungsabbau
connection establishment   Verbindungsaufbau
connection identifier   Verbindungskennung
connectionless   verbindungslos
connection network   Verbindungsnetz
connection of information   Informationsverbindung
connection oriented   verbindungsorientiert
connection timeout   Abfallzeit
connectivity   Anbindung
connector   Anschluß, Buchse, Steckbuchse, Stecker, Steckverbindung, Übergangsstelle
connector fastener   Steckerhalterung
connector ground   Masseverbinder

55

connector panel Anschlußfeld, Anschlußtafel
connector socket Anschlußstecker
connect time Anschaltdauer, Anschaltungsdauer, Anschaltzeit
connect to umverdrahten
consecutive hintereinander
consequence Konsequenz
consequential damages mittelbarer Schaden
consider berücksichtigen, erwägen
consideration Berücksichtigung, Betrachtung, Rücksicht
consignment Konsignation
consignment contract Konsignationskontrakt
consignment filling Konsignationsauffüllung
consignment goods Konsignationsware
consignment inventory Konsignationsbestand
consignment material Konsignationsmaterial
consignment movement Konsignationsbewegung
consignment order Konsignationsbestellung
consignment record Konsignationssatz
consignment replenishment order Konsignations-Auffüllauftrag
consignment stock Konsignationsbestand
consignment stock on order Konsignations-Bestellbestand
consignment stores Konsignationslager
consignment stores inventory Konsignations-Lagerbestand
consignment valuation price Konsignations-Bewertungspreis
consignment withdrawal order Konsignations-Entnahmeauftrag
consist bestehen
consistency error Konsistenzfehler
console Bildschirmkonsole, Konsole, Konsolterminal
console cartridge Konsolkassette
console command Konsolkommando
console emulator mode Konsolemulatorbetrieb
console logging Protokollieren von Konsolnachrichten
console operation Konsolbetrieb
console printer Kopiendrucker
console processor Bedienungsplatz-Prozessor
console serial line Konsolschnittstelle
console sheet Konsolprotokoll
console subsystem Konsolsubsystem
console terminal Konsole, Konsolterminal
console typewriter Fernschreiberkonsole
console workstation Systemkonsole
consolidate konsolidieren, verdichten, zusammenführen

consolidated data management zentrales Datenmanagement
consolidation instruction Konsolidierunganweisung
consolidation of divisions Geschäftsbereichs-Konsolidierung
consolidation of items Postenzusammenführung
constant Konstante, konstant
constant current source Konstantstromquelle
constant current transformer Drosseltransformator
constant data entry key Konstanteneingabetaste
constant data input key Konstanteneingabetaste
constant type Konstantentyp
constant voltage source Konstantspannungsquelle
constituent Bestandteil
constitution Beschaffenheit
construct bauen, errichten, fertigen, konstruieren
constructional bautechnisch
construction detail Konstruktionsmerkmal
construction of data Datenaufbau
consultation Abstimmung, Rücksprache
consumable resources Einweg-Betriebsmittel
consumables Verbrauchsmaterial
consumed verbraucht
consumer oriented kundenorientiert, verbrauchsorientiert
consumer substation Verbraucherstation
consumption Verbrauch
consumption account Verbrauchskonto
consumption data Verbrauchsdaten
consumption field Verbrauchsfeld
consumption list Verbrauchsliste
consumption marker Verbrauchskennzeichen
consumption of CPU time CPU-Zeitverbrauch
consumption posting Verbrauchsbuchung
contact Ansprechpartner, Kontakt, Schaltkontakt
contactor Steuerschütz
contact pressure Kontaktauflagedruck
contact relay Relaiskontakt
contain beinhalten, enthalten, umfassen
container Behälter
container rules Behältervorschrift
contaminate kontaminieren, verunreinigen
contamination Verunreinigung
cont down herunterzählen
contention mode Konkurrenzbetrieb
contents Feldinhalt, Inhalt, Inhaltsverzeichnis

contents of file Inhalt einer Datei
contents of the constant Konstanteninhalt
context Zusammenhang
contigency Fehlerzustand
contigency program Ausnahmezustand-Behandlungsprogramm
contiguous blocks fortlaufende Blöcke, zusammenhängende Blöcke
contiguous file Datei in zusammenhängenden Bereichen
contiguous files zusammenhängende Dateien
contiguous format fortlaufendes Format
continuation Fortführung, Fortsetzung, Programmfortsetzung, Weiterlauf
continuation call Fortsetzungsaufforderung
continuation card Folgekarte
continuation character Fortsetzungszeichen
continuation line Folgezeile
continuation marker Spurumschaltmerker
continuation number Folgenummer
continuation page Folgeseite
continuation screen Folgebild, Folgebildschirm
continuation sector Folgesektor
continuation sheet Folgeblatt
continuation tape Folgeband
continuation voucher Folgebeleg
continue fortfahren, fortsetzen, weiterarbeiten, weitermachen
continued processing Weiterverarbeitung
continue search weitersuchen nach gleichen Zeichenfolgen
continue to process weiterverarbeiten
continue to work weiterarbeiten
continue to write weiterschreiben
continuity data area Übergabebereich
continuous durchlaufend, fortlaufend, kontinuierlich, lückenlos, ständig
continuous fan-fold stock Endlosformularsatz
continuous form device Endlospapiereinrichtung
continuous operation Dauerbetrieb
continuous paper Endlospapier
continuous signal Dauersignal
continuous stationery Endlospapier
continuous test Dauerlauf
continuous tone Dauerton
contra contra-, gegen-
contra account Abstimmkonto, Gegenkonto
contract Kontrakt, Vertrag
contract accounting area Kontraktbuchungskreis
contract appendix Kontraktanhang
contract call offs Kontraktabrufe

contract change Kontraktänderung
contract data Kontraktdaten
contract date Kontraktabschlußdatum, Kontraktdatum
contract duration Kontraktlaufzeit
contract form Kontraktform
contract header Kontraktkopf
contraction segment Kürzelsegment
contraction table Kürzeltabelle
contract item Kontraktposition
contract item quantity Kontraktpositionsmenge
contract item type Kontraktpositionstyp
contract item voucher number Kontraktpositionsbelegnummer
contract monitoring Kontraktüberwachung
contract number Kontraktnummer
contractor Auftragnehmer
contract processing Kontraktabwicklung
contract text Kontrakttext
contract type Kontraktart
contractual penalty Vertragsstrafe
contract value Kontraktwert, Vertragswert
contract voucher Kontraktbeleg
contract voucher number Kontraktbelegnummer
contradict widersprechen
contradiction Widerspruch
contradiction sentence Widerspruchssatz
contra item Gegenposition, Gegenposten
contra post gegenbuchen
contra posting Gegenbuchung
contrast Gegensatz, Kontrast
contrast control Kontrastregler
contravene verstoßen
contribution Beitrag
control Aussteuerung, Bedienungselement, Regelung, Steuerung, ansteuern, kontrollieren, regeln, steuern, überwachen
control action Steuerungsfunktion
control and computer technology Regelungs- und Computertechnik
control area Steuerbereich
control bit Steuerbit
control block Kontrollblock, Steuerblock
control block format Steuerblockformat
control block process Steuerblockprozeß
control break Gruppenstufenwechsel, Gruppenwechsel
control bus Steuerbus
control byte Steuerbyte
control cabinet Steuerschrank
control cable Steuerkabel, Steuerleitung

control card

control card Steuerkarte, Vorhaltekarte, Vorlaufkarte
control card check Vorlaufkartenprüfung
control card description Vorlaufkartenbeschreibung
control card format Vorlaufkartenaufbau
control card identification Vorlaufkartenkennung
control card listing Steuerkartenübersicht
control character Steuerzeichen
control character sequence Steuerzeichenfolge
control code Steuercode, Steuerschlüssel, Steuerungsschlüssel
control command Steuerkommando
control computer Kontrollrechner, Steuerrechner
control data Steuerungsdaten
control desk Bedienpult
control device Steuergerät
control display Kontrollanzeige
control equipment Steuereinrichtung
control field Gruppenbegriffsfeld, Steuerfeld
control field contents Kontrollfeld-Inhalt
control field description Kontrollfeld-Beschreibung
control field processing Kontrollfeld-Verarbeitung
control file Steuerdatei
control file input Eingabe aus einer Steuerdatei
control flag Steuermarkierung, Steuerungskennzeichen
control format Kontrollformat
control function Steuerfunktion, Steuerungsfunktion
control ground bus bar Masseschiene
control identifier Steuerkennzeichen
control image Betriebsanweisung
control indicator Gruppenstufenbezugszahl
control indicator panel Bedienfeld, Wartungsfeld
control info Steuerungsinformation
control information Kontrollinformation, Steuerinformation
control instruction Steuerbefehl
control interrupt failure Fehler in der Interrupt-Steuerung
control job Koordinierungsauftrag
control key Steuertaste
control key number Steuerschlüssel-Nummer
control knob Drehknopf
controlled gesteuert

controlled line servicing bedienungsgesteuerte Leitungen
controller Controller, Regler, Steuereinheit, Steuermodul, Steuerung
controller board Controllerkarte, Steuerplatine, Steuerung
controller error Controllerfehler, Fehler im Steuermodul
controller memory Controllerspeicher
controller module Steuermodul
control level Gruppenstufe
control level indicator Gruppenstufenbezugszahl
control lever Einstellhebel
control line Steuerleitung
control line function Signalleitung-Funktion
control list Überwachungsliste
control logic Ablauflogik
control master data Steuerungs-Stammdaten
control mechanism Steuerungsmechanismus
control memory Steuerspeicher
control memory access Speicherzugriffssteuerung
control message Übertragungssteuerzeichenfolge
control of specific variable Steuerung einer bestimmten Variable
control of variables Variablensteuerung
control of variables for reference text Betreff-Variablensteuerung
control page Steuerabschnitt
control panel Bedienungsfeld, Bedienungspult, Steuerpult
control panel for ultrasonic treatment Bedienfeld für Ultraschall
control paragraph Kontrollabschnitt
control parameter Steuerungsparameter
control processor dispatching Verteilung von Rechenzeit
control product Kontrollprodukt
control program Steuerprogramm
control program for microprocessors CP/M (Betriebssystem)
control receiver Steuerempfänger
control record Steuersatz
control register Befehlsregister, Steuerregister
control room Steuerraum, Steuerwarte
control screen Kontrollbild
control section Codeabschnitt, Steuerabschnitt
control segment Steuersegment
control sequence Steuersequenz, Steuerungsablauf
control signal Führungsgröße, Steuersignal

correcting data

control statement Betriebsanweisung, Steueranweisung, Steuerstatement, Steuerungsangaben
control station Leitstation
control status register Kontrollstatusregister
control steering logic Steuerlogik
control storage code Steuerspeichercode
control stream Eingabestrom
control string Steuerzeichenfolge
control switch Steuerschalter
control symbol Steuerzeichen
control system Regelung
control system characteristic Regelungscharakteristik
control table Steuerungstabelle
control tape Steuerband
control technology Regelungstechnik
control theory Regelungstheorie
control total Kontrollsumme
control unit Leitwerk, Regler, Steuereinheit, Steuerwerk
control unit bit array Bitfolgenfeld der Steuereinheit
control unit end Ende der Übertragung zur Steuereinheit
control unit indicator Anzeige des Steuergerätes
control unit name Steuereinheitenbezeichnung, Steuereinheitenname
control variable Steuerungsvariable
control word Steuerwort
convenience Komfort
convenience outlet Steckdose
convention Konvention
conventional herkömmlich, konventionell
conventional access Standardzugriffsmethode
conversational interaktiv
conversational application Dialoganwendung
conversational mode Dialogbetrieb
conversational processing Dialogbearbeitung
conversational reply Antwort im Dialogbetrieb
conversational time sharing Dialogsystem
conversation number Konversationsnummer
conversation operation Umkehrbetrieb
conversely gegensätzlich
conversion Konvertierung, Umrechnung, Umsetzung, Umwandlung
conversion description Konvertierungsbeschreibung
conversion discrepancy Kursdifferenz
conversion factor Umrechnungsfaktor
conversion list Umwandlungstabelle
conversion option Umrechenmöglichkeit
conversion rate Umrechnungskurs

conversion table Umwandlungstabelle
convert konvertieren, umformen, umrechnen, umsetzen, umwandeln
converter Converter, Umsetzer, Wandler
converting Umrechnung
conveyed zugeführt
conveyor belt Förderband
cool kalt, kühl, kühlen
coolant Kühlmittel
coolant motor Kühlmittelpumpe
coolant pump Kühlmittelpumpe
coolant pump at pressure Kühlmittelpumpe unter Druck
coolant reservoir Kühlmittelbehälter
coolant return Kühlmittelrücklauf
coolant spray Kältespray
cooling unit Kühlanlage
coordinate Koordinate
coordinate resolver Koordinatenlöser
coordinates Koordinaten
coordination Koordination
copper wall Kupferwand
copy Duplikat, Durchschlag, Kopie, duplizieren, kopieren
copyable kopierbar
copy function Duplizierfunktion, Kopierfunktion
copy guide Papierableiter
copy holder Blatthalter, Formularhalter
copy operation Kopiervorgang
copy program Kopierprogramm
copy protection Kopierschutz
copy run Kopierlauf
cord Anschlußschnur, Leitungsschnur
core Core, Kern, Kernspeicher
core block Core-Block
core chain Warteschlange für Hauptspeicherbelegung
core image Core-Image
core memory Hauptspeicher, Kernspeicher
core memory work load Kernspeicherauslastung
core resident Core-resident
core storage Matrixspeicher
core storage surface Kernspeicher-Seite
corona Korona
corona-discharge tube Korona-Entladungsröhre
corporation Konzern
corporation group Konzerngruppe
correct berichtigen, korrekt, korrigieren, ordnungsgemäß, richtig
correcting data Berichtigungsdaten

59

correction Berichtigung, Korrektur, Verbesserung
correction facility Korrekturmöglichkeit
correction key Korrigiertaste
correction message Korrekturmitteilung
correction mode Korrekturmodus
correction number Korrekturnummer
correction of balance carried forward Saldovortragskorrektur
correction posting Korrekturbuchungen
correction status Korrekturstatus
correction system Korrektursystem
corrective action Abhilfemaßnahmen, Korrekturmaßnahme
corrective maintenance Reparatur, Wartung zur Beseitigung von Störungen
correctness Richtigkeit
correlatable access memory assoziativ abfragbarer Speicher
correlate in Beziehung stehen, zusammengehören
correspond entsprechen, übereinstimmen
correspondence Briefverkehr, Korrespondenz, Schriftverkehr, Übereinstimmung
corresponding entsprechend
correspondingly dementsprechend
corrosive korrosiv, ätzend
corrosive agent Ätzmittel
corrupt defekt, zerstören
corruption Verstümmelung, Zerstörung
cost Kosten, Preis
cost account Kostenkonto
cost accounting Betriebsabrechnung, Kostenrechnung
cost accounting procedure Kostenrechnungsverfahren
cost accounting report Kostenstellenauswertung
cost allocation Kostenverteilung
cost allocation file AVU-Datei
cost calculation Kostenermittlung
cost category Kostenart
cost centre Kostenstelle
cost centre accounting Kostenstellenrechnung
cost centre allocation Kostenumlage
cost centre number Kostenstellenumlage
cost control Kostenkontrolle, Kostenüberwachung
cost effective lohnend
cost flow Kostenfluß
cost function Kostenfunktion
cost objective Kostenträger

cost objective accounting Kostenträgerrechnung
cost of computation Rechenaufwand
cost price Einstandspreis
cost related kostenmäßig
cost type Kostenart
count Anzahl, Zähler, Zählung, zählen
count discrepancy Zähldifferenz
counter Zähler
counter account Gegenkonto
counterclockwise gegen den Uhrzeigersinn, im Gegenuhrzeigersinn
counter posting Gegenbuchung
counter reading Zählerstand
counter tube Zählrohr
counter variable Zählervariable
counting check Zählkontrolle
counting circuit Zählschaltung
counting error Zählfehler
counting tube Zählrohr
countries Länder
country code Landesvorwahl, Länderschlüssel
country key Länderschlüssel
country kit Landespaket
country name Länderbezeichnung, Ländername
count value Anzahl, Zählwert
count voucher Zählbeleg
couple koppeln
coupled circuit Verbundschaltung
coupler Kupplung
coupling Ankoppelung, Koppelung
coupling medium Koppelmedium
coupling pressure Ankoppeldruck
course of the project Projektverlauf
co-user Mitbenutzer
co-user designation Mitbenutzer-Bezeichnung
co-user directory Mitbenutzer-Verzeichnis
cover Abdeckung, Deckel, Gehäuseabdeckung, abdecken, bedecken, reichen
coverage Abdeckung, erfaßte Menge
coverage list Reichweitenliste
coverage time Reichweite
cover enclosure Gehäuse
cover release tab Feststellhebel, Feststellhebel der Abdeckung
cover up tape Korrekturband für abdeckendes Löschen
CPU architecture CPU-Architektur
crap Schrott
crash Absturz, Systemabsturz, Zusammenbruch, zusammenbrechen

crash imprinter Formular-Nachdruckeinrichtung
create anlegen, bilden, erstellen, erzeugen
create anew neuerstellen
create function Anlegefunktion, Erstellungsfunktion
create offline offline erstellen
creating a document Erstellen eines Dokuments
creating date Erstellungsdatum
creating text erstellen von Text
creating the delivery note Lieferscheinerstellung
creating the purchase order Bestellungserzeugung
creating the voucher Belegerstellung
creation Bildung, Erstellung
creation date Erstellungsdatum
creation of batches Chargenerstellung
creation of documents Dokumentenerstellung
creation period Erstellungsperiode
creation process Erstellungsprozeß
creation report Erstellungsreport
creation time Erstellungszeit
creator Ersteller
credit Entlastung, Kredit
credit account Entlastungskonto, Habenkonto
credit balance Habensaldo
credit check Kreditkontrolle
credit control Kreditüberwachung
credit item Habenposten
credit limit Kreditgrenze
credit limit check Kreditlimitprüfung
credit marker Habenkennzeichnen
credit note Gutschrift
credit note advice Gutschriftsankündigung
credit note quantity Gutschriftsmenge
credit note total Gutschriftsumme
credit note type Gutschriftsart
credit note value Gutschriftswert
creditor list Kreditorenliste
credit period Kreditlaufzeit
credit posting Habenbuchung
credit standing Bonität
credit status report Kreditstatusbericht
credit sum Habensumme
credit symbol Habenzeichen
credit to accounts receivable Debitorenhaben
credit total Habensumme
credit utilization Kreditorenanspruchnahme
crimp quetschen
crimped connector Quetschverbinder
criteria Kriterien

criteria file Argumentdatei
criterion Argument, Kriterium
critical kritisch
critical path method Ermittlung des kritischen Weges
critical section kritischer Abschnitt
criticism Kritik
cross quer
cross assembler Crossassembler
crossassembler machine programming Maschinenprogrammierung mit Crossassembler
cross compiler Crosscompiler
cross connected querverbunden
cross connection Querverbindung
cross filing Mehrfachablegung
crossfoot Querrechnen, Quersummenregister
cross linked file querverkettete Datei
cross out ankreuzen
cross reference Cross-Referenz, Querverweis
cross reference list Cross-Referenz-Liste
cross reference listing processor Querverweisprozessor
cross reference table Querverweistabelle
cross software Cross-Software
CRT controller Bildschirmsteuerbaustein, Bildschirmsteuereinheit
CRT control port Bildschirmsteueranschluß
CRT saver Dunkelschaltung, Einbrennschutz
cryogenic storage Tieftemperaturlagerung
cryostat Kryostat
cryotron Kryotron
crystal filter Quarzfilter
crystal holder Quarzhalter
cumulate kumulieren
cumulated field kumuliertes Feld
cumulative kumulativ
curly brace geschweifte Klammer
currency Aktualität, Kursivität, Währung, Währungseinheit
currency amount Währungsbetrag
currency code Währungsschlüssel
currency conversion Kursumrechnung, Währungsschutz
currency conversion discrepancy posting Kursdifferenzenbuchung
currency date Valutadatum
currency deviation Währungsabweichung
currency discrepancy Währungsdifferenz
currency exchange rate Währungskurs
currency format Währungsformat
currency item Währungsposten
currency ratios Währungsverhältnisse
currency requirement Währungsforderung

currency sign Währungszeichen
currency symbol Währungssymbol
currency table Währungstabelle
current Strom, aktuell, augenblicklich, derzeitig, gegenwärtig, laufend
current account Kontokorrent, Kontokorrentkonto
current account balance Kontokorrentsaldo
current account liability Kontokorrentobligo
current account management Kontokorrentverwaltung
current account posting Kontokorrentbuchung
current buffer aktueller Puffer
current carrying stromführend
current carrying capacity Belastbarkeit, zulässige Stromstärke
current cell aktuelles Feld
current collecting equipment Stromabnahmegerät
current count aktueller Zählerstand
current count value aktueller Zählerstand
current date Laufdatum, Tagesdatum, aktuelles Datum
current field aktuelles Feld
current file cabinet aktuelle Ablage
current instruction register aktuelles Befehlregister
current item aktueller Text
current item field Statusfeld
current loop Stromschleife, aktuelle Schleife
current loop supply Stromschleifen-Stromquelle
current message's originator Absender der aktuellen Nachricht
current number of lines aktuelle Zeilenzahl
current page number aktuelle Seitennummer
current program aktuelles Programm
current task aktuelle Funktion, aktuelles Programm
current text size aktuelle Zeilenanzahl
current time Uhrzeit, aktuelle Uhrzeit
current transformer Stromwandler, Transformator
current value Augenblickswert, aktueller Wert
current window aktuelles Fenster
cursor Cursor, Lichtpunkt, Schreibmarke, Zeiger
cursor addressing Cursoradressierung, Cursorsteuerung, Steuerung der Schreibmarke
cursor backward Cursor rückwärts
cursor control Cursorsteuerung
cursor control key Cursortaste, Schreibmarkentaste
cursor down Cursor nach unten
cursor forward Cursor vorwärts
cursor key Cursortaste
cursor left Cursor nach links
cursor line durch Cursor markierte Zeile
cursor movement key Taste zum Bewegen des Cursors
cursor positioning Cursorpositionierung
cursor position report Meldung der Cursorposition
cursor right Cursor nach rechts
cursor style Form des Cursors
cursor up Cursor nach oben
curtail abschneiden
curve Kurve
curve difference Kurvendifferenz
curve follower Kurvenleser
customer Auftraggeber, Klient, Kunde
customer address Warenempfängeradresse
customer area Kundenbezirk
customer authorization Kundenberechtigung
customer based debitorenabhängig
customer consignment Kundenkonsignation
customer credit Kundenkredit
customer credit check Kundenkreditkontrolle
customer data Anwenderdaten, Kundendaten
customer engineer Kundendiensttechniker
customer file Kundendatei
customer group Kundengruppe
customer grouping Kundengruppierung
customer home town Warenempfängerort
customer level Kundenebene
customer master Kundenstamm
customer master list Kundenstammliste
customer master record Kundenstammsatz
customer number Kundennummer
customer order Kundenauftrag, Kundenorder
customer parts for processing Kundenbeistellung
customer postcode Warenempfängerpostleitzahl
customer priority Kundenpriorität
customer record Kundensatz
customer related kundenbezogen
customer remark Kundenvermerk
customer set up Anwendereinstellung, vom Benutzer installiert
customer specific kundenspezifisch
customer statement Kundenkontenauszug
customers' turnover Kundenumsätze
customer's address Kundenadresse
customer's currency Kundenwährung
customer's processed-out material Kundenbeistellmaterial

customization Anpassung
customize anpassen
customized kundenspezifisch
customs Zoll
customs agreement Zollvereinbarung
customs number Zollnummer
customs tariff Zolltarif
customs term Verzollungskondition
custom tariff Brauchszolltarif
cut kürzen, schneiden, zwischenspeichern
cut off Abgrenzung, abgegrenzt
cut off option Abgrenzungsmöglichkeit
cut off press appliance Abschneidevorrichtung
cut out device ausgespartes Gerät
cycle Takt, Zyklus, zyklisch durchlaufen
cycle flowchart Zyklus-Ablaufplan
cycles per second Zyklen pro Sekunde
cycle time Zykluszeit
cyclic zyklisch
cyclic code zyklische Code
cyclic concatenation Kreisverkettung
cyclic processing zyklische Bearbeitung
cyclic redundancy check zyklische Blockprüfung, zyklische Redundanzprüfung
cyclic shift Stellenwertverschiebung
cylinder Zylinder
cylinder overflow area Zylinderüberlaufbereich

D

daily täglich
daily closing Tagesabschluß
daily ledger Journal
daily report Tagesauswertung
daisy chain Hintereinanderschaltung, Ring, Ringschaltung, Verkettung
daisy wheel Typenrad
daisy wheel printer Typenraddrucker
damage Beschädigung, Schaden, beschädigen, verletzen
damage number Schadensnummer
damping dämpfen
danger Gefahr
danger of deadlock Gefahr einer Systemblockade
dangerous gefährlich
dark dunkel
darken verdunkeln
dark screen Bildschirmhintergrund dunkel
dash Strich
dashed line gestrichelte Linie
data Daten, Datum
data access security Datenzugriffssicherheit
data acquisition Datenerfassung
data address Datenadresse
data administration Datenpflege, Datenverwaltung
data administration system Datenverwaltungssystem
data alteration Datenänderung
data analysis Datenanalyse
data and control bus Daten- und Steuerbus
data and text network Daten-/Textnetz
data area Datenbereich
data area address Datenbereichsadresse
data back up Datensicherung
data back up tape Datensicherungsband
data bank component Datenbankkomponente
data bank system Datenbanksystem
data base Datenbank, Datenbasis
data base access Datenbankzugriff
data base call Datenbankaufruf
data base description Datenbankbeschreibung
data base description language Sprache zur Datenbankbeschreibung
data base descriptor Datenbankbeschreibung
data base design Datenbankentwurf
data base diagram Datenbanksteuerprogramm

data base generator Datenbankgenerator
data base interface Datenbankschnittstelle
data base key logische Adresse
data base link Datenbankverknüpfung
data base machine Datenbankrechner
data base management Datenbankmanagement
database management system Datenbanksystem
database model Datenbankmodell
data base modification Datenbankveränderung
database organisator Datenbankorganisator
data base recovery Datenbankwiederherstellung
data base segment Datenbanksegment
data base service Datenbankdienstleistung
data base situation Datenbanksituation
data base structure Datenbankstruktur
data base system Datenbanksystem
data base transaction Datenbanktransaktion
data base use Datenbankverwendung
data batch Datenstapel
data bit Datenbit
data block Datenblock
data buffer Datenpuffer
data bus Datenbus, Datenübertragungsweg
data bus line Datensammelkanal
data cable Datenkabel
data card Datenkarte
data carrier Datenträger
data carrier address Datenträgeradresse
data carrier content Datenträgerinhaltsverzeichnis
data carrier end Datenträgerende
data carrier type Datenträgeraufbau
data category Datenkategorie
data center Datenzentrum
data chaining Datenverkettung
data change voucher Datenänderungsbeleg
data channel Datenkanal
data circuit Datenverbindung
data circuit module Direktanschlußmodul
data circuit terminating equipment Datenübertragungseinrichtung, Fernschaltgerät
data code Datencode
data collection Datensammlung
data communication Datenfernübertragung, Datenübermittlung, Datenübertragung
data communication equipment Datenübertragungseinrichtung, Übertragungseinrichtung
data communication interface Datenkommunikations-Schnittstelle
data communications Datenübertragung

data communication station Datenstation für Fernübertragung
data communication system Datenübermittlungssystem
data communication transaction Datenkommunikations-Transaktion
data compression Datenverdichtung
data concentrator Datenkonzentrator
data concept Datenkonzept
data connection Datenverbindung
data control block Dateisteuerblock
data control word Datenkontrollwort
data conversion Datenkonvertierung, Datenumwandlung, Konvertierung
data conversion regulation Datenkonvertierungsvorschrift
data convertor Datenwandler
data definition language processor Datenbank-Beschreibungsprozessor
data definition processor Datendefinitionsprozessor
data delivery program Datenübergabeprogramm
data description language Datenbankbeschreibungssprache, Datenbeschreibungssprache
data dictionary Datenverzeichnis
data disk Datendiskette
data diskette Datendiskette
data division Datenteil
data element Datenelement
data encryption standard Verschlüsselungsmuster
data entry Dateneingabe, Datenerfassung, Datenneuaufnahme
data entry system Datenerfassungssystem
data exchange Datenaustausch
data exchange identifier Datenaustauschkennzeichen
data exchange tape Datenaustauschband
data field Datenfeld
data field description Datenfeldbeschreibung
data figures Datenwerte
data file Benutzerdatei, Datei, Datenbestand, Datendatei
data flow Datenfluß
data flow chart Datenablaufplan
data flow control Datenflußsteuerung
data flow diagram Daten-Flußdiagramm
data format Datenformat
data gathering Datengewinnung
datagram Datagramm
data group Datengruppe
data handling Datenverarbeitung
data handling software Datenverarbeitungsprogramme
data independence Datenunabhängigkeit
data in line Dateneingabeleitung
data input Dateneingabe
data input bus Dateneingabebus
data input/output Datenein-/ausgabe
data inquiry Dateneingabe
data instruction Datenanweisung
data integration Datenintegration
data integrity Datensicherheit
data interchange code Code für Datenaustausch
data interchange format Datenaustauschformat
data interface Datenschnittstelle
data item Datenfeld, Datum
data layout Datenformat
data length Datenlänge
data line Datenzeile
data line escape character Zeichen zum Beenden einer Datenübertragung
data link Datenübertragungsanlage, Übermittlungsabschnitt, Übertragungsstrecke
data link channel state Übertragungskanalzustand
data link connection gesicherte Systemverbindung
data link control Übertragungssicherungs-Verfahren, Übertragungssteuerung
data link control procedure Übertragungssteuerungsverfahren
data link escape character Zeichen zur Umschaltung der Datenübertragung
data link layer Sicherungsschicht
data loopback self test Selbstdiagnose Datenrücklauf
data management system Datenbanksystem, Datenverwaltungssytem
data manipulation language Datenmanipulierungssprache
data manipulation processor Datenmanipulierungsprozessor
data medium Datenträger
data medium end label Datenträgerendekennsatz
data medium exchange Datenträgeraustausch
data merging Datenverknüpfung
data mode Datenmodus
data model Datenmodell
data modification Datenveränderung
data movement Datenverschiebung
data multiplexer Datenmultiplexer
data network Datennetz

data organisation

data organisation Datenorganisation
data out line Datenausgabeleitung
data output Datenausgabe
data packet Datenpaket
data parity bit Datenparitätsbit
data parity bits feature Auswahl der Datenparitätsbits
data path Datenpfad, Datenverbindung
data pool Datenbestand, Datenpool
data pooling system Datensammelsystem
data presentation Datendarstellung
data processing Datenverarbeitung
data processing area Datenverarbeitungsraum
data processing circuit Datenverarbeitungsschaltung
data processing development Datenverarbeitungsentwicklung
data processing equipment Datenverarbeitungsanlage
data processing system Datenverarbeitungssystem, Rechensystem
data processing unit Zentraleinheit
data processing utility Datenverarbeitungs-Dienstprogramm, Datenverarbeitungs-Hilfsprogramm
data processor Textmanipulator
data processor operating time Datenverarbeitungsanlagenbetriebszeit
data processor operation Datenverarbeitungsanlagenbetrieb
data protection Datensicherung
data rate Datenrate
data record Datensatz
data record definition Datensatzdefinition
data record description Datensatzbeschreibung
data record length Datensatzlänge
data release Datenfreigabe
data release key Datenfreigabetaste
data representation Datendarstellung, Informationsdarstellung
data requirement Datenbedarf
data requirement list Datenforderungsliste
data retention Datenhaltung
data routine Dateibearbeitungsroutine
data screen Datenbild
data security Datenschutz, Datensicherheit
data segment Datenteil
data sensitive fault datenabhängige Störung
data set Datensatz, Modem
data set archive Datenträgerarchiv
data set name Datensatzname
data set ready Modem bereit
data set ready off Modem nicht betriebsbereit
data sets Datenübertragungssteuerverfahren
data shift function Schiebefunktion
data shifting Datenverschiebung
data signal Datensignal
data signal concentrator Datensignalkonzentrator
data signalling rate Übertragungsgeschwindigkeit
data signal rate selector Auswahl der Übertragungsrate
data simulation Datensimulation
data sink Datenempfänger, Datensenke
data sorter Datensortiergerät
data sorting Datensortierung
data source Datenquelle
data station Datenstation
data status word Datenstatuswort
data storage position Datenspeicherplatz
data storage protection Schutz des Datenspeichers
data structure Datenstruktur
data tape Datenträgerband
data target Datenziel
data technical datentechnisch
data terminal Datenendgerät
data terminal equipment Datenendeinrichtung, Datenendgerät
data text station Daten-Text-Station
data text terminal Daten-Text-Endgerät
data transducer Datenwandler
data transfer Datentransfer, Datenübertragung, Phase der Datenübertragung
data transfer rate Übertragungsgeschwindigkeit
data transfer unit Transfereinheit
data translator Datenumsetzer
data transmission Datenübertragung, Verfahren zur Steuerung der Datenübertragung
data transmission block Datenübertragungsblock
data transmission method Datenübertragungsverfahren
data type Datentyp
data under voice Sprache über Daten
data unit control Formatsteuerung
data update Datenfortschreibung
data utilities dialog Datendienstroutinendialog
data utility Datendienstroutine
data validation Datenprüfung
data value Datenwert
data word Datenwort
date Datum, Termin
date and time Datum und Uhrzeit

date effective Gültigkeitsdatum
date for return of empties Leergutsrückgabedatum
date modified Änderungsdatum
date monitoring Terminkontrolle, Terminüberwachung
date of creation Erstellungsdatum
date of dispatch Absendedatum
date of entry Eingabedatum
date of expiry Verfalldatum
date of goods dispatch Warenausgangsdatum
date of issue Ausstellungsdatum
date of posting Buchungsdatum
date of purchase Einkaufsdatum
date separator Datumstrenner
date specified Datumsangabe
date the materials are required Materialbereitstellungsdatum
date time Datum Zeitangabe
date time of day Datum Uhrzeit
daughter company Tochtergesellschaft
day Kalendertag
daylight Tageslicht, taghell
daylock interrupt processor Zeitüberwachungsprozessor
days overdue Überfälligkeit
daytime work Tagesarbeit
day to day operation tägliche Benutzung
day's value Tageswert
DC component Gleichstromanteil
DCE call connected DÜE-Verbindung hergestellt
DCE fault condition DÜE-Störung
deactivate abschalten, deaktivieren, parken
deactivation Abschalten, Deaktivierung
deactivation date Deaktivierungsdatum
deactivation option Deaktivierungsmöglichkeit
deactivation process Deaktivierungsaktivität, Deaktivierungsvorgang
deactivation voucher Deaktivierungsbeleg
dead defekt, nicht stromführend, spannungslos
dead end Sackgasse
dead end insulator Endisolator
dead end job Datenstationsjob, Terminaljob
dead key Nulltaste, Tottaste
dead key override Tottastenausgleicher
dead letter nicht angekommene Nachricht
deadline Frist
deadline run Terminstapeljob
deadlock Stillstand, Systemblockade
deadlock recognition Deadlockerkennung
deadlock situation Deadlocksituation
dead mail nicht angekommene Nachricht
dead on arrival defekt geliefert
dead sector toter Sektor
deadtime Totzeit
deadtime compensation Totzeitkompensation
dead transmitter defekter Sender
deal befassen, behandeln
deallocate freigeben
deassign Zuordnung aufheben
debit Belastung, Soll, belasten
debit amount Lastschriftshöhe
debit balance Sollsaldo
debit entry Sollbuchung
debit header Lastschriftskopf
debit item Lastschriftsposition
debitor discount Kundenskonto
debit posting Lastschrift
debit registration Lastschrifterfassung
debit text Lastschriftstext
debit to accounts receivable Debitorensoll
debit type Lastschriftsart
debit value Lastschriftswert
debit voucher Lastschriftsbeleg
deblock entblocken
deblocking entblocken
debt Schuld
debug Fehler beheben, Fehler suchen, Fehler suchen und beheben, Testhilfe, austesten, testen
debugger Debugger, Testhilfe
debugger output Debuggerausgabe
debugging ausprüfen, austesten, Fehler suchen, Fehlerbehebung, Fehlerbeseitigung, Fehlersuche, testen
debugging aid Testhilfe
debugging feature Fehlererkennungshilfe
debugging setup Einstellung bei Fehlersuchbetrieb
debug mode Fehlererkennungshilfen, Fehlererkennungsmodus
debug monitor Testhilfe
debug program Fehlersuchprogramm
decalcified enthärtet
decatron dekadische Zählröhre
deceleration Abnahme, kangsamerwerden, Verlangsamung
decentralized dezentral
decentralized data entry dezentrale Datenerfassung
decentralized data processing dezentralisierte Datenverarbeitung
decibel Dezibel
decide entscheiden
decimal dezimal

decimal area Dezimalbereich
decimal comma Dezimalkomma
decimal constant Dezimalkonstante
decimal digit Dezimalstelle, Dezimalziffer
decimal fraction Dezimalbruchteil
decimal marker Kommamarke
decimal number Dezimalzahl
decimal place Dezimalstelle, Kommastelle
decimal point Dezimalkomma, Dezimalpunkt, Komma
decimal position Dezimalstelle
decimal symbol Dezimalzeichen
decimal system Dezimalsystem
decimal tabulator Dezimaltabulator
decimal to binary conversion Dezimal-Binär-Umwandlung
decimal zero Dezimalnull
decision Entscheidung, Verzweigung
decision box Entscheidungskästchen, Entscheidungssymbol
decision element Entscheidungselement
decision instruction Entscheidungsbefehl
decision making ability Entscheidungsfähigkeit
decision table Entscheidungstabelle
decisive ausschlaggebend, bestimmend, entscheidend
deck Mappe
deck identification Mappenidentifikation, Mappenkennung
deck index Mappenverzeichnis
deck name Mappenname
deck number Mappennummer
declaration Vereinbarung
declare deklarieren
declination magnetic magnetische Mißweisung
decode dekodieren, entschlüsseln
decoder Dekoder, Dekodierer, Entschlüssler, Meldungsentschlüsselungsroutine
decoding Dekodierung
decompress entkomprimieren
decompression Entkomprimierung
decrease Abnahme, Minderung, Verminderung, Verringerung, abnehmen, mindern, reduzieren, vermindern
decree Verordnung
decrement Verminderung, dekrementieren, herunterzählen
dedicate eigens zuordnen, widmen
dedicated fest zugeordnet
dedicated circuit eigener Stromkreis
dedicated computer dedizierter Rechner
dedicated connection Standverbindung
dedicated device fest zugeordnetes Gerät

dedicated line Standleitung
dedicated network Datenfestnetz
dedicated register fest zugeordnete Register
dedicated system maßgeschneidertes System
deduct abziehen, einbehalten
deduction Abzug
deduction posting Abgangsbuchung
deenergized unerregt
deenhancement Funktionsminderung
default Standard, Standardauswahl, Standardeinstellung, Standardvorgabe, Standardwert, vorgeben
default allocation Standardzuweisung
default assignment Standardzuordnung
default characteristics Standardmerkmale
default character set Standardzeichensatz
default combination Defaultkombination
default control command Standardsteuerkommando
default device name Name des Standardgerätes
default directory Standarddateiverzeichnis
default disk Standardplatte
default drive Standardlaufwerk, voreingestelltes Laufwerk, vorgegebenes Laufwerk
default editor Standardeditor
default extension Standarderweiterung
default file name Name der Standarddatei
default folder Standardordner
default import export terminator standardmäßiges Begrenzungszeichen
default interest Verzugszinsen
default key Standardtaste, Voreinstellungstaste
default language key Standardsprachenschlüssel
default library Standardbibliothek
default listing Standardausdruck
default mapping Standardbelegung
default memory Standardspeicher
default parameter Ausgangsparameter, Standardparameter
default partition Standardaufteilung
default printer Standarddrucker
default printer option Standarddruckeinstellung
default processing Standardverarbeitung
default program Standardprogramm
default record length Standardsatzlänge
default ruler standardmäßiges Zeilenlineal
default selection Standardauswahl
default setting Standardeinstellung, Voreinstellung
default start up menu Ausgangsmenü
default state Standardzustand

default system Standardsystem
default table Standardtabelle
default tabulator Standardtabulator
default value Defaultwert, Standardangabe, Standardvorgabe, Standardwert, Vorgabewert
deferment Aussetzung
deferred ausgesetzt, verzögert
deferred command verzögertes Kommando
deferred user service task zeitunkritische Servicefunktion
definable bestimmbar, definierbar
define beschreiben, besetzen, bestimmen, definieren, festlegen
define constant definiere Konstante
defined file definierte Datei
defined record management spezielle Satzverwaltung
definition Beschreibung, Definition, Festlegung
definition file Definitionsdatei
definition label Definitionskennsatz
definition language Definitionssprache
definition option Definitionsmöglichkeit
definition record Definitionssatz
definition section Definitionsteil
deformatting Deformatierung
degasify entgasen
degassed entgast
degassing Entgasung
degrade degenerieren, einschränken
degraded mode vermindertes Leistungspotential
degree Grad
degree of completion Erfüllungsgrad
degree of detail Detaillierungsgrad
degree of electrical protection Grad der elektrischen Sicherheit
degree of integration Integrationsgrad
degree of isochronous distortion Isochronverzerrungsgrad
degree of presorting Vorsortierungsgrad
degree of safety Sicherheitsgrad
degree of start-stop distortion Start-Stop-Verzerrungsgrad
degrees of freedom Freiheitsgrade
degressive degressiv
dehumidifier Trocknungsmittel
deinstall abbauen
deinstallation guide Abbauanweisungen
delay Aufschub, Verzug, Verzögerung, aufschieben, verzögern
delay circuit Verzögerungsschaltung
delay days Verzugstage
delayed verzögert

delayed internal succession indirekte interne Programmfolgesteuerung
delay line Verzögerungsleitung
delegate delegieren
delete löschen
deleteability Löschfähigkeit
delete a segment Löschen eines Segments
delete character Löschungszeichen
delete character buffer Zeichenlöschpuffer
delete character key Zeichenlöschtaste
delete criterion Löschkriterium
delete flag Löschzeichen
delete instruction Löschanweisung
delete key Korrekturtaste, Löschtaste
delete line Zeile löschen
delete line buffer Zeilenlöschpuffer
delete marker Löschkennmarke, Löschkennzeichen
delete operation Löschoperation
delete option Löschoption
delete procedure Löschvorgang
delete proposal Löschvorschlag
delete proposal list Löschvorschlagsliste
delete proposal program Löschvorschlagsprogramm
delete protected löschgeschützt
delete reservation Löschvormerkung
delete reservation marker Löschvormerkungskennzeichen
delete symbol Löschzeichen
delete text Text löschen
delete word buffer Wortlöschpuffer
deletion Löschung, Löschvorgang
deletion list Löschliste
deletion monitoring Löschüberwachung
deletion record Löschregister
deletion reservation Löschvermerk
deliberate gezielt
deliberately bewußt
delimiter Begrenzer, Begrenzungszeichen, Delimiter, Trennzeichen
deliver anliefern, ausliefern, liefern
deliverable lieferbar
delivery Anlieferung, Auslieferung, Belieferung, Lieferung
delivery agent Spediteur, Transportunternehmen
delivery arrangement Liefereinteilung
delivery commitment Lieferzusage
delivery costs Bezugskosten
delivery date Lieferdatum, Liefertermin
delivery instruction Auslieferungsanweisung
delivery monitoring Lieferüberwachung

69

delivery note Lieferschein
delivery note alteration Lieferscheinänderung
delivery note header Lieferscheinkopf
delivery note item Lieferscheinposition
delivery note item quantity Lieferscheinpositionsmengen
delivery note item weight Lieferscheinpositionsgewicht
delivery note number Lieferscheinnummer
delivery note processing Lieferscheinbearbeitung
delivery note remark Lieferscheinnotiz
delivery note text Lieferscheintext
delivery note type Lieferscheinart
delivery note voucher Lieferscheinbeleg
delivery note voucher record Lieferscheinbelegsatz
delivery order Lieferungsauftrag
delivery papers Lieferpapiere
delivery performance Liefermoral
delivery period Lieferzeitraum
delivery reminder Liefererinnerung, Liefermahnung
delivery schedule Lieferplan
delivery schedule date Lieferplandatum
delivery schedule end date Lieferplanendedatum
delivery schedule item Lieferplanposition
delivery schedule management Lieferplanverwaltung
delivery schedule monitoring Lieferplanüberwachung
delivery schedule number Lieferplannummer
delivery schedule printing Lieferplanschreibung
delivery schedule quantity Lieferplanmenge
delivery schedule start date Lieferplananfangsdatum
delivery schedule type Lieferplanart
delivery scheduling Lieferplaneinteilung
delivery stop Auslieferungsverbot, Liefersperre
delivery terms Lieferbedingung, Lieferkondition
delivery time Anlieferungszeitpunkt, Lieferzeit
delivery value Lieferwert
delivery voucher Lieferbeleg
delivery voucher number Lieferbelegnummer
delivery week Lieferwoche
delta Unterschied, Änderung
delta time Deltazeit
demand Anmahnung, Aufforderung, Bedarf, fordern
demand figures Bedarfszahlen

demand forecasting Bedarfsermittlung
demand for payment Zahlungsaufforderung
demand paging Seitenabruf
demand processing Teilnehmerbetrieb, Teilnehmerdialogbetrieb
demand schedule Bedarfsraster
demand site Dialogstation, Teilnehmerstation
demand submission Bedarfsanmeldung
demand user Dialogbenutzer
demo Demo, Präsentation, Vorführung
demodulator Demodulator, Empfangssignalumsetzer
demonstrate aufzeigen, demonstrieren
demultiplexer Demultiplexer
demultiplexing demultiplexen
density Schreibdichte
density control Konzentrationssteuerung
departement Amt
departement number Abteilungsnummer
department Abteilung, Fachabteilung
department affiliation Abteilungszugehörigkeit
department management Abteilungsleitung
department name Abteilungsbezeichnung
department related abteilungsbezogen
dependence Abhängigkeit
dependency Abhängigkeit
dependent abhängig
dependent on article artikelabhängig
dependent on financial year geschäftsjahresabhängig
dependent on item master record artikelstammsatzabhängig
dependent on item value positionswertabhängig
dependent on sign vorzeichenabhängig
dependent on supplier lieferantengebunden
depending on hardware hardwareabhängig
depending on the operating system betriebssystemabhängig
depict abbilden
depletion mode Abgangsart
deposit ablegen
deposit tray Depositeinrichtung
depreciate abschreiben
depreciation Abschreibung
depreciation adjustment Abschreibungskorrektur
depreciation amount Abschreibungsbetrag
depreciation calculation Abschreibungsrechnung
depreciation cancellation Abschreibungsstornierung
depreciation code Abschreibungsschlüssel

depreciation configuration Abschreibungskonstellation
depreciation control field Abschreibungssteuerungsfeld
depreciation costs Abschreibungskosten
depreciation field Abschreibungsfeld
depreciation forecast Abschreibungsprognose
depreciation list Abschreibungsliste
depreciation mode Abschreibungsmodalität
depreciation of buildings Gebäudeabschreibung
depreciation parameter Abschreibungsparameter
depreciation period Abschreibungsdauer
depreciation posting Abschreibungsbuchung
depreciation rate Abschreibungsprozent, Abschreibungsprozentsatz
depreciation record Abschreibungssatz
depreciation rule Abschreibungsregel
depreciation value Abschreibungswert
depth Tiefe
derivation Ableitung
derive ableiten, stammen
descending absteigend
descending order absteigende Reihenfolge
describe beschreiben
description Beschreibung, Darstellung
description file Kontobeschreibungsdatei
description mask Beschreibungsmaske
description medium Beschreibungsmittel
description of counter account Gegenkontobeschreibung
description of field name Feldnamenbeschreibung
description of operation Arbeitsgangbezeichnung
description of the materials Materialbeschreibung
description text Beschreibungstext
descriptor Deskriptor, Prädikat
descriptor block Deskriptorblock
descriptor file Beschreibungsdatei
descriptor list Deskriptorenliste
descriptor record Beschreibungssatz
descriptor section Deskriptorabschnitt
deselect abwählen, logisch abschalten
design Konzept
designate bezeichnen, kennzeichnen
designation Beschreibung, Bestimmung
designation of variables Variablenbezeichnung
design engineer Entwurfsingenieur
design guideline Entwurfsrichtlinie

design guideline program Programm der Entwurfsrichtlinien
design philosophy Entwurfsphilosophie
design voice Stimmkreation
desirable erwünscht, wünschenswert
desire Wunsch, wünschen
desk Arbeitstisch, Pult, Schreibtisch, Tisch
desk calculator Tischrechner
desk management Bürofunktionen
desktop calculator mode Tischrechnermodus
desktop computer Bürocomputer, Tischcomputer
desktop publishing Publizieren am Arbeitsplatz
destination Bestimmungsort, Ziel, Zielort
destination address Empfangsadresse, Zieladresse
destination address register Empfangsadreßregister, Zieladreßregister
destination area Zielbereich
destination device Zielgerät
destination diskette Kopiediskette, Zieldiskette
destination diskette drive Zieldiskettenlaufwerk
destination drive Ziellaufwerk
destination file Zieldatei
destination format Zielformat
destination group Zielgruppe
destination information Zielinformation
destination node Empfängerknoten, Zielknoten
destroy löschen, zerstören
destructive readout auslesen mit Zerstörung des Speicherinhalts, zerstörendes Lesen
detached abgesetzt
detached process unabhängiger Prozeß
detached program operation unabhängiger Programmlauf
detail Detail
detail calculation operation Einzelpostenberechnung
detail display Detailanzeige
detail display option Detailanzeigemöglichkeit
detailed ausführlich, detailliert
detailed account listing Kontenniederschrift
detailed information Detailinformation
detail file Einzelpostendatei
detail line Einzelpostenzeile
detail operation Einzelpostenoperation
detail output operation Einzelpostenausgabe
detail time Einzelpostenzeit
detect entdecken, feststellen, registrieren
detection bit Erkennungsbit
detection punch Kennlochung

detector Demodulator
detector circuit Detektorschaltung
determination of amortization Abschreibungsermittlung
determination of depreciation Abschreibungsermittlung
determination of variables Variablenermittlung
determine bestimmen, determinieren, ermitteln, feststellen
determining the net book value Restbuchwertermittlung
devaluated abgewertet
devaluation Abwertung
devaluation proposal Abwertungsvorschlagsliste
develop entwickeln
developed product erzeugtes Produkt
developing unit Entwicklungseinrichtung
development Entwicklung
development cycle Entwicklungszyklus
development number Entwicklungsnummer
development of consumption Verbrauchsentwicklung
development part Entwicklungsteil
development system Entwicklungssystem
development time Entwicklungszeit
development tool Entwicklungs-Tool, Entwicklungswerkzeug
development utility Dienstprogramm zur Programmentwicklung
device Apparat, Ein-/Ausgabeeinheit, Einrichtung, Gerät, Vorrichtung
device address Geräteadresse
device assignment set Gerätezuordnungsfolge
device attribute Geräteattribut
device configuration Geräteausstattung
device connector Geräteanschluß
device control Gerätesteuerung
device control interface Gerätesteuerungsschnittstelle
device controller Gerätesteuerung
device control routine Gerätesteuerroutine
device dependent geräteabhängig
device driver Gerätetreiber
device driver process Gerätetreiberprozeß
device function Gerätefunktion
device handler Gerätetreiber
device identification Gerätekennung
device identifier Gerätekennung
device instruction Gerätebefehl
device lock Gerätesperre
device macro Gerätemakro
device media control Gerätebeschreibung

device media control language Datenträgerbeschreibungssprache, Gerätebeschreibungssprache
device mnemonic logische Geräteadresse
device name Gerätename
device number Gerätenummer
device number input Gerätenummereingabe
device number plug Gerätenummernstecker
device operation Geräteoperation
device queue Gerätewarteschlange
device related gerätebezogen
device selection Geräteansteuerung
device selection code Geräteansteuerungscode
device specific geräteabhängig
device status Gerätezustand
device status report Gerätestatusanzeige, Meldung des Gerätestatus
device unique command gerätespezifisches Kommando
Diablo Diablo
diacritical mark diakritisches Zeichen
diagnose diagnostizieren
diagnosis Diagnose, Fehlerdiagnose
diagnostic area Diagnosebereich
diagnostic center Diagnosezentrum
diagnostic diskette Diagnosediskette, Wartungsdiskette
diagnostic display Diagnoseanzeige
diagnostic log Fehlerprotokoll
diagnostic log entry Diagnoselogeintrag
diagnostic message Diagnosemeldung
diagnostic program Diagnoseprogramm
diagnostic routine Diagnoseroutine, Fehlersuchprogramm
diagnostics Diagnoseroutine
diagnostic software Diagnosesoftware
diagnostic test Diagnose, Diagnoselauf, Test
diagram Diagramm
dial anrufen, anwählen, wählen
dial connection Wählverbindung
dial digit buffer Wählziffernpuffer
dial into anwählen
dialler mode Wählmodus
dialling Telefonwahl
dialling attempt Wählversuch
dialling code Vorwahl
dialling equipment Wähleinrichtung
dialling number Wählnummer
dialog Dialog
dialog answer Dialogantwort
dialog application program Dialoganwendungsprogramm
dialog based dialogunterstützt

dialog control Dialogsteuerung
dialog control indication Dialogsteuerungshinweis
dialog error Dialogfehler
dialog field Dialogfeld
dialog input Dialogeingabe
dialog memory limit Dialogspeichergrenze
dialog mode Dialogmodus
dialog page Dialogseite
dialog processing service Dialogverarbeitungsfunktion
dialog processor Dialogprozessor, Dialogsteuerungsprogramm
dialog program interface Dialogprogrammschnittstelle
dialog response Dialogantwort
dialog segment Dialogsegment
dialog sequence Dialogablauf
dialog session Dialogsitzung
dialog specification language Dialogbeschreibungssprache
dialog specification language translator Sprachübersetzer für die Dialogbeschreibungssprache
dialog structure Dialogstruktur
dial out automatischer Verbindungsaufbau
dial selection Nummernschalterwahl
dial tone Wählton
dial up equipment Wähleinrichtung
dial up number Wählnummer
dial up operation Anwählfunktion
dictionary Wörterbuch
dictionary manager Wörterbuchverwaltungssystem
diecast druckgießen
dielectric dielektrisch, nichtleitend
dielectric device nichtleitendes Gerät
dielectric material Dielektrikum
diesel electric power station dieselelektrisches Kraftwerk
diesel generator Dieselgenerator
differ abweichen, unterscheiden
difference Betragsabweichung, Differenz, Differenzbetrag, Differenzwert
difference quantity Differenzmenge
differential amplifier Differentialverstärker
differential analyser Differentialanalysator
differential relay Differentialrelais
differentiated differenziert
differentiating circuit Differenzierglied
differently unterschiedlich
differing abweichend
difficulty Schwierigkeit

diffuse diffus, unscharf
digit Kommastelle, Stelle, Ziffer
digital digital
digital analog converter Digital-Analog-Wandler
digital branch exchange Digitalvermittlung, digitale Vermittlung
digital circuit Digitalschaltung
digital computer Digitalrechner
digital cross-connect system digitales Querverbingungssystem
digital data bus digitaler Datenbus
digital data network digitales Datennetzwerk
digital filter digitales Filter
digital integrated circuit integrierte Digitalschaltung
digital line Digitalleitung
digital multimeter digitales Multimeter, digitales Vielfachmeßgerät
digital radar extractor digitaler Radarextraktor
digital readouts digitale Anzeigen
digital signal digitales Signal
digital signal distortion Schrittverzerrung
digital target extractor digitaler Zielextraktor
digital to analog converter Digital-Analog-Wandler
digitization Digitalisierung
digitizer Digitalisierer, Digitalisiergerät, Digitalisiertablett
digit position Ziffernstelle, Ziffernteil
digits of accuracy Genauigkeit von Dezimalstellen, Genauigkeit von Kommastellen
digraph Digraph
dim abgeblendet, dunkel
dimension Abmessung, Dimension
dimensioning Dimension
dimmed abgeblendet
dimmer switch Abblendschalter
diode Diode
dipole Dipol, Zweipol
dipole recording method Rückkehr-zu-Null-Verfahren
DIP switch DIP Schalter
direct direkt, leiten, richten, zuweisen
direct access Direktzugriff
direct access method Direktzugriffsmethode
direct access storage Direktzugriffsspeicher
direct adressing direkte Adressierung
direct bcd arithmetic direkte BCD-Arithmetik
direct cable connection Standleitung
direct call Direktruf
direct connection Direktverbindung, Standleitung

73

direct current Gleichstrom
direct current amplifier Gleichstromverstärker
direct current generator Gleichstromgenerator
direct current machine Gleichstrommaschine
direct current motor Gleichstrommotor
direct current power transmission Gleichstrom-Leistungsübetragung
direct current resistance Gleichstromwiderstand
direct current transformer Gleichstrom-Transformator
direct cursor address direkte Cursoradresse, direkte Schreibmarkenadresse
direct data capture direkte Datenerfassung
direct data interface Gerätesteuerungsschnittstelle
direct debit Bankeinzug, Einzug, Einzugsverfahren
direct debit authorization Einzugsermächtigung
direct debit date Einzugsdatum
direct debit list Bankeinzugsliste, Einzugsliste
direct debit type Einzugsart
direct dialling Direktanwahl, Direktwahl
direct dialling telephone Fernsprechhauptanschluß
direct distance dialing Direktrufverfahren
direct drive Direktantrieb, Direktsteuerung
direct energy conversion Energiedirektumwandlung
direct enquiry Direktabfrage
direct file Direktzugriffsdatei
direct inquiry Direktabfrage
direction Richtung
directional measurement Richtungsmessung
direction finder Peiler
direction key Pfeiltaste
directive Anweisung, Befehl, Betriebsanweisung, Direktive
directly heated cathode direkt geheizte Kathode
direct memory access Kanalsteuerung, direkter Speicherzugriff
direct memory access channel DMA-Kanal, Speicher-Direktzugriffskanal
direct memory access controller DMA-Steuerbaustein
direct operand Direktoperand
director card Steuerkarte
directory Adreßbuch, Dateiverzeichnis, Inhaltsverzeichnis, Verzeichnis
directory allocation sector Zuordnungssektor des Dateiverzeichnisses

directory area Dateiverzeichnisabschnitt
directory choice Verzeichnisauswahl
directory content Verzeichnisinhalt
directory display Anzeigen des Dateiverzeichnisses
directory entry Verzeichniseintrag
directory of internal messages Aktionsverzeichnis
directory of members Mitgliederverzeichnis
directory options Dateiverzeichnisaktionen
directory path Dateiverzeichnispfad, Verzeichnispfad
directory selection Verzeichnisauswahl
directory service Adreßauskunft, Adreßbuchdienst, Auskunft, Telefonauskunft
direct percentage prozentuale Auf- und Abschlagsrechnung
direct read after write Lesen nach Schreiben
direct robotic control direkt gesteuerter Roboter
direct selection Direktwahl
direct switching command Direktwahlkommando
direct value Direktwert
direkt access Direktzugriff
disable ausschalten, sperren
disabled gesperrt
disappear verschwinden
disassembly facility Depaketierer
discard nicht sichern
discharge Entladung, entladen
discharge time Entladezeit
disconnect Anschluß löschen, Verbindung trennen, trennen
disconnect character Zeichen »Verbindung abbrechen«
disconnect character enable Einschalten des Zeichens »Verbindung abbrechen«
disconnected nicht angeschlossen
disconnected mode Wartezustand
disconnectible abschaltbar
disconnection Trennen
discontinued item Auslaufartikel, Auslaufteil
discount Rabatt, Rabattgewährung, Rabattstufe, Skonto, diskontieren
discountable skontofähig
discount amount Rabattbetrag, Rabatthöhe, Skontobetrag
discount base Skontobasis
discount base amount Skontobasisbetrag
discount calculation Rabattrechnung, Rabattrechnungsverfahren
discount code Rabattschlüssel

disk formatting

discount conversion factor Rabattumrechnungsfaktor
discount credit note Rabattgutschrift
discount days Diskonttage, Skontotage
discount deduction Skontoabzug
discount due date Skontofälligkeit
discounted cash flow field interner Zinsfluß
discount expenses Diskontspesen
discount information Rabattangaben
discounting Abzinsung, Diskontierung
discount law Skontorecht
discount liabilities Diskontobligo
discount loss Skontoverlust
discount percentage Skontoprozentsatz
discount posting Diskontbuchung, Skontobuchung
discount price unit Rabattpreiseinheit
discount rate Rabattsatz, Skontosatz
discount record Diskontsatz
discount scale Rabattstaffel
discount settlement Skontoverrechnung
discount settlement account Skontoverrechnungskonto
discount structure Rabattgefüge
discount terms Rabattkonditionen
discount units Rabattmengeneinheit
discount yield Skontoertrag
discover auffinden, entdecken, finden
discrepancy Abweichung, Differenz
discrepancy advice Differenzmitteilung
discrepancy posting Differenzbuchen, Differenzbuchung
disc resident system plattenresidente Systemsteuerung, plattenresidentes System
discrete diskret
discrete addressing diskrete Adressierung
discrete components diskrete Bauteile
discrete data diskrete Daten
discrete memory diskreter Speicher
discriminating equipment Ausscheidungseinrichtung
discriminator Diskriminator
disjunction Disjunktion
disk Diskette, Magnetplatte, Platte
disk access method Plattenzugriffsmethode
disk address Plattenadresse
disk cartridge Plattenkassette
disk change Plattenwechsel
disk contents Platteninhalt
disk controller Plattensteuereinheit, Plattensteuerung
disk control unit Plattensteuereinheit
disk copy program Diskettenkopierprogramm
disk deck Plattenstapel
disk directory Dateiverzeichnis der Diskette
disk diskette services Platten-/Diskettendienste
disk drive Diskettenlaufwerk, Festplattenlaufwerk, Plattenlaufwerk
disk drive door Klappe des Diskettenlaufwerks, Laufwerksklappe
disk driver Plattentreiber
disk drive unit Plattenlaufwerk
disk dump restore Platten-Wiederherstellungsroutine
disk dump restore utility Datensicherungs- und Rückspeicherungsroutine
disk error Diskettenfehler, Plattenfehler
diskette Diskette
diskette based operating system Diskettensystem
diskette box Diskettenbox
diskette copy program Diskettenkopierprogramm
diskette cover Diskettenhülle, Kunststoffhülle
diskette device name Name des Diskettenlaufwerks
diskette drive Diskettenlaufwerk
diskette drive active Diskettenlaufwerk aktiv
diskette drive door Laufwerksklappe
diskette drive slot Einschub des Diskettenlaufwerks
diskette formatting program Diskettenformatierung
diskette initialization Disketteninitialisierung
diskette label Diskettenaufkleber
diskette maintenance Diskettenbearbeitung
diskette number Diskettennummer
diskette of suitable quality Diskette guter Qualität
diskette operating system Diskettenbetriebssystem
diskette preparation Diskettenvorformatierung
diskette services Diskettendienste
diskette side Diskettenseite
diskette stack reader Diskettenstapelleser
diskette system Diskettensystem
diskette type Diskettenart
diskette write error Fehler beim Schreiben auf Diskette
disk exchange Plattenwechsel
disk file Plattendatei
disk file management Plattendateiverwaltung
disk formatter Diskettenformatierer, Formatierprogramm
disk formatting Diskettenformatierung, Diskettenformatierung

disk handler Plattensteuerungsroutine, Plattentreiber
disk instruction Diskbefehl
disk label Plattenname
disk operating system DOS Betriebssystem, Plattenbetriebssystem
disk operation Diskettenoperation
disk order Plattenauftrag
disk pack Plattenstapel, Satz von Platten
disk pack well Plattenstapelaufnahme
disk partition data Plattenaufteilungsdaten, Plattenaufteilungsdaten
disk preformatting Diskettenvorformatierung
disk prep vorformatieren
disk processor Plattenspeicherprozessor
disk queuing facility Warteschlangenspeicherung auf Platte
disk quota Plattenquoten
disk sector Plattensektor
disk set Satz von Platten
disk side Diskettenseite
disk space Speicherplatz auf der Platte
disk specific plattenspezifisch
disk station Diskettenstation
disk storage Plattenspeicher
disk storage capacity Plattenspeicherkapazität
disk storage subsystem Plattenspeichersubsystem
disk work file Diskarbeitsdatei
dislocation Standortwechsel
dismantle demontieren
dismount logisch abmelden
dispatch Versand, absenden, versenden
dispatch advice Versandhinweis
dispatch control Versandpunktüberwachung
dispatch data Versanddaten
dispatch date Versanddatum
dispatch department Versandabteilung
dispatch documents Versandpapiere
dispatch due Versandfälligkeit
dispatcher Verteilerroutine
dispatch information Versandhinweis
dispatching Verteilung von Rechenzeit
dispatch lead time Versandvorlaufzeit
dispatch period Versandzeitraum
dispatch register Versandindex
dispatch release Versandanstoß
dispatch type Versandart
displacement Distanzadresse, Offset, Versatz
displacement address Distanzadresse, Offsetadresse
display Anzeige, Anzeige, anzeigen
displayable anzeigbar

display adapter Bildschirmadapter, Bildschirmkarte
display area Bildschirmbereich
display block Anzeigeblock
display capacity Bildschirmkapazität
display character darstellbares Zeichen
display code Anzeigencode
display console Bildschirmkonsole
display control Bildsteuerung
display control element Bildsteuerelement
display control format Bildsteuerformat
display control formatting Bildsteuerformatierung
display device Anzeigegerät, Sichtgerät
display device computer Rechner der Anzeigeeinheit
display field Anzeigefeld
display file Displaydatei
display format Anzeigeformat, Bildformat, Tabellenformat
display frame Bildschirmmaske, Maske
display function Anzeigefunktion
display information Anzeigeinformation
displaying individual item Einzelpostenanzeige
displaying individual record Einzelsatzanzeige
display instruction Anzeigebefehl
display invoice Rechnungsanzeige
display jitter Bildinstabilität
display limit Anzeigebeschränkung
display mask Anzeigemaske
display output Bildschirmausgabe
display output format Bildschirmausgabeformat
display output function Bildschirmausgabefunktion
display position Anzeigeposition
display program Anzeigeprogramm, Druckprogramm
display register Anzeigeregister
display rule Anzeigeregel
display screen Anzeigebild, Bildschirm
display screen keyboard Bildschirmsystem
display screen mask Bildschirmmaske
display screen page Bildschirmseite
display size Anzeigegröße
display test Anzeigetest
display text Anzeigentext
display types Anzeigentypen
disposable verfügbar, wegwerfbar
disposal Abgang
disposal month Abgangsmonat
disqualify aussteuern, disqualifizieren
dissipation Verlust

distance Entfernung
distance key Positionierungstaste
distant entfernt
distinction Unterscheidung
distinguish unterscheiden
distinguisher Unterscheidungsmerkmal
distortion Verzerrung
distortion degree Verzerrungsgrad
distribute verteilen
distributed abgesetzt, verteilt
distributed data entry dezentrale Datenerfassung
distributed data processing dezentrale Datenverarbeitung, vernetzte Datenverarbeitung, verteilte Datenverarbeitung
distributed end system gateway verteiltes Endsystemrelais
distributed intelligence system System mit verteilter Intelligenz
distributed inventory Teilbestände
distributed measurement network Meßnetzwerk-Konzept
distributed network architecture variable Netzwerkstruktur
distributed numeric control dezentrale numerische Maschinensteuerung
distributed processing Arbeitslastverteilung
distributed system dezentrales System
distributing center Verteilerstelle
distribution Verteilung
distribution basis Verteilungsbasis
distribution box Verteilerkasten
distribution channel Verteilerkanal
distribution circuit Verteilerkreis
distribution insert Anschlußplatte
distribution kit Originalsoftwarepaket
distribution list Verteilerliste
distribution media Programmträger
distribution panel Verteilerplatte
distribution panel assembly Verteilerplatteneinheit
distribution process Verteilungsprozeß
distribution totals Verteilungssummen
distribution transformer Verteilertransformator
distributor Distributor, Händler, Verteiler
disturb stören
disturbance Störung
divide aufgliedern, aufteilen, einteilen, teilen, unterteilen
divided into two parts zweigeteilt
divided up eingeteilt
division Division, Geschäftsbereich
divisional code Geschäftsbereichskennzeichen
divisional organisation Geschäftsbereichsaufteilung
divisional posting Geschäftsbereichskontierung
divisional turnover Geschäftsbereichsumsätze
DMA boundary error DMA Grenzwertfehler
DMA overrun error DMA-Überlauffehler
document Dokument, Schriftstück, Unterlage, dokumentieren, Übertragungsvorlage
documentation Dokumentation, Handbuch
documentation components Dokumentationsunterlagen
documentation entry Dokumentationseintrag
documentation index Dokumentationsübersicht
documentation map Dokumentationsübersicht
documentation paragraph Dokumentationsteil
documentation processor Dokumentationsprozessor
documentation section Dokumentationsteil
documentation text Dokumentationstext
document diskette Dokumentdiskette
document file Dokumentdatei
document identification Aktenzeichen-Kennzeichen
document indent Belegeinzug
document parting bar Abreißschiene
document processing Textverarbeitung
document recovery Dokumentrückgewinnung
document reference Aktenzeichen
document to be transmitted Übertragungsvorlage
document transfer mode Dokumentübertragung
dollar sign Dollarzeichen
domain Domäne
domain specification Domänenspezifikation
domestic connection Inlandsverbindung
domestic electrical installation elektrische Hausinstallation
dominate dominieren
done gemacht
door Klappe, Tür
door opening error Türtransportfehler
dot Bildpunkt, Pixel, Punkt
dot matrix printer Punktmatrixdrucker
dots per inch Punkte pro Zoll
double Doppel-, doppelt
double byte interleaved Zwei-Byte-Versatz
double connection Doppelverbindung
double current Doppelstrom
double density doppelte Dichte, doppelte Schreibdichte
double density diskette Diskette mit doppelter Schreibdichte

77

double density recording Aufzeichnung mit doppelter Dichte
double entry Doppelbelegung
double head drive assembly zweiseitiges Laufwerk
double height line Zeile mit doppelt hohen Zeichen
double integer doppelt genaue Ganzzahl
double precision doppelte Genauigkeit
double quote Anführungszeichen
double side zweiseitig
double sided diskette beidseitig beschreibbare Diskette, zweiseitige Diskette
double sided floppy zweiseitige Floppy
double strike print Drucken mit Doppelanschlag
double width doppelte Zeichenbreite
double width line Zeile mit doppelt breiten Zeichen
double word limit Doppelwortgrenze
down für nicht betriebsbereit erklären, nicht betriebsbereit
down arrow Pfeil nach unten, Pfeil vorwärts
down arrow key Pfeiltaste nach unten, Pfeiltaste vorwärts
down-key AB-Taste
downline load Laden eines Satellitenrechners
downline loading Fernladen, Satellitenrechner laden, downline laden
download laden, übertragen
down reserve list Liste der für nicht betriebsbereit erklärten und reservierten Betriebsmittel
downtime Ausfallzeit, Ausfallzeit, Standzeit, Totzeit
dp technical DV-technisch
draft Andruck, Entwurf, abfassen, verfassen
draft outbot schnelle Ausgabe
draft outline Grobstruktur
draft printer Punktmatrixdrucker, Schnelldrucker
draft quality printer Schnelldrucker
draining Entleerung
drain wire Masseleitung
draw aufnehmen, entnehmen, zeichnen, ziehen
drawer Aussteller, Fach
draw in einziehen
draw in facility Einzugseinrichtung
drawing Zeichnung
drawing in instruction Einzugsbefehl
drawing number Zeichnungsnummer
drawing type Zeichnungsart
drawing version Zeichnungsversion
draw in instruction Einzugsbefehl

draw up aufstellen, hinaufziehen
drill Bohrer
drill advance Vorschub
drill fixture Bohrerbefestigung
drill head Bohrkopf
drill head advance Bohrkopfvorschub
drill motor Bohrmotor
drive Antrieb, Laufwerk, Steuerung, antreiben, fahren, steuern
drive cable Laufwerkskabel
drive casing Fahrgehäuse
drive configurator Laufwerkskonfigurationsprogramm
drive coupling Antriebskopplung
drive door Laufwerksklappe
drive error Laufwerksfehler
drive ID Laufwerksbezeichnung, Laufwerksname, Laufwerksnummer
drive in use Laufwerk belegt
drive not ready Laufwerk nicht bereit
drive number Laufwerksnummer
drive on Diskettenlaufwerk aktiv
drive pin Mitnehmerstift
driver Treiber, Verstärker
driver process Treiberprozeß
driver receiver Sende- und Empfangsverstärker
drive select number Laufwerksnummer
drive speed out of range Laufwerksgeschwindigkeit falsch
drop fallen, sinken, sperren, tropfen
drop dead halt Maschinenstop
drop out Aussetzfehler, Dropout, herausfallen, kurzzeitiger Ausfall
drum Bildwalze, Schrittschaltwerk, Trommel
dry trocken
drying unit Trockeneinrichtung
dry run Blindversuch, Dunkellauf
dry running Blindversuch
dry type transformer Transformator mit Luftkühlung
DTE and DCE data DÜE und DEE-Daten
DTE call request DEE-Verbindungsanforderung
DTE controlled not ready DEE-gesteuert nicht bereit
DTE DCE waiting keine Änderung an der Schnittstelle
DTE repeat Wiederholungsaufforderung
DTE reset request DEE-Rücksetzanforderung
DTE restart request DEE-Restart-Anforderung
dual Doppel-, doppelt, zweifach
dual 8 bit interface erweiterte serielle Schnittstelle
dual access Zweifachzugriff

dual channel Zweikanalbetrieb
dual channel access Zweifachzugriff
dual cluster doppelte Funktionseinheitengruppe
dual diskette drive Doppeldiskettenlaufwerk
dual height module Zweifachkarte
dualing Datenmanagement, Zeichenaustausch
dual in line DIL
dual inline pin DIP
dual keyboard Zwillingstastatur
dual keyboard connection Zwillingstastaturanschluß
dual single feed Doppelvereinzelung
duct Kanal
due fällig
due date Fälligkeit, Fälligkeitsdatum, Taggrenze, Terminabgrenzung
due date entry Terminposition
due date item Terminposition
due day Abrechnungstag
dummy Blind-, Füllsignal, pseudo
dummy array Pseudofeldgruppe
dummy bit Leerbit
dummy block Leerblock
dummy condition Leerzustand
dummy entry Blindeingabe
dummy file Leerdatei, Testdatei
dummy fuse Blindsicherung
dummy instruction Blindbefehl
dummy key Leertaste
dummy message Blindnachricht
dummy record Leersatz
dummy section Blindabschnitt
dump Ausgeben des Speicherinhaltes, Speicherausdruck, Speicherauszug, abladen, dumpen, entladen
dump and restore facility Einrichtung zur Erstellung von Datenbankkopien mit anschließender Rückspeicherung
dump feature Dumpkennzeichen
dump file Speicherauszugsdatei
dump format Dumpformat
dumping code Auslagerschlüssel
dump routine Speicherauszugsroutine
duplex Duplex
duplex communication Duplexverkehr, Gegenverkehr
duplex mode Duplexbetrieb
duplex operation Duplexbetrieb
duplex transmission Gegenbetrieb
duplicate Doppel-, duplizieren, kopieren, vervielfältigen
duplicate control Duplikatsteuerung
duplicate field Duplizierfeld

duplicate key Doppelschlüssel, Dupliziertaste
duplicate print file Duplikatausdruckdatei
duplicate record Duplikatsatz
durability Bestand, Beständigkeit, Dauerhaftigkeit, Haltbarkeit, Stabilität
duration Anschaltdauer, Anschaltzeit, Dauer, Länge des Signals, Übertragungszeit
duration charge Zeitgebühr
during operation im laufenden Betrieb
duty Pflicht
dwell time Verweilzeit
dwell time check Verweilzeitprüfung
dwell timer Ruhezeitglied
dye laser Farbstofflaser
dynamic dynamisch
dynamic access dynamischer Zugriff
dynamic memory dynamischer Speicher
dynamic process dynamischer Prozeß
dynamic RAM dynamisches RAM
dynpro buffer Dynpropuffer
dynpro file Dynprodatei
dynpro language key Dynprosprachenschlüssel
dynpro maintenance Dynpropflege

E

early delivery   Frühlieferung
earmarked   vorgemerkt
earn   verdienen
earphone   Hörkapsel
earphones   Kopfhörer
earplug   Ohrhörer
earth   Masse
earth conductor   Masseleiter
earth electrode   Masseelektrode
earthing reactor   Erdschlußreaktanz
earthing switch   Masseschalter
earth terminal   Masseklemme
easy to use   handlich, leicht zu bedienen
echo   Echo, Zeichenecho, wiederholen, zurückmelden
echo effect   Echo
echo feature   Echofunktion
economical   wirtschaftlich
economize   sparen
economy   Wirtschaft
EDEC memory   EDEC-Speicher
edge   Flanke, Kante, Rand, Spaltenrand
edge connector   Kartenstecker
edge detection   Flankenerkennung
edge detector   Flankendetektor
edge of a column   Spaltenrand
edge sprocketed   kantenperforiert
edit   aufbereiten, bearbeiten, editieren, verändern
edit code   Aufbereitungscode
edit control character   Assembleraufbereitungszeichen
editing   Aufbereitung, Bearbeitung, Editieren
editing a document   Bearbeiten eines Dokuments
editing device   Editiergerät
editing key   Editiertaste
editing keypad   Editiertastenblock
editing method   Editierverfahren
editing mode   Editiermodus
editing option   Aufbereitungsoption
editing place   Editierplatz
editing possibility   Editiermöglichkeit
editing session   Editiersitzung
editing station   Editierstation
editing text   Bearbeiten von Text
edition date   Ausgabezeitpunkt
edit key feature   Merkmale der Editiertasten

edit line   Editierzeile
edit mask   Aufbereitungsformat, Ausgabemaske
edit menu   Editiermenü, Editmenü
edit mode   Editiermodus
edit offline   offline editieren
editor   Aufbereiter, Bearbeiter, Editor, Textverarbeitungsprogramm
editor menu   Editiermenü
editor workspace file   Arbeitsdatei des Editors
edit signal   Editzeichen
edit symbol   Editierzeichen
edit word   Aufbereitungsmaske
effect   Auswirkung, Wirkung
effective   effektiv, wirksam
effective address   effektive Adresse, wirksame Adresse
effective date   Wirksamkeitsdatum
effectiveness   Wirksamkeit
effect of freezing   Sperrwirkung
efficient operation   Leistungsbetrieb
e.g.   z.B.
EI status word   externes Unterbrechungsstatuswort
either way communication   wechselseitige Datenübermittlung
eject   Papiervorschub, Vorschub
ejection   Auswurf
ejection instruction   Auswurfbefehl
eject key   Auswurftaste
elapse   vergehen, verstreichen
elapsed time   Betriebszeit, vergangene Zeit, verstrichene Zeit
electric   elektrisch
electric actuator   elektrischer Auslöser
electrical   elektrisch
electrical block diagram   elektrisches Blockdiagramm
electrical bonding   feste elektrische Verbindung
electrical braking   elektrische Bremsung
electrical breakdown   elektrischer Durchschlag
electrical brush holder   Bürstenhalter, elektrischer Bürstenhalter
electrical component   Baugruppe, Bauteil, elektrisches Bauteil
electrical continuity test   Prüfung des elektrischen Durchgangs
electrical engineer   Elektroingenieur
electrical engineering   Elektrotechnik
electrical equipment   Elektrogeräte
Electrical Industries of America   Vereinigung der amerikanischen Elektroindustrie
electrical installation   Elektroinstallation, Installation

electrical insulating material elektrisches Isoliermaterial
electrical insulating paper elektrisches Isolierpapier
electrical insulation Isolierung, elektrische Isolierung
electrical insulation device Isolator
electrical insulation mat Isoliermatte, elektrische Isoliermatte
electrical insulation material Isolationsmaterial
electrical insulation paper Isolierpapier
electrically alterable programmable read only memory elektrisch veränderbarer programmierbarer Nur-Lese-Speicher
electrically alterable read only memory elektrisch veränderbarer Nur-Lese-Speicher
electrically erasable programmable read only memory elektrisch löschbarer programmierbarer Nur-Lese-Speicher
electrically erasable programmable ROM elektrisch löschbarer programmierbarer Nur-Lese-Speicher
electrically erasable read only memory elektrisch löschbarer Nur-Lese-Speicher
electrically insulated bushing Isolierscheibe, elektrisch isolierte Beilagscheibe
electrically operated device Elektrogerät
electrical network elektrisches Netzwerk
electrical outlet Netzsteckdose, Steckdose
electrical protection equipment elektrische Schutzeinrichtung
electrical value elektrischer Wert
electrical variable control elektrische Steuerung
electrical wiring Verdrahtung
electric ballast Belastung, Last, elektrische Last
electric box elektrische Box
electric cable elektrisches Kabel
electric cable system Verdrahtung, Verkabelung, elektrische Verkabelung
electric cell elektrische Zelle
electric coil Spule, elektrische Spule
electric conductor Leiter, elektrischer Leiter
electric conduit Installationsrohr
electric connector Anschluß, Stecker, elektrischer Anschluß
electric contact Kontakt, elektrischer Kontakt
electric contact protection Kontaktschutz, elektrischer Kontaktschutz
electric control equipment elektrische Steuereinheit

electric convertor Umformer, elektrischer Wandler
electric current control elektrische Stromregelung
electric filter Filter, elektrisches Filter
electric generator Elektrogenerator
electrician Elektriker
electric insulator Isolierstoff, Isolierung
electricity Elektrizität
electricity consumption Stromverbrauch
electricity worker Elektriker
electric lug elektrische Schleife
electric machine elektrische Maschine
electric motor Elektromotor
electric pin Steckstift
electric plug Stecker
electric power control elektrische Leistungssteuerung
electric power distribution Kraftstromverteilung
electric power distribution line Kraftstromfernleitung
electric power distribution point Kraftstromverteiler
electric power generation Kraftstromerzeugung
electric power network Kraftstromnetz
electric power station elektrisches Kraftwerk
electric power system Stromversorgungsnetz
electric power system control Steuerung des Stromversorgungsnetzes
electric power system disturbance Störung im Stromversorgungsnetz
electric power system measurement Messen im Stromversorgungsnetz
electric power system protection Schutz des Stromversorgungsnetzes
electric power transmission Kraftstromübertragung
electric power transmission line Kraftstromfernleitung, Kraftstromfernleitungsnetz
electric reactor Spule, elektrische Spule
electric regulator Regler, elektrischer Regler
electric rotor Läufer, Rotor, elektrischer Läufer
electric screen elektrischer Schirm
electric servomotor Hilfselektromotor
electric socket Fassung, elektrische Fassung
electric socket contact Kontakt in der Fassung
electric starter Elektrostarter
electric substation elektrische Unterverteilung
electric synchronisation elektrische Synchronisation
electric terminal Klemme

electric welding Elektroschweißen, Elektroschweißung
electric welding equipment Elektroschweißgerät
electric wire Draht, Leitung, elektrische Leitung
electric wiring system Verdrahtung
electroacoustic device elektroakustisches Gerät
electrochemical device elektrochemisches Gerät
electrode Elektrode
electrode change Elektrodenwechsel
electrode consumption Elektrodenabbrand
electrode holder Elektrodenhalterung
electrodeless discharge tube elektrodenlose Entladeröhre
electrolytic capacitor Elektrolytkondensator
electrolytic device Elektrolytgerät
electrolytic paper elektrolytisches Papier
electrolytic recording unit elektrolytische Schreibeinheit
electrolytic rectifier Elektrolytgleichrichter
electromagnet Elektromagnet
electromagnetic elektromagnetisch
electromagnetical interference elektromagnetische Beeinflussung
electromagnetic pulse elektromagnetischer Impuls
electromagnetic pulse effect Atomexplosionseffekt
electromechanical elektromechanisch
electromechanical device elektromechanisches Gerät
electromechanical filter elektromechanisches Filter
electromechanical output device elektromechanisches Ausgabegerät
electromechanical storage elektromechanischer Speicher
electromotive force elektromotorische Kraft
electron beam tube Elektronenstrahlröhre
electronic accounting machine elektronische Buchungsmaschine
electronically operated device elektronisches Gerät
electronic calculator Elektronenrechner, Rechner, Taschenrechner, Tischrechner
electronic crystal Quarz
electronic data processing elektronische Datenverarbeitung
electronic device elektronisches Gerät
electronic dialing system elektronisches Wählsystem

electronic engineering Elektronik
electronic file cabinet Ablagesystem, Ablagesystem im Rechner, elektronische Ablage
electronic mail E-Mail, Electronic Mail, elektronische Post
electronic mailbox Mailbox, Postbox, Postfach, elektronischer Briefkasten
electronic mail system E-Mail-System, Electronic-Mail-System
electronic message service elektronischer Nachrichtenübermittlungsdienst
electronic message system elektronisches Nachrichtenübermittlungssystem
electronic pen elektronischer Stift
electronic power supply Netzteil, elektronisches Netzteil
electronic private branch exchange elektronische private Nebenstellenanlage
electronics Elektronik
electronic storage elektronischer Speicher
electron multiplier Sekundärelektronenvervielfacher
electron tube Elektronenröhre
electron tube amplifier Röhrenverstärker
electron tube component Bauteil einer Elektronenröhre
electron tube holder Röhrenfassung, Röhrenhalterung
electron tube oscillator Röhrenoszillator
electron tube structure Aufbau einer Röhre
electron tube technology Röhrentechnik
electron wave tube Elektronenwellenröhre
electrophotographic paper elektrofotografisches Papier
electrophotographic recording unit elektrofotografische Schreibeinheit
electrosensitive paper elektrosensitives Papier
electrosensitive recording unit elektrosensitive Aufzeichnungseinheit
electrostatic device elektrostatisches Gerät
electrostatic recording unit elektrostatische Schreibeinheit
electrostatic storage elektrostatischer Speicher
electro technology Elektrotechnik
element Element, Glied, Teil
element chaining Elementverkettung
element processor Elementarprozessor
eligible befähigt, geeignet
eligible for bonus bonusberechtigt, bonusfähig
eliminate beheben, beseitigen, eliminieren
elimination of errors Fehlerbehebung, Fehlerbeseitigung
elite pitch Elite-Zeichenabstand

ellipsoid Ellipsoid
elongation at tear Reißdehnung
E-Mail E-Mail, elektronic Mail, elektronische Post
embed einlagern, einstreuen
embedded conduit eingebettetes Rohr
emergency circuit Notstromkreis
emergency electrical installation Notstrominstallation
emergency run activation Notlaufeinschaltung
emergency run code Notlaufschlüssel
emergency run reservation Notlaufbuchung
emergency shutdown Notabschaltung
emergency target Notfallziel
emitter Emitter
emitter coupled logic circuitry emittergekoppelte Halbleiterschaltungen
emphasize betonen, hervorheben
emphasized print Fettdruck, verstärkter Druck
emphasizing text Hervorheben von Text
emphatic stress Satzbetonung
employ beschäftigen, einstellen
employee Angestellter, Arbeitnehmer, Mitarbeiter
employees chamber code Arbeiter-/Angestelltenkammerschlüssel
empties Leergut, Leergutmaterial
empties outstanding Leergutaußenstände
empties quantity Leergutmenge
empties registration Leerguterfassung
empties submission Leergutbeistellung
empties values Leerwerte
empty entleert, leer
emulate emulieren
emulation Emulation
emulator Emulator
emulator generation Generieren eines Emulators
enable Freigabe, einschalten, ermöglichen, freigeben, zulassen
enable auto answerback Autoantwort einschalten, Einschalten des automatischen Answerback
enable condition Freigabebedingung
enabled freigegeben
enable disconnect character Einschalten des Unterbrechungszeichens
enable end of line Einschalten des Zeilenendezeichens
enable transmission Einschalten der Übertragungsfunktion
enamelled wire Lackdraht
enamelling Emaillieren

encapsuled transformer gekapselter Transformator
encashment period Einlösungsfrist
encode kodieren, verschlüsseln
encode/decode kodieren/dekodieren, verschlüsseln/entschlüsseln
encoder Kodierer, Verschlüssler
encoder shaft Kodiererwelle
encoding Kodieren, Verschlüsselung
encoding of mutated vowels Umlautverschlüsselung
encoding of umlauts Umlautverschlüsselung
encourage animieren, ermutigen
encumber beeinträchtigen
encumbered behaftet
end Ende, anhalten
end around carry Rückübertrag
end character Endezeichen
end criterion Endekriterium
end date Endedatum
end identifier Endkennzeichen
end indication Endekennzeichnung
ending label Endekennsatz, Endmarke, Endmarkierung
ending sentence Endsatz
end instruction Endeanweisung
end jump box Endesprungbox
end key Endetaste
end node Endknoten
end number Endnummer
end of address Adressenende
end of amortization Abschreibungsende
end of backup Beenden der Sicherung
end of block Blockende
end of block character Blockendezeichen, Satzendezeichen
end of buffer Pufferende
end of buffer address Pufferendadresse
end of card deck Kartenstapelende
end of character Zeichenende
end of contract Kontraktende, Vertragsende
end of data Datenende
end of date Datenende
end of deck Kartenstapelende, Stapelende
end of depreciation Abschreibungsende
end of field Feldende
end of field key Feldendetaste
end of file Dateiende, Ende Datei
end of file block Dateiendeblock
end of file code Dateiendecode, EOF-Code
end of file mark Dateiendmarkierung
end of financial year Geschäftsjahresende, Geschäftsjahreswechsel

83

end of form Formularende
end of input Eingabeende
end of job Auftragsende
end of line Zeilenende
end of line character Zeilenendezeichen
end of line signal Zeilenendsignal
end of log tape Logbandende
end of memory Speicherende
end of message Ende der Nachricht
end of message signal Nachrichtenendesignal
end of page Seitenende
end of paper indicator Papierendeanzeiger
end of partition Partitionsende
end of position status Positionierungsendestatus
end of posting Buchungsende
end of print position Druckendeposition
end of process Vorgangsende
end of record Satzende
end of reel Bandende, Spulenende
end of reel mark Spulenendmarkierung
end of sector Sektorende
end of selection Wählende
end of selection signal Wählendezeichen
end of session Sitzungsende
end of tape Bandende, Bandendemarke
end of tape mark Bandendemarke
end of text Textende
end of the month Monatsultimo, Monatswechsel
end of the program Programmende
end of the table Tabellenende
end of track Spurende
end of transaction Transaktionsende
end of transmission Übertragungsende, Übertragungsende
end of transmission block Ende des Übertragungsblocks
end of volume Datenträgerende
end of word Wortende
end of zone key Zonenendetaste
end page Endeseite
end procedure Endebehandlung
end product Enderzeugnis
end result Gesamtergebnis
end run Endlauf
end statement Endanweisung
end switch Endschalter
end system Endsystem
end to end Ende-Ende
end-to-end turn Schlußwindung
endurance Lebensdauer
endurance test Dauerprüfung

end user Anwender, Endbenutzer
end-user computing Endbenutzer-Datenverarbeitung
enforce erzwingen
engine Motor
engineer Ingenieur, Techniker
engineering change order Änderung, Änderungsanweisung
engraving Gravierung
enhance verbessern
enhanced graphics adapter erweiterte Grafikkarte, erweiterter Grafikadapter
enhancement Funktionsergänzung, Verbesserung
enhancement protocol Harmonisierungsprotokoll
enlargement Vergrößerung
enquire anfragen, erkundigen
enquiry Anfrage, Frage
enquiry delete list Anfragelöschliste
enquiry example Abfragebeispiel
enquiry generation Anfragengenerierung
enquiry header Anfragekopf
enquiry header text Anfragekopftext
enquiry item Anfrageposition
enquiry item text Anfragepositionstext
enquiry number Anfragenummer
enquiry option Abfragemöglichkeit
enquiry print program Anfrageschreibungsprogramm
enquiry processing Anfrageabwicklung, Anfragebearbeitung
enquiry registration Anfrageerfassung
enquiry text Anfragetext
enquiry voucher Anfragebeleg
ensure sicherstellen
enter betreten, eingeben, einreichen, einsteigen, eintragen, eintreten
enter file Eingabedatei
enter graphics mode Einschalten des Grafikmodus
enter in the ledger journalisieren
enter invoice Rechnungseingabe
enter key Returntaste
enterprise Unternehmen, Unternehmung
enter procedure Eingabeprozedur
enter process Eingabeprozeß, Enterprozeß
enter program Eingabeprogramm
entire vollständig
entire file Gesamtdatei
entitle berechtigen
entity Entität, Instanz, Objekt

entity relation   Entity Relation, Größengeneration
entity relationship   Objektbeziehung
entity relationship model   Entity-Relation-Modell, Objektbeziehungsmodell
entrepreneur   Unternehmer
entrepreneurial group   Unternehmensgruppe
entrust   betrauen
entry   Eingabe, Eingang, Einstieg, Eintrag, Eintragung, Eintritt, Erklärung
entry card   Eingabekarte
entry file   Eintragungsdatei
entry form   Eingabeformular
entry format   Eingabeformat
entry length   Eingabelänge, Eintragslänge
entry level members   Einstiegsmodelle
entry level model   Einstiegsmodell
entry level system   Einstiegsmodell
entry line   Eingabezeile
entry mode   Eingabemodus
entry name   Eintragsname
entry number   Eintragsnummer, Jobnummer
entry of variables   Variableneingabe
entry parameter   Eingangsparameter
entry phase   Eingabephase
entry point   Eingangspunkt
entry procedure   Eingabeprozedur
entry process   Eingabeprozeß
entry program   Eingabeprogramm
entry symbol   Eingabezeichen
entry syntax   Eingabeformalismus
entry type   Eingabeart
enumerate   aufzählen
enumeration   Aufzählung
envelope entry   Briefhülleneinzug, Kuverteinzug, Umschlagseinzug
envelope feeding device   Briefhüllenführung, Kuvertzuführung, Umschlagszuführung
envelope run   Briefhüllendurchlauf, Kuvertdurchlauf, Umschlagsdurchlauf
envelope setting   Briefhüllenanlage, Kuvertanlage, Umschlagsanlage
envelope stacker   Briefhüllenablage, Kuvertablage, Umschlagsablage
environment   Betriebsgegebenheiten, Betriebsumgebung, Umgebung, Umgebung
environmental condition   Umgebungsbedingung
environmental lost time   umgebungsbedingte Ausfallzeit
environmental requirement   Anforderungen an die Umgebung

environmental requirements   Umgebungsbedingung
environmental temperature   Umgebungstemperatur
EOT mark   Bandendemarke
epitaxial layer   epitaxiale Schicht
eprom card   EPROM-Karte
eprom programmer   EPROM-Programmiergerät
equal   gleich
equalizer   Ausgleichsverbindung, Entzerrer
equally   gleichermaßen
equal sign   Gleichheitszeichen
equal to   gleich
equate   gleichsetzen
equation   Gleichung
equijoin   Gleichverbindung
equip   ausrüsten, ausstatten
equipment   Ausrüstung, Gerät
equivalence name   Äquivalenzname
equivalent   äquivalent
erasable programmable read only memory   lösch- und programmierbarer Nur-Lese-Speicher
erasable storage   löschbarer Speicher
erase   löschen, radieren
eraseability   Löschbarkeit
erase in display   Löschen auf dem Bildschirm, Löschen im Bildschirm
erase in line   Löschen in Zeile
erase mode   Löschmodus
erase to end of line   Löschen bis Zeilenende
erase to end of screen   Löschen bis Bildschirmende
erase window   Fenster löschen, Löschfenster
erasing text   Text löschen
erasure   Löschung
erasure mode   Löschmodus
erasure procedure   Löschvorgang
ergonomics   Ergonomie
erroneous   falsch, fehlerbehaftet, fehlerhaft, irrtümlich
error   Fehler, Fehlfunktion, Störung
error activation   Fehleransteuerung
error amount   Fehlersumme
error analysis   Fehleranalyse
error analysis dump   Speicherauszug bei Fehlern
error checking and correction   Fehlerprüfung und Korrektur
error checking character   Fehlerkontrollzeichen

error clause Fehlerverzweigung
error code Errorcode, Fehlercode
error code list Fehlercodeliste
error condition Fehlerbedingung, Fehlerzustand
error control Fehlerkontrolle
error control procedure Fehlerüberwachung
error control unit Fehlerschutzeinheit, Fehlerüberwachungseinheit
error correcting Fehlerkorrektur
error correcting code Fehlerkorrektur, Fehlerkorrekturcode
error correcting program Fehlerkorrekturprogramm
error correction Fehlerbeseitigung, Fehlererkennung
error correction code Code zur Fehlerkorrektur, Fehlerkorrekturcode
error correction device Fehlerschutzgerät
error detecting code Fehlererkennungscode, Fehlersuchcode
error detection Fehlerbehebung
error detection and correction Fehlererkennung
error detection bit Fehlererkennungsbit
error diagnosis Fehlerdiagnose
error display Fehleranzeige
error estimation Fehlerabschätzung
error evaluation Fehlerauswertung
error exit Fehlerausgang
error file Fehlerdatei
error flag Fehlerkennzeichen
error free fehlerfrei
error from terminal Fehler am Terminal
error handler Fehlerbehandlungsprogrammm, Fehlerbehandlungsroutine, Fehlerunterprogramm
error handling Fehlerbehandlung
error handling routine Fehlerbehandlungsunterprogramm
error indication Fehlersymptom
error indicator Fehleranzeige, Störungsanzeige
error in partition Fehler im Bereich, Partitionsfehler
error inquiry Fehlerabfrage
error line Fehlerzeile
error list Fehlerliste, Fehlerverzeichnis
error listing Fehlerinhaltsverzeichnis, Fehlerliste, Fehlerverzeichnis
error listing file Fehlerprotokolldatei
error log Fehlerprotokoll
error log file Fehlerlogdatei, Fehlerprotokolldatei

error logging Fehlerprotokollierung
error message Fehlermeldung, Fehlernachricht
error message subroutine Fehlermeldungsunterprogramm
error note Fehlerhinweis
error number Fehlernummer
error off abbrechen, fehlerhafte Beendigung
error page Fehlerseite
error processing program Fehlerbehandlungsprogramm
error processing routine Fehlerbehandlungsroutine
error rate Fehlerhäufigkeit
error recognition Fehlererkennung
error recovery Wiederanlauf im Fehlerfall
error recovery sequence Wiederanlaufsequenz im Fehlerfall
error report Fehlerbericht, Fehlerliste, Fehlerreport
error report mask Fehlerreportmaske
error search Fehlersuche
error situation Fehlerkonstellation
error subroutine Fehlerunterprogramm
error text Fehlertext
error text number Fehlertextnummer
error value Fehlerwert
erstellen create
escape and control sequence Escape- und Steuersequenz
escape character Escapezeichen
escape mode Codeumschaltung
escape sequence Escapesequenz
especially besonders, eigens
essential wesentlich
estimate Schätzwert, einschätzen, schätzen, vermuten
estimated time of arrival voraussichtliche Ankunft
estimated value Schätzwert, Wertansatz
estimation Schätzung
ethernet file transfer protocol Ethernet Dateiübertragungsprotokoll
european article numbering europäische Artikelnummer
evaluable auswertbar
evaluate auswerten, ermitteln, feststellen
evaluate an expression Wert eines Ausdrucks ermitteln
evaluated according to average durchschnittliche Bewertung, durchschnittsbewertet
evaluate memory fit Speicherbelegung prüfen
evaluation Auswertung
evaluation utility Auswertungshilfsprogramm

even   gerade, geradzahlig, gleichmäßig
even parity   gerade Parität
event controlled   ereignisgesteuert
event drum   Ereignisschrittschaltwerk
event flag   Ereignismarke, Ereignismarkierung
event flag cluster   Gruppe von Ereignismarkierungen
event scheduling system   Ablaufsteuerung
eventuality   Eventualität, Möglichkeit
eventually   schließlich
every time   jedesmal
evidence   Nachweis
evidence of use   Teileverwendungsnachweis, Verwendungsnachweis
evident   ersichtlich
exact   genau
examination   Untersuchung
examine   durchsuchen, prüfen, untersuchen
examining variables   Überprüfen von Variablen
example   Beispiel, Musterbeispiel
example of control cards   Vorlaufkartenbeispiel
example of header cards   Vorlaufkartenbeispiel
exceed   überschreiten, übersteigen
exceeding end of form   Formularendeüberschreitung
exceeding the time   Zeitüberschreitung
exception   Ausnahme, Unterbrechung
exceptional   außerordentlich
exceptional condition   Ausnahmezustand
exception character   Ausschlußzeichen
exception condition   Ablaufunterbrechung, Ausnahmebedingung
exception file   Ausnahmedatei
exception handling   Ausnahmebehandlung
exception line   anwendergesteuerte Ausgabe
exception mask   Unterbrechungsmaske
exception record   anwendergesteuerter Satz
exception state   Unterbrechungsstatus
exception table   Ausnahmetabelle
exception validation   Ausnahmebewertung
excerpt   Ausschnitt, Extrakt
excerpt records   Extraktsätze
excerpt tape   Extraktband
excess   überlaufen, Überlauf
excess billing   Überrechnung
excess characters   überzählige Zeichen
excessive   übermäßig
excessive data   Überlaufdaten
excessive quantity   Überlieferung
exchange   Austausch, Vermittlung, Vermittlungsknoten, Wechsel, austauschen, tauschen, wechseln
exchange costs   Wechselspesen

exchange field   Austauschfeld
exchange rate   Kurs, Währungskurs
exchange rate discrepancy   Kursdifferenz
exchange rate fluctuation   Kursschwankung
exchange rate table   Kurstabelle, Währungskurstabelle
exchange rate value   Kurswert
excise tax   Gewerbesteuer, Verbrauchssteuer
exciter   Erreger, Steuersender
exclamation mark   Ausrufezeichen, Ausrufungszeichen
exclude   ausschließen
exclusion file specifier   Ausschlußdateispezifikation
exclusive   ausschließlich, exklusiv
exclusiveness character   Ausschließlichkeitszeichen
exclusive or   Exklusiv-ODER
exec   Systemsteuerung
executable   ausführbar, lauffähig
executable image   ausführbares Programm
executable program   ablauffähiges Programm, lauffähiges Programm
execute   ausführen, durchführen
execution time array   ladbare Feldgruppe
executing   Durchführung
execution   Ablauf, Ausführung
execution run   Ausführungslauf
execution time   Ablaufzeit, Ausführungszeit
executive   Systemsteuerung
executive mode   Executive-Modus
executive request   Anforderung an die Systemsteuerung
executive system   Systemsteuerung
exemplary   exemplarisch
exerciser   Prüfgerät
exhausted   erschöpft
exist   bestehen, existieren, vorhanden sein
existing   alt, vorhanden
exit   Ausgang, Austritt, austreten, beenden
exit code   Exitcode
exit from   beenden
exit graphics mode   Ausschalten des Grafikmodus
exit hub   Ausgangsbuchse
exit no save   beenden ohne Sichern
exit with changes   beenden mit Änderungen
expand   ausbauen, ausbauen, erweitern, expandieren, vergrößern
expandability   Ausbaubarkeit, Erweiterbarkeit
expanded metal   Streckgitter
expand escapement   Sperrschritt

expansion Ausbau, Dehnung, Erweiterung, Expandierung
expansion box Erweiterungsbox
expansion of partition control area Partitionssteuerbereichs-Ergänzung
expansion ram RAM-Erweiterung, Speichererweiterung
expansion register Erweiterungsregister
expansion slot Erweiterungssteckplatz
expansion unit Erweiterungseinheit
expect erwarten
expected time of response erwartete Antwortzeit
expected useful life Nutzungsdauer
expedited data Vorrangdaten
expendable ausgebbar
expendible entbehrlich
expenditure Aufwand
expense account Aufwandskonto, Kostenkonto
expenses Spesen
expenses charged Spesenbelastung
expenses flag Spesenkennzeichen
expenses posting Aufwandsbuchung, Spesenbuchung
experience Erfahrung, erfahren
experiment experimentieren
experimental gaming Planspiele
expiration Verfall
expiration date Verfalldatum
expire ablaufen, verfallen, verstreichen
expiry Verfall
expiry of warranty Garantieablauf
explain darlegen, darstellen, erklären, erläutern
explanation Erklärung, Erläuterung
explanation page Erläuterungsseite
explanatory erklärend, erläuternd
explanatory message erklärende Meldung
explicable erklärbar
explicit ausdrücklich, explizit
exploded view Explosionszeichnung
explosion proof drain explosionsgeschützter Kanal
explosion proof housing explosionsgeschütztes Gehäuse
explosion proof seal explosionsgeschützte Dichtung
exponent Exponent
exponentation Potenzierung
exponential exponentiell
exponential notation Potenz, Zahl als Mantisse und Potenz darstellen, exponentielle Schreibweise
exponent modifier Exponentenfaktor

export exportieren
exposed ausgesetzt, ausgestellt, frei, offen, ungeschützt
expound darlegen, darstellen
expression Ausdruck
expressive aussagefähig
extend erstrecken, erweitern, reichen, vergrößern, verlängern
extended access method direktsequentielle Zugriffsmethode
extended address register erweitertes Adreßregister
extended BASIC erweitertes BASIC
extended binary coded decimal interchange code EBCDIC-Code
extended bit map module Modul für Bitmustergrafik
extended control address Steueradreßerweiterung
extended control field Steuerfelderweiterung
extended file name erweiterter Dateiname
extended instruction set erweiterter Befehlssatz
extended main storage Sekundärhauptspeicher
extended memory monitor Monitor für erweiterten Speicher
extended precision erweiterte Genauigkeit
extended precision floating point Gleitpunktarithmetik mit doppelter Genauigkeit
extended result output erweiterte Resultatausgabe
extended selftest program erweiterte Selbstdiagnose
extended storage Ergänzungsspeicher
extended system software Erweiterungspaket zur Grundsoftware
extender card Erweiterungskarte
extension Ausbau, Erweiterung, Nebenstelle
extension cable Verlängerungskabel
extension code Erweiterungcode
extension function Erweiterungsfunktion
extension register Zusatzregister
extensive umfangreich, umfassend, weitgehend
extent Umfang
extention register Zusatzregister
extent mode Druckbereichsmodus
extent of the project Projektdauer
extent print Druckbereich
extents Dateibereiche
extent table Dateibereichstabelle
external außen, extern
external clocking externe Takterzeugung
external command externes Kommando

external computer externer Rechner
external data link Rechnerverbund
external device Peripheriegerät
external function acknowledgement Bestätigung bezüglich externer Funktion
external function request Anforderung bezüglich externer Funktion
external function word Funktionswort für Peripherie
external indicator externe Bezugszahl
external input externer Eingang
external interrupt Unterbrechung durch periphere Einheit
external item Systemkomponente
external loss time umgebungsbedingte Ausfallzeit
externally specified index hardwaremäßige Verteilung der Daten
external output externer Ausgang
external reset externes Rücksetzen
external speaker separater Lautsprecher
external storage Auslagerung, externer Speicher
external subroutine externe Subroutine, externes Unterprogramm
external table externe Tabelle
external trade Außenwirtschaft
external trade relations Außenwirtschaftsverkehr
external transmit clock externer Sendetaktgeber
extract Auszug, Extrakt, extrahieren
extract factory setting vom Hersteller eingestellt
extraction counter Indexmarkenzähler
extractor Ausziehvorrichtung
extraneous gebietsfremd
extra pay Zulage
extrapolate hochrechnen
extrapolation Hochrechnung
eyelet Kabelöse, Öse

F

face plate Frontplatte, Frontverkleidung
facilitate erleichtern, helfen
facilitation of work Arbeitserleichterung
facilities management Verwaltung der Systemeinrichtungen
facilities manager Leiter des Rechenzentrums
facility control Gerätedisposition
facility length Länge des Feldes zur Angabe von Leistungsmerkmalen
facility pool Tabelle der verfügbaren Geräte
facility request Leistungsmerkmalanforderung, Leistungsmerkmalaufruf
facility status Gerätestatus
facsimile Fernkopie, Telefax
facsimile communication equipment compatibility Fernkopiererkompatibilität
facsimile equipment Fernkopierer, Telefaxgerät
fact Fakt, Tatsache
factor Faktor, Operand
factorial notation Fakultätsdarstellung
factor of cooperation Kooperationsfaktor
factor total Faktorenaddition
factory Firma, Werk
factory acceptance test Werksabnahmetest
factory authorization Werksberechtigung
factory code Werksschlüssel
factory hardened für industriellen Einsatz
factory hardened keyboard Tastatur für industriellen Einsatz
factory information Werksangabe
factory inventory Werksbestand
factory level Werksebene
factory number Werksnummer
factory preset Voreinstellung vom Hersteller, Werkseinstellung, vom Hersteller eingestellt
factory records Werkssätze
factory segment Werkssegment
factory setting Voreinstellung vom Hersteller, Werkseinstellung, vom Hersteller eingestellt
factory supplies Betriebsstoffe
factory table Werkstabelle
fade out Verblassen der Anzeige, ausblenden
Fahrenheit Fahrenheit
fail code diagnostic Fehlercodeauswertung
failing bit fehlerhaftes Bit
failsafe ausfallsicher, fehlerunempfindlich
fail safe posting line Notlaufbuchungszeile
fail safe state Notlaufzustand

failure Ausfall, Einbruch, Fehler
failure analysis program Fehleranalyseprogramm, Programm zur Fehleranalyse
failure and malfunction report Störungsbericht
failure distribution Fehlerverteilung
failure to deliver Lieferverzug
fair Messe
fall entfallen, fallen
falling short Unterschreitung
fall short unterschreiten
fall time Flankenabfallzeit
false falsch, logisch falsch, nicht wahr
false drop Fehlantwort
fan Gebläse
fanfold paper Endlospapier
farewell page Abschiedsseite
fast schnell
fast auxiliary memory schneller Hilfsspeicher
fastening screw Befestigungsschraube
fast file scan schnelle Dateisuchoperation
fatal fatal, schwerwiegend
fatal error schwerwiegender Fehler
fatal error handling Behandlung von schwerwiegenden Fehlern
fatal error help Hilfe bei schwerwiegenden Fehlern
father Vater
father version Vaterversion
fault Fehler, Fehlfunktion, Störung
fault finding Fehlersuche
fault indicator Fehleranzeige
fault location by interpretive testing Fehlerlokalisierung durch interpretatives Testen
fault recovery path Fehlerbehebung
fault tolerant fehlertolerant
fault tolerant computer fehlertoleranter Computer, fehlertoleranter Rechner
favor begünstigen
fax Fax, Fernkopie, Telefax, faxen
fax box Faxbox
fax card Faxkarte
fax compatibility Faxkompatibilität, Fernkopiererkompatibilität
fax group 2 Fax Gruppe 2
fax group 3 Fax Gruppe 3
fax group 4 Fax Gruppe 4, ISDN-Fax
fax machine Fax, Fernkopierer
fax transmission Faxübertragung
FB monitor Vordergrund-/Hintergrundmonitor
feature Leistungsmerkmal, Merkmal, Möglichkeit, ausgestattet sein mit, verfügen über
feature memory Speicher für Terminalattribute

feature rich vielseitig
federal bank Bundesbank
federal legal gazette Bundesanzeiger
federal ministry Bundesministerium
federal post office Deutsche Bundespost
fee Gebühr, Honorar
feed Transport, Vorschub, eingeben
feedback control system Regelungssystem
feedback trim einstellbare Rückkopplung
feed connection Transportverbindung
feed control unit Auswahleinheit
feeder Zuführfach
feed error Zuführungsfehler
feed feature Vorschubeinrichtung
feeding for self-requirement Eigenbedarfseinspeisung
feed instruction Transportbefehl
feed scala Anlegeskala
feed table Anlegetisch
feed tape carriage Lochbandvorschub
feed unit Vorschubaggregat
feet Fuß
female weiblich
ferroelectric device ferroelektrisches Gerät
ferrous metal Eisenmetall
fetch Abruf, holen
fexible disk system Diskettensystem
fiber optic system Lichtwellenleitersystem
fibre optics Glasfaseroptik
fibre optique glasfaseroptisch
fictitious item Scheinposition
field Bereich, Datenfeld, Feld, Feldweiser, Kolonne
field address Feldadresse
field alignment Feldausrichtung
field attribute Feldattribut
field card Feldkarte
field change order Änderung beim Kunden
field characteristic Feldeigenschaft
field content Feldinhalt
field control Feldsteuerung
field control character Feldsteuerzeichen
field conversion Feldkonvertierung
field conversion description Feldkonvertierungsbeschreibung
field data Felddaten
field data format Feldformat
field declaration Felderläuterung
field declaration table Felderläuterungstabelle
field definition Feldbegrenzung, Felddefinition
field delimiter mode Feldendezeichenmodus
field description Feldbeschreibung
field description card Felddefinitionskarte

field description record Feldbeschreibungssatz
field description table Feldbeschreibungstabelle
field descriptor Feldbeschreibung
field dimension Felddimension
field effect transistor Feldeffekttransistor
field function Feldfunktion
field group Feldgruppe
field group mask Feldgruppenmaske
field group menu Feldgruppenauswahlmenü
field group number Feldgruppennummer
field group selection Feldgruppenauswahl
field length Feldlänge
field location Feldposition
field name Feldbezeichnung, Feldname
field name table Feldnamentabelle
field number Feldnummer
field of application Einsatzgebiet
field of variables Variablenfeld
field pole Feldpol
field related feldbezogen
field replaceable unit austauschbare Funktionseinheit, austauschbare Funktionseinheit, austauschbare Komponente, beim Kunden austauschbare Einheit, vor Ort austauschbare Einheit
field select Feldauswahl
field selection Feldansteuerung, Feldauswahl
field separation Feldtrennung
field seperator Feldtrenner
field service technischer Kundendienst
field size Feldgröße
field specification Feldangabe, Feldspezifikation
field specification character Feldspezifikationszeichen
field system System im Einsatz
field table Feldtabelle
field table generator Feldtabellengenerator
field test Betriebsversuch, Feldversuch
field type Feldart, Feldtyp
field value Feldwert
field wiring Verdrahtung vor Ort
FIFO memory FIFO-Speicher
figure Abbildung, Rechengröße, Zahl, auswerten
figures key Zifferntaste
filament power supply Heizstromversorgung
file Datei, Ordner, ablegen, archivieren, speichern
file access Dateizugriff
file access block Dateizugriffsblock
file access channel Dateizugriffskanal

file address register Dateiadreßregister
file administration Dateiverwaltung
file allocation Dateizuweisung
file allocation table Tabelle der Dateizuweisungen
file attribute Dateiattribut
file block Dateiblock
file cabinet Ablage, Ablagesystem
file cabinet maintenance Ablageverwaltung
file changing dateiverändernd
file command Dateikommando
file concatenation Dateiverkettung
file conception Dateikonzept
file content Dateiinhalt
file continuation value Fortsetzungswert für die Datei
file control block Dateisteuerungsblock, Datensteuerblock
file control block list Dateisteuerbereichsliste
file control group Dateisteuergruppe
file control program Dateisteuerungsprogramm, Programm zur Dateisteuerung
file convention Dateikonventionen
file converter Dateiumsetzer
file creation Dateianlage
file cycle Dateizyklus
file data read error Fehler beim Lesen der Datei
file data write error Fehler beim Schreiben auf die Datei
file definition Dateibeschreibung, Dateidefinition
file description Dateibeschreibung
file description module Dateibeschreibungsmodul
file descriptor Dateibeschreibung
filed message abgelegte Nachricht
file extension Dateierweiterung, Dateityp
file function Dateifunktion
file header Dateikopf, Dateikopfsatz
file header label Dateianfangskennsatz
file identification Dateiidentifizierung
file identifier Dateikennzeichen
file index Dateiindex
file information block Dateiinformationsblock
file initialisation Dateieröffnung
file input Dateieingabe
file input output Schreiben und Lesen von Dateien
file instruction Dateianweisung
file list Dateiliste
file locked Datei gesperrt
file maintenance Ablageverwaltung

file management Dateiverwaltung
file manipulation Dateibearbeitung
file modification Dateiänderung
file name Dateibezeichnung, Dateiname, Ordnername
filename directory Verzeichnis der Dateinamen
file number Dateianzahl, Dateinummer
file on the hard disk Festplattendatei
file open for update Datei geöffnet zum Verändern
file operation Dateioperation
file organisation Dateiart, Dateiorganisation
file overflow Dateiüberlauf
file overrun Dateiüberlauf
file protection Dateischutz
file register Dateiregister
file release Dateifreigabe
files catalog Verzeichnis der Dateinamen
file section end Dateiabschnittsende
file section number Dateiabschnittsnummer
file section sequence Dateiabschnittsfolge
file selection qualifier Dateiauswahlqualifizierer
file sequence number Dateifolgenummer
file server File Server
file sharing gemeinsamer Zugriff auf eine Datei
file size Dateigröße
file space Speicherkapazität
file specific dateispezifisch
file specification Dateispezifikation
file specifier Dateibezeichner, Dateispezifikation
file status variable Dateistatusvariable
file structure Dateistruktur
file system Dateisystem
file tape combination Datei-Bandkombination
file to file Datei zu Datei
file transfer Dateitransfer, Dateiübertragung
file transfer program Dateiübertragungsprogramm
file transfer programm Programm zur Dateiübertragung
file transfer protocol Dateiübertragungsprotokoll, Protokoll zur Dateiübertragung
file type Dateiart, Dateityp
file use Dateiverwendung
fill Füll-, füllen
fill character Füllzeichen
filled in ausgefüllt
filler Füllzeichen
filler byte Füllbyte
filler processing Füllzeichenbehandlung

filling level Füllungsgrad
film Film, aufnehmen, filmen, verfilmen
filter scheme Filterschema
fin Transportstachel
final endgültig
final balance Endsaldo
final billing flag Restrechnungskennzeichen
final delivery Endauslieferung, Endlieferung
final delivery flag Endlieferkennzeichen
final invoice Restrechnung
final line Schlußzeile
final line number Endzeilennummer
finally abschließend, schließlich
finally delivered endausgeliefert
final page Schlußseite
final position Endposition
final print position Enddruckposition
final program Schlußprogramm
final repayment Resttilgung
final stock Endbestand
final warning letzte Warnung
finances Finanzen
financial Finanz-, Geschäfts-, Wirtschafts-, finanziell
financial accounting Finanzbuchhaltung
financial asset Finanzanlage
financial institute Geldinstitut
financial institution Geldinstitut
financial month Geschäftsmonat
financial report Geschäftsbericht, Planungsübersicht
financial report analysis Auswerten eines Geschäftsberichtes
financial report generation Erstellen eines Geschäftsberichtes
financial transactions Wirtschaftsverkehr
financial year Geschäftsjahr, Wirtschaftsjahr
financial year before last Vorvorgeschäftsjahr
financing bill of exchange Finanzierungswechsel
find auffinden, finden
find again wiederfinden
findings Befund
fine fein
fine structure Feinstruktur
fine tuning Abgleich, Feinabstimmung
fine tuning variable Feinabstimmungsvariable
fin feed device Stacheltransporteinrichtung
finish abwickeln, beenden
finished article Fertigfabrikat
finished article warehouse Fertigproduktlager
finished product Fertigerzeugnis, Fertigprodukt
finishing Nachbearbeitung

finite element modeling Finite Elemente Modell
firm Firma
firm name Firmenname
firmware Firmware
firmware compatibility Firmware-Kompatibilität
first erstmalig
first address range erster Adreßbereich
first creating Ersterstellung
first installation Erstinstallation
first menu Ausgangsmenü
first named erstgenannt
first normal form erste Normalform
first time initialization Erstinitialisierung
fiscal year Geschäftsjahr
fit passen
fit for input eingebbar
fix definition Fixdefinition
fixed fest, festgelegt, feststehend, fix
fixed account Fixkonto
fixed accounts table Fixkontentabelle
fixed assets listing Sachanlagenbestandsliste
fixed block Block fester Länge, fester Block
fixed block format festes Blockformat
fixed capacitor Festkondensator
fixed decimal Festkommaautomatik
fixed disk Festplatte, Festplattenspeicher
fixed disk drive Festplattenlaufwerk
fixed disk write protect Schreibschutz für die Festplatte
fixed entry point feste Einsprungadresse
fixed format festes Format
fixed identifier Festname
fixed interest Festzins
fixed length block Block fester Länge
fixed line numbers feste Zeilennummern
fixed mass storage fest zugeordneter Massenspeicher
fixed mode festes Format
fixed point Festkomma
fixed point addition Festkommaaddition
fixed point arithmetic Festkommaarithmetik
fixed point operation Festkommabetrieb
fixed point representation Festkommadarstellung, Festpunktschreibweise
fixed point system Festkommasystem
fixed program flow fester Programmablauf
fixed resistor Festwiderstand
fixed time interval feste Zeitspanne
fixed value Festwert
fixed word length feste Wortlänge
fixing screw Befestigungsschraube

fixing unit Fixiereinrichtung
fixture Befestigung
flag Kennzeichen, Marke, Markierung, Schalter, Softwareschalter, kennnzeichnen, markieren
flag bit Fehlerkennzeichnungsbit, Kennzeichenbit
flag byte Kennzeichnungsbyte, Schalter
flameproof enclosure nichtentflammbares Gehäuse
flame-retardant flammenverzögernd
flame test Flammprobe
flammability Entflammbarkeit
flammability rating Flammbarkeitswert
flank Flanke
flash Blitz, Flash, blinken
flashing cycle Blinktakt
flashing signal Blinksignal
flat cable Flachbandkabel
flat washer Unterlegscheibe
flexibility Biegsamkeit, Universalität
flexible biegsam, flexibel
flexible cable biegsames Kabel
flexible conductor flexibler Leiter
flexible control block Dateisteuerblock
flexible control group Dateisteuergruppe
flexible disk Diskette, Floppy Disk
flexible manufacturing system flexibles Fertigungssystem
flicker flackern
flicker on flackern
flight control Flugregelung
flight simulator Flugsimulator
flight strip printer Kontrollstreifendrucker
flip chip device Flip-Chip-Bauteil
flip flop Flip-Flop
float gleiten, schwanken, schwimmen
floater Schwimmer
floating decimal Fließkomma, Gleitkomma, Gleitkommaautomatik
floating point Fließkomma, Gleitkomma
floating point adapter Fließkommaadapter, Gleitkommaadapter
floating point arithmetic Gleitkommaarithmetik, Gleitpunktarithmetik
floating point availability Fließkommaeinrichtung, Gleitkommaeinrichtung
floating point computation Fließkommarechnung, Gleitkommarechnung
floating point instruction Fließkommabefehl, Gleitkommabefehl
floating point multiplication Fließkommamultiplikation, Gleitkommamultiplikation

floating point number Fließkommazahl, Gleitkommazahl
floating point operation Fließkommaoperation, Gleitkommaoperation
floating point processor Gleitkommaprozessor
floating point representation Fließkommadarstellung, Fließkommaschreibweise, Gleitkommadarstellung, Gleitkommaschreibweise, Gleitpunktdarstellung
floating point routine Gleitkommaroutine
floating point unit Gleitkommaeinheit
floating point word Fließkommawort, Gleitkommawort
floating print number Gleitkommazahl
floor stand Standfuß
floor stand model Standmodell
floppy disk Diskette, Floppy, Floppy Disk
floppy disk controller Diskettencontroller, Floppy Disk-Steuerung
floppy disk drive Diskettenlaufwerk, Floppy Disk-Laufwerk
floppy diskette Floppy Disk
floppy disk storage Floppy-Disk-Speicher
floppy disk system Diskettensystem
floppy station Diskettenstation
flow Fluß
flow analysis program Ablaufanalysenprogramm
flow chart Ablaufplan, Flußdiagramm, Flußplan, Programmablaufplan
flow control Flußkontrolle, Flußregelung, Flußsteuerung
flow control ready Flußkontrolle bereit
flow structure Ablaufstruktur
flow text Fließtext
fluidic control equipment Fluidic-Steuergerät
fluidic control system Fluidic-Steuersystem
fluorescent screen Fluoreszenzschirm
flushed geflusht
flux changes per inch Flußwechsel pro Zoll
flyback regulation method Rücklauf-Regulierungsverfahren
flying head magnet drum FH-Trommel
flying spot store Lichtpunktspeicher
flyleaf Deckblatt
FM carrier recording Frequenzmodulationsaufzeichnung
foam Kunststoffschaum, Schaum
focal point Mittelpunkt
focal spot Brennfleck
focus Schärfe
focus control Schärferegler
folder Ablage, Ordner

folder name Ordnername
follow anschließen, folgen
following anschließend, folgend, nachstehend
following address Anschlußadresse
following page Folgeseite
following role Folgerolle
font Schriftart
foot Fuß
footage indicator Papierlängenanzeiger
footer Fußzeile, Seitenfuß
footer text Fußtext
foot text Fußtext
for all corporations mandantenübergreifend
forbid verbieten
force Kraft, zwingen
force attention Betriebsbereitschaft mitteilen
force attention interrupt Erzwingen der Betriebsbereitschaft
force control Kraftsteuerung
forced job startup programmierter Jobstart
force output Kraftausgang
forcibly zwangsläufig
forcibly terminate zwangsbeenden
forcing function erzwungene Funktion
forecast Prognose, Vorausschau, prognostizieren
forecast code Vorhersageschlüssel
foreground/background Vordergrund/Hintergrund
foreground/background operation Vordergrund-/Hintergrundbetrieb
foreground bit Vordergrundbit
foreground display Vordergrundanzeige
foreground program Vordergrundprogramm
foreign fremd, gebietsfremd, systemfremd
foreign currency Fremdwährung
foreign currency amount Fremdwährungsbetrag
foreign currency code Fremdwährungsschlüssel
foreign currency exchange rate Fremdwährungskurs
foreign currency item Fremdwährungsposition
foreign currency schedule Fremdwährungsdisposition
foreign currency sum Fremdwährungssumme
foreign currency valuation Fremdwährungsbewertung
foreign currency value Fremdwährungswert
foreign invoice Auslandsrechnung
foreign payment transactions Auslandszahlungsverkehr
foreign subsidiary Auslandstochtergesellschaft
foreign word Fremdwort

for free ohne Berechnung
forget vergessen
form Format, Formular, bilden, formen
form adjustment Formularjustierung
formal formal, formell
formal error Formalfehler
form alignment Formularjustierung
format Aufbau, Bett, Format, formatieren, umbrechen
format application Formateinsatz
format application file Formateinsatzdatei
format chaining Formatkettung
format control Formatsteuerung
format control data Formatsteuerungsdaten
format control language Formatsteuerungssprache, Sprache zur Formatsteuerung
format creation Formaterstellung
format creation function Formaterstellungsfunktion
format display editing Formatbildeditierung
format effector Formatsteuerzeichen
format effector layout character Formatsteuerzeichen
format field Formatfeld
format field creation Formatfelderstellung
format file Formatdatei
format file name Formatdateiname
format generation Formaterzeugung
format generator Formatgenerator
format handling system Format-Handling-System, Formatbehandlungssystem
format identifier Formatkennzeichen
format input Formateingabe
format instruction Formatanweisung
format interface Formatschnittstelle
format IO list interaction Angaben unter Format in der EA-Parameterliste
formation Bau, Entstehung
formation date Entstehungsdatum
formation of a library Bibliothekserstellung
format label Formatkennsatz
format library Formatbibliothek
format library application file Formatbibliothekseinsatzdatei
format library name Formatbibliotheksname
format list Formatliste
format management Formatverwaltung
format name Formatname
format notation Formatbeschreibung
format output Formatausgabe
format page Formatseite
format processing Formatbehandlung

95

format processing function Formatbehandlungsfunktion
format rule Formatvorschrift
format selector Formatwähler, Formularwähler
format service page Formatserviceseite
format specification Formatangabe
formatted formatiert
formatted diskette formatierte Diskette
formatter Formatierer
formatting Formatieren
formatting controlling formatierungssteuernd
formatting interface Formatierungsschnittstelle
formatting page mode Formatierungsseitenmodus
formatting system Formatierungssystem
format type Formatart
format word Formatanweisung
form card Formularkarte
form control Formularsteuerung
form description Formularbeschreibung
form description macro Formularbeschreibungsmakro
form description table Formularbeschreibungstabelle
form designator Formularkennzeichen
form document Formulardokument
former vorig
form feed Formularzuführung, Papiervorschub, Seitenvorschub
form feed control Seitenvorschubsteuerung
form feeding device Formularzuführungseinrichtung
form feed key Papiervorschubtaste
form feed mode Seitenvorschubmodus
form field Formularfeld
form file Formulardatei
form generator Formatgenerator
form guide Blattführung, Führung
form guide roller Führungsrolle
form holder Formularhalter
forming association numbers Zuordnungsnummernbildung
forming differences Differenzenbildung
form input Formulareingabe
form item Formularfeld
form length Seitenlänge
form letter Formbrief
form management system Maskengenerator
form overflow Formularende
form printing Formulardruck
form processing Formatbehandlung
form rack Formularhalter
forms creation Formaterstellung

forms description language Formularbeschreibungssprache, Sprache zur Formularbeschreibung
form selector Formularwähler
forms entry system Formulareingabesystem
form separator Formulartrenner
forms generation Formaterstellung
forms library Formatbibliothek
form specification Formatangabe
form table Formulartabelle
form tractor number Leporellonummer
form transport Formulartransport
form type Formularart
formula Formel
formula evaluation Formelauswertung
formulate formulieren
formulation Formulierung
formula translation Formelübersetzung
for the individual customer kundenindividuell, kundenspezifisch
for the master record stammsatzbezogen
for the record satzbezogen
forward vorwärts, weiterleiten
forward chaining Vorwärtskettung
forward channel Hauptkanal
forward declaration Vorwärtsdeklaration
forwarder Spediteur
forwarding address Nachsendeadresse
forwarding instruction Versandvorschrift
forward linkage Vorwärtsverkettung
forward linking Vorwärtsverkettung
forward positioning Vorwärtspositionierung
forward reference Vorwärtsverweis
forward space file Datei vorsetzen
forward supervision Vorwärtssteuerung
four address instruction Vieradressenbefehl
four character vierstellig
four digit vier Zeichen lang, vierstellig
four line binary code Vierkanalbinärcode
four port interface Schnittstelle mit vier Anschlüssen
fourth normal form vierte Normalform
four wire Vierdraht
fraction Bruch, Bruchzahl
fractional depreciation Teilwertabschreibung
fractional horsepower motor Motor mit Nennleistung unter 736 W
fractional part Bruchteil
fractional valuation Teilwertermittlung
fractional value Teilwert
fraction stroke Bruchstrich
fragility Zerbrechlichkeit

fragmented nicht aufeinanderfolgend, unzusammenhängend, zerstückelt
fragmented disk Platte mit Dateien in unzusammenhängenden Bereichen
fragmented file Datei in unzusammenhängenden Bereichen
fragmented sectors unzusammenhängende Sektoren
frame Block, Datenübertragungsblock, Rahmen, Steckrahmen
frame check sequence Rahmenprüffolge
frame heading Maskenüberschrift
frame of speech Sprachbaustein
frame reject Blockrückweisung
frames per second Rahmen pro Sekunde
frame start Rahmenanfang
frame structure Aufbau des Datenübertragungsblocks
framework Gerüst
frame yoke Rahmen
framing error Rahmenbitfehler, Rahmenfehler
free frei, unbelegt
free format Freiformat, freies Format
free from format formularunabhängiges Format
free line condition Freizustand
freely selectable frei wählbar
free memory freier Speicher
free sector list Tabelle der nichtbelegten Sektoren
free space list Freispeicherliste
freeze anhalten, einfrieren, einstellen, sperren
freeze date Sperrdatum
freeze entry Sperreintrag
freeze flag Sperrkennzeichen
freeze memory Speicherbelegung festhalten
freeze order Sperrbestellung
freezing Sperrung
freight Fracht
freight account Frachtkassenkonto
freight agreement Frachtvereinbarung
freight amount Frachtbetrag
freight bill Frachtabrechnung
freight charge quantity accruing Frachtverrechnungsmenge
freight charges Frachtkosten
freight charges accrued Frachtverrechnungswert
freight collect fund Frachtkasse
freight costs Frachtanteil
freight data input Frachterfassung
freight details Frachttext
freight dispatched Ausgangsfracht

freight distribution Frachtverteilung
freight element Frachtelement
freight expediting Frachterledigung
freight invoice Frachtrechnung
freight invoice validation Frachtrechnungsprüfung
freight inwards Eingangsfracht
freight item Frachtposition
freight marker Frachtkennzeichen
freight master segment Frachtmuttersegment
freight posting Frachtbuchung
freight process Frachtvorgang
freight reversal Frachtrückstellung
freight route Frachtroute
freight terms Frachtlieferbedingungen
frequency Frequenz, Häufigkeit, Taktfrequenz
frequency changer Frequenzwandler
frequency characteristic Frequenzkennlinie
frequency clock netztaktgesteuerte Uhr
frequency control Frequenzregelung, Frequenzsteuerung
frequency density Häufigkeitsdichte
frequency departure Frequenzablage
frequency distribution Häufigkeitsverteilung
frequency division multiplex equipment Frequenzmultiplex-Übertragungseinrichtung
frequency halver Frequenzhalbierschaltung
frequency instability Frequenzfehler
frequency modulated signal generator Signalgenerator mit Frequenzmodulation, Signalgenerator mit Frequenzmodulation
frequency modulation Frequenzmodulation
frequency modulator Frequenzmodulator
frequency multiplier Frequenzvervielfacher
frequency of use Benutzungshäufigkeit, Nutzungshäufigkeit
frequency response Frequenzantwort, Frequenzbereich
frequency selective filter Frequenzfilter
frequent häufig
fresh neu
fresh start Neubeginn, Neustart
fricative Reibelaut
from ab
from filename Herkunftsdatei
front end Vor-
front end capabilities Vorrechner- und Steuerfunktionen
front end computer Vorrechner
front end network processor Netzwerkvorrechner
front end procesor Vorrechner

front end processor Frontrechner, Netzwerkvorrechner, Vorschaltrechner
front feed device Vorsteckeinrichtung
frontier Grenzbereich
front panel Frontplatte
front panel indicators Anzeigen an der Bedienerkonsole
front panel switch Frontpanelschalter, Frontschalter, Schalter an der Frontplatte
front switch Frontschalter
frozen stock Sperrbestand
frozen stock stores Sperrlager
fulfill erfüllen
fulfillment Erfüllung
full voll
full adder Volladdierer
full checkpoint common bank gemeinsame Bank für Prüfpunkt
full delivery Vollauslieferung, Vollieferung
full delivery flag Bestlieferungskennzeichen
full delivery order Vollieferungsauftrag
full duplex Gegenbetrieb, Vollduplex
full duplex communication Vollduplexkommunikation
full key Gesamtschlüssel
full page transmit Übertragen von ganzen Seiten
full record sort Sortierung nach Sätzen
full restart common bank gemeinsame Wiederanlaufbank
full stop Punkt
full text Langtext
full text lines Langtextzeilen
full text messages Langtextnachrichten
full time circuit Dauerverbindung
fully integrated vollintegriert
fully operational mode Betriebsart mit voller Betriebsbereitschaft
function Funktion, Funktionsweise
functional funktional
functional description Beschreibung der Funktionsweise, Funktionsbeschreibung
functional element Funktionselement
functional module Funktionsbaugruppe
functional overview Funktionsübersicht
functional symbol Funktionssymbol
functional term funktioneller Ausdruck
functional test Funktionstest
functional unit Funktionseinheit
function block Funktionsbaustein
function call Funktionsaufruf
function card Funktionskarte
function character Funktionszeichen

function code Funktionscode, Funktionsnummer
function coded funktionscodiert
function code input Funktionscodeeingabe
function complete Funktion abgeschlossen
function control block Funktionssteuerblock
function defining funktionsbestimmend
function dependent funktionsabhängig
function description Funktionsbeschreibung
function descriptor Funktionsbeschreibung
function detail Funktionsdetail
function entry Funktionseintrag
function extent Funktionsumfang
function field Funktionsfeld
function group Funktionsgruppe
function identifier Funktionskennzeichen, Tastenkennzeichnung
function instruction Funktionsanweisung
function item Verweisfeld
function key Funktionstaste
function key row Funktionstastenreihe
function loader table Tabelle der transienten Steuerfunktionen
function loading Laden eines transienten Steuerprogramms
function module Funktionsmodul
function offer Funktionsangebot
function of representation Abbildungsfunktion
function oriented funktionsorientiert
function parameter Funktionsparameter
function preselection Funktionsvorwahl
function related funktionsbezogen
function selection Funktionsauswahl
function separation Funktionstrennung
function step Funktionsschritt
function table Funktionstabelle
function text Funktionstext
function type Funktionstyp
function value Funktionswert
function word Funktionswort
further details nähere Einzelheiten
further development Weiterentwicklung
furthermore weiterhin
further use Weiterverwendung
fuse Sicherung
fuse box Sicherungskasten
fuse carrier Sicherungskappe
fuse element Sicherungselement
fuse filter card Filtersicherungskarte
fuse holder Sicherungshalter
fuse link Schmelzeinsatz
fuse retainer Sicherungshalterung

G

gain control Verstärkungsregelung
galvanical galvanisch
galvanically insulated galvanisch isoliert
game control adapter Adapter für Computerspiele, Joystickanschluß
game function Spielfunktion
gang Gruppe, Kolonne
ganged condition Gleichlaufzustand
gang operation Verbundoperation
gang punch Folgestanzer
gap Lücke, Spalte
gape klaffen
garbage unsinniges Computerergebnis
garbage collection Reorganisationslauf
garbage in garbage out Mist rein Mist raus, Unsinn rein Unsinn raus
garbled unlesbar, verstümmelt
gas blast circuit breaker Gasstromschalter
gas discharge tube Gasentladungsröhre
gas filled switching tube Gasschaltröhre
gas filled transformer gasgefüllter Transformator
gas laser Gaslaser
gas plasma display Plasmaanzeige, Plasmabildschirm
gas turbine generator Gasturbinen-Generator
gas turbine power station Gasturbinen-Kraftwerk
gate verknüpfen
gateway Gateway, Haupteinfahrt, Relais
gateway entry Gateway-Eingang
gateway exchange Gateway-Wechsel
gateway instruction Gateway-Anweisung
gateway menu Gateway-Menü
gateway number Gateway-Nummer
gateway related Gateway-bezogen
gather ersehen, sammeln
gather write gesammelt schreiben
gauge Eichmaß, messen
gear column Getriebesäule
gear lever Ein-/Ausrückhebel, Ganghebel
general allgemein, generell
general communication subsystem Datenübertragungssteuereinheit
general comprehensive term Sammelbegriff
general default allgemeiner Standard
general editor Datenaufbereitungsprogramm, Editor
general format identifier Kennzeichen für Grundformat
general indicator allgemeine Bezugszahl
general ledger Hauptbuch, Sachbuch
general ledger account Hauptbuchkonto, Sachbuchkonto, Sachkonto
general ledger account area Hauptbuchkontenbereich
general ledger account code Hauptbuchkontenschlüssel
general ledger account group Hauptbuchkontengruppe
general ledger accounting Hauptbuchhaltung
general ledger account number Sachkontonummer
general ledger account register Sachkontenverzeichnis
general ledger alteration Sachkontenänderung
general ledger area Sachkontenbereich
general ledger authorization Sachkontenberechtigung
general ledger balance Sachkontensaldo
general ledger buffer Sachkontenpuffer
general ledger content Sachkonteninhalt
general ledger credit Sachkontenhaben
general ledger debit Sachkontensoll
general ledger file Sachkontendatei
general ledger group Sachkontengruppe
general ledger liability Hauptbuchverbindlichkeit
general ledger line Sachkontenzeile
general ledger master Sachkontenstamm
general ledger master file Sachkontenstammdatei
general ledger master record Sachkontenstammsatz
general ledger posting Hauptbuchschreibung, Hauptbuchung, Sachkontenbuchung, Sachkontenschreibung
general ledger prepayment account Anzahlungshauptbuchkonto
general ledger report Sachkontenauswertung
general ledger screen Sachkontenbild
general ledger special account Hauptbuchsonderkonto
general ledger table Sachkontentabelle
general ledger total Sachkontensumme
general ledger turnover Sachkontenumsatz
general poll allgemeiner Sendeaufruf
general process allgemeiner Prozeß
general purpose Allgemein-
general purpose character set universeller Zeichensatz

general purpose interface bus allgemeiner Schnittstellenbus
general purpose processor Universalrechner
general purpose programmer Universalprogrammiergerät
general purpose system simulator Simulation von diskretem dynamischen System
general register Mehrzweckregister
general register set allgemeiner Registersatz
general register stack allgemeiner Registersatz
general rule Faustregel
general set-up feature allgemeines Betriebsmodusmerkmal
generate aufbauen, erzeugen, generieren, schaffen
generate debug code Testhilfe generieren
generating a system Systemgenerierung
generating program erzeugendes Programm
generating the purchase order Bestellerzeugung
generation Generation, Generierungslauf
generation criterion Aufbaukriterium
generation error Generierungsfehler
generation file generierte Datei
generation interface Generierungsschnittstelle
generation of mask Maskengenerierung
generation process Generierungslauf
generator Generator
generator program Generatorprogramm
generic allgemein, generisch
generous großzügig
geneva disk Malteserscheibe
geneva drive Malteserantrieb
geothermal electric power station geothermisches Kraftwerk
German Bundespost Deutsche Bundespost
German PTT leased line service Direktrufnetz der DBP
German public data network Datex-P-Netz
gestation period Entwicklungsperiode
get bekommen, holen
get ahead weiterkommen
get confirmation before deleting Löschen bestätigen
get-process-put Eingabe-Verarbeitung-Ausgabe
get subroutine Get-Unterprogramm
getting started Einführung
gigabyte Gigabyte
giro posting line Giro-Buchungszeile
give angeben, vorgeben
given function Funktionsangabe
given line Zeilenangabe
given parameter Parameterangabe
given percentage Prozentangabe
given range of numbers Nummernkreisangabe
giving information Auskunftserteilung
glide gleiten
global allgemein, global
global address Generaladresse
global display Globalanzeige
global format Globalformat
global network weltweites Netz
global search globales Suchen
global search and replace globales Suchen und Ersetzen
global section globaler Abschnitt
global symbol globales Symbol
global symbol table globale Symboltabelle
global user service task globale Servicefunktion
glossary Glossar
glow discharge tube Glimmentladungsröhre
glow modulator tube Glimmmodulationsröhre
go gehen, laufen, reichen
gone vergangen
go-no-go test Ja-Nein-Kontrolle
good positiv
goods Güter, Waren
goods delivery Warenlieferung
goods directory Warenverzeichnis
goods dispatch Warenausgang, Warenversand
goods dispatched posting Warenausgangsbuchung
goods dispatched voucher Warenausgangsbeleg
goods inventory accounts Warenbestandskonten
goods issued voucher Warenausgabebeleg
goods liability Warenschuld
goods number Warennummer
goods received Warenannahme, Wareneingang
goods received clearance account Wareneingangsverrechnungskonto
goods received figure Wareneingangswert
goods received item Wareneingangsposition
goods received marker Wareneingangskennzeichen
goods received note Wareneingangsschein
goods received number Wareneingangsnummer
goods received posting Wareneingangsbuchung
goods received processing Wareneingangsabwicklung
goods received reversal Wareneingangsstorno
goods received valuation Wareneingangsbewertung
goods received voucher Wareneingangsbeleg
goods supplier Warenlieferant
good status positive Zustandsmeldung

goods withdrawal Warenentnahme
go out erlöschen, hinausgehen
gor identification burst Bitbündelkennung für Gruppenwechselschrift
go through durchlaufen
grand total Endsumme, Gesamtsumme
grant erteilen, gewähren
granting a bonus Bonus gewähren
granularity Modularität
graph Graphik, Kurve
graphic grafisch
graphic character Grafikzeichen
graphic display Grafikanzeige, grafische Anzeige
graphic editor Grafikeditor
graphic mode Grafikbetrieb
graphic plotter Kurvenschreiber
graphic rendition grafische Darstellung
graphic representation grafische Darstellung
graphics Grafik
graphics aspect ratio Grafikdruckverhältnis
graphics character Grafikzeichen
graphics mode Grafikmodus
graphics operating system Grafik-Betriebssystem
graphics printer Grafikdrucker
graphics workstation Graphik-Arbeitsstation, Graphik-Workstation
graphic symbol Grafiksymbol
gray code Gray-Code
great groß
greater than größer als
greater than or equal größer oder gleich
greatest common divisor größter gemeinsamer Teiler
greek character griechischer Buchstabe
greeting page Begrüßungsseite
greeting paragraph Grußabschnitt
grey scale Grauskala
grid Punktraster, Raster, Rasterung
grid leak resistor Gitterableitwiderstand
grid line Rasterzeile
grid parameter Rasterparameter
grid voltage Gitterspannung
grip Griff, Halt
grip ring Haltering
grommet isolierte Durchführung
groove Einkerbung, Rille
gross Brutto
gross amount Bruttobetrag
gross entry Bruttobuchung
gross price Bruttopreis
gross processing Bruttoverfahren

gross purchase order price Bruttobestellpreis
gross purchase order value Bruttobestellwert
gross revenue Bruttoerlös
gross sales order value Bruttoauftragswert
gross unit price Bruttoeinzelpreis
gross value Bruttowert
gross weight Bruttogewicht
ground Erde, Erdung, Masse, Masseelektrode, erden
ground bus bar Erdsammelschiene
grounded grid circuit Gitterbasisschaltung
grounding conductor Schutzleiter
ground point Massepunkt
ground terminal Erdklemme, Masseklemme
ground wire Erdungskabel, Massekabel
group Gruppe, gruppieren
group account Gruppenkonto
group account file Gruppenkontendatei
group account list Gruppenkontenliste
group address Gruppenadresse
group card Gruppenkarte
group coded recording gruppencodierte Datenaufzeichnung
group control change Gruppenwechsel
group encoded recording Gruppenwechselschrift
group end routine Gruppenende-Routine
group field Gruppenfeld
group field description Gruppenfeldbezeichnung
group identification Gruppenkennung
group identifier Gruppenmerkmal
group indicator Gruppenanzeige
group key Gruppenschlüssel
group leader Gruppenleiter
group level Gruppenstufe
group management Gruppenverwaltung
group menu Gruppenmenü
group number Gruppennummer
group of files Dateigruppe
group of letters Briefgruppe
group processing Gruppenverarbeitung
group related gruppenbezogen
group selection Gruppenselektion
group selector Gruppenschalter
group specification Gruppenangabe, Gruppenspezifikation
group start routine Gruppen-Anfangsroutine
group table Gruppentabelle
group total Gruppensumme
growth potential Erweiterungsfähigkeit
guarantee Gewähr, Gewährleistung, gewährleisten

guaranteed entry point feste Einsprungadresse
guard abschirmen, schützen
guard digit Hilfsziffer
guarded area transfer Übertragen von geschütztem Abschnitt
guidance system Leitsystem
guide Führung, Führungsschiene, einweisen, führen, leiten
guideline Leitfaden, Richtlinie
guide mode Unterweisungsmodus
guide plate Führungsplatte
guide to operations Bedienerhandbuch, Bedienungshandbuch
gunn diode Gunn-Diode

# H

half halb
half adder Halbaddierer
half adjust runden
half duplex Halbduplex
half duplex operation Halbduplexbetrieb, Simplexbetrieb
half duplex transmission Wechselbetrieb
half screen Bildhälfte
half section Halbglied
half space key Halbschrittaste
half subtractor Halbsubtrahierer
half time digit emitter Halbpunktzahlenverteiler
half word Halbwort
half yearly halbjährlich
halt Halt, Stop, anhalten, stoppen
halt and proceed instruction Anweisung »Halt mit Anzeige«
halt background mode Hintergrundmodus anhalten
halt indicator Stopbezugszahl
hamming code Hamming-Code
Hamming distance Hamming-Abstand
handbook Anleitung, Handbuch
hand held terminal Taschenterminal, tragbares Terminal
handicapped behindert
handle Griff, Handgriff, abwickeln, bearbeiten, behandeln, handhaben
handled in a random manner randombearbeitet
handler Handler, Hantierer, Steuerprogramm, Treiber
handler device Gerätesteuerprogramm
handling Behandlung, Handhabung
handling instance Bearbeitungsvorfall
handover Übergabe
handshake Protokoll
handshake procedure Verständigungsprozedur
handshaking Quittungsbetrieb
hand signal Handsignal
handswitch Handtaster
hangup Blockierung des Arbeitsablaufes
hardcopy Ausdruck, Hardcopy, Kopie, Papierausdruck
hard copy printer Copydrucker, Kopiendrucker
hardcopy terminal druckendes Terminal

hard disk Festplatte
hard disk controller Festplattencontroller
hard disk controller board Festplattencontroller
hard disk drive Festplattenlaufwerk
hard disk drive name Name des Festplattenlaufwerks
hard disk installation guide Installationshandbuch der Festplatte
hard disk option Festplatte
hard disk parameter Festplattenparameter
hard disk status Festplattenstatus
hard disk storage Festplattenspeicher
hard disk system Festplattensystem
hard disk upgrade zusätzlich installierte Festplatte
hard disk utility program Festplattenhilfsprogramm
hard format hart formatieren, vorformatieren
hard return festes Wagenrücklaufzeichen
hard sectorcd hartsektoriert
hardware Hardware
hardware compatibility Hardware-Kompatibilität
hardware confidence message Hardware-Betriebsbereitschaftsmeldung
hardware conversion Hardwareumrüstung
hardware error Fehler in der Hardware, Hardwarefehler
hardware error recovery system Hardware-Fehlerbeseitigungssystem
hardware failure Hardwarefehler
hardware implemented fault tolerance auf Hardware basierende Fehlertoleranz
hardware initiated error message Hardwarefehlermeldung
hardware maintenance Hardwarewartung
hardware maintenance and service manual Hardware Service und Diagnose Handbuch
hardware master bit table Kontrolltabelle für Geräteverfügbarkeit
hardware message Hardwaremeldung
hardware overview Hardwareübersicht
hardware priority interrupt hardwaremäßig nach Prioritäten gesteuerte Unterbrechung
hardware specific hardwareabhängig
hardware supported hardwareunterstützt
hardwire fest verdrahten, hartgezogener Draht
hard wired festverdrahtet
harmful schädlich
harmless harmlos, unschädlich
harmonic distortion Klirrfaktor

harmonic oscillator Sinusoszillator
hash algorithm library Hash-Bibliothek
hash error Kontrollsummenfehler
hazard category sheet Gefahrenklassenmerkblatt
hazardous gefährlich
HDLC protocol HDLC-Protokoll
head Kopf, Schreib-/Lesekopf
head and cylinder specification half word Kopf-Zylinder-Halbwort
head crash Kopflandung
head data Kopfdaten
head data field in job Auftragskopffeld
head data of job Auftrag-Kopfdaten
header Briefkopf, Job-Informationsvorspann, Kopfzeile, Kennsatz, Kopf, Seitenkopf, Vorspann
header card Vorlaufkarte
header card check Vorlaufkartenprüfung
header card description Vorlaufkartenbeschreibung
header card file Vorlaufkartendatei
header card format Vorlaufkartenaufbau
header card identification Vorlaufkartenkennung
header data Kopfdaten
header discount Kopfrabatt
header dump Kennsatzdump
header entry Kennsatzeintrag
header file Kennsatzdatei
header information Ablageinformation eines Schriftstückes, Anfangsinformation, Vorlaufinformation
header label Bandanfangskennsatz
header line Kopfzeile
header operation Kopfzeilenoperation
header record Kopfsatz, Vorsatz
header record type Kopfsatzart
header screen Kopfbild
header text Briefkopftext, Kopftext
header time operation Kopfzeilenoperation
head gap Luftspalt
heading Kopfzeile, Überschrift
heading time Kopfzeilenzeit
head label erster Dateianfangskennsatz
headline Überschriftszeile
head number Kopfnummer
head of a list Listenkopf
head office Zentrale
head-on collision Belegungszusammenstoß
headphone jack Kopfhörerbuchse
headphones Kopfhörer

head positioner flag Signalgeber für die Kopfposition
headset Kopfhörer
head-to-tape contact Bandkontakt
health insurance company Krankenkasse
heap overflow Heap-Überlauf
heat dissipation Wärmeabgabe
heavy schwer
heavy duty für schwere Belastung
heavy duty power cable Starkstromleitung
Hebraic character hebräisches Zeichen
height Höhe
height of the form Formularhöhe
hektowriter Hektoschreiber
help Help, Hilfe
help call Helpaufruf, Hilfeaufruf
help file Hilfedatei
help frame Hilfetext
helpful behilflich
help function Helpfunktion, Hilfefunktion
help library Hilfebibliothek
help line Hilfezeile, zentraler Telefonservice
help message Hilfemeldung
help page Hilfeseite
help screen Hilfsanzeige
help text Hilfetext
hermetically sealed transformer hermetisch gekapselter Transformator
Hertz Hertz
Hertzian line Hertz'sche Linie
hexadecimal Hexadezimal, hexadezimal
hexadecimal character Hexadezimalzeichen
hexadecimal code Hexadezimalcode, Hexadezimalverschlüsselung, Hexverschlüsselung
hexadecimal key Hexadezimaltaste
hexadecimal number Hexadezimalzahl, Hexzahl
hexadecimal number system hexadezimales Zahlensystem
hexadecimal representation Hexadezimaldarstellung
hexadecimal system Sedezimalsystem
hex display Hexanzeige
hi High
hidden system file versteckte Systemdatei
hierarchical compression Hierarchieverdichtung
hierarchy Hierarchie, Rangordnung
hierarchy display Hierarchieanzeige
hierarchy level Hierarchieebene
hierarchy number Hierarchienummer
hierarchy report Hierarchiebericht
high hoch, logisch hoch

high collar insulator Kragenisolator
high density hohe Aufzeichnungsdichte, hohe Dichte, hohe Schreibdichte
high density date storage device Speicher mit hoher Packungsdichte
high density digital magnetic recording HDDR-Verfahren
higher level übergeordnet
high frequency Hochfrequenz
high frequency amplifier Hochfrequenzverstärker
high frequency transformer Hochfrequenztransformator
high high sehr hoch
high impedance hochohmig
high level compiler Übersetzer für höhere Programmiersprachen
high level data link bitorientiertes Steuerungsverfahren
high level data link control HDLC-Steuerung
high level language Hochsprache, höhere Programmiersprache
highlight hervorheben
highlighted hellleuchtend, leuchtend
highlighting feature Möglichkeit zum Hervorheben von Text, Texthervorhebungsfunktion
highlighting key Taste zum Hervorheben von Text
highly hochgradig
high order harmonics Oberwellen mit höherer Ordnungszahl
high pass filter Hochpassfilter
high performance Hochleistungs-, leistungsfähig
high performance computer Hochleistungsrechner
high performance control storage schneller Steuerspeicher
high resolution hochauflösend, hohe Auflösung
high resolution color farb-hochauflösend
high resolution color graphics hochauflösende Farbgrafik
high speed Hochgeschwindigkeit
high speed arithmetic unit Hochgeschwindigkeits-Rechenwerk
high speed buffer Hochgeschwindigkeitspuffer
high speed code Hochgeschwindigkeitscode
high speed computation hohe Rechengeschwindigkeit
high speed machine Hochgeschwindigkeitsmaschine
high speed memory Hochgeschwindigkeitsspeicher, sehr schneller Speicher
high speed printer Schnelldrucker
high speed pulse train schnelle Impulsfolge
high speed response schnelle Antwort
high speed rewind Schnellrücklauf
high speed scan Schnellabtastung, schnelle Abtastung
high speed scan area Bereich schneller Abtastung
high speed scan function schnelle Abtastfunktion
high speed scan instruction Befehl zur schnellen Abtastung
high speed scanning Schnellabtastung
high speed scanning area Bereich schneller Abtastung
high voltage equipment Hochspannungsgeräte
high voltage installation Hochspannungsinstallation
high volume timesharing system Schnelldrucker
hihi sehr hoch
hihigh sehr hoch
hinged plastic window Kippfenster
hint Hinweis
histogram computer Histogrammrechner
historical auf der Basis von Vergangenheitsdaten
historical record Prüfpunkt
history Entwicklung, Entwicklungsgeschichte
history record Entwicklungssatz
history report Historieauswertung
hit Treffer
hit counter Trefferzähler
hit probability Trefferwahrscheinlichkeit
hit ratio Trefferquote
hold Wartezustand, fassen, festhalten, halten
holder Halterung
holding area Zwischenspeicherbereich
holding circuit Halteschaltung
holding interlock Haltesperre
holding time Belegungsdauer, Haltezeit
hold queue Haltewarteschlange
Hollerith width Hollerithlängenfaktor
home Anfangsposition, Ausgangsposition, linke obere Bildschirmecke
home address Spuranfangsadresse
home currency Landeswährung
home key Taste Ausgangsposition
home paper position Grundstellung Blattanfang
home position Ausgangsposition, Grundstellung, linke obere Bildschirmecke
home screen Startanzeige

home town Wohnort
homogeneous homogen
homologate zulassen
homologation Zulassung
homologation regulation Zulassungsbedingungen
homopolar generator Gleichpolgenerator
homopolar machine Gleichpolmaschine
homopolar motor Gleichpolmotor
honor akzeptieren
hopper Eingabefach, Kartenmagazin
horizontal and vertical position horizontale und vertikale Position
horizontal drive horizontale Steuerung
horizontal tab Horizontaltabulator, Tabulator, horizontaler Tabulator
horizontal tabulation set Horizontaltabulatoren
horizontal tabulator key Horizontaltabuliertaste
horizontal title horizontaler Titel
host Hostrechner, Zentralrechner, Zentralsystem
host adapter Anschluß an Zentralrechner, Multiplexkanalanschluß
host computer Entwicklungsrechner, Hostrechner, Zentralrechner
host data processing system zentrales Computersystem
hosted ablaufen auf
host language Hauptsprache
host line Verbindung zum Hostrechner
host line control loopback test Steuerungs-Echo-Test auf der Hostleitung
host line data loopback test Daten-Echo-Test auf der Hostleitung
host processor Zentralrechner
host software Zentralrechnersoftware
host speak command Kommando für Sprachausgabe vom Host
host support facility Dienstprogramm für das Zentralsystem
host system Zentralrechner, Zentralsystem
hot stromführend
hot back-up hot back-up
hot cathode Glühkathode
hot cathode gas-filled tube Schaltröhre
hot start Wiederherstellungsstart
hour Stunde
house Haus
housekeeping Verwaltung
housekeeping track Verwaltungsspur
house language Haussprache
house number Hausnummer
housing Gehäuse

human factor ergonomischer Faktor, menschlicher Faktor
human interface Mensch-Maschine-Schnittstelle
human sounding voice menschlich klingende Stimme
humidity Feuchtregelung, Luftfeuchtigkeit
humidity control Feuchtesteuerung
hybrid Verbund
hybrid computer Hybridrechner
hybrid integrated circuit integrierte Hybridschaltung
hydraulic control equipment hydraulisches Steuergerät
hydraulic control system hydraulische Steuerung
hydroelectric power station Wasserkraftwerk
hyphen Bindestrich, Gedankenstrich, Trennzeichen
hysteresis loop Magnetisierungsschleife
hysteresis motor Hysteresemotor

I

icon Grafiksymbol
iconocenter Ikonozentrum
id Anmeldecode, Identifikation, Kennung, Merkmal
idea Absicht
ideal case Idealfall
identical gleichlautend, identisch
identification Ermittlung, Gruppenkennung, Identifikation, Kennung
identification data Identifikationsdaten
identification file Identifikationsdatei
identification message Identifikationsmeldung
identification number Identifikationsnummer
identification of variables Variablenidentifikation
identification process Identifikationsablauf
identification proposal Identifikationsvorschlag
identification table Identifikationstabelle
identification transmitter Nachrichtenkopfsender
identifier Bezeichner, Idenfikation, Identifikationsmerkmal, Kennung, mnemonische Bezeichnung
identifier block Identifikationsblock
identifier transmitter Nachrichtenkopfsender
identify ausweisen, identifizieren, kennzeichnen
identifying number Kennzahl
identity of names Namensgleichheit
idle Leerlauf, leerlaufen, sich in einer Warteschleife befinden
idle probe Sendeaufrufsignal
idle state Ruhezustand
idle time Leerlaufzeit
id number Identifikationsnummer
if wenn
if necessary notfalls
if-then-else if-then-else, wenn-dann-sonst
ignition transformer Zündspule, Zündtransformator
ignore ignorieren
ignore parity Parität ignorieren
illegal illegal, nicht zulässig, unberechtigt, unerlaubt, ungültig
illegal address nicht zulässige Adresse, ungültige Adresse, unzulässige Adresse
illegal argument ungültiges Argument
illegal call ungültiger Verbindungsaufbau
illegal character nicht zulässiges Zeichen, ungültiges Zeichen
illegal data ungültige Daten, ungültige Daten
illegal file name ungültiger Dateiname, unzulässiger Dateiname
illegal frame ungültiger Block
illegal frame structure ungültiger Blockaufbau
illegal operation unzulässige Operation
illegal separator ungültiges Trennzeichen
illegal value nicht zulässiger Wert, ungültiger Wert, unzulässiger Wert
illogical unlogisch
illuminating intensity Leuchtintensität
illustrate veranschaulichen
illustration Abbildung, Bild
image Abbild, Bild, Kartenbild, lauffähiges Programm
image intensifier Bildverstärker
image jitter Bildinstabilität
image journal file Nachrichten-Protokolldatei
image mode Normalmodus
image orthicon Superorthikon
image response Spiegelfrequenzverhalten
immediate direkt, unmittelbar, unverzüglich
immediate addressing unmittelbare Adressierung
immediate mode Direktmodus, Kommandomodus
immediate operand Direktoperand
impact printer Anschlagdrucker, Drucker, Impact-Drucker, mechanischer Drucker
impatt diode IMPATT Diode
impedance Impedanz
impedance switch Impedanzschalter
implausible unplausibel
implementation phase Implementationsphase
implement implementieren, realisieren
implementation Implementation, Implementierung
implementation aid Implementationshinweis
implementation phase Realisierungsphase
implementation support Implementationsunterstützung
implementing Realisation
implicit implizit
implicit array implizite Matrix
implicit job startup impliziter Jobstart
imply unterstellen
import importieren, übernehmen
important bedeutend
imprint Impressum
improperly defined symbol ungültig definiertes Symbol

107

improve verbessern
improvement Verbesserung
improvement in performance Leistungsverbesserung
imputed kalkulatorisch
imputed data Kalkulationsdaten
inactive inaktiv
in addition zusätzlich
inadmissible unzulässig
inbound ankommend, eingehend
inbound line Eingangsleitung, ankommende Leitung, hereinführende Leitung, zum Prozessor führende Leitung
incandescent lamp Glühlampe
inch Zoll
inches per second Zoll pro Sekunde
inch per second Zoll pro Sekunde
include aufnehmen, einfügen, hinzutreten, verfügen über, zurechnen, übernehmen
inclusive inclusiv
inclusive phase freie Abschnitte
inclusive reference gewöhnlicher Verweis
income Ertrag
incoming ankommend, eingehend
incoming call ankommender Ruf
incoming call barred ankommender Ruf blockiert
incoming goods function Wareneingangsfunktion
incoming inspection Wareneingangskontrolle
incoming line hereinführende Leitung
incoming order list Auftragseingangsliste
incompatibility Unverträglichkeit
incompatible inkompatibel, unverträglich
incomplete unerledigt, unvollständig
incorporate einbauen, eingliedern
incorrect falsch
incorrect input Fehleingabe
increase Erhöhung, Steigerung, erhöhen, steigern, vergrößern, zunehmen
increment Erhöhung, Inkrement, erhöhen, inkrementieren
incremental schrittweise, stufenweise
incremental backup änderungsbezogene Datensicherung
incremental encoder Inkrementalkodierer
increment growth konstantes Wachstum
increment printer Serielldrucker
indefinable undefinierbar
indefinite unbestimmt
indentation Eindrückung, Einzug, Vertiefung
indentation level count Eindrückungsfaktor

independent eigenständig, selbständig, unabhängig
independently unabhängig
independent of accounting area buchungskreisunabhängig
independent run Einzeljob
in detail ausführlich, detailliert
indeterminable unübersehbar
index Index, Stichwortverzeichnis, Verzeichnis, hochindizieren, indizieren
index block identifier Indexblockkennung
index display Verzeichnisanzeige
indexed indiziert
indexed file indizierte Datei
indexed file organisation indexsequentielle Dateistruktur
indexed random access file indizierte Direktzugriffsdatei
indexed random access method indexdirekte Zugriffsmethode
indexed sequential access file indexsequentielle Zugriffsdatei
indexed sequential access method indexsequentielle Zugriffmethode
index field Sortierfeld
index file Indexdatei
index hole Indexloch, Indexöffnung
indexing instruction Indexregisterbefehl
index level Indexebene
index marker Indexmarke
index matrix compare Indexmatrixvergleich
index of cooperation Kooperationsmodul
index of documents Dokumentverzeichnis
index of files Dateiregister, Dateiverzeichnis
index parameter Indexparameter
index pawl Indexklinke
index record Indexsatz
index register Indexregister
index row Indexreihe
index row key Indexreihenschlüssel
index section Indexteil
index selection Verzeichnisauswahl
index sequence Ordnungsfolge
index sequential indexsequentiell
index sequential file indexsequentielle Datei
index table Indextabelle
index track Indexspur
index tree description Indexbaumbeschreibung
index type Indexart
indicate anzeigen, aufweisen, auszeichnen, hinweisen
indication Anzeige, Kennzeichnung
indication of charges Gebührenangabe

indicator Anzeige, Anzeige, Indikator, Kennnummer, Statuszeile
indicator function Anzeigefunktion, Signalfunktion
indicator half-value Merker-Halbwort
indicator initialization Vorgaben für das Setzen der Bezugszahlen
indicator light Anzeige, Kontrolllampe
indicator position Merkerstellung
indicator tube Anzeigeröhre
indirect indirekt, mittelbar
indirect addressing indirekte Adressierung
indirect command file indirekte Kommandodatei
indirect file indirekte Datei, indirekte Dateispezifikation
indirectly heated cathode indirekt geheizte Kathode
indispensable unabdingbar
individual einzeln, individuell, spezifisch
individual account Einzelkonto
individual budget Einzelbudget
individual case Einzelfall
individual checking Einzelprüfung
individual conception Individuallösung
individual display Einzelanzeige
individual field Einzelfeld
individual format of cells Format der einzelnen Felder
individual function Einzelfunktion
individual invoice Einzelrechnung
individual item Einzelposten
individual items daily ledger Einzelpostenjournal
individual keyboard Einzeltastatur
individual line Einzelzeile
individual management Einzelverwaltung
individual program Einzelprogramm
individual proof Einzelnachweis
individual record Einzelsatz
individual request Einzelanforderung
individual table Einzeltabelle
individual terms Einzelbedingungen
individual text Individualtext
individual transaction Einzelbewegung
individual value Einzelwert
individual voucher Einzelbeleg
individual voucher item Einzelbelegposition
indoor innerhalb geschlossener Räume
indoor electric equipment elektrische Innenraumanlage
induction generator Induktionsgenerator
induction machine Induktionsmaschine
induction motor Induktionsmotor
induction voltage regulator Induktions-Spannungsregler
inductive proximity switch induktiver Näherungsschalter
inductor Induktivität
inductor generator Induktionsgenerator
inductor machine Induktionsmaschine
industrial company Industriebetrieb
industrial control Industriesteuerung, industrielle Steuerung
industrial control application industrielle Steuerung
industry Industrie
industry's leading applications marktführende Anwendungen
ineffective unwirksam
in error fehlerhaft
inertial navigation Trägheitsnavigation
inevitable unumgänglich
in fact allerdings, tatsächlich
in favor of zugunsten
inferior geringwertig
infinitely unendlich
infinitely variable stufenlos
influence Beeinflussung, Einfluß, beeinflussen
influenced by tendency trendbeeinflußt
influencing turnover umsatzwirksam
info file Infodatei
info record Infosatz
inform benachrichtigen, informieren, mitteilen
informal formlos
information Aufschluß, Auskunft, Hinweis, Information, Nutzdaten, in Gründung
information area Informationsbereich
information basis Informationsbasis
information code Informationscode
information content Informationsgehalt, Informationsinhalt
information data Informationsdaten
information display planner Informationsanzeigeplaner
information field Datenfeld, Textfeld
information file Informationsdatei
information file user Informationsdateien-Benutzer
information flow Informationsfluß
information flow rate Datendurchsatz
information function Auskunftsfunktion
information gap Informationslücke
information header Mitteilungskopf
information hierarchy Informationshierarchie
information indication Informationsanzeige

information length Informationslänge
information level Informationsebene
information line Informationszeile
information list Hinweisliste
information management software Informationsverwaltungssystem
information management system Informations-Management-System
information message Übertragungssteuerzeichenfolge, Übertragungszeichenfolge
information offer Informationsangebot
information operation Auskunftsbetrieb
information output Informationausgabe
information page Informationsseite
information processing system System zur Informationsverarbeitung, informationsverarbeitendes System
information program Auskunftsprogramm
information provider Informationsanbieter
information record Informationssatz
information relation Informationsbeziehung
information representation Informationsdarstellung
information retrieval Informationserschließung
information segment Informationssegment
information selection Informationsselektion
information separator Trennzeichen
information service Auskunftsdienst
information storage Nachrichtenspeicherung
information storage and retrieval Informationsspeicherung und -gewinnung
information supplier Informationsanbieter
information supplier format Informationsanbieterformat
information system Informationssystem
information technology Informationstechnik, Informationstechnologie
information value Informationswert
information work file Informationsarbeitsdatei
informative informativ
informative message Hinweisaktion
info text Infotext
infrared infrarot
in front of the decimal point im Ganzteil einer Zahl, vor dem Dezimalpunkt
in functional terms funktionell ausgedrückt
in general generell
inhibit hindern, sperren
inhibiting input Sperreingang
inhibit pulse Sperrimpuls
in house betriebsintern, firmenintern, hausintern, inhouse
in house system Inhouse-System

in house table Inhouse-Tabelle
initial anfangs, initial
initial bootstrap Erstladen
initial construction Erstanlegen
initial direction anfängliche Richtung
initial facility hold Wartezustand im Augenblick der Arbeitsablauferöffnung
initial failure Einsatzbeginnausfall
initial file continuation value Initialfortsetzungswert für Datei
initialisation Formatierung
initialization Initialisierung, Neuanlage, Systemeröffnung
initialization data Initialisierungsdaten
initialization mode Initialisierungsmodus, Vorbereitungsphase
initialization pattern Initialisierungsmuster
initialization phase Eröffnungsphase, Initialisierungsphase
initialization process Initialisierungsprozeß
initialization routine Initialisierungsroutine
initialization segment Standarderöffnungssegment
initialization type Eröffnungsart
initialize durchstarten, einleiten, eröffnen, formatieren, initialisieren, neuanlegen, rücksetzen, starten
initializer and utility Initialisierungs- und Dienstprogramm
initializing Initialisierung
initializing diskettes Dokumentdiskette vorbereiten
initial keyword Initialschlüsselwort
initial load Erstladen
initial name Startname
initial occupancy Anfangsbelegung
initial page number Anfangsseitennummer, Seitennummer der ersten Seite
initial parameter Ausgangsparameter
initial picture Anfangsbild
initial position Ausgangsposition
initial program load Startladen
initial program loader Urlader
initial record layout Initialsatz
initial run Erstlauf
initial selection sequence erstmalige Gerätansteuerung
initial statement Anfangsstatement
initial status word Anfangszustandswort
initial track Anfangsspur
initial value Anfangswert, Initialwert
initiate einleiten, initialisieren, verursachen
ink jet printer Tintenstrahldrucker

inline transducer Inline-Transducer
innermost operation am tiefsten verschachtelte Operation
inoperable time Funktionsunfähigkeitszeit
inoperative program ruhendes Programm
in- or output Ein-/Ausgabe
in parallel parallel
in progress im Ablauf
in proportion to quantity mengenproportional
input Eingabe, Eingang, Relaiseingang, eingeben, einspielen
input area Eingabebereich
input authorization Eingabeberechtigung
input block Eingabeblock
input block length Eingabeblocklänge
input block size Eingabeblockgröße
input buffer Eingabepuffer, Eingabespeicher
input buffer full Eingabepuffer voll, Eingangspuffer voll
input buffer overflow Überlauf des Eingabepuffers
input buffer register Eingabepufferregister
input call Eingabeaufruf
input card Eingabekarte
input character Eingabezeichen
input combination Eingabekombination
input condition Eingangsbedingung
input control Eingabekontrolle
input data Eingabedaten
input data acknowledge Bestätigung der Eingabedaten
input date Eingabedatum, Eingabetag
input device Eingabegerät, Geber
input error Eingabefehler
input field Eingabefeld
input field description Eingabefeldbeschreibung
input file Eingabedatei
input file destination Eingabedateibestimmung
input form Eingabeformular
input formal operand Eingangsformaloperand
input format Eingabeformat
input formatting Eingabeformatierung
input fuse Eingangssicherung
input fuse rating Wert der Eingangssicherung
input gate Eingabeeingang
input impedance Eingangsimpedanz
input in einlesen
input instruction Erfassungsvorschrift
input job Eingabeauftrag
input job stream Eingabedatenfluß
input keyboard Eingabetastatur
input led Eingangs-LED

input length Eingabelänge
input level Eingangspegel
input library Eingabebibliothek
input line Eingabezeile
input memory Eingabespeicher
input message Eingabenachricht
input message area Bereich für Eingabenachrichten
input method Eingabeart
input mode Eingabemodus
input module Eingangsmodul
input operation Eingabeoperation
input option Eingabemöglichkeit
input/output Ein-/Ausgabe, Ein-/Ausgang
input/output adapter Ein-/Ausgabeadapter
input/output block Ein-/Ausgabeblock
input/output buffer Ein-/Ausgabepuffer
input/output bus Ein-/Ausgabe-Bus, Ein-/Ausgabebus
input/output channel Ein-/Ausgabekanal
input/output control Ein-/Ausgabesteuerung
input/output controller Ein-/Ausgabeprozessor, Ein-/Ausgabesteuereinheit, Ein-/Ausgabesteuerung
input/output control system modules Ein-/Ausgabesteuersystem
input/output device Ein-/Ausgabe-Gerät, Ein-/Ausgabegerät
input/output devices Ein-/Ausgabegeräte
input/output features Leistungsmerkmale der E/A-Einheit
input/output interrupt handler Ein-/Ausgabeinterrupthandler
input/output microprocessor Ein-/Ausgabemikroprozessor, Ein-/Ausgabeprozessor
input/output module Ein-/Ausgabemodul
input/output processor Ein-/Ausgabeprozessor
input/output program Ein-/Ausgangsprogramm
input/output queue Ein-/Ausgabequeue, Ein-/Ausgabewarteschlange
input/output register Ein-/Ausgaberegister
input/output request block Ein-/Ausgabe-Anforderungsblock
input/output screen format ausgefüllte Masken, deren Einträge veränderbar sind
input/output supervisor Ein-/Ausgabeüberwachung
input/output system Ein-/Ausgabesystem
input/output trap Ein-/Ausgabeunterbrechung
input/output unit Ein-/Ausgabeprozessor
input parameters Eingabeparameter
input phase Eingabephase
input program Eingabeprogramm

input program load Startladen
input reader Systemeingaberoutine
input record Eingabesatz
input sequence Eingabesequenz
input signal Eingangssignal
input slot Eingabeschlitz
input source Eingabequelle
input specification Eingabeformat
input speed Eingabegeschwindigkeit
input statement Eingabestatement
input status Eingabestatus
input syntax Eingabeformalismus, Eingabesyntax
input tape Eingabeband
input template Eingabeschablone
input translator Eingabeübersetzer
input type Eingabetyp
input value Eingabewert
input voltage Eingangsspannung
inquire abfragen, anfragen, erfragen
inquiring Abfragen
inquiry Abfrage, Anfrage, Frage
inquiry command Abfragebefehl
inquiry delete list Anfragelöschliste
inquiry example Abfragebeispiel
inquiry function Abfragefunktion
inquiry generation Anfragengenerierung
inquiry header Anfragekopf
inquiry header text Anfragekopftext
inquiry item Anfrageposition
inquiry item text Anfragepositionstext
inquiry mode Abfragemodus
inquiry number Anfragenummer
inquiry option Abfragemöglichkeit
inquiry print program Anfrageschreibungsprogramm
inquiry processing Anfrageabwicklung, Anfragebearbeitung
inquiry program Abfrageprogramm
inquiry registration Anfrageerfassung
inquiry service Abfragedienst
inquiry station Abfrageeinheit
inquiry terminal Abfrageterminal
inquiry text Anfragetext
inquiry voucher Anfragebeleg
insert Einsatz, Einschub, einfügen, einschieben, hinzufügen, vorschalten, zwischenschalten
insert character Zeichen einfügen
inserting and replacing Einfügen und Ersetzen
inserting text Text einfügen
insertion Einfügung
insertion area Einfügungsbereich

insertion mode Einfügemodus
insert line Zeile einfügen
insert mode Einfügefunktion, Einfügemodus
insert operation Einfügeoperation
insert position Einfügestelle
insert procedure Einfügeprozedur
inside the program programmintern
insignificant unbedeutend, unerheblich
inspect untersuchen, überprüfen
inspection Inspektion, Untersuchung
inspection marker Inspektionskennzeichen
install generieren, installieren
installation Einbau, Installation, Installierung
installation card Anlagenkarte
installation code Aufbaucode
installation dependent anlagenspezifisch
installation guide Installationsanweisung, Installationshandbuch
installation instruction Installationsanweisung
installation internal anlagenintern
installation manual Installationshandbuch
installation planning Anlagenplanung
installation procedure Installationsprozedur, Installationsvorgang
installation specific anlagenspezifisch
installation verification program Konfigurationsprüfprogramm
instance of deadlock Deadlock-Fall
instance of dialog Dialogfall
instance of repetition Wiederholungsfall
instantaneous value Augenblickswert
instigate veranlassen
instigation Veranlassung
institute Institut
instruct befehlen
instruction Anleitung, Anweisung, Befehl, Instruktion, Kommando
instruction address Befehlsadresse
instruction address register Befehlsadreßregister
instruction block Befehlsblock
instruction bus Befehlsbus
instruction counter Befehlszähler
instruction counter status Befehlszählerstand
instruction cycles Befehlszyklen
instruction distribution channel Befehlsverteilerkanal
instruction field Befehlsfeld
instruction format Befehlsaufbau
instruction issue unit Befehlsausgabeeinheit
instruction length Befehlslänge
instruction list Befehlsliste
instruction modification Befehlsänderung

instruction parameter Befehlsparameter
instruction pipelining Befehlsansteuerung
instruction pointer Befehlszeiger
instruction pre-processor Befehlsaufbereitungsprozessor
instruction processor Befehlführungsprozessor
instruction register Befehlsregister
instruction repertoire Befehlsrepertoire
instruction repetition Befehlswiederholung
instruction retry facility Befehlswiederholungs-Einrichtung
instructions Beschreibung
instruction set Befehlssatz, Befehlsvorrat
instruction stack Anweisungspuffer
instruction table Befehlstabelle
instruction time Befehlszeit
instruction word Befehlswort
instrument shunt Nebenwiderstand
instrument transformer Meßwandler
insufficient ungenügend
insulated cable isoliertes Kabel
insulated wire isolierter Draht
insulating coating Isolierschicht
insulating enclosure isoliertes Gehäuse
insulating film Isolierfilm
insulating material Isoliermaterial, Isolierstoff
insulating oil Isolieröl
insulating substrate isolierendes Substrat
insurance Versicherung
insurance base value Versicherungsbasiswert
insurance company Versicherungsgesellschaft
insurance index Versicherungsindex
insurance premium Versicherungsbeitrag
insurance terms Versicherungskonditionen
insure versichern
insured value Versicherungswert
intact intakt
integer Ganzzahl, ganzzahlig
integer constant Ganzzahlkonstante
integer digit Vorkommastelle
integer division Ganzzahldivision
integerize umwandeln in Ganzzahl
integer operation Ganzzahloperation
integer ratio aufgehendes Verhältnis
integer seed Keimzahl
integer variable Ganzzahlvariable
integrable integrierbar
integral integral
integral modem Integralmodem
integrate integrieren, übernehmen
integrated circuit integrierte Schaltung, integrierter Schaltkreis

integrated circuit technology Technik der integrierten Schaltung
integrated communication access method Datenübertragungssteuerprogramm
integrated communication adapter feater integrierte Datenübertragungsanschlußeinrichtung
integrated communication rack integriertes Datenübertragungsmodul
integrated control register Steuerregister
integrated disk adapter Plattenspeicherdirektanschluß
integrated logic circuit integrierte Logikschaltung
integrated memory circuit integrierte Speicherschaltung
integrated modem Einbaumodem, integriertes Modem
integrated network processor integrierter Netzwerkprozessor
integrated peripheral channel integrierte Gerätesteuerung
integrated software Verbundsoftware
integrated switching circuit Schalt-IC
integrated test Verbundtest
integrated text and data network integriertes Text- und Datennetz
integration Übernahme (von Betriebssoftware in eigenes System)
integration ability Integrationsfähigkeit
integration level Integrationsstufe
integration marker Verbundkennzeichen
intelligence layer Intelligenzebene
intelligent communications interface intelligente Kommunikationsschnittstelle
intelligent keyboard intelligente Tastatur
intelligent memory manager intelligente Speicherverwaltung
intelligent network processor intelligenter Netzwerkprozessor
intelligent terminal system intelligentes Terminalsystem
intelligent transmitter intelligenter Sender
intend beabsichtigen, vorhaben
intensified display Intensivanzeige
intensive intensiv
intensive display Intensivanzeige
intention Absicht
interact ineinandergreifen
interaction Nachrichtenaustausch
interaction management Dialogkontrolle
interactive dialogmäßig, interaktiv
interactive buffer Wechselpuffer

interactive computer graphics interaktive Computergrafik
interactive data entry interaktive Datenerfassung
interactive debugging aid Dialogtesthilfe
interactive file processing Dateiverarbeitung im Dialog, interaktive Dateiverarbeitung
interactive health care system Krankenhausverwaltungssystem
interactive job control dialogorientierte Jobsteuerung
interactive level Dialogstufe
interactive message Dialognachricht
interactive mode Dialog, Dialogbetrieb, Dialogmodus
interactive processing Dialogbetrieb
interactive processor Dialogprogramm
interactive program Dialogprogramm
interactive program generator Dialogprogrammgenerator
interactive region Dialogregion
interactive segment Dialogteil
interactive services dialogorientierte Dienstleistungen
interactive session Dialogsitzung
interactive step Dialogschritt
interactive system Dialogsystem
interactive task Dialogtask
interactive terminal Dialogdatenstation, Dialogeinheit, interaktives Terminal
interactive user Dialogbenutzer
interactive videotext Bildschirmtext
interactive videotext center Bildschirmtext-Zentrale
interactive videotext computer network Bildschirmtext-Rechnerverbund
interblock gap Zwischenraum zwischen zwei Blöcken
interblock space Blockabstand
intercept Nulldurchgang, abfangen
intercept data storage position Abfangspeicherstelle
interchange Austausch
interchange circuit Schnittstellenstromkreis
interchange point Übergabestelle
interconnection Zusammenschaltung
intercouple zusammenkoppeln
interest Interesse, Zins, interessieren
interest accrual Verzinsung
interest due Zinsforderung
interested customer Interessent
interested party Interessent
interest payment Zinszahlung

interest rate Zinsprozentsatz, Zinssatz
interest type Verzinsungsart
interest value Zinswert
interface Anschalteinrichtung, Anschluß, Ausgang, Nahtstelle, Port, Schnittstelle, Verbindung
interface bus Schnittstellenbus
interface condition Schnittstellenbedingung
interface data unit Schnittstellendateneinheit
interface description Schnittstellenbeschreibung
interface equipment Nahtstellenanordnung
interface field strength Störstrahlung
interface flow control Schnittstellenflußkontrolle
interface module Schnittstellenmodul
interface movement Schnittstellenbewegung
interface problems Schnittstellenproblematik
interface register Schnittstellenregister
interface signalling state diagram Zustandsdiagramm zum Verbindungsaufbau-Steuerverfahren
interface signalling (sequence) diagram Signalablaufdiagramm
interface time filler Füllzeichen zwischen Datenübertragungs-Blöcken
interface to Schnittstelle bilden zu
interface transfer switch Schnittstellenschalter
interface types Schnittstellentypen
interface voltage Funkstörung
interfault interval Zeitspanne zwischen Ausfällen, Zeitspanne zwischen Fehlern
interfere einmischen
interfering radiation Störstrahlung
interim measure Zwischenlösung
interlace Bildzeilendichte, Zwischenzeile
interlaced mit Zeilensprung
interlaced storage assignment Verschachtelungszuordnung
interlacing Verschachtelung
interleave Versatz, versetzen, verzahnen
interleaved modules Module, auf die verschränkt zugegriffen wird
interleaved set verschränkt organisierter Satz
interleaving Interleaving
interlink verzahnen
interlock Sperre, Verriegelung, sperren
interlock bypass Aufheben einer Verriegelung
interlocking signal Blocksignal
interlock routine Verriegelungsroutine
intermediate conversion Zwischenkonvertierung
intermediate field Zwischenfeld

intermediate file Zwischenspeicherdatei
intermediate frequency amplifier Zwischenfrequenzverstärker
intermediate level Zwischenstufe
intermediate output file Druckausgabezwischendatei
intermediate storage area Zwischenspeicherbereich
intermediate system Transitsystem
intermediate total Zwischensumme
intermediate transmission block Blockzwischenprüfung
in terms of value wertmäßig
internal eigen, hauseigen, intern
internal billing Nachkalkulation
internal bus interner Bus
internal code interner Code
internal command internes Kommando
internal communication switch interner Kommunikationsschalter
internal control bit internes Steuerbit
internal control word internes Steuerwort
internal data processing innere Datenverarbeitung
internal error Systemfehler
internal file interne Datei
internal format internes Format
internal indicator interne Bezugszahl
internal loopback test interner Test mit Rückkopplung
internally produced eigengefertigt
internal message code Aktionscode
internal message list Aktionsliste
internal message number Aktionsnummer
internal message record Aktionssatz
internal message text Aktionstext
internal message type Aktionsart, Aktionstyp
internal node interner Knoten
internal output interner Ausgang
internal production Eigenfertigung, Eigenherstellung
internal register internes Register
internal speaker eingebauter Lautsprecher
internal table interne Tabelle
internal to purchasing einkaufsintern
internal turnover Binnenumsatz
internal word output interner Wortausgang
international international
international alphabet internationales Alphabet
international credit transfer Auslandsüberweisung
international help line zentraler Telefonservice

international language keyboard internationale Tastatur
international payment transaction Auslandszahlungsverkehr
international standard internationale Norm, internationaler Standard
International Standardization Organization Internationaler Normungsausschuß
international telegraph alphabet internationales Telegrafenalphabet
international transfer list Auslandsüberweisungsliste
interoffice network büroübergreifendes Netz
interpartition-move Interpartitions-Verschiebung
interpret interpretieren
interpretation Aufschlüsselung
interpreter Interpreter, Interpretierer
interpreter administration area Interpreter-Verwaltungsbereich
interpreter obsolence area Interpreter-Verwaltungsbereich
interprocess communication Kommunikation zwischen Prozessen
interrogate abfragen, befragen
interrogating magnetic tape Abfragemagnetband
interrogation Stationsaufforderung
interrupt Interrupt, Unterbrechung, unterbrechen
interrupt acknowledge Interruptbestätigung, Unterbrechungsbestätigung
interrupt acknowledgement Unterbrechungsantwort
interrupt address register Interruptadreßregister, Unterbrechungsadreßregister
interrupt confirmation Unterbrechungsbestätigung
interrupt criterion Unterbrechungskriterium
interrupt driven unterbrechungsgesteuert
interrupted abgebrochen, unterbrochen
interrupter Schalter, Unterbrecher
interrupt facility Programmunterbrechungs-Einrichtung
interrupt handler Interrupthandler
interrupt lockout Unterbrechungssperre
interrupt mask Interruptmaske, Unterbrechungsmaske
interrupt protocol Unterbrechungsprotokoll
interrupt register Interruptregister, Unterbrechungsregister
interrupt request Interruptanforderung, Unterbrechungsanforderung

115

interrupt service routine Interrupt Service Routine, Interruptroutine, Unterbrechungsroutine
interrupts off Interrupts Aus
interrupts off instruction Anweisung »Interrupts Off«
interrupt stack Interrupt-Stack
interrupt state Unterbrechungsstatus
intersection Durchschnitt, Schnittpunkt
intersperse einstreuen
interval Intervall, Zeitabstand
interval timer Intervallzeitgeber
intervention Eingriff
interworking zusammenarbeitend
in the correct position stellenrichtig
initial record layout Initialsatzbett
in time slices zeitscheibenweise
intrinsical eigentlich
introduction Einführung
introductory know-how Einführungs-Know-how
in turn turnusmäßig
invalid fehlerhaft, ungültig, unzulässig
invalid address ungültige Adresse, unzulässige Adresse
invalid argument ungültiges Argument
invalid call ungültiger Verbindungsaufbau
invalid character ungültiges Zeichen
invalid data ungültige Daten
invalid field Fehlerkennzeichen
invalid frame ungültiger Block, ungültiger Blockaufbau
invalid operation unzulässige Operation
invalid reception ungültiger Empfang
invalid separator ungültiges Trennzeichen
inventorial inventurmäßig
inventory Inventar, Inventur, Lagerbestand, Materialbestand
inventory account Bestandskonto
inventory adjustment Bestandsberichtigung
inventory alteration Bestandsveränderung
inventory analysis Inventurauswertung
inventory check Bestandskontrolle
inventory coverage Bestandsdeckung
inventory credit entry Bestandsentlastung
inventory data Bestandsdaten
inventory date Inventurdatum
inventory debit entry Bestandsbelastung
inventory devaluation Bestandsabwertung
inventory development Bestandsentwicklung
inventory difference Inventurdifferenz
inventory difference list Inventurdifferenzliste
inventory display Bestandsanzeige

inventory entry file Inventureingabedatei
inventory evidence Bestandsnachweis
inventory field Bestandsfeld
inventory file Bestandsdatei
inventory item Bestandspostion
inventory list Bestandsliste
inventory listing Lagerbestandsliste
inventory maintenance Lagerbestandsführung
inventory monitoring Bestandsüberwachung
inventory neutral lagerbestandsneutral
inventory posting Bestandsbuchung
inventory program Inventurprogramm
inventory quantity Lagerbestandsmenge
inventory record Bestandsatz
inventory register Inventarverzeichnis
inventory reservation Bestandsreservierung
inventory result Inventurbestand
inventory result list Inventurbestandsliste
inventory revaluation Bestandsaufwertung, Bestandsumbewertung
inventory schedule Inventurplan
inventory situation Bestandssituation
inventory status Bestandsstatus
inventory summary Bestandsübersicht
inventory tape Bestandsband
inventory update flag Bestandsführungskennzeichen
inventory valuation Bestandsbewertung, Inventurbewertung
inventory value Bestandswert, Lagerwert
inventory value correction Bestandswertkorrektur
inventory value posting Bestandswertbuch
inventory value simulation Bestandswertsimulation
invert invertieren, umdrehen, umkehren, umstellen, umstülpen
inverted invers dargestellt
inverter Inverter
investment Investition
investment budgeting Investitionsplanung
investment costs Investitionsabgabe
investment installment Investitionsanzahlung
investment order Investitionsbestellung
investment payment Investitionszahlung
investment premium Investitionszulage
investment premium key Investitionszulagenschlüssel
investment year Investitionsjahr
invisible unsichtbar
invisible hyphen unsichtbares Trennzeichen
invitation to clear Aufforderung zur Verbindungsauslösung

invitation to send Aufforderung zum Senden, Sendeaufforderung
invoice Faktura, Rechnung, Rechnungsbeleg, fakturieren
invoice accompanying delivery Lieferzeitrechnung
invoice address Rechnungsadresse
invoice addressee Rechnungsempfänger
invoice addressee number Rechnungsempfängernummer
invoice amount Rechnungsbetrag, Rechnungswert
invoice cancellation Rechnungsstorno
invoice controller Rechnungsprüfer
invoice currency Fakturawährung
invoice data Rechnungsdaten
invoice date Fakturadatum, Rechnungsdatum
invoice due date Fälligkeitsdatum, Rechnungstermin
invoice function Fakturierung
invoice index Fakturaindex
invoice item Rechnungsposition, Rechnungsposten
invoice item value Rechnungspositionswert
invoice module Fakturierungsmodul
invoice net Fakturanetto
invoice number Rechnungsbelegnummer
invoice posting Rechnungsverbuchung
invoice price Rechnungspreis
invoice program Fakturaprogramm
invoicer Rechnungslieferant
invoice receipt number Rechnungseingangsnummer
invoice received settlement account Rechnungseingangsverrechnungskonto
invoice sheet Rechnungsseite
invoice text Fakturatext
invoice validation Rechnungsprüfung
invoicing Fakturierung
invoicing date Fakturierungsdatum
invoicing program Fakturierungsprogramm
invoicing record Fakturierungssatz
invoke aufrufen
invoke confidence test Funktionstest starten
I/O code E/A-Code
I/O device E/A-Gerät
I/O device address E/A-Einheitenadresse
I/O facility E/A-Routinen des Supervisors
I/O forcing E/A erzwingen
I/O operation E/A-Operation
I/O order E/A-Auftrag
I/O requirement E/A-Bedürfnis
I/O trace E/A-Befehlsprotokollierung

I/O word E/A-Wort
iram file IRAM-Datei
iron Eisen
iron core Eisenkern
isam access statements Befehle zum Zugriff auf ISAM-Datei
isam key ISAM-Schlüssel
iso character ISO-Zeichen
isochronous isochron
isolating capacitor Sperrkondensator, Trennkondensator
isolating transformer Isoliertransformator
isolation transformer Isoliertransformator
isolator switch Trennschalter
iso seven-bit coded character set 7-bit-kodierter Zeichensatz nach ISO
issue Abgang, Ausgabe, Ausgang, Ausstellung, Problemstellung, Thema, abgeben, ausgeben, ausstellen
issue date Abgangsdatum
issue of invoice Rechnungsausgang
issue of materials Materialausgabe
issues list Abgangsliste
issues of materials Materialabgang, Materialausgabe
issue unit Ausgabeeinheit
item Aktion, Artikel, Artikelbezeichnung, Element, Position, Posten, Punkt, Teil
item account number Artikelkontonummer
item amount Positionsbetrag
item character Artikelcharakter
item credit Artikelgutschrift
item data Positionsdaten
item description Artikelbezeichnung
item discount Positionsrabatt
item display Postenanzeige
item freight Positionsfracht
item grouping Artikelgruppierung
item history file Artikelkontodatei
item information Posteninformationen
itemize aufschlüsseln
itemized list aufgeschlüsselte Liste
item level Postenebene
item line Postenzeile
item list Artikelübersicht
item marker Postenkennzeichen
item master Artikelstamm
item number Artikelnummer, Positionsnummer
item oriented artikelorientiert
item price Artikelpreis
item processing Postenbearbeitung
item record Postensatz
item related artikelbezogen, positionsbezogen

item report

item report Artikelübersicht
item screen Positionsbild
item selection Postenauswahl, Postenselektion
item sorting Postensortierung
item specific artikelabhängig
item statistics Artikelstatistik
item summary Artikelkurztext, Positionsübersicht
item text Positionstext
item total Postensumme
item type Positionsart, Positionstyp
item value Positionswert
item weight Positionsgewicht
iteration Durchlauf, Iteration, Schleifendurchlauf
iteration count Iterationszähler
iteration index Iterationsindex
iteration loop Iterationsschleife

J

jack Buchse, Klinkenstecker, Schaltfeld
jack plug Klinkenbuchse
jack plug cable Kabel mit Klinkenstecker
jarring test Erschütterungstest
jitter Jitter, Phasenzittern
job Auftrag, Job, Programm
job accounting facility Jobabrechnungseinrichtung
job accounting reporting facility Jobabrechnungs-Protokollierungseinrichtung
job backlog Bestand nicht eröffneter Jobs
job box Jobkasten
job classification Arbeitseinstufung, Jobeinteilung
job control command Jobbetriebsanweisung
job control dialog Jobsteuerungsdialog
job control language Jobbetriebssprache
job control statement Jobbetriebsanweisung
job control stream Jobeingabestrom
job distribution facility Jobverteilungsprozessor
job distribution processor Jobverteilungsprozessor
job information line Auftragskopfdaten
joblog report program Routine zum Ausdrucken des Jobabrechnungsprotokolls
job name Jobname
job order Arbeitsauftrag
job oriented aufgabenorientiert
job processing Jobbearbeitung
job processing command Befehl für die Jobverarbeitung
job region Jobbereich
job remote initiation Jobfernstart
job rescheduling Änderung der Jobablaufplanung
job scheduler Jobablaufplanung
job shop system control Jobverarbeitungssteuerung
job slot Jobtabellenplatz
job slot number Jobtabellenplatznummer
job step Jobschritt
job step control Jobschrittsteuerung
job step initializer Jobschrittsteuerung
job stream Jobeingabestrom
job transfer facility Jobverteilungsprozessor
jogger Rüttler
join verbinden

join file Teilnehmerdatei
joint Gelenk, Verbindung
join table Teilnehmertabelle
josephson junction Josephson-Element
journal date Journaldatum
journal file Journaldatei
journal teleprinter Journalfernschreiber
journal type Journalart
joystick Joystick, Spielpult, Steuerknüppel
joystick position Spielpultposition
judder zittern
judge befinden, beurteilen
judgement Beurteilung
jump Sprung, springen, überspringen
jump address register Sprungadreßregister
jump back Rücksprung
jumper Brücke, Kontaktbrücke, Springer, Steckbrücke, Verbindungsdraht
jumper clip Steckbrücke
jumper terminal Brückenklemme
jumping around timer Sprung-Zeitglied
jump instruction Sprungbefehl
jump routine Sprungprogramm
jump scroll schneller Bilddurchlauf
jump sequential sprungsequentiell
jump to anspringen
junction Zusammenführung
junction box Abzweigdose
junction diode Flächendiode
junction line Verbindungsleitung
junction temperature Sperrschichttemperatur
junction transistor Flächentransistor
just gerade
justification Ausrichtung, Blocksatz
just in time Just-in-Time, gerade rechtzeitig
just in time delivery Just-in-Time-Lieferung

119

K

Kansas City Standard   Kansas-City-Standard
kbyte   kByte (Kilobyte)
keep   aufbewahren, halten, sichern
keep back   zurückhalten
keep secret   geheimhalten
kept in parallel   mitgeführt
kept secret   geheimgehalten
kernel   Kern, Systemkern
kernel mode   Kernel-Modus
key   Schlag, Schlüssel, Taste
key argument   Schlüsselparameter
key assignment   Tastendefinition
keyboard   Bedientastatur, Tastatur
keyboard access code   Tastaturschlüssel
keyboard action mode   Tastaturfunktionsmodus
keyboard beep   Tastatursignal
keyboard bell   Tastatursignal
keyboard cable   Tastaturkabel
keyboard cable socket   Anschluß für Tastaturkabel
keyboard command   Tastaturkommando
keyboard control   Tastatursteuerung
keyboard data   Daten von der Tastatur, Tastaturdaten
keyboard data station   Datenstation mit Tastatur
keyboard driver   Tastaturanpassung, Tastaturtreiber
keyboard encoder   Tastaturcodierer
keyboard entry   Eintastung, Tastatureingabe
keyboard feature   Tastaturmerkmal
keyboard feet   Tastaturfuß
keyboard file   Tastaturdatei
keyboard handling   Tastaturbedienung
keyboard indicator   Tastaturanzeige
keyboard instruction   Tastaturbefehl
keyboard interface failure   Fehler in der Tastaturschnittstelle
keyboard key   Taste
keyboard key with special use   Sonderfunktionstaste
keyboard label strip   Funktionstastenstreifen
keyboard language   Tastatursprache
keyboard locked   Tastatur gesperrt
keyboard mapping   Tastaturumkodierung
keyboard mode   Tastaturmodus
keyboard monitor   Tastaturmonitor
keyboard process   Tastaturbearbeitung
keyboard release   Tastaturfreigabe
keyboard section   Tastaturteil
keyboard selection   Tastaturauswahl
keyboard selection menu   Tastaturauswahlmenü
keyboard setting   Einstellung der Tastatur
keyboard shift level   Umschaltebene
keyboard task   Tastaturaufgabe
keyboard test   Tastaturtest
keyboard transmit buffer   Tastaturzeichenpuffer
keycap   Tastenkappe
keyclick   Tastenklick
key code   Schlüsselcode
key data   Schlüsseldaten
key dependant   schlüsselabhängig
key directory   Schlüsselverzeichnis
keyed   indiziert
keyed access   Zugriff über Schlüssel
key editing   Schlüsselaufbereitung
keyed plug   kodierter Stecker
key entry   Schlüsseleintrag
key field   Schlüsselfeld, Sortierfeld
key field location   Schlüsselfeldposition
key field starting location   Schlüsselfeldanfang
keyfile   indizierte Datei
key function   Tastenfunktion
key information   Schlüsselinformation
keying   Kodierung
key input   Tasteneingabe
key length   Schlüssellänge
key lock   Tastensperre
key of reference   Bezugsschlüssel
key option   Schlüsseloption
keypad   Tastenblock, numerisches Tastenfeld
keypad application mode   anwendungsorientierter Funktionstastenmodus
keypad area   Tastaturbereich
keypad key codes   Kodierung der Funktionstasten
keypad numeric mode   numerischer Tastenblock
key plug   Stecker mit Einsteckmarkierung, kodierter Stecker
key repeat   Tastenwiederholung
key row   Tastenreihe
key strip   Funktionsstreifen
key stroke   Tastenanschlag, Tastenbetätigung
keyswitch   Schlüsselschalter
key symbol   Tastenzeichen
key term   Schlüsselbegriff
key to error text   Fehlertextschlüssel
keytop touch area   Tastfläche

key touch selector Tastenbetätigungskrafteinsteller
key type Schlüsselart
key-type file indizierte Datei
keyword Kürzel, Schlagwort, Schlüsselwort, Stichwort
key word class Schlüsselwortklasse
key word file Stichwortdatei
key word flag Schlüsselwortkennzeichen
key word generator Stichwortgenerator
key word input Stichworteingabe
key word line Schlüsselwortzeile
key word list Stichwortliste
key word operand Schlüsselwortoperand
key word parameter Schlüsselwortparameter
key word search Stichwortrecherche, Stichwortsuche
key word table Schlüsselworttabelle
kilobaud Kilobaud
kilobyte Kilobyte
kilogram Kilogramm
kilopacket Kilopaket
kiloword Kilowort
kind Art
kind of document modification Aktenzeichenart
kind of source device Quellgeräteart
kit Baukasten, Bausatz, Satz
klystron Klystron
knowledge Kenntnis
knowledge about the system Systemkenntnis

L

label Aufkleber, Dateikennzeichnung, Etikett, Kennsatz, Kennzeichner, Label, Marke, Markierung, Merker, Text
label cross reference table Kennsatz-Querverweistabelle
label handling routine Kennsatzroutine
label identifier Kennsatzname
label modifier Adreßmodifikator
label name Kennsatzname
label number Kennsatznummer
label parameter Namensparameter
label printing Etikettendruck
label set Kennsatzfamilie
label strip Funktionsstreifen
label table listing Kennsatztabellen-Ausdruck
label type Kennsatztyp
labial labial
lace factor Versatzfaktor
lack of storage Speichermangel
ladder diagram Stromlaufplan
ladder logic Logikprogramm, Stromlaufplan
ladder logic circuit Stromlaufplan
ladder logic diagram Stromlaufplan
ladder logic element Element im Stromlaufplan
ladder logic instruction Anweisung im Stromlaufplan
ladder logic program Logikprogramm
ladder logic syntax Logiksyntax
ladder rung Leiterholm
lag Verzögerung
lagged verzögert
laid down festgehalten, festgelegt
laminated core Blechkern
lamp Lampe
lampholder Lampenfassung
land register Grundbuch
land register entry Grundbucheintrag
landscape Querformat
landscape format Querformat
language Sprache
language editor Datenaufbereitungsprogramm, Sprachen-Editor
language element Sprachelement
language identifier Sprachkennzeichen
language key Sprachenschlüssel, Sprachkennzeichen
language of a country Landessprache

language pool Sprachenpool
language processing Sprachverarbeitung
language processor Sprachprozessor, Sprachübersetzer
language processor output module Zielcodeelement
language processor source module Quellcodeelement
language ROM Sprach-ROM
language selection menu Menü zur Auswahl der Sprache, Sprachauswahlmenü
language selection quantity Sprachenauswahlmenge
language statement Sprachanweisung
language symbol Sprachsymbol
language system support Programmtesthilfe
language table Sprachentabelle
language translation Sprachenübersetzung
lap of honour Ehrenrunde
large groß
large computer installation Großrechenanlage
large core memory Großkernspeicher
large machine Großmaschine
large scale integration Hochintegrationstechnik, hochintegriert
large scale module Großmodul
laser Laser
laser printer Laserdrucker
last but one vorletzter
last character input letztes eingegebenes Zeichen
last character keyed letztes eingegebenes Zeichen
last day of posting month Buchungsmonatsultimo
last day of the month Ultimo
last in - first out Kellerspeicher
last input letzte Eingabe, letzteingeben
last line Schlußzeile
last line lock up Schlußzeilensperre
last mentioned letztgenannt
last record indicator Programmende-Bezugszahl
last track Servospur
latch Auffang-Flipflop, Einschnappklinke, Latch, Zwischenspeicher, rasten
latch circuit Latch-Schaltung
latch down key rastbare Taste
latching circuit Latch-Schaltung
latching relay Stromstoßrelais
latch out tabulator Hafttabulator
late acknowledge condition EA-Rückmeldung
late line storage Speicherung der letzten Zeile

122

latency Latenz, Wartezeit
later nachträglich
Latin character lateinisches Zeichen
law Gesetz, Gesetzgeber, Recht
law of formation Bildungsgesetz
lay Lage, legen
lay down festlegen
layer Ebene, Lage, Schicht
layered product zusätzliche Software
layered storage Speicherhierarchie
layout Anordnung, Briefgestaltung, Layout, bereitlegen
layout character Formatsteuerzeichen
layout control Layout-Steuerung
layout file Layoutdatei
layout record Layoutsatz
lead Vorlauf, führen
lead acid battery Bleiakkumulator
leader Vorlauf, Vorspann
leader file Vorlaufdatei
leader record Vorlaufsatz
leader tape Vorlaufband, Vorspannband
leading führend
leading edge führende Flanke
leading minus sign führendes Minuszeichen
leading tape mark Bandanfangsmarke
leading zero Vornull, führende Null
leading zeroes führende Nullen
lead lag Vor-/Nacheilung
lead lag computation Berechnung der Vor-/Nachteilung
lead lag dynamic compensation dynamische Kompensation der Vor-/Nachteilung
lead pencil Bleistift
lead protrusion Auskragung
lead time Vorlaufzeit
leakage current Kriechstrom
leapfrog test Bocksprung-Test
lease Miete, Pacht, mieten, pachten, verpachten
leased circuit Mietleitung, Standverbindung
leased common carrier Fernmeldemietleitung
leased line Mietleitung
leased line network Mietleitungsnetz
leased line service Mietleitungsdienst
leased out verleast
leased point-to-point line festgeschaltete Punkt-zu-Punkt-Leitung
leased private line private Mietleitung
leasing Leasing
leasing status Leasingstatus
least significant bit Bit mit dem niedrigsten Stellenwert, niedrigstwertiges Bit, wertniedrigstes Bit

least significant digit Ziffer mit niedrigstem Stellenwert, niedrigstwertige Stelle, wertniedrigste Ziffer
leave verlassen, überlassen
leave blank freilassen
leave out auslassen
leaving the backup program Beenden der Sicherung
LED display LED-Anzeige
ledger Debitorenverzeichnis
LED indicator LED-Anzeige
left links, überlassen
left arrow Pfeil nach links
left arrow key Pfeiltaste nach links
left hand margin Anfangsanschlag, linker Rand
left hand side links
left justify linksbündig formatieren
left margin linker Rand
left margin adjustment Setzen des linken Schreibrandes
left margin set Anfangsrandsteller
leftmost character am weitesten links stehendes Zeichen
leftmost character position erste Zeichenposition
left shift Verschieben nach links
left to right von links nach rechts
legal gerichtlich, gesetzlich, juristisch, rechtlich
legal department Rechtsabteilung
legal standard Rechtmäßigkeit
legend strip Funktionsstreifen
legibility Lesbarkeit
legitimately transacted transaktionsberechtigt
lend leihen, verleihen
length Länge
length byte Längenbyte
length field Längenfeld
length of defining argument Länge des Ordnungsbegriffs
length of the constant Konstantenlänge
length of variables Variablenlänge
length parameter Längenparameter
length specification Längenangabe
length specification bit Längenangaben-Bit
length statistics Längenstatistik
length sum Längensumme
less or equal kleiner oder gleich
less than kleiner als
let vermieten
letter Brief, Buchstabe, Schreiben
letter address Briefanschrift
letter area Briefbereich

letter bottom Brieffuß
letter catalog Briefkatalog
letter content Briefinhalt
letter creation Brieferstellung
letter creation file Brieferstellungsdatei
letter date Briefdatum
letter design Briefgestaltung
letter end Briefende
letter form Briefform
letter generation Brieferstellung
letter head Briefkopf
letter head text Briefkopftext
letter information record Briefinformationssatz
letter name Briefname
letter number Briefnummer
letter number area Briefnummernbereich
letter number file Briefnummerndatei
letter number record Briefnummernsatz
letter of apprenticeship Lehrzeugnis
letter of intent Vorvertrag
letter of understanding Vorvertrag
letter output Briefausgabe
letter page Briefseite
letter print Briefausdruck
letter processing Briefverarbeitung
letter quality printer Korrespondenzdrucker
letter request Briefanforderung
letter request generation Briefauftragserstellung
letter request record Briefauftragssatz
letter row Buchstabentastenreihe
letter selection mask Briefauswahlmaske
letter shift Buchstabenumschaltung
letter skeleton Briefgerüst
letter skeleton data Briefgerüstdaten
letter skeleton mask Briefgerüstmaske
letter spacing mechanism Schreibschritteinrichtung
letter stock Briefvorrat
letter structure Briefaufbau
letter symbol Buchstabensymbol
letter text Brieftext
letter to phoneme conversion Umwandlung von Buchstaben in Phoneme
letter-to-sound module Modul für die Umwandlung von Buchstaben
letter transaction Brieftransaktion
letter type Briefart
letter variable Briefvariable
letter writing Briefschreibung
letter writing procedure Briefschreibungsprozedur

level 1 indicator Bezugszahl Gruppenstufe 1
level Ebene, Niveau, Prioritätsebene, Schicht, Stufe, Version
level control Niveauregelung
level header Stufenvorsatz
level header entry Eintrag in Stufensatz
level identification Stufenkennzeichen
level identifier Gruppenstufenmerkmal
level measurement Niveaumeßgerät
level network Ebenenverbund
level of language Sprachebene
level storage interner Zwischenspeicher
level switch Niveauschalter, Pegelschalter
level transducer Niveaugeber
lever Hebel, Schalthebel
lexical stress Wortbetonung
lexicon Lexikon
liabilities Bilanzpassiva, Passiva
liability Gewähr, Gewährleistung, Obligo, Verbindlichkeit
liability for damages Haftung auf Schadenersatz, Schadenersatzhaftung
liable for -pflichtig
liable for wealth tax vermögenssteuerpflichtig
liable to pay entgeltpflichtig
librarian Bibliotheksprogramm, Bibliotheksverwalter, Bibliotheksverwalter, Librarian
librarian programm Bibliotheksprogramm
library Bibliothek
library administration Bibliotheksverwaltung
library administrator Bibliotheksverwalter
library directory Bibliotheksverzeichnis
library document Bibliotheksdokument
library function Bibliotheksfunktion
library maintenance Bibliothekspflege
library organisation Bibliotheksaufbau
library output type Bibliotheksausgabetyp
library program Bibliotheksprogramm
library register Bibliothekstabelle
library routine Bibliotheksprogramm
library tape Bibliotheksband
library type Bibliothekstyp
lie liegen
life insurance Lebensversicherung
lifetime Nutzungsdauer
lifetime period Nutzungsdauer
lift heben
lift off tape Korrekturband
light Licht, hell
light bulb Glühbirne, Glühlampe
light code Anzeigencode
light cyan helles Kobaltblau
light emitting diode Leuchtdiode

lighter leichter
lighting device Leuchteinheit
lightning conductor Blitzableiter
lightning generator Blitzgenerator
lightning protection Blitzschutz
light pen Lichtgriffel, Lichtgriffel, Lichtschreiber, Lichtstift
lightpen adjustment Lightpenabgleich
light screen heller Bildschirm
light shielding Lichtschutz
light up aufleuchten
limit Grenze, Grenzwert, Schranke, begrenzen
limit amount Grenzbetrag
limitation Beschränkung
limiter circuit Begrenzungsschaltung
limit switch Grenzschalter
limit switch wiring Verdrahtung des Grenzschalters
line Leitung, Linie, Zeile, Übertragungsleitung
line adapter Leitungsendgerät
linear linear
linear distance Luftlinie, kürzester Abstand
linear equation lineare Gleichung
linear fit lineare Interpolation
linear integrated circuit integrierte Linearschaltung
linear interpolation Geradeninterpolation
linear motor Linearmotor
linear programming lineare Programmierung
line attribute Zeilenattribut
line beginning Zeilenanfang
line buffer Zeilenlöschpuffer, Zeilenpuffer
line by line zeilenweise
line clearing Leitungsabbau
line connecting equipment Leitungsanschlußeinrichtung
line control table Leistungskontrolltabelle
line counter Zeilenzähler
line counter file zwischengespeicherte Druckdatei
line counter specification Druckzeilenbestimmung
line current feed Leitungsspeisung
line designation Leitungsbezeichnung, Leitungskennzeichnung, Zeilenbezeichnung
line diagram Liniendiagramm
line distance Zeilenabstand
line driver Signalverstärker
line echo Zeichenecho
line editing Editieren im Zeilenmodus
line editor Zeileneditor
line end Zeilenende
line end control key Zeilenendsteuertaste

line splitter

line end lock Zeilenendsperre
line end signal Zeilenendsignal
line fall-out Leitungsausfall
line feed Zeilenschaltung, Zeilenvorschub
line feed control Vorschubsteuerung
line feed key Zeilenvorschubtaste
line feed new line Zeilenvorschub neue Zeile
line feed speed Zeilenvorschubgeschwindigkeit
line frequency Netzfrequenz
line frequency clock netztaktgesteuerte Uhr
line frequency tolerance Netzfrequenztoleranz
line graph Liniendiagramm
line identification Anschlußkennung
line identification letter Zeilenkennbuchstaben
line indication Zeilenangabe
line insert Zeile einfügen
line interface Leitungsschnittstelle
line interference Leitungsstörung
line key Zeilenstoptaste
line makeup Zeilenumbruch
line margin Zeilenrand
line mode Zeilenmodus
line network Leitungsnetz
line number Leitungsnummer, Positionsnummer, Zeilennummer
line number sequence Zeilennummersequenz
line occurrence Leitungsereignis
line of print Druckzeile
line oriented protocol zeilenorientiertes Protokoll
line outage Leitungsausfall
line position Zeilenposition
line printer Systemdrucker, Zeilendrucker
line printer spooler program Zeilendruckerspooler
line propagation time Leitungslaufzeit
line protocol handler Leitungsprotokoll-Steuerprogramm
line range Zeilenbereich
line remainder Zeilenrest
line ruler Liniereinrichtung, Tabulatorzeile
line selection Zeilenauswahl
line skip Zeilensprung, Zeilentransport
line space key Zeilenschalttaste
line space preset key Zeilenvoreinsteller
line space selector Zeilenabstandeinsteller
line spacing Zeilenabstand
line speed Übertragungsgeschwindigkeit, Übertragungsrate
lines per inch Zeilen pro Zoll
lines per minute Zeilen pro Minute
lines per second Zeilen pro Sekunde
line splitter Kanalaufteiler

125

line structure Zeilenaufbau
line switching Durchschalten, Leitungsvermittlung, leitungsvermitteln
line tapping Leitung anzapfen
line terminal Leitungsendgerät
line terminator Leitungsabschluß, Zeilenendezeichen
line time Übertragungszeit
line-to-store transfer Einspeicherung
line transmit zeilenweises Übertragen
line type Zeilenart, Zeilentyp
line up Inbetriebnahme, aufreihen
line voltage Netzspannung
line wrap Zeilenumbruch
link Anschluß, Verknüpfung, binden, ketten, linken, verknüpfen, Überleitung, Übertragungsstrecke
linkable linkbar, verknüpfbar
link address Anschlußadresse
linkage Bindung
linkage editor Verknüpfungsprogramm
linkage procedure Bindeprozedur
linkage register Verknüpfungsregister
linkage removal Verbindungsabbau
linkage set-up Verbindungsaufbau
link control procedure Übertragungssteuerungsverfahren
link edit map Verknüpfungsprotokoll
linker Binder, Linker, Verknüpfungsprogramm
linker map Verknüpfungsausgabeliste
link error Linkfehler
link field Kettungsfeld
link field indicator Kettungsfeldbezugszahl
linking loader Bindelader
linking module Verbindungsmodul
linking sequence Anschlußbefehlsfolge
link macro Linkmakro
link map Bindertabelle
link name Linkname
link operand Linkoperand
link protocol Übermittlungsprotokoll, Übermittlungsvorschrift
link run Linklauf
link set Bindeelementmenge
link statement Bindeanweisung
liquid Flüssigkeit
liquid controller Flüssigkeitsregulierung
liquid crystal display Flüssigkristallanzeige
liquid electrical insulating flüssiges Isolationsmaterial
liquid film Flüssigkeitsfilm
liquid laser Flüssigkeitslaser
liquid starter flüssiger Starter

list Liste, Tabelle, aufführen, listen
list analysis Listenauswertung
list composition Listenzusammenstellung
list contents Listeninhalt
list definition Listendefinition
list dependant listenabhängig
list designation Listenbezeichnung
list device Druckgerät
list display Listenanzeige
list document Listendokument
list draft Listenentwurf
list editing Listenaufbereitung
listener Empfänger
list file Listendatei
list flag Listenkennung
list form Listenform
list format Listenform, Tabellenformat
list function Listenfunktion
list generation program Listenerstellungsprogramm
list group Listengruppe
list headline Listenüberschrift
listing Liste
listing file Druckdatei, Listendatei
listing line Nutzzeile
listing version Protokollversion
list item Listenposition
list length Listenlänge
list line Listenzeile
list name Listenbezeichnung, Listenname
list number Listennummer
list of balances Saldenliste
list of money denominations Geldsortenliste
list of options Auswahlliste
list of user control blocks Teilnehmersteuerbereichsliste
list of variants Variantenliste
list output Listenausgabe
list parameter Listenparameter
list printout Listenausdruck
list processing Listenverarbeitung
list processing feature Listenverarbeitungspaket
list program Listenprogramm
list report Listenauswertung
list screen Listenbild
list screen definition Listenbilddefinition
list section Listenabschnitt, Listenteil
list structure Listenaufbau
list summary Listenzusammenfassung, Listenübersicht
list type Listenart, Listentyp
list value Tabellenwert
literal Literal

literal subscript absoluter Index
literature Literatur
literature module Literaturmodul
lithium Lithium
live line spannungsführende Leitung
live part unter Spannung stehendes Teil
load Belastung, Last, laden
load call Bereitstellungsaufruf
load code buffer Codepuffer
load directory Ladeverzeichnis
load disk Programmdiskette, Startdiskette, Systemdiskette
loader Ladeprogramm, Lader
loader area Ladebereich
loader input sector Ladeversorgungssektor
load exclusion factor Ladeausschlußfaktor
loading access Ladezugriff
loading error Einspeicherungsfehler
loading time Ladezeit
load LED Ladeanzeige
load list Ladeliste
load mode Lademodus
load module Lademodul, ladbares Programm
load name Phasenname
load operation Ladevorgang
load path Ladepfad
load pointer Einräumzeiger
load program Ladeprogramm
load regulator Lastregelung
load resistor Ballastwiderstand, Belastungswiderstand
load voltage Ladespannung
loan Darlehen, leihen
loan account Darlehenskonto
loan amount Darlehensbetrag
loan discount Disagio
loan information Darlehensangaben
loan master record Darlehensstammsatz
local lokal
local address lokale Adresse
local area network lokales Netzwerk
local call Ortsgespräch
local call number örtliche Rufnummer
local copy Eigenkopie
local digital sales office Geschäftsstelle
local echo lokales Zeichenecho
local editing lokales Editieren
localize lokalisieren
local line lokaler Anschluß
local loop Teilnehmerleitung, lokale Prüfschleife, nahe Prüfschleife
local loopback lokale Prüfschleife
local mode Lokalbetrieb

local node lokaler Knoten
local number örtliche Rufnummer
local office Geschäftsstelle
local procedure error lokaler Ablauffehler
local speak command Kommando für lokale Sprachausgabe
local symbol lokales Symbol
local symbol table Tabelle der lokalen Symbole
local syntax lokale Syntax
local telecommunication authority Fernmeldeamt
local terminal controller lokale Terminal-Steuereinheit
local virtual address lokale virtuelle Adresse
locate feststellen, suchen
locating arm Ortungsarm
locating arm transducer Ortungsarm-Transducer
locating key Führungssteg
locating slot Plazierungseinschnitt
locating system Ortungssystem
location Adresse, Aufstellungsort, Lage, Ort, Ortung, Position, Speicherplatz, Stelle
location counter Adreßzähler, Positionszähler
location mode Ablagemodus, Lokalisierungsmodus
lock Sperre, sperren
locked eingerastet
locked file gesperrte Datei
locked in place eingerastet
locked-unlocked gesperrt-ungesperrt
locking plate Befestigungsplatte
lock key Feststelltaste
lock key ejection Rasttastenauswurf
lock key indicator Rasttastenanzeige
lock mode Feststellmodus
lock out blockieren
lock request Sperranforderung
lock table Locktabelle, Sperrtabelle
log Log, Protokoll, aufzeichnen, protokollieren
log byte Protokollbyte
log counter Protokollzähler
log data Protokolldaten
log database Protokolldatenbank
log device Protokollgerät
log document Protokolldokument
log file Logdatei, Protokolldatei
log file editor Abrechnungsprotokollierung
log function Protokollfunktion
logging device selection/deselection Protokolliergeräte-An-/Abwahl
logging on again Neuanmeldung

log header Protokollheader
logic Logik
logical logisch
logical add logische Addition
logical address logische Adresse
logical and logisch und, logisches »UND«
logical block logischer Block
logical channel logischer Kanal
logical circuit logische Schaltung
logical comparison logischer Vergleich
logical condition logische Bedingung
logical construct logische Adresse
logical control Logiksteuerung
logical control contact Logiksteuerkontakt
logical decision logische Entscheidung
logical device logisches Gerät
logical element Verknüpfungsglied
logical end of media logisches Ende des Datenträgers
logical false logisch falsch
logical file definition logischer Dateiname
logical high logisch hoch
logical input ouput control system logisches Ein-/Ausgabe-Steuersystem
logical instruction Logikbefehl
logical looping capability logische Schleifenfunktion
logically independent logisch voneinander unabhängig
logical name logischer Name
logical not logisches »NICHT«
logical operation block Logikblock
logical or logisch oder, logisches »ODER«
logical page number logische Seitennummer
logical record logischer Datensatz
logical record access logischer Datensatzzugriff
logical record length logische Datensatzlänge
logical relationship logische Beziehung
logical sequence indexsequentiell
logical true logisch wahr
logical unit number logische Gerätenummer
logical value Aussagenwert
logic analyser Logikanalysator
logic board Logikplatine
logic circuit Logikschaltung
logic device Logikgerät
logic diagram Logikdiagramm
logic element Verknüpfungsglied
logic gate Logikgatter
logic ground logische Masse
logic instruction logischer Befehl
logic level Logikpegel, logischer Zustand

logic operation logische Verknüpfung
logic pages logische Seiten
logic printed circuit board Schaltkreisplatine
logic state logischer Zustand
login Anmeldung, Einloggen, Login, Logon, anmelden, einloggen
login flag Anmeldemarkierung
log information Loginformation
login procedure Anmeldeprozedur
login to sich beim System anmelden
logistics Logistik
logistics group Disponentengruppe
logoff Abmeldung, abmelden
logon Anmeldung, Einloggen, Login, Logon, anmelden, einloggen
logon again neuanmelden
logon procedure Anmeldeformalismus
logout Abmeldung, abmelden
logout from sich beim System abmelden
logout of sich beim System abmelden
log printout device Protokollierdruckgerät
log record Protokollsatz
log record type Protokollsatzart
log sheet Protokoll für Maschinenvorgänge
log statement Protokollanweisung
log tape Logband, Protokollband
log utilities Protokollausführung
long lang
long distance Fern-, Weit-
long distance call Ferngespräch
long distance data transmission Datenfernübertragung
long distance xerox Fernkopie, Telefax
long recovery Vorwärtswiederherstellung
long term langfristig
long term data Langzeitdaten
long term storage Langzeitspeicher
longword Langwort
longword integer Ganzzahllangwort
look ahead field Vorgriffsfeld
look ahead record Vorgriffssatz
look up nachlesen, nachschlagen, nachsehen
look up operation Suchoperation
look up table Suchtabelle, Tabellensuche
loop Programmschleife, Regelkreis, Schleife
loopback Prüfschleife
loopback connector Prüfschleifenstecker
loopback self test Rücklaufselbstdiagnose
loop block Schleifenblock
loop current Schleifenstrom
loop gain Schleifenverstärkung
loop test Testschleife
loss Verlust

loss account Verlustkonto
loss accounting Verlustrechnung
loss of use Nutzungsausfall, Nutzungsschaden
lost verloren
lost time Verlustzeit
lot size Losgröße
loudspeaker Lautsprecher
low end configuration Minimalkonfiguration
lower address range unterer Adreßbereich des Speichers
lower bound Untergrenze
lower bus module Modul für den unteren Bus
lowercase letter Kleinbuchstabe
lowering tiefstellen
lower letter row untere Buchstabentastenreihe
lower level Unterstufe
lower limit Betragsuntergrenze, Untergrenze
lower margin Untergrenze
lower threshold Untergrenze
low frequency amplifier Niederfrequenzverstärker
low income earner Geringverdiener
low level format vorformatieren
low level language Maschinensprache, niedrige Programmiersprache
low order niederwertig
low order bit niedrigstwertiges Bit
low order digit Zeichen in der niederwertigen Position, niederwertige Ziffer
low order storage unterer Adreßbereich des Speichers
low pass filter Tiefpaßfilter
low speed langsam
low speed operation Betrieb mit niedriger Geschwindigkeit
low voltage equipment Niederspannungseinrichtungen, Niederspannungsgerät
lug Kabelschuh, Lötfahne, Nase

M

machine Apparat, Automat, Gerät, Maschine
machine aided cognition maschinengestützte Erkennung
machine capacity Maschinenbelastung
machine code Maschinenbefehl, Maschinencode
machine cycle Maschinenzyklus
machine data Gerätedaten, Maschinendaten
machine date Maschinendatum
machine dependant geräteabhängig
machine function Maschinenfunktion
machine ID Anlagennummer
machine independent maschinenunabhängig
machine language Maschinensprache
machine language debugger Maschinensprachen-Debugger
machine language program Maschinensprachen-Programm, Programm in Maschinensprache
machine language programming Programmierung in Maschinensprache
machine number Anlagennummer
machine program Maschinenprogramm
machine readable maschinenlesbar
machine readable material maschinenlesbares Material
machinery Maschinen
machine speed Maschinengeschwindigkeit
machine tool Werkzeugmaschine
machine tool control Werkzeugmaschinensteuerung
machine variable Maschinengröße
machine word length Maschinenwortlänge
machining head Maschinenkopf
macro Makro
macroassembler Makroassembler
macroassembly program Makroassemblerprogramm
macro call Makroaufruf
macro coding Makrocodierung
macrogenerating program Makrogenerierprogramm
macro instruction Makrobefehl
macroinstruction storage Makrobefehlsspeicher
macro language Makrosprache
macro library Makrobibliothek
macroprocessor Makroprozessor

magenta violett
magnet Magnet
magnetic magnetisch
magnetic amplifier Magnetverstärker
magnetic bubble memory Magnetblasenspeicher
magnetic card Magnetkarte
magnetic card reader Magnetkartenleser
magnetic character recognition magnetische Zeichenerkennung
magnetic character set magnetischer Zeichensatz
magnetic circuit Eisenkreis
magnetic circuit air gap Luftspalt im Eisenkreis
magnetic compass Magnetkompaß
magnetic computer Magnetfeldrechner
magnetic core Magnetkern
magnetic core stack modules Magnetkernspeichermodule
magnetic device magnetisches Gerät
magnetic disc Magnetplatte
magnetic disc storage Magnetplattenspeicher
magnetic disc unit Magnetplatteneinheit
magnetic disk drive Magnetplattenlaufwerk
magnetic drum Magnettrommel
magnetic film memory Magnetfilmspeicher
magnetic head Magnetkopf
magnetic head mount Magnetkopfhalterung
magnetic ledger card Magnetkontokarte
magnetic ledger card device Magnetkontokarteneinrichtung
magnetic ledger card dispenser Magnetkontokartenzuführgerät
magnetic memory magnetischer Speicher
magnetic plate storage Magnetplattenspeicher
magnetic reading Magnetschriftabtastung
magnetic recording magnetische Aufzeichnung
magnetic recording data magnetisch aufgezeichnete Daten
magnetic recording techniques Magnetaufzeichnungsverfahren
magnetic state Magnetisierungszustand
magnetic storage magnetische Speicherung
magnetic store Magnetspeicher
magnetic surface magnetische Oberfläche
magnetic tape Magnetband
magnetic tape controller Magnetbandsteuereinheit
magnetic tape control unit Magnetbandsteuereinheit
magnetic tape device Magnetbandgerät
magnetic tape equipment Magnetbandgerät

magnetic tape form Magnetbandbegleitzettel
magnetic tape handler Magnetbandtreiber
magnetic tape processing Magnetbandverarbeitung
magnetic tape reader Magnetbandleser
magnetic tape standard Magnetbandnorm
magnetic tape storage Magnetbandspeicherung
magnetic tape transport Magnetbandtransport
magnetic tape unit Magnetbandeinheit
magnetic thin film device magnetisches Dünnfilmgerät
magnetic track Magnetspur
magnetic variable control magnetische Steuerung
magnetohydrodynamic conversion magnetohydrodynamische Umwandlung
magnetostriction Magnetostriktion
magnetostrictive device magnetostriktives Gerät
magnetron Magnetron
magnitude Größenordnung
magtape Magnetband
mail Post, elektronische Post
mail address Postanschrift
mailbox Briefkasten, Mailbox, Postfach
mailbox administrator Mailboxverwalter
mailbox service Mailboxdienst
mailing address Postanschrift
mail message Nachricht
main Haupt-
main account Zentralkonto
main account number Stammhausnummer
main board Hauptplatine
main buffer Hauptpuffer
main command menu Hauptmenü
main component Hauptkomponente
main contract voucher Kontrakthauptbeleg
main cost centre Hauptkostenstelle
main field Hauptfeld
main file Hauptdatei
mainframe Großrechenanlage, Großrechner, Zentralrechner
mainframe computer Großrechenanlage, Großrechner
mainframe software Zentralrechnersoftware
main header Hauptoberbegriff
main key Hauptschlüssel
main keyboard Haupttastatur, Haupttastenblock
main keypad Haupttastatur, Haupttastenblock
main library Hauptbibliothek
main memory Hauptspeicher
main memory area Hauptspeicherbereich

main memory extension Hauptspeichererweiterung
main memory extract Hauptspeicherauszug
main memory register Hauptspeicherregister
main memory request Hauptspeicheranforderung
main memory table Hauptspeichertabelle
main menu Ausgangsmenu, Hauptmenü
main menu option Option im Hauptmenü
main mode Hauptmodus
main module Hauptmodul
main number Hauptnummer
main program Hauptprogramm
main screen Hauptbild
main selection Hauptauswahl
main station Hauptkonsole, Konsole
mainstay of sales Hauptumsatzträger
main storage Hauptspeicher
main storage consolidation service Hauptspeicherreorganisation
main storage interface facility Hauptspcicheranschlußeinheit
main storage partition Hauptspeicherpartition
main storage processor Hauptspeicherzugriffseinheit
main storage unit Hauptspeicher
main storage unit bank Hauptspeicherbank
main store Hauptspeicher
main system menu Systemhauptmenü
maintain pflegen, warten
maintainability Wartbarkeit
maintainance operation Wartung
maintained in parallel mitgepflegt
main task Hauptaufgabe
maintenance Instandhaltung, Nacharbeit, Pflege, Wartung
maintenance access channel Wartungskanal
maintenance condition Pflegezustand
maintenance controller Wartungsprozessor
maintenance control unit Wartungskontrolleinheit
maintenance entry Wartungseintrag
maintenance interface Wartungsschnittstelle
maintenance log Wartungsprotokoll
maintenance schedule Wartungskalender, Wartungsplan
maintenance shutdown wartungsbedingtes Abschalten
main voucher Hauptbeleg
main voucher head Hauptbelegkopf
main voucher item Hauptbelegposition
main warehouse Hauptlager
major component Hauptfunktionseinheit

131

make tun
make access zugreifen
make a partial delivery teilbeliefern
make a standing entry dauerbuchen
make do behelfen
make sure verifizieren
make the final delivery endausliefern
make up konstruieren
make zero nullen
making use of Ausnutzung
male contact Stecker
male plug Buchsenstecker
male plus Stecker
malfunction Fehlfunktion, Störung
malfunction indicator Störungsanzeige
manage leiten, verwalten
management Leitung, Verwaltung
management area Verwaltungsbereich
management file Verwaltungsdatei
management identifier Verwaltungskennzeichen
management information system Management-Informationssystem
management module Verwaltungsmodul
management of basic data Grunddatenverwaltung
management of internal messages Aktionsverwaltung
management option Verwaltungsmöglichkeit
management program Verwaltungsprogramm
management record Verwaltungssatz
management system Verwaltungssystem
manager Betreuer, Leiter, Manager, Verwalter
manchester encoding Manchester-Code, Manchester-Kodierung
mandatory obligatorisch, zwingend
mandatory entry Mußeingabe
mandatory instruction Muß-Anweisung
manipulate bearbeiten, bedienen, verarbeiten
manipulating variables Bearbeiten von Variablen
manipulation Bedienung, Hantierung, Manipulation, Veränderung
maniupulate verändern
man machine Mensch-Maschine
man machine conversation Mensch-Maschine-Dialog
man machine model Mensch-Maschinen-Modell
manner of processing Verarbeitungsweise
mantissa Mantisse
manual Anleitung, Bedienungsanleitung, Handbuch, händisch, manuell, manuell, von Hand

manual answer manuelle Antwort
manual call manueller Anruf
manual control system Handeinstellsystem
manual data input manuelle Dateneingabe
manual function manuelle Funktion
manual input device Handeingabegerät
manual network Handvermittlungsnetz
manual positioning remote control Handsteuergerät
manual swivelling enabled manuelles Schwenken frei
manual swivelling locked manuelles Schwenken gesperrt
manufacture herstellen
manufacturer Hersteller
manufacturer independent herstellerunabhängig
manufacturer software Herstellersoftware
manufacturing automation protocol Industriesteuerungsprotokoll
manufacturing control Fertigungskontrolle
manufacturing costs Herstellkosten
manufacturing inspection Fertigungskontrolle
manufacturing line Fließband
manufacturing method Herstellungsverfahren
manufacturing process Herstellungsverfahren
man week Mannwoche
map Abbildung, Adressenbelegung, Hauptspeicherauszug, Karte, Plan, Speicherbelegungsplan, abbilden
map area Belegungsbereich
map assembler Verknüpfungsassembler
mapped memory process Speicherauszugsprozeß
mapping Abbild, Abbildung, Adreßumsetzung, Belegung, Umsetzung
mapping facility Aufzeichnungsmöglichkeit
mapping function Abbildungsfunktion
mapping pointer Bitbelegungszeiger
mapping procedure Abbildungsprozedur
mapping program Adreßinformationsprogramm
mapping routine Speicheradressenroutine
margin Rand, Schreibrand
marginal amount Grenzbetrag
marginal check Randwertkontrolle
marginal condition Randwertbedingung
marginal test Grenzprüfung
margin bell Randsignal
margin release key Randlösetaste
margin scale Randstellerskala
margin setting Randeinstellung
margin stop Randsteller

margin stop indicator Randanzeiger
margin stop scale Randstellerskala
margin stop setting key Randstelltaste
margin width Randzonenbreite
marine navigation Schiffsnavigation
mark kennzeichnen, markieren
mark channel Markierkanal
mark down als nicht betriebsbereit kennzeichnen
marker Indexregisterstelle, Kennzeichen, Merker
marker byte Merkerbyte
marker half word Merkerhalbwort
marker letter Kennbuchstabe
market analysis Marktanalyse
marketing Vertrieb
marketing data Vertriebsdaten
marketing department Vertriebsabteilung
marketing system Vertriebssystem
marking term Aufschrift, Kennzeichnung
marking zone Markierzone
mark with a cross ankreuzen
maser Maser
mask Formular, Maske
maskable interrupt maskierbare Unterbrechung, maskierbarer Interrupt
mask data Maskendaten
mask definition Maskendefinition
mask description Maskenbeschreibung
mask field Maskenfeld
mask generator Maskengenerator
mask heading Maskenüberschrift
masking Maskieren
mask name Maskenname
mask positioning Maskenpositionierung
mask preparation Maskenaufbereitung
mask programmable read only memory maskenprogrammierbare Festwertspeicher
mask programmed read only memory maskenprogrammierter Nur-Lese-Speicher
mask register Maskenregister
mask set Maskensatz
mask symbol Maskenzeichen
mask text Maskentext
mass Groß-, Masse, Massen-, en gros
mass copy Massenkopie
mass initialisation Masseninitialisierung
mass memory Massenspeicher
mass storage Massenspeicher
mass storage subsystem Massenspeichereinheit, peripherer Direktzugriffsspeicher
mass storage system Massenspeicher
mass storage unit Hauptspeichereinheit

master Haupt-, Master, Stamm
master account Hauptkonto
master account number Hauptkontonummer
master account system Hauptkontensystem
master administration Stammverwaltung
master bit table interne Bit-Tabelle
master card Hauptkarte
master clear in Ausgangsstellung bringen
master clock Haupttaktgeber
master configuration table Konfigurationshaupttabelle
master console exchange Masterplatzwechsel
master control Hauptschalter, Hauptsteuerung, Steuerschalter
master control relay Hauptsteuerrelais, Steuerrelais
master control unit Steuereinheit
master copy Original
master data Stammdaten
master data administration Stammdatenverwaltung
master data alteration Stammdatenänderung
master data area Stammdatenbereich
master database Stammdatenbank
master data list display Stammdatenlistenanzeige
master data management Stammdatenverwaltung
master data organisation Stammdatenorganisation
master data printout Stammdatenausdruck
master data structure Stammdatenaufbau
master data transfer Stammdatenübernahme
master directory Hauptdateiverzeichnis
master disk Stammsystemplatte
master file Hauptdatei, Stammdatei
master file alteration Stammdatenänderung
master file alteration voucher Stammdatenänderungsbeleg
master file directory Hauptdateikatalog, Hauptdateiverzeichnis
master hold Totalstop, übergeordneter Stop
master key Hauptschlüssel
master list Stammliste
master log file Hauptprotokolldatei
master logging device Masterplatz-Protokollgerät
master long file Hauptprotokolldatei
master menu Hauptmenü
master processor Hauptprozessor
master record Artikelstammsatz, Hauptsatz, Stammsatz
master record alteration Stammsatzänderung

133

master record asset Stammsatzanlage
master record authorization Stammsatzberechtigung
master record data screen Stammsatzdatenbild
master record display Stammsatzanzeige
master record field Stammsatzfeld
master record information Stammsatzinformationen
master record level Stammsatzebene
master record maintenance Stammsatzpflege
master record screen Stammsatzbild
master record type Stammsatzart
master record value field Stammsatzwertfeld
master segment Muttersegment
master set Originalsatz
master station Hauptstation, Sendestation, übergeordnete Station
master system diskette Originalsystemdiskette
master tape Stammband
master terminal Sendestation
master workstation Masterplatz
match vergleichen, übereinstimmen, Übereinstimmung
matchcode Matchcode, Suchcode, Vergleichscode
matchcode acquisition Matchcode-Erfassung
matchcode display Matchcode-Anzeige
matchcode search word Matchcode-Suchbegriff
matching passend, vergleichsgesteuerte Verarbeitung, zutreffend
matching character set passender Zeichensatz
matching field Paarigkeitsfeld, Vergleichsfeld
matching pairs Vergleichspaare
matching record Vergleichssatz
matching record file Vergleichsdatensatzdatei
matching record function Vergleichsfunktion auf Satzbasis
matching record indicator Paarigkeitsbezugszahl
matching record technique Vergleichssatztechnik
material Material, Stoff, Werkstoff
materials account class Materialkontenklasse
materials acquisition Materialzugang
materials allocation Materialbereitstellung
materials area Materialbereich
materials authorization Materialberechtigung
materials availability Materialverfügbarkeit
materials brief designation Materialkurzbezeichnung
materials code Materialschlüssel
materials consumption Materialverbrauch

materials consumption report Materialverbrauchsliste
materials control code Materialsteuerbyte
materials data Materialdaten
materials database Materialdatenbank
materials delivery Materiallieferung
materials entry Materialaufnahme
materials group Materialgruppe
materials information Materialinformation
materials inventory Materialbestand
materials inventory update Materialbestandsführung
materials management Materialwirtschaft
materials management record Materialverwaltungssatz
materials master Materialstamm
materials master data Materialstammdaten
materials master data update Materialstammdatenpflege
materials master file Materialstammdatei
materials master management Materialstammverwaltung
materials master marker Materialstammkennzeichen
materials master record Materialstammsatz
materials master segment Materialstammsegment
materials month Materialmonat
materials name Materialbezeichnung
materials number Materialnummer
materials number allocation Materialnummernvergabe
materials posting Materialbuchung
materials price Materialpreis
materials price change Materialpreisänderung
materials register Materialverzeichnis
materials-related materialbezogen
materials requirement Materialbedarf
materials reservation Materialreservierung
materials segment Materialsegment
materials shortfall report Materialunterdeckungsliste
materials submitted Beistellmaterial, Materialbeistellung
materials submitted line item Beistellposition
materials submitted record Beistellmaterialsatz
materials summary Materialkurztext
materials text Materialtext
materials type Materialart
materials type table Materialartentabelle
materials used Einsatzstoffe
materials utilization Materialeinsatz

materials valuation account Materialbewertungskonto
materials value Materialwert
materials value monitoring Materialwertkontrolle
materials voucher Materialbeleg
materials withdrawal Materialentnahme
materials withdrawal note Materialentnahmeschein
mate with zusammenpassen mit
mathematical mathematisch
mathematical function mathematische Funktion
mathematical operation mathematische Operation
matrix Matrix, Matrize
matrix algebra Matrix-Algebra, Matrizenrechnung
matrix form Matrixform
matrix inversion Matrixinversion
matrix line Matrixzeile
matrix notation Matrizenschreibweise
matrix printer Matrixdruck, Matrixdrucker, Mosaikdrucker
matrix size Matrixgröße, Matrizengröße
matrix (enhanced) Matrix (Briefqualität)
matrix (normal) Matrix (Manuskriptqualität)
maturity interval Fälligkeitsintervall
maximum Maximum, maximal
maximum length Maximalumfang
maximum limit Maximalgrenze
maximum memory requirements maximaler Speicherbedarf
maximum number Maximalzahl
maximum occupancy state Maximalbelegung
maximum stock Höchstbestand
maximum value Maximalwert
MByte MByte (Megabyte)
mean bedeuten
meaning Bedeutung
meaningful aussagekräftig, bedeutend
meaningless unbedeutend
mean repair time mittlere Reparaturzeit
means Mittel
mean service time mittlere Wartungszeit
means of access Zugriffsweg
means of communication Kommunikationsmittel
means of payment scheduling Zahlungsmittelterminierung
means of payment type Zahlungsmittelarten
mean time between errors mittlere Zeit zwischen Fehlern

mean time between failure durchschnittliche Zeit zwischen zwei Ausfällen, durchschnittliche störungsfreie Zeit, mittlere fehlerfreie Rechenzeit
mean time between failures mittlere Zeit zwischen Ausfällen
mean time between maintenance mittlere Zeit zwischen Wartungen
mean time to failure mittlere Zeit bis zum Ausfall
mean time to repair mittlere Reparaturzeit
mean time to restore mittlere Instandsetzungszeit, mittlere Wiederherstellungszeit
mean up-time mittlere Produktivzeit
measure Maßnahme, Satzbreite, messen
measurement Abmessung, Messung
measurement system Meß- und Analysesystem
measuring Messung
measuring of performance Geschwindigkeitsmessung
measuring relay Meßrelais
mechanical control equipment mechanische Steuerung
mechanical control system mechanisches Steuersystem
mechanical variable control mechanische Steuerung
mechanism Mechanismus
media Medium
media and documentation Software und Dokumentation
media and documentation box Software- und Dokumentationspaket
media copy Ausdrucken des Bildschirminhalts
media drive selector Stationswähler
medium Datenträger, Medium, mittel, mittlere
medium bright halbhell
medium scale integration mittlere Integrationsdichte
medium term mittelfristig
medium voltage installation Mittelspannungs-Installation
meet erfüllen, treffen
meeting Besprechung, Meeting, Treffen
meeting agenda Besprechungsprotokoll
megabyte Megabyte
megainstructions per second Millionenbefehle pro Sekunde
megaword Megawort
member Mitglied
member count Kettsatzzähler
member entry Mitgliedseintrag
member record Kettsatz

135

member type Mitgliedsart
memo Memorandum, Mitteilung
memorandum Mitteilung, Notiz, Vermerk
memory Arbeitsspeicher, Hauptspeicher, Speicher, Speicherkapazität
memory access Speicherzugriff
memory access control Speicherzugriffssteuerung
memory access controller Speicherzugriffssteuereinheit
memory access logic Speicherzugriffslogik, Speicherzugriffsschaltkreis
memory access unit Speicherzugriffssteuerung
memory address Speicheradresse, Speicheradresse
memory address counter Speicheradressenzähler
memory address extension Speicheraddreßerweiterung
memory address register Speicheradreßregister
memory allocation Speicherplatzzuweisung
memory allocation map Speicherbelegungsplan
memory allocation processor Verknüpfungsprogramm
memory allocation unit Speicherzuordnungseinheit
memory area Speicherbereich
memory bank Speicherbank
memory base register Speicher-Basisregister
memory board Speicherplatine
memory bus Speicherbus
memory bus controller Speicherbussteuereinheit
memory capacity Speichergröße, Speicherkapazität
memory card Speicherkarte
memory cell Speicherzelle, binäre Speicherzelle
memory consolidation Speicherbelegungsverdichtung
memory control Speicheransteuerung
memory controller Speichersteuereinheit
memory control unit Speichersteuereinheit
memory cycle Speicherzyklus
memory data register Speicherregister
memory definition Speicherdefinition
memory drive Pseudofloppy, virtuelle Platte, virtuelles Laufwerk
memory dump Speicherabzug
memory expansion Speichererweiterung
memory expansion option Speichererweiterung
memory extension Speichererweiterungsmodul

memory extension option Speichererweiterungsmodul
memory failure Speicherdefekt, Speicherfehler
memory fault Speicherfehler
memory initiation Speicherinitiierung
memory interface Speicherschnittstelle
memory location Speicheradresse
memory lockout register Register für Speicherzugriffssteuerung
memory management Speicherverwaltung
memory management system Speicherverwaltungssystem
memory management unit Speicherverwaltungsbaustein, Speicherverwaltungschip
memory map Hauptspeicherauszug, Speicherbelegungsplan
memory module Speichermodul
memory oriented system speicherorientiertes System
memory parity error Paritätsfehler im Speicher
memory protected speichergeschützt
memory protection Speicherschutz
memory read Lesezugriff auf Speicher, Speicher-Lesezugriff, Speicher-Schreibzugriff
memory request controller Steuerung für Speicherzugriffe
memory requirement Speicherplatzanforderung
memory resident speicherresident
memory select register Speicherauswahlregister
memory size Speichergröße, Speicherkapazität
memory space Speicherplatz
memory structure Speicherstruktur
memory table Speichertabelle
memory test Speichertest
memory timing and control module Speichertakt- und Steuermodul
memory unit Speichereinheit
memory upgrade option Speichererweiterungsoption
mentioned below siehe unten, untengenannt
menu Auswahl, Auswahlmaske, Menu, Menü
menu display Menüanzeige
menu driven menügeführt, menügesteuert
menue Menü
menu end Auswahlende
menu indication Menüanzeige
menu item Menüaktion, Menüpunkt
menu keyword Menükürzel
menu level Menüebene
menu name Menüname
menu offer Menüangebot
menu option Menüoption

menu organisation Menüorganisation
menu page Menüseite
menu position Menüposition
menu screen Menübildschirm
menu selection Menüauswahl
menu structure Menüstruktur
menu technology Menütechnik
menu term Menübegriff
menu tree Menübaum
menu tree access routine Menübaumzugriffsroutine
menu tree definition Menübaumdefinition
menu tree file Menübaumdatei
menu tree generator Menübaumgenerator
menu tree instruction Menübaumanweisung
menu tree instruction language Menübaumanweisungssprache
menu tree instruction sequence Menübaumanweisungsfolge
menu tree key Menübaumschlüssel
menu tree process Menübaumverfahren
menu tree structure Menübaumstruktur
menu tree structure list Menübaumstrukturliste
merchandise Handelsware
merchantability handelsübliche Qualität
mercury Quecksilber
mercury arc rectifier Quecksilberdampf-Gleichrichter
mercury switch Quecksilberschalter
merely lediglich
merge einbinden, mischen
merge processing Mischverarbeitung
merge run Mischlauf
meshed network Maschennetz
message Meldung, Mitteilung, Nachricht
message beginning character Meldungsbeginnzeichen
message communication Nachrichtenkommunikation
message confirmation indicator Empfangsbestätigungsanzeige
message control level Nachrichtensteuerungsebene
message control program Nachrichtensteuerprogramm
message control table Nachrichtensteuertabelle
message delay Sendungsverzug
message display Meldungsanzeige
message editing Nachrichtenaufbereitung
message ending character Nachrichtenschlußzeichen
message exchange Mitteilungsaustausch

message format Meldungsformat
message formatting Nachrichtenformatierung
message handling system Mitteilungs-Übermittlungsdienst
message header prefix Vorspann einer Nachricht
message identification Nachrichtenkennung
message interchange protocol Nachrichtenaustausch-Protokoll
message length Nachrichtenlänge
message line Meldungszeile, Statuszeile
message network Rechnernetzwerk
message number Mitteilungsnummer, Nachrichtennummer
message output Nachrichtenausgabe
message queuing Aufbau von Nachrichtenwarteschlangen
message recipient Nachrichtenempfänger
message scope Nachrichtenbereich
message select register Speicherauswahlregister
message staging Nachrichtenpufferung
message status display Meldungs-Statusanzeige
message storage Nachrichtenspeicherung
message switching Nachrichtenübermittlung, Sendungsvermittlung
message text Mitteilungstext
message transfer time Mitteilungs-Übertragungszeit
message transmission Übertragung
message type Mitteilungsart, Nachrichtenart
message waiting time Nachrichtenwartezeit
mess up verwechseln
meta assembler Metaassembler
metal Metall
meta language Metasprache
metal case Blechgehäuse
metal clad cable Metallmantelkabel
metal film resistor Metallschichtwiderstand
metal housing Blechgehäuse
metal oxide silicon MOS
metals discount Metallrabatt
metals surcharge Metallzuschlag
metal tab Metallasche
metasyntax Metasyntax
meter Meßgerät, messen
metering failure Zählstörung
metering station Meßstation
method Methode, Verfahren
method of approach Annäherungsmethode
method of depreciation Abschreibungsmethode
method of handling Bearbeitungsart
method of operation Wirkungsweise

method of payment Zahlungsart, Zahlungsmodus, Zahlungsweise
methodology Vorgehensweise
metropolitan networks Netze in Großstädten
mica Glimmer
mica capacitor Glimmerkondensator
micro klein, millionstel
microassembling Mikroassemblierung
microcode Mikrocode, Mikroprogramm
microcoded line adapter Datenübertragungssteuerteil
microcomputer Mikrocomputer
microcomputer application Mikrocomputer-Anwendungen
microcomputer software Mikrocomputer-Software
microcontroller Programmschaltwerk
microinstruction Mikrobefehl
micrologic expansion feature erweiterter Befehlsvorrat
micrometer drive Mikrometerantrieb
microminiature circuit Mikrominiaturbaugruppe
micromodule Kleinstbaugruppe
microphone Mikrofon
microprocessor Mikroprozessor
microprocessor chip Mikroprozessorbaustein
microprocessor classification Mikroprozessorarten
microprocessor development system Mikroprozessor-Entwicklungssystem
microprocessor instruction set Mikroprozessorbefehlssatz
microprocessor slices Mikroprozessorelemente
microprogram Mikroprogramm
microprogrammability Möglichkeit zur Mikroprogrammierung
microprogramming Mikroprogrammierung
microprogramming advantages Vorteile der Mikroprogrammierung
microprozessor Mikroprozessor
Microsoft disk operating system Microsoft Betriebssystem
microswitch Mikroschalter
microwave amplifier Mikrowellenverstärker
microwave circuit Mikrowellenschaltung
microwave filter Mikrowellen-Filter
microwave integrated circuit integrierter Mikrowellenbaustein
microwave microelectronic Mikrowellen-Mikroelektronik
microwave oscillator Mikrowellenoszillator
microwave transistor Mikrowellentransistor

microwave tube Mikrowellenröhre
middle letter row mittlere Buchstabentastenreihe
midrange mittlere Einstellung
migrate ausbauen, migrieren
migration Ausbau, Migration
migration path Erweiterungsalternative
military militärisch
milli tausendstel
mineral insulated cable Kupfermantelkabel
mini Mini-, klein
miniature Mini-
miniature circuit breaker Miniatur-Leistungsschalter
miniature relay Miniaturrelais
minicomputer Minicomputer, Rechner der Mittleren Datentechnik
minicomputer display Minicomputer-Sichtgerät
mini control unit Nebensteuereinheit
minimum Mindest-, Minimum, minimal
minimum access programming Bestzeitprogrammierung
minimum access routine Bestzeitprogramm
minimum amount Mindestbetrag
minimum availability time Mindesteindeckungszeit
minimum balance Saldomindestbetrag
minimum contents level Mindestfüllrand
minimum length Mindestlänge
minimum number Mindestanzahl
minimum order Mindestbestellung
minimum order quantity Mindestauftragsmenge, Mindestbestellmenge
minimum purchase order quantity Mindestbestellmenge
minimum quantity Mindestmenge
minimum reminder amount Mahngrenzbetrag
minimum run configuration Minimallaufkonfiguration
minimum selection Minimalauswahl
minimum stock Mindestbestand
minimum stock level Mindestbestand
minimum stock quantity Mindestbestandsmenge
minimum valuation principle Niederstbewertungsprinzip
minimum value Minimalwert
mini operating system Systemsteuerprogramm
Ministry of International Trade and Industry (Japan) Außenhandels- und Außenwirtschaftsministerium von Japan
minor gering, geringwertig, kleiner
minus abzüglich, minus

138

minus sign Minuszeichen
minute Minute
mirror Spiegel
mirror disk gespiegelte Platte
mirror field Spiegelfeld
mismatch Disparität, Fehlanpassung
missing fehlend
missing parts list Fehlteileliste
mistake Fehler, verwechseln
mistype vertippen
mix mischen, mixen
mix array Mix-Array
mix data Mix-Daten
mixer circuit Mischkreis
mixer tube Mischröhre
mix file Mix-Datei
mix record Mix-Satz
mix up verwechseln
mnemonic Abkürzung, Gedächtnisstütze, Kurzbezeichnung, Mnemonic, mnemonisch, symbolischer Name
mnemonic address mnemonische Adresse
mnemonic addressing Kurzadressierung
mnemonic code Buchstabencode, mnemonischer Code
mnemonic table Kürzeltabelle
mode Betriebsart, Modus
mode conversion Moduswechsel
mode execute ready pushbutton Ausschalter
model Ausführung, Kalkulationsmodell, Modell, Muster, Typ
modem Anpassungseinrichtung, Modem
modem control Modemsteuerung
modem data parity bit Modemdaten-Paritätsbit
mode menu display Anzeige des Modusmenüs
modem evaluation board Modem-Testkarte
modem printer select key Modem-/Drucker-Taste
modem receive speed Empfangsgeschwindigkeit des Modems
modem transmit speed Übertragungsgeschwindigkeit des Modems
mode of consumption Verbrauchsart
mode of data access Datenzugriffsverhalten
mode of operation Betriebsart, Betriebsmodus
mode of payment Zahlungsmodus
mode of processing Verarbeitungsform, Verarbeitungsmodus
mode parameter Modusparameter
mode point Verknüpfungspunkt
moderate mäßig
mode select Betriebsartauswahl
mode setting Formatwahl

modicon Modikon
modification Modifikation, Veränderung, Änderung
modification code Modifikationscode, Veränderungscode, Veränderungsschlüssel
modification constant Modifikationskonstante
modification data Änderungsdaten
modification error Modifikationsfehler
modification function Änderungsfunktion
modification key Änderungsschlüssel
modification order Änderungsauftrag
modification procedure Änderungsprozedur
modification range Änderungsbereich
modification section Modifikationsteil
modification service Änderungsdienst
modification status Veränderungsstatus
modified frequency modulation modifizierte Frequenzmodulation
modifier Modifizierer
modify modifizieren, verändern, ändern
modular Baukastenprinzip, elementweise, modular
modular plug Telefonstecker, modularer Telefonstecker
modular plug on telephone Telefonstecker
modulator Modulator, Sendesignalumsetzer
module Baukasten, Baustein, Element, Modul, Programmbaustein, Programmsegment
module component Modulkomponente
module form Modulform
module length Bausteinlänge
module library Modulbibliothek
module menu Modulmenü
module name Modulname
module part Modulteil
module parts list Baukastenstückliste
module parts usage Baukastenteileverwendung
module pool Modulpool
module population Modulbestückung
module puller Modulzieher
module status Modulstand
module type Art des Elements
modulo Modulo, Prüfziffer
modulo n-check Modulo-n-Prüfung
moisture control Feuchteregelung
moisture resistance Feuchtigkeitsverhalten
moisture resistant feuchtigkeitsbeständig
moment Augenblick
momentary toggle switch Wippschalter
monaural headphones Monokopfhörer
monetary balance Währungssaldo
monetary transaction Geldverkehr

139

monitor Bildschirm, Monitor, verfolgen, überwachen
monitor cable Bildschirmkabel
monitor display Dienstaufsichtsbildschirmgerät
monitor function Überwachungsfunktion
monitor image Monitorprogramm
monitoring period Überwachungszeit
monitoring time Überwachungszeit
monitor interrupt Monitorunterbrechung
monitor mode Programmüberwachung
monitor program Monitorprogramm, Überwachungsprogramm
monitor routine Monitorroutine
monitor system Monitorsystem
monochrome einfarbig, monochrom
monochrome display Monochrombildschirm
monochrome monitor Monochrombildschirm
monolithic monolithisch
monolithic integrated circuit monolithisch integrierte Schaltung
monostable trigger circuit monostabiler Multivibrator
month Berichtsmonat, Kalendermonat, Monat
month area Monatsbereich
month end balance rollover Monatsverschiebung
month end balance rollover program Monatsverschiebeprogramm
month end closing Monatsabschluß
month evaluated Auswertmonat
month field Monatsfeld
monthly balance Monatssaldo
monthly consumption Monatsverbrauch
monthly rental charge Monatsmiete
monthly statistics Monatsstatistik
month to date seit Monatsanfang
month value Monatswert
month's balance Monatssaldo
month's end Monatsabgrenzung
more detailed näher
moreover überdies
more precise genauer
more significant höherwertiger
morpheme morphem
mortgage Hypothek
mosaic printer Matrixdrucker
MOS-technologies MOS-Technologien
most frequent häufigst
most significant höchstwertig
most significant bit höchstwertige Bit, höchstwertiges Bit
most significant digit Ziffer mit höchstem Stellenwert, werthöchste Ziffer

mother company Dachgesellschaft, Muttergesellschaft
motion stop switch Bewegungsstopp-Schalter
motor Antrieb, Motor
motor alternator Motorgenerator
motor convertor Kaskadenumformer
motor generator set Umformergruppe
moulding Formteil
mount anbringen, befestigen, einsetzen, laden, logisch anmelden
mounting hole Befestigungsloch
mounting socket Montagesockel
move fahren, verfahren, verschieben, versetzen, übertragen
move backward rücksetzen
move forward vorsetzen
movement factor Bewegungsfaktor
movement of empties Leergutbewegung
movement record Bewegungssatz
movement test Mechaniktest
move statement Verschiebebefehl
moving in opposite directions gegenläufig
moving text Verschieben von Text
muldex Muldex
multi Mehrfach-
multi access line Mehrfachanschluß
multi address calling Rundsenden
multi address message Rundschreibnachricht
multi-axis table Mehrachsentisch
multibus memory design Mehrfachbus-Speicherdesign
multi channel access line Mehrfachanschluß
multichip carrier Platine
multicolumn printing mehrspaltiges Drucken
multicolumn total Summe mehrerer Spalten
multicomputer system Mehrrechnersystem
multi copy form Formularsatz
multicopy forms Durchschlagformulare
multicore cable mehradriges Kabel
multi destination routing Mehrstationsadressierung
multidrop connection Mehrpunktverbindung
multi-endpoint connection Mehrpunkt-Verbindung
multi environment processing vielfältige Konfigurations- und Verarbeitungsmöglichkeiten
multi firm processing Mehr-Firmen-Verarbeitung
multijobbing Mehrjobverarbeitung
multi key sort Mehrfachschlüssel-Sortierung, Sortieren mit mehreren Schlüsseln

multi language tool Internationalisierungs-Werkzeug
multilayer board Mehrschichtleiterplatte
multilayer fabrication Herstellung in Mehrschichttechnik
multilayer production Herstellung in Mehrschichttechnik
multi level mehrstufig
multilingual mehrsprachig
multilink Bündel
multinational multinational
multinational 8-bit character set multinationaler 8-Bit-Zeichensatz
multinational character set multinationaler Zeichensatz
multi partitioned file mehrfach partionierte Datei
multiple Mehrfach-, mehrfach, vielfach
multiple bit error Fehler über mehrere Bits
multiple character sort Mehrzeichen-Sortierlauf
multiple column selection device Mehrspaltensucheinrichtung
multiple command Mehrfachkommando
multiple depreciation Mehrschichtabschreibung
multiple destination routing Rundsendebetrieb
multiple file Mehrfachdatei
multiple indexed random access method mehrfach indexdirekte Zugriffsmethode
multiple insertion operation Vielfach-Einfügeoperation
multiple linear regression lineare Mehrfachregression
multiple line read selection Mehrzeilenabfühlsteuerung
multiple package basis Gebindebasis
multiple package inventory Gebindebestand
multiple package marker Gebindekennzeichen
multiple package number Gebindenummer
multiple package record Gebindesatz
multiple package record marker Gebindesatzkennzeichen
multiple partitioned file mehrfach partionierte Datei
multiple precision mehrfache Genauigkeit
multiple step sizes Mehrschrittgrößen
multiple system Mehrlingssystem
multiple use Mehrfachnutzung
multiplex Mehrkanal-, mehrfach, multiplex
multiplex equipment Mehrkanal-Übertragungseinrichtung
multiplexer Multiplexer

multiplexing multiplexen
multiplexing equipment Mehrkanalgerät
multiplex line Multiplex-Leitung, mehrfach genutzte Leitung
multiplex mode Multiplexbetrieb
multiplex operation Mehrfachausnutzung
multiplex printing telegraphy Multiplex-Fernschreibverfahren
multiplication Multiplikation
multiplicity Vielzahl
multiplier Multiplikator
multiplying circuit Multiplizierer
multipoint Mehrfach-, mehrfach
multipoint connection Mehrpunktverbindung
multipoint feature Mehrfachspeicherzugriffssteuerung
multipoint network Knotennetz
multiport feature Mehrfachspeicherzugriffssteuerung
multiport memory interface Speicherschnittstelle für Mehrfachzugriff
multiprocessing Mehrprogrammbetrieb, Mehrprozessorbetrieb
multiprocessing program Simultanverarbeitungs-Programm
multiprocessing system Simultanverarbeitungs-System
multiprocessor Mehrprozessor, Multiprozessor
multiprocessor system Mehrprozessorsystem
multiprogramming Mehrprogrammbetrieb, Simultanverarbeitung
multiprogramming priority Multiprogramm-Priorität
multi roll file Mehrrollen-Datei
multi stage mehrstufig
multi-subsystem adapter Adapter für byteorientierte Geräte, Adapter zur Steuereinheit
multitasking Multitasking, Simultanbetrieb
multi task operation Mehr-Prozeß-Betrieb
multiuser Mehrbenutzer
multiuser system Mehrplatzsystem
multivariable control Mehrfachregelung
multivendor installation Konfiguration mit Produkten verschiedener Hersteller
multivibrator oszillator Multivibrator
multivolume file Datei auf mehreren Datenträgern, Mehrdatenträgerdatei

N

name Name, benennen
name field Namensfeld
name of mask set Maskensatzname
name of the month Monatsname
name specified Namensangabe
naming documents Dokumentnamen vergeben
narrow band Schmalband
nasal Nasallaut
national national
native systemeigen
native mode Normalbetriebsart, Normalmodus
nature Beschaffenheit
navigation Navigation
navigational measurement Navigationsmessung
nean time to repair mittlere Instandsetzungszeit
necessary benötigt, erforderlich, notwendig
necessity Notwendigkeit
need Bedarf, brauchen
needle printer Nadeldrucker
needle printer head Nadeldrucker-Druckkopf
negate verneinen
negation Negativwert
negative negativ
negative acknowledge nicht erkannt
negative acknowledgement negative Rückmeldung
negative amount Negativbetrag
negative entry Eingabe negativer Zahlen
negative going negativ
negative going error negativer Fehler
negative logic negative Logik
negative-positive negativ-positiv
negative value Negativwert
negative value indication Darstellung des negativen Vorzeichens
nest schachteln, verschachteln
nested program verschachteltes Programm
nesting Schachtelung, Verschachtelung
nesting jump function geschachtelte Sprungfunktion
nesting jump instruction geschachtelte Sprunganweisung
nesting level Verschachtelungsebene
net Netto, Netz, Netzwerk
net amount Nettobetrag
net asset calculation Vermögensermittlung
net assets Vermögenswert
net balance volume Nettoausgleichsvolumen
net book value Restbuchwert
net costs Nettokosten
net date Nettodatum
net due date Nettofälligkeit
net invoice amount Rechnungsnettowert
net order value Bestellnettowert
net posting Nettobuchung
net price Nettopreis
net price calculation Nettopreisermittlung
net purchase order price Nettobestellpreis
net purchase order value Bestellnettowert
net record length Nettosatzlänge
net requisition planning Nettobedarfsermittlung
net terms Nettobedingung
net turnover Nettoumsatz
net value Nettowert
network Netz, Netzwerk, Verbindungsnetz
network access contoller Netzwerkzugangssteuereinheit
network access machine Netzwerkzugangsrechner
network access method Netzwerkzugangsverfahren
network access protocol Netzwerkzugangsprotokoll
network address Endsystemadresse, Netzadresse
network analyser Netzwerkberechner
network analysis Netzwerkanalyse
network analyzer Netzanalysator, Netzwerkanalysator
network bias current Netzeingangsstrom
network congestion Netzüberlastung
network connection Endsystemverbindung, Netzverbindung
network control Netzwerksteuerung, Netzkontrolle, Netzsteuerung
network control block Netzwerksteuerungsblock
network control center Netzkontrollzentrum
network control language Netzsteuerungssprache
network control module Netzsteuerungsmodul
network control node Netzhauptknoten
network control process Netzsteuerungsprozess
network control program Netzsteuerungsprogramm
network control system Netzsteuersystem
network description language Netzbeschreibungssprache

network file access method Netzwerkdateizugriffsverfahren
network file access protocol Netzwerkdateizugriffsprotokoll
network file transfer Netzwerkdateiübertragung
network front end Netzwerkvorrechner
network generation Netzgenerierung
network identification Netzkennung
network information Netzinformation
network information services Netzwerkinformationsdienste
network interface task Netzwerkschnittstellenprozess
network layer Netzschicht, Vermittlungsschicht
network maintenance Datennetzwartung, Netzwartung
network management Netzführung, Netzmanagement
network management center Netzkontrollzentrum
network manager Netzmanager, Netzwerkmanager
network native mode formatgebundener Netzwerkmodus
network parameter Netzwerkparameter
network path Netzwerkpfad
network performance management Netzwerktuning
network resource Netzwerkelement
network security center Netzsicherheitszentrum
network switching center Netzvermittlung
network synthesis Netzwerksynthese
network system software Netzwerksoftware
network termination unit Datenfernschaltgerät
network topology and routing Netzwerk-Topologie und Wegeauswahlverfahren
network transmission system Netzübertragungssystem
network user Netzteilnehmer
neutral conductor Nulleiter
new neu
new acquisition Neuzugang
new addition Neuhinzufügung
new call Neuaufruf
new entry Neueingabe
new installation Neuinstallation
new line neue Zeile
new page neue Seite
new selection Neuauswahl, Neuselektion
new start Neustart
new structure Neuaufbau

next folgend, nächst
next higher nächsthöher
next larger nächstgrößer
next line nächste Zeile
next lower nächstniedrig
next screen Folgebild
next user Folgebenutzer
nibble Halbbyte
nibs Nadelspitzen
nicad Nickel-Cadmium-Akku
nickel cadmium battery Nickel-Cadmium-Akkumulator
nitrogen Stickstoff
nitrogen flow-rate meter Stickstoffüberwachung
no charge ohne Berechnung
no connection frei
nodal equipment Knoteneinrichtung
nodal switching center Knotenvermittlung
node Knoten, Netzwerkknoten
node control centre Netzkontrollzentrum
node equipment Knoteneinrichtung
no forced parity keine automatische Paritätsprüfung
noise Geräusch, Rauschen
noise block Störblock
noise filter Rauschfilter
noise generator Rauschgenerator
noise ratio Störpegelabstand
nokeypad command Nokeypad-Kommando
nokeypad editing Editieren im Nokeypad-Modus
nokeypad mode Nokeypad-Modus
no load interruption leistungsloses Schalten
nominal coordinate Sollkoordinate
nominal value Sollwert
non blocking switching matrix blockierungsfreies Koppelfeld
non bootable nicht bootfähig, ohne System
nonconducting isolierend, nichtleitend
non contiguous nicht aufeinanderfolgend
nondestructive read nichtzerstörender Lesezugriff
non destructive readout zerstörungsfreies Lesen
nonferrous metal Nichteisen-Metall
nonfunctional nicht-funktionsbeteiligt
non impact printer anschlagfreier Drucker
non intelligent nicht intelligent
non interchangeable nicht austauschbar, unverwechselbar
non interlaced ohne Zeilensprung

nonmaskable interrupt nichtmaskierbare Unterbrechungsanforderung, nichtmaskierbarer Interrupt
non operating humidity Luftfeuchtigkeit im ausgschaltetem Zustand
non operating temperature Umgebungstemperatur im ausgeschalteten Zustand
nonoperative im Ruhezustand
non return to zero Richtungsschrift
nonstandard device nichtexistierendes Gerät
non volatile nichtflüchtig
non volatile memory nichtflüchtiger Speicher
no parity keine Parität
normal üblich
normal form Normalform
normally closed Ruhekontakt, im Ruhezustand geschlossen
normally open Arbeitskontakt, im Ruhezustand geöffnet
not AND negiertes UND
not available nicht verfügbar
note Kommentar, Notiz
not equal ungleich
notice Notiz, bemerken, wahrnehmen
null password leeres Passwort
number Anzahl, Nummer, Zahl
number of shots Schußzahl
number representation Zahlendarstellung
number system Zahlensystem
numeral Numeral
numeric numerisch
numerical numerisch
numerical control numerische Steuerung
numerical controlled numerisch gesteuert

O

object Gegenstand, Objekt
object code Maschinencode, Objektcode
object code library Objektcode-Bibliothek
object file Objektdatei
objection Beanstandung
object language Objektsprache
object module Objektmodul
object module library Objektmodul-Bibliothek
object program Objektprogramm
object related objektbezogen
obligation Verpflichtung, Zwang
obligatory verbindlich
oblige verpflichten
observation channel Beobachtungskanal
observe beachten, beobachten
obtain erhalten
obviously offensichtlich
occasion Gelegenheit
occupancy Belegung
occupancy size Belegungsgröße
occupancy state Belegungsstand
occupied cell belegtes Feld
occupy belegen, besetzen
occur auftreten, entstehen, vorkommen
octal oktal
octal address Oktaladresse
octal code Oktalcode
octal digit Oktalziffer
octal figure Oktalziffer
octal system Oktalsystem
odd ungerade
odd parity ungerade Parität
offer Angebot, Einkaufsangebot, Offerte, anbieten, bieten
offer due date monitoring Angebotsterminüberwachung
offer generation Angebotserstellung
offer header Angebotskopf
offer input Angebotsaufnahme
offer inventory Angebotsbestand
offer item Angebotsposition
offer management Angebotsverwaltung
offer number Angebotsnummer
offer processing Angebotsbearbeitung
offer procurement Angebotseinholung
offer quantity Angebotsmenge
offer reminder Angebotserinnerung
offer storage Angebotsspeicherung
offer text Angebotstext
offer text processing Angebotstextbearbeitung
offer type Angebotsart, Angebotstyp
offer value Angebotswert
offer voucher Angebotsbeleg
office Amt, Büro
office area Betriebsumgebung
office editing place Büroeditierplatz
office environment Arbeitsplatzumgebung
office-size package mit der Größe eines Bürorechners
official amtlich
offline Off-Line-Verarbeitung, lokal, nicht angeschlossen, offline, rechnerunabhängig
offline editing Offline-Editierung
offline edit method Offline-Editierverfahren
offline mode Offline-Modus
offline operation Lokalbetrieb, Off-Line-Betrieb
offline step Offline-Schritt
offline switching Offline-Umschalten
off-normal contact Arbeitskontakt
offset Distanzadresse, Offset, Startpunkt, Versatz, versetzen
offset address Distanzadresse
offset pointer Relativzeiger
offsetting Verrechnung
offset value Offset-Wert
off switch Ausschalter
off-the-shelf ab Lager
oil circuit breaker Ölschalter
oil-immersed transformer ölgekapselter Transformator
oil switch Ölschalter
old alt
omission Auslassung
omit auslassen, verzichten, weglassen
on board refresh integrierter Refresh
once einmal
on delay timer Verzögerungszeitglied
one after another nacheinander
one-chip microcomputer Einchip-Mikrocomputer
one dimensional eindimensional
one letter einbuchstabig
one level einstufig
one line einzeilig
one million floating-point operations per second eine Million Gleitkommaoperationen pro Sekunde
ones-complement Einerkomplement
one shot Einkreis, monostabil
one shot circuit monostabile Schaltung

145

one state Eins-Zustand
one task operation Ein-Task-Betrieb
one time job Einzelproblem
one-to-one eindeutig
one way communication einseitige Datenübermittlung
online On-Line, im Onlinebetrieb, online, rechnergekoppelt
online account information Online-Konteninformation
online debugging technique Online-Fehlersuche
online diagnostic Online-Diagnose
online diagnostic and maintenance programs Diagnostik- und Wartungsprogramme
online help Online-Hilfstext
online indicator Online-Anzeige
online mode Online-Modus
online operation Online-Betrieb
online printer Online-Drucker
online program Online-Programm
online scenario controller Online-Ablaufsteuerung
online session Online-Session
online system Online-System
online transaction processing Teilhaberbetrieb
only einzig
on off Ein Aus
on off code Ja-Nein-Code
on off key Ein-/Ausschalttaste
on/off-line on/off-line
on off switch Netzschalter
onsite device lokal angeschlossenes Gerät
onsite peripheral equipment lokal angeschlossene Peripherie
on stock auf Lager, lieferbar
opcode Betriebsanweisungscode, Opcode
open einleiten, eröffnen, offen, öffnen
open circuit voltage Ruhespannung
open electrical equipment offene elektrische Einrichtung
opening Eröffnung, Öffnung
opening balance Eröffnungsbilanz
opening book value Anfangsbuchwert
opening status Eröffnungsstatus
opening stock entry Erstübernahme
open line Leitungszusammenbruch, nicht angeschlossene Leitung, offene Leitung
open mode Open-Modus
open run eröffneter Job
open shop Bedarfsbetrieb
operable time Betriebsbereitschaftszeit
operand Operand

operand address Operandenadresse
operand error Operandenfehler
operand error code Operandenfehlercode
operand input Operandeingabe
operand part Operandenteil
operand section Operandenteil
operand value Operandenwert
operate bedienen, betreiben, handhaben
operating code Befehlscode
operating command Betriebssystemkommando
operating diskette Betriebssystemdiskette
operating environment Betriebsumgebung
operating feature Betriebsmerkmale
operating frequency Betriebsfrequenz
operating humidity Luftfeuchtigkeit während des Betriebs
operating information Betriebsinformation
operating instruction Bedienerhandbuch
operating instruction text Bedientext
operating language Betriebssprache
operating manual Bedienungshandbuch
operating mechanism Betätigungseinrichtung
operating memory Arbeitsspeicher, Betriebsspeicher
operating method Arbeitsmethode
operating mode Betriebsart
operating module Betriebsmodul
operating phase Arbeitsphase
operating procedure Betriebsanleitung
operating register Register
operating statement Ergebnisrechnung
operating statement item Ergebnisposition
operating statement version Ergebnisrechnungsversion
operating system Betriebssystem
operating system command level Kommandoebene des Betriebssystems
operating system dependent betriebssystemabhängig
operating system diskette Systemdiskette
operating system file Betriebssystemdatei
operating system kit Betriebssystempaket
operating system menu Betriebssystemmenü
operating system message Betriebssystemmeldung, Meldung des Betriebssystems
operating system specific betriebssystemabhängig
operating threshold Ansprechschwelle
operating time Anzugszeit, Betriebszeit
operating voltage Betriebsspannung
operation Ablauf, Arbeitsgang, Arbeitsweise, Betrieb, Betätigung, Eingriff, Operation
operational betrieblich, betriebsbereit

operational amplifier Operationsverstärker
operational mode Betriebsart mit voller Betriebsbereitschaft, Betriebsbereitschaft
operational software Systemsoftware
operational test Funktionstest
operation code Operationscode, Operationsteil
operation cycle Operationszyklus
operation exception unzulässige Operation
operation line Arbeitsgangzeile
operation method indicator Betriebsartanzeige
operation method switch Betriebsartschalter
operation mode Betriebsweise
operation name Operationsname
operation option Funktion
operation oriented ablauforientiert
operation part Operationsteil
operation possibility Bedienungsmöglichkeit
operation procedure Betriebsablauf
operations Betrieb
operations guide Bedienungshandbuch, Benutzerhandbuch
operations manager technischer Leiter
operations manual Bedienungshandbuch
operations on files Dateien bearbeiten
operation time Betriebszeit
operation's guide Bedienerhandbuch
operator Bediener, Benutzer, Operator, Sachbearbeiter
operator checklist Checkliste für den Bediener
operator code Bedienerschlüssel
operator console Bedienungsplatz, Operatorkonsole
operator console typewriter Bedienungsblattschreiber
operator control Bedienereingriff, Bedienerführung
operator control indicator Bedienungsanzeigetafel
operator control panel Bedienungsfeld
operator identification Operatoridentifikation
operator identification table Sachbearbeiteridentifikationstabelle
operator interface Bedienerkonsole
operator log file Operatorprotokolldatei
operator maintenance panel Bedienungs-/Wartungsfeld
operator manual Bedienungsanleitung
operator message Bedienermeldung
operator number Sachbearbeiternummer
operator oriented bedienerorientiert
operator panel Bedienfeld
operator request Anfrage an den Operator
operator table Sachbearbeitertabelle

operator's communication process Dialog mit dem Bediener
oppose gegenüberstellen
opposite gegenüber, gegenübergestellt
opposite direction Gegenrichtung
opposition Gegenüberstellung
optical Bar Code Reader Strichcodeleser
optical channel cable Lichtleiter
optical character Klarschriftzeichen
optical character recognition Beleglesung, Klarschriftleser, Schriftenerkennung, Schrifterkennung, Zeichenerkennung
optical character recognition-ANSI standard Schrifterkennung nach ANSI-Norm
optical character recognition-international standard Schrifterkennung nach internationaler Norm
optical data links Datenübertragungstechnik über Lichtleiter, Lichtleiter
optical data transmission optische Datenübertragung
optical fiber engineering Lichtleitertechnik
optical interface optische Schnittstelle
optical isolation optische Abschirmung, optische Isolation
optical isolator optische Einwegleitung
optically isolated optisch abgeschirmt, optisch isoliert
optical mark reader optischer Markierungsleser
optical variable control Optiksteuerung
optimization Optimierung
optimization criterion Optimierungskriterium
optimum optimal
option Erweiterung, Möglichkeit, Option, Schalter, Variation, Wahlmöglichkeit, Zusatzgerät, Option
optional auf Wunsch, optional
optional communications port zusätzlicher Kommunikationsanschluß
optional entry Kanneingabe
optional feature optionales Merkmal
optional field Kannfeld
optional floor stand Standfuß
optional input Wahleingabe
optional memory board Speichererweiterungsmodul
optional printer optionaler Drucker
optional specification Wahlangabe
optional stop wahlweiser Halt
optional variable Kannvariable
option keyword Kürzel
option module Erweiterungsmodul

option position Modulsteckplatz
options list Auswahlliste
options menu Auswahlmenu
opto-coupled optogekoppelt
optoelectronic device optoelektronisches Gerät
opto isolator Optokoppler
or logisch oder
order Anordnung, Auftrag, Befehl, Bestellung, Ordnung, Reihenfolge, befehlen, bestellen, ordnen
order acquisition Auftragsgewinnung
order advice quantity Bestellvorschlagsmenge
order alteration Auftragsänderung
order assembly Auftragszusammenlegung
order authorization Bestellungszulässigkeit
order backlog Auftragsbestand
order backlog list Auftragsbestandsliste
order confirmation Auftragsbestätigung
order confirmation check Auftragsbestätigungskontrolle
order confirmation number Auftragsbestätigungsnummer
order confirmation report Auftragsbestätigungsliste
order confirmation requirement Auftragsbestätigungspflicht
order costs Bestellkosten
order crediting Auftragsgutschrift
order currency Auftragswährung
order data bank Auftragsdatenbank
order date Auftragsdatum, Bestelldatum
order development Auftragsentwicklung
order development record Auftragsentwicklungssatz
order entry Auftragseingabe, Auftragserfassung
orderer Auftraggeber
order file Auftragsdatei
order form Auftragsformular
order gross Auftragsbrutto
order handling Bestellabwicklung
order header Auftragskopf
order header discount Auftragskopfrabatt
order heading Auftragskopfsatz
ordering Bestellwesen
ordering guide Bestellanweisung
ordering information Bestellinformationen
ordering price Bestellpreis
ordering units Bestellmengeneinheit
order insertion Auftragshinzufügung
order issue Auftragsausstellung
order item Auftragsposition
order item mask Auftragspositionsmaske
order item record Auftragspositionssatz

order lead date Bestellzeitpunkt
order lead time Bestellzeitraum
order list Auftragsliste
order list withdrawal Auftragslistenentnahme
order management Auftragsverwaltung
order net amount Auftragsnetto
order number Auftragsnummer
order number change Auftragsnummernänderung
order of columns Spaltenreihenfolge
order of execution Ausführungsreihenfolge
order of precedence Rangordnung, Reihenfolge
order of program execution Ausführungsreihenfolge
order oriented auftragsorientiert
order planning Bestelldisposition
order point Bestellpunkt
order point monitoring Bestellpunktüberwachung
order policy Bestellpolitik
order printing Auftragsschreibung
order processing Auftragsabwicklung, Auftragsbearbeitung, Auftragsverarbeitung
order processing function Auftragsbearbeitungsfunktion
order proposal Bestellvorschlag
order proposal program Bestellvorschlagsprogramm
order quantity Auftragsmenge, Auftragspositionsmenge
order register Auftragsverzeichnis
order registration Auftragserfassung
order-related auftragsbezogen
order remark Auftragsnotiz
order reservation Auftragsreservierung
order scheduling Auftragseinplanung
orders on hand Auftragsbestand
order-specific bestellspezifisch
order statistics Auftragsstatistik
order summary Auftragszusammenführung
order text Auftragstext
order type Auftragsart
order value Auftragswert
order voucher Auftragsbeleg
order voucher record Auftragsbelegsatz
ordinal number Ordnungsnummer, Ordnungszahl
ordinary differential equation normale Differentialgleichung
organisation Organisation
organisational organisatorisch
organisational level Organisationsebene
organisational module Organisationsmodul

organisation expenditure Organisationsaufwand
organisation form Organisationsform
organisation of core storage Kernspeicherverwaltung
organisation program Organisationsprogramm
organization block Organisationsbaustein
orient orientieren
orientation Orientierung
orientation aid Orientierungshilfe
orientation display Orientierungsanzeige
oriented bit orientiertes Bit
origin Ausgangsbereich, Herkunft, Ursprung
original originär, ursprünglich
original acquisition Ersterfassung
original data Originaldaten
original equipment manufacturer Hersteller von Fremdfabrikaten, Konfektionär
original state Originalzustand
original value Ausgangswert, Ursprungswert, Urwert
original voucher Originalbeleg, Ursprungsbeleg
original voucher type Originalbelegart
originate erstellen
originator of the voucher Belegautor
origin code Erstellungskennzeichen
orthography Rechtschreibung
oscillator Oszillator
other andere, anders, fremd
other partition Fremdpartition
other vendors' system Fremdsystem, System eines Drittanbieters
otherwise andernfalls, ansonsten
outband signaling Außerbandsignalisierung
outbound abgehend
outbound line Ausgangsleitung, abgehende Leitung, zur Peripherie führende Leitung
outdoor electrical equipment Freiluft-Elektrogeräte
outer insulation äußere Isolierung
outgoing abgehend
outgoing amount Abgangsbetrag
outgoing call abgehende Verbindung
outgoing call barred nur ankommende Verbindung
outgoing line Ausgangsleitung, abgehende Leitung
outlay auslagern
outlet Steckdose, Wandsteckdose
out of außerhalb
out-of-phase interruption phasenverschobene Unterbrechung

outperform übertreffen
output Ausgabe, Ausgang, Ausgangssignal, Relaisausgang, ausgeben
output acknowledge Ausgangsbestätigung, Signal auf einem EA-Kanal
output buffer Ausgabepuffer, Ausgabespeicher, Ausgangspuffer
output capacity Ausgabekapazität
output chute Ausgabeschacht
output circuit Ausgangskreis
output coil Ausgangsrelais
output connector Ausgang, Ausgangsanschluß, Ausgangsbuchse
output data Ausgabedaten, Ausgangsdaten
output data acknowledge Ausgabedatenbestätigung
output data request Ausgabedatenanfrage
output device Ausgabegerät, Ausgangsgerät
output error Ausgabefehler
output field Ausgabefeld
output file Ausgabedatei
output file identification and control Ausgabedateikennzeichen und -steuerung
output format specification Ausgabeformat
output formatting Ausgabeformatierung
output fuse Ausgangssicherung
output impedance Ausgangsimpedanz
output indicator Ausgabebezugszahl
output initialization Ausgabeeröffnung
output instruction Ausgabebefehl
output intensive ausgabeintensiv
output job Ausgabeauftrag
output led Ausgangs-LED
output length Ausgabelänge
output macro Ausgabemakro
output matching Ausgangsanpassung
output message Ausgabenachricht
output message area Ausgabebereich
output module Ausgabemodul
output multiplier Datenvervielfacher
output off switch Schalter zum Ausschalten eines Ausgangs
output parameter Ausgabeparameter
output position Ausgabefeld
output printer spacing Druckausgabeformatsteuerung
output rate Ausgabegeschwindigkeit
output record Ausgabesatz
output record size Ausgabesatzlänge
output register Ausgaberegister
output result Ausgangsergebnis
output screen Ausgabebild
output signal Ausgangsimpuls

149

output stacker Ausgabefach
output step Ausgabeschritt
output structure Ausgabestruktur
output suppression Ausgabeunterdrückung
output tape Ausgabeband
output terminal Ausgabeterminal, Ausgangsanschluß
output threshold Ausgangsschwelle
output time Ausgabezeit
output to printer Ausgabe auf den Drucker
output type Art des Ausgangs
output voltage Ausgangsspannung
output work queue Ausgabewarteschlange
output writer Systemausgaberoutine
outside außerhalb
outside processing Lohnverarbeitung
outstanding ausstehend, hervorragend
overall gesamt
overall concept Gesamtkonzept
overall discount Gesamtrabatt
overall discount flag Gesamtrabattkennzeichen
overall display Gesamtdarstellung
overall invoice discount Gesamtrechnungsrabatt
overall project Gesamtprojekt
overall response delay Gesamtantwortverzug
overall simulation value Gesamtsimulationswert
overall system Gesamtsystem
overcompensation Überkompensation
overcurrent circuit-breaker Überstromschalter
overcurrent detector Überstromsensor
overcurrent limiter Überstrombegrenzer
overcurrent protection Überstromschutz
over delivery Überlieferung
over descriptor Überdeskriptor
overdraft Überziehungskredit
overdraft period Überzugstage
overdue überfällig
overflow Bereichsüberlauf, Überhang, Überlauf
overflow control Kapazitätsüberwachung
overflow control indicator Formularwechselanzeige
overflow ejection Übertragsvorschub
overflow heading record group Überlaufkopf
overflow indicator Formularüberlaufbezugszahl
overflow line Formularüberlaufzeile
overhead Gemeinkosten, Overhead, Zusatz-, Überhang
overhead cable oberirdisches Kabel
overhead category Gemeinkostenart
overhead cost centre Gemeinkostenstelle
overhead factor Gemeinkostenfaktor
overhead line oberirdische Leitung

overhead power line Freileitung
overhead segment Briefkopfteil
overhead surcharge Gemeinkostenzuschlag
overhead table Gemeinkostentabelle
overlap überschneiden, Überlappung
overlapping überlappen, Überschneidung
overlapping in terms of time zeitverzahnt
overlay überlagern, Überlagerung
overlay area Überlagerungsbereich
overlay level Overlaystufe
overlay operation Overlay
overlay origin Überlagerungsursprung
overlay segment Überlagerungssegment
overlay transaction Overlay-Transaktion
overleaf umseitig
overload überladen
overload indicator Überlastanzeiger
overload protection Überlastschutz
overlook übersehen
overplay überspielen
overprinting übereinander drucken
overprint lock Überschreibsperre
overpunch Überlochzeichen
overpunch sign Überlochzeichen
override außer Kraft setzen, überschreiben, überspringen
overrun nicht aufnehmen können, überlaufen, Überlauf
overrun error Überlauffehler
overspool Überspulen
overstrike editing Editieren im Überschreibemodus
overtake überholen
overtype überschreiben
overview Übersicht
overview display Übersichtsanzeige
overvoltage protection Überspannungsschutz
overwrite überschreiben
own eigen
owner Besitzer, Eigentümer
owner identification Eigentümervermerk
owner process identification Kennummer des Benutzerprozesses
owner record Stammsatz
ownership Besitz, Eigentum
owner's manual Benutzerhandbuch, Systemhandbuch

P

pack Packung, packen, verdichten, verpacken
package Gehäuse, Paket, verpacken
package letter Ganzbrief
package size Packungsgröße
packaging Verpackungsmittel
packed number gepackte Zahl
packet Datenpaket, Paket
packet assembler disassembler PAD, Paketvermittlungsstation
packet assembly Paketierer
packet assembly disassembly facility Paketvermittlungsstation
packet count Paketzähler
packet level Paketebene
packet mode paketorientiert
packet mode operation Datenpaketübermittlung
packet of characters Zeichenpaket
packet receive sequence number Paketempfangslaufnummer
packet send sequence number Paketsendelaufnummer
packet sequencing Paketreihung
packet switched paketvermittelt
packet switched network Paketnetz, paketvermitteltes Netz, paketvermitteltes Netzwerk
packet switched services Datex-P, Paketnetz, paketvermittelter Dienst, paketvermitteltes Netzwerk
packet switching Paketvermittlung, Paketvermittlungsdienst, Paketübertragung, paketvermittelt
packet switching data network paketvermitteltes Datennetz
packet switching network Datex-P-Netzwerk, Paketnetz, paketvermitteltes Netz, paketvermitteltes Netzwerk
packet switching network in Germany Datex-P-Netz
packet switching processor Paketvermittlungsrechner
packet switching services Paketnetz, Paketvermittlungsdienste, paketvermittelter Dienst, paketvermitteltes Netzwerk
packet type Pakettyp
packet type identifier Bestimmungskennzeichen für Pakettyp
pack identification Datenträgernummer

packing agreement Verpackungsvereinbarung
packing delivery terms Verpackungslieferbedingungen
packing density Packungsdichte
packing material Verpackungsmaterial
packing materials number Verpackungsmaterialnummer
packing procedure Verpackungsanleitung
packing record Packungssatz
packing terms Verpackungskonditionen
pack verification Datenträgerüberprüfung
pad anfügen, auffüllen
padding characters Füllzeichen, zusätzliche Zeichen
paddle Spielkonsole, Spielregler
PAD-Host protocol PAD-Rechner-Protokoll
page Blatt, Seite, blättern, umblättern
page accounting Seitenverrechnung
page address field Seitenadreßfeld
page addressing Seitenadressierung
page address register Seitenadreßregister
page area Seitenbereich
page back zurückblättern
page backwards rückblättern, rückwärtsblättern, zurückblättern
page base Seitenbasis
page break Seitenvorschub
page buffer Seitenpuffer
page control block Seitensteuerungsblock
page control register Seitensteuerungsregister
page delimiter Seitentrennzeichen
page display Seitenanzeige
page editing Seitenaufbereitung
pagefault Seitenfehler
page feed Seitenvorschub
page formatting Blatteinteilung
page forward vorwärtsblättern
page function Blätterfunktion
page handling Blattbehandlung
page header Seitenkopf
page header information Seitenkopfinformation
page height Blatthöhe
page layout Seitenlayout
page length Blatthöhe, Seitenlänge
page length field Seitenlängenfeld
page makeup Seitenumbruch, Umbruch
page margin Blattrand
page mark Seitenmarke
page marker Seitenmarke
page mode Seitenmodus
page name Seitenname
page number Blattnummer, Seitennummer

151

page number assignment Seitennummernvorgabe
page number direct choice Seitennummerdirektwahl
page number field Seitennummerfeld
page number mask Seitennummermaske
page number range Seitennummernbereich
page number text Seitenzahlentext
page over überblättern
page overflow Seitenüberlauf
page parameter Seitenparameter
page price Seitenpreis
page range Seitenbereich
page request Seitenanforderung
page scrolling seitenweises Blättern
page selection Seitenauswahl
page size Seitengröße
page specific seitenspezifisch
page table Seitentabelle
page type Seitentyp
pagewrite printer Kopiendrucker
pagewriter Blattschreiber
paginate umbrechen
paginating from the print menu Seitenumbruch im Druckmenü
paginating stamp Paginierstempel
pagination Paginierung, Seitenumbruch
paging Paging, Seitenwechselverfahren
paging command Blätterkommando
paging function Blätterfunktion
paging width Umbruchbreite
pair Paar
panel Bedienfeld, Konsole
panel connector Anschluß am Gehäuse
panic dump Speichersofortauszug
pan scrolling kontinuierliches Abrollen
paper Papier
paper adjust routine Papiereinlegeautomat
paper brake Papierbremse
paper capacitor Papierkondensator
paper capacity Papierdurchlaßdicke
paper clamp Papierbefestigung
paper clamping lever Papierspanner
paper copy Ausdruck
paper cover Papierabdeckung
paper cradle Papierrollenhalter
paper ejection Papierauswurf
paper ejection device Papierauswerfeinrichtung
paper feed Blattführung, Papiervorschub
paper feed aperture Papierdurchlaß, Papierdurchlaßvorrichtung
paper feed device Papiereinzugsvorrichtung
paper feed unit Papiereinzugsvorrichtung

paper guide Blattführung
paper guide mark Anlegemarkierung
paper guide stop Anschlagleiste
paper holding tension Papierspannung
paper insertion Papierzufuhr
paper jam Papierstau
paper path Papierführung
paper release Papierlöser
paper release lever Papierfreigabehebel, Papierlösehebel
paper runaway Papierdurchlauf
paper sensor Papierfühler
paper stripe ejection Papierstreifenauswurf
paper stripe stacker Papierstreifenablage
paper support Papierauflage
paper table Papierauflage
paper tape Papierstreifen
paper tape punch Lochstreifenstanzer
paper tape reader Lochstreifenleser
paper thickness lever Papierstärke-Einstellhebel
paper transport group Papiertransportgruppe
paper transport mechanism Papiertransporteinrichtung
paper window Papierfenster
paragraph Absatz, Abschnitt
paragraph buffer Abschnittspuffer
paragraph card Abschnittskarte
paragraph file management Abschnittsdateiverwaltung
paragraph group Abschnittsgruppe
paragraph key Absatzstoptaste
paragraph letter Abschnittsbrief
paragraph letter number Abschnittsbriefnummer
paragraph list Abschnittsliste
paragraph marker Absatzmarke
paragraph number Abschnittsnummer
paragraph numbering field Absatznumerierungsfeld
paragraph protection Absatzschutz
paragraph record Abschnittssatz
paragraph region Abschnittsbereich
paragraph selection Abschnittauswahl
paragraph selection letter Abschnittsselektionsbrief
paragraph selection list Abschnittsauswahlliste
paragraph selection table Abschnittsauswahltabelle
paragraph work file Abschnittsarbeitsdatei
parallel parallel
parallel arithmetic unit Parallelrechenwerk
parallel by character zeichenparallel

parallel circuit Nebenschlußleitung, Parallelstromkreis
parallel input/output parallele Ein-/Ausgabe
parallel-posted account Mitbuchkonto
parallel posting Mitbuchung
parallel posting marker Mitbuchungskennzeichen
parallel printer Paralleldrucker
parallel processor Parallelprozessor
parallel transmission Parallelübergabe, Parallelübertragung, parallele Übertragung
parameter Parameter
parameter adminstration Parameterverwaltung
parameter block Parameterblock
parameter call Parameterabruf
parameter card Parameterkarte
parameter contents Parameterinhalt
parameter control Parametersteuerung
parameter data Parameterdaten
parameter dependent parameterabhängig
parameter description Parameterbeschreibung
parameter driven tabellengesteuert
parameter field Parameterfeld
parameter indication Parameterangabe
parameterize parametrieren, parametrisieren
parameter line Parameterleiste
parameter list Parameterliste
parameter number Parameternummer
parameter processor Parameterprüfprogramm
parameter record Parametersatz
parameter sequence Parameterfolge
parameter test mode Parametertestbetrieb
parameter value Parameterwert
parametric amplifier parametrischer Verstärker
parent company Muttergesellschaft
parent directory übergeordnetes Datenverzeichnis
parenthesis runde Klammer
parenthetical remark Einschub
parity Parität
parity bit Paritätsbit, Prüfbit
parity character Paritätszeichen
parity check Paritätskontrolle, Paritätsprüfung
parity checking Paritätsprüfung
parity control Paritätskontrolle
parity error Paritätsfehler
parity odd ungerade Parität
parity rear panel error Paritätsrückwandfehler
parity setting Paritätseinstellung
park parken
park position Parkstellung
parse analysieren

parse filename Dateiname abfragen
parser Analyseprogramm, Analysesystem, Befehlsanalyseprogramm, Kommandoprozessor
part Bestandteil, Stück, Teil, teilen, trennen
part area Teilbereich
partial teilweise
partial checkpoint Teilprüfpunkt
partial checkpoint common bank gemeinsame Teilprüfpunktbank
partial decrease Teilabgang
partial delivery Teillieferung
partial delivery flag Teillieferungskennzeichen
partial field Teilfeld
partial format Teilformat
partial format name Teilformatname
partial formatting Teilformatierung
partial issue Teilabgang
partial key Teilschlüssel
partial lot Teilcharge
partial message Teilnachricht
partial page transmit Übertragen von Teilseiten
partial problem Teilproblem
partial project Teilprojekt
partial restart common bank gemeinsame Teilwiederanlaufbank
partial starting address partielle Startadresse
partial statement Teilauszug
partial word Teilwort
participant Beteiligter, Teilnehmer
participate beteiligen, teilnehmen
particular bestimmt
particular operation bestimmte Funktion
parting bar Trennschiene
partition Bereich, Partition, Plattenbereich, logische Unterteilung
partition abort Partitionsabbruch
partition administration Partitionsverwaltung
partition administration segment Partitionsverwaltungssegment
partition alternate sector Bereichsersatzsektor
partition arrangement Aufteilung in Bereiche
partition assignment Partitionszuordnung
partition control area Partitionsadresse
partition control block extension Partitionssteuerbereichs-Ergänzung
partition end Partitionsende
partition error Fehler bei Neuaufteilung
partition extension Partitionsvergrößerung
partition independent partitionsunabhängig
partitioning Aufteilung
partitioning program Systemkonfigurierungsprogramm

partition input/partition output Partitions-ein-/ausgabe
partition menu Bereichsmenü, Partitionsmenü
partition network Partitionsverbund
partition number Partitionsnummer
partition of program under test Prüfpartition
partition of unknown type Fremdpartition
partition parameter record Partitionsparametersatz
partition plan Aufteilungsschema
partition requirement Partitionsbedarf
partition side Seite einer Unterteilung
partition size Partitionsgröße
partition specific partitionsspezifisch
partition state Partitionsstatus
partition structure Partitionsaufbau
partition table Partitionstabelle, Tabelle der Plattenbereiche
partition table entry Eintrag in der Partitionstabelle
partition utility Dienstprogramm zum Aufteilen der Festplatte
part list Stückliste
part list maintenance Stücklistenpflege
part message Teilnachricht
partner program Partnerprogramm
part number Teilenummer
part of program Programmanteil, Programmteil
part quantity Teilmenge
parts list Stückliste
parts list file Stücklistendatei
parts list management Stücklistenverwaltung
parts list master Stücklistenstamm
parts list withdrawal Stücklistenentnahme
parts structure Teilstrukturen
parts submitted Beistellteile
part to be bought Kaufteil
pass Arbeitsgang, Durchgang, Durchlauf, durchlaufen, vergehen
pass across übergeben
passbook chute Sparbuchschacht
passbook ejection Sparbuchauswurf
passbook motion Sparbuchbewegung
passbook processing Sparbuchverarbeitung
passed vergangen
passenger Fahrgast, Fluggast, Passagier
passenger name record Passagierliste
passive filter passives Filter
passive station Wartestation
pass number Durchlaufnummer
pass on weitergeben, weiterschalten
pass through weitergeben

pass-thru processing rechnerübergreifende Verarbeitung
password Anmeldecode, Benutzercode, Kennwort, Passwort
password check Passwortprüfung
password input Passworteingabe
password processing Passwortverarbeitung
password protection Kennwortschutz, Passwortschutz
password test Kennwortprüfung
password validation Passwortprüfung
past Vergangenheit, vergangen, zurückliegend
paste einfügen, einschieben, einsetzen
paste area Zwischenspeicher
paste buffer Einfügungspuffer, Zwischenpuffer
paste operation Einfügeoperation
paste position Einfügestelle
past field Vergangenheitsfeld
patch Korrektur
patch area Bereich zur freien Verdrahtung, Klemmfeld, Kreuzschienenverteiler, Patchbereich, Steckfeld, Änderungsbereich für Betriebssystem
patch card Einschub
patch panel Klemmfeld, Kreuzschienenverteiler, Kreuzsteckfeld, Schaltfeld, Steckfeld
patch processor Änderungsroutine
patch record Korrektursatz
path Pfad, Weg, Zweig
path for cable Kabelverlauf
path specification Pfadangabe, Pfadspezifikation
patient data Patientendaten
patient positioning Patientenpositionierung
patient table Patientenliege
patient table movement Liegenbewegung
patient table rotation Liegenbewegung
pattern Muster
pattern recognition Mustererkennung
pause warten
pay entrichten, zahlen
payables account Kreditorenauszüge
payee Zahlungsempfänger
payer Zahlender
payment Auszahlung, Bezahlung, Zahlung, Zahlungsausgang, Zahlungsvorgang, Zahlungswesen
payment account Zahlungsmittelkonto
payment advice Zahlungsmitteilung
payment amount Zahlungsbetrag
payment code Zahlungsschlüssel
payment condition Zahlungskondition
payment control Zahlungssteuerung

payment date Zahldatum, Zahlungsdatum, Zahlungstermin
payment deadline Zahlungsfrist
payment deadline base Zahlungsfristenbasis
payment habits Zahlungsgewohnheiten
payment history Zahlungsverhalten
payment history analysis Zahlungsverhaltensanalyse
payment list Zahlungsliste
payment method Zahlungsweg
payment of taxes Steuerentrichtung
payment order Zahlungsauftrag
payment posting Zahlungsbuchung
payment program Zahlungsprogramm
payment proposal Zahlungsvorschlag
payment proposal list Zahlungsvorschlagsliste
payment received Zahlungseingang
payment record Zahlungsgepflogenheit
payment reminder Zahlungserinnerung
payment run Zahlungslauf
payment status Zahlungsstatus
payment term Zahlungsbedingung, Zahlungskondition
payment terms code Zahlungsbedingungsschlüssel, Zahlungskonditionsschlüssel
payment transaction Zahlungsverkehr
payment type Zahlungsart
payment voucher Zahlungsbeleg, Zahlungsträger
payment voucher file Zahlungsträgerdatei
payment voucher program Zahlungsträgerprogramm
payoff period Abschreibungszeitraum
payroll Gehaltsliste
payroll format program Formatprogramm für Lohn
peak Peak, Spitze
peak-to-peak Spitze-zu-Spitze
peak voltage Spitzenspannung
peak voltmeter Spitzenspannungsmesser
pedestrian Fußgänger
pedestrian-controlled system fußgängergesteuertes System
pend anstehen, zurückstellen
pending anhängig
pentad Fünfergruppe
pentode Pentode
per je, pro
percent Prozent
percentage Prozentsatz
percentage figure Prozentangabe
percentage limit Prozentschranke
percentage scale Prozentstaffel

percentage sign Prozentzeichen
percent key Prozenttaste
percent sign Prozentzeichen
perform ausführen, leisten, verrichten
performance Geschwindigkeit, Leistung, Leistungsfähigkeit
performance activity Leistungsaktivität
performance degradation Leistungsabfall
performance dialog Leistungsdialog
performance improvement Leistungsverbesserung
performance management Leistungssteuerung, Leistungsverteilung, Netzwerktuning
performance screen Leistungsmonitor
performance test Eignungsprüfung, Funktionsprüfung
perform a read-after-write check kontrollesen
period Berichtsperiode, Laufzeit, Periode, Punkt, Zeitabschnitt, Zeitraum
period field Periodenfeld
periodical invoice Periodenrechnung
periodic time Schwingungsdauer
period of grace Kulanztage
period spent Verweildauer
peripheral peripher
peripheral control block Peripheriegerät-Steuerblock
peripheral controller Peripheriesteuerung
peripheral device Peripherie, Peripheriegerät, peripheres Gerät
peripheral equipment periphere Einheit
peripheral handling Peripheriebehandlung
peripheral interface Parallelschnittstelle
peripheral interface adapter peripherer Schnittstellenadapter
peripheral marker Peripheriemerker
peripheral system Peripheriesystem
peripheral unit control aerea Peripheriegerät-Steuerbereich
periphery Peripherie
permanent fest, permanent
permanent magnet Dauermagnet, Permanentmagnet
permanent magnet generator Generator mit Permanentmagnet
permanent memory Festwertspeicher, Permanentspeicher
permanent storage Dauerspeicher
permanent virtual circuit feste virtuelle Verbindung
permill Promille
permill key Promilletaste
permissable zulässig

155

permissibility Zulässigkeit
permit erlauben, zulassen
perpetually laufend, ständig
person Person
personal account number persönliche Kontonummer
personal computer PC, Personalcomputer, Rechner
personal computing persönlicher Rechnerzugriff
personal identification device Gerät zur Personenidentifikation
personal identification number persönliche Geheimnummer
personal programmable calculator programmierbarer Taschenrechner
person in charge Betreuer
personnel information Personalinformation
personnel number Personalnummer
person registering Personenerfassung
pertinent relevant, sachdienlich
perusal Kenntnisnahme, Stellungnahme
phantom cursor Phantomcursor, Phantomschreibmarke
phase Phase, einphasen
phase changer Phasenschieber
phase changing circuit Phasenschieberschaltung
phase characteristic Phaseneigenschaft, Phasenverhalten
phase control Phasenregelung
phase detector Phasendemodulator
phase deviation Phasenabweichung
phase encoded Richtungstaktschrift
phase encoded tape Band mit Richtungstaktschrift
phase error Phasenfehler
phase inverter circuit Phaseninvertierschaltung
phase modulation recording Phasenmodulationsaufzeichnung
phase name file Phasennamendatei
phase program Phasenprogramm
phase reference Phasenbeziehung
phase reversal Phasenumkehr
phase shifter Phasenschieber
phase shifting transformer Phasenschiebertransformator
phase shifting unit Phasenglied
phase shift oscillator Phasenkettenoszillator
phase variable Phasenvariable
ph control pH-Wert-Steuerung
philosophy Gesamtkonzept, Gesamtkonzeption, Konzept, Konzeption, Philosophie

phone Telefon
phone call Telefonat
phone conversation Telefonat
phonem Phonem
phonemic code Phonemcode
phonemic inventory Phoneminventar
phonemics Phonemik
phonemic text phonemischer Text
phonemic transcription phonemische Umschreibung
phone number Telefonnummer
phone plug Telefonstecker
phone switch Telefonschalter
photocathode Fotokathode
photoconductive cell Fotozelle
photoconductive device fotoleitendes Gerät
photodiode Fotodiode
photoelectric cell Fotozelle, Sonnenzelle
photoelectric device lichtelektrisches Gerät
photoelectric relay fotoelektrisches Relais
photomultiplier Sekundärelektronenvervielfacher
phototransistor Fototransistor
phototube Fotoröhre
phototypesetter Lichtsatzanlage
photovoltaic cell Fotoelement
phrase Ausdruck, Phrase, Satzteil
phrase structure module Satzteilgenerator, Satzteilmodul
physical physikalisch
physical access Hardwarezugriff, direkter Gerätezugriff, direkter Zugriff, hardwarenaher Zugriff, physikalischer Zugriff
physical block number physikalische Blocknummer
physical connection ungesicherte Systemverbindung
physical device Hardware, physikalisches Gerät
physical dimensions Abmessungen
physical record pysikalischer Datensatz
physical sequential physikalisch aufeinanderfolgend
pica Pica
pica pitch Pica-Teilung
pick selektieren
pick off brush Abnahmebürste
pickup interval Verteilungsintervall
picture Bild
picture control Bildschirmregler
picture tube Bildröhre
pie chart Kreisdiagramm, Tortendiagramm
piezoelectric device piezoelektrisches Gerät
pigeonhole number Ablagefachnummer

pile processing Stapelverarbeitung
pin Nadel, Pin, Stachel, Steckerstift, Verbindung
pinfeed paper Endlospapier
pin insulator Stiftisolator
pinout Stiftbelegung
pipeline Pipeline
pipe thread Gegengewinde
pitch Tonhöhe, Zeichenabstand
pixel Bildpunkt, Pixel, Punkt
place Stelle, legen, setzen, stellen
place before voransetzen
place in the table Tabellenplatz
place of malfunction Störstelle
plain einfach, klar
plain text Klarschrift, Klartext
plain text designation Klartextbezeichnung
plan Disposition, Plan, disponieren, planen
plan controlled plangesteuert
plane Ebene
planned availability time Solleindeckungszeit
planned delivery time geplante Lieferzeit
planned quantity Planmenge
planned stock Sollbestand
planning data Plandaten
planning for Einplanung
planning horizon Planungshorizont
planning level Planungsebene
planning manager Disponent
planning phase Planungsstadium
plant Firma, Werk
plant wide firmenweit
plasma Plasma
plasma diode Plasmadiode
plasma display Plasmaanzeige, Plasmabildschirm
plasma display unit Plasmabildschirm
plastic Kunststoff, Plastik
plastic film capacitor Kunststoffolienkondensator
plastic foam Kunststoffschaum
plastic handle Kunststoffgriff
plate Anode, Platte, Scheibe
plate dissipation Anodenverlustleistung
plated through hole durchkontaktierte Bohrung
plate efficiency Anodenwirkungsgrad
plate modulation Anodenmodulation
platen Druckwalze, Walze
platen knob Walzendrehknopf, Walzenknopf
plausibility check Plausibilitätskontrolle
plausible plausibel
play spielen
play back abspielen
play back routine Umspielroutine
plot Grundstück, plotten
plot data Grundstücksdaten, Zeichendaten
plotter Kurvenschreiber, Plotter, Zeichengerät
plug adaptor Adapterstecker
plug board Rangierfeld
plug box Steckerkasten
plug compatible manufacturer Hersteller von steckerkompatiblen Geräten
plug compatible mainframe steckerkompatibler Großrechner
plug compatible memory steckerkompatibles Speichermodul
plug-in Einsteck-
plug-in module Einsteckmodul
plug-in tabulator Stecktabulator
plug-in-unit Einschub
plug-on Anschraub-
plug-on screw terminal Schraubklemme
plug pipe plastic Kunststoffeinsteckrohr
plug square head Stecker mit quadratischem Kopf
plus Plus
pneumatic pneumatisch
pneumatic control system pneumatisches Steuersystem
pneumatic valve Luftventil
point Gesichtspunkt, Punkt, deuten, hinweisen, zeigen
pointer Zeiger
pointer array Feld von Zeigern, Zeigerbereich, Zeigermatrix
pointer reference Zeigerreferenz
pointer state Zeigerstand
point in time Zeitpunkt
pointless sinnlos
point of entry Einstiegspunkt
point of interruption Unterbrechungsstelle
point of sale Verkaufsort
point of sales terminal Kassenterminal
point out bemerken, erklären, hervorheben, hinweisen auf, klarmachen, verdeutlichen
point setting Kommaeinstellung
point to zeigen auf
point to point Punkt-zu-Punkt
point to point connection Punkt-zu-Punkt-Verbindung
point to point positioning system Einzelpunktsteuerungssystem
point where the error occurred Fehlereingangsstelle
polarity Polarität, Polung
polarized relay polarisiertes Relais

pole Pol
polish notation polnische Notation
poll abfragen, abrufen, pollen
poll call Pollaufruf
poll frequency Pollfrequenz
polling Abfragetechnik
polling mode Aufrufverfahren
polling station abfragende Stelle
pollute verunreinigen
pollution Verunreinigung
polynom Polynom
polynomial polynom
polyphase motor Mehrphasenmotor
polyphase transformer Mehrphasentransformator
pool Pool
pooling file Sammeldatei
pool key Poolschlüssel
pool name Poolname
pool parameter Poolparameter
pool size Poolgröße
pop-up menu Fenstermenü
porosity Durchlässigkeit
port Anschluß, Ausgang, Eingang, Port, Schnittstelle, portieren, übertragen
port connector Anschlußverbindung
port expansion unit Schnittstellenvervielfacher
portion Abschnitt, Partie
portion of text Textteil
portion of the text Zeichenfolge
portrait Hochformat
portrait format Hochformat
position Lage, Position, Stelle, Stellung, positionieren, setzen, stellen
positional qualifier Positionsqualifizierer, positionsabhängiger Qualifizierer
position control Positionssteuerung
position display Positionsanzeige
position for reference text Betreffposition
position independent relozierbar
position independent code relozierbarer Code
position indication Positionsangabe
positioning Positionierung
positioning device Positionierung
position parameter Stellungsparameter
position report Meldung der Cursorposition
position switch Positionsschalter
positive positiv
positive going error positiver Fehler
positive logic positive Logik
positive number positive Zahl
possess besitzen, verfügen
possibility of error Fehlermöglichkeit

possible etwaig
possibly eventuell
post Kippständer, Post, buchen, kontieren, verbuchen nach
postable buchbar
postal postalisch
postal address Adresse, Postanschrift
postal code Postleitzahl
postal marker Postkennzeichen
postal telephone and telegraph Postverwaltung
postal transfer Postüberweisung
postbox Postfach
postcode Postleitzahl
post decimal position Nachkommastelle
post entry Nacherfassung
posting area Verbuchungsbereich
posting base date Buchungsstichtag
posting block Kontierungsblock
posting control Verbuchungssteuerung
posting counter Verbuchungszähler
posting cycle Buchungszeitraum
posting data Buchungsdaten, Kontierungsdaten
posting data balancing Buchungsdatenabstimmung
posting data extract Buchungsdatenextrakt
posting deck Buchungsmappe
posting display Buchungsanzeige
posting field Kontierungsfeld
posting instruction Kontierungsvorschrift
posting key Buchungsschlüssel
posting line Kontierungszeile
posting message Verbuchungsmeldung
posting method Buchungsweise
posting module Verbuchungsmodul
posting month Buchungsmonat
posting of costs Kostenbuchung
posting of invoice received Rechnungseingangsbuchung
posting of voucher items Buchungszeilenkontierung
posting page Verbuchungsseite
posting process Buchungsvorgang, Verbuchungsvorgang
posting program Verbuchungsprogramm
posting record Buchungssatz
posting run Buchungslauf
posting screen Buchungsbild
posting segment Buchungssegment
postings of invoices received Rechnungseingangsbuchungen
posting step Buchungsschritt
posting string Buchungsstring
posting text Buchungstext

posting time Buchungszeit
posting to Bebuchung, Zubuchung
posting transaction Buchungstransaktion, Buchungsvorfall, Verbuchungstransaktion
posting type Buchungsart
posting year Buchungsjahr
post installation nach Installation
post insulator Stützisolator
post mortem Postmortem
post mortem dump Postmortemdump
post office Postamt, Postscheckamt
post office giro account Postscheckkonto
post office giro cheque Postscheck
post office giro transfer Postschecküberweisung
postpone aufschieben
post regulator Nachregler
potential transformer Spannungswandler
potentiometer Potentiometer
pound Pfund
pound sign Pfundzeichen
power Kraft, Netz, Netzstrom, Stromversorgung
power amplifier Leistungsverstärker
power cable Netzkabel
power capacitor Leistungskondensator
power connection Netzanschluß
power connector Netzanschluß
power consumption Energieverbrauch, Leistungsaufnahme, Stromverbrauch
power control Leistungssteuerung
power cord Netzkabel
power cord plug Netzkabelstecker
power divider Leistungsverteiler
power electronics Leistungselektronik
power factor Leistungsfaktor
power fail restart Neustart nach Stromausfall
power failure Ausfall der Stromversorgung, Netzausfall
power failure marker Netzausfallmerker
power failure protected netzausfallsicher
power flow path Leistungsfluß
power fluctuation Schwankung in der Netzspannung
powerful kräftig, leistungsfähig, mächtig
power indicator Netzanzeige, Stromanzeige
power interruption Ausfall der Stromversorgung
power lead Stromzuführung
power line Starkstromleitung
power line filter Starkstromleitungsfilter
power line voltage Netzspannung
power off key Ausschalttaste
power off switch Ausschalter
power OK indicator Betriebsbereitschaftsanzeige
power on Netz ein
power on key Einschalttaste
power-on mode Einschaltart
power-on self-test Selbsttest beim Einschalten
power oscillator Leistungsoszillator
power receptacle Netzanschluß, Steckdose
power regulator Spannungsstabilisator
power requirement Netzanschlußwert
power requirements Stromversorgung
power resistor Leistungswiderstand
power source Stromquelle
power source fault Netzausfall
power supply Netzteil, Stromversorgung
power supply module Netzteil, Stromversorgung, Stromversorgungsmodul
power supply transformer Transformator des Netzteils
power supply type Netzteiltyp
power switch Leistungsschalter, Netzschalter
power transformer Leistungstransformator
power transistor Leistungstransistor
power-up Einschaltvorgang, einschalten
power-up and checkout procedure Einschalten und Überprüfen
power-up self-test Selbsttest beim Einschalten
power up sequence Einschaltvorgang
power wiring Netzverkabelung
preallocate vorbelegen
preamplifier Vorverstärker
preboot program Vorladeprogramm
precedence Vorrang
precedence sequence Vorrangreihenfolge
preceding vorangestellt, vorhergehen
preceding tape Vorgängerband
preceding zero suppression Vornullenunterdrückung
precious metal Edelmetall
precise genau, präzise
precision Genauigkeit, Präzision
precision resistor Präzisionswiderstand
pre-contract Vorvertrag
predate vordatieren
predating table Vordatierungstabelle
predecessor Vorgänger
predefine vordefinieren, vorherbestimmen
predialog Prädialog
predicate Aussage
preemptible resources entziehbare Betriebsmittel
preemption Vorbelegung

preemptive priority Ausnahmepriorität
preexecution time table Warteschlange
prefer bevorzugen
preference Präferenz
preference list Präferenzliste
prefix Präfix, Satzvorspann, Vorsatz
prefix file Präfixdatei
prefix indication Präfixangabe
preformat vorformatieren
preoccupy vorbesetzen
preorder Vorausanordnung
preparation Vorbereitung
preparation list Vorbereitungsliste
prepare bereiten, präparieren, vorbereiten
prepayment Anzahlung
prepayment equipment Münzeinrichtung
prepayment posting Anzahlungsbuchung
prepayment request Anzahlungsanforderung
preposition Präposition
prepping (disk) Vorformatieren
preprocess vorarbeiten
preprocessing work Vorbereitungsarbeit
preproduce vorfertigen
prerequisite Voraussetzung
preselect vorauswählen, vorselektieren
preselected vorgemerkt
preselection number Ortskennzahl
preselection prefix Ortskennzahl
presence Anwesenheit, Vorhandensein
present Gegenwart, vorhanden
presentation entity Darstellungsinstanz
presentation layer Darstellungsebene, Darstellungsschicht
presentation plan Manualbaum
present value Augenblickswert, Kapitalwert
preset voreinstellen, vorgeben
preset actual value Istwertvorgabe
preset count value voreingestellter Zählerstand
preset nominal value Sollwertvorgabe
preset symbol Vorgabezeichen
preset value Vorgabewert
presort vorsortieren
press betätigen, drücken, pressen
pressure control Druckregelung
pressure plate Anpressbügel
pressure sensitive adhesive Trockenklebeband
pressure switch Druckkontakt, Druckschalter
presumably vermutlich
presume vermuten
presumed mutmaßlich, voraussichtlich
pretable Vortabelle
prevent verhindern
prevention Verhinderung

preventive maintenance routinemäßige Wartung, vorbeugende Wartung
preview Eingangsvorschau, Vorschau
preview of due dates Fälligkeitsvorschau
preview of payments received Zahlungseingangsvorschau
previous vorangegangen, vorherig
previous financial year Vorgeschäftsjahr
previously ehemals, vorhergehend
previous month Vormonat
previous month field Vormonatsfeld
previous period Vorperiode
previous stock level Altbestand
previous year Vorjahr
previous year indexed vorjahresindiziert
previous year's transaction Vorjahresbewegung
price Preis, Staffelpreis
price agreement Preisvereinbarung
price category Preisart
price change Preisänderung
price change tape Preisänderungsband
price code Preissteuerung
price code flag Preissteuerungskennzeichen
price code marker Preissteuerungskennzeichen
price code variable Preissteuerungsvariable
price configuration Preiskonstellation
price curve Preiskurve
price data Preisdaten
price deviation Preisabweichung
price discrepancy Preisdifferenz
price discrepancy account Preisdifferenzkonto
price discrepancy posting Preisdifferenzbuchung
price field Preisfeld
price group Preisgruppe
price history Preisentwicklung
price history element Preisentwicklungselement
price history file Preisentwicklungsdatei
price history number Preisentwicklungsnummer
price history period Preisentwicklungszeitraum
price history record Preisentwicklungssatz
price information Preisauskunft
price information function Preisauskunftsfunktion
price inquiry Preisanfrage
price list Preisliste
price list contents Preislisteninhalt
price list credit note Preislistengutschrift
price list group Preislistengruppe
price list level Preislistenstaffel
price list master record Preislistenstammsatz

price list number Preislistennummer
price list record Preislistensatz
price list type Preislistentyp
price monitoring list Preisüberwachungsliste
price quantity scale Preismengenstaffel
price scale Preisstaffel
price section Preisteil
price situation Preissituation
price structure Preisgefüge
price terms Preiskonditionen
price unit Preiseinheit
price validity Preisgültigkeit
price validity date Preisgültigkeitsdatum, Preiswirksamkeitsdatum
price validity period Preisgültigkeitszeitraum
pricing quantity unit Preismengeneinheit
pricing unit Preiseinheit
pricing unit of measurement Preismengeneinheit
primary Leitsteuerung, primär
primary battery Primärbatterie
primary computer system Primärcomputersystem
primary control Leitsteuerung
primary control panel Bedienungsfeld
primary drive erstes Laufwerk
primary entry Ersteintrag
primary file Primärdatei
primary header Hauptordnungsbegriff
primary implementation Erstimplementation
primary index Primärindex
primary initialize Erstinitialisieren
primary input Ersteingabe, Primäreingabe
primary key Hauptordnungsbegriff
primary memory Primärspeicher
primary start-up program Primärstartprogramm
primary storage Hauptspeicher
primary store Arbeitsspeicher
primary track Originalspur
prime route Kurzweg
primitive buffer Primitivpuffer
primitive type Primitivtyp
principle Methode, Prinzip, Verfahren
print Andruck, Druck, drucken
print actuator carriage Druckwagen
print area Druckabschnitt
print attempt Schreibversuch
print buffer Druckpuffer
print cartridge Farbbandkassette
print chain Druckerkette
print control character Drucksteuerzeichen

printer port

print control command Drucksteuerkommando
print control language Sprache zur Drucksteuerung
print controller Druckersteuerung
print density Druckqualität, Zeilendichte
printed circuit gedruckte Schaltung
printed circuit base gedruckte Schaltung
printed circuit board gedruckte Leiterplatte, gedruckte Schaltung
printed copy Ausdruck
print editing Druckaufbereitung
printed page gedruckte Seite
printed text gedruckter Text
printed wiring gedruckte Leiterbahn, gedruckte Schaltung
printer Drucker
printer adapter Druckeradapter
printer baud rate Druckerbaudrate, Übertragungsgeschwindigkeit zum Drucker
printer cable Druckerkabel
printer carriage width Druckerbahnbreite, Druckerbreite
printer characteristics Druckermerkmale
printer communication cable Druckeranschlußkabel
printer configuration Druckerkonfiguration
printer connector Druckeranschluß
printer control Druckersteuerung
printer control information Druckeranweisungen
printer controls Bedienungselemente des Druckers
printer data parity bit Druckerdaten-Paritätsbit
printer format chart Formular für Druckanordnung
printer form control tape Druckvorschub-Steuerlochstreifen
printer handling Druckerbearbeitung
printer identification Druckerkennung
printer installation manual Installationshandbuch des Druckers
printer instruction Druckerbefehl
printer interface Druckerschnittstelle
printer layout Listenbild
printer mechanism Druckwerk
printer menu Druckermenü
printer mismatch Druckzeichendisparität
printer mount Druckerständer
printer output Druckerausgabe
printer paper Druckerpapier
printer port Druckeranschluß

printer port failure Fehler im Druckeranschluß
printer power cord Druckernetzkabel
printer sharing Druckersharing
printer speed Druckgeschwindigkeit
printer stand Druckerständer
printer terminal Druckerstation
printer test Druckertest
printer type Druckertyp
printer width Druckerbreite
print extent Druckbereich
print file Druckdatei
print file name Druckdateiname
print function Druckfunktion
print head Druckkopf, Druckstock
printhead retainer clip Befestigungsclip des Druckkopfes
print identifier Druckkennzeichen
printing control Drucksteuerung
printing cycle Druckdurchgang, Druckvorgang
printing delivery notes Lieferscheindruck, Lieferscheinschreibung
printing disturbance Druckstörung
printing element type Druckwerksart
printing key Drucksteuertaste, Schreibtaste, Zeichentaste
printing mask format Druckmaskenaufbau
printing of enquiries Anfrageschreibung
printing of inquiries Anfrageschreibung
printing of vouchers Belegschreibung
printing position Druckposition
printing purchase orders Bestellschreibung
printing station Druckstation
printing unit Druckeinheit, Druckwerk
print job Druckauftrag
print lock Schreibsperre
print menu Druckmenü
print menu option Druckmenüauswahl
print method Druckverfahren
print name Druckname
print number Drucknummer
print out Ausdruck, andrucken, ausdrucken
print output Druckausgabe
print page heading Kopfzeilenanweisung
print parameter Druckparameter
print patch history table utility Programm zur Ausgabe der Korrekturliste
print pointer Schreibzeiger
print position Druckposition, Druckstelle
print preparation Druckaufbereitung
print program Druckprogramm
print quality Druckqualität

print queue Druckerwarteschlange
print request Druckauftrag
print ribbon Farbband
print screen Ausdruck des Bildschirminhaltes, Drucken des Bildschirminhaltes
print section Druckabschnitt
print selection Druckauswahl
print setting Druckeinstellung
print speed Druckgeschwindigkeit
print subsequently nacheinander drucken
print symbiont Drucksymbiont
print termination character Druckendezeichen
print unit Druckeinheit
print unit parameter Druckwerksparameter
print unit type Druckwerkart
print utility Dienstprogramm für Druckausgaben
printwheel Typenrad
priority Priorität
priority grant Prioritätszuteilung
priority message Prioritätsnachricht
private benutzereigen, privat
private account Personenkonto
private automatic branch exchange automatische Nebenstellenanlage
private branch exchange Nebenstellenanlage
private branch number Nebenstellennummer
private common carrier private Telefongesellschaft
private leased line private Mietleitung
private line Standleitung
private packet exchange private Paketvermittlung
privilege Berechtigung, Privileg
privilege check Berechtigungsprüfung
privileged process privilegierter Prozeß
privilege mask Berechtigungsmaske
privilege tax Konzessionsabgabe, Konzessionsgebühr
probability Wahrscheinlichkeit
probability of acceptance Annahmewahrscheinlichkeit
probable cause mögliche Ursache
probably wahrscheinlich
probe Abfragen, Status abfragen, Versuchsteil
problem Fragestellung, Problem, Problematik
problem category Problemklasse
problem determination Problemanalyse
problem determination procedure Problemanalyseprozedur
problem free fehlerfrei
problem isolation chart Tabelle zur Fehlerbestimmung

problem language Problemsprache
problem message Fehlermeldung
problem mode Problemmodus
problem oriented problemorientiert
problem oriented language problemorientierte Programmiersprache, problemorientierte Sprache
procedure Methode, Prozedur, Routine, Verfahren, Vorgang
procedure calling standard Standardprozeduraufruf
procedure code Vorgangsschluß
procedure course Prozedurablauf
procedure definition processor Prozedurdefinitionsprozessor
procedure dependent prozedurabhängig
procedure description Prozedurbeschreibung
procedure documentation Verfahrenserläuterung
procedure name Prozedurname
procedure selection Verfahrensauswahl
procedure statement Prozeduranweisung
procedure status Abwicklungsstand
procedure type Vorgangsart
proceed vorgehen, weiterarbeiten, weiterschalten
proceedings Protokoll, Tätigkeitsbericht, Veranstaltung
proceeds Erlös
proceeds posting Erlösbuchung
proceed to select Wahlaufforderung
proceed to select signal Wahlaufforderungszeichen
process Prozeß, Verarbeitung, Verfahren, abarbeiten, abwickeln, bearbeiten, erledigen, verarbeiten, verfahren
process area Verarbeitungsbereich
process automation Prozeßautomatisierung
process communication Prozeßkommunikation
process control Prozeßsteuerung
process control application Prozeßsteuerungsanwendung
process control block Prozeßsteuerblock, Prozeßsteuerungsblock
process control language Prozeßsteuersprache
process data Prozeßdaten, Vorgangsdaten
process dependent vorgangsabhängig
process descriptor block Prozeßbeschreibungsblock
processed-out purchase order Lohnauftragsbestellung
process function Prozeßfunktion
process further weiterbearbeiten

process identification Prozeßkennnummer, Prozeßkennzeichen
process image Prozeßabbild
processing Bearbeitung
processing computer Verarbeitungscomputer
processing condition Bearbeitungsbedingung
processing error Bearbeitungsfehler, Verarbeitungsfehler
processing file Verarbeitungsdatei
processing form Verarbeitungsform
processing function Bearbeitungsfunktion
processing indicator Verarbeitungszeiger
processing information Bearbeitungsinformation
processing level Verarbeitungsstufe
processing marker Verarbeitungskennzeichen
processing module Verarbeitungsmodul
processing note Bearbeitungshinweis
processing option Bearbeitungsmöglichkeit
processing output Verarbeitungsleistung
processing path Verarbeitungspfad
processing pattern Bearbeitungsschema
processing procedure Bearbeitungsvorgang, Verarbeitungsprozedur
processing program Bearbeitungsprogramm
processing run Verarbeitungsablauf, Verarbeitungsgang
processing sequence Bearbeitungsfolge
processing state Bearbeitungsstand
processing station Datenverarbeitungsstelle
processing status Bearbeitungsstatus
processing step Verarbeitungsschritt
processing structure Verarbeitungsstruktur
processing time Rechenzeit
processing unit Prozessoreinheit
process level Vorgangsebene
process loop Prozeßschleife
process macro Prozeßmakro
process mode Verarbeitungsmodus
process name Prozeßname
process of exchange Austauschverfahren
processor Prozessor
processor common input output system PCIOS-System
processor control panel Prozessorbedienungsfeld
process-oriented vorgangsorientiert
processor interrupt facility Prozessorunterbrechungsmöglichkeit
processor library Systemprogrammbibliothek
processor number Prozessornummer
processor stall timer Prozessorzeitüberschreitung

163

processor status word Prozessorstatuswort
process priority Prozeßpriorität
process proceeding Vorgangsverarbeitung
process-related vorgangsbezogen
process selection Prozeßwahl
process-specific vorgangsspezifisch
process state Prozeßzustand
process table Prozeßtabelle
process type Prozeßtyp
procure beschaffen, besorgen
procurement Beschaffung
procurement costs Beschaffungskosten
procurement data bank Beschaffungsdatenbank
procurement price Beschaffungspreis
procurement quantity Beschaffungsmenge
procurement risk Beschaffungsrisiko
procurement time Beschaffungszeit
produce erstellen, erzeugen, fertigen, herstellen, produzieren, schaffen
producer independent herstellerunabhängig
product Erzeugnis, Produkt
product group Produktgruppe
production Erstellung, Fertigung, Herstellung, Produktion
production batch Charge
production batch splitting Chargensplitting
production completion Fertigungsabschluß
production control Fertigungskontrolle, Fertigungsorganisation
production control system System zur Fertigungssteuerung
production lot Fertigungslos
production mode Produktionsmodus
production order Betriebsauftrag, Fertigungsauftrag
production order number Betriebsauftragsnummer
production order processing Betriebsauftragsabwicklung
production plan Produktionsplan
production planning system Produktionsplanung und -steuerung
production program Erstellungsprogramm
production run Produktionsjob
production unit Produktionseinheit
productive produktiv
product name Produktname
product plan Produktplan
product range Sortiment
product-related produktbezogen
products master Produktstamm
product status Produktstatus

profit Gewinn
profitability Rentabilität
profit account Gewinnkonto
profit accounting Gewinnermittlung
profit and loss Gewinn- und Verlustrechnung
profit calculation Gewinnrechnung
prognosis Prognose
prognosticate prognostizieren
program Programm, programmieren
program abort Programmabbruch
program address Programmadresse
program address counter Befehlsadreßregister
program address register Programmadreßregister
program advance Programmfortschaltung
program area Programmbereich
program block Programmbaustein
program body Programmkomplex
program call Programmaufruf
program carrier Programmträger
program check Programmüberprüfung
program circle Programmkreis
program code Programmcode
program communication block Programmverständigungsblock
program complex Programmpaket
program constant Programmkonstante
program construction Programmkonstruktion
program continuation Programmfortsetzung
program control Programmsteuerung
program control block Programmsteuerblock, Programmsteuerungsblock
program controlled vom Programm gesteuert
program controlled interrupt programmgesteuerte Unterbrechung, programmgesteuerter Interrupt
program control table Programmsteuerungstabelle
program correction Programmkorrektur
program counter Befehlszähler, Programmzähler
program cycle Programmzyklus
program data buffer Programmdatenpuffer
program description Programmbeschreibung
program design Ablaufstruktur, Programmentwurf
program development system Programmentwicklungssystem
program disk Programmplatte
program end Programmende
program error Programmfehler
program execution Programmablauf, Programmausführung

program fault Programmfehler
program flow Programmablauf, Programmfluß
program flow chart Programmablaufplan
program flow control Programmablaufsteuerung
program frame Programmrahmen
program function Programmfunktion
program generator Programmgenerator
program group Programmverbund
program header Programmkopf
program identification Programmidentifikation, Programmname
program independence Programmunabhängigkeit
program indicator Programmbezugszahl
program information block Programminformationsblock
program instruction Programmanweisung, Programmbefehl
program interface Programmschnittstelle
program interrupt Programminterrupt
program jump Programmverzweigung
program keyin Programmeingabe
program layout Programmaufbau, Programmentwurf
program level key Programmstufentaste
program library Programmbibliothek
program linking Programmverknüpfung
program listing Programmprotokoll
program logic Programmlogik
program logon Programmaufbau
programmable controller speicherprogrammierbare Steuerung
programmable front end processor programmierbarer Vorrechner
programmable multiplexer programmierbarer Multiplexer
programmable point of sales terminal programmierbares Kassenterminal
programmable read only memory programmierbarer Lesespeicher
program management Programmverwaltung
programmed learning programmiertes Lernen
programmer Programmierer, Programmiergerät
programmer error Fehler des Programmiers
programmer manual Programmierhandbuch
programmer reference manual Programmierhandbuch
programmer unit Programmiergerät
programmer's handbook Programmierhandbuch
programming Programmierung

programming consideration Programmierhinweis
programming device Programmiergerät
programming effort Programmieraufwand
programming error Programmierfehler
programming error abort Programmierfehlerabbruch
programming instruction Programmieranweisung
programming knowledge Programmierkenntnisse
programming language Programmiersprache
programming language types Arten von Programmiersprachen
programming note Programmierhinweis
programming rule Programmierrichtlinie
programming standard Programmierstandard
programming system Programmiersystem
programming technique Programmiertechnik
program mode Programmodus
program module Programmodul
program name Programmbezeichnung, Programmname
program network chart Programmnetzwerkplan
program number Programmnummer
program organization Programmorganisation
program parameter Programmparameter
program processor Programmprozessor
program product Softwareprodukt
program production time Programmproduktivzeit
program region address Programmbezirksadresse
program register Programmregister
program run Programmablauf, Programmlauf
program scan Programmabtastung
program scan time Programmabtastzeit
program section Programmabschnitt
program segment Programmsegment
program segmentation Programmsegmentierung
program select key Programmwahltaste
program selector Programmverteiler
program sequence Programmfolge
program size Programmgröße
program skip Programmsprung
program specific programmspezifisch
program specification Programmspezifikation
program start Programmanfang
program status Programmstatus

165

program status doubleword Programmstatus-Doppelwort, Programmzustands-Doppelwort
program status longword Programmstatus-Langwort, Programmzustands-Langwort
program status word Programmstatuswort, Programmzustandswort
program step Programmschritt
program stop Programmstop, programmierter Halt
program storage Programmspeicher
program structure Programmaufbau, Programmstruktur
program summary Programmübersicht
program switch Programmschalter
program system Programmsystem
program tape Programmband
program termination Programmabbruch
program testing Prüfen eines Programmes
program test time Programmtestzeit
program type Programmtyp
program under test Prüfling
program variable Programmvariable
program version Programmversion
program writing Schreiben eines Programmes
progress Fortschritt
project Projekt, projektieren
project accounting Projektkontierung
project authorization Projektberechtigung
project budget Projektbudget
project control Projektkontrolle, Projektsteuerung, Projektüberwachung
project group Projektgruppe
project level Projektebene
project master Projektstamm
project master data Projektstammdaten
project master record Projektstammsatz
project number Projektnummer
project record Projektsatz
project related projektbezogen
project scheduling Projektplanung
project summary Projektübersicht
project text Projekttext
prolong verlängern
prompt Aufforderung, Aufforderungszeichen, Bedienungsführung, Bereitschaftsmeldung, Eingabeaufforderung, Prompt, Systemmeldung, auffordern
prompt character Aufforderungszeichen
prong Kontaktzunge
pronunciation mark Aussprachezeichen
proper ordnungsgemäß, richtig, sauber
proper inventory Eigenbestand

property Besitz, Eigentum
property accounting Anlagenbuchhaltung
property flag Eigentumskennzeichen
proportion Anteil
proportional proportional
proportional band Proportionalband
proportional spacing Proportionaldruck
proportional spacing mechanism Proportionalschritt-Schalteinrichtung
proportional value Wertanteil
proposal Vorschlagsliste
proposal due date Angebotstermin
proposal program Vorschlagsprogramm
proposed value Vorschlagswert
proprietary item area Markenartikelbereich
proprietory gesetzlich geschützt
prospect Interessent
protect schützen
protected geschützt
protected electrical equipment geschützte elektrische Einrichtung
protected memory address Adresse im geschützten Speicherbereich
protected mode Protected Mode
protected motor geschützter Motor
protect feature Zeichenschutz
protect field attribute Attribut »geschütztes Feld«
protect field transmission Übertragung von geschützten Feldern
protection Schutz, Zeichenschutz
protection feature Sicherungskennzeichen
protection in edit mode Schutz im Editiermodus
protection of data privacy Datenschutz (für natürliche Personen)
protection status Dateischutz
protective Schutz-, schützend, sichernd
protective capacitor Schutzkondensator
protective coil Schutzspule
protective conduit Schutzrohr
protective cover Plastikhülle, Schutzabdeckung, Schutzmantel
protective device Schutzvorrichtung
protective enclosure Schutzgehäuse
protective envelope Schutzhülle
protector Schutz, Schutzeinrichtung
protocol Protokoll, Übertragungssicherungs-Verfahren
protocol control Protokollsteuerung
protocol control information Protokollheader
protocol data unit Protokolldateneinheit
protocol function Protokollfunktion

166

protocol layer Protokollebene
protocol manual Protokollhandbuch
prototype card Prototypkarte
protrusion Vorsprung
prove beweisen, erweisen
provide bereitstellen, bieten, versehen, zur Verfügung stellen
provided for vorgesehen
provider Anbieter
provision Bereitstellung
proximity switch Näherungsschalter
pseudo pseudo
pseudocode Deckname, Pseudocode
pseudo execution Quasiausführung
pseudo instruction Quasibefehl
pseudo routine Pseudoroutine
pseudo statement Pseudoanweisung
public öffentlich
public data network öffentliches Datennetz
public dial-up connection Post-Wählverbindung
public key öffentlicher Schlüssel
public key algorithm Verschlüsselungsalgorithmus mit öffentlichem Schlüssel
public services öffentliche Dienste
public switched data network öffentliches Datennetz
public switched network öffentliches Netz
public switched telephone network Fernsprechnetz, öffentliches Fernsprechnetz, öffentliches Telefonnetz
public telephone network öffentliches Fernsprechnetz, öffentliches Telefonnetz
publisher Verlag
publishing company Verlag
pull hinwegziehen, ziehen
pulley Führungsrolle
puls code modulation Puls-Codemodulation
pulse Impuls
pulse amplifier Impulsverstärker
pulse amplitude modulation Puls-Amplitudenmodulation
pulse circuit Stoßkreis
pulse dialing Impulswahlverfahren
pulse dialling Impulswahl
pulse generator Impulsgenerator
pulse modulator tube Impulsmodulationsröhre
pulse period Impulsperiode
pulse regenerating circuit Impulsregenerationsschaltung
pulses per second Impulse pro Sekunde
pulse train Impulsfolge
pulse transformer Impulstransformator

pulse with Impulsbreite
pump Pumpe
punch lochen, stanzen
punch card Lochkarte
punch card file Lochkartendatei
punch card instruction Lochkartenbefehl
punch card operation Lochkartenoperation
punched card Lochkarte
punched card equipment Lochkartengerät
punched card reader Lochkartenleser
punched card reproducer Lochkartenkopierer
punched card sorter Lochkartensortierer
punched card to magnetic tape Lochkarten-Magnetband-Umsetzer
punched card to punched tape Lochkarten-Lochstreifen-Umsetzer
punched tape Lochstreifen
punched tape equipment Lochstreifengerät
punched tape punch Lochstreifenlocher
punched tape reader Lochstreifenleser
punched tape reproducer Lochstreifenkopierer
punched tape to magnetic tape Lochstreifen-Magnetband-Umsetzer
punched tape to punched card Lochstreifen-Lochkarten-Umsetzer
puncher Locher, Stanzer
punch image Kartenbild
punch out ausstanzen
punch tape Lochstreifen
punch track Lochspur
punctuation Triadenmarkierung
punctuation mark Satzzeichen
purchase Einkauf, Kauf, einkaufen, kaufen
purchase activity Bestelltätigkeit
purchase area Einkaufsbereich
purchase authorization Einkaufsberechtigung
purchase data Einkaufsdaten
purchase date Bezugsdatum, Einkaufsdatum
purchase field Einkaufsfeld
purchase group master Einkaufgruppenstamm
purchase info record Einkaufsinfosatz
purchase information Einkaufsinformationen
purchase information record Einkaufsinformationssatz
purchase invoice Eingangsrechnung
purchase item Kaufartikel
purchase option Bezugsmöglichkeit, Vorkaufsrecht
purchase order Bestellbeleg, Bestellung, Einkaufsbestellung
purchase order alteration Bestelländerung
purchase order appendix Bestellanhang

purchase order appendix text Bestellanhangstext
purchase order appendix type Bestellanhangsart
purchase order change print-out Bestelländerungsschreibung
purchase order completion Bestellabschluß
purchase order concluding text Bestellabschlußtext
purchase order data Bestelldaten
purchase order data base Bestelldatenbank
purchase order date Bestellungstermin
purchase order document Bestellungsanlage
purchase order entry Bestelleingabe, Bestellungsbuchung
purchase order file Bestellauftragsdatei
purchase order form Bestellformular
purchase order header Bestellkopf
purchase order history Bestellentwicklung
purchase order history element Bestellentwicklungselemente
purchase order history flag Bestellentwicklungskennzeichen
purchase order history record Bestellentwicklungssatz
purchase order history source Bestellentwicklungstyp
purchase order in Bestelleingang
purchase order item Bestellposition
purchase order item completion Bestellpositionserfüllung
purchase order item extract Bestellpositionsextraxt
purchase order item type Bestellpositionstyp
purchase order letter Bestellschreiben
purchase order monitoring Bestellüberwachung
purchase order net value Nettobestellwert
purchase order note Bestellnotiz
purchase order number Bestellnummer
purchase order pricing unit Bestellpreiseinheit
purchase order processing Bestellabwicklung, Bestellbearbeitung
purchase order proposal Bestellvorschlag
purchase order proposal list Bestellvorschlagsliste
purchase order remark Bestellnotiz
purchase order request Bestellabforderung
purchase order request file Bestellanforderungsdatei
purchase order request number Bestellanforderungsnummer

purchase order request record Bestellanforderungssatz
purchase order statistics Bestellstatistik
purchase order text Bestelltext
purchase order type Bestellart, Bestelltyp
purchase order value Bestellwert
purchase order volume Bestellvolumen
purchase price Einkaufspreis, Kaufpreis
purchase price unit Einkaufspreiseinheit
purchase quantity Bezugsmenge
purchase transaction Einkaufstransaktion
purchase unit Kaufmengeneinheit
purchase voucher Einkaufsbeleg
purchasing Einkauf
purchasing budget Einkaufsbudget
purchasing commitment Bestellobligo
purchasing data Einkaufsdaten
purchasing department Einkaufsabteilung
purchasing group Einkaufsgruppe
purchasing group code Einkaufsgruppenschlüssel
purchasing group master Einkaufsgruppenstamm
purchasing group master record Einkaufsgruppenstammsatz
purchasing negotiation Einkaufsverhandlung
purchasing source Bezugsquelle
purchasing statistics Einkaufsstatistik
pure rein
purpose Funktion, Verwendungszweck, Zweck
pushbutton Druckknopf
pushbutton control Druckknopfsteuerung
push button selection Tastenwahl
pushbutton switch Druckknopfschalter, Druckschalter
push down storage Kellerspeicher
put aufsetzen, legen, setzen, stellen
put in front voransetzen
put into hineinstellen
put out ausgeben
pyhsical layer Bitübertragungsschicht

Q

quad height module   Vierfachkarte
quadrature   Phasenverschieber, Quadratur
quadrature component   Blindkomponente
quadrature output   Phasenverschieberausgang
quadword   Quadwort
qualifier   Gruppenmerkmal, Kennzeichen, Merkmal, Qualifizierer
qualifier filename   vollständige Dateikennung
qualify   qualifizieren
qualify for bonus   bonusfähig
qualifying option   Einschränkungsmöglichkeit
quality   Beschaffenheit, Güte, Qualität
quality assurance   Qualitätskontrolle, Qualitätssicherung
quality check   Programmüberprüfung, Qualitätsprüfung
quality control   Qualitätskontrolle
quality faults   Qualitätsmängel
quality of service   Dienstgüte
quality of services   Dienstgüte
quality parameter   Dienstgüteparameter
quantitative   mengenmäßig
quantity   Materialmenge, Menge, Positionsmenge, Warenmenge
quantity acquired   Zugangsmenge
quantity alteration   Mengenänderung
quantity amendment   Mengenveränderung
quantity called off   Abrufmenge
quantity cancelled   Stornomenge
quantity column   Mengenspalte
quantity consumed   Verbrauchsmenge
quantity contract   Mengenkontrakt
quantity contracted   Kontraktmenge
quantity control   Mengenprüfung, Mengenüberprüfung
quantity counted   Zählmenge
quantity credit note   Mengengutschrift
quantity delivered   Liefermenge
quantity discrepancy   Mengenabweichung
quantity dispatched   Versandmenge
quantity field   Mengenfeld
quantity for delivery   Lieferumfang
quantity given   Mengenangabe
quantity informed   Mitteilungsmenge
quantity invoiced   Fakturamenge
quantity issued   Entnahmemenge
quantity lock table   Mengensperrtabelle
quantity of data   Datenmenge

quick information

quantity of frozen stock   Sperrbestandsmenge
quantity on order   Bestellbestand
quantity optimisation   Bestellobligation
quantity ordered   Bestellmenge, Ordermenge
quantity oriented   mengenorientiert
quantity posting   Mengenbuchung
quantity purchased   Abnahmemenge
quantity received   Eingangsmenge, Wareneingangsmenge
quantity reference   Mengenbeziehung
quantity reserved   Reservierungsmenge
quantity returned   Rückgabemenge
quantity scale   Mengenstaffel
quantity shortfall   Mengenunterdeckung
quantity situation   Mengensituation
quantity sold   Verkaufsmenge
quantity submitted   Beistellmenge
quantization level   Quantisierungsstufe
quantization noise   Quantisierungsrauschen
quarantine   Quarantäne
quarantine period   Quarantänezeit
quarantine service   Quarantänedienst
quarter   Quartal, Viertel
quarter word mode   Viertelwortverarbeitung
quartz   Quarz
quartz crystal   Quarzkristall
quartz oscillator   Quarzoszillator
quasi execution   Quasiausführung
quasi instruction   Quasibefehl
quasi special depreciation   Quasisonderabschreibung
query   Abfrage, Frage, Rückfrage, abfragen, rückfragen
query command   Abfragebefehl
query example   Abfragebeispiel
query language   Abfragesprache
query language processor   Abfrageprozessor
query message   Frageaktion
query mode   Abfragemodus
query name   Abfragename
question   Frage, Fragestellung, Rückfrage, erfragen, fragen
question mark   Fragezeichen
queue   Queue, Warteschlange
queue control block   Queue-Kontrollblock, Warteschlangen-Kontrollblock
queued input/output   Ein-/Ausgabe über Warteschlange
queue entry   Warteschlangeneintrag
queue file   Warteschlangendatei
queue full   Queue voll, Warteschlange voll
queue manager   Warteschlangenverwalter
quick information   Schnellinformation

169

quick lookup guide Benutzerhandbuch
quick recovery Sofortwiederherstellung
quit abbrechen, beenden, beenden ohne Sichern
quittieren acknowledge
quota Quote
quotation Kostenvoranschlag, Preisstellung
quotation mark Anführungszeichen
quotation marks Hochkommata
quote Angebot, Kostenvoranschlag, zitieren

R

race Rennen, rennen
race condition Rennzustand
rack Einbaurahmen, Gestell
rackmount Einbaurahmen, Gestellrahmen
rackmount assembly Einbaurahmen
rackmount model Einbaumodell
radar antenna Radarantenne
radar data extractor Radardatenextraktor, Zieldatenextraktor
radar receiver Radarantennenempfänger
radar scan rate Antennenumlaufgeschwindigkeit
radial chart recorder Polarkoordinatenschreiber
radiation absorbed dosis absorbierte Strahlendosis
radio Rundfunk
radio control Funkfernsteuerung
radio direction finding Funkpeilung
radio frequency Funkfrequenz
radiofrequency amplifier Hochfrequenzverstärker
radio frequency interference Empfangsstörung
radiofrequency signal amplifier Hochfrequenzverstärker
radioguidance Funkleitung
radio link Richtfunkstrecke
radiolocation Funkortung
radionavigation Funknavigation
radix Basis, Radix
radix conversion Elementarumwandlung
radix notation Radixschreibweise
radix point Dezimalpunkt, Radixpunkt
rail Montageschiene, Schiene
rail transport Bahntransport
railway Bahn
railway station Bahnstation
RAM disk Pseudofloppy
RAM enable RAM-Freigabe
ramp Rampe
ramp voltage linearer Spannungsanstieg
RAM refresh operation RAM-Auffrischoperation
random random, wahlfrei, willkürlich
random access wahlfreier Zugriff
random access device Gerät mit wahlfreiem Zugriff
random access memory Direktzugriffsspeicher, Randomspeicher, Schreib-/Lesespeicher
random access processing Direktzugriffsverarbeitung
random access storage Speicher mit wahlfreiem Zugriff
random access store Direktzugriffsspeicher
random code Zufallsschlüssel
random function Zufallsfunktion
random number Zufallszahl
random number generator Zufallsgenerator
random processing Randomverarbeitung
random seek wahlfreier Zugriff
random value Zufallswert
range Bereich, Kreis
range clamping switch Bereichsumschalter
range level Bereichsebene
range of characters Zeichenbereich
range of information Informationsumfang
range of lines Zeilenbereich
range of numbers Nummernintervall, Nummernkreis, Zahlenbereich
ranges of master record numbers Stammnummernkreise
range specification Bereichsangabe
rapid schnell
rapid alteration schnelle Änderung
rapid input Schnellerfassung
rapid input mask Schnellerfassungsliste
raster Punktraster
raster graphics Bitmustergrafik
raster image mode Bitabbildmodus
ratchet Ratsche
rate Geschwindigkeit, Kurs, Rate, bewerten, einschätzen
rated frequency Nennfrequenz
rated output Nennleistung
rated speed Nenndrehzahl
rate of change Änderungsgeschwindigkeit
rate of duty Zollsatz
rate of personnel expenditure Personalkostenanteil
rating Bewertung, Nennleistung
ratio Verhältnis
ratio control Verhältnisregelung
rationalization effect Rationalisierungseffekt
rationalization potential Rationalisierungspotential
ratio of exchange rates Kursverhältnis
raw roh, unbearbeitet
raw clock Grobtakt
raw material Rohstoff
reach erreichen

react reagieren
reaction Reaktion
reactivate reaktivieren, wiederbeleben, wiedereinschalten
reactivation Nachaktivierung, Reaktivierung, Wiederbelebung
read Lesen, ablesen, einlesen, lesen
readable lesbar
read after write Hinterbandkontrolle, Lesen nach Schreiben, Prüflesen, Schreibkontrolle
read area Lesebereich
read attempt Leseversuch
read backwards zurücklesen
read buffer storage Abfühlpufferspeicher
read call Leseaufruf
read cycle time Lesezykluszeit
reader Leser, Systemleseroutine
read error Fehler beim Lesen, Lesefehler
read head Lesekopf
read in einlesen, einspielen, hereinlesen
readiness Bereitschaft
readiness for data transmission Übertragungsbereitschaft
reading-printing-sorting Lesen-Drucken-Sortieren
reading-sorting Lesen-Sortieren
reading station Abfühlstation
read in operation Einleseoperation
read in unit Lesestation
readjustment Neueinstellung
read mode Lesemodus
read on zulesen
read only Nur-Lese-
read only file Nur-Lese-Datei
read-only memory Festspeicher nur zum Lesen, Festwertspeicher, Nur-Lese-Speicher
readout Ausgabe
read over überlesen
read pulse Abfühlimpuls
read routine Leseroutine
read through durchlesen
read unit Lesestation
read winding Abtastwicklung
read/write Schreib/Lese
read write access slot Schreib-/Leseöffnung
read write board Schreib-/Lesekarte
read write error Schreib-/Lesefehler
read/write/execute Schreiben/Lesen/Ausführen
read write head Schreib-/Lesekopf
read write slot Schreib-/Leseöffnung
ready bereit
ready busy protocol Bereit/Belegt-Protokoll
ready condition Bereitzustand

ready for data Übertragungsbereitschaft
ready for input eingabebereit
ready for occupancy schlüsselfertig
ready for output ausgabebereit
ready for sending Sendebereitschaft
ready for use benutzungsfertig
ready indicator Anzeige READY (Bereit)
ready prompt Bereitmeldung
ready state Bereitzustand
ready station Wartestation
ready status Betriebsbereitschaft
ready to be printed druckfertig
ready to receive Empfangsbereitschaft, empfangsbereit
ready to transmit Übetragungsbereitschaft
real real, reell
real address effektive Adresse
real constant reelle Konstante
realisable verwertbar
realistic realistisch
realm Gebiet
real number reelle Zahl
real number division Division einer reellen Zahl, reelle Division
realtime Echtzeit, Realtime
realtime clock Echtzeituhr, Realzeituhr
realtime clock failure Fehler in der Systemuhr
realtime common bank im Realtimebetrieb benutzte gemeinsame Bank
realtime device Echtzeitgerät
realtime input/output Echtzeit Ein-/Ausgabe
realtime language Echtzeitsprache
realtime library Echtzeitbibliothek
realtime operating system Realtimeverarbeitungssystem
realtime operation Realtimeverarbeitung, Realzeitbetrieb
realtime processing Echtzeitverarbeitung, Realtimeverarbeitung
realtime processing system Realzeitverarbeitungssystem
realtime status Echtzeitstatus
realtime system Echtzeitsystem
real variable reelle Variable
rear hinterer
rearrange neu ordnen, umsortieren
rear side Rückseite
rear side of voucher Belegrückseite
rear view Rückseite
reason Anlaß, Grund, Ursache, Veranlassung
reason for discount Rabattgrund
reason for freezing Sperrgrund
reason for performance Performancegrund

reason for release Freigabegrund
reason of space Platzgrund
reassemble reassemblieren
reassembling vereinigen
reboot System neu laden, erneut laden, neu laden
rebuild neuaufbauen
recalculate neu berechnen, neurechnen
recalculation Neuberechnung
recalculation mode Modus der Neuberechnung
recalculation order Reihenfolge der Neuberechnung
recall Wiederaufruf, abrufen, wiederaufrufen, zurückrufen
receipt Quittung
receipt list Empfangsliste
receipt of invoice Rechnungseingang
receipt of payment Zahlungseingang
receipt printing Quittungsdruck
receivable account Debitorenkonto
receive Empfang, eingehen, empfangen, erhalten
receive block Empfangsblock
receive buffer Empfangspuffer
receive circuit Empfangsschaltung
receive copy Empfangskopie
received characters empfangene Zeichen
received line Empfangsleitung
receive job Empfangsauftrag
receive mode Empfangsbetrieb
receive only nur Empfang
receive parity Empfangsparität, Empfangssignalpegel
receive parity feature Auswahl der Empfangsparität
receive processor Empfangsprozessor
receiver Datenempfänger, Empfangsgerät, Empfänger
receive rate Empfangsgeschwindigkeit
receiver card Empfängerkarte
receiver dependent empfängerabhängig
receiver ready empfangsbereit
receiver margin Empfangsspielraum
receiver not ready nicht empfangsbereit
receiver ready Empfangsbereitschaft
receiver signal element timing Empfängersignal-Elementzeitgeber
receive sequence number Empfangsfolgenummer
receive speed Empfangsgeschwindigkeit
receive speed feature Einstellen der Empfangsgeschwindigkeit
receive state variable Empfangsfolgezähler

receive timing Empfangszeittakt
receiving device for paper stripes Abschnittsammelbehälter
receiving end Empfangsseite
receiving point Empfangsstelle
receiving station Gegenstelle
receiving warehouse Zugangslagerort
reception point Empfangsstelle
recheck wiederprüfen
recipient Empfänger, Warenempfänger
recipient department Empfangsabteilung
recipient of the internal message Aktionsempfänger
recode umschlüsseln
recognition Erkennung
recognize anerkennen, erkennen
recommence wiederanfangen
recommend empfehlen
reconciliation Debitorenverrechnung
reconciliation list Abstimmliste
reconciliation of accounts Kontenabstimmung
reconfiguration Neukonfigurierung, Rekonfigurierung
reconfiguration error Rekonfigurierungsfehler
reconfiguration error detection unit Rekonfigurierungs-Fehlererkennungseinheit
reconfiguration fault Rekonfigurierungsfehler
reconstruct neu aufbauen, zurückladen
record Datensatz, Protokoll aufnehmen, Satz, aufnehmen, aufzeichnen
record address field Satzadreßfeld
record address file Satzadreßdatei
record address type Adressierungsart
record by record satzweise
record cell Satzzeile
record contents Satzinhalt
record counter Satzzähler
record definition Datensatzbeschreibung, Datensatzdefinition, Satzdefinition
record definition field Datensatzbeschreibungsfeld
record description Datensatzbeschreibung
record description word Satzbeschreibungswort
record descriptor Satzbeschreibung
record descriptor word Satzbeschreibungswort
record designation Satzbezeichnung
recorded surface beschriebene Fläche
recorder Aufnahmegerät, Schreiber
record field Satzfeld
record fill Füllzeichen
record form Erfassungsformular, Satzform
record format Satzbett, Satzformat

record format value Satzbettwert
record group Satzgruppe
record head Aufnahmekopf
record identification Satzbeschreibung, Satzidentifikation
record indicator Satzbezugszahl
recording comb Aufzeichnungskamm
recording date Aufnahmedatum
recording density Aufzeichnungsdichte, Schreibdichte
recording device Aufzeichnungseinrichtung
recording head Schreib-/Lesekopf, Schreibkopf
recording jack plug cable Aufnahmekabel
recording line Schreibzeile
recording method Aufzeichnungsverfahren
recording mode Schreibverfahren
recording procedure Schreibvorgang
recording record Aufzeichnungssatz
recording stylus Brennadel
record key Aufzeichnungstaste, Satzschlüssel
record layout Satzaufbau
record length Datensatzlänge, Satzbreite, Satzlänge
record length field Satzlängenfeld
record level Aufnahmepegel
record line Aufzeichnungszeile
record management service Datensatzverwaltungsdienst
record management system Datensatzverwaltungssystem
record mark Satzgrenze
record number Datensatznummer, Satznummer
record segment Satzsegment
record selection expression Satzauswahlphrase
record sequence Satzfolge
record size Aufzeichnungsgröße
records per sector Datensätze pro Sektor, Sätze pro Sektor
records per track Datensätze pro Spur, Sätze pro Spur
record stream Datenfluß
record structure Satzaufbau
record text Schreibtext
record type Satzart
record type description Satzartbeschreibung
record type specification Satzartenangabe
record width Satzbreite
recover beheben, wiederherstellen
recoverable error edit Fehlerstatistikprogramm
recovery Rückgewinnung
recovery bootstrap Wiederherstellungsladen
recovery procedure Wiederherstellungsvorgang

recovery program Fehlerbehandlungsprogramm, Reparaturprogramm
recovery result Ergebnis der Reparatur
recovery software Wiederanlaufsoftware
recovery voltage Wiederkehrspannung
recreate neu einrichten, neu errichten, neu erstellen, neu anlegen
rectangle Rechteck
rectangular rechteckig
rectifier Gleichrichter
rectifier diode Gleichrichterdiode
rectifier substation Gleichrichterstation
rectifier transformer Gleichrichter-Transformator
rectifier tube Gleichrichterröhre
recursion Rekursion, Schleife
recursive rekursiv
recursive check Rekursivitätsprüfung
redefine erneut definieren, neu belegen, neu definieren, redefinieren, umbelegen, umdefinieren
redistribution Umverteilung
reduce abbauen, abnehmen, ermäßigen, reduzieren, vermindern
reduced intensity reduzierte Helligkeit
redundancy Redundanz
redundancy check Redundanzprüfung
redundancy code generator Sicherheitscode-Generator
redundancy group Redundanzgruppe
redundancy reduction Redundanzverminderung
redundant redundant
reed relay Reedrelais, Schutzgasrelais
reel Spule
reel holddown Bandtellerbefestigung
reel number Spulennummer
reenter Neueingabe, Neueinsprung, nachbuchen
reentrant routines eintrittsinvariante Routinen
reentry Wiedereingabe, Wiedereintritt
refer beziehen, verweisen
reference Ansprechen, Bezug, Bezugnahme, Referenz, Verweis
reference account Referenzkonto
reference accounting area Referenzbuchungskreis
reference asset Referenzanlage
reference ballast Normalvorschaltgerät
reference card Befehlsübersicht, Faltkarte zum Nachschlagen, Übersichtskarte
reference date Journaldatum
referenced relation Bezugsrelation

reference filter Bezugsfilter
reference format Programmbildformat
reference handbook Referenzhandbuch
reference information Nachschlaginformationen
reference level Bezugspegel
reference listing Referenz-Auflistung
reference manual Befehlsreferenz, Nachschlagewerk, Referenzhandbuch
reference master record Referenzstammsatz
reference material Referenzmaterial
reference message Hinweismeldung
reference model Referenzmodell
reference modifier Bezugsfaktor
reference number Referenznummer
reference operand Bezugsoperand
reference relationship Referenzbeziehung
references Verweise
reference sign Diktatzeichen
references to cell Feldreferenz, Feldverweis
reference table Adreßzuordnungstabelle
reference text Betrefftext, Referenztext
reference to function Funktionsaufruf
reference value Anhaltewert
reference work Nachschlagewerk
referencing bezugnehmend, in Bezug auf
referencing attribute Referenzattribut
referring to bezüglich
referring to an accounting area buchungskreisbezogen
refind wiederauffinden
refinement Feinheit, Verfeinerung
reformat neu formatieren, reformatieren, umformen, umgestalten
refresh Auffrischen, auffrischen, erfrischen
refresh circuit Auffrisch-Schaltung
refresh memory Speicher auffrischen
refresh screen Bildschirmanzeige neu aufbauen
refusal of offer Angebotsabsage
refuse verweigern
regain wiederfinden
regard anschauen, ansehen, betrachten
regarding bezugnehmend, in Bezug auf
regardless ohne Rücksicht
regenerate aufbereiten
regeneration Aufbereitung, Regenerierung
regenerative interface converter regenerierende Schnittstellenanpassungen
region Bereich, Region
regional regional
register Kasse, Register, Verzeichnis, erfassen, verzeichnen
register computer Registerrechner

register contents Registerstand
register convention Registerkonvention
registered offices Betriebsstätte
registered quantity erfaßte Menge
registering posting data Buchungsstofferfassung
registering process Erfassungsvorgang
registering single items Einzelpositionserfassung
registering the purchase order Bestellerfassung
registering the voucher Belegerfassung
register length Registerstellenzahl
register position Registerstelle
register safeguard Registersicherung
registration Erfassung
registration block Erfassungsblock
registration effort Erfassungsaufwand
registration form Erfassungsform
registration number Registriernummer
registration period Erfassungsperiode, Erfassungszeitraum
registration screen Erfassungsbild
registration technique Erfassungstechnik
regular geregelt, regelmäßig
regular customer field Kundenstammfeld
regular customer record Kundenstammsatz
regularity Regelmäßigkeit
regulate regulieren
regulated service regulierter Dienst
regulation Regelung, Richtlinie, Vorschrift
reimburse vergüten
reimbursement Vergütung
reinitialization Neuinitialisierung
reinitialize neu initialisieren
reject Absage, ablehnen, abweisen, zurückweisen
reject drawer Rejectfach
rejection Aussteuerung
reject page Rejectseite
relate beziehen
related to article artikelmäßig
related to customers kundenbezogen
related to order item auftragspositionsbezogen
related to polarity symbol vorzeichengerecht
related to statistics statistikmäßig
relation Beziehung, Verhältnis
relational data Bezugsdaten
relational data base relationale Datenbank
relational decimal array Vergleichsdezimalfeld
relation condition Vergleich
relation operator Vergleichsoperator
relative relativ

relative address relative Adresse
relative addressing relative Adressierung
relative addressing method relative Zugriffsmethode
relative address register relatives Indexregister
relative file organization relative Dateistruktur
relative humidity relativ, relative Luftfeuchtigkeit
relative record number relative Datensatznummer, relative Satznummer
relative reference relativer Verweis
relative virtual address relative virtuelle Adresse
relay Relais, weiterleiten
relay circuit breaker Relaisschalter
relay control function Relaissteuerung
relay element Relaiselement
relay function Relaisfunktion
relay ladder logic Relaislogikprogramm
relay ladder logic programming Relaislogikprogrammierung
relay output Relaisausgang
relay storage Relaisspeicher
release Freigabe, Version, auslösen, entsperren, freigeben
release button Auslöseknopf
release date Freigabedatum
release diskette Systemdiskette
release identifier Freigabekennzeichen
release interrupt lockout Freigabe der Unterbrechungssperre
release key Freigabetaste
release lock Freigabesperre
release media Datenträger für Software-Dokumenatation
release notes Versionshinweise
release notice Freigabemitteilung
release switch Auslösetaste
release tab Entriegelungsklammer, Feststellhebel
release version Releaseversion
relevance Relevanz
relevant betreffend, relevant
reliability data Zuverlässigkeitsangaben
reliable zuverlässig
relief Erleichterung
relieving the load on the system Systementlastung
reload System neu laden, erneut laden, neu laden, rückladen, zurückladen
reload the system System neu laden
relocatable adreßunabhängig, relozierbar, verschiebbar

relocatable code relozierbarer Code
relocatable data Verschiebedatensätze
relocatable element Zielprogrammelement
relocate umlagern
relocated stock Umlagerungsbestand
relocating loader Lader für verschiebbare Programme
relocation Standortwechsel, Verschieben, Wiederauffindung
relocation register Basisadreßregister
reluctance motor Magnetmotor
remain verbleiben, verweilen, zurückbleiben
remainder Ergänzungswert, Restanzahl
remaining amount Restbetrag
remaining time Restlaufzeit
remap neu belegen, umbelegen, umdefinieren
remark Anmerkung, Vermerk
remind erinnern, mahnen
reminder Erinnerung, Gedächtnisstütze, Mahnung
reminder address Mahnadresse, Mahnanschrift
reminder code Mahnschlüssel
reminder control Mahnsteuerung
reminder counter Mahnzähler
reminder criterion Mahnkriterium
reminder date Mahndatum
reminder frequency Mahnrhythmus
reminder list Mahnliste
reminder period Mahnperiode
reminder print file Mahnungsdruckdatei
reminder print program Mahnungsdruckprogramm
reminder procedure Mahnablauf, Mahnverfahren
reminder program Mahnprogramm
reminder stage Mahnstufe
reminder statistics Mahnstatistik
reminder status Mahnstatus
reminder system Erinnerungssystem
reminder text Mahntext
reminder total Erinnerungswert
reminding type Mahnart
remote Fern-, abgesetzt, dezentral, entfernt
remote base controller dezentraler Montageplatten-Controller
remote batch processing Stapelfernverarbeitung
remote batch processor Prozessor für Stapelfernverarbeitung
remote batch terminal Stapelfernverarbeitungsstation
remote channel controller Kanalfernsteuerung

remote communications terminal Datenfernübertragungsstation
remote computer Fernrechner, entfernter Rechner
remote control Fernsteuerung
remote control interface Fernsteuerungsanschluß
remote controlled vehicle ferngesteuertes Fahrzeug
remote control system Fernsteuersystem
remote control unit Fernsteuerung
remote data processing system Datenfernverarbeitungssystem
remote data station Ferndatenstation
remote device Datenstation
remote device handler Stationssteuerroutine, Steuerroutinen für Datenstationen
remote diagnostics link Ferndiagnoseanschluß
remote identification Fremdknotenkennummer
remote identifier Stationsgruppenkennung
remote input output control Kanalsteuerung
remote job initiation Jobfernstart
remote loop entfernte Prüfschleife, ferne Prüfschleife
remote node indentification Fremdknotenkennummer
remote port Fernanschluß
remote power controller Spannungsfernbedienung
remote print dezentraler Druck
remote printer dezentraler Drucker
remote procedure call Fernprozeduraufruf
remote procedure error Ablauffehler der Gegenstelle
remote processor error Ablauffehler der Gegenstelle
remote radar tracking Flugzielverfolgung über entfernte Radarstationen
remote site Datensichtstation
remote spoolout processor Spool-Fernverarbeitungsprogramm
remote station dezentrale Station, entfernte Station, verteilte Station
remote switching-on Ferneinschaltung
remote symbiont Stapelfernverarbeitungssymbiont
remote symbiont interface Fernverarbeitungs-Symbiontenschnittstelle
remote system Hostrechner
remote technical assistance Fernwartung
remote terminal Datenstation
remote terminal interface Datenfernübertragungs-Schnittstelle

remote terminal processor Datenstationsprozessor
remote testing Fernprüfung
remote transaction I/O Datenübertragungs-E/A-Programm
remote user Datenstationsbenutzer, Fremdbenutzer, entfernter Benutzer
remote workstation dezentraler Arbeitsplatz
remount erneut montieren, wieder montieren, wieder mounten
removable auswechselbar
removable disk drive Diskettenlaufwerk, Wechselplattenlaufwerk
removable disk write protect Schreibschutz für die Diskette
removal Aufhebung, Entfernung
removal criterion Räumkriterium
removal date Räumdatum
removal of document Belegentnahme
remove aufheben, entfernen, löschen, räumen
remove a drive Laufwerk aufheben
remove a ruler Zeilenlineal löschen
rename neubenennen, umbenennen
rendering of invoice Rechnungsstellung
renew erneuern
renewal Erneuerung
renounce verzichten
rent Miete, mieten
renumber neunumerieren
reorganization Reorganisation
reorganization program Reorganisationsprogramm
reorganization run Reorganisationslauf
reorganize reorganisieren
repaginate umformen
repagination Neunumerierung, Neuumbruch
repair Reparatur, reparieren
repair advice Reparaturhinweis
repair material Reparaturmaterial
repair order Reparaturauftrag
repartitioning Neuaufteilen der Festplatte
repayment Tilgung
repayment invoice Tilgungsrechnung
repayment plan Tilgungsplan
repeal Aufhebung, aufheben
repeat Wiederholung, wiederholen
repeat count Wiederholungsfaktor
repeat key Dauertaste
repeat request Wiederholungsanforderung
repertoire Vorrat
repetition Wiederholung
repetition of input field Eingabefeld-Wiederholung

177

repetitive wiederkehrend
repetitive funktion Wiederholfunktion
replace austauschen, auswechseln, ersetzen, substituieren
replaceable auswechselbar
replaceable parameter austauschbarer Parameter
replacement Austausch, Ersatz, Ersetzung
replacement battery Ersatzbatterie
replacement character Ersatzzeichen
replacement cost Wiederbeschaffungswert
replacement costs Wiederbeschaffungskosten
replacement costs per article Wiederbeschaffungsstückkosten
replacement proposition Wiederbeschaffungsvorschlag
replacement string Ersatzzeichenfolge
replacement time Wiederbeschaffungszeit
replacement unit Ersatzgerät
replace mode Ersetzmodus
replacement part Ersatzteil
replay record interner Arbeitssatz
replicated system approach Minimalkonfiguration
reply Antwort, antworten
reply message Quittungsnachricht
report Befund, Bericht, Liste, Zustandsmeldung, berichten, melden
report address Folgeadresse anzeigen
report analysis Berichtsauswertung
report data Berichtsdaten
report data administration Berichtsdatenverwaltung
report data bank Berichtsdatenbank
report definition Berichtsdefinition
report file Listendatei
reporting period Berichtszeitraum
report level Berichtsstufe
report line level Berichtszeilenebene
report month Berichtsmonat
report number Berichtsnummer
report period Berichtsperiode
report preparation Berichtschreibung
report program Berichtsprogramm, Listenprogramm
report program generator Listenprogrammgenerator
report table Berichtstabelle
report time Berichtszeitpunkt
report writer Listengenerator
report year Berichtsjahr
reposition Rückpositionieren, wiederaufsetzen

reposition backward rückwärts neu positionieren
reposition forward vorwärts neu positionieren
represent darstellen, vertreten
representation Darstellung
representational form Darstellungsform
representation control Darstellungssteuerung
representation feature Darstellungseigenschaft
representation layer Darstellungsebene
representation level Darstellungsebene
representation method Darstellungsverfahren
representation of character Zeichendarstellung
representation symbol Darstellungszeichen
representative Vertreter, Vertriebsbeauftragter
representative number Vertreternummer
representative's visit Vertreterbesuch
reprint Rücksetzen der Druckdatei
reproduce utility routine Kartendopplerroutine
reproducible reproduzierbar
reprogrammable ROM reprogrammierbares ROM
repurchase value Rückkaufswert
request Anforderung, Anfrage, Rückfrage, Wunsch, anfordern, wünschen
request acknowledge system Anforderungsbestätigungssystem
request block Anforderungsblock
request button Rückfrageknopf
request data Anforderungsdaten
request date Anforderungsdatum
requested delivery date Wunschlieferdatum
requested item Bestellanforderungsgegenstand
requested quantity Anforderungsmenge
request for posting Verbuchungsanforderung
request information Anforderungsinformationen
request key Rückfragetaste
request number Anforderungsnummer
request scheme Anforderungsprinzip
request signal Rückfragesignal
request type Anforderungsart
require benötigen, erfordern, fordern
required benötigt, erforderlich, notwendig
required by the system systemnotwendig
requirement Bedarf
requirement calculation Bedarfsauflösung
requirement list Bedarfsliste
requirement planning Bedarfsplanung
requirement report Bedarfsmeldung
requirements data bank Bedarfsdatenbank
requirements report Bedarfsmeldung
requirements report number Bedarfsmeldungsnummer

resulting indicator

requisition voucher Bedarfsmeldungsschein
reregistration document Nacherfassungsbeleg
rerun time Wiederholungszeit
research and development Forschung und Entwicklung
reselection Neuauswahl
resequence neu numerieren
reservation Reservierung, Vormerkung
reservation block Reservierungsblock
reservation center Buchungszentrum
reservation chain Vormerkkette
reservation date Reservierungsdatum, Vormerkdatum
reservation field Vormerkfeld
reservation list Reservierungsübersicht
reservation management Reservierungsverwaltung
reservation monitoring Reservierungsüberwachung
reservation number Reservierungsnummer
reservation quantity Vormerkmenge
reservation record Reservierungssatz
reservation status Reservierungsstatus
reservation type Reservierungskennzeichen
reserve reservieren, vormerken
reserve cheque Ausnahmescheck
reserved vorgemerkt
reserved instruction nicht ausführbare Anweisung
reserved stock Vormerkbestand
reserved word reserviertes Wort
reserve entry Ausnahmeposition
reservoir Behälter, Speicher
reset Rücksetzen, in den Ausgangsmodus zurücksetzen, neu starten, normieren, rücksetzen, rückstellen, zurücksetzen
reset condition Nullstellungszustand
reset key Rückstelltaste
reset pulse Resetsignal
resetting device rücksetzendes Gerät
resetting total field Summenfeld rücksetzen
reset to initial state in den Ausgangsmodus zurücksetzen
residency Residenz
residency percentage Residenzprozentsatz
resident geladen, resident
resident compiler residenter Kompilierer
resident macroassembler residenter Makroassembler
resident part residenter Teil
resident program residentes Programm
residual buffer Restpuffer

residual error probability Restfehlerwahrscheinlichkeit
residual memory Restspeicher
resolution Auflösung, Rasterfeinheit
resolution indicator Rasteranzeige
resolution selector Rasterschalter
resolve auflösen
resonant frequencies Resonanzfrequenzen
resource Einsatzmittel, Ressource
resource allocation Einsatzmittelplanung
resource combination Betriebsmittelkombination
resource lock Betriebsmittelsperre
resource macro Betriebsmittelmakro
resources Betriebsmittel
respect achten
respond antworten
respondent Verklagter
response Antwort
response possibility Antwortmöglichkeit
response time Antwortzeit, Reaktionszeit
responsibility Verantwortung
responsible verantwortlich, zuständig
restart Neubeginn, Neustart, Wiederanlauf, Wiederaufnahme, erneuter Start, neu starten, wiederanfangen
restart arrangement Restartvorkehrung
restart error Restartfehler
restart logic Restartlogik
restate erneut definieren
restoration Rückstellung, Wiederherstellung
restore wiedereinlesen, wiederherstellen, zurückladen
restore cursor Cursor wiederherstellen
restore over überschreiben
restoring files Wiedereinlesen von Dateien
restraining cable Sicherungsschnur
restrict abgrenzen, beschränken, eingrenzen
restricted distribution eingeschränkter Verteiler
restriction Einschränkung, Restriktion
restriction card Begrenzungskarte
restriction option Eingrenzungsmöglichkeit
restructure neustrukturieren
resubmission day Wiedervorlagetag
resubmission period Wiedervorlagezeit
resubmitting Wiedervorlage
result Ergebnis, Resultat, entstehen, erbringen, ergeben, resultieren
result area Ergebnisbereich
result code Ergebnisschlüssel
result document Ergebnisdokument
resulting indicator Ergebnisbezugszahl

result number Ergebnisnummer
result number input Ergebnisnummereingabe
result of check Ergebnis der Prüfung
result of comparison Vergleichsergebnis
result of computation Rechenergebnis
result of handling Bearbeitungsergebnis
result of the count Zählergebnis
result page Ergebnisseite
results high Ergebnis größer
results low Ergebnis kleiner
result statement item Ergebnisposition
result statement version Ergebnisrechnung
retailer Einzelhändler
retail price Endbenutzerpreis, Verkaufspreis
retail trade Einzelhandel
retain beibehalten, halten, weiterbenutzen, zurückhalten
retainer bracket Haltebügel
retainer ring Sicherungsring
retaining screw Befestigungsschraube, Sicherungsschraube
retention Beibehaltung
retentive dicht
retentive area dichter Bereich
retrace zurückverfolgen
retract einziehen
retransfer zurückkopieren
retransmission erneute Übermittlung
retrieval Wiederauffindung, Zugriff
retrieval file Abrufdatei
retrieve abrufen, einlesen, nachholen, zugreifen
retrieve stored print settings Druckeinstellungen einlesen
retroactive effect Rückwirkung
retry Wiederholung, wiederholen
retry operation Operation nochmals ausführen
return Aussprung, Rückkehr, Rücklieferung, ausgeben, zurückkehren
returnable packaging Leihverpackung
returnable packing Leihpackung
return address Rücksprungadresse
return address register Rücksprungadreßregister
return a value Ergebniswert liefern
return branch Rücksprung
return cheque Rückscheck
return code Returncode
return date Rückgabedatum, Rücksendedatum
returned status Rückkehrstatus
return field Rückgabefeld
return function Rücksendefunktion
return information Returninformation
returning error Fehlerzustand dem Programm melden
return jump Rücksprung
return key Returntaste, Rückführtaste, Wagenrücklauftaste
return message Rückaktion
return program Rücksendeprogramm
return the delivery zurückliefern
return ticket Rückschein
return to header Kopfrückzug
return to zero method Rückkehr-zu-Null-Verfahren
return transfer Rücküberweisung
return value Rückgabewert
reuse Wiederverwendung
revaluation Aufwertung, Umbewertung
revaluation account Umbewertungskonto
revaluation discrepancy Umbewertungsdifferenz
revaluation voucher Umbewertungsbeleg
revalue aufwerteten, umwerten
reversal Rückstellung, Umkehr
reverse channel Hilfskanal
reverse charging acceptance Gebührenübernahme
reverse interrupt erzwungene Unterbrechung
reverse line feed Zeilenvorschub rückwärts
reverse polish notation umgekehrte polnische Notation
reverse protect Zeichenschutz für invertierte Zeichen
reverse screen invertierter Bildschirm
reverse video Umkehranzeige, invertierte Bilddarstellung
reversible counter Zweirichtungszähler
revert umkehren
review technique Überprüfungstechnik
revised amount Korrekturbetrag
revision Änderung
revision level Änderungsstand
revision modification Änderungsmitteilung
rewind zurückspulen
rewind key Rückspultaste
rewind with interlock Rückspulen mit Sperre
rheostat Regelwiderstand
rhythm Rhythmus
ribbon Farbband
ribbon cable Flachbandkabel
ribbon cartridge Farbbandkassette
ribbon feed Farbbandtransport
ribbon shield Farbtuchschutzleiste
right rechts
right angle connector Winkelstecker

right hand side rechts
right justified rechtsbündig
right justified margin rechtsbündiger Rand
right justified repeating label rechtsbündiger Wiederholungstext
right justify rechtsbündig formatieren
right margin rechter Rand
rightmost digit am weitesten rechts stehende Ziffer
right shift Rechtsshift, Verschieben nach rechts
rigid cable starres Kabel
rigid conductor starrer Leiter
rigid conduit Leitungsrohr, Stahlpanzerisolierrohr, Stahlpanzerrohr
ring Ring, klingeln
ring buffer Ringpuffer
ring counter Ringzähler
ring indicator Aufrufsignal, akustisches Signal
ripple Brummspannung
rise time Anstiegszeit, Flankenanstiegszeit
rising edge steigende Flanke
risk covering risikodeckend
risk of theft Diebstahlgefahr
roentgen equivalent man Maßeinheit für biologische Strahlungsdosis
roll Rolle, rollen, umschlagen
roll area Rollbereich
roll back Rücksetzen, zurückrollen
rollback attempt Wiederholungsversuch
roll buffer Rollpuffer
roll in zurückspeichern
roll out auslagern
rollover Mehrfachbetätigung
roll over program Verschiebeprogramm
roll scrolling zeilenweises Abrollen
ROM organization Organisation eines Festwertspeichers
room Büro, Platz, Raum, Zimmer
root Stamm, Wurzel
root directory Stammdateiverzeichnis
root element Wurzelelement
root mean square voltage Effektivspannung
root phase Urabschnitt
rotary Impulswahl, Impulswahlverfahren, Wählscheibe
rotary convertor Umrichter
rotary switch Drehschalter
rotate rotieren
rotating amplifier Drehverstärker
rotating electric machine drehende elektrische Maschine
rotating generator drehender Generator
rotating patient table frame Rahmendrehung

rotational delay time Umdrehungswartezeit
rotational latency Drehwartezeit
rotor winding Läuferwicklung
round Runde, Tour, rund, runden
roundabout route Umweg
rounded off gerundet
rounding error Rundungsfehler
round of honor Ehrenrunde
route Führung, Leitweg, Route, Tour, Weg
route control Leitwegsteuerung
route number Tourennummer
routine Routine
routine task Routinearbeit
routing Leitwegsplanung, Netzwerk-Topologie und Wegeauswahlverfahren, Routing, Wegewahl
routing information Leitinformation
routining scope Prüfbereich
row Reihe, Zeile
row number Zeilennummer
row pitch Sprossenteilung
rows per inch Spalten pro Zoll
row wise order zeilenweise
RS232-Interface RS232-Schnittstelle
RS flipflop RS-Flip-Flop
rubber insulated gummiisoliert
rubber plug Gummistecker
ruggedized computer für erschwerte Umweltbedingungen gebauter Computer
rule Regel
ruler Zeilenlineal
ruler change Tabuloränderung
ruler line Tabellierzeile
ruler setting Einstellung im Zeilenlineal
ruling part Regelteil
run Ablauf, Betrieb, Job, Lauf, Verlauf, ablaufen, betreiben, fahren, starten
runaway check Zeitüberschreitungsfehler
run card Laufkarte
run control Ablaufsteuerung
run identification Jobkennung, Jobname
run indicator light Kontrollampe RUN
run length Lauflänge
run library Systemjoblaufbibliotheksdatei
run mode Ablaufmodus, Abspielmodus
run procedure Ablaufbeschreibung, Ablaufschema
run processing Jobverarbeitungssteuerung
run processor Betriebssprachenprozessor
run state Ablaufzustand
runstream Jobeingabestrom
run through durchlaufen, einspielen
runtime Ausführungszeit, Laufzeit

runtime check Laufzeitprüfung
runtime error Laufzeitfehler
runtime library Laufzeitbibliothek
runtime package Laufzeitpaket
runtime system Laufzeitsystem
run unit Verarbeitungsabschnitt
run unit rollback Rücksetzen des Verarbeitungsabschnitts
rural electric power network Überlandleitung
rush current Stromanstieg
rush draft schnelle Ausgabe

S

safe gesichert, sicher
safeguarded transmission mode gesichertes Übermittlungsverfahren
safeguarding point Sicherungspunkt
safekeeping sichern
safe throwover switch Tresorschalter
safety Sicherheit
safety code Schutzcode
safety isolating transformer Trenntransformator
safety measure Sicherheitsmaßnahme
safety officer Sicherheitsverantwortlicher
salaried employees' insurance Angestelltenversicherung
salary Gehalt
sale Umsatz, Verkauf
sales accounting Verkaufsabrechnung
sales area Verkaufsbezirk
sales data Verkaufsdaten
sales department Verkaufsabteilung
sales field Verkaufsfeld
sales group Verkaufsgruppe
sales group code Verkaufsgruppenschlüssel
sales group record Verkaufsgruppensatz
sales info Verkaufsinfo
sales information Verkaufsinformationen
sales information record Verkaufsinformationssatz
sales negotiation Verkaufsverhandlung
sales order Kundenauftrag
sales order net value Nettoauftragswert
sales order number Kundenauftragsnummer
sales order record Kundenauftragssatz
salesperson Vertreter, Vertriebsbeauftragter
sales price list Verkaufspreisliste
sales product Verkaufsartikel, Verkaufsprodukt
sales remark Verkaufsvermerk
sales representative Vertreter, Vertriebsbeauftragter
sales specific verkaufsspezifisch
sales support Vertriebsunterstützung
sales table Verkaufstabelle
sales talk Verkaufsgespräch
sales tax Ausgangssteuer, Umsatzsteuer
sales tax type Ausgangssteuerart
sales text Verkaufstext
sales transaction Verkaufstransaktion
sales unit Verkaufsmengeneinheit
sales value Verkaufswert
sales voucher Verkaufsbeleg
salient pole ausgeprägter Pol
same gleich
sample Beispiel, Muster, Probe
sample and hold Sample and Hold
sample chart Diagrammbeispiel
sample data record Musterdatensatz
sample diagram Diagrammbeispiel
sample formula Beispiel
sample frequency Abtastrate
sample item Musterartikel
sample job Musterjob
sample master Musterstamm
sample master record Musterstammsatz
sample offer Musterangebot
sample program Beispielprogramm
sample record Mustersatz
sample voucher Musterbeleg
sampling Abtastung
sampling control Abtastregelung
sampling date Aufnahmedatum
sampling rate Abtastfrequenz
sandblast sandstrahlen
satellite Satellit
satellite computer Satellitenrechner, Verbundrechner
satellite link Satellitenstrecke, Satellitenverbindung
satellite network Satellitennetz
satisfy befriedigen
saturable core reactor Magnetverstärker
saturate sättigen
saturation Sättigung
save retten, sichern, sparen, speichern, zwischenspeichern
save area Sicherstellungsbereich
save cursor Cursorposition speichern, Schreibmarkenposition speichern
saved job control modules zwischengespeicherte Jobeingabeströme
save operation Sicherung
save procedure Sicherungsprozedur
save set Sicherungsset
savings book balance Sparbuchsaldo
savings deposit Sparbuchung
scalar Skalar
scale Größe, Größenordnung, Staffel, staffeln
scale modifier Präzisionfaktor
scale number Staffelnummer
scale value Staffelwert
scaling circuit Flip-Flop, bistabiler Multivibrator

scan Programmzyklus, abtasten
scan converter Radarsignalumsetzer
scan encoder Abtastungskodierer
scan matrix compare Abtast-Matrixvergleich
scanner Abtasteinrichtung, Abtaster, Scanner
scanner computer Scannercomputer
scanning carriage Abtastwagen
scanning density Zeilendichte
scanning electronic microscope Rasterelektronenmikroskop
scanning line Abtastzeile
scanning line frequency Zeilenabtastfrequenz
scanning line period Zeilenabtastzeit
scanning pitch Zeilenteilung
scanning speed at reception Aufzeichnungsgeschwindigkeit
scanning speed at transmission Abtastgeschwindigkeit
scanning spot at reception Aufzeichnungspunkt
scanning spot at transmission Abtastpunkt
scanning track direction Abtastrichtung
scan plane Scanebene
scan rate Antennenumlaufgeschwindigkeit
scan time Abtastzeit, Zykluszeit
scan unit Abfrageschaltung
scatter gram value Streuungsmaß
scatter plot Steuerdiagramm
scatter read gestreut lesen
schedule Raster, Terminplan, disponieren, terminieren
schedule code Rasterkennzeichen
scheduled maintenance planmäßige Wartung
scheduled stocktaking Stichtaginventur
scheduled time of arrival planmäßige Ankunft
scheduled time of departure planmäßige Abfahrt, planmäßiger Start
schedule file Rasterdatei
schedule level Dispositionsstufe
scheduler Disponent
scheduling Jobablaufplanung
scheduling aid Dispositionshilfe
scheduling code Dispositionsmerkmal
scheduling data Dispositionsdaten
scheduling office Dispositionsstelle
scheduling step Dispositionsstufe
schematic representation schematische Darstellung
scheme Gesamtschema der Datenbank, Schema
scheme language Schemasprache
schottky-barrier diode Schottky-Diode
science Wissenschaft

scientific accelerator module beschleunigte Gleitpunktarithmetik
scientific modeling wissenschaftliche Kalkulationsmodelle
scientific notation wissenschaftliche Darstellung, wissenschaftliche Zahlendarstellung
scope Anwendungsbereich, Geltungsbereich, Rahmen, Ziel
scope terminator Bereichsabschlußzeichen
scored card Kurzlochkarte
scrap Schrott, verschrotten
scrap value Schrottwert
scratch character Schmierzeichen
scratch file Arbeitsdatei, temporäre Datei
scratch pad Notizblock
scratch pad area Pufferbereich
scratchpad memory Notizblock-Speicher
screen Anzeige, Bildschirm, Menü, überwachen
screen alignment display Anzeige zur Bildschirmjustierung
screen background Bildschirmhintergrund
screen brightness Bildschirmhelligkeit
screen bypass Bildschirmumgehungspuffer
screen cleaner Bildschirmreiniger
screen clearing procedure Bildschirmlöschung
screen copy Ausdruck des Bildschirminhalts, Bildschirmausdruck, Bildschirmduplikat
screen display Anzeige, Bildschirmanzeige
screen dump facility Bildschirmdruckausgabe
screen enquiry Bildschirmabfrage
screen field Bildschirmfeld
screen format Bildaufbau, Bildschirmformat, Bildschirmlayout, Bildschirmmaske
screen format coordinator Maskenkoordinator, Maskenverwaltungsprogramm
screen format editor Maskenaufbereitungsprogramm
screen format generator Maskengenerator
screen format program Maskenaufbereitungsprogramm
screen format service maskenspezifisches Dienstprogramm
screen group Bildgruppe
screen group selection Bildgruppenauswahl
screen image Bildschirmabbild
screen inquiry Bildschirmabfrage
screen layout Bildaufbau, Bildgestaltung, Bildschirmlayout
screen line Bildschirmzeile
screen mask Bildschirmbild, Bildschirmmaske
screen message Bildschirmnachricht
screen mode Bildschirmmodus

screen modification Bildmodifikation, Bildschirmmodifikation
screen of information Bildschirminhalt
screen page Bildschirmseite
screen page number Bildschirmseitennummer
screen print Bildschirmausdruck
screen prompt Anweisung auf dem Bildschirm
screen saver Dunkelschaltung, automatische Bildschirmabschaltung
screen selection Bildauswahl
screen sequence Bildfolge
screen size Bildschirmgröße, Bildumfang
screen symbol Bildschirmsymbol
screen terminal Bildschirmterminal
screen width Bildschirmbreite
screen window Bildausschnitt
screw Schraube, schrauben
screw drive Spindel
screwdriver Schraubenzieher
scroll verrollen, verschieben
scroll down nach unten rollen
scrolling Bilddurchlauf, Verschieben
scrolling function Scrollingfunktion
scrolling region Bilddurchlaufbereich
scroll mode Bilddurchlaufmodus
scroll up nach oben rollen
sculptured key array ergonomische Tastenanordnung
seal Dichtung
seal bearing Dichtlager
search Suche, aufsuchen, suchen
search argument Suchargument, Suchbegriff
search for catchwords Schlagwortsuche
search logic Suchlogik
search-logical suchlogisch
search mask Suchmaske
search query Suchfrage
search routine Suchroutine
search run Suchlauf
search string Sachzeichenfolge, Suchfolge
search time Suchzeit
search tree Suchbaum
search tree procedure Suchbaumverfahren
search value Suchbegriff
search word Suchbegriff
seasonal saisonal
second Sekunde, zweite
secondary Folgesteuerung, sekundär
secondary boot program sekundäres Ladeprogramm, zweite Ladestufe
secondary clear to send zweite Sendebereitschaft
secondary control Folgesteuerung

secondary file Sekundärdatei
secondary function Nebenfunktion
secondary index Sekundärindex
secondary input Sekundäreingabe
secondary station Folgestation
secondary storage area Sekundärspeicherbereich
secondary surveillance radar Sekundär-Rundsichtradar
second normal form zweite Normalform
second order statistics Kovarianzmatrix
second source Zweitanbieter
second stacker zweites Ausgabefach
section Abschnitt, Arbeitsgebiet
section file Abschnittsdatei
section number Abschnittsnummer
sector Branche, Sektor
sector end Sektorende
sector number Sektornummer
sector number register Sektornummernregister
sector of a circle Kreisausschnitt
sector sequence Sektorfolge
sectors per track Sektoren pro Spur
secure sichern, sicherstellen
securing Absicherung
securities Wertpapiere
Securities and Exchange Commission amerikanische Börsenaufsicht
security Geheimhaltung, Sicherheit
security arrangements Sicherungsvereinbarung
security auditing Sicherheitsprüfung
security feature Sicherheitsvorrichtung
security measures Sicherheitsvorkehrungen
see ersehen
see appendix siehe Anhang
seed Ausgangszahl
see figure siehe Abbildung
seek error Positionierfehler, Zugriffsfehler
seek time Positionierzeit
see section siehe Abschnitt
segment Segment, aufteilen, segmentieren
segment address register Segmentadreßregister
segmentation Aufteilung, Unterteilung, Zerstückelung
segmentation file Zerlegungsdatei
segment beginning Segmentanfang
segment category Segmenttyp
segment category selection Segmentypenauswahl
segment control Segmentsteuerung
segment control byte Segmentsteuerbyte
segment control flag Segmentsteuerkennzeichen

segment definition

segment definition Segmentdefinition
segment descriptor Segmentbeschreibung
segment descriptor block Segmentbeschreibungsblock
segment descriptor table Segmentbeschreibungstabelle, Segmenttabelle
segment format Segmentformat
segment header Segmentkopf
segment identification Segmentkennung
segmenting Fragmentierung
segment key Segmentschlüssel
segment length Segmentlänge
segment level Segmentstufe
segment library Segmentbibliothek
segment prefix Segmentpräfix
segment prefix table Segmentpräfixtabelle
segment sequence Segmentreihenfolge
segments in message file Segmente in der Meldungsdatei
segment start Segmentanfang
segment text Segmenttext
segment type Segmentart, Segmentidentifikation, Segmenttyp
select anwählen, aussuchen, auswählen, markieren, selektieren, wählen
select block symbol Blockauswahlsymbol
select character set Zeichensatz auswählen
selected drive aktuelles Laufwerk, gewähltes Laufwerk
selected line gewählte Zeile
select graphic rendition grafische Darstellung wählen
selecting Empfangsaufruf
selecting features Auswählen von Merkmalen
selecting mode Aufrufbetrieb
selecting signals Wählzeichenfolge
selection Auswahl, Selektion, Wahl
selection algorithm Auswahlalgorithmus
selection alternative Auswahlalternative
selection card Auswahlkarte, Selektionskarte
selection condition Selektionsbedingung
selection control Auswahlsteuerung
selection criterion Auswahlkriterium, Selektionskriterium
selection date Selektionsdatum
selection digit Auswahlziffer
selection end Auswahlende, Selektionsende
selection feature Selektionsmerkmal
selection field Selektionsfeld
selection flag Selektionskennzeichen
selection group Selektionsgruppe
selection input Selektionseingabe

selection instruction Selektionsanweisung, Wahlaufforderung
selection key word Auswahlschlüsselwort
selection letter Selektionsbrief
selection level Auswahlstufe
selection limit Selektionsgrenze
selection list Auswahlliste
selection marker Auswahlkennzeichen
selection menu Auswahlmenü
selection mode Auswahlmodus
selection node Auswahlknoten
selection number Auswahlnummer
selection of files Dateiauswahl
selection of key words Schlagwortauswahl
selection of suppliers Lieferantenauswahl
selection of variables Variablenselektion
selection option Auswahlmöglichkeit, Selektionsmöglichkeit
selection page Auswahlseite
selection parameter Auswahlparameter
selection program Selektionsprogramm
selection quantity Auswahlmenge
selection report group Auswahlleiste
selection restriction Selektionsrestriktion
selection run Selektionslauf
selection screen Selektionsbild
selection signal Wählzeichen
selection signal sequence Wählzeichenfolge
selection specification Auswahlspezifikation
selection statement Selektionsangabe
selection table Auswahltabelle
selection term Auswahlbegriff, Selektionsbegriff
selection vector Auswahlvektor
selective selektiv
selective core memory dump Kernspeicherauszug
selective criterion Auswahlkriterium
select mark Selektiermarke
select mode Betriebsart auswählen
selector Auswahlvorrichtung
selector control card Selektorkarte
selector facility Wählereinrichtung
selector switch Wahlschalter
select range Auswahlbereich, Bereich, Selektierbereich
select symbol Auswahlsymbol
self-adjusting system selbsteinstellendes System
self-checking Selbstprüfung
self-chosen selbstgewählt
self-correcting selbstkorrigierend
selfdefined in sich definiert

self-describing selbsterklärend
self-diagnosed problem durch Selbsttest festgestelltes Problem
self-diagnostic Selbsttest
self-diagnostics Selbsttest
self-manufactured part Eigenfertigungsteil
self-paced instruction course Selbststudienkurs
self-searching selbstsuchend
self-service centre Selbstbedienungszentrum
selftest Selbstdiagnose
selftest device Testlaufeinrichtung
sell verkaufen
seller Verkäufer
selling price Verkaufspreis
selling price calculation Preisfindung
selling price unit Verkaufspreiseinheit
selling rate Briefkurs
semaphor Semaphor
semiautomatic system halbautomatisches System
semi-closed system halbgeschlossenes System
semiconductor Halbleiter
semiconductor amplifier Halbleiterverstärker
semiconductor device Halbleiterbauelement
semiconductor diode Halbleiterdiode
semiconductor modulator Halbleitermodulator
semiconductor rectifier Halbleitergleichrichter
semiconductor relay Halbleiterrelais
semiconductor resistor Halbleiterwiderstand
semiconductor storage Halbleiterspeicher
semiconductor switch Halbleiterschalter
semiconductor technology Halbleitertechnologie
semi-finished material Halbzeug
send absenden, senden, versenden
send buffer Sendepuffer
send data Sendedaten
sender Absender, Sender
sender identification Senderidentifikation
sender marker Absenderkennzeichnung
sender of the internal message Aktionsabsender
send off absenden
send only password Kennwort »nur Senden«
send/receive Sende-/Empfangs-
send receive mode Übertragungs-/Empfangsmodus
send sequence number Sendefolgenummer
send state variable Sendefolgezähler
senior Senior
sense Sinn
sense byte Zustandsbyte
sense command Abfragebefehl

sense data Zustandsdaten
sensible sinnvoll, vernünftig
sensing contact Abfühlkontakt
sensing head Abtastkopf
sensor Radarantenne, Sensor
sensor processor Radarantennenprozessor
sensor receiver Radarantennenempfänger
sensor receiver and processor Radarantennenempfänger und -prozessor
sentence parser Satzanalysesystem
separate gesondert, separat, separieren, trennen
separate clock unit Synchronadapter
separation Trennen, Trennung
separation accuracy Trenngenauigkeit
separation character definition Trennerdefinition
separation code Trenncode
separator Trennzeichen
sequence Folge, Reihenfolge, Sequenz, Sortierfolge
sequence address Folgeadresse
sequence chain Ablaufkette
sequence check control card Steuerkarte für Folgekontrolle
sequence checking routine Folgeprüfprogramm
sequence counter Programmschrittzähler
sequence error Folgefehler
sequence file Sequenzdatei
sequence file name Sequenzdateiname
sequence input Folgeeingabe
sequence name Sequenzname
sequence number Folgenummer
sequence number generator Laufnummerngeber
sequence of charts Bildablauf
sequence of functions Funktionsablauf
sequence of instructions Befehlsfolge
sequence of screens Bildablauf
sequence of slides Bildablauf
sequence screen Folgebildschirm
sequence statement Folgeanweisung
sequence string Ordnungsfolge
sequence transaction code Folgetransaktionscode
sequencing sequentialisieren
sequencing hold Folgesuspendierung
sequential sequentiell
sequential access sequentieller Zugriff
sequential access method sequentielle Zugriffsmethode, sequentieller Zugriff
sequential access storage digitaler Speicher mit sequentiellem Zugriff

187

sequential circuit Schaltwerk
sequential control Folgesteuerungsfunktion
sequential data table sequentielle Datentabelle
sequential file sequentielle Datei
sequential file organization sequentielle Dateiorganisation
sequential logic sequentielle Logik, sequentielle Logikschaltung
sequential operation sequentielle Arbeitsweise
sequential program area aufeinanderfolgender Programmbereich
sequential program scan lineare Programmabtastung
sequential shift register sequentielles Schieberegister
sequential storage sequentieller Speicher
serial seriell
serial access serieller Zugriff
serial adder serieller Addierer
serial character serielles Zeichen
serial communication controller Controller für serielle Kommunikation, serielle Schnittstellensteuerung
serial data serielle Daten
serial input/output serielle Ein-/Ausgabe
serialization Serialisierung
serialization name Serialisierungsname
serial letter Serienbrief
serial letter command Serienbriefauftrag
serial letter creation Serienbrieferstellung
serial letter demand Serienbriefanforderung
serial line serielle Verbindung
serial line unit serielle Leitungseinheit
serial number Seriennummer
serial printer Seriendrucker
serial printer interface serielle Druckerschnittstelle
serial storage Speicher mit seriellem Speicherzugriff
serial transmission Serienübergabe, serielle Übertragung
series Reihe, Serie
series circuit Serienstromkreis
series contact in Reihe geschaltete Kontakte
series of bell tones mehrere Tastatursignale
series reactor Vorschaltdrossel
serve dienen, servieren
service Dienst, Dienstleistung, Wartung
service access point Dienstzugangspunkt
service capability Dienstfähigkeit
service computing center Dienstleistungsrechenzentrum
service contract Serviceabkommen

service data unit Dienstdateneinheit
service engineer Kundendiensttechniker
service function Servicefunktion
service off-time Dienstunterbrechungsdauer
service primitive Dienstprimitiv
service provider Dienstanbieter, Diensterbringer
service request Dienstanforderung
service routine Dienstprogramm
services diskette Systemdienstdiskette
services enterprise Dienstleistungsbetrieb
service technician Kundendiensttechniker
service user Dienstbenutzer
servicing Bedienung, bedienen
servicing contract Wartungsvertrag
servo axis Achse des Hilfsmotors
servo axis module Servosteuerungs-Modul
servo board Regelplatine
servo clamp Klemme des Hilfsmotors
servo-controlled system Nachlaufregelsystem
servo controller Folgesteuerkette
servo-driven potentiometer Nachlaufpotentiometer
servomechanism Nachlaufwerk
servomotor Hilfsmotor, Stellmotor
servosystem Folgesteuerungssystem
session Anschaltdauer, Sitzung
session address Sitzungsadresse
session begin Sessionbeginn
session connection Sitzungsverbindung
session continuation Sitzungsfortsetzung
session control Sitzungssteuerung
session layer Kommunikationssteuerungsschicht, Sitzungsschicht
session log Sitzungsprotokoll
session structure Sitzungsaufbau
session variable Sessionvariable
set Gruppe, Menge, einstellen, setzen
set as well mitsetzen
set asynchronous balanced mode Aufforderung zum Übergang in gleichberechtigten Asynchronbetrieb
set asynchronous response mode Aufforderung zum Übergang in asynchronen Antwortbetrieb
set bit Bit setzen
set date and time Eingeben von Datum und Zeit
set foot betreten
set mode Betriebsart wählen, Modus auswählen
set of arrow keys Pfeiltastenblock
set of backup diskettes Satz von Sicherungsdisketten, Sicherungsdiskettenset

set of key words Schlagwortmenge
set order interne logische Set-Ordnung
set program mask Programmaske setzen (Befehl)
set relation Set-Beziehung, in Beziehung setzen
sets of data Datensätze
setting Anzeige, Einstellung
setting margin Einstellung der Schreibränder
setting regulator Einstellregler
setting treshold Polarisationsschwelle
settle abrechnen, verrechnen
settlement Abrechnung, Verrechnung, Verrechnungsverfahren
settlement date Abrechnungsdatum, Abrechnungstermin
settlement marker Verrechnungskennzeichen
settlement of a bill Wechselabrechnung
settlement of freight charges Frachtkostenabrechnung
settlement of invoice Fakturaverrechnung
settlement of order Auftragsverrechnung
settlement period Abrechnungszeitraum, Regulierungsdauer, Zieltage
settlement type Abrechnungsart
set to setzen auf
set top and bottom margin oberen und unteren Rand festlegen
set transmit state Übertragungsstatus einstellen
set up Betriebsmodus, Einrichtung, Einstellungen ändern, anlegen, aufgebaut, aufsetzen, einrichten, errichten
set up costs Rüstkosten
set up display Betriebsmodusanzeige
set up feature Betriebsmodusmerkmal
set up field Betriebsmodusanzeige
set up marker Aufsetzkennzeichen
set up memory Betriebsmodusspeicher
set up mode Auswahlmodus, Betriebsmodus
set up option Betriebsmoduseinstellung
set up point Aufsetzpunkt
set up reset Betriebsmodus rücksetzen
set up save Betriebsmodus speichern
set up screen Auswahlbild
set up selection Betriebsmoduseinstellung
several times mehrmals
severity Fehlergrad
shade Schatten
shaded-pole motor Spaltpolmotor
shaded symbol unterlegtes Symbol
shade print Schattendruck
shaft coupler Wellenkupplung
shaft rotation Wellendrehung
shaft support Stützlager, Wellenlager

shank Kegel
shank of the shaft drive pin Kegel des Wellenstumpfs
share Anteil, teilen
shareability Mitbenutzbarkeit
shareable image gemeinsam nutzbares Programm
shared access gemeinsamer Zugriff
shared access unit Aufteilungseinheit für EA-Geräte
shared code capability gemeinsam benutzbares Coding
shared direct memory access gleichzeitiger direkter Speicherzugriff
shared line printer operation gemeinsamer Zugriff auf den Zeilendrucker
shared mass storage Massenspeicher im Mehrfachzugriff
shared memory interface Speicherzuordnungseinheit
shared peripheral interface Mehrkanalanschlußeinheit
shared resource gemeinsame Betriebsmittel
shared terminal operation gemeinsamer Zugriff auf ein Terminal
sheated cable ummanteltes Kabel
sheated conductor ummantelter Leiter
sheet Einzelblatt
sheet chaining Blattkettung
sheet feeder Einzelblatteinzug, Einzelblattzufuhreinheit, Einzelblattzufuhrgerät
sheet feeding Einzelblatteinzug
sheet feeding device Einzelblattzufuhrgerät
sheet feeding unit Einzelblattzufuhreinheit
sheet identifier Blattkennzeichen
sheet metal case Blechgehäuse
shelf life Lagerfähigkeit
shell type transformer Manteltransformator
sherardizing Sherardisieren
shield Abschirmung, Schild, abschirmen
shielded conduit bewehrter Kanal
shielded signal cable abgeschirmtes Datenkabel, isoliertes Datenkabel
shielded terminal ummantelte Klemme
shield plate Bodenplatte
shift schieben, shiften, verschieben
shift data Schiebedaten
shifted character umgeschaltete Belegung einer Taste
shift from word control Abgabe-Stellenversetzung
shifting down nach unten rollen
shifting up nach oben rollen

shift instruction Shiftbefehl
shift key Umschalttaste
shift left Verschieben nach links, nach links verschieben
shift lock Umschaltfeststeller, Umschaltfeststelltaste, Zeichen umschalten
shift mode Umschaltmodus
shift operation Schiebeoperation
shift recovery Rückwärtswiederherstellung
shift register Schieberegister
shift right Verschieben nach rechts, nach rechts verschieben
shift word Wort verschieben
ship versenden
shipment Versand
shipment label Versandkennzeichen
shipping address Lieferanschrift
shipping block Transportrahmen
shipping box Versandkarton
shock Schlag, Schock, elektrischer Schlag
shock hazard Gefahr eines Schlages
shock wave Stoßwelle
shock wave generation Stoßwellenerzeugung
shock wave generator Stoßwellengenerator
shock wave release Stoßwellenauslösung
shock wave release handswitch Handtaster, Handtaster für Stoßwellenauslösung
shock wave release switch Stoßwellenauslösetaste
short kurz
short circuit Kurzschluß
short circuit plug Kurzschlußstecker
short cut Kurzform
short dialog Kurzdialog
shortfall Deckung, Fehlbestand, Fehlmenge, Unterdeckung
shortfall quantity Unterdeckungsmenge
shortfall record Unterdeckungssatz
short form Kurz-, Kurzform
short form address Kurzadresse
short format Kurz-
shorthand Kurz-
shorthand macro Abkürzung
short information Kurzinformation
short key Kurzschlüssel
short message Kurzbrief
short name Kurzbezeichnung
short range modem Nahbereichsmodem
short term kurzfristig
short term filing Kurzzeitarchivierung
short term monitoring Kurzzeitüberwachung
short time storage Kurzspeicher
shot Schuß

shot release Schußauslösung
shove out ausschieben
show anzeigen, aufweisen, zeigen
shunt Nebenschluß, im Nebenschluß anlegen
shunt reactor Nebeninduktivität
shutdown Ausschalten des Systems, abschalten, herunterfahren
shutdown error Fehler beim Herunterfahren, Shutdown-Fehler
shutdown error message Shutdown-Fehlermeldung
shutdown phase Shutdown-Phase
shutdown signal Abschaltsignal
shutting down System anhalten
sight Sicht, Sichtfenster
sight verification Sichtprüfung
sigma memory Resultataddition
sign Vorzeichen, Vorzeichensymbol
signal Signal
signal cable Signalkabel
signal diode Signaldiode
signal distance Hamming-Abstand
signal distribution board Signalverteilerplatte
signal element Schritt
signal element timing Schrittakt
signal generator Signalgenerator
signal ground Signalerde, Signalmasse
signaling information Signalisierungsinformation
signal level Impulsebene
signal light Signallicht
signal line Signalleitung
signal receiver Signalempfänger
signal time Länge des Signals
sign bit Vorzeichenbit
sign handling Vorzeichenbearbeitung
significance Bedeutung
significant signifikant, wertig
signify bedeuten
sign on Anwählen des Systems
signon indication Signon-Angabe
silence phoneme Pausenphonem
silencing Geräuschdämpfung
silica gel Silikagel
silicon disk Pseudofloppy, virtuelle Platte, virtuelles Laufwerk
Silicon Valley Siliziumtal
silicon wafer Siliziumplättchen
silkscreen marking Siebdruck
similar analog, gleichartig, ähnlich
simple einfach
simplex simplex

simplex communication Richtungsverkehr, Simplexverkehr
simplex mode Simplexbetrieb
simplex operation Richtungsbetrieb
simplex transmission Richtungsbetrieb
simplification Vereinfachung
simplification rule Vereinfachungsregel
simplify erleichtern, vereinfachen
simply einfach
simulate simulieren
simulated amortization Abschreibungssimulation
simulated depreciation Abschreibungssimulation
simulation Simulation
simulation base value Simulationsbasiswert
simulation data Simulationsdaten
simulation equipment Nachbildungsgerät
simulation of the public switching center Vermittlungssimulation
simulation purpose Simulationszweck
simulation status Simulationsstatus
simulation value Simulationswert
simulator Simulator
simultaneous gleichzeitig, simultan
simultaneous execution Simultanablauf
simultaneous operation Simultanbetrieb
simultaneous run Simultanlauf
simultaneous time Simultanzeit
since da
single alleine, einfach, einzel, einzeln
single address instruction Einadreß-Befehl
single address machine Einadreß-Maschine
single area Einzelbereich
single bit error Ein-Bit-Fehler
single board computer Einplatinencomputer, Einplatinenrechner
single buffering Einzelpufferung
single byte interleaved mit Byteversatz
single character einstellig
single check Einzelnachweis
single core cable Einleiterkabel
single cycle Einzelgang
single density einfache Dichte, einfache Schreibdichte
single display Einzelanzeige
single document Einzelbeleg
single feeder Vereinzeler
single feed function Vereinzelungsfunktion
single feed instruction Vereinzelungsbefehl
single feed job Vereinzelungsauftrag
single feed motor Vereinzelungsmotor
single feed process Vereinzelungsvorgang
single feed tape Vereinzelungsband
single file Einfachdatei
single form chute Einzelformulareinzug
single head running gear Einkopflaufwerk
single item display Einzelpositionsanzeige
single item ejection Einzelpostenvorschub
single key sort Sortieren mit einem Schlüssel
single key stroke Einzelanschlag
single letter Einzelbrief
single level einstufig
single level bill of materials Baukastenstückliste
single line Einzelzeile
single message Einzelmitteilung
single page Einzelseite
single partition Einzelpartition
single phase einphasig
single phase motor Einphasenmotor
single phase power einphasiger Stromanschluß
single phase transformer Einphasentransformator
single position Einzelposition
single precision einfache Genauigkeit
single quote Hochkomma
single record Einzelsatz
single scan box execution Ausführung eines Boxbefehls bei einmaliger Abtastung
single sheet Einzelblatt, Einzelformular
single sheet feeder Einzelblatteinzug
single sheet feeding Einzelblattzufuhr
single sheet paper Einzelblattpapier
single shot pulse Einzelimpuls
single shot timer monostabiles Zeitglied
single sideband Einseitenband
single sided einseitig beschreibbar
single sided diskette einseitige Diskette
single specification Einzelangabe
single step Einzelschritt
single step mode Einzelgang
single step posting Einzelschrittverbuchung
single step procedure Einzelschrittverfahren
single transitition time einfacher Übergang
single use Einzelbenutzung
single user print spooler Druckerspooler für Einzelbenutzer
single user system Einplatz-System
single value einfacher Wert
single volume file Einzelpostendatei
single voucher Einzelbeleg
single width line Zeile mit einfach breiten Zeichen
sink sinken
sister company Schwestergesellschaft

site Anlage, Installation
site consideration Wahl des Aufstellungsortes
site internal anlagenintern
site layout Anlagenplanung
site number Anlagennummer
site specific anlagenspezifisch
situation Situation
size Größe
size of program Programmgröße
sizing Dimensionierung
skeleton sales order Rahmenauftrag
sketch skizzieren, zeichnen
skew Schräglauf
skid plate Einschubplatte
skilful geschickt
skill Erfahrung, Geschick
skilled erfahren
skip übergehen, überspringen
skip function Sprungfunktion
skip instruction Überspringbefehl
skip key Sprungtaste
skip through durchblättern
skirting Scheuerleiste
slack size Schlupfgröße
slash Schrägstrich
slave computer Satellitenrechner
slave monitor Hilfsbildschirm
slave station Tochterstation
slave system Untersystem
slice Scheibe
slide Bild, gleiten
slide group Bildgruppe
slide layout Bildaufbau, Bildgestaltung
slide rule Rechenschieber
sliding average price Verrechnungspreis
slight gering
slip ring Schleifring
slip ring motor Schleifringmotor
slo blo träge
slope Flanke
slot Einschub, Steckplatz
slow langsam
slow and dead stock Lagerhüter
slowing-down time Nachlaufzeit
small gering, klein
small computer Kleincomputer
small computer system Kleinrechner
small power transformer Kleinleistungstransformator
small punch card Kleinlochkarte
small scale integration niedriger Integrationsgrad
smoothing factor Glättungsfaktor

smoothness Weichheit
smooth scroll weicher Bilddurchlauf, weicher Bildlauf
snap ring retainer Sicherungsringaufnahme
snap switch Federschalter, Schnappschalter
society Gesellschaft
socket Anschluß, Buchse, Fassung, Lampenfassung, Netzanschluß, Sockel, Steckdose
soft sectored softsektoriert
software Software
software characteristic Software-Identifizierungsmerkmal
software compatible softwarekompatibel
software component Softwarekomponente
software configuration Softwarekonfiguration
software controlled softwaregesteuert, vom Programm gesteuert
software development process Software-Entwicklungsverfahren
software development system Software-Entwicklungssystem
software engineering Softwareentwicklung
software error Softwarefehler
software function Softwarefunktion
software interface Programmschnittstelle
software interrupt programmgesteuerte Unterbrechung, programmgesteuerter Interrupt, softwaregesteuerter Interrupt
software mailbox Programmverständigungsblock
software maintenance package Softwarepflegepaket
software message Softwaremeldung
software package Softwarepaket
software performance report Softwarefehlerbericht
software problem report Fehlerbericht für Software
software product Softwareprodukt
software product description Softwareproduktbeschreibung
software related softwarebezogen
software routine Programmroutine
software side Softwareseite
software switch Programmschalter
software technique Programmiertechnik
software tool Softwarewerkzeug
software version Softwareversion
solar cell Solarzelle, Sonnenzelle
solder Lötzinn, löten
soldered connector gelötete Verbindung
soldering iron Lötkolben
soldering lug Lötfahne

solderless connector Klemmvorrichtung für nichtgelötete Drahtverbindungen
solderless wrapped connector lötfreie Wickelverbindung
solder mask Lötmaske
solely einzig, lediglich
solenoid operated valve Magnetventil
solid conductor Volleiter, fester Leiter, massiver Leiter
solid core insulator fester Isolator
solid laser Feststofflaser
solid state circuit Festkörperschaltung
solid state device transistorbestücktes Gerät
solid state relay Halbleiterrelais
solid wire Volldraht
solvent Lösungsmittel
son Sohn
sonar Sonar
sophisticated hochentwickelt
sort Art, Sortierung, sortieren
sort break Sortierbruch
sort code Sortierschlüssel
sort control record Sortiersteuersatz
sort criterion Sortierkriterium
sort direction Sortierrichtung
sort error Sortierfehler
sort field Sortierfeld
sort file Sortierdatei
sort information Sortierinformation
sorting drawer Sortierfach
sorting term Ordnungsbegriff, Sortierbegriff
sorting time Sortierzeit
sort instruction Sortieranweisung
sort notion Sortierbegriff
sort possibility Sortiermöglichkeit
sort procedure Sortiervorgang
sort program Sortierprogramm
sort program switch Sortierweiche
sort run Sortierlauf
sort sequence Sortierfolge
sort specification Sortierspezifikation
sound Geräusch, Klang, Ton, fundiert, klingen, vernünftig
sound feature Klangmerkmal
sounding the buzzer Signal ausgeben
sound representation Klangdarstellung
sound system Klangsystem
source Quelle, Source
source address Quelladresse
source address register Quelladreßregister
source archive number Quellarchivnummer
source area Quellbereich
source buffer Quellpuffer

source byte Quellbyte
source code Quellcode
source code control system System zur Quellcodeverwaltung
source code data carrier Quellcodedatenträger
source code file Quellcodedatei
source code unit Quellcodeelement
source data Quelldaten
source deck Quelldeck
source device Quellgerät
source device number Quellgerätenummer
source disc Quellplatte
source diskette Ausgangsdiskette, Originaldiskette
source document Erfassungsbeleg, Erfassungsliste, Originalbeleg, Urbeleg
source drive Ausgangslaufwerk
source file Ausgangsdatei, Quelldatei
source file list Quelldateiliste
source format file Quellformatdatei
source impedance Quellimpedanz
source language Quellsprache
source library Quellbibliothek
source name Quellname
source of error Fehlerquelle, Fehlerursache
source of supply Lieferbeziehung
source operand Quelloperand
source pack serial number Quellarchivnummer
source position Quellposition
source program Primärprogramm, Quellprogramm
source program library Quellprogrammbibliothek
source record Quellsatz
source segment Quellsegment
source statement Quellstatement
source text Quellcode
source text file Quellcodedatei
source voucher Urbeleg
space Leerzeichen, Platz, Raum, Zwischenraum
space back rückschalten
space bar Leertaste
space capacity Speicherplatz
space-charge-controlled tube Raumladungsröhre
space-charge-limited device raumladungsbegrenztes Gerät
space compression Leerzeichenkomprimierung
space compression mode Leerzeichenkomprimierungsmodus
space condition Raumbedingung

spacecraft navigation Raumschiff-Navigation
space expand key Leerschritterweiterungstaste
space key Leerzeichentaste
space reasons Platzgründe
space saving platzsparend
spare Ersatzteil
spare part Ersatzteil, Reparaturteil
speak sprechen
speaker Lautsprecher
special Sonder-, besonders, speziell
special accounting period Sonderbuchungsperiode
special agreement Nebenabrede, besondere Vereinbarung
special balance Sondersaldo
special case Ausnahmefall, Sonderfall
special character Sonderzeichen, Sonderzeichen
special character function Sonderzeichenfunktion
special character table Sonderzeichentabelle
special code Sonderschlüssel
special condition Sonderkondition
special depreciation Sonderabschreibung
special depreciation code Sonderabschreibungsschlüssel
special feature Besonderheit
special flag Sonderkennzeichen
special form Sonderform
special function Sonderfunktion
special function key Sonderfunktionstaste
special general ledger Sonderhauptbuch
special general ledger account Sonderhauptbuchkonto
special general ledger balance Sonderhauptbuchsaldo
special general ledger field Sonderhauptbuchfeld
special general ledger posting Sonderhauptbuchung
special general ledger turnover field Sonderhauptbuchumsatzfeld
special graphics Grafiksonderzeichen
special interest committee Sonderausschuß
special inventory Sonderbestand
special inventory file Gebindedatei
special inventory marker Gebindekennzeichen
special inventory master record Gebindestammsatz
special inventory record Gebindesatz
special inventory remark Gebindevermerk
special inventory segment Gebindesegment
special inventory type Gebindeart

specialist area Fachbereich
specialist department Fachabteilung
specialist use Fachnutzung
special key Sondertaste, Spezialtaste
special list Sonderliste
special material Sondermaterial
special position Sonderstellung
special posting Sonderbuchung
special program Sonderprogramm
special quote character Begrenzungszeichen
special rate Sonderkurs
special record Spezialsatz
special regulation Sonderregelung
special status Sonderstatus
special term Sonderkondition
special text Sondertext
special treatment Sonderbehandlung
special treatment parameter Sonderbehandlungsparameter
special turnover Sonderumsatz
special use besondere Funktion
special voucher type Sonderbelegart
specific spezifisch
specification Angabe, Spezifikation, Spezifizierung, technische Daten
specification of amount posted Buchungsbetragsangabe
specify angeben, bezeichnen, spezifizieren, vorschreiben
specimen Probe, Versuchsteil
spectacular eklatant
speech module Sprachmodul
speech processor Sprachprozessor
speech recognition Spracherkennung
speech sound Sprachklang
speech synthesis Sprachsynthese
speech synthesizer Sprachsynthesizer
speech waveform Sprachwellenform
speed Baudrate, Geschwindigkeit, Schnelligkeit
speed control Geschwindigkeitsregelung
speed distortion Drehzahlverzerrung
speed in using files schnelle Zugriffszeit auf Dateien
speed of operation Verarbeitungsgeschwindigkeit
spill verschütten
spindle Spindel
spindle hole Spindelöffnung
splice Spleiße, Spleißstelle, Spleißung
split aufteilen, splitten
split phase motor Einphasenmotor mit Anlaßhilfsphase
split screen geteilter Bildschirm

splitting aufspalten
spoken output Sprachausgabe
spoken response Sprachausgabe
spool spoolen, spulen
spool component Spoolkomponente
spooler Spooler
spread card feature Kompaktkarteneinrichtung
spread out ausspreizen
spreadsheet Arbeitsblatt, Tabellenkalkulation
spreadsheet program Kalkulationsprogramm, Tabellenkalkulation, Zahlenverwaltungsprogramm
sprocket Zahnrad
sprocket hole Lochung, Transportloch
square Quadrat
square bracket eckige Klammer
square plug quadratischer Stecker
square root Quadratwurzel
square wave generator Rechteckgenerator
squirrel cage motor Kurzschlußläufermotor
Stack Stack
stack Kellerspeicher, Kellerspeicher, Stack, Stapel, Stapelspeicher
stack access block Stackzugriffsblock
stack control block Stackkontrollblock
stack empty Stack leer
stack entry Stackeintragung
stacker Ablagefach
stacker selection Ablagesteuerung
stack feed Stapelzuführung
stack feeder Stapelzuführungseinrichtung
stack frame Stapelrahmen
stack full Stack voll
stack overflow Stacküberlauf, Stacküberschreitung
stack parameter Stackparameter
stack pointer Stackzeiger, Stapelzeiger
stack requirement Stackbedarf
stage Stand
stamp Stempel
stand Stand
standalone einzelstehend, standalone, unabhängig
standalone arrangement Standalone-Anordnung
standalone operation Standalone-Operation, unabhängiger Betrieb
standalone program Standalone-Programm, unabhängiges Programm
standard Norm, Regel, Standard, serienmäßig
standard access method Standardzugriffsmethode
standard acquisition Standarderfassung
standard address Standardanrede
standard allocation Standardzuweisung
standard assignment Standardzuordnung
standard backup option Standardaktion für die Sicherung
standard card enclosure Normkartengehäuse
standard character Standardzeichen
standard condition Standardkondition
standard continuation Standardfortsetzung
standard data Standarddaten
standard default Standardvorgabe
standard depreciation Regelabschreibung
standard display control format Standardbildsteuerformat
standard dump Standarddump
standard error handling routine Standardfehlerbehandlung
standard error message Standardfehlermeldung
standard error routine Standardfehlerroutine
standard format Standardformat
standard format handling system Standardformat-Handlingsystem
standard input Standardeingabe
standard interface Standardschnittstelle
standardisation Standardisierung
standard key Standardtaste
standard letter Standardbrief
standard listing Standardausdruck
standard mapping Standardbelegung
standard page number Standardseitennummer
standard parameter Standardparameter
standard plant power supply firmenübliches Netzteil
standard position Standardposition
standard price Normalpreis, Standardpreis
standard processing Standardverarbeitung
standard program Standardprogramm
standard reactor Normspule
standard record Standardsatz
standard record length Standardsatzlänge
standard register convention Standardregisterkonvention
standard report Standardauswertung
standard restore option Standardaktion für das Wiedereinlesen
standard routine Standardroutine
standard ruler standardmäßiges Zeilenlineal
standard selection Standardauswahl
standards office Normungsbüro
standard stamp Standardstempel
standard state Normalzustand, Standardzustand
standard system Standardsystem

standard system setting

standard system setting Standardeinstellung
standard table Standardtabelle
standard target file Standardzieldatei
standard text Standardtext
standard text management Standardtextverwaltung
standard text module Standardtextbaustein
standard text number Standardtextnummer
standard text size Standardtextzeilen
standard value added tax Standardmehrwertsteuer, normaler Mehrwertsteuersatz
standby Bereitschaft, Bereitschaftsbetrieb, Betriebsbereitschaft, Ersatz
standby battery Ersatzbatterie, Reservebatterie
standby unit Ersatzgerät
standing entry Dauerbuchung
standing entry voucher Dauerbuchungsbeleg
standing purchase order Dauerbestellung
standing voucher Dauerbeleg
star Sternchen
starred mit Sternchen versehen
start Anfang, Beginn, anfangen, anregen, beginnen, einschalten, starten
start address Anfangsadresse
start again neustarten
start clock Einschalten der Uhr
start column Anfangsspalte
start date Beginndatum
start distance Anlauflänge
start element Startbit
starter supervisor Ladesteuerprogramm
starting a program Aufruf eines Programms
starting mask Startmaske
starting motor Anlasser
starting procedure Startprozedur
start instruction Startbefehl
start jump box Startsprungbox
start key Anlaufschlüssel
start number Anfangsnummer
start of amortization Abschreibungsbeginn
start of block Blockanfang
start of chain Kettenanfang
start of contract Kontraktanfang
start of depreciation Abschreibungsbeginn
start of file Dateianfang
start of frame Rahmenanfang
start of header Kopfanfang
start of line Zeilenanfang
start of memory Speicheranfang
start of message Nachrichtenanfang, Nachrichtenbeginn
start of posting Buchungsbeginn, Verbuchungsbeginn

start of process Vorgangsbeginn
start of program Programmanlauf, Programmstart
start of record Satzanfang, Satzbeginn
start of sector Abschnittsanfang
start of tape Bandanfang
start of text Textanfang
start of transmission Übertragungsanfang
start partial program Startteilprogramm
start pulse Anlaufschritt
start-stop transmission intermittierende Übermittlung
start the system System starten
start time Anfangszeit
start transaction code Starttransaktionscode
startup anlassen, einschalten, initialisation, anfangen, hochfahren
startup command file Startkommandoprozedur
startup message Startmeldung
startup module name Startup-Modulname
start up picture Anfangsbild
startup procedure installieren des Systems, Systemstart
startup program Startprogramm
startup value Initialisierungswert
star type network Sternnetz
star washer Zahnscheibe
state Stand, Zustand, behaupten, besagen
statement Anweisung, Aussage, Auszug, Debitorenauszug, Niederschrift
statement format Anweisungsformat
statement jump Anweisungssprung
statement list Befehlsliste
statement number Auszugsnummer
statement of account Kontoauszug
statement of totals Summenbericht
statement period Auszugsberichtzeitraum
statement printer Kontoauszugsdrucker
statement text Anweisungstext
state of account Kontenstand
state of operating system Betriebssystem-Stand
static balancer Mittelpunktstransformator
static convertor Stromrichter
static inverter statischer Umrichter
static memory statischer Speicher
static process statischer Prozeß
station address Stationsadresse
stationery Büromaterial
station group identification Stationsgruppenkennung
station identification Stationskennung
station name Stationskennung, Stationsname

196

statistical package for social sciences Statistikpaket für Sozialwissenschaften
statistical posting Statistikbuchung
statistical time division multiplexer statistischer Zeitmultiplexer
statistical value Statistikwert
statistics Statistik
statistics pooling file Statistiksammeldatei
statistics record Statistiksatz
stator Ständer
stator frame Ständergehäuse
stator winding Ständerwicklung
status Materialstatus, Status, Zustand
status bit Zustandsbit
status bulletin Statusprotokoll
status byte Statusbyte, Zustandsbyte
status change Statusänderung
status code Statuscode, Statuskennzeichen
status data Statusdaten, Zustandsdaten
status designator Statusbezeichner
status display Statusanzeige
status field Statusfeld
status led Status-LED
status line Statuszeile
status register Statusregister, Zustandsregister
status report Zustandsbericht
status transfer Statusübertragung
status word Zustandswort
status word register Statuswortregister
steam electric power station Dampfkraftwerk
steel Stahl
steel rod Rundstahl
steering control device Richtungssteuerungsgerät
stencil Schablone
step Impuls, Schritt
step address Schrittadresse
step block Schrittbaustein
step by step im Einzelschritt
stepdown spannungserniedrigend
stepdown configuration spannungserniedrigende Einstellung
step-down transformer Abwärtstransformator
step extent Schrittweite
step mode Schrittmodus, Stepmodus
stepped depreciation Stufenabschreibung
stepping motor Schrittmotor
step response Impulsantwort
step sequence Schrittfolge
step size Schrittgröße
stereophonic stereophonisch
sterility Sterilität
sticker Aufkleber, Bandleuchtmarke

still noch
stipulat vorschreiben
stochastic stochastisch
stock Bestand, Vorrat
stock account Materialbestandskonto
stock availability Lieferbereitschaft
stock category Warengruppe
stock control Lagersteuerung, Lagerwesen
stock control parameter Lagerwirtschaftsparameter
stock count Zählbestand
stock data Lagerbestandsdaten
stock data bank Lagerbestandsdatenbank
stock file Bestandsdatei
stock in hand Materialbestand
stock in quality control Qualitätskontrollbestand
stock issue unit Ausgabemengeneinheit
stock level monitoring Punktüberwachung
stock location tariff Lageortsatz
stock management Lagerbewirtschaftungsmethode, Lagerverwaltung
stock managing clerk Lagerdisponent
stock material Lagermaterial
stock movement Lagerbewegung, Materialbewegung, Warenbewegung
stock movement report Lagerbewegungsliste
stock on order Bestellbestand
stockpiling Vorrat schaffen, Vorratsanlegung, Vorratsschaffung
stock processing Lagerabwicklung
stock quantity Bestandsmenge, Lagermenge
stock quantity issued Lagerausgabemenge
stock query Lagerabfrage
stock read interface Bestandleseschnittstelle
stock read routine Bestandleseroutine
stock receipt program Lagerzugangsprogramm
stock relocation Umlagerung
stock relocation code Umlagerschlüssel
stock requisition Entnahmeschein
stock situation Lagersituation
stock survey Lagerübersicht
stocktaking Inventur, Inventurzählkontrolle
stocktaking data Inventurdaten
stocktaking date Aufnahmedatum
stocktaking discrepancy Inventurdifferenz
stocktaking line Inventurzeile
stocktaking list Inventurzählliste
stocktaking procedure Inventurabwicklung
stocktaking proposal Inventurvorschlagsliste
stocktaking returns Inventuraufnahmeprotokoll
stocktaking returns input Inventurerfassung
stocktaking sheet Inventurblatt

stocktaking sheet number Inventurblattnummer
stocktaking transaction Inventurtransaktion
stocktaking value Aufnahmewert
stocktaking voucher Inventurbeleg
stocktaking voucher posting Inventurbelegsbuchung
stock transaction processing Lagerbewegungsverarbeitung
stock turnover Lagerumschlagshäufigkeit
stock updating function Lagerbestandsführungsfunktion
stock variable Bestandsvariable
stock variable name Bestandsvariablenname
stock weight Lagergewicht
stock withdrawal Auslagerung
stock with sub-contractor Lohnveredlerbestände
stop Halt, Stop, anhalten, stoppen, unterbrechen
stop address Halteadresse, Stopadresse
stop bit Endbit, Stopbit
stop distance Stopplänge
stop indicator Anzeige Stop, Stopanzeige
stop key Stoptaste
stoppage of payment Zahlungssperre
stopping Abbrechen
stopping programs Unterbrechen von Programmen
stopping the system Arbeit mit dem System beenden, System anhalten, System herunterfahren
stop printer menu Druckstopmenü
storage Aufbewahrung, Speicher, Speicherung
storage access channel Speicherzugriffskanal
storage access control Speicherzugriffssteuerung
storage address Speicheradesse
storage address register Speicheradreßregister
storage administration Speicherplatzverwaltung
storage area Speicherbereich
storage battery Akkumulator
storage battery electrode Akkumulatorelektrode
storage capacity Fassungsvermögen, Kapazität, Speicherkapazität
storage card Speicherkarte
storage cycle time Speicherzykluszeit
storage device Datenträger, Speichereinheit, Speichergerät
storage element Speicherelement
storage form Speicherungsform

storage information Lagerplatzauskunft
storage instruction Speicherbefehl
storage interface unit Speicherzugriffseinheit
storage life Lagerfähigkeit
storage limit Speicherlimit
storage malfunction Speicherdefekt
storage medium Datenträger
storage period Lagerzeit
storage point Speicherstelle
storage problem Platzschwierigkeit, Speicherproblem
storage request Speicheranforderung
storage requirement Speicherbedarf
storage software Platzsoftware
storage space Lagerplatz, Speicherkapazität, Speichermakro in Konfigurationsdatei
storage terms Lagerbedingungen
storage tube Speicherröhre
storage unit Speichereinheit
store abspeichern, aufbewahren, lagern, nachlagern, speichern
store and forward Speichervermittlung, zwischenspeichern
store and forward system Puffersystem, Speichervermittlungssystem, System mit Zwischenspeicherung, gepuffertes System
store and forward technique Teilstreckenverfahren
stored messages gespeicherte Meldungen
stored program computer speicherprogrammierter Rechner
store externally auslagern
store management Speicherverwaltung
store print settings Druckeinstellungen speichern
stores Lager, Lagerort, Lagerstätte
stores acquisitions Lagerzugänge
stores basis Lagerbasis
stores description Lagerplatzbeschreibung
stores information Lagerauskunft
stores inventory Lagerortbestand
stores issue unit Lagerausgabemengeneinheit
stores level Lagerortebene
stores location Lagerort
stores location table Lagerorttabelle
stores number Lagerortnummer
stores price Lagerpreis
stores-related lagerortsbezogen
stores segment Lagerortsegment
stores-specific lagerortspezifisch
stores unit Lagermengeneinheit
storing properties Lagerfähigkeit
straight gerade

198

straight angle connector   gerader Stecker
straightforward   direkt, gerade
strain relief   Zugentlastung
strain relief clip   Zugentlastungsklammer
strand   Einzeldraht
stranded conductor   verseilter Leiter
strap   Band
strategy   Gesamtkonzept
stream   Strom, fortlaufendes Format
streamer   Bandlaufwerk
streamer tape   Magnetband
street name   Straßenname
stretch out   erstrecken
stricker fuse   Sicherung
striker   Klöppel
string   Aneinanderreihung, String, Zeichenfolge
string argument   Stringargument, Zeichenfolgeargument
string constant   Stringkonstante, Zeichenfolgekonstante
string of symbols   Zeichenfolge
string tie   Kabelbinder
string value   Wert des Strings, Wert einer Zeichenfolge
string variable   Stringvariable, Zeichenfolgevariable
strip   Band
strip instrument   Bandskaleninstrument
strip light   Bandleuchte
stripwound cut core   Flachkupfer
strobe   Takt
stroke   Anschlag, Schlag, Strich
stroke counter   Anschlagzähler
structure   Aufbau, Beschaffenheit, Struktur, aufbauen
structure administration   Strukturverwaltung
structure data   Strukturdaten
structure description   Strukturbeschreibung
structure designation   Strukturbezeichnung
structure display   Strukturanzeige
structured programming   strukturierte Programmierung
structure field   Aufbaufeld
structure independence   Strukturunabhängigkeit
structure instruction   Strukturanweisung
structure number   Strukturnummer
structure parts list   Strukturstückliste
structure parts use   Strukturteileverwendung
structure representation   Strukturdarstellung
structure rule   Strukturregel
structuring of information   Informationsstrukturierung

stuck   festgefahren, festgeklemmt, stecken bleiben
stylus belt   Nadelträgerriemen
subaccount   Unterkennung, Unterkonto
subacquisition   Teilerfassung
subarea   Teilbereich
subcommand   Unterkommando
subcommittee   Unterausschuß
subcontractor   Lohnveredler
subdirectory   Unterverzeichnis
subdivided   untergliedern
subdivision   Aufteilung
subfunction   Teilfunktion
subfunction selection   Unterfunktionsanwahl
subject   Sachgebiet
sublayer   Teilschicht, Unterschicht
subledger   Abrechnungskreis
sublist   Teilliste
submarine cable   Unterseekabel
submarine power line   Untersee-Starkstromkabel
submenu   Untermenü
subminiature phone plug   Klinkenstecker
submission   Vorlage
submission date   Vorlagedatum
submission period   Vorlagezeit
submit   bereitstellen, vorlegen, übergeben
subnetwork   Teilnetz
subnode   Zwischenknoten
subnumber   Unternummer
subordinate   unterordnen, unterordnen
subpool   Subpool
subprocess   Unterprozeß
subprogram   Unterprogramm
subquantity   Untermenge
subroutine   Subroutine, Unterprogramm
subroutine branch   Unterprogrammrücksprung
subroutine call   Unterprogrammaufruf
subroutine control   Unterprogrammsteuerung
subroutine function   Unterprogrammfunktion
subroutine level   Unterprogrammstufe
subroutine traceback   Zurückverfolgen der Subroutine
subschema   Teilschema
subscriber   Teilnehmer
subscriber control area   Teilnehmersteuerungsbereich
subscriber identification   Teilnehmerkennung
subscript   Index, Tiefstellung, tiefgestelltes Zeichen
subscript character   tiefgestelltes Zeichen
subscripted variable   indizierte Variable
subscript modifier   Indexfaktor

199

subscript value Indexgröße
subsection Teilabschnitt, Unterabschnitt
subsegment Folgesegment
subsegment number Untersegmentnummer
subsequent nachfolgend, nachträglich
subsequent call Folgeaufruf
subsequent dynpro Folgedynpro
subsequent page Folgeblatt
subsequent processing Folgeverarbeitung
subsequent program Folgeprogramm
subsequent section Folgeabschnitt
subset Teilmenge
subsidiary Konzerntochter, Organschaft, Tochterfirma
subsidiary accounting Nebenbuchhaltung
subsidiary balance Nebensaldo
subsidiary company Konzerntochter, Tochtergesellschaft
subsidiary relation Nebenrelation
subsidiary voucher Hilfsbeleg
substitute Ersatz, Substitut, ersetzen, substituieren
substitute form Ersatzformular
substitute material Ersatzmaterial, Substitutionsmaterial
substitute material number Ersatzmaterialnummer
substring Teilstring, Teilzeichenfolge
substructure Unterstruktur
subsystem Subsystem, Untersystem
subsystem availability unit Peripheriekonfigurierungseinheit
subtable Subtabelle
subtest Testlauf
subtopic Unterthema
subtotal Zwischensumme
subtract abziehen
subtraction Subtraktion
subvoucher Unterbeleg
subvoucher header Unterbelegkopf
subwarehouse Unterlager
succeed darauffolgen, folgen
succeeding darauffolgend
success Erfolg
success message Erfolgsmeldung
successor Nachfolger
such solch
suffice ausreichen, genügen, reichen
suffix Anhang, Endung, Erweiterung, Nachsilbe, Suffix
suggest erkennen lassen, vorbringen, vorschlagen
suggested value Vorschlagswert

suggestion Vorschlag
suitable geeignet, passend
sum Summe, addieren, summieren
summary Kurztext, Zusammenfassung, Überblick, Übersicht
summary account Sammelkonto
summary account file Gesamtabrechnungsdatei
summary account posting Sammelbuchung
summary advice Sammelnachweis
summary file Übersichtsdatei
summary invoice Sammelrechnung
summary line Kurztextzeile
summary management Sammelverwaltung
summary page Übersichtsseite
summary screen Übersichtsbild
summary voucher Sammelbeleg
summation Aufsummierung, Summierung
summation check Längssummenkontrolle
summation criterion Summationskriterium
summing circuit Summierschaltung
sum subtotal Zwischensumme aufaddieren
superconducting supraleitend
superconducting device supraleitendes Gerät
superconductor Supraleiter, Supraleiter
superfluous überflüssig
superior übergeordnet
superscript Hochstellung, Hochzahl, hochgestelltes Zeichen, hochindiziert
supervisor Organisator
supervisor station Beobachterplatz
supervisory and executive program Überwachungsprogramm
supervisory control Überwachungssteuerung
supplement Ergänzung, ergänzen
supplementary code Zusatzschlüssel
supplementary function Ergänzungsfunktion
supplementary graphic set zusätzlicher Grafikzeichensatz
supplementary module Ergänzungsmodul
supplementary text Hilfstext
supplier Lieferant, Zulieferer
supplier authorization Lieferantenberechtigung
supplier master record Lieferantenstammsatz
supplier number Lieferantennummer
supplier-related lieferantenbezogen
suppliers file Lieferantendatei
suppliers level Lieferantenebene
suppliers master Lieferantenstamm
suppliers master file Lieferantenstammdatei
supplier specification Lieferantenspezifikation
suppliers register Lieferantenverzeichnis
supplier's installment Lieferantenanzahlung
supplier's invoice Lieferantenrechnung

supplier's name Lieferantennamen
supplier's offer Lieferantenangebot
supplies Zubehör
supply Lieferung, Versorgung, beistellen, liefern, versorgen
supply circuit Speisestromkreis
supply reel Ablaufbandteller
support unterstützen
suppose vermuten
supposed separation point Sollbruchstelle
suppress unterdrücken
suppression Unterdrückung
suppressor Entstörgerät
suppressor grid Bremsgitter
surcharge Zuschlag, zuschlagen
surcharge unit Zuschlagmengeneinheit
surface Oberfläche
surface mounted device oberflächenmontierbares Bauelement
surface scan Platte auf Fehler prüfen
surge current Stromstoß
surge detector Überstromsensor
surge limiter Überstrombegrenzer
surge protection Überstromschutz
surge quenching circuit Stromstoß-Löschschaltung
surge suppressor Überstromschutz
surplus participation Überschuß-Beteiligung
susceptance Blindleitwert
suspect Verdacht
suspended process suspendierter Prozeß
suspense account Interimskonto
suspension insulator Hängeisolator
suspension of spooling Beenden des Spoolens
suspicion Verdacht
swap auslagern, auslagern und nachladen, austauschen, tauschen
swap out auslagern
swim schwimmen
switch Minischalter, Schalter, schalten, umschalten
switch back rückschalten
switchboard Schaltfeld, Schalttafel, Vermittlung
switch configuration Schalterstellung
switch directory Verteilerverzeichnis
switched line Wählleitung
switched network Wählnetzwerk
switched telecommunications network Wählnetz für Telekommunikation
switch fuse Trennsicherung
switchgear Schaltvorrichtung
switch hook character Anschlußzeichen

switching Wählbetrieb
switching center Vermittlungsknoten, Vermittlungsstelle
switching circuit Verteilerschaltung
switching computer Vermittlungsrechner
switching contact Schaltkontakt
switching control Vermittlungssteuerung
switching device Schaltvorrichtung
switching equipment Vermittlungseinrichtung
switching exchange Vermittlungsknoten
switching function Schaltfunktion
switching node Vermittlungsknoten
switching off Ausschalten
switching on Einschalten
switching substation Verteilstation
switching time Schaltzeit
switching unit Vermittlung
switch jump Steuerleiste
switch off abschalten, ausschalten
switch on einschalten
switch-on reaction Einschaltverhalten
switch position Schalterstellung
switch tabs Schalthebel
swivel schwenken
syllabic consonant Silbenkonsonant
syllabification Silbentrennung
syllabification module Silbentrenn-Modul
syllabification program Silbentrenn-Programm
symbiont Symbiont
symbiont device Papierperipheriegerät
symbiont loader technique Symbiontenladetechnik
symbiont name Symbiontenname
symbol Symbol, Zeichen
symbol cross-reference table Symbolquerverweistabelle
symbolic adressenfrei, symbolisch
symbolic address symbolische Adresse
symbolic assembler symbolischer Assembler
symbolic code symbolischer Code
symbolic debugger symbolische Testhilfe
symbolic language symbolische Sprache
symbolic name symbolischer Name
symbol key Symboltaste
symbol substitution Symbolsubstitution
symbol table Symboltabelle
symbol table listing Symboltabellenausdruck
symptom Symptom
symptom menu Symptommenü
sync character Synchronisationszeichen
synchronisation Synchronisierung
synchronisation character Synchronisationszeichen

synchronization Synchronisation
synchronization error Synchronisationsfehler
synchronization point Synchronisationspunkt
synchronizer Synchronisierer
synchronize windows Fenster synchronisieren
synchronous synchron
synchronous data link control synchrone Datenverbindungskontrolle
synchronous generator Synchrongenerator
synchronous induction motor Synchronmotor
synchronous line module Synchronmodul
synchronous mode Gleichlaufzustand
synchronous motor Synchronmotor
synchronous transmission synchrone Übertragung
syntactic marker syntaktische Leseanweisung
syntax Syntax
syntax check Formalprüfung, Syntaxüberprüfung
syntax error Formalfehler, Syntaxfehler, syntaktischer Fehler
syntax notation Syntaxschreibweise
syntax requirement Syntaxvorschrift
sysop Mailboxverwalter
system Anlage, Einheit, System
system administrator Systemverwalter
system analyst Systemanalytiker
system application diskette Systemanwendungsdiskette
system application indicator Rekonfigurationsanzeige
systematic Systematik, systematisch
system attendant Systembetreuer
system attribute Systemattribut
system based systemunterstützt
system block diagram Systemblockdiagramm
system board Systemplatine
system board memory switch settings Setzen der Hauptspeicherschalter
system box Systemeinheit
system cabinet Systemablage
system cable Datenkabel
system carrier change Systemträgerwechsel
system checkout Systemüberprüfung
system code Systemschlüssel
system command Systembefehl
system computer Systemrechner
system configuration Systemkonfiguration
system console Masterterminal, Systemkonsole
system console command Konsolkommando
system console message Konsolnachricht
system constant Systemkonstante
system consultant Systemberater

system control Systemsteuerung
system control center Systemkontrollzentrum
system controller Leitrechner
system control section Systemsteuerabschnitt
system crash Systemabsturz, Systemausfall
system data Systemdaten
system data base Systemdatenbank
system dependent anlagenspezifisch, systembedingt
system description Systembeschreibung
system design Systementwurf, Systemplanung
system development Systementwicklung
system directory Systemdateiverzeichnis, Systemverzeichnis
system disk Systemplatte
system diskette Betriebssystemdiskette, Systemdiskette
system dump file Systemspeicherauszugsdatei
system engineering Systementwicklung
system environment Systemumgebung
system error Systemfehler
system error data Systemfehlerdaten
system error message Systemfehlermeldung
system extension Systemerweiterung
system feature Systemmerkmal
system file Systemdatei
system firmware Systemfirmware
system floppy Systemdiskette
system function Systemfunktion
system gain Gesamtverstärkung
system generation Systemgenerierung
system image Systemprogramm
system independent maschinenunabhängig
system initialization Systemstart
system input file Systemeingabedatei
system inspection Systemüberprüfung
system integrity verification Überwachung der Integrität des Systems
system internal systemintern, systemseitig
system kit Systempaket
system language Systemsprache
system language translator Systemsprachenübersetzer
system load incomplete System nicht vollständig geladen
system logic Systemlogik
system maintenance diskette Systemwartungsdiskette
system manager Systemmanager, Systemspezialist
system manager's manual Systemverwalter-Handbuch
system message Systemmeldung

system module Systemmodul
system monitoring station Systemüberwachungsstation
system network Systemverbund
system nucleus Systemkern
system of accounts Kontenrahmen
system of components Komponentensystem
system operation Systembetrieb
system operator Systembetreuer
system options menu Betriebsmodusmenü
system outline Systemübersicht
system overload Systemüberlastung
system overview Systemübersicht
system parameter Systemparameter
system partition Systempartition
system patch routine Systemkorrekturroutine
system performance Leistung, Leistung des Systems, Systemgeschwindigkeit
system printer Systemdrucker
system process Systemprozeß
system program Systemprogramm
system program function Systemprogrammfunktion
system program library Systemprogrammbibliothek
system prompt Eingabeaufforderung, Eingabeaufforderung des Systems
system proposal Systemvorschlag
system reaction Systemreaktion
system-related systembezogen
system residence pack Systemträger
system resource Systemresource
system run Systemablauf
systems analyst Systemanalytiker
system scheduler Systemplaner
system service Systemdienst
system setup Systemeinstellung, Systemgrundeinstellung, Systemmerkmal
system size Systemgröße
systems management Systemverwaltung
systems management file Systemverwaltungsdatei
systems manual Systemhandbuch
system software Betriebssoftware, Systemsoftware
system software component Systemsoftwarekomponente
system software diskette Systemsoftwarediskette
system startup Systemstart
system startup program Systeminitialisierungsprogramm
system status Systemstatus

system status report Systemzustandsbericht
system supervisor Systemverwalter
system table Systemtabelle
system termination Systemabbruch
system test Systemtest
system testing Testen des Systems
system transaction Systemtransaktion
system transfer Systemübertragung
system under test getestetes System
system unit Systemeinheit
system unit cover Abdeckung der Systemeinheit
system unit power switch Systemnetzschalter
system unit test Systemeinheitstest
system user Systembenutzer
system variable Systemvariable
system variable field Systemvariablenfeld
system warning Systemwarnung
system-wide keyboard definitions Tastendefinitionen der Arbeitsplatzstation
system's internal test Selbstdiagnose des Systems

T

tab   Einrückung, Tabulator
tab connector   Kabelschuh
tabel driven   tabellengesteuert
tab end   Tab-Ende
tab field   Tabulatorfeld
tab key   Tabulatortaste
table   Tabelle
table access   Tabellenzugriff
table alteration   Tabellenänderung
table argument   Tabellenargument
table beginning   Tabellenanfang
table book   Tabellenbuch
table buffer   Tabellenpuffer
table compiler   Tabellenkompilierer
table composition   Tabellenaufbau
table contents   Tabelleninhalt
table definition   Tabellendefinition
table dependent   tabellenabhängig
table designation   Tabellenbezeichnung
table display   Tabellenanzeige
table element   Tabellenelement
table entry   Tabelleneintrag
table error   Tabellenfehler
table file   Tabellendatei
table function   Tabellenfunktion
table generation   Tabellengenerierung
table group   Tabellengruppe
table index   Tabellenverzeichnis
table linkage field   Tabellenverknüpfungsfeld
table list   Tabellenliste
table look-up   Tabellensuche
table maintenance   Tabellenpflege
table management system   Tabellenverwaltungssystem
table manual   Tabellenhandbuch
table modification   Tabellenmodifikation
table name   Tabellennamen
table number   Tabellennummer
table of contents   Inhaltsverzeichnis, Verzeichnis
table of samples   Mustertabelle
table of variables   Variablentabelle
table overflow   Tabellenüberlauf
table read   Tabellenlesen
table record   Tabellensatz
table reservation   Tabellenvormerkung
tabletop model   Tischmodell
table transfer   Tabellentransport

table use   Tabellenbenutzung
tab level   Einrückungsebene
tab level count   Einrückungsfaktor
tab mark   Tabulatormarke
tab position   Tabulator
tab setting   Tabulatoreinstellung
tab size   Tabulatorweite
tab stops   Tabulatoren
tabular technology   Tabellentechnik
tabulator   Tabulator
tabulator set key   Tabulatorsetztaste
tabulator stop   Tabulatorstop
tabulator value   Tabulatorwert
tag   Etikett, Kennzeichen, Markierung
tag sort   Kennzeichensortierung
tailor   anpassen
take   entnehmen
take care of   betreuen
take from   entnehmen
take into account   berücksichtigen
taken for   aufgefaßt
taken in   vereinnahmt
taken into account   mitgerechnet
take out   austragen
take over   aufkaufen, übernehmen, Übernahme
takeover year   Übernahmejahr
take place   erfolgen
take precedence   dominieren
take up   annehmen
take up reel   Aufwickelrolle
talker   Sender
talk mode   Sprechmodus
talon   Kartenstapel, Talon
tandem device   Tandemgerät
tangent   Tangens
tangible asset   Anlagegut
tank circuit   Parallelresonanzkreis
tank number   Tanknummer
tantalum capacitor   Tantalkondensator
tap   anzapfen
tap a line   Leitung anzapfen
tap changing device   Anzapfeinrichtung
tape   Band, Trockenklebeband
tape cartridge   Bandkassette, Magnetbandkassette
tape contents   Bandinhalt
tape controller   Bandcontroller, Bandsteuereinheit, Bandsteuerung
tape drive   Bandlaufwerk, Magnetbandlaufwerk
tape dump   Bandabtastung
tape feed   Bandtransport
tape file   Banddatei
tape format   Bandformat

tape input Bandeingabe
tape leader Vorlaufband
tape loop Bandschleife
tape mark Bandkennzeichen, Bandmarke
tape number Bandnummer
tape output Bandausgabe
tape output record Bandausgabesatz
tape positioning Bandpositionierung
tape reader Bandlesegerät
tape read register Bandleseregister
tape receiver Bandempfänger
tape record Bandsatz
tape recorder Bandaufzeichnungsgerät, Tonbandgerät
tape rewind function Rückspulfunktion
tape rewind mode Rückspulmodus
tape servo Bandservosteuerung
tape set Satz von Bändern
tape speed Bandgeschwindigkeit
tape start Bandanlauf
tape station Bandstation
tape structure Bandstruktur
tape threading Bandeinfädelung
tape transport mechanism Bandtransportmechanismus
tape unit Bandeinheit
tape write register Bandschreibregister
target Ziel, Zielangabe
target archive number Zielarchivnummer
target area Zielbereich
target delivery time Sollieferzeit
target device Zielgerät
target device number Zielgerätenummer
target device type Zielgerätetyp
target file Zieldatei
target format Zielformat
target group Zielgruppe
target indication Zielangabe
target information Zielinformation
target language Zielsprache
target library Zielbibliothek
target line Zielzeile
target node Zielknoten
target positioning Zielpositionierung
target quantity Sollmengen
target serial number Sollarchivnummer
target trail history Radardatenrückverfolgung
task Aufgabe, Auftrag, Funktion, Programm, Rechenprozeß, Task
task area Taskbereich
task builder Programmgenerator
task control Tasksteuerung
task control block Tasksteuerblock

task end Taskende
task image lauffähiges Programm
task management Taskverwaltung
task number Aufgabennummer
task operation Taskbetrieb
task specific taskspezifisch
task switching priority Taskverarbeitungspriorität
task type Tasktyp
tax Steuer
taxable steuerpflichtig
tax amount Steuerbetrag
tax assessment Steuerveranlagung
tax balance Steuerbilanz
tax calculation Steuerverrechnung
tax category Steuerkategorie
tax control statement Steueranweisung
tax correction Steuerkorrektur
tax declaration Steuererklärung
tax deduction Steuereinbehaltung
tax flag Steuerkennzeichen
tax law Steuerrecht
tax listing Steueraufstellung
tax marker Steuerkennzeichen
tax posting Steuerbuchung
tax rate Steuersatz
tax rectification Steuerberichtigung
tax type Steuerart
technical technisch
technical committee technischer Ausschuß
technical documentation kit technisches Dokumentationspaket
technical manual technisches Handbuch
technical reference manual technisches Handbuch
technical specialist Wartungstechniker
technical term Fachwort
technician Techniker
technique Technik
telecommunications Datenfernübertragung
telecommunications installation Telekommunikationsanlage
telecommunications law Telekommunikationsordnung
telecommunications monitor DFÜ-Überwachungseinheit
telecommunications system Datenfernübertragungssystem, Telekommunikationssystem
telefax Telefax
telefax service Telefaxdienst
telegraph character Fernschreibzeichen
telegraph leased circuit Fernschreibstandverbindung

telegraph line Fernschreibleitung
telegraph message Fernschreibnachricht
telemetry Telemetrie
telephone Telefon
telephone call Fernruf, Telefonat
telephone dialling Telefonwahl
telephone network Fernsprechnetz
telephone number Fernsprechnummer, Telefonnummer
telephone service Telefondienst
telephone support zentraler Telefonservice
telephone type modular connectors modulare Telefonstecker
telephone wall jack Telefonanschlußdose
teleprocessing Datenfernverarbeitung, Fernverarbeitung
teletext Teletextsystem
teletext machine Teletextgerät
teletext service Teletextdienst
teletext terminal Teletextgerät
teletype Fernschreiber
teletype interface Interface-Schaltung für Fernschreibanschluß
teletype line Fernschreibleitung, Telexleitung
teletypewriter Fernschreiber, Fernschreibmaschine
teletypewriter exchange Telex
television Fernsehen
telex Fernschreiber, Telex
telex and datex service network Fernschreib- und Datexdienst
telex machine Fernschreibmaschine, Telexgerät
telex message Fernschreibnachricht
telex network Telexnetz
telex service Telexdienst
temex service Temexdienst
temperature Temperatur
temperature condition Temperaturbedingung
temperature control Temperaturregelung
temperature controller Temperaturregler
temperature measurement Temperaturmessung
template Muster, Schablone, Skelett, Speicherschablone
template pool Schablonenpool
temporary Hilfs-, temporär, vorübergehend
temporary buffer Zwischenpuffer
temporary delivery note Vorablieferschein
temporary document Zwischendokument
temporary electrical installation elektrische Behelfsinstallation
temporary file Arbeitsdatei, temporäre Datei
temporary storage Zwischenspeicher
tension Zugspannung

term Begriff, Term
terminal Anschluß, Bildschirm, Datensichtgerät, Datensichtstation, Datenstation, Endgerät, Klemme, Sichtgerät, Terminal
terminal access controller Terminalsteuereinheit
terminal block Anschlußblock, Klemmleiste
terminal connection Datenstationsanschluß
terminal controller board Terminalsteuerplatine
terminal dimension Abmessungen des Terminals
terminal emulation Bildschirmemulation, Terminalemulation
terminal entry Terminaleingang
terminal equipment Bildschirmausstattung
terminal extension Anschlußerweiterung
terminal file Terminaldatei
terminal input Eingabe über Terminal
terminal interface Anschalteinrichtung, Terminalanschluß, Terminalinterface, Terminalschnittstelle
terminal job Terminaljob
terminal junction Anreihverteiler
terminal message Terminalnachricht
terminal mode Terminalmodus
terminal name Terminalname
terminal number Terminalnummer
terminal operation Betrieb des Terminals
terminal plate Anschlußklemme, Klemmenblock
terminal printer Terminaldrucker
terminal specific bildschirmspezifisch, terminalspezifisch
terminal status block Terminalstatusblock
terminal type Terminaltyp
terminal user Bildschirmbenutzer
terminate abbrechen, beenden, schließen
termination Abbruch, Beenden
termination character Endezeichen
termination error Abbruchfehler
termination message Abbruchmeldung, Abschiedsmeldung
termination of the program Programmbeendigung
termination procedure Beendigungsverfahren
termination program Abschlußprogramm
termination segment program Abschlußteilprogramm
terminator Endbegrenzer, Endezeichen
terminator point Endpunkt
terminator socket Abschlußsockel
terms Frachtkonditionen, Konditionen

terms and conditions Geschäftsbedingungen
terms marker Konditionsartenkennzeichen
terms record Konditionensatz, Konditionssatz
test Diagnose, Diagnoselauf, Prüfung, Test,
  Testlauf, austesten, prüfen, testen, überprüfen,
  Überprüfung
test accounting area Testbuchungskreis
test activity Testaktivität
test aid Testhilfe
test bit Bit prüfen, Prüfbit, Testbit
test button Testlauftaste, Testschalter
test certificate Prüfzeugnis
test character Prüfzeichen
test chart Testvorlage
test code Prüfschlüssel
test document Prüfdokument
tester Prüfgerät
test feature Prüfkennzeichen
test file Prüfdatei
testing variables Überprüfen von Variablen
test input/output Test-Ein-/Ausgabe
test instruction Prüfanweisung
test key Prüfschlüssel
test kit Testkit
test letter Testbrief
test letter production Testbrieferstellung
test log Prüfprotokoll, Testprotokoll
test loop Testschleife
test mode Prüfmodus, Testmodus
test module Prüfmodul
test phase Testphase
test point Testpunkt
test program Testprogramm
test provision Prüfvorschrift
test purpose Testzweck
test record Testsatz
test report Testbericht
test report definition Testberichtsdefiniton
test result Prüfungsergebnis
test run Testablauf
test sample Prüfling
test section Testabschnitt
test setup Meßanordnung, Meßaufbau
test state Teststand
test system partition Testsystem-Partition
tetrad Tetrade
tetrode Tetrode
texid control block Texid-Steuerblock
text Text
text area Textbereich
text blank line Textleerzeile
text block Textblock
text buffer Textpuffer

text catalog Textkatalog
text code Textschlüssel
text constant Textkonstante
text control character Textsteuerzeichen
text correspondence Textkorrespondenz
text descriptor Textbeschreibung
text document Textdokument
text editing Textaufbereitung
text editor Texteditor
text entry Texteingabe
text field Textfeld
text file ASCII-Datei, Textdatei
text generation Textgenerierung
text group Textgruppe
text identifier Textkennzeichen
textile-covered wire umsponnener Draht
text input Texteingabe
text insertion Einfügen von Text
text letter Textbrief
text line Textzeile
text line number Textzeilennummer
text maintenance Textverwaltung
text manager Textverwalter
text manual Texthandbuch
text module Textbaustein
text network Textnetz
text number Textnummer
text number range Textnummernkreis
text paragraph Textabschnitt
text position Textposition
text preservation Textkonserve
text processing Textbearbeitung, Textverarbeitung
text processing function Textverarbeitungsfunktion
text processing market Textverarbeitungsmarkt
text processing system Textverarbeitungssystem
text processor Textmanipulator, Textverarbeitungsprogramm
text quantity Textaufkommen, Textmenge
text record Textsatz
text recording Textaufzeichnung
text registration Texterfassung
text screen Textbild
text system Textsystem
text table Texttabelle
text type Textart
text variable Textvariable
text variable designation Textvariablenbezeichnung
text variable name Textvariablenname
text volume Textvolumen
text voucher Textbeleg

theoretically theoretisch
therapy data Therapiedaten
therapy head Therapiekopf
therapy mode Therapiemodus
therapy unit Therapieeinheit
thermal electric power station Wärmekraftwerk
thermal printer Thermodrucker
thermal variable control thermische Steuerung
thermionic conversion thermionische Umwandlung
thermionic rectifier Glühkathodengleichrichter
thermionic valve Diodenröhre
thermistor Thermistor
thermoelectric conversion thermoelektrische Umwandlung
thermoelectric device thermoelektrisches Gerät
thermopile Thermokette
thermoplastic thermoplastischer Kunststoff
thermostat Thermostat
thick-film capacitor Dickschichtkondensator
thick-film circuit Dickschichtschaltung
thick-film resistor Dickschichtwiderstand
thin-film circuit Dünnschichtschaltung
thin-film device Dünnschichtgerät
third normal form dritte Normalform
third party herstellerunabhängig
third party business Streckengeschäft
third party order Streckenauftrag
third party purchase order Streckenbestellung
third party sales order Streckenauftrag
third party supplier Streckenlieferant
thousand position indicator Tausenderpunkt
thousands separator Trennzeichen für Tausendereinheiten
thread Draht, Faden, einfädeln
thread into einführen
three address code Dreiadressencode
three character dreistellig
three dimensional dreidimensional
three-key operation Dreitasten-Bedienung
three line dreizeilig
three phase motor Dreiphasenmotor
three phase rectifier Dreiphasen-Gleichrichter
three phase transformer Dreiphasen-Transformator
three state output Drei-Zustands-Ausgang
three-word pipeline Drei-Wort-Pipeline
threshold Grenzwert, Schwelle
threshold value Schwellwert
throughput Durchsatz, Informationsdurchsatz
throughput class Durchsatzklasse
throughput performance Durchsatzleistung
throughput ratio Durchsatz
thumb screw Rändelschraube
thyristor Thyristor
ticket Fahrkarte
tidal power station Gezeitenkraftwerk
tie wrap Kabelbinder
tight eng, fest
tighten festziehen
tilt leg Kippfuß
timbre Klangfarbe
time Zeit, Zeitpunkt
time base Zeitgeber
time base generator Ablenkgenerator
time base value Zeitgeberwert
time between failures Ausfallabstand
time calculation Zeitrechnung
time charge Zeitgebühr
time check Zeitprüfung
time control Zeitüberwachung
time critical zeitkritisch
time delay Totzeit, Verzögerung
time delay relay Verzögerungsrelais
time division multiplexer Zeitmultiplexer
time gate Zeitgatter
time interval Zeitintervall
time of day Tageszeit, Uhrzeit
time of notice Kündigungszeitpunkt
time of transfer Übernahmezeit
time origin Zeitursprung
time out Timeout, Zeit überschreiten, Zeitablauf, Zeitüberschreitung, Zeitüberwachung
time out error Zeitüberschreitung, Zeitüberschreitungsfehler
time performance Zeitverhalten
time-proportional zeitanteilig
time proven bewährt
time pulse Zeitimpuls
timer Zeitgeber
timer accuracy Genauigkeit des Zeitgebers
timer counter Zeitgeberzähler
timer function Zeitgeberfunktion
timer interrupt Uhr-Interrupt
timer partition Uhr-Partition
timer processing zeitgesteuerte Bearbeitung
timer queue Zeitgeberwarteschlange
time saver Abkürzung
time share Timesharing
time sharing Mehrbenutzerbetrieb, Teilnehmerbetrieb
time sharing computer Rechner im Time-Sharing-Betrieb
time sharing control Timesharing-Steuerung
time sharing cycle Timesharing-Zyklus

time sharing mode Timesharing-Modus
time sharing program Timesharing-Programm
time sharing service Timesharing-Service
time sharing system Timesharing-System
time slice Zeitscheibe
time slice duration Zeitscheibendauer
time slice period Zeitscheibenanteil
time slice remainder Zeitscheibenrest
time slicing Zuordnen von Zeitscheiben
time spent Verweilzeit
time stamp Uhrzeiteindruck, Zeitmarke, Zeitstempel
time switch Zeitschalter
time track Zeitschiene
time unit Zeiteinheit
timing Elementzeitgeber, Synchronisierung, Zeitmessung
timing chart Zeitdiagramm
timing circuit Zeitgeber, Zeitkreis
timing generator Synchronisiereinheit
timing pulse Taktimpuls
tip off Anstoß
title Anrede, Name, Titel, Titulierung
today's date Tagesdatum
together miteinander, zusammen
tolerance Toleranz
tolerance day Toleranztag
tolerance limit Toleranzgrenze
tool Tool, Werkzeug
toolkit Softwareentwicklungswerkzeug
too low zu niedrig
top Anfang, oben
top and bottom margin oberer und unterer Rand
top cover Abdeckung
top-down Top-Down
top down development Top-Down-Entwicklung
top edge oberer Rand
topic Stichwort, Thema
top margin oberer Rand
top menu Ausgangsmenü
top of a document Anfang eines Dokuments
top of page Blattanfang
top of stack Stackspitze
top row of keys oberste Tastenreihe
torn tape condition Bandriß
torque motor Drehmomentmotor
total Gesamtanzahl, Gesamtsumme, Gesamtzahl, Summe, addieren, summieren
total account Gesamtkonto
total acquisition value Gesamtanschaffungswert
total allocation Gesamtzuweisung
total amount Endbetrag

total balance Gesamtsaldo
total cancellation Vollstorno
total capacity Gesamtkapazität
total configuration Gesamtkonfiguration
total deduction Gesamtabzug, Summenabzug
total depreciation Vollabschreibung
total export Totalexport
total field Summenfeld
total file size Gesamtdateigröße
total freight charges Gesamtfrachtkosten
total length Gesamtlänge
total liabilitiy Gesamtobligo
total line Absummierungszeile, Summenzeile
total line length Gesamtzeilenlänge
totalling account Absummierungskonto
total loss Vollabgang
totally depreciated voll abgeschrieben
total memory Gesamtspeicher
total menu Gesamtmenü
total message Gesamtnachricht
total net value Gesamtnettowert
total number Gesamtanzahl, Gesamtzahl
total protocol Absummierungsprotokoll
total quantity Gesamtmenge
totals according to country Ländersummen
total sales Gesamtumsatz
totals block Summenblock
totals column Summenspalte
totals counter Summenzähler
totals display Summenanzeige
totals list Summenliste
totals management Summenverwaltung
totals output Summenausgabe
totals page Summenblatt
totals section Summenteil
totals summary Summenübersicht
total stocks Gesamtbestand
totals to date Periodensummen
total structure Gesamtaufbau
total summary Gesamtübersicht
total system Gesamtsystem
total transfer rate Gesamtübertragungsrate
total value Gesamtwert
total value consumed Gesamtverbrauchswert
total volume Gesamtgröße
total weight Gesamtgewicht
touch berühren
touch switch Berührungsschalter
trace verfolgen
trace back Ablaufverfolgung, zurückführen, zurückverfolgen
trace function Tracefunktion
tracepoint Meldepunkt

trace possibility Tracemöglichkeit
tracing Ablaufverfolgung
track Spur
track address register Spuradreßregister
track condition table Spurzustandstabelle
tracking index Index zur Rekonstruktion
track number Spurnummer
track pitch seitlicher Spurabstand
track row Spur
track selector Spurenwähler
tracks per inch Spuren pro Zoll
track width Spurbreite
tractor Traktor
tractor feed Traktorvorschub
trade Handel, handeln
trade draft Warenwechsel
trade fair Messe
trade mark Warenzeichen
trade name Handelsbezeichnung
trading Handel
traffic Verkehr
traffic signal Verkehrssignal
trailer Nachsatz
trailer card Nachlaufkarte
trailer page Nachspannseite
trailer tag Dateiende-Etikett
trailing cable Steuerkabel
trailing edge nachfolgende Flanke
trailing minus sign abschließendes Minuszeichen
trailing space nachfolgendes Leerzeichen
training Schulung
training mode Schulungsmodus
training purpose Schulungszweck
transaction Bewegung, Transaktion
transaction account Bewegungskonto
transaction amount Bewegungsbetrag
transaction authorization Transaktionsberechtigung
transaction automation Vorgangsautomatisierung
transaction call Transaktionsaufruf
transaction code Transaktionscode
transaction control Transaktionssteuerung
transaction control selector Übertragungsselektor
transaction count field Verkehrszahlenfeld
transaction data Bewegungsdaten
transaction data record Bewegungsdatensatz
transaction dependent transaktionsabhängig
transaction descriptor Transaktionsbeschreibung
transaction document Transaktionsdokument

transaction figure Verkehrszahl
transaction file Transaktionsdatei
transaction function Transaktionsfunktion
transaction monitor Transaktionsmonitor
transaction name Transaktionsbezeichnung
transaction period Bewegungszeitraum
transaction procedure Transaktionsablauf
transaction processing Transaktionsbetrieb, Transaktionverarbeitung, Vorgangsbearbeitung
transaction process line Vorgangszeile
transaction program Transaktionsprogramm
transaction record Bewegungssatz
transaction report Bewegungsliste
transaction request Transaktionsauftrag
transaction selection Transaktionsauswahl
transaction sequence Transaktionsfolge
transaction sequence number Transaktionsfolgenummer
transaction simulation Bewegungssimulation
transaction specific transaktionsspezifisch
transaction stage Transaktionsstufe
transaction status Transaktionsstatus
transaction step Transaktionsschritt
transaction table Transaktionstabelle
transaction text Transaktionstext
transaction type Bewegungsart, Transaktionsart
transaction type code Bewegungsartenschlüssel
transaction type entry Bewegungsarteneintrag
transaction type table Bewegungsartentabelle
transaction work area Transaktionsarbeitsbereich
transceiver Sender/Empfänger, Übertragungsgerät
transceiver cable Übertragungskabel
transfer Transfer, Transport, umbuchen, weitergeben, übertragen, Übergabe, Übertragung, Überweisung
transfer back rücküberweisen, zurückübergeben
transfer control Übertragssteuerung
transfer function Übergangsfunktion
transfer interface Übergabeschnittstelle
transfer key Übertragungstaste
transfer list Umbuchungsliste
transfer page Übergabeseite
transfer page format Übergabeseitenformat
transfer page number Übergabeseitennummer
transfer page processing Übergabeseitenbearbeitung
transfer page record Übergabeseitensatz
transfer phase Phase der Datenübertragung
transfer posting Umbuchung
transfer program Übernahmeprogramm

transfer rate Übertragungsgeschwindigkeit
transferring numbers Werte übertragen
transfer switch Umschalteinheit
transfer syntax Transfersyntax
transfer target Ansprungziel
transfer termination mode Übertragungsendemodus
transfer time Transferzeit, Übertragungszeit
transfer total Umbuchungssumme
transfer voucher Umbuchungsbeleg
transform umformen, umsetzen, umwandeln, wandeln
transformation Umwandlung
transformation list Umwandlungsliste
transformation table Umsetztabelle
transformer phase shifter Phasenschieber-Transformator
transformer substation Transformatorstation
transient command externes Kommando
transient program Überlagerungsprogramm
transient response Einschwingverhalten
transition Übergang
transit time device Laufzeitgerät
translation procedure Übersetzungsablauf
translation register Umsetzungsregister
translation table Übersetzungstabelle
translator program Übersetzungsprogramm
transmission Übertragung
transmission channel Übertragungskanal
transmission control Übertragungssteuerung
transmission control character Übertragungs-Steuerzeichen
transmission control unit Datenübertragungskontrolleinheit
transmission data Sendedaten
transmission date Sendedatum
transmission device Übertragungsgerät
transmission enable Einschalten der Übertragungsfunktion
transmission equipment Übertragungsgerät
transmission information block Datenübertragungsblock
transmission job Sendeauftrag
transmission line Übertragungsleitung
transmission message Sendenachricht
transmission occurence Übertragungsereignis
transmission path Übertragungsweg
transmission possibility Übertragungsmöglichkeit
transmission queue Sendewarteschlange
transmission rate Übertragungsrate
transmission request Sendeanforderung

transmission speed Baudrate, Übertragungsgeschwindigkeit, Übertragungsrate
transmission time Übertragungszeit
transmit senden, übertragen
transmit and receive Senden/Empfangen
transmit block size Sendeblockgröße
transmit buffer Sendepuffer, Übertragungspuffer
transmit data Sendedaten
transmit execution feature Einstellen des Übertragungsbeginns
transmit mode Übertragungsmodus
transmit speed Übertragungsgeschwindigkeit
transmitter Sender
transmitter clock pulse Sendeschrittaktimpuls
transmitter housing Sendergehäuse
transmit termination Beenden der Übertragung
transmit termination character Übertragungsendezeichen
transmitter off Sender aus
transmitter on Sender an
transmitter shaft Übertragungswelle
transmitter signal element Sendesignalelement
transmitter signal element timing Sendesignalelementzeitgeber
transmit time Übertragungszeit
transmitting characters Übertragung von Zeichen
transmitting procedure Übertragungsprozedur
transparency Overheadfolie, Transparenz
transparency mode Transparenzmodus
transport Transport
transport acknowledgement Transportquittung
transport address Teilnehmeradresse
transport connection Teilnehmerverbindung
transport costs Rollgeld
transport date Transportdatum
transport department Verkehrsabteilung
transporting characters Zeichen austauschen
transport layer Transportschicht
transport medium Transportmedium
transport network Teilnehmernetz, Transportnetz
transport perforation Transportlochung
transport system Transportsystem
transport unit Transporteinheit
transpose umsetzen
transposition error Austauschfehler
transposition mode Umsetzmodus
transposition program Umsetzprogramm
transreceiver Sender
trapatt Trapatt-Diode

trash Schrott
travel fahren, verfahren
travelling wave tube Wanderwellenröhre
travel range Verfahrbereich
treatable behandelbar
treatment Behandlung
treatment log Behandlungsbericht
treatment of errors Fehlerbehandlung
treatment session Behandlung
tree procedure Baumverfahren
tree structure list Baumstrukturliste
trend setting zukunftsweisend
trial part Versuchsteil
trial sort Probevereinzelung
tributary station Trabantenstation
trickle charge Erhaltungsladen
trigger Trigger, auslösen
trigger circuit Kippschaltung
trigger criterion Auslösekriterium
triggering function Auslösefunktion
trigger tube Glimmrelaisröhre
trimmer capacitor Trimmkondensator
triple zero Dreifachnull
tri-pole circuit-breaker dreipoliger Schalter
tripping mechanism Schnellauslöser
trouble Fehler, Problem
trouble location Fehlerortsuche
trouble report Fehlerbericht
trouble shoot Fehler beheben, Fehlersuche, reparieren
trouble shooting Fehlerbehebung, Fehlersuche
true logisch wahr
truncate abbrechen, abschneiden, kürzen
truncation Abbrechen, Abschneiden
truncation error Abbrechfehler
trunking Fernleitungsbetrieb
trust Konzern
truth table Wahrheitstabelle, Wahrheitstafel
try versuchen
try another Vorgang wiederholen
tube Rohrleitung
tube socket Röhrenfassung
tube technology Röhrentechnik
tubing Rohrleitung
tune abstimmen, einstellen
tuning Abgleich
tuning indicator tube Abstimmröhre
tunnel diode Tunneldiode
turbo generator Turbogenerator
turing machine Turing-Maschine
turn drehen, wenden
turnaround character Umkehrzeichen

turning off the system Ausschalten des Systems
turning on the system Einschalten des Systems
turnkey schlüsselfertig
turnkey system schlüsselfertiges System
turnkey system vendor Vertreiber von schlüsselfertigen Systemen
turn off ausschalten
turn on einschalten
turnover Umsatz, Umschlagsdauer
turnover display Umsatzanzeige
turnover field Umsatzfeld
turnover figure Umsatzzahl
turnover marker Umsatzkennzeichen
turnover-related umsatzbezogen
turnover segment Umsatzsegment
turnover tax Umsatzsteuer
turnover type Umsatzart
turnover update Umsatzfortschreibung
tutor Lehrprogramm, Lotse, lotsen
tutoring Lotsenfunktion
twenty-four hour clock Vierundzwanzig-Stundenmodus
twice zweimal
twisted pair cable verdrillte Doppelleitung
twisted wire pair verdrillte Doppelleitung
two address instruction Zwei-Adreßbefehl
two address machine Zwei-Adreßmaschine
two character zweistellig
two digit zweistellig
two dimensional zweidimensional
two fold doppelt
two line zweizeilig
two phase motor Zweiphasenmotor
two phase servomotor Zweiphasen-Servomotor
two stage zweistufig
two tier abtrennbar, zweistufig
two wire Zweidraht
two wire direct interface Zweidrahtschnittstelle
two's complement Zweierkomplement
typamatic key stroke Tastenwiederholung
type Art, Typ, eingeben, tippen
typeahead buffer Eingabepuffer
typeface Schrifttyp
type number Typennummer
type of acquisition Erfassungsart
type of application program Anwendungsprogrammtyp
type of claim Forderungsart
type of display Anzeigetyp
type of error Fehlertyp
type of file to save Dateityp der Sicherungsdatei

type of form Formularart
type of format Formattyp
type of letter Briefart
type of mask Maskenart
type of output Ausgabenart
type of paragraph numbering Absatznumerierungstyp
type of price list Preislistentyp
type of print Drucktyp
type of printer Druckertyp
type of processing Verarbeitungsart
type of record Satztyp
type of source device Quellgerättyp
type of statistics Statistikart
type of system residence pack Systemträgerart
type of terminal Datenstationstyp
type of text identifier Textartkennzeichen
type of use Verwendungsart
type of variable Variablenart
type specification Typangabe
type wheel Typenrad
typewriter Fernschreiber, Schreibmaschine
typewriter keyboard Schreibmaschinentastatur
typical Standard, typisch
typically typisch
typical of cartridges kassettentypisch

U

ultra fast cpu Hochgeschwindigkeits-CPU
ultra high frequency amplifier UHF-Verstärker
ultra high frequency tube UHF-Röhre
ultrasonic location Ultraschall
ultrasonic storage cell Ultraschallspeicher
ultraviolet erasable PROM UV-löschbares PROM
ultraviolet light erasing Löschen mit ultraviolettem Licht
umlaut dot Umlaut-Punkt
umlaut encoding Umlautverschlüsselung
unallowed unzulässig
unauthorized unberechtigt
unavoidably zwangsläufig
unblanked hellgetastet
unblock entsperren
unchanged unverändert
unchecked ungeprüft
uncompressed unverdichtet
unconcatenated nicht verkettet
unconditional unbedingt
unconditional end absolutes Ende, unbedingtes Ende
unconditional jump unbedingter Sprung
unconditionally bedingungslos
unconditional transfer unbedingte Übertragung
undamaged fehlerfrei
undefined nicht definiert, undefiniert, ungeklärt
undefined command nicht definierter Befehl
undeliverable unzustellbar
under control unter Kontrolle
under delivery Unterlieferung
underflow Minimalwertunterschreitung, Unterlauf
underground cable unterirdische Stromverteilung, unterirdisches Kabel
underground power line unterirdische Starkstromleitung
underline Unterstreichung, unterstreichen
underline protect Zeichenschutz für unterstrichene Zeichen
underline protected geschützte Unterstreichung
under program control vom Programm gesteuert
underscore Unterstreichungszeichen
understocking Unterdeckung
understocking quantity Unterdeckungsmenge
underwater navigation Unterwassernavigation
unequal ungleich, unterschiedlich
unexpected unerwartet
unfit ungeeignet
unfix the title Aufheben eines definierten Titels
unformatted unformatiert
unformatted media unvorbereiteter Datenträger
unfortunately leider
unfulfillable unerfüllbar
ungenerated ungeneriert
unidirectional in einer Richtung wirkend
uniform einheitlich
unintentional unbeabsichtigt
uninterruptable computer power unterbrechungsfreie Stromversorgung
uninterruptable power supply Stromausfallsicherung, unterbrechungsfreie Stromversorgung
uninterruptable power system unterbrechungsfreie Stromversorgung
uninterrupted ununterbrochen
union Vereinigung
unipolar modulation Unipolar-Tastung
unique eindeutig, einmalig
unique menu keyword eindeutiges Menükürzel
uniqueness Einmaligkeit
unit Aggregat, Anlage, Einheit, Maßeinheit
unit basis Einheitenbasis
unit control block Einheitensteuerblock
unit control word Einheitensteuerwort
unit counter Einheitenzähler
unite vereinigen
unit element Einheitsschritt
unit of measurement Maßeinheit
unit price Einzelpreis, Stückpreis
unit processor Einprozessorsystem
unit register Einheitenregister
unit valuation Einheitsbewertung
unit valuation code Einheitsbewertungsschlüssel
unit value Einheitswert
universal asynchronous receiver/transmitter universeller asynchroner Schnittstellenbaustein
universal character set universeller Zeichensatz
universal input/output universelle Ein-/Ausgabe
universal motor Universalmotor
universal peripheral controller universelle Peripheriesteuereinheit

universal programmer Universalprogrammiergerät, universeller Programmierer
universal programmer unit universelle Programmiereinheit
universal synchronous/asynchronous receiver/transmitter universeller synchroner/asynchroner Schnittstellenbaustein
unload entladen
unloading point Abladestelle
unloading the tape Band entladen
unlock freigeben
unlocked cell ungeschütztes Feld
unlocking lever position Entriegelungshebel
unmatched angle brackets falsche spitze Klammern, unpaarige spitze Klammern
unnecessary unnötig, überflüssig
unnumbered acknowledge Unnumbered Acknowledge, nichtnumerierte Bestätigung
unoccupied unbelegt
unpack auspacken, entpacken
unplanned ungeplant
unplug ausstecken
unposted unverbucht
unprocessed unbearbeitet
unprogrammed nicht programmiert
unreadable nicht lesbar, unlesbar
unrealistic unrealistisch
unrecovered sector nicht reparierter Sektor
unscheduled außerplanmäßig
unsolicited unaufgefordert
unsuccessful erfolglos
unsynchronize windows Synchronisierung der Fenster aufheben
unused leer, unbenutzt
unvalued unbewertet
unwind Stapelspeicher zurücksetzen
up arrow Pfeil nach oben
up arrow key Pfeiltaste nach oben
update Pflege, Update, aktualisieren, fortschreiben, pflegen
update posting Nachbuchung
update procedure Update-Prozedur
update program Update-Programm
update run Update-Lauf
update state Aktualität
update value Fortschreibungswert
update version number Fortschreibungsversionsnummer
updating file Fortschreibungsdatei
updating file records Verändern von Sätzen in Datei
updating of accounts Kontenfortschreibung

updating the base values Basiswertfortschreibung
up down counter Auf-/Abwärtszähler, Vorwärts-/Rückwärtszähler
upfront payment Anzahlung
upgrade Ausbau, ausbauen, erweitern
up-key AUF-Taste
upper and lower case Groß- und Kleinschreibung
upper and lower case printing Groß- und Kleinschreibung
upper bound Obergrenze
upper bus module Modul für den oberen Bus
upper case Großschreibung, Großschrift
upper case letter Großbuchstabe
upper half word oberes Halbwort
upper left links oben
upper letter row obere Buchstabentastenreihe
upper limit Obergrenze
upper limit for date Datumsobergrenze
upper limit of numbers Nummernobergrenze
upper/lower Unter-/Ober-
upper/lower case Groß-/Kleinschrift
uptime Betriebszeit, Verfügbarkeit
upward compatible aufwärtskompatibel
urgent order Eilauftrag
usable brauchbar, verwendbar, verwendungsfähig
usable line length nutzbare Zeilenlänge
usable partition funktionsfähiger Bereich
usage Brauch
use Benutzung, Funktion, benutzen, einsetzen, heranziehen, verwenden
useability Einsatzfähigkeit
useable einsetzbar, verwertbar
useful nützlich, sinnvoll
useful life related nutzungsdauerbezogen
use of parts Teileverwendung
use of parts master Teileverwendungsstamm
user Anwender, Bediener, Benutzer, Nutzer, Teilnehmer
user acknowledgement Benutzerquittung
user action Benutzereingriff
user area Benutzerbereich
user attribute benutzerspezifisches Attribut
user authorization Teilnehmerberechtigung
user authorization file Benutzerberechtigungsdatei
user available storage Anwenderspeicher
user behaviour Teilnehmerverhalten
user class of service Benutzerklasse
user code Anwenderschlüssel
user comfort Benutzerkomfort

215

user communication Bedienerkommunikation
user control Anwendersteuerung
user control block Parameterblock
user controlled anwendergesteuert
user customization Benutzeranpassung
user data Anwenderdaten
user data base Benutzerdatenbank
user data set Anwenderbestand
user default Benutzervorgabe
user definable comment vom Benutzer definierbarer Kommentar
user defined vom Benutzer festgelegt
user defined key programmierbare Taste
user dependent benutzerabhängig
user dictionary Benutzerwörterbuch
user element Benutzerelement
user entry Anwendereintrag
user environment Benutzerumgebung
user equipment Teilnehmereinrichtung
user error Anwenderfehler
user exit Benutzerausgang
user exit connection module Benutzerausgang-Anschlußmodul
user facility Leistungsmerkmal
user field Bedienerfeld
user file Anwenderdatei, Teilnehmerdatei
user format Benutzerformat
user friendly benutzerfreundlich
user function Anwenderfunktion
user group Benutzergruppe
user guide Benutzerführung
user identification Benutzeridentifikation
user identification code Benutzerkennnummer
user independent anwenderneutral
user individual benutzerindividuell
user information Benutzerinformation
user input Benutzereingabe
user installed vom Benutzer installiert
user interest Benutzerbelang
user interface Bedienungsführung, Benutzeroberfläche, Benutzerschnittstelle
user interrupt code subroutine Unterbrechungsbehandlungsroutine des Benutzers
user interrupt service routine Unterbrechungsbehandlungsroutine des Benutzers
user key Benutzertaste
user label Benutzerkennzeichen
user list Benutzerliste, Benutzertabelle
user manual Benutzerhandbuch
user master Benutzerstamm
user master date Anwenderstammdatum
user master master Benutzerstammstamm
user master record Benutzerstammsatz

user memory Benutzerspeicher
user memory area Benutzerspeicherbereich
user menu Benutzermenü
user message Benutzernachricht
user name Anmeldecode, Benutzername
user number Benutzernummer
user operation Teilnehmerbetrieb
user oriented anwenderorientiert
user profile Benutzerdaten
user program Anwenderprogramm
user programmed vom Benutzer programmiert
user programmer Anwenderprogrammierer
user record Benutzersatz
user related benutzerbezogen
user relation Teilnehmerverhältnis
user request Teilnehmeranforderung
user routine Benutzerroutine
user section Benutzerabschnitt
user segment Benutzersegment
user session Teilnehmersitzung
user set up Anwendereinstellung, vom Benutzer installiert
user side Benutzerseite
user software Anwender-Software
user source Benutzersource
user specific teilnehmerspezifisch
user specified vom Benutzer festgelegt
user storage area Benutzerspeicherbereich
user structure Anwenderstruktur
user suffix Benutzersuffix
user support Bedienerunterstützung
user surface Benutzeroberfläche
user system Teilnehmersystem
user table Benutzerliste, Benutzertabelle
user terminal Anwenderendgerät, Benutzerstation
user training Anwenderschulung
user variable Benutzervariable
user workstation Benutzer-Workstation
user's guide Benutzerhandbuch
user's manual Benutzerhandbuch
use tax Gebrauchssteuer
use up Aufbrauchen
usually üblich
utility Dienstprogramm
utility and service routine Dienst- und Serviceroutine
utility component Dienstkomponente
utility diskette Dienstprogrammdiskette
utility function Dienstprogrammfunktion
utility modifier card Datendienstbetriebsanweisung
utility processor Dienstprogramm

utility program Dienstprogramm, Hilfsprogramm
utility program diskette Dienstprogrammdiskette
utility register Hilfsregister
utility routine Serviceprogramm
UV light UV-Licht

V

vacuum capacitor Vakuumkondensator
vacuum circuit breaker Vakuum-Stromkreisunterbrecher
vacuum tube Vakuumröhre
valency Wertigkeit
valid gültig, zulässig
validate auf Gültigkeit überprüfen
validate bit Gültigkeitsbit
validation Gültigkeitsprüfung
validation statement Anweisung zur Gültigkeitsprüfung
valid date Wertstellungsdatum
validity Gültigkeit, Valuta
validity feature Gültigkeits-Kennzeichen
validity period Gültigkeitsdauer, Gültigkeitszeitraum
valid memory address gültige Speicheradresse
valid time gültige Zeit
valid time period gültiger Zeitabschnitt
valuation Bewertung, Wertermittlung, Wertung
valuation account Bewertungskonto
valuation basis Bewertungsgrundlage
valuation code Wertungsschlüssel
valuation criterion Bewertungskriterium
valuation data Bewertungsdaten
valuation discrepancy Bewertungsdifferenz
valuation forecast Bewertungsvorschau
valuation list Bewertungsliste
valuation price Bewertungspreis
valuation rate Bewertungskurs
valuation run Wertungslauf
value Berichtwert, Rechngröße, Wert, Wertgröße, Werthöhe, bewerten
value added Mehrwert
value added network Mehrwert-Netz, Netz mit Mehrwertdiensten
value added network service Mehrwert-Netzwerkdienst, Netz mit Mehrwertdiensten
value added service Mehrwertdienst
value added tax Mehrwertsteuer
value added tax account Mehrwertsteuerkonto
value added tax amount Mehrwertsteuerbetrag
value added tax bill Mehrwertsteuerberechnung
value added tax category Mehrwertsteuerklasse
value added tax code Mehrwertsteuerkennzeichen, Mehrwertsteuerschlüssel
value added tax correction Mehrwertsteuerkorrektur
value added tax identification Mehrwertsteuerkennung
value added tax marker Mehrwertsteuerkennzeichen
value added tax posting Mehrwertsteuerbuchung
value added tax rate Mehrwertsteuersatz
value added tax record Mehrwertsteuersatz
value added tax settlement account Mehrwertsteuerverrechnungskonto
value added tax type Mehrwertsteuerart
value adjustment Wertberichtigung
value adjustment posting Wertberichtigungsbuchung
value allocation Wertzuweisung
value base date Wertstellungsdatum
value carried forward Wertvortrag
value consumed Verbrauchswert
value consumed in the year Jahresverbrauchswert
value contract Wertkontrakt
value credit note Wertgutschrift
value days Valutatage
value delivered Lieferwert
value field Wertfeld
value field update Wertfeldfortschreibung
value lock table Wertesperrtabelle
value of the discrepancy Abweichungswert
value of the number Zahlenwert
value of variable Variablenwert
value received Wareneingangswert
value registration Werterfassung
value relationship Wertbeziehung
value tax Wertsteuer
value transfer Wertübertragung
value updated Wertfortschreibung
valve cooling unit Ventilkühlanlage
varactor Reaktanzdiode
varec gauge Varec-Norm
variable Rechngröße, Variable, variabel
variable ambient temperature test Prüfung bei unterschiedlichen Umgebungstemperaturen
variable assignment Variablenzuordnung
variable block format variable Satzlänge, variables Blockformat
variable capacitor variabler Kondensator
variable content Variableninhalt
variable data field Variablenfeld
variable for reference text Betreffvariable
variable frequency oszillator durchstimmbarer Oszillator

variable identification Variablenkennzeichen
variable label Variablenzeichen
variable memory Variablenspeicher
variable name Variablenname
variable name for reference text Betreffvariablenname
variable resistor veränderlicher Widerstand
variant Variante
variation Abweichung
variety Vielfalt
various divers
vary variieren
vector Vektor
vector address Vektoradresse
vector data buffer Vektordatenpuffer
vectored interrupt gerichteter Interrupt
vector generator Vektorgenerator
vector length Vektorlänge
vector processor Vektorprozessor
vector switch Vektorschalter
vehicle control Fahrzeugsteuerung
vehicle management Fuhrparkverwaltung
velocity Geschwindigkeit
velocity control Geschwindigkeitsregelung
velocity modulated tube Laufzeit-Triftröhre
vendor Lieferant
ventilating opening Lüftungsöffnung
ventilation opening Lüftungsschlitz
verb Kommandowort, Tätigkeitswort, Verb
verbal verbal
verbose abgekürzt, kurz, verkürzt
verb phrase Verbalphrase
verification Verifikation
verifier Prüflocher
verify prüfen, verifizieren
verify a diskette Diskettenstruktur verifizieren
verify disk drive Diskettenlaufwerk verifizieren
verify indicator Prüfkennzeichen
versatile interface adapter universelle Schnittstelle
version Fassung, Variante, Version
version limit Versionsbegrenzung
version number Versionsnummer
vertical senkrecht, vertikal
vertical adjustment lock lever Schubhebel
vertical drive vertikale Steuerung
vertical format buffer Vorschubsteuerungspuffer
vertical format unit Vorschubsteuermechanismus
vertical format unit tape Vorschubsteuerlochstreifen
vertical positioning Vertikalpositionierung

vertical redundancy check Querprüfung
vertical spacing Zeilenschaltung
vertical tab Vertikaltabulator
vertical tabulator key Vertikaltabuliertaste
vertical title vertikaler Titel
very different sehr unterschiedlich
very high sehr hoch
very large scale integration Größtintegration
V format V-Format
via mittels
vibration control Vibrationsregelung
vice versa und umgekehrt
video Video
video amplifier Bildfrequenzverstärker, Bildverstärker
video cable Bildschirmkabel
video communications system Videokommunikationsanlage, Videokommunikationssystem
video control Bildschirmregler
video data terminal Bildschirmterminal
video display controller Videocontroller
video display generator Videogenerator
video display unit Bildschirm, Videosichtgerät
videofrequency amplifier Bildfrequenzverstärker
video monitor Bildschirm, Bildschirmgerät
video monitor controls Bildschirmregler
video output Videoausgang
video output connector Videoausgang
video page Anzeigeseite
video programming unit Bildschirm-Programmiergerät
video random access memory Bildschirmspeicher
video signal cable Videosignalkabel
video terminal Bildschirm, Bildschirmgerät, Bildschirmterminal
video test Anzeigetest
videotext Bildschirmtext
videotext center Bildschirmtext-Zentrale
view ansehen, prüfen
viewing angle Neigungswinkel
viewing text Text prüfen
view mode Prüfmodus
viewport Grafikfenster
viewport coordinates Koordinaten des Grafikfensters
violation Verletzung
virgin media unvorbereiteter Datenträger
virtual virtuell
virtual address virtuelle Adresse
virtual address translator Umsetzer für virtuelle Adressen

virtual array virtuelle Matrix
virtual call virtuelle Verbindung, virtuelle Wählverbindung
virtual computer virtueller Rechner
virtual connection virtuelle Verbindung
virtual data virtuelle Daten
virtual disk virtuelles Diskettenlaufwerk
virtual memory virtueller Speicher
virtual memory timer Systemzeitgeber
virtual overlay virtueller Overlay
virtual processor virtueller Prozessor
virtual storage virtuelle Speicherung
virtuel page number virtuelle Seitennummer
virual memory virtueller Speicher
visibly sichtbar
vision Sicht
visual optisch, visuell
visual indication optische Anzeige
vocal folds Stimmbänder
vocal tract Artikulationsorgane
vocoder Vocoder
voice advisary Sprachauskunft
voice band Sprachband
voice channel Fernsprechkanal
voice quality Stimmeigenschaft
volatile memory flüchtiger Speicher
volatile storage flüchtiger Speicher
volt Volt
voltage Netzspannung, Spannung
voltage amplifier Spannungsverstärker
voltage caution label Warnaufkleber
voltage change Spannungswechsel
voltage control Spannungsregelung
voltage controlled filter spannungsgesteuertes Filter
voltage controlled gain spannungsgesteuerte Verstärkung
voltage controlled oscillator spannungsgesteuerter Oszillator
voltage divider Spannungsteiler
voltage monitoring Spannungsüberwachung
voltage reference diode Zenerdiode
voltage regulator Spannungsregler
voltage selection switch Spannungswahlschalter
voltage selector switch Spannungswahlschalter
voltage setting Spannung, Spannungseinstellung
voltage stabilizer tube Spannungsstabilisierungsröhre
voltage switch Spannungswahlschalter
voltage tolerance Spannungstoleranz
volt alternating current Volt-Wechselspannung
volt ampere Voltampere
volume Datenträger, Lautstärke, Volumen

volume charge Volumengebühr
volume control Lautstärkeregler
volume header label Datenträgerkennsatz
volume identifier Datenträgerkennzeichen
volume label Datenträgerkennsatz, Datenträgername, Kennsatz
volume name Datenträgername
volume of data Datenbestand
volume of traffic Verkehrsbelastung
volume serial number Datenträgernummer
volume set Bandmenge, Bändersatz, Plattengruppe, Plattensatz, Satz von Bändern, Satz von Platten
volume table of contents Datenträgerinhaltsverzeichnis
vote out abwählen
voucher Beleg, Buchungsbeleg
voucher address Belegadresse
voucher adjustment Belegabstimmung
voucher age Belegalter
voucher alteration Belegänderung
voucher amount Belegbetrag
voucher analysis Belegauswertung
voucher archive Belegarchiv
voucher availability Belegverfügbarkeit
voucher balance Belegsaldo
voucher-by-voucher belegweise
voucher category Belegtyp
voucher category selection Belegtypenauswahl
voucher correlation Belegzusammenhang
voucher currency Belegwährung
voucher daily ledger Belegjournal
voucher data Belegdaten
voucher data base Belegdatenbank
voucher data volume Belegdatenvolumen
voucher date Belegdatum
voucher directory Belegverzeichnis
voucher display Beleganzeige
voucher display screen Beleganzeigebild
voucher duration Beleglaufzeit
voucher file Belegdatei
voucher foot Belegfuß
voucher form Belegform
voucher head Belegkopf
voucher header Belegkopf
voucher header data Belegkopfdaten
voucher header display Belegkopfanzeige
voucher header screen Belegkopfbild
voucher header segment Belegkopfsegment
voucher header text Belegkopftext
voucher hold duration Belegverweildauer
voucher holding time Belegverweilzeit

voucher holding time check Belegverweilzeitprüfung
voucher index Belegindex
voucher index block Belegindexblock
voucher input Belegeingabe
voucher item Belegposition, Buchungsposition, Buchungszeile
voucher item data Belegpositionsdaten
voucher item number Belegpositionsnummer
voucher item segment Belegpositionssegment
voucher level Belegebene
voucher line Belegzeile
voucher master index Belegmasterindex
voucher number Belegnummer
voucher number allocation Belegnummernvergabe
voucher number file Belegnummerndatei
voucher number range Belegnummernkreis
voucher posting Belegkontierung
voucher posting deck Belegbuchungsmappe
voucher processing Belegbearbeitung
voucher rapid belegschnell
voucher rapid change belegschnell ändern
voucher reading beleglesen
voucher record Belegsatz
voucher registration Belegerfassung
voucher re-org Belegreorganisation
voucher re-organization Belegreorganisation
voucher re-org run Belegreorganisationslauf
voucher residency Belegresidenz
voucher segment Belegsegment
voucher selection Belegauswahl
voucher specific belegspezifisch
voucher start Beleganfang
voucher total Belegsumme
voucher type Belegart
voucher type duration Belegartenlaufzeit
voucher type text Belegartentext
voucher volume Belegvolumen
vulcanized fiber Vulkanfiber

W

wafer Scheibe, Siliziumplättchen
wait warten
waiting period Wartezeit
waiting program wartendes Programm
wall outlet Netzsteckdose, Steckdose
want wünschen
warm up phase Aufwärmphase
warm up time Aufwärmzeit
warning Warnung
warning beep Warnton
warning label Warnaufkleber
warranty Garantie
watch dog timer Watchdog Timer
water circulation control unit Wasserkreislaufsteuergerät
water cushion Wasserkissen
water spray test Sprühwasserprüfung
watt Watt
wattage Wattleistung
way Weg
week to date seit Wochenanfang
weigh in einwiegen
weigh out auswiegen
welcome page Begrüßungsseite
welcome picture Anfangsbild
width Breite
wildcard Platzhalter
winchester disk Festplatte, Winchester-Platte
window Fenster
window plotting Plotten von Ausschnitten
wire Draht, Leitung
wire printer Nadeldrucker
wirewound resistor Drahtwiderstand, Wickelwiderstand
wire wrap wire wrap
wiring diagram Schaltbild, Schaltplan, Stromlaufplan
word Wort
word count Anzahl der Wörter
word length Wortlänge
word processing Textverarbeitung, Textbearbeitung
word processing system Textverarbeitung
word processor Textverarbeitung, Textverarbeitungsprogramm
words per minute Worte pro Minute
word value Wortwert
working group Arbeitsgruppe
working register Arbeitsregister
working storage Arbeitsspeicher
worksheet Arbeitsblatt
work space Arbeitsbereich
workstation host Workstation-Host
write schreiben
write attempt Schreibversuch
write enable ohne Schreibschutz
write fault Schreibfehler
write lock Schreibsperre
write off abschreiben
write protect Schreibschutz
writer Autor

X

XAB address Adresse des erweiterten Attributblocks
xoff transmit off XOFF Übertragung aus
xon transmit on XON Übertragung ein
xon xoff XON/XOFF
xon xoff feature Funktion XON/ XOFF
xy recorder XY-Schreiber

Y

yardstick Maßzahl
year Berichtsjahr, Jahr, Jahreszahl
year before last Vorvorjahr
year-end Jahresende
year-end closing Jahresabschluß
year-end closing program Jahresabschlußprogramm
year-end closing rate Jahresabschlußkurs
year-end program Jahreswechselprogramm
year field Jahresfeld
year to date seit Jahresanfang
year-to-date balance Periodensaldo
year-to-date figure Jahresverkehrszahl
year (yy) Jahr (jj)
year's balance Jahressaldo
year's end Jahreswechsel
year's result Jahresergebnis
year's result account Jahresergebniskonto
year's turnover Jahresumsatz
yield einbringen
yield request Wartezustand anfordern
yymmdd (year month day) jjmmtt (Jahr Monat Tag)
yymm (year month) jjmm (Jahr Monat)
yy (year) jj (Jahr)

Z

zero Null, Nullstelle
zero access Nullzugriff
zero amount Blankanzahl
zero balancing Nullkontrolle
zero check Nullstellenprüfung
zero compression Nullunterdrückung beim
Speichern von Daten
zero defect Nullfehler
zero entry Nulleintrag
zero error Nullpunktfehler
zero flag Nullkennzeichen
zero indicator Feldbezugszahl bei Null
zeropoint Zeropoint
zeropoint offset Zeropoint-Offset
zero potential Nullpotential
zero shift Nullpunktverschiebung
zero state Nullzustand
zero suppression Nullenunterdrückung
zip code Postleitzahl
zone Zone

ABKÜRZUNGEN

ABKÜRZUNGEN

A	Abschnitt	Abtl.	Abteilung
A	Abteilung	Abtlg.	Abteilung
A	Aggregat	Abw.	Abweichung
A	Alarm	Abzw.	Abzweigung
A	Alphabet	ACA	automatisches Codeauswertungs-
A	Ampere		system
A	Amplitude	AD	Ablaufdiagramm
A	analog	AD	Adresse
A	Anpassungsschaltung	AD	Adressendefinition
A	Anschluß	AD	Arbeitsplatzdatei
A	Anweisung	AD	Archivdatei
A	Arbeit	ADA	allgemeine Dienstanweisung
A	Aufgabe	ADABAS	adaptierbares Datenbanksystem
A	Aufzeichnung	ADABAS	allgemeines Datenbanksystem
A	Ausgabe	ADAP	Adapter
A	Ausgang	ADD	Addierer
A	Auslösung	ADD	Addition
A	Auswertung	Add.	Additionswerk
AA	Absolutadresse	ADD	Adressendekoder
AA	Anfangsadresse	ADE	allgemeine Datenerfassung
AA	Ausführungsanweisung	ADE	Anschlußeinheit für Datenendplatz
AA	Automatik aus	ADEM	Anwendungsdaten-Erfassungsmatrix
AAB	automatische Angebots- und Auf-	ADF	adaptives Digitalfilter
	tragsbearbeitung	ADF	automatische Datenerfassung in Fer-
AÄ	Adressänderung		tigungsbetrieben
AAE	automatische Antworteinheit	ADPT	Adapter
AAE	automatische Anrufeinrichtung	ADPTR	Adapter
AAE	automatische Anrufbeantworte-	Adr.	Adresse
	einheit	ADR	Adressenregister
AAnw.	Ausführungsanweisung	ADR	Adressenteil
AAP	automatischer Arbeitsplatz	ADR	Adreßkonstante
AAR	Anfangsadreßregister	ADRU	Ausgabe Druckliste
AAS	Ausnutzung des Arbeitsspeichers	ADS	Adressensteuerung
Ab	Abtaster	ADS	Adresse Spalte
AB	allgemeine Bedingungen	ADS	Auftragsdatenspeicher
AB	Amplitudenbegrenzer	ADS	automatisiertes Datenerfassungs-
AB	Anfangsbedingung		system
AB	Arbeitsbereich	ADSUM	Adressensuchmethode
AB	Ausführungsbestimmung	ADU	Analog-Digital-Umwandlung
AB	Ausgangsblock	ADU	Analog-Digital-Umschalter
AB	Ausnahmebedingung	ADU	Analog-Digital-Umsetzung
Abf.	Abfertigung	ADU	Analog-Digital-Umsetzer
Abfr.	Abfrage	ADU	automatischer Datenumsetzer
Abfr.	Abfrageeinrichtung	ADV	allgemeine Datenverarbeitung
Abl.	Ablenkung	ADV	Arbeitsgemeinschaft für Daten-
Abl.	Ablesung		verarbeitung
abn.	abnehmend	ADV	automatische Datenverarbeitung
Abs.	Absatz	ADVA	automatische Datenverarbeitungs-
Abs.	Abschnitt		anlage
abs.	absolut	ADVE	automatische Datenverarbeitungs-
ABS	Anschlußsteuerung Bildschirmein-		einheit
	heit	ADVS	automatisches Datenverarbeitungs-
Abt.	Abteilung		system

225

ABKÜRZUNGEN

ADW	Analog-Digital-Wandler	AIVS	automatisiertes Informationsverarbeitungssystem
ADW	Analog-Digital-Wandlung		
ADxVerz	amtliches Datexverzeichnis	AIZ	Arzneimittel-Informationszentrum
ADZ	Adresse Zeile	AK	Adreßkonstante
AE	Abfrageeinheit	AK	Anschlußkosten
AE	Ablenkeinheit	AK	Arbeitkreis
AE	Abstimmeinheit	AK	Arbeitskarte
AE	Adreßeingang	AK	Arbeitskontakt
AE	Anwendungsentwicklung	AKO	automatisierte Korrespondenz
AE	Anzeigeeinheit	AKS	Ausgang für Kontrollsignal
AE	Arbeitseinheit	AL	Adressenleitung
AE	Auftragseingang	AL	Anfangslader
AE	Auftragselement	AL	Auftragsliste
AE	Automatik Ein	AL	Ausgang löschen
Ä	Ämter	ALE	arithmetisch-logische Einheit
ÄA	Änderungsauftrag	alg.	algebraisch
ÄndV	Änderungsverordnung	ALI	Autofahrer-Lenkungs- und Informationssytem
ÄndVTKO	Änderungsverordnung zur Telekommunikationsordnung		
		ALK	Ausgabelochkarte
äq.	äquivalent	ALLA	allgemeine Anweisung
AER	Adressenerweiterungsregister	ALM	Alarm
Af	Abfrage	Alph.	Alphabet
Af	Arbeitseffektivität	alph.	alphabetisch
AF	ausführen	ALR	automatische Lautstärkeregelung
AFC	automatische Frequenzregelung	ALS	automatisches Leitungssystem
AFD	automatisierte Fernbedienung	ALZ	Alarmzentrale
AfDl	Auftragsdienstleistung	AM	Abrechnungsmaschine
AFE	Auftragseingabe	AM	Abschnittsmarke
AFeB	amtliches Fernsprechbuch	AM	Amperemeter
AFM	Anschlußsteuerung Fernschreibmaschine	AM	Amplitude
		AM	Amplitudenmodulation
AFR	automatische Frequenzregelung	AM	Anfangsmarke
AFU	Analog-Frequenz-Umsetzer	Am	Anmeldestelle für Fernmeldeeinrichtungen
AFZ	Aufzeichnung		
AG	Arbeitsgang	AM	arithmetisches Mittel
AG	Arbeitsgruppe	AM	arithmetischer Mittelwert
AG	Auftraggeber	AM	astabiler Multivibrator
AG	Ausgabegerät	AM	Auslösemagnet
AGRU	Ansage geänderter Rufnummern	AM	Aussteuerungsmesser
AGV	Ausgabeverteiler	AMB	Ausgabe Magnetband
AH	Abtast und Halte	AMD	Arbeitskreis mittlere Datentechnik
AHR	Adreßhilfsregister	AME	Ausgabeeinheit Meldungen
AID	Anmeldeidentifikation	Amn	Anschlußmöglichkeiten
AID	Auftragsbearbeitung im Dialog	AMP	Ausgabe Magnetplatte
AIDOS	automatisiertes Informations- und Dokumentationssystem	Amtsbl	Amtsblatt
		AmtsblVfg	Amtsblattverfügung
AIF	Anweisungen für den internationalen Fernsprechdienst	AMV	astabiler Multivibrator
		A/N	alphanumerisch
AIS	automatisiertes Informationsverarbeitungssystem	AN	Anlage
		An	Anzeige
AIV	automatische Informationsverarbeitung	AN	Auftragnehmer
		anal.	analog
		ANAU	Analogausgabe

ABKÜRZUNGEN

ANAU	Analogausgabegerät	AR	Adreßregister
ANDEP	alphanumerischer Datenerfassungsplatz	AR	allgemeines Register
		AR	Analogrechner
AnDig	Analog-Digital	AR	Anzeigeröhre
ANF	Anfang	AR	Arbeitsrechner
ANF	Anforderung	AR	Arbeitsregister
ANFADR	Anfangsadresse	AR	Ausgaberegister
ANG	automatischer Nummergeber	AR	automatische Regelung
anh.	anhalten	AR	automatscher Regler
ANIS	allgemeines nichtnumerisches Informationssystem	ArbAnw	Arbeitsanweisungen
		ArbAnw Am	Arbeitsanweisung für den Anmeldedienst für Fernmeldeeinrichtungen
Anl.	Anlage		
Anl.	Anlauf	ArbAnw N	Arbeitsanweisung für den Abnahmedienst für private Fernmeldeeinrichtungen
Anl.	Anleitung		
AnlfdB	Anleitung für die Bedienung		
Anl. f. d. Bed.	Anleitung für die Bedienung	ArbAnw ÜvÜ	Arbeitsanweisung für das Überlassen von Übertragungswegen
ANR	Advisornummer	arch.	archivieren
ANR	Auftragsnummer	ARD	Arbeitsgemeinschaft der öffentlich-rechtlichen Rundfunkanstalten
ANS	Ansatz		
anst.	ansteuern	AREG	Adreßregister
AnSw	Anwender-Software	ARNR	Artikelnummer
AnT	Anlaßtaste	ARP	Arithmetikprozessor
ANW	Anweisung	ARS	automatisches Reservierungssystem
Anw.	Anweisung	ARZ	Ausbildungsrechenzentrum
Anz.	Anzeige	A/s	Anschläge pro Minute
AO	Abfrageoperation	AS	Abfragesignal
AP	Abrufprogramm	AS	Anwendungssimulation
AP	Adreßpuffer	AS	Arbeitsspeicher
AP	Anpassungsschaltung	AS	Assemblersprache
AP	Anschlußplatte	AS	Ausgang setzen
AP	Anwenderprogramm	AS	Ausgangssignal
AP	Applikationsprogramm	AS	Ausschalter
AP	Arbeitsplatzdatei	AS	automatische Steuerung
AP	Arbeitsprogramm	ASB	Arbeitssteuerblock
AP	automatische Programmierung	ASD	Auftragsteuerdaten
APD	Arbeitsplatzdatei	ASE	Anschlußsteuereinheit
APE	Anpassungseinheit	ASIM	Analogsimulation
APE	automatische Prüfeinrichtung	ASK	Anschlußkabel
APG	allgemeiner Programmgenerator	ASL	Anschlußleitung
A-Phase	Ausführungsphase	ASP	Ablaufsteuerprogramm
API	Anwendungsprogramm-Interface	ASP	Adreßspeicher
Apl.	Arbeitsplan	ASP	Arbeitsspeicher
ApM	Anschläge pro Minute	ASR	Ablaufsteuerrechner
APR	Ausgabe-Pufferregister	ASS	Assembler
APS	Anwenderprogrammsystem	ASS	Assemblersprache
APS	Applikationsprogrammsystem	ASS	Außendienst-Steuerungssystem
APS	automatische Produktionssteuerung	ASt	Abfragestelle
APU	automatische Programmunterstützung	ASt	Amtsstelle
		AST	Asynchronsteuergerät
AR	Abfrageregister	AST	Aufgabenstellung
AR	Abschreibungsrate	AST	Auftragssteuerung
AR	Abstimmanzeigeröhre	ASVO	Arbeitsschutzverordnung

ABKÜRZUNGEN

ASW	Auswahl	AWE	automatische Wähleinrichtung
AT	Abfragetaste	AWG	Adreßwort-Generator
At.	Abtaster	AWR	automatischer Wagenrücklauf
AT	Adreßteil	AWS	Ausgabewarteschlange
AT	alphanumerische Tastatur	AZ	Aktenzeichen
AT	Anpaßteil	AZ	Arbeitszeit
AT	Anzeigeteil	AZG	Alarmzeichengeber
AT	Ausgangstext	AZR	Adressenzählregister
ATE	automatische Testeinrichtung	AZRE	Ausnutzung der Zentralrechen-
ATS	automatisches Testsystem		einheit
ATZ	Abtastzyklus		
ATZ	automatische Telefonzentrale	B	Band
AUD	Auftragsdatei	B	Bandbreite
AÜ	Additionsübertrag	B	Befehlsregister
AÜ	Adreßübertrag	B	Block
AUF	Auftragsabwicklung	B	Breite
Aufh.	Aufhebung	B	Bus
Auftr.	Auftrag	BA	Betriebsart
Aufz.	Aufzeichnung	BA	Bildaustastung
AUSB	Ausgabe binär	BAG	Bildaufzeichnungsgerät
Ausg.	Ausgabe	BAL	Balance
Ausg.	Ausgang	BAM	Belegartmerkmal
Aus-lDVST-P	Auslandsvermittlungsstelle mit Paketvermittlung	BANF	Blockanfangsadresse
		BAP	Branchenanwendungsprogramm
Aus-lTKGebO	Auslandstelekommunikations-gebührenordnung	BAR	Basisadreßregister
		Bat.	Batterie
Aus-lTKGebV	Auslandstelekommunikations-gebührenvorschriften	Batt.	Batterie
		BB	Bandblock
AuslTKO	Auslandstelekommunikationsordnung	BB	Bereitschaftsbetrieb
ausw.	auswählen	BB	Breitband
Ausw.	Auswahl	BB	Buchungsbeleg
Ausw.	Auswertung	BBK	Breitbandkommunikation
Ausz.	Auszug	Bbl	Bibliothek
aut.	automatisch	BBS	Bandbetriebssystem
Autom.	Automatik	BBS	Basis-Betriebssystem
autom.	automatisch	BC	Bedienungscode
AV	Ablaufverfolger	BC	Befehlscode
AV	Addierverstärker	BC	Binärcode
AV	Audiovision	BC	Bürocomputer
AV	audiovisionell	BCD	binär codierte Dezimalzahl
AVerz-TxTtx	Amtliches Telex- und Teletexver-zeichnis	BCK	Block
		b/cm	Bit pro Zentimeter
AVLS	automatisches Verkehrserfassungs-und Lenkungs-System	BD	Band
		Bd	Band
AVR	automatische Verstärkungsregelung	Bd	Bandgerät
A/W	Aufnahme/Wiedergabe	BD	Begrenzer/Demodulator
AW	Abtastwert	BD	binärer Dekoder
AW	Addierwerk	BD	Bitdichte
AW	Anfangswort	BD	Blockdiagramm
AW	Anwendung	Bde	Bände
AW	Ausweisleser	BDE	Bedieneinheit
AWD	automatische Wähleinrichtung für Datenverbindungen	BDE	Betriebsdatenerfassung
		BDSG	Bundesdatenschutzgesetz

ABKÜRZUNGEN

BDT	Bürodatentechnik		Bl	Blockade
BE	Basiseinrichtung		BL	Blocklänge
BE	Bauelement		BLC	Blocklängencode
BE	Bedienereingriff		BLF	Blockungsfaktor
BE	Betriebseinheit		BLK	Belastungskapazität
BE	Betriebselektronik		BLK	Block
BE	Bezugserde		BLMUX	Blockmultiplexkanal
BE	Bildschirmeinheit		BM	bistabiler Multivibrator
bed.	bedienen		BM	Blockmarke
BEDA	Bearbeitungsdauer		BM	Bytemaschine
Bef.	Befehl		BM	bytemultiplex
BefC	Befehlscode		BMA	Benutzermaschine
BefReg	Befehlsregister		BMF	Betriebsmittelfond
BefW	Befehlswort		BND	Band
BefZ	Befehlszähler		BNF	Backus-Normalform
BefZReg	Befehlszählregister		BO	boolean
BefZyk	Befehlszyklus		BP	Bandpaß
Beisp.	Beispiel		BP	Bauprinzip
BES	besetzt		BP	Bedienpult
Bestpr-DrFA	Bestimmungen über private Drahtfernmeldeanlagen		BP	Bedienungsprozessor
			BP	Bedienungspult
Betr.	Betrieb		BP	Benutzerprozeß
Betr.-Sp.	Betriebsspannung		BP	Berechnungsprotokoll
Betr.-Spg.	Betriebsspannung		BP	Bibliotheksprogramm
Betr.-Spgn	Betriebsspannungen		BP	Bildpunkt
Bez.	Bezeichnung		BPB	Benutzer-Programmbibliothek
BF	Bandfilter		BPF	Bandpaßfilter
BF	Blockfaktor		BPM	Bundesministerium für das Post- und Fernmeldewesen
BG	Bandgerät			
BG	Bandgeschwindigkeit		BR	Basisregister
BG	Baugruppe		BR	Baureihe
BG	Bitgruppe		BR	Bedienrechner
BGB	Bürgerliches Gesetzbuch		BR	Betriebsrechner
BGBL	Bundesgesetzblatt		BRT	bereit
BGBl.	Bundesgesetzblatt		BS	Bandsperre
BGR	Begrenzungsregelung		BS	Bandsystem
BH	Befehl Holen		BS	Baustein
BH	Buchhaltung		BS	Betriebssystem
BIB	Bildungszentrum für informationsverarbeitende Berufe		BS	Bildschirm
			BS	Bildschirmeinheit
BIFOA	Betriebswirtschaftliches Institut für Organisation und Automation		BS	Bildschirmsteuereinheit
			BS	Bildsender
BIGFON	breitbandiges integriertes Glasfaser-Fernmeldeortsnetz		BS	Blockstruktur
			BSC	Bandsystem
Bit/s	Bit pro Sekunde		BS	Baustein
bit/s	Bit pro Sekunde		BS	Betriebssystem
BK	Block		BS	Bildschirm
BKO	Betriebskosten		BS	Bildschirmeinheit
BKS	Baukastensystem		BS	Bildschirmsteuereinheit
BKZ	Benutzerkennzeichen		BS	Bildsender
BL	Befehlslänge		BS	Blockstruktur
BL	Blatt		BSC	binär synchroner Code
Bl	Block		BSE	Betriebsschutzerde

229

ABKÜRZUNGEN

BSE	Bussteuereinheit	DAGÖ	Anweisungen für den Fernmeldedienst bei gemeindlichen öffentlichen Sprechstellen
BSHG	Bundessozialhilfegesetz		
Bsp.	Beispiel		
BSP	Bruttosozialprodukt	DAGt	Datenanschlußgerät
BSR	Betriebssystem für reale Adressierung	DAK	Dateienkatalog
		DAN	Datenübertragungsanschluß
BSS	Bausteinsystem	DaNzKo	Datennetzkoordinator
BSS	Bildschirmsteuergerät	DaO	Dateiorganisation
BSS	Bildschirmsystem	DAPU	Datenpuffer
BST	Befehlssteuerwerk	DAR	Datenausgaberegister
BST	Bildschirmtastatur	DAR	Datenregister
BSV	Betriebssystem für virtuelle Speicherung	DAS	Datenausgabesteuerung
		DAS	Datenstation
BSV	Betriebssystem für virtuelle Adressierung	DAS	Digitalausgabe
		DAS	direktes Abfragesystem
BT	Bittakt	DASI	Datensicherungsgerät
BTX	Bildschirmtext	DASI	Datensiebprogramm
BU	Bandumsetzung	DATORG	Datenorganisation
BU	Bandumsetzer	DAU	Digital-Analog-Umsetzer
BU	Buchstabenumschaltung	DAU	dynamische Adreßumsetzung
BV	Bandverstärker	DAW	Digital-Analog-Wandler
BWS	Bildwiederholspeicher	DB	Datenbank
BZ	Befehlszähler	DB	Datenbus
BZ	Binärzähler	DB	Durchschnittsbestand
BZR	Befehlszählregister	DBBS	Datenbankbetriebssystem
		DBG	Datenbankgenerator
CCITT	Comité Consultatif International Télégraphique et Téléfonique	DBMS	Datenbank-Management-System
		DBP	Deutsche Bundespost
CMV	Computer-Mißbrauch-Versicherung	DBS	Datenbankbetriebssystem
COLA	Computerladen	DBS	Datenbank-Software
CPH	computergestützte Programmierhilfe	DBS	Datenbanksystem
CUU	computerunterstützter Unterricht	DCT	Decoderteil
CW	Codewort	DD	Datendarstellung
		DD	Datendefinition
D	Dämpfung	DDA	digitaler Differentialanalysator
D	Daten	DDM	dezentraler Datenmultiplexer
D	digital	DDT	dezentrale Datentechnik
D	Diode	DE	Dämpfungsentzerrer
D	Drucker	DE	Dateneingabe
DA	Datenanalysator	DE	Datenerfassung
DA	Datenausgang	DE	Digitaleingabe
DA	Dienstanweisung	DEE	Datenendeinrichtung
DA	Differentialanalysator	DEF	Datenerfassung
DA	Digitalausgabe	DEF	Definition
DABA	Datenbank	DEG	Datenendgerät
DAE	Datenanschlußeinheit	DEP	Datenerfassungsplatz
DAER	Datenerfassung	DES	Dateneingabesystem
DA F-Buchd	Dienstanweisung für den Fernmeldebuchdienst	DES	Datenendstelle
		DES	Datenerfassungssystem
DAFÜ	Datenfernübertragung	DEV	Dioden-Erd-Verfahren
DAG	Datenanschlußgerät	DF	Datenfeld
		DF	Datenfernübertragung
		DF	Differenzfrequenz

ABKÜRZUNGEN

DFE	Datenfernübertragungseinrichtung	DPCM	Differenz-Pulscodemodulation
DFG	Datenfreigabe	DPS	Datenparametersatz
DFGt	Datenfernschaltgerät	DPS	Druckpufferspeicher
DFM	digitaler Frequenzmesser	DQ	Datenquelle
DFP	Datenflußplan	DQV	Differenzquotientenverfahren
DFS	digitaler Frequenzsynthesizer	DR	Digitalrechner
DFT	diskrete Fouriertransformation	DRA	Druckausgabe
DFT	Dünnfilmtechnik	DS	Datensatz
DFÜ	Datenfernübertragung	DS	Datensenke
DFV	Datenfernverarbeitung	DS	Datensichtstation
DG	doppelte Genauigkeit	DS	Datensichtgerät
DGL	Differentialgleichung	DS	Datensystem
DGS	Differentialgleichungssystem	DSA	dezentrale Systemarchitektur
DH	Diensthabender	DSB	Dateisteuerblock
DIDI	digitales Diffusionsprogramm	DSB	Datenschutzbeauftragter
DIF	Differential	DSB	Datensteuerblock
DIFF	Differential	DSE	Datensicherungseinheit
diff.	differential	DSE	Drucksteuereinheit
Diff.	Differenz	DSG	Datenschutzgesetz
Diff.-Gl.	Differentialgleichung	DSN	Datensatzname
Diff.-Quot	Differentialquotient	DSR	Datensammelrechner
DIM	Dimension	DSR	Datenstationsrechner
DIMDI	Deutsches Institut für medizinische Dokumentation und Information	DSS	Datensichtstation
		DST	Datenstation
DIMU	Digital-Multimeter	DSt	Dienststelle
DIN	Deutsches Institut für Normung	DT	Datentechnik
Dir.-Übert	Direktübertragung	DT	Datenteil
Dir.-Verb.	Direktverbindung	DT	Datenträger
DISPOS	Dienstprogrammsystem	DTA	Datenträgeraustausch
DIV	Dividend	DTF	Dateidefinition
DKR	Datenkoordinierungsrechner	DTN	digitales Telefonnetz
DKZ-Nl	D-Kanal-Zeichengabe auf Endstellenleitungen	DTP	Dateiparameter
		DU	Datenumsetzer
DL	Datenfeld-Länge	DÜ	Datenüberträger
DL	Datenlänge	DÜ	Datenübertragung
DLG	Datenlesegerät	DÜE	Datenübertragungseinrichtung
DLM	Datenleitungsmeßgerät	DÜE	Datenübertragungseinheit
DLS	Datenleitstelle	DÜGO	Datenübertragungs-Gebührenordnung
DLS	Dialogsystem		
DLZ	Durchlaufzeit	DÜN	Datenübermittlungsnetz
DMM	digitales Multimeter	DÜO	Datenübertragungsordnung
DMS	Datenmanagementsystem	DÜS	Datenübermittlungssystem
DN	Dateiname	DÜS	Datenübertragungssystem
DNA	Deutscher Normenausschuß	DÜST	Datenübertragungs- und Steuereinheit
DNF	disjunktive Normalform		
DNKZ	Datennetzkontrollzentrum	DÜST	Datenübertragungssteuerung
DNST	Datennebenstelle	DUET	Datenübertragungseinrichtung
DOTAN	Digitales optisches Teilnehmer-Anschlußnetz	DÜVO	Datenübertragungsverordnung
		DÜVO	Datenübermittlungsverordnung
DP	Datenpuffer	DUG	digitales Umschaltgerät
DP	Datenübertragungsprogramm	DUPL	Duplizierprogramm
DP	Dienstprogramm	DurchfVO	Durchführungsverordnung
DP	dynamisches Programmieren	DV	Datenverarbeitung

ABKÜRZUNGEN

DV	Druckvorschrift	EBD	Empfangsbezugsdämpfung
DVA	Datenverarbeitungsanlage	EBE	einheitliches Betriebsereignis
DV-AH	Datenverarbeitung außer Haus	EBM	Einseitenbandmodulation
DVD	Datenverarbeitungsdienst	EBS	Echtzeitbetriebssystem
DVE	Datenverarbeitungseinrichtung	ED	Einschaltdauer
DVE-P	Datenvermittlungseinrichtung mit Paketvermittlung	EDK	elektronische Datenkommunikation
		EDO	einheitliche Dateiorganisation
DVL	Datenverbundleitung	EDS	elektronisches Datenvermittlungs-System
DVP	Datenverarbeitungsperipherie		
DVR	Datenübertragungsvorrechner	EDS	elektronisches Datenverarbeitungssystem
DVR	Datenverarbeitungsvorrechner		
DVS	Dateiverwaltungssystem	EDS	elektronische Datenverarbeitungsstation
DVS	Datenverarbeitungssystem		
DVS	Datenvermittlungssystem	EDV	elektronische Datenverarbeitung
DVST-L	Datenvermittlungsstelle mit Leitungsvermittlung	EF	Eingabefilter
		EF	Empfangsfilter
DVST-P	Datenvermittlungsstelle mit Paketvermittlung	EG	Eingabegerät
		EHKP	Einheitliche Höhere Kommunikationsprotokolle
DVT	Datenverteiler		
DVZ	Datenverarbeitungszentrum	EI	Eingangsinformation
DW	Doppelwort	EIDN	einheitliches integriertes digitales Netz
DW	Druckwerk		
DWE	digitale Wahleinheit	EIR	Einschaltroutine
Dx	Datex	ELE	Element
DZ	Datenzentrale	EM	Einbaumodem
DZ	Dezimalzähler	EM	Elektromotor
DZA	dezentrale Abfrageeinheit	EMA	elektromagnetischer Antrieb
		EMD	Edelmetall-Drehwähler
E	Ein	EMD	Edelmetall-Motor-Drehwähler
E	Eingabe	EMD-VSt	Vermittlungsstelle mit Edelmetall-Drehwählern
E	Eingang		
E	Elektrode	EML	Emulator
E	Elektron	EN	Europa-Norm
E	Empfänger	EO	Elementaroperation
E	Erde	EOS	Echtzeitoperationssystem
E/A	Ein-/Ausgabe	EP	Eingabeprogramm
EA	elektronischer Analogrechner	EPR	Echtzeit-Prozeßrechner
EA	endlicher Automat	EPR	Eingabe-Pufferregister
EAE	Ein-/Ausgabeeinheit	EPS	Einprozessorsystem
EAK	Ein-/Ausgabekanal	ER	Eingaberegister
EAN	europäische Artikelnummer	ER	Entscheidungsregel
EAO	Ein-/Ausgabe-Operation	ER	Ergänzungsrechner
EAP	Ein-/Ausgabeprogramm	ER	Ersatzrechner
EAP	Ein-/Ausgabeprozessor	ERA	elektronische Rechenanlage
EAR	Ein-/Ausgaberegister	ERM	elektronische Rechenmaschine
EAR	elektronischer Analogrechner	ERS	Einzelrechnersystem
EAS	Ein-/Ausgabe-Steuerung	ERT	elektronische Rechentechnik
EAS	Ein-/Ausgabe-Steuerungssystem	ERZ	elektronisches Rechenzentrum
EAS	Ein-/Ausgabe-System	ES	Eingangsschalter
EAST	Ein-/Ausgabe-Steuerung	ES	elektromagnetischer Speicher
EAW	Ein-/Ausgabewerk	ES	Elektronenrechnersystem
EB	Eingangsblock	ES	elektronische Steuerung
EB	Einseitenband	ES	Energiesystem

ABKÜRZUNGEN

ES	entfernte Station		FD	freier Deskriptor
ES	Erkennungssignal		FDM	Finite Differenzen Methode
ESB	Einseitenband		Fe-	Fernsprech-
ESP	Echtzeitspeicher		FeAfD	Fernsprechauftragsdienst
ESP	Eingangsspeicher		FED	Fernsprechhauptanschluß für Daten-
ESP	Externspeicher			übertragung
EST	Eingangssteuerung		FeE	Fernsprechentstörung
ET	Einschaltetaste		FEI	Funktionseinheit
ET	Einzeltakt		FEM	Finite Elemente Methode
ET	Elektronik		FeN	Fernsprechnetz
ET	Elektrotechnik		FER	Fehlerregister
ET	Empfangstakt		FFE	formatfreie Eingabe
ET	Entscheidungstabelle		FFS	flexibles Fertigungssystem
ETAB	Entscheidungstabelle		FGNr.	Fernmeldegebührennummer
ETD	Ersatzteildienst		FGT	Fernschaltgerät
ETR	elektronischer Tischrechner		FGV	Fernmeldegebührenvorschrift
ETS	Entscheidungstabellensystem		FIBU	Finanzbuchhaltung
ETT	Entscheidungstabellentechnik		FIS	Fachinformationssystem
ETVÜ	Entscheidungstabellenvorübersetzer		FIS	Flughafen-Informationssytem
ETZ	elektronische Zeitung		FIZ	Fachinformationszentrum
EV	Eigenvektor		FK	Fehlerklasse
EV	Empfangsverstärker		FK	Festkomma
EVSt	Erdvermittlungsstellen		FK	Flüssigkristall
EVz	Endverzweiger		FKA	Flüssigkristallanzeige
EW	Eigenwert		FKD	Filekopierdienst
EWR	Eingabewortregister		FKG	Fehlerkorrekturgerät
EWS	elektronisches Wählsystem		FKTO	Fernmeldegebührenkonto
EWS-VSt	Vermittlungsstelle mit Elektroni-		FKZ	freies Kennzeichen
	schem Wähl-System		FL	Filter
EZÜ	elektronische Zahlungsüberweisung		FM	Fehlermenge
			FM	Frequenzmodulation
F	Fernmeldewesen		FMR	Fehlermusterregister
F	Festformat		FMT	Format
F	Frequenz		FO	Fernmeldeordnung
F	Fühler		FP	Festpunkt
FA	Fehleranzeige		FP	freie Pufferzeit
FA	Fernmeldeamt		FP	Funktionsprinzip
FÄ	Fernmeldeämter		FPS	Festplattenspeicher
FAG	Gesetz über Fernmeldeanlagen		FRD	Fernmelderechnungsdienst
FB	Fehlerbedingung		FRS	File rücksetzen
FB	Fehlerbyte		FRZ	Fachrechenzentrum
FB	Funktionsblock		FS	Fernschreiber
FBE	Fernbedienungseinheit		FS	Fernschreiben
FBG	Fernbediengerät		Fs-	Fernschreib-
Fbl	Formblatt		FS	Festspeicher
FBO	Fernmeldebauordnung		FS	Festwertspeicher
FBP	Formularbeschreibungsprogramm		FSE	Fernschalteinrichtung
FBS	Fernbetriebssystem		FSE	Fernschalteinheit
FBS	Finanzbuchhaltungssystem		FSPRO	Fehlersuchprogramm
FBV	Funkbetriebsvorschrift		FST	Fertigungssteuerung
FCS	Blockprüfzeichenfolge		FST	Funktionsteuerung
FD	Flußdiagramm		FT	Fouriertransformation
FD	Formulardrucker		FT	Frequenzteiler

ABKÜRZUNGEN

FTA	Familientelefonanlage	GT	Grundtext
FTZ	Fernmeldetechnisches Zentralamt	GTBK	geschlossene Teilnehmerbetriebsklasse
FUR	Fehlerunterbrechungsroutine		
FVS	File vorsetzen	GÜ	Geräteübersicht
FVV	feste virtuelle Verbindung	GUm	Gemeinschaftsumschalter
FW	Festwort	GVV	gewählte virtuelle Verbindung
FW	Finanzwesen	GW	Ganzwort
FW	Firmware	GZR	Gerätezustandsregister
FWA	Festwortadresse		
FWE	Fernwirkempfänger	H	Halbaddierer
FWG	Fernwirkgerät	H	Hersteller
FWR	Fehlerwortregister	H	Hundert
FWT	Fernwirktechnik	HA	Hauptabschnitt
FZA	Fernmeldezeugamt	HA	Hauptadresse
		HA	Hauptanschluß
G	Geber	HA	Hauptaufgabe
GAA	Geldausgabeautomat	HAB	Hauptbuch
GAP	Grundlagen für Anwendungsprogrammierung	HADES	halbautomatisches Datenerfassungssystem
GAR	Geräteadreßregister	HADR	Hilfsadressregister
GB	Gigabyte	HAPRO	Hauptprogramm
GBK	Großbaukasten	HAR	Host-Anpassungsrechner
GBS	Grundbetriebssystem	HAs	Hauptanschluß
GD	Große Datentechnik	HB	Handbuch
GDV	grafische Datenverarbeitung	HBG	Hauptbaugruppe
GEN	Generator	HD	Hochleistungsdrucker
GEP	Gebührenerfassungsplatz	HeimG	Heimgesetz
GF	Grundform	HfD	Hauptanschluß für Direktruf
GG	Grundgerät	HiP	Hilfsprogramm
GGT	größter gemeinsamer Teiler	HL	Halbleiter
GK	Gleitkomma	HL	Hauptleitung
GKR	Gleitkommaregister	HOK	Hauptordnungskriterium
GKT	Gültigkeit	HP	Hilfsprogramm
GL	Glied	HPS	höhere Programmiersprache
GM	Gruppenmarke	HR	Hauptrechner
GN	Gerätenummer	HR	Hilfsrechner
GÖ	gemeindliche öffentliche Telefonstellen	HR	Hilfsregister
		HR	Hintergrundrechner
GR	Gesamtregister	HR	Hybridrechner
GR	Gleichrichter	HS	Hauptspeicher
GR	Großrechner	HS	Hilfsspeicher
GR	Gruppe	HSB	Hauptsteuerblock
GR	Gruppe rücksetzen	HSP	Hauptspeicher
GRA	Großrechenanlage	HSTP	Hauptsteuerprogramm
GRZ	Großrechenzentrum	HT	Hauptteil
GS	Gebersignal	HVSt	Hauptvermittlungsstelle
GS	Geschäftsstelle	HW	Halbwort
GS	Grundsektor	HW	Hauptwort
GS	Gruppensignal	HZ	Hauptzentrale
GS	Gruppe setzen	Hz	Hertz
GSE	Gerätesteuereinheit		
GSS	gesteuertes Stapelfernübertragungssystem	I	Indexregister
		I	Information

ABKÜRZUNGEN

IA	Impulsanzahl	KD	Kette von Daten
IA	Informationsausgabe	KDEC	Kanaldekodierung
IA	Inkrementalausgabe	KE	Kanaleingangsschaltung
IA	Internationales Alphabet	KE	Kanalende
IB	Informationsbank	KE	Karteneinheit
IBFN	integriertes Breitband-Fernmeldenetz	KE	Kern
ICG	interaktive Computergrafik	KES	Karteneinschub
ID	Identifizierer	KF	Kontrollfeld
ID	Informationsdarstellung	KFS	Kontrollfernschreiber
IDA	indirekte Datenadressierung	KG	Kennungsgeber
IDD	Identifikationsdatei	KG	Kennzeichengruppe
IDENT	Identifikation	kHz	Kilohertz
IDN	integriertes Datennetz	KIS	Kundeninformationssystem
IDN	integriertes Text- und Datennetz	KIS	kundenintegrierte Schaltung
IDX	Index	KK	Karteikarte
IE	Informationseingabe	KK	Kartenkennzeichen
IE	Informationseinheit	KL	Kartenleser
IEB	integrierte elektronische Baugruppe	KL	Kartenlocher
IF	Impulsformer	KL	Kommalampe
IF	Information	KLE	Kassettenleser
IF	Instruktionsfluß	KMR	Kommandoregister
IFF	Impulsfolgefrequenz	KOK	Kontrollkarte
IFN	Information	KON	Konsole
IFO	Information	KOR	Kontrollregister
IG	Impulsgeber	KR	Kleinrechner
IGA	integrierter Geräteanschluß	KRA	Kleinrechenanlage
IGS	interaktives grafisches System	KRS	Kleinrechnersystem
IKZ	Impulskennzeichen	KS	Kartenstanzer
ILN	interne Leitungsnummer	KS	Kellerspeicher
IM	Impulsmodulation	KS	Kernspeicher
IMP	Impuls	KS	Kontrollsignal
IMS	intelligenter Matrix-Schalter	KSE	Kanalsteuereinheit
INPR	Initialisierungsprogramm	KSP	Kernspeicher
INT	Interpreter	KSR	Kleinsteuerrechner
IR	Interpolationsrechner	KST	Kanalsteuerung
i. S.	im Sinne	KSt	Kartenstanzer
IS	Informationssystem	KTN	Kontrollnummer
ITA	Internationales Telegrafenalphabet	KU	Kanalumschalter
IÜ	Informationsübertragung	KU	Kanalumsetzer
IUR	internes Unterbrechungsregister	KU	Kurzunterbrechung
IV	Informationsverarbeitung	KVSt	Knotenvermittlungsstelle
IVS	informationsverarbeitendes System	KVz	Kabelverzweiger
IWV	Impulswahlverfahren	kW	Kilowatt
IZ	Informationszentrum	KZR	Kanalzustandsregister
		KZU	Kennzeichenumsetzer
K	Kontrolle		
K	Konzentrator	L	Lampe
K	Korrektur	L	Leistung
KAD	Kanaladressendekoder	L	Leseleitung
KAG	Kassettengerät	L	Lichtgriffel
KAG	Kassettengerät-Treiber	L	Liste
KAR	Kleinanalogrechner	L	lochen
kbit/s	Kilobit pro Sekunde	L	Locher

ABKÜRZUNGEN

LAB	Leitungsanschlußbaugruppe	MA	Meßausgang
LAD	laufende Adresse	MABU	Maschinenbuchhaltung
LBE	Lochbandeingabe	MACRO	Makrobefehl
LBK	Lochbandkarte	MADA	maschinelle Datenanalyse
LBL	Lochbandleser	MARO	Magnetbandroutine
LE	Leitungsanschlußeinheit	MARS	Magnetstreifenschreiber
LK	Leitungskonzentrator	MAS	Makrosprache
LK	letzte Karte	MAS	modulares Anwendungssystem
LK	Lochkarte	MAZ	magnetische Aufzeichnung
LKE	Lochkarteneingabe	MB	Magnetbandgerät
LKG	Lochkartengerät	MB	Magnetband
LKL	Lochkartenleser	MB	Makrobefehl
LKL	Lochkartenlocher	MB	mechanische Bauelemente
LKM	Lochkartenmaschine	MBC	Magnetbandcassette
LKSt.	Lochkartenstanzer	MBE	Magnetbandeinheit
LKV	Lochkartenverarbeitung	MBE	Magnetbandeingabe
LL	Lochkartenleser	MBG	Magnetbandgerät
LL	Lochstreifenleser	MBG	Magnetbandsteuergerät
LLF	Lichtleitfaser	MBK	Magnetbandkassette
LMR	lineare Mehrfachregression	MBKG	Magnetbandkassettengerät
LOG	logisch	MBR	Mikrobefehlsregister
LP	Ladeprogramm	MBS	Magnetbandsteuerung
LP	Leiterplatte	MBS	Magnetbandspeicher
LP	lineare Programmierung	MBS	Magnetbandsteuergerät
LP	Linearprogrammierung	MBSE	Magnetbandsteuereinheit
LP	Lizenzprogramm	MBST	Magnetbandsteuerung
LP	logische Ports	MC	Maschinencode
LR	Leseregister	MCS	Microcomputersystem
LS	Leistungsschalter	MD	Magnetdrahtspeicher
LS	Lochstreifen	MDE	Maschinendatenerfassung
LSA	Lochstreifenausgabe	MDE	mobile Datenerfassung
LSE	Lochstreifeneingabe	MDS	Magnetdrahtspeicher
LSK	Lochstreifenkarte	MDSP	Magnetdrahtspeicher
LSR	Lese-/Schreibregister	MDT	mittlere Datentechnik
LSS	Lochstreifenstanzer	MDV	mittlere Datenverarbeitung
LST	Lochstreifenstanzer	MEK	Mehrfacheinzelkanal
LUG	Lohn und Gehalt	MES	Management-Entscheidungssystem
LV	Leitungsverstärker	MES	Messung
LV	Leitungsvermittlung	MESP	Meldespeicher
LW	Laden Wort	MF	Maschinenfehler
LW	Laufwerk	MF	Mikrofilm
LW	Leitwerk	MFB	Multifunktionsbaustein
LWI	Laden Wort Indirekt	MFG	Mehrfrequenzgenerator
LWL	Lichtwellenleiter	MFT	Mikrofilmtechnik
LZ	Leerzeichen	MFV	Mehrfrequenzverfahren
LZS	Langzeitspeicher	MFV	Mehrfrequenzwahlverfahren
LZZ	Lesezwangszyklus	MG	Magnetbandgerät
		MGK	Magnetkarte
M	Markierer	MI	Maschineninventarnummer
M	Menge	MIK	Mikroelektronik
M	Monitor	MINIC	Minicomputer
MA	Maschinenaufarbeitung	MIP	Mikroprozessor
MA	Maschinenauftrag	MIS	Management-Informationssystem

ABKÜRZUNGEN

MK	Magnetkarte	NDZ	nicht druckbares Zeichen
MK	Magnetkopf	NE	Nachrichteneinheit
MK	Morsekode	NF	Normalform
MKA	Magnetbandkassetten-Aufnahmegerät	NF	Normalformat
MKS	Magnetkartenspeicher	NG	Nachrichtengröße
MKS	Magnetkernspeicher	NK	Netzknoten
ML	Markierungsleser	NKZ	Netzkontrollzentrum
ML	Mehrfachlochung	NMI	nicht maskierbarer Interrupt
MLT	Monolithtechnik	NNB	Netznachbildung
MM	mathematisches Modell	nöbL	nichtöffentlicher beweglicher Landfunk
MM	mittleres Management		
MM	monostabiler Multivibrator	NPSW	neues Programmstatuswort
MODEM	Modulator-Demodulator	NPT	Netzplantechnik
MOS	maschinenorientierte Sprache	NRMUe-g	Notrufmeldeübertragung für abgehenden Verkehr
MOS	maschinenorientiertes System		
MP	Magnetplatte	NRMUe-k	Notrufmeldeübertragung für ankommenden Verkehr
MP	Mehrprozessorsystem		
MP	Mikroprozessor	NS	Nebenspeicher
MP	Multiplexer	NS	numerische Steuerung
MPS	Magnetplattensteuereinheit	NSt	Nebenstelle
MPS	Magnetplattenspeicher	NSTA	Nebenstellenanlage
MPS	Magnetplattenstapel	NSZ	Netzsicherheitszentrum
MPS	Maschinenprogrammsprache	NT	Nachrichtentechnik
MPS	Mikroprogrammsystem	NT	Netztakt
MPS	Mikroprogrammspeicher	NT	Netzteil
MPS	Mikroprozessorsystem	NT	Normaltakt
MPSE	Magnetplattensteuereinheit	NÜ	Nachrichtenübertragung
MR	Mehrrechnersysten	NV	Nachrichtenverarbeitung
MR	Mikrorechner	NWS	Nachrichten-Warteschlange
MRS	Mehrrechnersystem		
MS	Magnetstreifen	O	Oszillator
MS	Makrosprache	OA	Organisationsanweisung
MS	Maschinensteuerung	OB	Ordnungsbegriff
MS	Maschinensprache	OB	Ortsbatterie
MSS	Massenspeichersystem	OBL	optischer Belegleser
MT	Magnettrommel	OD	Ordnungsdaten
MT	Magnettrommelspeicher	ODA	optischer Dokumentenabtaster
MT	Maschinentyp	ODS	optischer Dokumentensortierer
MT	Meßtaste	Ö	öffentliche Telekommunikationsstellen
MTB	Maschinentagebuch		
MTS	Magnettrommelspeicher	öbL	öffentlicher beweglicher Landfunk
MTSP	Magnettrommelspeicher	ÖTel	öffentliche Telefonstellen
MW	Maschinenwort	ÖTx	öffentliche Telexstellen
MZ	Maschinenzeit	OG	Operationsgruppe
MZZA	mittlere Zeit zwischen zwei Ausfällen	OK	oberer Kanal
		OK	Optokoppler
		OK	Ordnungskriterium
N	Nachricht	OLFU	on line Feldunterstützung
N	Netz	OLL	optischer Lochstreifenleser
N	Netzgerät	OLZ	on line Zusatz
N	Netzwerk	ON	Ortsnetz
NA	numerische Adressendatei	ONB	Ortsnetzbereich
NAR	Netzwerkadreßregister	ONDA	on line Datenverarbeitung

237

ABKÜRZUNGEN

OP	Objektprogramm	PDT	Prozeßdatentechnik
OP	Operationscode	PDV	Prozeßdatenverarbeitung
OP	Operationsregister	PE	periphere Einheit
OP	Opertaionsverstärker	PE	periphere Einrichtung
OPD	Oberpostdirektion	PE	Platteneinheit
OPR	Operand	PE	Programmende
OPR	Operation	PE	Programmentwicklung
OPREG	Operationsregister	PE	Prozeßeinheit
OPT	Option	PE	Prozeßelement
OR	Operandenregister	PEA	Prozeßein-/-ausgabe
OR	Operationsregister	PERSIS	Personalinformationssystem
OReg	Operationsregister	PFK	Phasenfrequenzkennlinie
OS	oberes Seitenband	PFM	Pulsfrequenzmodulation
OS	Operationssystem	PFN	Pulsformungsnetzwerk
OSB	oberes Seitenband	PFS	programmierbarer Festwertspeicher
OST	Operationssteuerung	PG	peripheres Gerät
OV	Operationsverstärker	PG	Peripheriegerät
OVk	Ortsverbindungskabel	PG	Programmgenerator
OVl	Ortsverbindungsleitung	PG	Programmiergerät
OVSt	Ortsvermittlungsstelle	PGS	Programmgeneratorsystem
OZ	Operationszentrum	PIB	Programminformationsblock
OZL	optischer Zeilenleser	PIP	Programm im Programm
		PK	Personalkennzeichen
P	Parität	PK	Personenkennzeichen
P	Perforation	PK	programmierter Kanal
P	Prozessor	PK	Programmkapazität
P	Puls	PK	Programmkarte
PA	Programmausnahme	PL	programmiertes Lernen
PA	Prüfadapter	PLA	programmierbare logische Arrays
PAE	Programmausgabeeinheit	PLIS	Planungsinformationssystem
PAE	Prozeßausgabeeinheit	PLK	Parameterlochkarte
PAG	Programmablaufgraph	PLK	Plastik-Lochkarte
PAISY	Personal-Abrechnungs- und Informationssystem	PlL	Planungsstelle für Linien
		PLM	Pulslängenmodulation
PAM	Pulsamplitudenmodulation	PLS	Prozeßleitsystem
PAP	Papierende	PLZ	Postleitzahl
PAP	Programmablaufplan	PM	Pegelmesser
PAR	Parameter	PM	Phasenmodulation
PAS	Programmablaufsteuerung	PM	Problemmaschine
PAS	Prozeßautomatisierungssprache	PM	Pulsmodulation
PB	Parameterblock	PN	Personalnummer
PB	Paritätsbit	PNK	programmierter Netzknoten
PB	Programmbibliothek	PNW	Prioritäten-Netzwerk
PB	Programmblock	POR	problemorientierte Routine
PB	Prüfen auf Bereich	PostO	Postordnung
PBM	Pulsbreitenmodulation	PostÖKart	öffentliche Telefonstellen mit Bedienung des Telefons durch den Benutzer bei Ä u
PBS	Plattenbetriebssystem		
PBS	Programmbaustein		
PCM	Pulscodemodulation	PostÖ-Münz	öffentliche Telefonstellen mit Bedienung des Telefons durch den Benutzer bei Ä u
PD	Pulsdauer		
PDM	Primärdatenmenge		
PDM	Pulsdauermodulation	PP	Produktionsprozeß
PDS	Personaldatensystem	PP	Programmpaket

ABKÜRZUNGEN

PP	Pseudoprogramm	PZR	Programmzustandsregister
PPM	Pulsphasenmodulation	PZU	Peripheriezugriff
PPM	Pulspositionsmodulation		
PPP	Produktionsprogrammplanung	QG	Quarzgenerator
PPS	computerunterstützte Produktions-	QIS	Qualitätsinformationssystem
	planung und -steuerung	QO	Quarzoszillator
PPS	problemorientierte Programmier-	QS	Qualitätssteuerung
	sprache	QS	Quellensprache
PR	Prozeßrechner	QUPR	Quellenprogramm
PR	Pseudoregister	Qvl	Querverbindungsleitungen
PRA	Prozeßrechneranlage		
PRAP	Programmablaufplan	R	Rasterdruck
PRB	Programmaufrufblock	R	Rechenwerk
PRF	Prozeßrechnerfunktion	R	Rechnung
Prt	privatöffentliche Telefonstellen	R	Redundanz
PROP	Produktionsplanung	R	Regelung
PROSI	Prozeß-Simulation	R	Register
PRS	Prozeßrechnersystem	R	Rückmeldung
PRT	Prozeßdatentechnik	RA	Rechenanlage
PRT	Prozeßrechentechnik	RA	relative Adresse
PS	Plattenspeicher	RA	Resultatausgabe
PS	Programmiersystem	RAS	Rückkehradressenspeicher
PS	Programmschlüssel	RBA	relative Byteadresse
PS	Programmsteuerung	RDC	Rufdekodierer
PS	Programmstatus	Re	Fernmelderechnungsstellen
PS	Programmsystem	RE	Rechner
PS	Projektsteuerungssystem	RE	Regelungselement
PSB	Programmspezifikationsblock	REF	Referenz
PSD	Programmstatusdoppelwort	REG	Register
PSE	programmierbare Steuereinheit	REW	Rechenwerk
PSE	programmierbare Steuereinrichtung	RF	Rechnerfamilie
PSG	Programmsteuergerät	Rf-	Rundfunk-
PSP	Plattenspeicher	RGB	rot/grün/blau
PSP	Programmspeicher	RGR	rechnergeführte Steuerung
PSP	Pufferspeicher	RGU	rechnergestützer Unterricht
PSS	Plattenspeichersteuerung	Richtl.	Richtlinie
PSS	Prozeßsteuerungssystem	RIR	relatives Indexregister
PST	Programmstruktur	RIS	rechnerunterstütztes Informations-
PST	Programmsteuerung		system
PSW	Programmstatuswort	RK	Randlochkarte
PT	programmierbares Terminal	RK	Rechnerkern
PT	Programmtechnik	RKS	Rückspulen
PTAB	Programmzustandstabelle	RL	Rückwärtslesen
PTS	Puffertaktsteuerung	RLK	Randlochkarte
PTV	programmierte Textverarbeitung	RM	Rechenmaschine
PU	programmierter Unterricht	RM	Rückmeldesignal
PU	Programmunterbrechung	RN	Rechnernetz
PUS	Programmunterbrechungssignal	RO	Rechenoperation
PV	Papiervorschub	RP	Rechenprozessor
PVSt	Paketvermittlungsstelle	RPL	Rechenplan
PW	Programmwechsel	RR	Rechenregister
PWS	Programmwarteschlange	RR	Resultatregister
PZ	Prüfzustand	RRZ	regionales Rechenzentrum

239

ABKÜRZUNGEN

RS	Rechnersystem	SF	Signalformer
RS	Referenzsignal	SF	Signalfrequenz
RS	Rücksetzen	SFT	schnelle Fourier-Transformation
RSE	Rechner-Statuseinheit	SI	Signalinformation
RSE	Ruf- und Signalstromerzeuger	SI	Standardinterface
RSM	Rücksetzen manuell	SIA	Standardinterface-Anschluß
RTS	rechnergestütztes Textsystem	SIAG	Signalausgabe
RU	rechnerunterstützter Unterricht	SIEG	Signaleingabe
RUU	rechnerunterstützter Unterricht	SIG	Sichtgerät
RVS	Rechner-Verbundsystem	SIG	Signal
RW	Rechenwerk	SIP	selbstinterpretierender Programmgenerator
RZ	Rechenzentrum		
		SK	Satzkennzeichen
s.	siehe	SK	Schaltkontakt
S	Satz	SK	Schnellkanal
S.	Seite	SK	Senderkennung
S	setzen	SK	Sortierkriterium
S	Sortierung	SK	Standardkanal
S	Speicher	SKE	Satelliten-Kommunikations-Empfangseinrichtungen
S	Start		
SA	Satzadresse	SKZ	Satzkennzeichen
SA	Schreibautomat	SL	Satzlänge
SA	Sortierautomatik	SL	Signallampe
SAB	Signalaufbereitung	SL	Signalleitung
SAP	Satellitenprogramm	SL	Steuerlogik
SAR	Speicheradreßregister	SL	Streifenleser
SAR	Speicherauswahlregister	SL	Streifenlocher
SAS	Speicheranschlußsteuerung	SM	Schreibmaschine
SAS	Steuerwertausgabesystem	SM	Servomotor
SB	Servicebüro	SM	Sortiermaschine
SB	Systemberater	SNT	Schaltnetzteil
SB	Systemberatung	SO	Speicherorganisation
SB	Systembereich	SOP	Sortierprogramm
SBD	Sendebezugsdämpfung	SP	Schnittstelle parallel
SBN	Standard-Buchnummer	SP	Speicher
SBS	Speicherbereichsschutz	SP	Speicherplatz
SC	Strichcode	SP	Speicherung
SD	Schnelldrucker	SP	strukturierte Programmierung
SD	Streifendrucker	SP	Systemprozeß
SDG	Steuerdifferentialgeber	SPA	Speicheradresse
SDP	Sinnbilder für Datenflußpläne	SPB	Speiseblock
SDR	Schnelldrucker	SPE	Speichereinheit
SDR	Sender	SPE	Speichererweiterung
SDR	Speicherdatenregister	SPO	Speicherorganisation
SDS	Stammdatenspeicher	SPR	Speicherprüfroutine
SDÜ	schnelle Datenübertragung	SPR	Systemprogramm
SE	Sortiereinheit	SPS	Steuerprogrammsystem
SE	Speichereinheit	SPS	symbolisches Programmiersystem
SE	Steuereinheit	SPSW	steuerndes Programmstatuswort
SE	Steuereinrichtung	SPU	seriell-parallel-Umsetzer
SE	Systemeinheit	SPU	Sprung ins Unterprogramm
SEG	Sende- und Empfangsgerät	SR	Satellitenrechner
SEU	Sende-/Empfangsumsetzer	SR	Schwenkrahmen

ABKÜRZUNGEN

SR	Speicherregister	TD	Testdaten
SRE	Spannungsregeleinrichtung	TD	Text- und Datensysteme
SRegelF	Sonderregelung über Aufwandsvergütungen im Bereich der Ämter des Fernmeldewesens	TDG	Testdatengenerator
		TE	Takteinheit
		Tel.	Telefon
SS	Speicher-Speicher	Tel	Telefondienst
SSI	System Status Information	TEPOS	Testprogrammsystem
ST	Startsignal	TES	Teilnehmereinrichtungsschaltung
ST	Systemtechnik	TESPOS	Testprogrammsystem
STA	Steueralgorithmus	TESY	Testsystem
STE	Steuereinheit	TF	Trägerfrequenz
STE	Systemsteuereinheit	Tfx	Telefaxdienst
STP	Steuerprogramm	TG	Taktgeber
STR	Startadreßregister	TG	Taktgenerator
STV	Stapelverarbeitung	TIB	technische Informationsbibliothek
STV	Stromversorgung	TIS	Totalinformationssystem
STZ	Steuerzeichen	TK	Typenerkennung
SU	Systemunterstützung	TKAnl	Telekommunikationsanlage
SUSY	Subsystem	TKO	Telekommunikationsordnung
SV	Seitenvorschub	TKSys	Telekommunikationssystem
SV	Systeme und Verfahren	TL	Transistorlogik
SVE	Stromversorgungseinheit	Tmx	Temexdienst
SVG	Stromversorgungsgerät	Tn-	Ton-
SVGR	Stromversorgungsgerät	TN	Transportnetzwerk
SWFD	Selbstwählferndienst	TP	Testprogramm
SYN	Synchronisierung	TPR	Teilprogramm
SYP	Systemprogramm	TR	Taschenrechner
SZ	Satzzeichen	TR	Tischrechner
SZ	Servicezentrum	TR	Transferregister
SZ	Suchzeit	TRS	Transkription
SZA	Speicherzyklusanforderung	TS	Teilnehmersystem
		TS	Teilnehmerschaltung
T	Tabelle	TSE	Test- und Simuliereinrichtung
T	Tastatur	TSP	Transponder
T-	Telegrafen-	TSP	Trommelspeicher
T	Trommel	TST	Transportsteuerung
TA	Tastatur	TT	Transistortechnik
TA	Teilantwort	TTU	Teletex-Telex-Umsetzer
TAB	technischer Arbeitsbericht	Ttx	Teletextdienst
TAD	Tagesdatei	TÜ	Terminalübersicht
TAE	Telekommunikationsanschlußeinheit	TV	Teilnehmerverbinder
TAG	Telexteilnehmer-Anschaltgerät	TV	Textverarbeitung
TAGDAT	Tagesdaten	TVArb	Tarifvertrag für Arbeiter
TAP	Terminalanpassungsprozessor	TVP	Telex-Verschlüsselungs-Paket
TAR	temporäres Adreßregister	TVS	Taktversorgung
TAR	Terminalanpassungsrechner	Tx	Telex
TAS	Tastatur	Tx	Telexdienst
TAS	Terminabrufsystem	TxNstA	Telex-Nebenstellenanlage
TB	Tonbandgerät	TZ	Taktzentrale
TbF	technische und betriebliche Funktionsbedingungen		
		U	Umschalter
TBG	Testbaugruppe	UB	Umschaltbaugruppe
TBS	Teilnehmer-Betriebssystem	UDB	universelle Datenbank

ABKÜRZUNGEN

UDR	Unterdrücken	VL	Vorwärtslesen
UDS	universelles Datenbanksystem	VM	virtuelle Maschine
Ü	Überlauf	VMM	virtueller Maschinenmonitor
Ü	Übertrag	VMS	Vermittlungssystem
Ü	Übertrager	VN	Verteilernetzwerk
ÜAS	Übertragungsablaufsteuerung	VO	Vollzugsordnung
Üb.	Übersetzung	VOFe	Vollzugsordnung für den Fernsprechdienst
ÜD	Überspringen von Daten		
ÜE	Übertragungseinheit	VOFunk	Vollzugsordnung für den Funkdienst
ÜE	Übertragungseinrichtung	VorlArb-Anw	vorläufige Arbeitsanweisung für den handvermittelten Fernsprechdienst
ÜLE	Überleiteinrichtung		
ÜP	Übersetzungsprogramm	VOT	Vollzugsordnung für den Telegrafendienst
ÜST	Übertragungssteuerung		
ÜW	Überwachung	VP	Verarbeitungsprogramm
UIT	Union Internationale des Télécommunications	VP	Verarbeitungsperiode
		VP	Versuchsprogramm
UK	unterer Kanal	VR	Vermittlungsrechner
UKW	Ultrakurzwelle	VR	Vorrechner
UL	Urlader	VRZ	Verkehrsrechenzentrum
ULE	universelle logische Einheit	VRZ	Vorwärts-/Rückwärtszähler
ULS	universelle Logikschaltung	VS	Verarbeitungssystem
UP	Unterprogramm	VS	virtueller Speicher
UPN	umgekehrte polnische Notation	VS	virtuelles System
UPRO	Unterprogramm	VSS	Verbundsteuersystem
UPS	Unterprogrammsprung	VSt	Vermittlungsstelle
US	Unterbrechungssystem	VT	Vertikaltabulation
US	unteres Seitenband	VT	Videotext
US	Untersystem	VV	Vorverstärker
USP	Unterprogrammsprung	VVDi	Verbindungs- und Verteilungsdose Innenausbau
Ust	Umsatzsteuer		
UStG	Umsatzsteuergesetz	VwAnw	Verwaltungsanweisung
USV	unterbrechungsfreie Stromversorgung	VwVfG	Verwaltungsverfahrensgesetz
		VZ	Verarbeitungszeit
UTA	Universal-Telex-Adapter	VZ	Verhältniszähler
UTC	universaler Teletex Controller	VZ	Verzweigung
UZ	Universalzähler	VZ	Vorzeichen
		VZZ	Verzögerungszähler
V	Variable		
V	Verbindung	W-	Wähl-
V	Verkehr	W	Wählleitung
V	Verstärker	W	Wechselspannung
V	Verstärkung	W	Wort
V	Voltmeter	WAL	Wiederanlauf
VA	Voltampere	WAR	Wortausgaberegister
VC	Volkscomputer	WAZ	Wahlaufforderungszeichen
VD	Verdrahtung	WD	Warndienst
VDE	Verband Deutscher Elektrotechniker	WDB	Werkstoffdatenbank
VDI	Verein Deutscher Ingenieure	WDV	wissenschaftliche Datenverarbeitung
VE	Verarbeitungseinheit	WEX	Wortexpander
VE	Verkehrseinheit	WEZ	Wahlendezeichen
VGF	Vergleichsfehler	WF	Walshfunktion
VIS	Vorstandsinformationssystem	WGR	Wiedergaberegister
VKS	visuelles Kommunikationssystem	WGR	wiedergeben rückwärts

ABKÜRZUNGEN

WGV	wiedergeben vorwärts	ZVOFunk	Zusatz-Vollzugsordnung für den Funkdienst
Wh	Wattstunde	ZVSt	Zentralvermittlungsstelle
WHP	Wiederholungsprüfung	ZW	Zählwerk
WI	wiederholen	ZT	Zyklustakt
WIS	Wertpapierinformationssystem	ZZF	Zentralamt für Zulassungen im Fernmeldewesen
WL	Wortlänge		
WM	wortorganisierte Maschine		
WPL	Wechselplatte		
WPM	Wörter pro Minute		
WR	Wagenrücklauf		
WS	Warteschlange		
WStE	Wählsterneinrichtung		
WT	Wählton		
WT	Wechselstromtelegrafie		
Z	Zähler		
Z	Zahl		
Z	Zeichen		
Z	Zentralregister		
Z	Zuverlässigkeit		
ZA	Ziffernanzeige		
ZB	Zentralbatterie		
ZD	Zahlendarstellung		
ZD	Zusatzdrucker		
ZDB	zentrale Datenbank		
ZDF	Zweites Deutsches Fernsehen		
ZDM	zentraler Datenmultiplexer		
ZDR	Zeichendrucker		
ZDR	Zeilendrucker		
ZDV	zentrale Datenverarbeitung		
ZE	Zeilenende		
ZE	Zentraleinheit		
Zeichen/s	Zeichen pro Sekunde		
ZI	Ziffernumschaltung		
ZM	Zeitmarke		
ZP	Zykluspuffer		
ZR	Zentralrechner		
ZR	Zwischenregister		
ZRA	zentrale Rechenanlage		
ZS	Zufallssignal		
ZS	Zustandsspeicher		
ZS	Zwischenspeicher		
ZSP	Zwischenspeicher		
ZST	Zentralsteuerung		
ZT	Zieltext		
ZTE	Zentraleinheit		
ZÜ	Zeichenübertragung		
ZÜP	zeitüberwachtes Programm		
ZulB	Zulassungsbedingungen		
ZV	Zeilenvorschub		
ZVEI	Zentralverband der Elektrotechnischen Industrie e.V.		

000-Taste 000-key
10-Sekundentakt 10 seconds cycle
15-Pin D-Stecker weiblich 15-pin female D-connector
16-Bit-Rechner 16-bit processor
1-Block 1 block
1-Zeichen-Block 1 character block
20mA-Option 20mA option
20mA-Schalter 20mA switch
2stufig 2-step
4-20 mA Verdrahtung 4-20mA instrument wiring
4adriges Kabel 4-wire cable
4-Bit-Anzeige 4-bit-display
4 Byte lang 4 byte long
4polig 4-pin
4poliges Spiralkabel 4-pin coiled cord
50-Pin-Anschluß 50-pin connector
760m-Band 760m tape
80 Byte lang 80 byte long
80spaltige Lochkarte 80-column punched card

A

á commercial at
ab from
abarbeiten process
Abbauanweisungen deinstallation guide
abbauen deinstall, reduce
Abbild image, mapping
abbilden depict, map
Abbildung figure, illustration, map, mapping
Abbildungsfunktion function of representation, mapping function
Abbildungsprozedur mapping procedure
Abblendschalter dimmer switch
Abbrechen aborting, stopping, truncation
abbrechen abandon, abort, cancel, error off, quit, terminate, truncate
abbrechen ohne Änderungen abort without change
Abbrechfehler truncation error
Abbruch abort, cancel, termination
Abbruchcode abort code
Abbruchfehler termination error
Abbruchmakro abort macro
Abbruchmeldung termination message
Abbruchstelle breakpoint
abdecken cover
Abdeckung access cover, cover, coverage, top cover
Abdeckung der Systemeinheit system unit cover
Abfallzeit connection timeout
abfangen intercept
Abfangspeicherstelle intercept data storage position
abfassen draft
Abfertigung am Kassenplatz checkout
Abfrage inquiry, query
Abfragebefehl inquiry command, query command, sense command
Abfragebeispiel enquiry example, inquiry example, query example
Abfragedienst inquiry service
Abfrageeinheit inquiry station
Abfragefunktion inquiry function
Abfragemagnetband interrogating magnetic tape
Abfragemodus inquiry mode, query mode
Abfragemöglichkeit enquiry option, inquiry option

Abfragen inquiring, probe
abfragen inquire, interrogate, poll, query
Abfragename query name
abfragende Stelle polling station
Abfrageprogramm inquiry program
Abfrageprozessor query language processor
Abfrageschaltung scan unit
Abfragesprache query language
Abfragesystem mit Parallelzugriff concurrent inquiry system condition
Abfragetechnik polling
Abfrageterminal inquiry terminal
Abfühlimpuls read pulse
Abfühlkontakt sensing contact
Abfühlpufferspeicher read buffer storage
Abfühlstation reading station
Abgabe-Stellenversetzung shift from word control
Abgang disposal, issue
Abgangsart depletion mode
Abgangsbetrag outgoing amount
Abgangsbuchung deduction posting
Abgangsdatum issue date
Abgangsliste issues list
Abgangsmonat disposal month
abgeben issue
abgeblendet dim, dimmed
abgebrochen interrupted
abgegrenzt cut off
abgehend outbound, outgoing
abgehende Leitung outbound line, outgoing line
abgehende Verbindung outgoing call
abgekürzt brief, verbose
abgekürzte Adressierung abbreviated addressing
abgekürztes Tastaturkommando abbreviated keyboard command
abgelegte Nachricht filed message
abgerufen called off, called up
abgeschirmtes Datenkabel shielded signal cable
Abgeschlossenheit compartmentation
abgesetzt detached, distributed, remote
abgespeicherte Testmeldung canned test message
abgesprochen agreed
abgewertet devaluated
Abgleich adjustment, fine tuning, tuning
abgrenzen restrict
Abgrenzung cut off
Abgrenzungsmöglichkeit cut off option
abhängig dependent

245

Abhängigkeit dependence, dependency
Abhilfemaßnahmen corrective action
Abkürzung abbreviation, mnemonic, shorthand macro, time saver
abladen dump
Abladestelle unloading point
Ablage cabinet, file cabinet, folder
Ablagefach stacker
Ablagefachnummer pigeonhole number
Ablageinformation eines Schriftstückes header information
Ablagemodus location mode
Ablagename cabinet file name
ab Lager off-the-shelf
Ablagesteuerung stacker selection
Ablagesystem electronic file cabinet, file cabinet
Ablagesystem im Rechner electronic file cabinet
Ablageverwaltung file cabinet maintenance, file maintenance
Ablauf execution, operation, run
Ablaufanalysenprogramm flow analysis program
Ablaufbandteller supply reel
Ablaufbeschreibung run procedure
ablaufen expire, run
ablaufen auf hosted
ablauffähiges Programm active program, executable program
Ablauffehler der Gegenstelle remote procedure error, remote processor error
Ablaufkette sequence chain
Ablauflogik control logic
Ablaufmodus run mode
ablauforientiert operation oriented
Ablaufplan flowchart
Ablaufschema run procedure
Ablaufsteuerung event schenduling system, run control
Ablaufstruktur flow structure, program design
Ablaufunterbrechung exception condition
Ablaufverfolgung trace back, tracing
Ablaufzeit execution time
Ablaufzustand run state
ablegen deposit, file
ablehnen reject
ableiten derive
Ableitung derivation
Ablenkgenerator time base generator
ablesen read
abmelden logoff, logout
Abmeldung logoff, logout

Abmessung dimension, measurement
Abmessungen physical dimensions
Abmessungen des Terminals terminal dimension
Abnahme acceptance, deceleration, decrease
Abnahmebedingungen acceptance terms
Abnahmebürste pick off brush
Abnahmemenge quantity purchased
abnehmen accept, decrease, reduce
Abnehmer client
abnormal abnormal
abnormales Ende abnormal end
Abnormalitätsprüfung abnormal test
abrechnen settle
Abrechnung accounting, settlement
Abrechnungsart settlement type
Abrechnungsdatei accounting file
Abrechnungsdatum settlement date
Abrechnungskreis subledger
Abrechnungsperiode accounting period
Abrechnungsprotokolldatei accounting log file
Abrechnungsprotokollierung log file editor
Abrechnungstag due day
Abrechnungstermin settlement date
Abrechnungszeitraum accounting period, settlement period
Abreißschiene document parting bar
Abruf call, fetch
Abrufauftrag call-off
Abrufdatei retrieval file
Abrufdatum call-off date
Abrufdokumentation call-off documentation
abrufen call, poll, recall, retrieve
Abrufkommando calling command
Abrufkriterium call criterion
Abrufmenge quantity called off
Abrufnummer call-off number
Abrufwerte call-off values
Absage cancellation, reject
absagen cancel
Absageschreiben cancellation notice
Absageschreibung cancellation notice
Absatz paragraph
Absatzmarke paragraph marker
Absatznumerierungsfeld paragraph numbering field
Absatznumerierungstyp type of paragraph numbering
Absatzschutz paragraph protection
Absatzstoptaste paragraph key
abschaltbar disconnectible
Abschalten deactivation
abschalten deactivate, shutdown, switch off

Abschaltsignal shutdown signal
Abschiedsmeldung termination message
Abschiedsseite farewell page
abschirmen guard, shield
Abschirmung shield
Abschlag adjustment, anticipated payment
abschließen close, conclude
abschließend finally
abschließendes Minuszeichen trailing minus sign
Abschluß closing, completion
Abschlußbuchung closing entry
Abschlußposten close off item
Abschlußprogramm termination program
Abschlußsockel terminator socket
Abschlußstatus completion status
Abschlußteilprogramm termination segment program
Abschlußtermin closing date
Abschlußtext closing text
Abschneiden truncation
abschneiden curtail, truncate
Abschneidevorrichtung cut off press appliance
Abschnitt block, paragraph, portion, section
Abschnittauswahl paragraph selection
Abschnittsammelbehälter receiving device for paper stripes
Abschnittsanfang start of sector
Abschnittsarbeitsdatei paragraph work file
Abschnittsauswahlliste paragraph selection list
Abschnittsauswahltabelle paragraph selection table
Abschnittsbereich paragraph region
Abschnittsbrief paragraph letter
Abschnittsbriefnummer paragraph letter number
Abschnittsdatei section file
Abschnittsdateiverwaltung paragraph file management
Abschnittsgruppe paragraph group
Abschnittskarte paragraph card
Abschnittsliste paragraph list
Abschnittsnummer paragraph number, section number
Abschnittspuffer paragraph buffer
Abschnittssatz paragraph record
Abschnittsselektionsbrief paragraph selection letter
abschreiben amortize, depreciate, write off
Abschreibung amortization, depreciation
Abschreibungsart amortization type
Abschreibungs-Basiswert base value for amortization

Abschreibungsbeginn start of amortization, start of depreciation
Abschreibungsberechnung calculation of amortization, calculation of depreciation
Abschreibungsbetrag amortization amount, amount of depreciation, depreciation amount
Abschreibungsbuchung amortization posting, depreciation posting
Abschreibungsdauer amortization period, depreciation period
Abschreibungsende end of amortization, end of depreciation
Abschreibungsermittlung determination of amortization, determination of depreciation
Abschreibungsfeld amortization field, depreciation field
Abschreibungshöhe amount of the amortization
Abschreibungskonstellation amortization configuration, depreciation configuration
Abschreibungskorrektur amortization adjustment, depreciation adjustment
Abschreibungskosten amortization costs, depreciation costs
Abschreibungslauf amortization
Abschreibungsliste amortization list, depreciation list
Abschreibungsmethode amortization method, method of depreciation
Abschreibungsmodalität amortization mode, depreciation mode
Abschreibungsparameter amortization parameter, depreciation parameter
Abschreibungsprognose amortization forecast, depreciation forecast
Abschreibungsprozent amortization rate, depreciation rate
Abschreibungsprozentsatz amortization rate, depreciation rate
Abschreibungsrechnung amortization calculation, depreciation calculation
Abschreibungsregel amortization rule, depreciation rule
Abschreibungssatz amortization record, depreciation record
Abschreibungsschlüssel amortization code, depreciation code
Abschreibungssimulation simulated amortization, simulated depreciation
Abschreibungssteuerungsfeld amortization control field, depreciation control field
Abschreibungsstornierung amortization cancellation, depreciation cancellation

Abschreibungswert amortization value, depreciation value
Abschreibungszeitraum payoff period
Absendedatum date of dispatch
absenden dispatch, send, send off
Absender sender
Absender der aktuellen Nachricht current message's originator
Absenderkennzeichnung sender marker
Absicherung securing
Absicht idea, intention
absolut absolute
Absolutadreßbereich absolute address area
Absolutadresse absolute address
Absolutaktenzeichen absolute file reference
Absolutauswahl absolute selection
Absolutdatei absolute file
absolute Adresse absolute address
absolute Adressierung absolute addressing
Absoluteintragung absolute entry
absolute Programmierung absolute programming
absoluter Index literal subscript
absolutes Ende unconditional end
absolute virtuelle Adresse absolute virtual address
Absolutlader absolute loader
Absolutname absolute name
Absolutnummer absolute number
Absolutsteuerblock absolute control block
Absoluttext absolute text
absorbierte Strahlendosis radiation absorbed dosis
abspeichern store
abspielen play back
Abspielmodus run mode
Absprache agreement
absteigend descending
absteigende Reihenfolge descending order
abstimmen adjust, tune
Abstimmkonto contra account
Abstimmliste reconciliation list
Abstimmröhre tuning indicator tube
Abstimmung adjustment, consultation
Abstimmzähler check off counter
abstrakte Syntax abstract syntax
Absturz crash
Absummierungskonto totalling account
Absummierungsprotokoll total protocol
Absummierungszeile total line
Abszisse abscissa
AB-Taste AB-key, down-key
Abtasteinrichtung scanner

abtasten scan
Abtaster scanner
Abtastfrequenz sampling rate
Abtastgeschwindigkeit scanning speed at transmission
Abtastkopf sensing head
Abtast-Matrixvergleich scan matrix compare
Abtastpunkt scanning spot at transmission
Abtastrate sample frequency
Abtastregelung sampling control
Abtastrichtung scanning track direction
Abtastung sampling
Abtastungskodierer scan encoder
Abtastwagen scanning carriage
Abtastwicklung read winding
Abtastzeile scanning line
Abtastzeit scan time
Abteilung department
Abteilungsbezeichnung department name
abteilungsbezogen department related
Abteilungsleitung department management
Abteilungsnummer departement number
Abteilungszugehörigkeit department affiliation
abtrennbar two tier
Abtretung assignment
abwählen deselect, vote out
Abwärtstransformator step-down transformer
abweichen differ
abweichend differing
abweichende Sortierfolge alternate collation sequence
abweichende Zeichen character mismatch
Abweichung discrepancy, variation
Abweichungsmenge amount of the discrepancy
Abweichungswert value of the discrepancy
abweisen reject
Abwertung devaluation
Abwertungsvorschlagsliste devaluation proposal
abwickeln finish, handle, process
Abwicklungsstand procedure status
abziehen deduct, subtract
Abzinsung discounting
abzüglich minus
Abzug deduction
Abzweigdose junction box
Achse des Hilfsmotors servo axis
achten respect
Achtung caution
acknowledge quittieren
Adapter für byteorientierte Geräte multi-subsystem adapter

Adapter für Computerspiele game control adapter
Adapterstecker plug adaptor
Adapter zur Steuereinheit multi-subsystem adapter
adaptieren adapt
Addendenregister addend register
Addiereinrichtung adder
addieren accumulate, add, add up, sum, total
Addierer adder
Addiergeschwindigkeit accumulation speed
Addierglied adder
Addiermaschine adding machine
Addiermodus add mode
Addierwerk adder unit
Addition addition
Additionsbefehl add instruction
Additionsregister adding register
Additionsübertrag add carry
Additionswert addend
Administration administration
Administrations-Befehl administration command
Administrations-Kommando administration command
Administrationskomponente administrative component
Administrationsplatz administration place
Administrationsprogramm administrative program
Administrator administrator
administrieren administer
Adreßanhängung address enable
Adressarithmetik-Einheit address arithmetic unit
Adressatennummer addressee number
Adreßaufbau address structure
Adreßauskunft directory service
Adreßauswahl address repertoire
Adreßbereich address space
Adreßbit address bit
Adreßbuch directory
Adreßbuchdienst directory service
Adreßbuchstatistik address book statistic
Adreßbus address bus
Adreßdaten address data
Adreßdatenverarbeitung address data processing
Adreßdekodierung address decode logic
Adresse address, location, postal address
Adresse der gerufenen Station called address
Adresse der rufenden Station calling address

Adresse des erweiterten Attributblocks XAB address
Adresse im geschützten Speicherbereich protected memory address
Adreßeingabe address input
Adressenänderung address modification
Adressen-Ansteuerungssystem address selecting system
Adressenbearbeitung address calculating
Adressenbelegung map
Adressendefinition address definition
Adressenende end of address
adressenfrei symbolic
Adressen-Leerstelle address blank
Adressenmarke address mark
Adressenschreibung address printing
Adreßfehler address error
Adreßfeld address field
Adreßgenerator address generator
adressierbar addressable
Adressierbarkeit addressability
adressieren address
Adressierung addressing
Adressierungsart addressing mode, record address type
Adressierungsdomäne addressing domain
Adressierungsverwaltung addressing authority
Adreßimpulseingang address strobe input
Adreßinformationsprogramm mapping program
Adreßkennzeichen address identification
Adreßliste address list
Adreßmodifikator label modifier
Adreßraum address space, addressing space
Adreßrechnung address arithmetic
Adreßregister address register
Adreßrepertoire address repertoire
Adreßschlüssel address code
Adreßteil address part
Adreßüberschreitung address overflow
Adreßübersetzer address translator
Adreßumsetzung address translation, mapping
adreßunabhängig relocatable
Adreßverriegelung address latch enable
Adreßzähler address counter, location counter
Adreßzuordnung address assignment
Adreßzuordnungstabelle reference table
ähnlich similar
änderbar alterable
ändern alter, change, modify
Ändern der Tastatur change keyboard
Änderung alteration, delta, engineering change order, modification, revision

249

Änderung beim Kunden field change order
Änderung der Jobablaufplanung job rescheduling
Änderungsanweisung engineering change order
Änderungsart alteration type
Änderungsauftrag modification order
Änderungsbeleg change voucher
Änderungsbelegnummer change voucher number
Änderungsbereich modification range
Änderungsbereich für Betriebssystem patch area
Änderungsbestätigung change acknowledgement
änderungsbezogene Datensicherung incremental backup
Änderungscode alteration code
Änderungsdaten modification data
Änderungsdatum alteration date, amendment date, date modified
Änderungsdienst modification service
Änderungsfolge change string
Änderungsfunktion modification function
Änderungsgeschwindigkeit rate of change
Änderungshinweise change marker
Änderungsindex amendment index
Änderungskennzeichen change bar
Änderungsmitteilung change message, revision modification
Änderungsprotokoll amendment cog
Änderungsprozedur modification procedure
Änderungsrate alteration rate
Änderungsroutine patch processor
Änderungsschlüssel modification key
Änderungsschreibung change posting
Änderungsstand revision level
Änderungsvormerkung change note
Änderungszeile alteration line
Änderungszeit alteration time
äquivalent equivalent
Äquivalenzname equivalence name
ätzend corrosive
Ätzmittel corrosive agent
äußere Isolierung outer insulation
Affrikat affricate
Aggregat aggregate, unit
Aggregatnummer aggregate number
Aiken-Code Aiken-Code
Akkumulator accumulator, storage battery
Akkumulatorelektrode storage battery electrode
Akkumulator-Platte battery plate
Akkumulator-Rechner accumulator computer

akkumulieren accumulate
Akkumulierungsfeld accumulation field
Akronym acronym
Akt act
Aktenzeichen document reference
Aktenzeichenart kind of document modification
Aktenzeichen-Kennzeichen document identification
Aktion action, item
Aktionsabsender sender of the internal message
Aktionsart internal message type
Aktionscode internal message code
Aktionsempfänger recipient of the internal message
Aktionsliste internal message list
Aktionsnummer internal message number
Aktionsprogramm action program
Aktionssatz internal message record
Aktionstext internal message text
Aktionstyp internal message type
Aktionsverwaltung management of internal messages
Aktionsverzeichnis directory of internal messages
aktiv active
Aktiva assets
aktiver Arbeitsbereich active work space
aktiver Filter active filter
aktives Laufwerk active drive
aktiv für anderen Kanal busy to other channel
aktivieren activate
Aktivierung activation
Aktivierungsbeleg activation voucher
aktivierungsfähig activatable
Aktivierungskennzeichen activation marker
Aktivierungsnummer activation number
Aktivierungsschalter activation switch
Aktivität activity
Aktivitätensteuerteil activity request packet
Aktivitätensteuerung activity control
Aktivitätskette activity chain
Aktivitätskettenfeld activity chaining field
aktualisieren update
Aktualität currency, update state
aktuell current
aktuelle Ablage current file cabinet
aktuelle Daten actual data
aktuelle Funktion current task
aktueller Ordner active folder
aktueller Puffer current buffer

aktueller Text current item
aktueller Wert current value
aktueller Zählerstand actual count, current count, current count value
aktuelles Befehlregister current instruction register
aktuelle Schleife current loop
aktuelles Datum current date
aktuelle Seitennummer current page number
aktuelles Feld active cell, active field, current cell, current field
aktuelles Fenster active window, current window
aktuelles Laufwerk active drive, selected drive
aktuelles Programm active program, active task, current program, current task
aktuelle Uhrzeit current time
aktuelle Zeile actual line
aktuelle Zeilenanzahl current text size
aktuelle Zeilenzahl current number of lines
Akustikkoppler acoustic coupler
akustisches Meldegerät annunciator
akustisches Signal alarm message, audible indicator, beep, ring indicator
akustische Steuerung acoustic variable control
akustisches Zeichen beep
Akzeptanz acceptance
akzeptieren accept, honor
alarmierend alarming
Algorithmus algorithm
Alias alias
Alkali-Mangan-Batterie alkaline batterie
alleine alone, single
allerdings in fact
alles löschen clear all
Allgemein- general purpose
allgemein general, generic, global
allgemeine Bezugszahl general indicator
allgemeine Querverweistabelle common cross-reference table
allgemeiner Prozeß general process
allgemeiner Registersatz general register set, general register stack
allgemeiner Schnittstellenbus general purpose interface bus
allgemeiner Sendeaufruf general poll
allgemeiner Standard general default
allgemeines Betriebsmodusmerkmal general set-up feature
Alphabet alphabet
Alphabet-Mischeinrichtung alphabetic collating device
Alpha-Eingabe alpha input

alphanumerisch alphanumeric
alphanumerische Anzeigearchitektur alphanumeric display architecture
alphanumerischer Farbmodus A/N color mode
alphanumerischer Tastenbereich alphanumeric area
alphanumerischer Zeichensatz alphanumeric character set
Alphazeichen alpha, alpha character, alphabetic character
als nicht betriebsbereit kennzeichnen mark down
alt existing, old
Altbestand previous stock level
Alter age
Altern aging
altern age
Alternativangebot alternative offer
Alternative alternative
alternativer Programmpfad alternate program path, alternative program path
alternative Sortierfolge alternate collation sequence
Alternativmodus alternative mode
Alternativsprache alternative language
alternativ zu alternative to
Altersgrenze age limit
Aluminium aluminium
Aluminiumkondensator aluminium capacitor
alveolar alveolar
am besten best
amerikanische Börsenaufsicht Securities and Exchange Commission
amerikanische Normbehörde American National Standardization Institute
Amerikanischer Standard-Code American Standard Code
amerikanischer Standardcode für Informationsaustausch American Standard Code for Information Interchange
Amerikanische Vereinigung der Mikroprozessor-Ingenieure American Association of Microprocessor Engineers
Amortisation amortization
Amortisationsprozentsatz amortization rate
Amortisationsüberwachung amortization control
Amplidyne amplidyne
Amplitudenmodulation amplitude modulation, amplitude shift keying
amplitudenmoduliertes Signal amplitude-modulated signal

Amt departement, office
am tiefsten verschachtelte Operation innermost operation
amtlich official
am weitesten links stehendes Zeichen leftmost character
am weitesten rechts stehende Ziffer rightmost digit
analog analog, analogous, similar
Analogalarm analog alarm
Analogausfall analog failure
Analog-Digital-/Digital-Analog-Wandler analog to digital/digital to analog convertor
Analog-Digital-Umsetzer analog digital converter
Analog-Digital-Wandler analog digital converter, analog to digital convertor
analoge Phasenverriegelungsschleife analog phase locked loop
Analog-Hilfseingang auxiliary analog input
Analogie analogy
Analogquelle analog supply
Analogrechenwerk analog processing unit
Analogrechner analog computer
Analogschaltung analog circuit
Analogverstärkung analog gain
Analysator analyzer
Analyse analysis
Analysedatei analysis file
Analysefunktion analysis function
Analyseprogramm analysation program, analysis program, parser
Analysesystem parser
analysieren analyse, parse
Analytiker analyst
Anbaugerät accessory equipment
anbieten offer
Anbieter provider
Anbindung connectivity
anbringen mount
andere other
andere Zeichenfolge alternate collation sequence
andernfalls otherwise
anders other
Andruck draft, print
andrucken print out
Aneinanderreihung string
anerkennen recognize
anfängliche Richtung initial direction
anfallen accrue, come up
Anfang begin, beginning, start, top
Anfang eines Dokuments top of a document

anfangen begin, start, start up
anfangs initial
Anfangsadresse start address
Anfangsanschlag left hand margin
Anfangsbelegung initial occupancy
Anfangsbild initial picture, start up picture, welcome picture
Anfangsbuchwert opening book value
Anfangsinformation header information
Anfangskennzeichnung beginning mark
Anfangsnummer start number
Anfangsposition home
Anfangsrandsteller left margin set
Anfangsseitennummer initial page number
Anfangsspalte start column
Anfangsspur initial track
Anfangsstatement initial statement
Anfangswert initial value
Anfangszeit start time
Anfangszustandswort initial status word
anfordern request
Anforderung request
Anforderung an die Systemsteuerung executive request
Anforderung bezüglich externer Funktion external function request
Anforderungen an die Umgebung environmental requirement
Anforderungsart request type
Anforderungsbestätigungssystem request acknowledge system
Anforderungsblock request block
Anforderungsdaten request data
Anforderungsdatum request date
Anforderungsinformationen request information
Anforderungsmenge requested quantity
Anforderungsnummer request number
Anforderungsprinzip request scheme
Anfrage enquiry, inquiry, request
Anfrageabwicklung enquiry processing, inquiry processing
Anfrage an den Operator operator request
Anfragebearbeitung enquiry processing, inquiry processing
Anfragebeleg enquiry voucher, inquiry voucher
Anfrageerfassung enquiry registration, inquiry registration
Anfragekopf enquiry header, inquiry header
Anfragekopftext enquiry header text, inquiry header text
Anfragelöschliste enquiry delete list, inquiry delete list

Anlagenfeldgröße

anfragen ask for, call for, enquire, inquire
Anfragengenerierung enquiry generation, inquiry generation
Anfragenummer enquiry number, inquiry number
Anfrageposition enquiry item, inquiry item
Anfragepositionstext enquiry item text, inquiry item text
Anfrageschreibung printing of enquiries, printing of inquiries
Anfrageschreibungsprogramm enquiry print program, inquiry print program
Anfragetext enquiry text, inquiry text
anfügen append, attach, pad
anführen cite
Anführungszeichen double quote, quotation mark
Angabe specification
Angaben unter Format in der EA-Parameterliste format IO list interaction
angeben give, specify
Angebot offer, quote
Angebotsabsage refusal of offer
Angebotsart offer type
Angebotsaufnahme offer input
Angebotsbearbeitung offer processing
Angebotsbeleg offer voucher
Angebotsbestand offer inventory
Angebotseinholung offer procurement
Angebotserinnerung offer reminder
Angebotserstellung offer generation
Angebotskopf offer header
Angebotsmenge offer quantity
Angebotsnummer offer number
Angebotsposition offer item
Angebotsspeicherung offer storage
Angebotstermin proposal due date
Angebotsterminüberwachung offer due date monitoring
Angebotstext offer text
Angebotstextbearbeitung offer text processing
Angebotstyp offer type
Angebotsverwaltung offer management
Angebotswert offer value
angebracht appropriate
angehören associate
angeschlossene Operation connected operation
angeschlossenes DELNI-Netz connected DELNI LAN
Angestelltenversicherung salaried employees' insurance
Angestellter employee
angewandte Funktion applied function

angewandter Befehl applied instruction
angezogen attracted
angleichen approximate
anhängen append
anhängig pending
anhalten end, freeze, halt, stop
Anhaltewert reference value
Anhang addendum, appendix, suffix
Anhangbereich append area, appendix
animieren encourage
an-isochron anisochronous
Anker armature
Ankerwicklung armature winding
ankommen arrive
ankommend inbound, incoming
ankommende Leitung inbound line
ankommender Ruf incoming call
ankommender Ruf blockiert incoming call barred
Ankoppeldruck coupling pressure
Ankoppelung coupling
ankreuzen cross out, mark with a cross
ankündigen announce
Ankunft arrival
Anlage arrangement, asset, site, system, unit
Anlageanweisung asset advice
Anlagegut tangible asset
Anlagenabgang asset disposal
Anlagenabgangsbuchung asset disposal posting
Anlagenbeleg asset voucher
Anlagenberechtigung assets authorization
Anlagenberechtigungsgruppe assets authorization group
Anlagenbereich assets area
Anlagenbestände asset investments
Anlagenbestand asset investment
Anlagenbestandskonto asset investment account
Anlagenbewegungen asset transactions
Anlagenbewegungssatz asset transaction record
Anlagenbuch asset ledger
Anlagenbuchhaltung assets accounting, property accounting
Anlagenbuchhaltungsbeleg assets accounting voucher
Anlagenbuchhaltungssystem assets accounting system
Anlagenbuchung asset posting
Anlagenbuchungszeilen asset posting lines
Anlagendatei asset file
Anlagenentwicklung asset development
Anlagenfeldgröße asset field size

253

Anlagenfertigstellung

Anlagenfertigstellung asset completion
Anlagengegenstand asset
Anlagenhauptbuchkonto assets general ledger account
anlagenintern installation internal, site internal
Anlagenjournal assets daily ledger
Anlagenkarte assets card, installation card
Anlagenklasse asset category
Anlagenkonto assets account
Anlagenkurztext asset summary
Anlagennummer asset number, machine ID, machine number, site number
Anlagenplanung installation planning, site layout
Anlagensatz assets record
Anlagenschlüssel asset key, assets code
anlagenspezifisch installation dependent, installation specific, site specific, system dependent
Anlagenspiegel assets analysis
Anlagenstamm asset master
Anlagenstammdaten asset master data
Anlagenstammdatenübernahme asset master data transfer
Anlagenstammsatz asset master record, assets master record
Anlagentext asset text
Anlagenumbuchungen asset re-postings
Anlagenumsetzung asset transfer
Anlagenverwaltung assets management
Anlagenwertführung assets management
Anlagenzugänge additions to assets
Anlaß cause, reason
Anlassen startup
Anlasser starting motor
Anlauflänge start distance
Anlaufschlüssel start key
Anlaufschritt start pulse
Anlegefunktion create function
Anlegemarkierung paper guide mark
anlegen create, set up
Anlegeskala feed scala
Anlegetisch feed table
Anleitung handbook, instruction, manual
anliefern deliver
Anlieferung delivery
Anlieferungszeitpunkt delivery time
Anmahnung demand
Anmeldecode id, password, user name
Anmeldeformalismus logon procedure
Anmeldemarkierung login flag
anmelden login, logon
Anmeldeprozedur login procedure
Anmeldung login, logon
Anmerkung comment, remark
annähern approach
annähernd approximately
Annäherung approximation
Annäherungsmethode method of approach
Annahme acceptance
Annahmewahrscheinlichkeit probability of acceptance
Annahmewert assumed value
annehmen accept, assume, take up
annullieren cancel
Anode anode, plate
Anodenmodulation anode modulation, plate modulation
Anodenverlustleistung anode dissipation, anode loss, plate dissipation
Anodenwirkungsgrad plate efficiency
Anordnung arrangement, layout, order
anpassen adapt, customize, tailor
Anpassung adaptation, adjustment, customization
Anpassung der Software bei Systemgeneration adaptation generation
Anpassungseinrichtung modem
anpassungsfähig adaptive
anpassungsfähige Regelung adaptive control
anpassungsfähige Steuerung adaptive control
Anpassungsgebühr adaptation charge
Anpassungsmöglichkeit adaptability
Anpressbügel pressure plate
Anrede title
Anredeschlüssel address code
Anredetext address text
anregen start
Anreihverteiler terminal junction
Anrufanforderung attention request
Anrufbeantwortung answering
Anrufbestätigung call confirmation
anrufen call, dial
Anrufsignal calling signal
anschaffen acquire
Anschaffung acquisition
Anschaffungswert acquisition value
Anschaltdauer connect time, duration, session
Anschalteinrichtung activate facility, interface, terminal interface
Anschaltmodul access module
Anschaltnetz access network
Anschaltungsdauer connect time
Anschaltverteilungsmodul access distribution module
Anschaltzeit connect time, duration

254

anschauen regard
Anschlag alignment, stroke
Anschlagdrucker impact printer
anschlagfreier Drucker non impact printer
Anschlagleiste paper guide stop
Anschlagzähler stroke counter
anschließen connect, follow
anschließend following
Anschluß adapter, adjustment, connection, connector, electric connector, interface, link, port, socket, terminal
Anschlußadresse following address, link address
Anschluß am Gehäuse panel connector
Anschluß an Zentralrechner host adapter
Anschlußbefehlsfolge linking sequence
Anschlußblock terminal block
Anschlußerweiterung terminal extension
Anschlußfeld connector panel
Anschluß für Tastaturkabel keyboard cable socket
Anschlußkabel connecting cable
Anschlußkennung line identification
Anschlußkennung gerufene Station called line identification
Anschlußkennung rufende Station calling line identification
Anschlußklemme terminal plate
Anschluß löschen disconnect
Anschlußplatte distribution insert
Anschlußschnur cord
Anschlußstecker attachment plug, connector socket
Anschlußtafel connector panel
Anschlußverbindung port connector
Anschlußzeichen switch hook character
Anschraub- plug-on
Anschrift address
Anschriftenkennzeichen address identification
Anschriftsfeld address field
Anschriftsteil address part
ansehen regard, view
ansonsten otherwise
ansprechbar addressable
Ansprechen reference
ansprechen address
Ansprechpartner contact
Ansprechschwelle operating threshold
anspringen access, branch to, jump to
Anspruch claim
Ansprung access
Ansprungziel transfer target
anstehen be present, pend

ansteuern activate, call, control
Ansteuerung activation
Anstiegszeit rise time
Anstoß tip off
Anteil proportion, share
Antennenumlaufgeschwindigkeit radar scan rate, scan rate
antreiben drive
Antrieb drive, motor
Antriebskopplung drive coupling
Antriebswelle capstan
Antwort answer, reply, response
antworten answer, reply, respond
Antwort im Dialogbetrieb conversational reply
Antwortmöglichkeit response possibility
Antwortzeit response time
anwählen call, dial, dial into, select
Anwählen des Systems sign on
Anwählfunktion dial up operation
Anweisung directive, instruction, statement
Anweisung auf dem Bildschirm screen prompt
Anweisung im Stromlaufplan ladder logic instruction
Anweisungsformat statement format
Anweisungspuffer instruction stack
Anweisungssprung statement jump
Anweisungstext statement text
Anweisung zur Gültigkeitsprüfung validation statement
Anweisung »Halt mit Anzeige« halt and proceed instruction
Anweisung »Interrupts Off« interrupts off instruction
anwendbar applicable
Anwendbarkeit applicability
anwenden applicate, apply
Anwender end user, user
anwenderabhängig application dependent
Anwenderbestand user data set
Anwenderdatei user file
Anwenderdaten customer data, user data
Anwendereinstellung customer set up, user set up
Anwendereintrag user entry
Anwenderendgerät user terminal
Anwenderfehler user error
Anwenderfunktion user function
anwendergesteuert user controlled
anwendergesteuerte Ausgabe exception line
anwendergesteuerter Satz exception record
anwenderneutral user independent
anwenderorientiert user oriented

Anwenderprogramm application program, user program
Anwenderprogrammierer user programmer
Anwenderschlüssel user code
Anwenderschulung user training
Anwender-Software user software
Anwenderspeicher user available storage
Anwenderstammdatum user master date
Anwendersteuerung user control
Anwenderstruktur user structure
Anwendung application
Anwendungsberechtigung authorization
Anwendungsbereich scope
anwendungsbezogene Funktionstastenbelegung application keypad mode
Anwendungsdatei application file
Anwendungsdaten application data
Anwendungsdienstelement application service element
Anwendungsdiskette application diskette
Anwendungsdokumentation application documentation
Anwendungsentwicklungssystem application documentation
Anwendungsfehler application error
Anwendungsfunktion application function
Anwendungsgebiet areas of application
Anwendungsinformation application information
Anwendungskontext application context
anwendungsorientierter Funktionstastenmodus keypad application mode
anwendungsorientierte Sprache application oriented language
Anwendungspaket application kit
Anwendungsprogramm application program
Anwendungsprogramm-Aufruf call for application program
Anwendungsprogrammierer application programmer
Anwendungsprogramm-Schnittstelle application program interface
Anwendungsprogrammtyp application program type, type of application program
Anwendungsprotokoll application log
Anwendungsschicht application layer
Anwendungsschnittstelle application interface
Anwendungssoftware application software
Anwendungssystem application system
Anwendungsverarbeitung application processing
Anwesenheit presence

Anwesenheitsbeleg attendance sheet
Anzahl count, count value, number
Anzahl der Wörter word count
Anzahlung advance payment, prepayment, upfront payment
Anzahlungsanforderung prepayment request
Anzahlungsbuchung prepayment posting
Anzahlungshauptbuchkonto general ledger prepayment account
Anzapfeinrichtung tap changing device
anzapfen tap
anzeigbar displayable
Anzeige display, indication, indicator, indicator light, screen, screen display, setting
Anzeigebefehl display instruction
Anzeigebeschränkung display limit
Anzeigebild display screen
Anzeigeblock display block
Anzeige des Modusmenüs mode menu display
Anzeige des Steuergerätes control unit indicator
Anzeigefeld display field
Anzeigeformat display format
Anzeigefunktion display function, indicator function
Anzeigegerät display device
Anzeigegröße display size
Anzeigeinformation display information
Anzeigemaske display mask
anzeigen display, indicate, show
Anzeigen an der Bedienerkonsole front panel indicators
Anzeigencode display code, light code
Anzeigen des Dateiverzeichnisses directory display
Anzeigentext display text
Anzeigentypen display types
Anzeigeposition display position
Anzeigeprogramm display program
Anzeige READY (Bereit) ready indicator
Anzeigeregel display rule
Anzeigeregister display register
Anzeigeröhre indicator tube
Anzeigeseite video page
Anzeige Stop stop indicator
Anzeigetest display test, video test
Anzeigetyp type of display
Anzeige zur Bildschirmjustierung screen alignment display
Anzeige »Bereit zum Übertragen« clear to send indicator
Anzugszeit operating time
Aperturverzerrung aperture distortion

Apostroph apostrophe
Apparat device, machine
Applikation application
arabisches Zeichen arabic character
Arbeiter/ Angestelltenkammerschlüssel employees chamber code
Arbeit mit dem System beenden stopping the system
Arbeitnehmer employee
Arbeitsauftrag job order
Arbeitsbereich work space
Arbeitsbereichsegment closely defined work area
Arbeitsblatt spreadsheet, worksheet
Arbeitsdatei scratch file, temporary file
Arbeitsdatei des Editors editor workspace file
Arbeitseinstufung job classification
Arbeitserleichterung facilitation of work
Arbeitsgang operation, pass
Arbeitsgangbezeichnung description of operation
Arbeitsgangzeile operation line
Arbeitsgebiet section
Arbeitsgruppe working group
Arbeitskontakt normally open, off-normal contact
Arbeitslastverteilung distributed processing
Arbeitsmethode operating method
Arbeitsphase operating phase
Arbeitsplatzumgebung office environment
Arbeitsregister working register
Arbeitsspeicher memory, operating memory, primary store, working storage
Arbeitstisch desk
Arbeitsweise operation
Arbeitszustand des Übertragungskanals active data link channel
Architektur architecture
Archiv archive
Archivband archive tape
archivieren archive, file
Archivnummern-Vergleich archive number comparison
Arcuscosinus arc cosine
Arcussinus arc sine
Arcustangens arc tangent
Argument argument, criterion
Argumentdatei criteria file
Argumententeil argument section
Argumenttabelle argument table
Arithmetik-Einheit arithmetic unit
Arithmetikprozessor arithmetic processor
Arithmetikrechenwerk arithmetic processing unit
Arithmetikregister arithmetic register
arithmetisch arithmetic
arithmetische Funktion arithmetic function
arithmetische Gleichung arithmetic expression
arithmetische Operation arithmetic operation
arithmetischer Befehl arithmetic instruction, arithmetical instruction
arithmetischer Block arithmetic block
arithmetischer Überlauf arithmetic overflow
arithmetisch-logische Einheit arithmetic logic unit
Arm arm
AR-Register ar register
Art kind, sort, type
Art des Ausgangs output type
Art des Elements module type
Arten von Programmiersprachen programming language types
Artikel article, item
artikelabhängig dependent on article, item specific
Artikelart article type
Artikelbezeichnung article description, item, item description
artikelbezogen item related
Artikelcharakter article character, item character
Artikelgruppe article group
Artikelgruppierung item grouping
Artikelgutschrift item credit
Artikelkatalog article catalog
Artikelkonto article account
Artikelkontodatei article history file, item history file
Artikelkontonummer article account number, item account number
Artikelkurztext item summary
artikelmäßig related to article
Artikelnummer item number
Artikelnummerkriterium article number criterion
artikelorientiert item oriented
Artikelpreis item price
Artikelsperre article immobilisation
Artikelstamm item master
Artikelstammdatei article master file
Artikelstammdaten article master data
Artikelstammerweiterung article master extension
Artikelstammfeld article master field

Artikelstammkonvertierung article master conversion
Artikelstammsatz master record
artikelstammsatzabhängig dependent on item master record
Artikelstammwartung article master maintenance
Artikelstatistik article statistics, item statistics
Artikelübersicht article report, item list, item report
Artikulationsorgane vocal tract
ASCII-Datei ascii file, text file
Aspekt aspect
Assembler assembler, assembler language
Assembleraufbereitungszeichen edit control character
Assembler-Definition assembler definition
Assemblerdirektive assembler directive
Assemblerformat assembler format
Assembler-Konvention assembler convention
Assemblermodul assembler module
Assembler-Primärprogramm assembler primary program
Assemblerprogramm assembler program, assembly program
Assembler-Programmierer assembler language programmer, assembler programmer
Assembler-Programmverknüpfung assembler program link
Assemblersprache assembler language
assemblieren assemble
Assemblierer assembler
assemblierte Programmstelle assembled program count
Assemblierung assembly
Assemblierungsprozedur assembly procedure
Assoziation association
Assoziationskontrolldienstelement association control service element
assoziativ abfragbarer Speicher correlatable access memory
Assoziativ-Relation associative relation
Assoziativspeicher associative memory, associative storage
Assoziativ-Speicher associative storage
AST-Tabelle alternate sector table
asymmetrisch asymmetric
asymmetrisch Vollduplex asymmetric full duplex
asynchron asynchronous
Asynchronanwendungsprogramm asynchronous application program

asynchrone Arbeitsweise asynchronous operation
asynchroner Kommunikationsanschluß asynchronous communications adapter
asynchroner Schnittstellenbaustein asynchronous communications interface adapter
asynchroner Systemsprung asynchronous system trap
asynchroner Übertragungsadapter asynchronous communications adapter
asynchroner Zeitmultiplexer asynchronous time division multiplexor
asynchrones Modem asynchronous modem
asynchrone Start/Stop-Verbindung asynchronous start stop interface
asynchrone Übertragung asynchronous transmission
Asynchronmaschine asynchronous machine
Asynchronmotor asynchronous motor
Asynchronmultiplexer asynchronous multiplexer
Asynchronprogramm asynchronous program
Atomexplosionseffekt electromagnetic pulse effect
Attribut attribute
Attributaktualisierung attribute update
Attributbyte attribute byte
Attributkennzeichen attribute identifier
Attributmodifikation attribute modification
Attributverwendung attribute use
Attribut/Wert attribute value
Attributzeichen attribute sign
Attribut »fettgedruckt« bold attribute
Attribut »geschütztes Feld« protect field attribute
Audiokommunikationssysteme audio communication equipment
Audioverstärker audio amplifier
Auditdatei audit file
Auf-/Abwärtszähler up down counter
Aufbau format, structure
Aufbaucode installation code
Aufbau des Datenübertragungsblocks frame structure
Aufbau einer Röhre electron tube structure
aufbauen build, build up, generate, structure
Aufbaufeld structure field
Aufbaukriterium generation criterion
Aufbau von Nachrichtenwarteschlangen message queuing
aufbereiten edit, regenerate
Aufbereiter editor
Aufbereitung editing, regeneration

Aufbereitungscode edit code
Aufbereitungsformat edit mask
Aufbereitungsmaske edit word
Aufbereitungsoption editing option
aufbewahren keep, store
Aufbewahrung storage
Aufbrauchen use up
auf der Basis von Vergangenheitsdaten historical
auf die verschränkt zugegriffen wird interleaved modules
aufeinanderfolgender Programmbereich sequential program area
Auffang-Flipflop latch
auffinden discover, find
auffordern prompt
Aufforderung demand, prompt
Aufforderungszeichen prompt, prompt character
Aufforderung zum Senden invitation to send
Aufforderung zum Übergang in asynchronen Antwortbetrieb set asynchronous response mode
Aufforderung zum Übergang in gleichberechtigten Asynchronbetrieb set asynchronous balanced mode
Aufforderung zur Verbindungsauslösung invitation to clear
Auffrischen refresh
auffrischen refresh
Auffrisch-Schaltung refresh circuit
aufführen list
auffüllen pad
Aufgabe task
Aufgabennummer task number
aufgabenorientiert job oriented
aufgebaut built up, set up
aufgebläht blown up
aufgefaßt taken for
aufgehendes Verhältnis integer ratio
aufgerufen called up
aufgeschlüsselte Liste itemized list
aufgliedern break down, divide
Aufgliederung breakdown
auf Gültigkeit überprüfen validate
auf Hardware basierende Fehlertoleranz hardware implemented fault tolerance
aufheben remove, repeal
Aufheben einer Verriegelung interlock bypass
Aufheben eines definierten Titels unfix the title
Aufhebung removal, repeal

aufkaufen buy out, take over
Aufkleber label, sticker
auf Lager on stock
auflaufen accumulate
auf Leerzeichen setzen blank, blank out
aufleuchten light up
auflösen close, resolve
Auflösung closing, resolution
aufmerksam aware
Aufmerksamkeit attention
Aufnahme accommodation
Aufnahmedatum recording date, sampling date, stocktaking date
Aufnahmegerät recorder
Aufnahmekabel recording jack plug cable
Aufnahmekopf record head
Aufnahmepegel record level
Aufnahmewert stocktaking value
aufnehmen draw, film, include, record
aufreihen line up
Aufruf call
Aufrufadresse calling address
aufrufbare Nachrichten canned messages
Aufrufbetrieb selecting mode
Aufruf eines Programms starting a program
aufrufen call, call up, invoke
Aufrufkennzeichen calling identifier
Aufruflänge call length
Aufrufmechanismus calling mechanism
Aufruf-Reihenfolge calling sequence
Aufrufsignal ring indicator
Aufrufverfahren polling mode
aufschieben delay, postpone
aufschlüsseln break down, itemize
Aufschlüsselung interpretation
Aufschluß information
Aufschrift marking term
Aufschub delay
aufsetzen put, set up
Aufsetzkennzeichen set up marker
Aufsetzpunkt set up point
aufspalten splitting
aufsteigend ascending
aufsteigende Reihenfolge ascending order
aufstellen draw up
Aufstellungsort location
aufsuchen search
Aufsummierung summation
AUF-Taste up-key
aufteilen block, categorize, divide, segment, split
Aufteilung partitioning, segmentation, subdivision

259

Aufteilung in Bereiche partition arrangement
Aufteilungseinheit für EA-Geräte shared access unit
Aufteilungsschema partition plan
Auftrag job, order, task
Auftraggeber client, customer, orderer
Auftrag-Kopfdaten head data of job
Auftragnehmer contractor
Auftragsabwicklung order processing
Auftragsänderung order alteration
Auftragsart order type
Auftragsausstellung order issue
Auftragsbearbeitung order processing
Auftragsbearbeitungsfunktion order processing function
Auftragsbeleg order voucher
Auftragsbelegsatz order voucher record
Auftragsbestätigung order confirmation
Auftragsbestätigungskontrolle order confirmation check
Auftragsbestätigungsliste order confirmation report
Auftragsbestätigungsnummer order confirmation number
Auftragsbestätigungspflicht order confirmation requirement
Auftragsbestand order backlog, orders on hand
Auftragsbestandsliste order backlog list
Auftragsbetrieb closed shop (operation)
auftragsbezogen order-related
Auftragsbrutto order gross
Auftragsdatei order file
Auftragsdatenbank order data bank
Auftragsdatum order date
Auftragseingabe order entry
Auftragseingangsliste incoming order list
Auftragseinplanung order scheduling
Auftragsende end of job
Auftragsentwicklung order development
Auftragsentwicklungssatz order development record
Auftragserfassung order entry, order registration
Auftragsformular order form
Auftragsgewinnung order acquisition
Auftragsgutschrift order crediting
Auftragshinzufügung order insertion
Auftragskopf order header
Auftragskopfdaten job information line
Auftragskopffeld head data field in job
Auftragskopfrabatt order header discount
Auftragskopfsatz order heading

Auftragsliste order list
Auftragslistenentnahme order list withdrawal
Auftragsmenge order quantity
Auftragsnetto order net amount
Auftragsnotiz order remark
Auftragsnummer order number
Auftragsnummernänderung order number change
auftragsorientiert order oriented
Auftragsposition order item
Auftragspositionsmenge order quantity
auftragspositionsbezogen related to order item
Auftragspositionsmaske order item mask
Auftragspositionssatz order item record
Auftragsreservierung order reservation
Auftragsrückstand back orders
Auftragsschreibung order printing
Auftragsstatistik order statistics
Auftragstext order text
Auftragsverarbeitung order processing
Auftragsverrechnung settlement of order
Auftragsverwaltung order management
Auftragsverzeichnis order register
Auftragswährung order currency
Auftragswert order value
Auftragszusammenführung order summary
Auftragszusammenlegung order assembly
auftreten appear, occur
Auftrieb buoyancy
Auftritt appearance
Aufwärmphase warm up phase
Aufwärmzeit warm up time
aufwärtskompatibel upward compatible
Aufwand expenditure
Aufwandsbuchung expenses posting
Aufwandskonto expense account
aufweisen indicate, show
aufwerten revalue
Aufwertung revaluation
Aufwickelrolle take up reel
auf Wunsch optional
aufzählen enumerate
Aufzählung enumeration
aufzeichnen log, record
Aufzeichnung mit doppelter Dichte double density recording
Aufzeichnungsdichte recording density
Aufzeichnungseinrichtung recording device
Aufzeichnungsgeschwindigkeit scanning speed at reception
Aufzeichnungsgröße record size
Aufzeichnungskamm recording comb
Aufzeichnungsmöglichkeit mapping facility

Aufzeichnungspunkt scanning spot at reception
Aufzeichnungssatz recording record
Aufzeichnungstaste record key
Aufzeichnungsverfahren recording method
Aufzeichnungszeile record line
aufzeigen demonstrate
Aufzinsung compound growth
Augenblick moment
augenblicklich actual, at present, current
Augenblickswert actual value, current value, instantaneous value, present value
Ausbau expansion, extension, migration, upgrade
Ausbaubarkeit expandability
ausbauen expand, migrate, upgrade
ausblenden blank out, fade out
Ausdruck expression, hardcopy, paper copy, phrase, print out, printed copy
Ausdruck des Bildschirminhalts media copy, print screen, screen copy
ausdrucken print out
ausdrücklich explicit
auseinandergesteuert categorize
Ausfall failure
Ausfallabstand time between failures
Ausfall der Stromversorgung power failure, power interruption
ausfallsicher failsafe
Ausfallzeit down time, downtime
ausführbar executable
ausführbares Element absolute element
ausführbares Programm executable image
ausführen execute, perform
ausführlich detailed, in detail
Ausführung execution, model
Ausführung eines Boxbefehls bei einmaliger Abtastung single scan box execution
Ausführungslauf execution run
Ausführungsreihenfolge order of execution, order of program execution
Ausführungszeit execution time, runtime
Ausgabe issue, output, readout
Ausgabe auf den Drucker output to printer
Ausgabeauftrag output job
Ausgabeband output tape
Ausgabebefehl output instruction
Ausgabebereich output message area
ausgabebereit ready for output
Ausgabebezugszahl output indicator
Ausgabebild output screen
Ausgabedatei output file

Ausgabedateikennzeichen und -steuerung output file identification and control
Ausgabedaten output data
Ausgabedatenanfrage output data request
Ausgabedatenbestätigung output data acknowledge
Ausgabeeinheit issue unit
Ausgabeeröffnung output initialization
Ausgabefach output stacker
Ausgabefehler output error
Ausgabefeld output field, output position
Ausgabeformat output format specification
Ausgabeformatierung output formatting
Ausgabegerät output device
Ausgabegeschwindigkeit output rate
ausgabeintensiv output intensive
Ausgabekapazität output capacity
Ausgabelänge output length
Ausgabemakro output macro
Ausgabemaske edit mask
Ausgabemengeneinheit stock issue unit
Ausgabenachricht output message
Ausgabenart type of output
Ausgabeparameter output parameter
Ausgabepuffer output buffer
Ausgaberegister output register
Ausgabesatz output record
Ausgabesatzlänge output record size
Ausgabeschacht output chute
Ausgabeschritt output step
Ausgabespeicher output buffer
Ausgabestruktur output structure
Ausgabeteil des Systemdatenpfades busout
Ausgabeterminal output terminal
Ausgabeunterdrückung output suppression
Ausgabewarteschlange output work queue
Ausgabezeit output time
Ausgabezeitpunkt edition date
Ausgang exit, interface, issue, output, output connector, port
Ausgangsanpassung output matching
Ausgangsanschluß output connector, output terminal
Ausgangsbereich origin
Ausgangsbestätigung output acknowledge
Ausgangsbuchse exit hub, output connector
Ausgangsdatei source file
Ausgangsdaten output data
Ausgangsdiskette source diskette
Ausgangsergebnis output result
Ausgangsfracht freight dispatched
Ausgangsgerät output device
Ausgangsimpedanz output impedance

261

Ausgangsimpuls output signal
Ausgangskreis output circuit
Ausgangslaufwerk source drive
Ausgangs-LED output led
Ausgangsleitung outbound line, outgoing line
Ausgangsmenu main menu
Ausgangsmenü default start up menu, first menu, top menu
Ausgangsmodul output module
Ausgangsparameter default parameter, initial parameter
Ausgangsposition home, home position, initial position
Ausgangspuffer output buffer
Ausgangsrelais output coil
Ausgangsschwelle output threshold
Ausgangssicherung output fuse
Ausgangssignal output
Ausgangsspannung output voltage
Ausgangssteuer sales tax
Ausgangssteuerart sales tax type
Ausgangswechsel bill of exchange
Ausgangswert base value, original value
Ausgangszahl seed
ausgebbar expendable
ausgeben issue, output, put out, return
Ausgeben des Speicherinhaltes dump
ausgedehnt big
ausgefüllt filled in
ausgefüllte Masken, deren Einträge veränderbar sind input/output screen format
ausgenommen apart from
ausgeprägter Pol salient pole
ausgerichtet aligned
ausgesetzt deferred, exposed
ausgespartes Gerät cut out device
ausgestattet sein mit feature
ausgestellt exposed
Ausgleich balance
ausgleichen balance
Ausgleichsanzeige balance display
Ausgleichsbetrag balancing amount
Ausgleichsbuchung balance posting
Ausgleichsdaten balancing data
Ausgleichsdatum balancing date
Ausgleichsinformation balancing info
Ausgleichsperiode balancing period
Ausgleichsprüfung balance checking
Ausgleichssaldo balance
Ausgleichsschlüssel balancing code
Ausgleichsstoff balancing data
Ausgleichssumme balance total
Ausgleichsverbindung equalizer

Ausgleichsvolumen balancing volume
Ausgleichsvorgang balancing procedure, balancing process
Ausgleichswert balancing value
Ausgleichsziffer balancing code
Auskragung lead protrusion
Auskunft directory service, information
Auskunftsbetrieb information operation
Auskunftsdienst information service
Auskunftserteilung giving information
Auskunftsfunktion information function
Auskunftsprogramm information program
auslagern checkpoint, outlay, roll out, store externally, swap, swap out
auslagern und nachladen swap
Auslagerschlüssel dumping code
Auslagerung external storage, stock withdrawal
Auslandsrechnung foreign invoice
Auslandstochtergesellschaft foreign subsidiary
Auslandsüberweisung international credit transfer
Auslandsüberweisungsliste international transfer list
Auslandszahlungsverkehr foreign payment transactions, international payment transaction
auslassen leave out, omit
Auslassung omission
Auslassungszeichen caret letter
Auslastung capacity
Auslaufartikel discontinued item
Auslaufteil discontinued item
Auslesen mit Zerstörung des Speicherinhalts destructive readout
ausliefern deliver
Auslieferung delivery
Auslieferungsanweisung delivery instruction
Auslieferungsverbot delivery stop
auslöschen blank out
Auslöseanforderung clear request
Auslösebestätigung clear confirmation
Auslösefunktion triggering function
Auslöseknopf release button
Auslösekriterium trigger criterion
Auslösemechanismus circuit breaker
Auslösemeldung clear indication
auslösen clear, release, trigger
Auslösetaste release switch
Auslösung clearing
Ausnahme exception
Ausnahmebedingung exception condition
Ausnahmebehandlung exception handling
Ausnahmebewertung exception validation
Ausnahmedatei exception file

Ausnahmefall special case
Ausnahmeposition reserve entry
Ausnahmepriorität preemptive priority
Ausnahmescheck reserve cheque
Ausnahmetabelle exception table
Ausnahmezustand exceptional condition
Ausnahmezustand-Behandlungsprogramm contigency program
Ausnutzung making use of
auspacken unpack
Ausprüfen debugging
Ausräumzeiger clear indicator
ausreichen suffice
ausrichten align
Ausrichtung alignment, justification
Ausrichtung auf Speichergrenze boundary alignment
ausrüsten equip
Ausrüstung equipment
Ausrufezeichen exclamation mark
Ausrufungszeichen exclamation mark
Aussage predicate, statement
aussagefähig expressive
aussagekräftig meaningful
Aussagenwert logical value
Ausschalten switching off
ausschalten disable, switch off, turn off
Ausschalten des Grafikmodus exit graphics mode
Ausschalten des Systems shutdown, turning off the system
Ausschalter access standby switch, mode execute ready pushbutton, off switch, power off switch
Ausschalttaste power off key
Ausscheidungseinrichtung discriminating equipment
ausschieben shove out
ausschlaggebend decisive
ausschließen exclude
ausschließlich exclusive
Ausschließlichkeitszeichen exclusiveness character
Ausschlußdateispezifikation exclusion file specifier
Ausschlußzeichen exception character
Ausschnitt excerpt
Aussehen appearance
außen external
Außenhandels- und Außenwirtschaftsministerium von Japan Ministry of International Trade and Industry (Japan)
Außenstände accounts receivable

Außenwirtschaft external trade
Außenwirtschaftsverkehr external trade relations
Außerbandsignalisierung outband signaling
außerhalb out of, outside
außer Kraft setzen override
außerordentlich exceptional
außerplanmäßig unscheduled
außerplanmäßige Beendigung abnormal termination
Aussetzfehler dropout
Aussetzung deferment
Aussprachezeichen pronunciation mark
ausspreizen spread out
Aussprung return
ausstanzen punch out
ausstatten equip
ausstecken unplug
ausstehend outstanding
ausstellen issue
Aussteller drawer
Ausstellung issue
Ausstellungsdatum date of issue
aussteuern disqualify
Aussteuerung control, rejection
aussuchen select
Austausch exchange, interchange, replacement
austauschbare Funktionseinheit field replaceable unit
austauschbare Komponente field replaceable unit
austauschbarer Parameter replaceable parameter
austauschen exchange, replace, swap
Austauschfehler transposition error
Austauschfeld exchange field
Austauschverfahren process of exchange
Austesten checkout, debugging
austesten debug, test
austragen take out
austreten exit
Austritt exit
auswählen choose, select
Auswählen von Merkmalen selecting features
Auswahl menu, selection
Auswahlalgorithmus selection algorithm
Auswahlalternative selection alternative
Auswahlbegriff selection term
Auswahlbereich select range
Auswahlbild set up screen
Auswahl der Datenparitätsbits data parity bits feature

263

Auswahl der Empfangsparität receive parity feature
Auswahl der Übertragungsrate data signal rate selector
Auswahleinheit feed control unit
Auswahlende menu end, selection end
Auswahlkarte selection card
Auswahlkennzeichen selection marker
Auswahlknoten selection node
Auswahlkriterium selection criterion, selective criterion
Auswahlleiste selection report group
Auswahlliste list of options, options list, selection list
Auswahlmaske menu
Auswahlmenge selection quantity
Auswahlmenu options menu
Auswahlmenü selection menu
Auswahlmodus selection mode, set up mode
Auswahlmöglichkeit choice, selection option
Auswahlnummer selection number
Auswahlparameter selection parameter
Auswahlschlüsselwort selection key word
Auswahlseite selection page
Auswahlspezifikation selection specification
Auswahlsteuerung selection control
Auswahlstufe selection level
Auswahlsymbol select symbol
Auswahltabelle selection table
Auswahlvektor selection vector
Auswahlvorrichtung selector
Auswahlziffer selection digit
auswechselbar removable, replaceable
auswechseln change, replace
ausweichen bypass
Ausweichleitung bypass line
Ausweichpfad alternative path, bypass
ausweisen identify
Ausweisleser badge card reader
auswertbar evaluable
auswerten analyse, evaluate, figure
Auswerten eines Geschäftsberichtes financial report analysis
Auswertmonat month evaluated
Auswertung analysis, evaluation
Auswertungshilfsprogramm evaluation utility
Auswertungsprogramm analysis program
Auswertungszweck analysis purpose
auswiegen weigh out
Auswirkung effect
Auswurf ejection
Auswurfbefehl ejection instruction
Auswurftaste eject key

Auszahlung payment
auszeichnen indicate
Ausziehvorrichtung extractor
Auszifferinformation balancing info
ausziffern balance
Ausziffertabelle balance table
Auszug extract, statement
Auszugsberichtzeitraum statement period
Auszugsnummer statement number
Authorisation authorization
Auto... auto
Auto-Antwortbetrieb auto answer mode
Autoantwort einschalten enable auto answerback
Automat machine
Automatik automatism
automatisch automatic
automatische Anrufbeantwortung auto answer
automatische Anschaltleitungstrennung automatic answer disconnect, automatic answer hang up
automatische Antwort automatic answer, automatic answering
automatische Bildschirmabschaltung auto screen blank, screen saver
automatische Datenträgererkennung automatic volume recognition
automatische Datenverarbeitung automatic data processing
automatische Einheit für ankommende und/oder abgehende Rufe automatic calling and/or answering equipment
automatische Frequenzregelung automatic frequency control
automatische Funktion automatic function
automatische Kassiermaschine automated teller machine
automatische Nebenstellenanlage private automatic branch exchange
automatische Papierzuführung automatic feed
automatische Quellprogrammgenerierung auto report facility
automatischer Einzelblatteinzug automatic sheet feeder
automatischer Jobstart auto job startup
automatischer Programmgenerator automatic code generator, automatic program generator
automatischer Seitenumbruch automatic pagination
automatischer Verbindungsaufbau dial out
automatischer Zeilenumbruch auto wrap, automatic word wrap
automatisches Answerback auto answerback

automatisches Answerback einschalten auto answerback enable
automatische Schirmbildverschiebung auto offset
automatisches Drucken auto print
automatisches Erstellen auto create
automatisches Steuerungssystem automatic control system
automatisches Sytem zur Fehlersuche automatic interactive debugging system
automatisches XON/XOFF-Protokoll auto XON XOFF
automatische Übertragung automatic transfer mode
automatische Umkehr auto turnaround
automatische Verstärkungsregelung automatic gain control
automatische Wählvorrichtung auto dialler
automatische Wahl auto select, automatic dialling
automatische Wiederherstellung autorecovery
automatische Wiederherstellung der Systemsteuerung autorecovery bootstrap
automatische Wiederholung des Tastendrucks auto key repeat
automatische Zufuhr auto feed
Automatisierung automation
Autor author, writer
Autostart auto boot
Autotransformator autotransformer
Autowiederholung autorepeat
Avalance-Diode avalance diode
Avis advice
Avishinweis advice
Avistexte advice texts
AVU-Datei cost allocation file

B

Badewannenkurve bathtub curve
Bändersatz volume set
Bahn railway
Bahnstation railway station
Bahntransport rail transport
Bake beacon
Balken bar, beam
Balkendiagramm bar chart
Balkenmusteranzeige bar pattern display
Ballastwiderstand load resistor
Band band, strap, strip, tape
Bandabtastung tape dump
Bandanfang beginning of tape, start of tape
Bandanfangskennsatz header label
Bandanfangsmarke beginning of tape, leading tape mark
Bandanlauf tape start
Bandaufzeichnungsgerät tape recorder
Bandausgabe tape output
Bandausgabesatz tape output record
Bandbreite bandwidth
Bandcontroller tape controller
Banddatei tape file
Banddeflektor band deflector
Bandeinfädelung tape threading
Bandeingabe tape input
Bandeinheit tape unit
Bandempfänger tape receiver
Bandende end of reel, end of tape
Bandendemarke EOT mark, end of tape, end of tape mark
Band entladen unloading the tape
Bandformat tape format
Bandgeschwindigkeit tape speed
Bandinhalt tape contents
Bandkassette cassette tape, tape cartridge
Bandkassetteneinheit cassette tape unit
Bandkennzeichen tape mark
Bandkontakt head-to-tape contact
Bandlaufwerk streamer, tape drive
Bandlesegerät tape reader
Bandleseregister tape read register
Bandleuchte strip light
Bandleuchtmarke sticker
Bandmarke tape mark
Bandmatrix band matrix
Bandmatrize band matrix
Bandmenge volume set

Band mit Richtungstaktschrift phase encoded tape
Bandnummer tape number
Bandpaßverstärker bandpass amplifier
Bandpositionierung tape positioning
Bandriß torn tape condition
Bandrücksetzen backspace
Bandsatz tape record
Bandschalter band selector
Bandschleife tape loop
Bandschreibregister tape write register
Bandservosteuerung tape servo
Bandskaleninstrument strip instrument
Bandsperre band suppressor, bandstop filter
Bandstation tape station
Bandsteuereinheit tape controller
Bandsteuerung tape controller
Bandstruktur tape structure
Bandtellerbefestigung reel holddown
Bandtransport tape feed
Bandtransportmechanismus tape transport mechanism
Bank bank
Bankadresse bank address
Bankangaben bank details
Bankanschrift bank address
Bankbuchung bank posting
Bankbuchungsbetrag bank posting amount
Bankdaten bank data
Bankeinzug direct debit
Bankeinzugsliste direct debit list
Bankkonto bank account
Bankkontoschlüssel bank account code
Bankkunde banking client
Bankländerschlüssel bank country code
Banklastschrift bank debit entry
Bankleitzahl bank number
Banknummer bank code
Bankquittung bank receipt
Bankquittungsverfahren bank receipt
Banksammler collective bank remittance
Bankschlüssel bank code
Bankspesen bank charges
Banküberweisung bank credit transfer
Bankverbindung bank details
Bankverbindungen bank data
Baritt-Diode Baritt diode
Barverkauf cash sale
BASIC-Modul basic module
basieren base
Basis base, basis, radix
Basisadresse base address

Basisadreßregister base register, relocation register
Basisband baseband
Basisband-Übertragungseinrichtung baseband transmission equipment
Basisbetrag basic amount
Basisblatt basic sheet
Basisdaten basic data
Basisdatum base date
Basisformatliste basic format list
Basisformatname basic format name
Basisfunktion basic function
Basisgrenzwert base limit
Basisjahr base year
Basiskonstante basic constant
Basis-Parameterdatei base parameter file
Basispreis base price
Basispreisermittlung basic price calculation
Basispreistabelle basic price table
Basisprogramm checkbox program
Basisprogrammierung checkbox programming
Basisrabatt basic discount
Basisrabattabelle basic discount table
Basissystem basic system
Basisteilformat basic part format
Basisversion basic version
Basiswert base value
Basiswertfortschreibung updating the base values
Basiszahl base number
Basiszyklus basic time state
Batch batch
Batchaufteilung batch splitting
Batchauswertungsübersicht batch evaluation monitoring
Batchbearbeitung batch processing
Batchbetrieb batch operating
Batchbuchen batch posting
Batchbuchungsflag batch posting flag
Batchdatei batch file
Batch-Dateiverarbeitung batch file processing
Batchdruckausgabe batch print output
Batcherfassung batch entry
Batcherstellung batch generation
Batchgenerierung batch generation
Batchinput batch input
Batchjob batch job
Batchkommando batch command
Batchlauf batch run
Batchmerkmal batch qualifier
Batchmodus batch mode
batchorientiert batch oriented
Batchprogramm batch program

Batchprozedur batch procedure
Batchrahmen batch mode
Batchteil batch part
BAT-Tabelle bad address table
Batterie battery
batteriebetriebenes Gerät battery powered device
batteriegepuffert battery buffered
Batterieladegerät battery charger
Batterienotversorgung battery backup
Bau formation
Baud baud
Baudrate baud rate, speed, transmission speed
Bauelement component
bauen build, construct
Baugruppe component, electrical component
Baukasten kit, module
Baukastenprinzip modular
Baukastenstückliste module parts list, single level bill of materials
Baukastenteileverwendung module parts usage
Baumstrukturliste tree structure list
Baumverfahren tree procedure
Bausatz kit
Baustein block, building block, component, module
Bausteinlänge module length
bautechnisch constructional
Bauteil component, electrical component
Bauteil einer Elektronenröhre electron tube component
BCD-Arithmetikfunktion BCD arithmetic function
beabsichtigen intend
beachten observe
Beam-Lead-Gerät beam-lead device
beanspruchen claim
Beanstandung claim, objection
beantworten answer
Beantwortung answering
bearbeiten edit, handle, manipulate, process
Bearbeiten eines Dokuments editing a document
Bearbeiten von Text editing text
Bearbeiten von Variablen manipulating variables
Bearbeiter editor
Bearbeitung editing, processing
Bearbeitungsart method of handling
Bearbeitungsbedingung processing condition
Bearbeitungsergebnis result of handling
Bearbeitungsfehler processing error
Bearbeitungsfolge processing sequence

Bearbeitungsfunktion processing function
Bearbeitungshinweis processing note
Bearbeitungsinformation processing information
Bearbeitungsmöglichkeit processing option
Bearbeitungsprogramm processing program
Bearbeitungsschema processing pattern
Bearbeitungsstand processing state
Bearbeitungsstatus processing status
Bearbeitungsvorfall handling instance
Bearbeitungsvorgang processing procedure
Bebuchung posting to
Bedarf demand, need, requirement
Bedarfsanmeldung demand submission
Bedarfsauflösung requirement calculation
Bedarfsbetrieb open shop
Bedarfsdatenbank requirements data bank
Bedarfsermittlung demand forecasting
Bedarfsliste requirement list
Bedarfsmeldung requirement report, requirements report
Bedarfsmeldungsnummer requirements report number
Bedarfsmeldungsschein requisition voucher
Bedarfsplanung requirement planning
Bedarfsraster demand schedule
Bedarfszahlen demand figures
bedecken cover
bedeuten mean, signify
bedeutend important, meaningful
Bedeutung meaning, significance
bedienen manipulate, operate, servicing
Bediener operator, user
Bedienereingriff operator control
Bedienerfeld user field
Bedienerführung operator control
Bedienerhandbuch guide to operations, operating instruction, operation's guide
Bedienerkommunikation user communication
Bedienerkonsole operator interface
Bedienermeldung operator message
bedienerorientiert operator oriented
Bedienerschlüssel operator code
Bedienerunterstützung user support
Bedienfeld operator panel, panel
Bedienfeld für Ultraschall control panel for ultrasonic treatment
Bedienpult control desk
Bedientastatur keyboard
Bedientext operating instruction text
Bedienung manipulation, servicing
Bedienungsanleitung manual, operator manual

Bedienungsanzeigetafel operator control indicator
Bedienungsblattschreiber operator console typewriter
Bedienungselement control
Bedienungselemente des Druckers printer controls
Bedienungsfeld control indicator panel, control panel, operator control panel, primary control panel
Bedienungsführung prompt, user interface
Bedienungsgesteuerte Leitungen controlled line servicing
Bedienungsgrundlagen basic system operation
Bedienungshandbuch guide to operations, operating manual, operations guide, operations manual
Bedienungsmöglichkeit operation possibility
Bedienungsplatz operator console
Bedienungsplatz-Prozessor console processor
Bedienungspult control panel
Bedienungs-/Wartungsfeld operator maintenance panel
bedingt conditional
bedingte Befehlsausführung conditional execution of commands
bedingter Sprung conditional jump
bedingtes Ende conditional end
Bedingung condition
bedingungslos unconditionally
Bedingungsschlüssel condition code
Bedingungstext condition text
Bedingungstyp condition type
Bedingung: keine Operation condition no operation
beeinflussen influence
beeinträchtigen encumber
Beenden termination
beenden exit, exit from, finish, quit, terminate
Beenden der Sicherung end of backup, leaving the backup program
Beenden der Übertragung transmit termination
Beenden des Spoolens suspension of spooling
Beenden einer Pufferoperation buffer termination
beenden mit Änderungen exit with changes
beenden ohne Sichern abandon, exit no save, quit
Beendigungsverfahren termination procedure
Beendigungszeit completion time
befähigt eligible
befassen deal

Befehl command, directive, instruction, order
befehlen instruct, order
Befehle zum Zugriff auf ISAM-Datei ISAM access statements
Befehlsführungsprozessor instruction processor
Befehl für die Jobverarbeitung job processing command
Befehlsadresse instruction address
Befehlsadreßregister instruction address register, program address counter
Befehlsänderung instruction modification
Befehlsanalyseprogramm parser
Befehlsansteuerung instruction pipelining
Befehlsaufbau instruction format
Befehlsaufbereitungsprozessor instruction preprocessor
Befehlsausführung command execution
Befehlsausgabeeinheit instruction issue unit
Befehlsbehandlung command processing
Befehlsblock instruction block
Befehlsbus instruction bus
Befehlscode operating code
Befehlsdatei command file
Befehlsebene command level
Befehlseingabe command input
Befehlsergänzung command complement, command modifier
Befehlserweiterung command extension
Befehlsfeld command field, instruction field
Befehlsfolge command sequence, sequence of instructions
Befehlsinterpreter command interpreter, command language interpreter
Befehlslänge instruction length
Befehlsliste instruction list, statement list
Befehlsoption command option
Befehlsparameter instruction parameter
Befehlsprozedur command procedure
Befehlsprozessor command processor
Befehlsqualifizierer command qualifier
Befehlsreferenz reference manual
Befehlsregister control register, instruction register
Befehlsrepertoire instruction repertoire
Befehlsrückweisung command reject
Befehlssatz command record, command set, instruction set
Befehlssatz zur Arrayverarbeitung array processing instruction set
Befehlsschlüsselwort command keyword
Befehlssprache command language
Befehlssteuerblock command control block
Befehlstabelle instruction table
Befehlstaste command key
Befehlsübersicht reference card
Befehlsverkehr command communication
Befehlsverteilerkanal instruction distribution channel
Befehlsvorrat instruction set
Befehlswiederholung instruction repetition
Befehlswiederholungs-Einrichtung instruction retry facility
Befehlswort command word, instruction word
Befehlszähler address counter, instruction counter, program counter
Befehlszählerstand instruction counter status
Befehlszeiger instruction pointer
Befehlszeile command line
Befehlszeilenform command line form
Befehlszeit instruction time
Befehlszusatz command option
Befehlszyklen instruction cycles
Befehl zur schnellen Abtastung high speed scan instruction
befestigen mount
Befestigung fixture
Befestigungsclip des Druckkopfes printhead retainer clip
Befestigungsloch mounting hole
Befestigungsplatte locking plate
Befestigungsschraube fastening screw, fixing screw, retaining screw
befinden judge
befragen interrogate
befriedigen satisfy
Befund findings, report
Beginn beginning, start
Beginndatum start date
beginnen begin, start
Beglaubigung authentication
Begleitliste accompanying list
Begleitmeldung accompanying message
begrenzen limit
Begrenzer delimiter
Begrenzungskarte restriction card
Begrenzungsschaltung limiter circuit
Begrenzungszeichen delimiter, special quote character
Begriff term
Begriffsvariante conceptual variant
Begriffszuordnung conceptual allocation
Begrüßungsseite greeting page, welcome page
begünstigen favor
Behälter container, reservoir
Behältervorschrift container rules

behaftet encumbered
behandelbar treatable
behandeln deal, handle
Behandlung handling, treatment, treatment session
Behandlungsbericht treatment log
Behandlung von schwerwiegenden Fehlern fatal error handling
behaupten claim, state
beheben eliminate, recover
behelfen make do
behilflich helpful
behindert handicapped
beibehalten retain
Beibehaltung retention
beidseitig beschreibbare Diskette double sided diskette
beidseitige Datenübermittlung both way communiction
beim Kunden austauschbare Einheit field replaceable unit
Beinflussung influence
beinhalten contain
Beispiel example, sample, sample formula
Beispielprogramm sample program
beistellen supply
Beistellmaterial materials submitted
Beistellmaterialsatz materials submitted record
Beistellmenge quantity submitted
Beistellposition materials submitted line item
Beistellteile parts submitted
Beistellung auxiliary order materials submission
beistimmen agree
Beitrag contribution
bekommen get
Belastbarkeit current carrying capacity
belasten debit
Belastung debit, electric ballast, load
Belastungen charges
Belastungsanforderung charge request
Belastungswiderstand load resistor
Beleg voucher
Belegabstimmung voucher adjustment
Belegadresse voucher address
Belegänderung voucher alteration
Belegalter voucher age
Beleganfang voucher start
Beleganzeige voucher display
Beleganzeigebild voucher display screen
Belegarchiv voucher archive
Belegart voucher type
Belegartenlaufzeit voucher type duration

Belegartentext voucher type text
Belegauswahl voucher selection
Belegauswertung voucher analysis
Belegautor originator of the voucher
Belegbearbeitung voucher processing
Belegbetrag voucher amount
Belegbuchungsmappe voucher posting deck
Belegdatei voucher file
Belegdaten voucher data
Belegdatenbank voucher data base
Belegdatenvolumen voucher data volume
Belegdatum voucher date
Belegebene voucher level
Belegeingabe voucher input
Belegeinzug document indent
belegen occupy
Belegentnahme removal of document
Belegerfassung registering the voucher, voucher registration
Belegerstellung creating the voucher
Belegform voucher form
Belegfuß voucher foot
Belegindex voucher index
Belegindexblock voucher index block
Belegjournal voucher daily ledger
Belegkontierung voucher posting
Belegkopf voucher head, voucher header
Belegkopfanzeige voucher header display
Belegkopfbild voucher header screen
Belegkopfdaten voucher header data
Belegkopfsegment voucher header segment
Belegkopftext voucher header text
Beleglaufzeit voucher duration
beleglesen voucher reading
Beleglesung optical character recognition
Belegmasterindex voucher master index
Belegnummer voucher number
Belegnummerndatei voucher number file
Belegnummernkreis voucher number range
Belegnummernvergabe voucher number allocation
Belegposition voucher item
Belegpositionsdaten voucher item data
Belegpositionsnummer voucher item number
Belegpositionssegment voucher item segment
Belegreorganisation voucher re-org, voucher re-organization
Belegreorganisationslauf voucher re-org run
Belegresidenz voucher residency
Belegrückseite rear side of voucher
Belegsaldo voucher balance
Belegsatz voucher record
belegschnell voucher rapid

beobachten

belegschnell ändern voucher rapid change
Belegschreibung printing of vouchers
Belegsegment voucher segment
belegspezifisch voucher specific
Belegsumme voucher total
belegtes Feld occupied cell
Belegtyp voucher category
Belegtypenauswahl voucher category selection
Belegtzustand busy condition
Belegung mapping, occupancy
Belegungsbereich map area
Belegungsdauer holding time
Belegungsgröße occupancy size
Belegungsstand occupancy state
Belegungszusammenstoß head-on collision
Belegverfügbarkeit voucher availability
Belegverweildauer voucher hold duration
Belegverweilzeit voucher holding time
Belegverweilzeitprüfung voucher holding time check
Belegverzeichnis voucher directory
Belegvolumen voucher volume
Belegwährung voucher currency
belegweise voucher-by-voucher
Belegzeile voucher line
Belegzusammenhang voucher correlation
beliebig any, any desired
Belieferung delivery
belüften aerate, air
bemerken notice, point out
bemessen apportion
benachrichtigen inform
benennen call, name
benötigen require
benötigt necessary, required
benutzen use
Benutzer operator, user
benutzerabhängig user dependent
Benutzerabschnitt user section
Benutzerangaben call user data
Benutzeranpassung user customization
Benutzerausgang user exit
Benutzerausgang-Anschlußmodul user exit connection module
Benutzerbelang user interest
Benutzerberechtigungsdatei user authorization file
Benutzerbereich user area
benutzerbezogen user related
Benutzercode password
Benutzerdatei data file
Benutzerdaten call user data, user profile
Benutzerdatenbank user data base

benutzereigen private
Benutzereingabe user input
Benutzereingriff user action
Benutzerelement user element
Benutzerformat user format
benutzerfreundlich user friendly
Benutzerführung user guide
Benutzergruppe user group
Benutzerhandbuch operations guide, owner's manual, quick lookup guide, user manual, user's guide, user's manual
Benutzeridentifikation user identification
benutzerindividuell user individual
Benutzerinformation user information
Benutzerkennummer user identification code
Benutzerkennzeichen user label
Benutzerklasse user class of service
Benutzerkomfort user comfort
Benutzerkonto account
Benutzerkonto-Name account name
Benutzerliste user list, user table
Benutzermenü user menu
Benutzernachricht user message
Benutzername user name
Benutzernummer user number
Benutzeroberfläche user interface, user surface
Benutzerquittung user acknowledgement
Benutzerroutine user routine
Benutzersatz user record
Benutzerschnittstelle user interface
Benutzersegment user segment
Benutzerseite user side
Benutzersource user source
Benutzerspeicher user memory
Benutzerspeicherbereich user memory area, user storage area
benutzerspezifisches Attribut user attribute
Benutzerstamm user master
Benutzerstammsatz user master record
Benutzerstammstamm user master master
Benutzerstation user terminal
Benutzersuffix user suffix
Benutzertabelle user list, user table
Benutzertaste user key
Benutzerumgebung user environment
Benutzervariable user variable
Benutzervorgabe user default
Benutzerwörterbuch user dictionary
Benutzer-Workstation user workstation
Benutzung use
benutzungsfertig ready for use
Benutzungshäufigkeit frequency of use
beobachten observe

Beobachterplatz supervisor station
Beobachtungskanal observation channel
Beratungsfirma business consultancy
berechnen bill, calculate, charge
Berechnung billing, calculation
Berechnung der Vor-/Nacheilung lead lag computation
Berechnungsverfahren arithmetic technique
berechtigen authorize, entitle
Berechtigung authorization, clearance, privilege
Berechtigungsgruppe authorization group
Berechtigungskennzeichen authorization flag, authorization identification
Berechtigungsklasse authorization category
Berechtigungsmaske authorization mask, privilege mask
Berechtigungsprüfung authorization check, privilege check
Berechtigungsstufe clearance level
Bereich area, field, partition, range, region, select range, zone
Bereich für Eingabenachrichten input message area
Bereichsabschlußzeichen scope terminator
Bereichsanfang area start, beginning of extent
Bereichsangabe range specification
Bereichsauflösung area deallocation
Bereich schneller Abtastung high speed scan area, high speed scanning area
Bereichsebene range level
Bereichsersatzsektor partition alternate sector
Bereichskennzeichen area flag
Bereichsmenü partition menu
Bereichsüberlauf overflow
Bereichsumschalter range clamping switch
Bereichszuweisung area allocation
Bereich zur freien Verdrahtung patch area
bereinigen clean up
Bereinigungsmaßnahmen cleaning up measures
bereit ready
Bereit/Belegt-Protokoll ready busy protocol
bereiten prepare
bereitlegen layout
Bereitmeldung ready prompt
bereits already
Bereitschaft readiness, standby
Bereitschaftsbetrieb standby
Bereitschaftsmeldung prompt
Bereitschaftssignal attention interrupt
Bereitschaftssystem backup system
bereitstellen provide, submit

Bereitstellung provision
Bereitstellungsaufruf load call
Bereitzustand ready condition, ready state
Bericht report
berichten report
berichtigen correct
Berichtigung correction
Berichtigungsdaten correcting data
Berichtsauswertung report analysis
Berichtschreibung report preparation
Berichtsdaten report data
Berichtsdatenbank report data bank
Berichtsdatenverwaltung report data administration
Berichtsdefinition report definition
Berichtsjahr report year, year
Berichtsmonat month, report month
Berichtsnummer report number
Berichtsperiode period, report period
Berichtsprogramm report program
Berichtssaldo balance
Berichtsstufe report level
Berichtstabelle report table
Berichtszeilenebene report line level
Berichtszeitpunkt report time
Berichtszeitraum reporting period
Berichtwert value
Bers-Anschluß bers type connector
berücksichtigen consider, take into account
Berücksichtigung consideration
berühren touch
Berührungsschalter touch switch
beruhen base
besagen state
beschädigen damage
Beschädigung damage
beschäftigen employ
beschaffen procure
Beschaffenheit condition, constitution, nature, quality, structure
Beschaffung procurement
Beschaffungsdatenbank procurement data bank
Beschaffungskosten procurement costs
Beschaffungsmenge procurement quantity
Beschaffungspreis procurement price
Beschaffungsrisiko procurement risk
Beschaffungszeit procurement time
beschleunigen advance
beschleunigte Gleitpunktarithmetik scientific accelerator module
Beschleunigungsregelung acceleration control
Beschleunigungszeit acceleration time

**beschlossene Bardividende auf Stamm-
aktien** cash dividends declared
beschränken restrict
Beschränkung limitation
beschreiben define, describe
Beschreibung definition, description, designation, instructions
Beschreibung der Funktionsweise functional description
Beschreibungsdatei descriptor file
Beschreibungsmaske description mask
Beschreibungsmittel description medium
Beschreibungssatz descriptor record
Beschreibungstext description text
beschriebene Fläche recorded surface
beseitigen eliminate
besetzen define, occupy
Besetztfall busy condition
Besetztmeldung busy response
Besitz ownership, property
besitzen possess
Besitzer owner
besondere Funktion special use
besondere Vereinbarung special agreement
Besonderheit special feature
besonders especially, special
besorgen procure
Besprechung meeting
Besprechungsprotokoll meeting agenda
besser better
Beständigkeit durability
bestätigen acknowledge, confirm
Bestätigen des Fehlers acknowledge the error
Bestätigung ack, acknowledge, acknowledgement, confirmation
Bestätigung bezüglich externer Funktion external function acknowledgement
Bestätigung der Eingabedaten input data acknowledge
Bestätigungsliste confirmation list
Bestätigungs-Maske acknowledgement mask
Bestätigungsmeldung acknowledgement message, confirmation message
Bestätigungspflicht confirmation requirement
Bestätigungs-Taste acknowledgement key
Bestand durability, stock
Bestandleseroutine stock read routine
Bestandleseschnittstelle stock read interface
Bestand nicht eröffneter Jobs backlog, backlog of jobs, job backlog
Bestandsabwertung inventory devaluation
Bestandsanzeige inventory display
Bestandssatz inventory record

Bestandsaufwertung inventory revaluation
Bestandsband inventory tape
Bestandsbelastung inventory debit entry
Bestandsberichtigung inventory adjustment
Bestandsbewertung inventory valuation
Bestandsbuchung inventory posting
Bestandsdatei inventory file, stock file
Bestandsdaten inventory data
Bestandsdeckung inventory coverage
Bestandsentlastung inventory credit entry
Bestandsentwicklung inventory development
Bestandsfeld inventory field
Bestandsführungskennzeichen inventory update flag
Bestandskonto inventory account
Bestandskontrolle inventory check
Bestandsliste inventory list
Bestandsmenge backlog, stock quantity
Bestandsnachweis inventory evidence
Bestandspostion inventory item
Bestandsreservierung inventory reservation
Bestandssituation inventory situation
Bestandsstatus inventory status
Bestandsübersicht inventory summary
Bestandsüberwachung inventory monitoring
Bestandsumbewertung inventory revaluation
Bestandsvariable stock variable
Bestandsvariablenname stock variable name
Bestandsveränderung inventory alteration
Bestandswert inventory value
Bestandswertbuch inventory value posting
Bestandswertkorrektur inventory value correction
Bestandswertsimulation inventory value simulation
Bestandteil component, constituent, part
bestehen consist, exist
Bestellabforderung purchase order request
Bestellabruf call-off
Bestellabschluß purchase order completion
Bestellabschlußtext purchase order concluding text
Bestellabwicklung order handling, purchase order processing
Bestelländerung purchase order alteration
Bestelländerungsschreibung purchase order change print-out
Bestellanforderungsdatei purchase order request file
Bestellanforderungsgegenstand requested item
Bestellanforderungsnummer purchase order request number

Bestellanforderungssatz

Bestellanforderungssatz purchase order request record
Bestellanhang purchase order appendix
Bestellanhangsart purchase order appendix type
Bestellanhangstext purchase order appendix text
Bestellanweisung ordering guide
Bestellart purchase order type
Bestellauftragsdatei purchase order file
Bestellbearbeitung purchase order processing
Bestellbeleg purchase order
Bestellbestand quantity on order, stock on order
Bestellbetrag amount of the order
Bestelldaten purchase order data
Bestelldatenbank purchase order data base
Bestelldatum order date
Bestelldisposition order planning
Bestelleingabe purchase order entry
Bestelleingang purchase order in
bestellen order
Bestellentwicklung purchase order history
Bestellentwicklungselemente purchase order history element
Bestellentwicklungskennzeichen purchase order history flag
Bestellentwicklungssatz purchase order history record
Bestellentwicklungstyp purchase order history source
Bestellerfassung registering the purchase order
Bestellerzeugung generating the purchase order
Bestellformular purchase order form
Bestellinformationen ordering information
Bestellkopf purchase order header
Bestellkosten order costs
Bestellmenge quantity ordered
Bestellmengeneinheit ordering units
Bestellnettowert net order value, net purchase order value
Bestellnotiz purchase order note, purchase order remark
Bestellnummer purchase order number
Bestellobligation quantity optimisation
Bestellobligo purchasing commitment
Bestellpolitik order policy
Bestellposition purchase order item
Bestellpositionserfüllung purchase order item completion
Bestellpositionsextrakt purchase order item extract
Bestellpositionstyp purchase order item type

Bestellpreis ordering price
Bestellpreiseinheit purchase order pricing unit
Bestellpunkt order point
Bestellpunktüberwachung order point monitoring
Bestellschreiben purchase order letter
Bestellschreibung printing purchase orders
bestellspezifisch order-specific
Bestellstatistik purchase order statistics
Bestelltätigkeit purchase activity
Bestelltext purchase order text
Bestelltyp purchase order type
Bestellüberwachung purchase order monitoring
Bestellung order, purchase order
Bestellungsanlage purchase order document
Bestellungsbuchung purchase order entry
Bestellungserzeugung creating the purchase order
Bestellungstermin purchase order date
Bestellungszulässigkeit order authorization
Bestellvolumen purchase order volume
Bestellvorschlag order proposal, purchase order proposal
Bestellvorschlagsliste purchase order proposal list
Bestellvorschlagsmenge order advice quantity
Bestellvorschlagsprogramm order proposal program
Bestellwert purchase order value
Bestellwesen ordering
Bestellzeitpunkt order lead date
Bestellzeitraum order lead time
bestimmbar definable
bestimmen define, determine
bestimmend decisive
bestimmt certain, particular
bestimmte Funktion particular operation
Bestimmung designation
Bestimmungskennzeichen für Pakettyp packet type identifier
Bestimmungsort destination
Bestlieferungskennzeichen full delivery flag
Bestzeitprogramm minimum access routine
Bestzeitprogrammierung minimum access programming
betätigen press
Betätigung operation
Betätigungseinrichtung operating mechanism
beteiligen participate
Beteiligter participant
betonen emphasize
betrachten regard
Betrachtung consideration

Betrag amount
Betragsabweichung amount deviation, difference
Betragsaufbereitung amount editing
Betragsausrechnung amount calculation
Betragsberechtigung amount authorization
Betragsberichtigung amount adjustment
Betragseingabe amount input
Betragserteilung apportionment
Betragskontierung amount posting
Betragskorrektur amount correction
betragsmäßig according to amount
Betragsuntergrenze lower limit
Betragszuordnung amount allocation
betrauen entrust
betreffen concern
betreffend concerning, relevant
Betreffposition position for reference text
Betrefftext reference text
Betreffvariable variable for reference text
Betreffvariablenname variable name for reference text
Betreff-Variablensteuerung control of variables for reference text
betreiben operate, run
betreten enter, set foot
betreuen care, take care of
Betreuer manager, person in charge
Betreuung care
Betrieb business, company, operation, operations, run
Betrieb des Terminals terminal operation
betrieblich business, operational
Betrieb mit niedriger Geschwindigkeit low speed operation
Betriebsablauf operation procedure
Betriebsabrechnung cost accounting
Betriebsanleitung operating procedure
Betriebsanweisung control image, control statement, directive
Betriebsanweisungscode opcode
Betriebsart mode, mode of operation, operating mode
Betriebsartanzeige operation method indicator
Betriebsart auswählen select mode
Betriebsartauswahl mode select
Betriebsart mit voller Betriebsbereitschaft fully operational mode, operational mode
Betriebsartschalter operation method switch
Betriebsart wählen set mode
Betriebsauftrag business order, production order

Betriebsauftragsabwicklung production order processing
Betriebsauftragsnummer production order number
betriebsbereit operational
Betriebsbereitschaft operational mode, ready status, standby
Betriebsbereitschaft mitteilen force attention
Betriebsbereitschaftsanzeige power OK indicator
Betriebsbereitschaftszeit operable time
Betriebsfrequenz operating frequency
Betriebsgegebenheiten environment
Betriebsinformation operating information
betriebsintern in house
Betriebsmerkmale operating feature
Betriebsmittel resources
Betriebsmittelkombination resource combination
Betriebsmittelmakro resource macro
Betriebsmittelsperre resource lock
Betriebsmodul operating module
Betriebsmodus mode of operation, set up, set up mode
Betriebsmodusanzeige set up display, set up field
Betriebsmoduseinstellung set up option, set up selection
Betriebsmodusmenü system options menu
Betriebsmodusmerkmal set up feature
Betriebsmodus rücksetzen set up reset
Betriebsmodusspeicher set up memory
Betriebsmodus speichern set up save
Betriebssoftware system software
Betriebsspannung operating voltage
Betriebsspeicher operating memory
Betriebssprache operating language
Betriebssprachenprozessor run processor
Betriebsstätte registered offices
Betriebsstoffe factory supplies
Betriebssystem computer operating system, operating system
betriebssystemabhängig depending on the operating system, operating system dependent, operating system specific
Betriebssystemdatei operating system file
Betriebssystemdiskette operating diskette, system diskette
Betriebssystemkommando operating command
Betriebssystemmeldung operating system message
Betriebssystemmenü operating system menu
Betriebssystempaket operating system kit

Betriebssystem-Stand state of operating system
Betriebsumgebung environment, office area, operating environment
Betriebsversuch field test
Betriebsweise operation mode
betriebswirtschaftlich business
Betriebszeit elapsed time, operating time, operation time, up time
Betrug mit Computerunterstützung computer assisted fraud
Bett format
beurteilen judge
Beurteilung judgement
bevorzugen prefer
bewährt time proven
Bewegung transaction
Bewegungsart transaction type
Bewegungsarteneintrag transaction type entry
Bewegungsartenschlüssel transaction type code
Bewegungsartentabelle transaction type table
Bewegungsbetrag transaction amount
Bewegungsdaten transaction data
Bewegungsdatensatz transaction data record
Bewegungsfaktor movement factor
Bewegungskonto transaction account
Bewegungsliste transaction report
Bewegungssatz movement record, transaction record
Bewegungssimulation transaction simulation
Bewegungsstopp-Schalter motion stop switch
Bewegungszeitraum transaction period
bewehrter Kanal shielded conduit
beweisen prove
bewerten rate, value
Bewertung rating, valuation
Bewertungsdaten valuation data
Bewertungsdifferenz valuation discrepancy
Bewertungsgrundlage valuation basis
Bewertungskonto valuation account
Bewertungskriterium valuation criterion
Bewertungskurs valuation rate
Bewertungsliste valuation list
Bewertungspreis valuation price
Bewertungsprogramm benchmark program
Bewertungsvorschau valuation forecast
bewirken cause
bewußt deliberately
bezahlbar affordable
Bezahlung payment
bezeichnen designate, specify
Bezeichner identifier
beziehen refer, relate
Beziehung relation

Bezirk area
bezüglich referring to
Bezug reference
Bezugnahme reference
bezugnehmend referencing, regarding
Bezugsart acquisition type
Bezugsdaten acquisition data, relational data
Bezugsdatum purchase date
Bezugsfaktor reference modifier
Bezugsfilter reference filter
Bezugskosten delivery costs
Bezugskostenbetrag amount of delivery costs
Bezugsmenge purchase quantity
Bezugsmöglichkeit purchase option
Bezugsnebenkosten additional delivery costs
Bezugsoperand reference operand
Bezugspegel reference level
Bezugsperiode acquisition period
Bezugsquelle purchasing source
Bezugsrelation referenced relation
Bezugsschlüssel key of reference
Bezugswert acquisition value
Bezugszahl Gruppenstufe 1 level 1 indicator
Bibliothek library
Bibliotheksaufbau library organisation
Bibliotheksausgabetyp library output type
Bibliotheksband library tape
Bibliotheksdokument library document
Bibliothekserstellung formation of a library
Bibliotheksfunktion library function
Bibliothekspflege library maintenance
Bibliotheksprogramm librarian, librarian programm, library program, library routine
Bibliothekstabelle library register
Bibliothekstyp library type
Bibliotheksverwalter librarian, librarian, library administrator
Bibliotheksverwaltung library administration
Bibliotheksverzeichnis library directory
bidirektional bidirectional
bidirektionales Drucken bidirectional printing
bidirektional mit Vorwärts-/Rückwärtssuche bidirectional lookahead
biegsam flexible
biegsames Kabel flexible cable
Biegsamkeit flexibility
bieten offer, provide
Bilanz balance sheet
Bilanzaktiva assets
Bilanzbewertung balance sheet valuation
Bilanzkonto balance account
Bilanzpassiva liabilities
Bilanzposition balance sheet item

Bilanzprüfung balance check
Bilanzsteuerschlüssel balance control code
Bilanzsteuerung balance control
Bilanzstichtag balance sheet date
Bilanzvortrag balance carried forward
Bild chart, illustration, image, picture, slide
Bildablauf sequence of charts, sequence of screens, sequence of slides
Bildaufbau screen format, screen layout, slide layout
Bildaufnahmeröhre camera tube
Bildausschnitt screen window
Bildauswahl screen selection
Bilddurchlauf scrolling
Bilddurchlaufbereich scrolling region
Bilddurchlaufmodus scroll mode
bilden create, form
Bildfolge screen sequence
Bildformat aspect ratio, display format
Bildfrequenzverstärker video amplifier, videofrequency amplifier
Bildgestaltung chart design, screen layout, slide layout
Bildgruppe chart group, screen group, slide group
Bildgruppenauswahl screen group selection
Bildhälfte half screen
Bildinstabilität display jitter, image jitter
Bildmodifikation screen modification
Bildpunkt dot, pixel
Bildröhre cathode ray tube, picture tube
Bildschirm cathode ray tube, cathode ray unit display, display screen, monitor, screen, terminal, video display unit, video monitor, video terminal
Bildschirmabbild screen image
Bildschirmabfrage screen enquiry, screen inquiry
Bildschirmadapter display adapter
Bildschirmanzeige screen display
Bildschirmanzeige neu aufbauen refresh screen
Bildschirmausdruck screen copy, screen print
Bildschirmausgabe display output
Bildschirmausgabeformat display output format
Bildschirmausgabefunktion display output function
Bildschirmausstattung terminal equipment
Bildschirmbenutzer terminal user
Bildschirmbereich display area
Bildschirmbild screen mask
Bildschirmbreite screen width

Bildschirmdruckausgabe screen dump facility
Bildschirmduplikat screen copy
Bildschirmemulation terminal emulation
Bildschirmfeld screen field
Bildschirmformat screen format
Bildschirmgerät video monitor, video terminal
Bildschirmgröße screen size
Bildschirmhelligkeit brightness, screen brightness
Bildschirmhintergrund background, screen background
Bildschirmhintergrund dunkel dark screen
Bildschirminhalt screen of information
Bildschirmkabel monitor cable, video cable
Bildschirmkapazität display capacity
Bildschirmkarte display adapter
Bildschirmkonsole console, display console
Bildschirmlayout screen format, screen layout
Bildschirm löschen clear screen
Bildschirmlöschung screen clearing procedure
Bildschirmmaske display frame, display screen mask, screen format, screen mask
Bildschirmmodifikation screen modification
Bildschirmmodus screen mode
Bildschirmnachricht screen message
Bildschirm-Programmiergerät video programming unit
Bildschirmregler picture control, video control, video monitor controls
Bildschirmreiniger screen cleaner
Bildschirmseite display screen page, screen page
Bildschirmseitennummer screen page number
Bildschirmspeicher video random access memory
bildschirmspezifisch terminal specific
Bildschirmsteueranschluß CRT control port
Bildschirmsteuerbaustein CRT controller
Bildschirmsteuereinheit CRT controller
Bildschirmsymbol screen symbol
Bildschirmsystem display screen keyboard
Bildschirmterminal screen terminal, video data terminal, video terminal
Bildschirmtext interactive videotext, videotext
Bildschirmtext-Rechnerverbund interactive videotext computer network
Bildschirmtext-Zentrale interactive videotext center, videotext center
Bildschirmumgehungspuffer screen bypass
Bildschirmzeile screen line
Bildseitenverhältnis aspect ratio
Bildsteuerelement display control element
Bildsteuerformat display control format

277

Bildsteuerformatierung display control formatting
Bildsteuerung display control
Bildumfang screen size
Bildung creation
Bildungsgesetz law of formation
Bildverstärker image intensifier, video amplifier
Bildwalze drum
Bildzeilendichte interlace
binär binary
Binärbaum binary tree
Binärcode binary code
binär codiertes Dezimalsystem binary coded decimal
Binärdarstellung binary notation
Binärdatei binary file
Binär-Dezimal-Umsetzung binary to decimal conversion
Binär-/Dezimal-Umwandlung binary decimal conversion, binary to decimal conversion
binäre Arithmetikfunktion binary arithmetic function
Binäreinheit binary digit
binärer Fehlererkennungscode binary error detecting code
binärer Fehlerkorrekturcode binary error correcting code
binäre Speicherzelle binary cell, memory cell
binäres Semaphor binary semaphor
Binärkartencode column binary card data format
binär kodierte Dezimalzahl binary coded decimal
binär kodierte Oktalzahl binary coded octal
Binärkomma binary point
Binärmodus compressed card mode
Binäroperator binary operator
Binärrelation binary relation
Binärschlüssel binary code
Binärstelle binary digit
Binärsumme binary total
binärsynchrones Übertragungsprotokoll binary synchronous communications protocol
binärsynchrone Übertragung binary synchronous communications
Binärtext binary text
Binärumwandlung binary conversion
Binärzähler binary counter
Binärzahl binary number
Binärziffer binary digit
Bindeanweisung link statement
Bindeelementmenge link set

Bindelader linking loader
binden link
Bindeprozedur linkage procedure
Binder linker
Bindertabelle link map
Bindestrich hyphen
Bindung linkage
Binnenumsatz internal turnover
bipolar bipolar
bipolarer Transistor bipolar transistor
Bipolar-Tastung bipolar modulation
Biprozeßrechner bi-processor
Biquinärkode biquinary code
bistabil bistable
bistabiler Multivibrator bistable trigger unit, scaling circuit
bistabiles Kippglied bistable trigger unit
Bit binary digit, bit
Bitabbildmodus bit image mode, raster image mode
Bitbelegungsplan bit map
Bitbelegungszeiger mapping pointer
Bitbündelkennung für Gruppenwechselschrift gor identification burst
Bitbündel-Übertragung burst transmission
Bitdichte bit density
Bitfehlerrate bit error rate
Bitfehlerratenmonitor bit error rate monitor
Bitfehlerratentester bit error rate tester
Bitfolge an der Übergabestelle bit order of transmission
Bitfolgenfeld der Steuereinheit control unit bit array
Bitfrequenz bit rate
Bitgeschwindigkeit bit rate
Bit löschen bit clear, clear bit
Bit-Map bit map
Bit-Map-Sektor bit map sector
Bit-Map-Zugriff bit map access
Bitmaske bit mask
Bit mit dem niedrigsten Stellenwert least significant bit
Bitmuster bit pattern
Bitmustergrafik bit map graphics, raster graphics
bitorientiertes Protokoll bit oriented protocol
bitorientiertes Steuerungsverfahren high level data link
bitparallel bit-parallel
Bitposition bit position
Bit pro Sekunde bits per second, bits per second
Bit pro Zeichen bits per character

Bit pro Zoll bit per inch, bits per inch
Bit prüfen bit check, bit pick, bit test, check bit, test bit
Bit-Schieberegister bit shift register
Bit setzen bit set, set bit
Bit-Slice-Mikroprozessor bit slice microprocessor
Bitsummenfehler bit total error
bitsynchrone Kommunikation binary synchronous communications, bit synchronous communications
bitsynchrone Schnittstelle bit synchronous adapter, bitsynchronous communications adapter
Bittabelle bit map
Bitübertragungsschicht pyhsical layer
Bit-Vollgruppe bit envelope
Bit-Wert bit value
Bitzellenzeit bit cell time
Bitzuordnung bit assignment
Blackbox black box
Blätterfunktion browse function, page function, paging function
Blätterkommando paging command
blättern browse, page
Blankanzahl zero amount
Blatt page
Blattanfang beginning of page, top of page
Blattbehandlung page handling
Blatteinteilung page formatting
Blattführung form guide, paper feed, paper guide
Blatthalter copy holder
Blatthöhe page height, page length
Blattkennzeichen sheet identifier
Blattkettung sheet chaining
Blattnummer page number
Blattrand page margin
Blattschreiber pagewriter
Blechgehäuse metal case, metal housing, sheet metal case
Blechkern laminated core
Bleiakkumulator lead acid battery
Bleistift lead pencil
Blind- dummy
Blindabschnitt dummy section
Blindbefehl dummy instruction
Blindeingabe dummy entry
Blindkomponente quadrature component
Blindleitwert susceptance
Blindnachricht dummy message
Blindsicherung dummy fuse
Blindversuch dry run, dry running

blinken blink, blink, flash
Blinksignal flashing signal
Blinktakt flashing cycle
Blitz flash
Blitzableiter lightning conductor
Blitzgenerator lightning generator
Blitzschutz lightning protection
Block block, frame
Blockabbruch abort
Blockabstand interblock space
Blockanfang start of block
Blockansteuerung block selection
Blockanweisung block statement
Blockauswahlsymbol select block symbol
Blockbeschreibungswort block descriptor word
Blockbild block screen
Blockcursor block cursor
Blockebene block level
Block-Empfangsbestätigung block acknowledgement
Blocken blocking
blocken block
Blockende end of block
Blockendezeichen end of block character
Blockfehlerrate block error rate
Blockfehlerratenprüfung block error rate test
Block fester Länge fixed block, fixed length block
Blockformat block format
Blockgeschwindigkeit block-to-block speed
Blockieren blocking
blockieren block, lock out
blockiert blocked
blockierter Prozeß blocked process
Blockierung blocking
Blockierung des Arbeitsablaufes hangup
blockierungsfreies Koppelfeld non blocking switching matrix
Blockkennung block identification
Blockkopf block header
Blocklänge block length
Blocklücke block gap
Blockmarkierspur block marker track
Blocknummer block number
Blockprüfung block check
Blockprüfzeichen block check character
Blockprüfzeichenfolge block check sequence
Blockrückweisung frame reject
Blocksatz justification
Blockschreibmarke block cursor
Blocksicherungsverfahren block securing
Blocksignal interlocking signal
Blocksortierung block sort

blockstrukturiert block structured
Blockzeichen block characters
Blockzugriffsmethode block access method
Blockzwischenprüfung intermediate transmission block
Bocksprung-Test leapfrog test
Bodenplatte base plate, shield plate
Bogen arc
Bogenentladungsröhre arc discharge tube
Bohrer drill
Bohrerbefestigung drill fixture
Bohrkopf drill head
Bohrkopfvorschub drill head advance
Bohrmotor drill motor
Bonität credit standing
Bonus bonus
Bonusabrechnung bonus settlement
bonusberechtigt eligible for bonus
Bonusermittlung bonus calculation
bonusfähig eligible for bonus, qualify for bonus
Bonus gewähren granting a bonus
Bonusgutschrift bonus credit note
Bonuskennzeichen bonus flag
Bonusmerkmal bonus flag
Bonusstaffel bonus scale
Bonusüberwachung bonus monitoring
boolesche Algebra boolean algebra
boolesche Operation boolean operation
boolesche Verknüpfung boolean operation
Bool'sch boolean
bootbarer Datenträger bootable medium
booten boot
Boot-ROM boot ROM
Box box
Box-Einschaltzustand box enable condition
Boxfunktion box function
Branche sector
Brandbreitenkompression bandwidth compression
Brauch usage
brauchbar usable
brauchen need
Brauchszolltarif custom tariff
Braunsche Röhre cathode ray tube
Breitband- broadband
Breitband-Koaxialkabel broadband coaxial cable
Breitbandvermittlung broadband exchange
Breite width
Bremse brake
bremsen brake
Bremsgitter suppressor grid

Brennadel recording stylus
Brennfleck focal spot
Brief letter
Briefanforderung letter request
Briefanschrift letter address
Briefart letter type, type of letter
Briefaufbau letter structure
Briefauftragserstellung letter request generation
Briefauftragssatz letter request record
Briefausdruck letter print
Briefausgabe letter output
Briefauswahlmaske letter selection mask
Briefbereich letter area
Briefdatum letter date
Briefende letter end
Brieferstellung letter creation, letter generation
Brieferstellungsdatei letter creation file
Briefform letter form
Brieffuß letter bottom
Briefgerüst letter skeleton
Briefgerüstdaten letter skeleton data
Briefgerüstmaske letter skeleton mask
Briefgestaltung layout, letter design
Briefgruppe group of letters
Briefhüllenablage envelope stacker
Briefhüllenanlage envelope setting
Briefhüllendurchlauf envelope run
Briefhülleneinzug envelope entry
Briefhüllenführung envelope feeding device
Briefinformationssatz letter information record
Briefinhalt letter content
Briefkasten mailbox
Briefkatalog letter catalog
Briefkopf header, letter head
Briefkopfteil overhead segment
Briefkopftext header text, letter head text
Briefkurs selling rate
Brief-Kurzinhalt brief letter content
Briefname letter name
Briefnummer letter number
Briefnummernbereich letter number area
Briefnummerndatei letter number file
Briefnummernsatz letter number record
Briefschreibung letter writing
Briefschreibungsprozedur letter writing procedure
Briefseite letter page
Brieftext letter text
Brieftransaktion letter transaction
Briefvariable letter variable
Briefverarbeitung letter processing
Briefverkehr correspondence

Briefvorrat letter stock
Brillianz brilliance
Broschüre booklet
Bruch breakage, fraction
Bruchstrich fraction stroke
Bruchteil fractional part
Bruchzahl fraction
Brücke bridge, jumper
Brückenklemme jumper terminal
Brückenschaltung bridge circuit
Brummspannung ripple
Brutto gross
Bruttoauftragswert gross sales order value
Bruttobestellpreis gross purchase order price
Bruttobestellwert gross purchase order value
Bruttobetrag gross amount
Bruttobuchung gross entry
Bruttoeinzelpreis gross unit price
Bruttoerlös gross revenue
Bruttogewicht gross weight
Bruttopreis gross price
Bruttoverfahren gross processing
Bruttowert gross value
Buch book
buchbar postable
Buchbestand book inventory
buchen book, charge, post
Buchführung accounting, bookkeeping
Buchgewinn book profit
Buchhalter accountant
Buchhaltung accounting, bookkeeping
Buchhaltungsabschluß accounts closing
Buchhaltungsbeleg accounting voucher
Buchhaltungsbereich accounting field
Buchhaltungsdaten accounting data
Buchhaltungsfeld accounting field
Buchhaltungsleiter chief accountant
Buchhaltungssachbearbeiter accounts clerk
Buchhaltungssegment accounting segment
Buchhaltungsstruktur accounting structure
Buchhaltungssystem accounting system, business accounting system
Buchhaltungstransaktion accounting transaction
Buchse connector, jack, socket
Buchsenstecker male plug
Buchstabe alphabetic character, letter
Buchstabencode alpha code, mnemonic code
Buchstabeneingabe alpha input
Buchstabensymbol alpha symbol, letter symbol
Buchstabentastenreihe letter row
Buchstabenumschaltung letter shift
Buchungsanzeige posting display

Buchungsart posting type
Buchungsbeginn start of posting
Buchungsbeleg voucher
Buchungsbereich accounting field
Buchungsbetrag amount posted
Buchungsbetragsangabe specification of amount posted
Buchungsbild posting screen
Buchungsdaten posting data
Buchungsdatenabstimmung posting data balancing
Buchungsdatenextrakt posting data extract
Buchungsdatum date of posting
Buchungsende end of posting
Buchungsjahr posting year
Buchungskontrolle audit trail
Buchungskreis accounting area
Buchungskreisangabe accounting area specification
Buchungskreisberechtigung accounting area authorization
buchungskreisbezogen referring to an accounting area
Buchungskreisdaten accounting area data
Buchungskreisdatenbank accounting area database
Buchungskreisebene accounting area level
Buchungskreiseintrag accounting area entry
Buchungskreisgruppe accounting area group
Buchungskreiskonsolidierung accounting area consolidation
Buchungskreisnummer accounting area number
Buchungskreisschlüssel accounting area code
Buchungskreistabelle accounting area table
Buchungskreistext accounting area text
buchungskreisunabhängig independent of accounting area
Buchungskreisverwaltung accounting area management
Buchungskreisverwaltungssatz accounting area management record
Buchungskreiswechsel change of accounting area
Buchungslauf posting run
Buchungsmappe posting deck
Buchungsmaschine accounting machine
Buchungsmonat posting month
Buchungsmonatsultimo last day of posting month
Buchungsperiode accounting period
Buchungsposition voucher item
Buchungssatz posting record

Buchungsschema accounting schedule
Buchungsschlüssel posting key
Buchungsschluß close of posting
Buchungsschritt posting step
Buchungssegment posting segment
Buchungsstichtag posting base date
Buchungsstofferfassung registering posting data
Buchungsstring posting string
Buchungstext posting text
Buchungstransaktion posting transaction
Buchungsvorfall posting transaction
Buchungsvorgang posting process
Buchungsweise posting method
Buchungszeile voucher item
Buchungszeilenkontierung posting of voucher items
Buchungszeit posting time
Buchungszeitraum posting cycle
Buchungszentrum reservation center
Buchwert book value
Budget budget
Budgetkontrolle budget control
Budgetliste budget list
Budgetnummer budget number
Budgetumverteilung budget re-distribution
Bündel bundle, burst, multilink
Büro office, room
Bürocomputer business computer, desktop computer
Büroeditierplatz office editing place
Bürofunktionen desk management
Büromaterial stationery
büroübergreifendes Netz interoffice network
Bürste brush
Bürstenhalter brush rocker, electrical brush holder
Bürstenvergleichsprüfung brush compare check
Bundesanzeiger federal legal gazette
Bundesbank federal bank
Bundesministerium federal ministry
Burstmodus burst mode
Bus bus
Busanforderung bus request
Bus-Arbitrator bus arbitrator
Busbelastung bus load
Busquittierungsleitung bus grant
Busschiene bus
Busschnittstelle bus interface
Bussystem bus system
Bustreiber bus driver
Bus verfügbar bus available

Byte byte
Byteanzahl byte count
Bytebearbeitung byte handling
Bytekanalumschalter byte channel transfer switch
Bytelänge byte length

C

Cache-Speicher   cache memory
Cartridge-Datei   cartridge file
Cartridge-Laufwerk   cartridge drive assembly
C-Bogen   C-arm
Celsius   celsius
charakterisieren   characterize
charakteristisch   characteristic
Charge   batch, production batch
Chargenerstellung   creation of batches
Chargennummer   batch number
chargenpflichtig   always batched
Chargensatz   batch record
Chargensplitting   batch splitting, production batch splitting
Chassis   chassis
Checkliste für den Bediener   operator checklist
Chemie   chemics
chemisch   chemical
chemischer Laser   chemical laser
chemische Steuerung   chemical variable control
Chiffre   code
chiffrieren   code
Chip   chip
Chip-Auswahl   chip select
Chip-Freigabe   chip enable
chronologisch   chronological
circa   about, approximately
Clip   clip
Cluster   cluster
Cobol-Programm   COBOL program
Code   code
Codeabschnitt   control section
Codeangabe   code specification
codeaufwendig   code intensive
Codeausgabefehler   code output error
Codeausgabefeld   code output field
Codebereich   code block
Codec   codec
Codeerweiterung   code extension
Codeerzeugung   code creation
Code für Datenaustausch   data interchange code
Codepuffer   load code buffer
Codesegment   code segment
Codesharing-Bearbeitung   code sharing operation
Codesteuerzeichen   code extension character
codetransparente Datenübermittlung   code transparent data communication
Codeumschaltung   escape mode
Codeumsetzer   code converter
Codeumwandler   code converter
Codeumwandlung   code conversion
codeunabhängige Datenübermittlung   code independent data communication
codeunabhängige Übertragung   code independent transmission
Codeungleichheit   character mismatch
Code zur Fehlerkorrektur   error correction code
codieren   code
Compiler   compiler, compiling program
Compilersprachen   compiler level languages
Computer   computer
Computerausgabe auf Mikrofilm   computer output microfilm
Computer-Ausweicheinrichtung   computer backup
Computerbauteil   computer component
Computerbestandteil   computer component
Computerbetriebssystem   computer operating system
Computercode   computer code
Computerdatei   computer file
Computerdrucker   computer printer
computergesteuertes Lernprogramm   computer based instruction
computergestütztes Lernen   computer based learning
computergestütztes Management (CAM)   computer assisted management
Computerhardware   computer hardware
Computerkriminalität   computer criminality
Computerlauf   computer run
Computermodus   computer mode
Computernetz   computer network, computer network system
Computernetzwerk   computer network
computerorientiert   computer oriented
computerorientierte Sprache   computer oriented language
Computerperipherie   computer peripheral equipment
Computerprogramm   computer program
Computersoftware   computer software
Computerspeichereinheit   computer storage device
Computer-Sprachauskünfte   computer voice advisories
Computerstraftat   computer aided crime

Computersystem computer system
Computersystemkonfiguration computer system configuration
Computertechnik computer technology
Computertechnologie computer technology
Computerterminal computer terminal
computerunterstützter Entwurf (CAD) computer aided design
computerunterstütztes Lernen computer assisted learning
Computerwort computer word
contra- contra
Controller controller
Controllerfehler controller error
Controller für serielle Kommunikation serial communication controller
Controllerkarte controller board
Controllerspeicher controller memory
Converter converter
Copydrucker hard copy printer
Core core
Core-Block core block
Core-Image core image
Core-resident core resident
CP/M (Betriebssystem) control program for microprocessors
CPU central processing unit
CPU-Architektur CPU architecture
CPU-Zeitverbrauch consumption of CPU time
create erstellen
Crossassembler cross assembler
Crosscompiler cross compiler
Cross-Referenz cross reference
Cross-Referenz-Liste cross reference list
Cross-Software cross software
CR-Taste carriage return key
Cursor cursor
Cursoradressierung cursor addressing
Cursor nach links cursor left
Cursor nach oben cursor up
Cursor nach rechts cursor right
Cursor nach unten cursor down
Cursorpositionierung cursor positioning
Cursorposition speichern save cursor
Cursor rückwärts cursor backward
Cursorsteuerung cursor addressing, cursor control
Cursortaste cursor control key, cursor key
Cursor vorwärts cursor forward
Cursor wiederherstellen restore cursor

D

da since
Dachgesellschaft mother company
dämpfen damping
Dämpfung attenuation
Dämpfungsglied attenuator
Dampfkraftwerk steam electric power station
darauffolgen succeed
darauffolgend adjacent, succeeding
daraus schließen conclude
darlegen explain, expound
Darlehen loan
Darlehensangaben loan information
Darlehensbetrag loan amount
Darlehenskonto loan account
Darlehensnehmer borrower
Darlehensstammsatz loan master record
darstellbares Zeichen display character
darstellen explain, expound, represent
Darstellung description, representation
Darstellung des negativen Vorzeichens negative value indication
Darstellungsebene presentation layer, representation layer, representation level
Darstellungseigenschaft representation feature
Darstellungsform representational form
Darstellungsinstanz presentation entity
Darstellungsschicht presentation layer
Darstellungssteuerung representation control
Darstellungsverfahren representation method
Darstellungszeichen representation symbol
Datagramm datagram
Datei data file, file
Dateiabschnittsende file section end
Dateiabschnittsfolge file section sequence
Dateiabschnittsnummer file section number
Dateiadreßregister file address register
Dateiänderung file modification
Dateianfang beginning of file, start of file
Dateianfangskennsatz file header label
Dateianlage file creation
Dateianweisung file instruction
Dateianzahl file number
Dateiart file organisation, file type
Dateiattribut file attribute
Datei auf mehreren Datenträgern multivolume file
Dateiauswahl selection of files

Dateiauswahlqualifizierer file selection qualifier
Datei-Bandkombination file tape combination
Dateibearbeitung file manipulation
Dateibearbeitungsroutine data routine
Dateibereiche extents
Dateibereichstabelle extent table
Dateibeschreibung file definition, file description, file descriptor
Dateibeschreibungsmodul file description module
Dateibezeichner file specifier
Dateibezeichnung file name
Dateiblock file block
Dateidefinition file definition
Dateieingabe file input
Dateien computer based files
Dateien bearbeiten operations on files
Dateiende end of file
Dateiendeblock end of file block
Dateiendecode end of file code
Dateiende-Etikett trailer tag
Dateiendmarkierung end of file mark
Dateien koppeln concatenate files
Dateien verketten concatenate files
Dateieröffnung file initialisation
Dateierweiterung file extension
Dateifolgenummer file sequence number
Dateifreigabe file release
dateiführend at the head of the file
Dateifunktion file function
Datei geöffnet zum Verändern file open for update
Datei gesperrt file locked
Dateigröße file size
Dateigruppe group of files
Dateiidentifizierung file identification
Dateiindex file index
Dateiinformationsblock file information block
Dateiinhalt file content
Datei in unzusammenhängenden Bereichen fragmented file
Datei in zusammenhängenden Bereichen contiguous file
Dateikennzeichen file identifier
Dateikennzeichnung label
Dateikommando file command
Dateikonventionen file conventions
Dateikonzept file conception
Dateikopf file header
Dateikopfsatz file header
Dateiliste file list
Dateiname file name

285

Dateiname abfragen

Dateiname abfragen parse file name
Dateinummer file number
Dateioperation file operation
Dateiorganisation file organisation
Dateiregister file register, index of files
Dateirücksetzen backward space file
Dateischutz file protection, protection status
Dateispezifikation file specification, file specifier
Dateispezifikation der nicht zu sichernden Datei backup exclusion file specifier
Dateispezifikation der zu sichernden Datei backup file specifier
dateispezifisch file specific
Dateistatusvariable file status variable
Dateisteuerbereichsliste file control block list
Dateisteuerblock data control block, flexible control block
Dateisteuergruppe file control group, flexible control group
Dateisteuerungsblock file control block
Dateisteuerungsprogramm file control program
Dateistruktur file structure
Dateisystem file system
Dateitransfer file transfer
Dateityp file extension, file type
Dateityp der Sicherungsdatei backup file type, type of file to save
Dateiüberlauf file overflow, file overrun
Dateiübertragung file transfer
Dateiübertragungsprogramm file transfer program
Dateiübertragungsprotokoll file transfer protocol
Dateiumsetzer file converter
dateiverändernd file changing
Dateiverarbeitung im Dialog interactive file processing
Dateiverarbeitung im Stapelbetrieb batch file processing
Dateiverkettung file concatenation
Dateiverwaltung file administration, file management
Dateiverwendung file use
Dateiverzeichnis directory, index of files
Dateiverzeichnisabschnitt directory area
Dateiverzeichnisaktionen directory options
Dateiverzeichnis der Diskette disk directory
Dateiverzeichnispfad directory path
Datei vorsetzen forward space file
Datei zu Datei file to file
Dateizugriff file access

Dateizugriffsblock file access block
Dateizugriffskanal file access channel
Dateizuweisung file allocation
Dateizyklus file cycle
Daten data
datenabhängige Störung data sensitive fault
Datenablaufplan data flow chart
Datenadresse data address
Datenänderung data alteration
Datenänderungsbeleg data change voucher
Datenanalyse data analysis
Datenanweisung data instruction
Datenaufbau construction of data
Datenaufbereitungsprogramm general editor, language editor
Datenausgabe data output
Datenausgabeleitung data out line
Datenaustausch data exchange
Datenaustauschband data exchange tape
Datenaustauschformat data interchange format
Datenaustauschkennzeichen data exchange identifier
Datenbank data base
Datenbankaufruf data base call
Datenbankbeschreibung data base description, data base descriptor
Datenbank-Beschreibungsprozessor data definition language processor
Datenbank-Beschreibungssprache data description language
Datenbankdienstleistung data base service
Datenbankentwurf data base design
Datenbankgenerator data base generator
Datenbankkomponente data bank component
Datenbankmanagement data base management
Datenbankmodell data base model
Datenbankorganisator data base organisator
Datenbankrechner data base machine
Datenbankschnittstelle data base interface
Datenbanksegment data base segment
Datenbanksituation data base situation
Datenbanksteuerprogramm data base diagram
Datenbankstruktur data base structure
Datenbanksystem data bank system, data base system, data management system, data base management system
Datenbanktransaktion data base transaction
Datenbankveränderung data base modification
Datenbankverknüpfung data base link
Datenbankverwendung data base use
Datenbankwiederherstellung data base recovery
Datenbankzugriff data base access

Datenbasis data base
Datenbedarf data requirement
Datenbereich data area
Datenbereichsadresse data area address
Datenbeschreibungssprache data description language
Datenbestand data file, data pool, volume of data
Datenbild data screen
Datenbit data bit
Datenblock data block
Datenbus data bus
Datencode data code
Datendarstellung data presentation, data representation
Datendatei data file
Datendefinitionsprozessor data definition processor
Datendienstbetriebsanweisung utility modifier card
Datendienstroutine data utility
Datendienstroutinendialog data utilities dialog
Datendiskette data disk, data diskette
Datendurchsatz information flow rate
Daten-Echo-Test auf der Hostleitung host line data loopback test
Datenein-/ausgabe data input/output
Dateneingabe data entry, data input, data inquiry
Dateneingabebus data input bus
Dateneingabeleitung data in line
Datenelement data element
Datenempfänger data sink, receiver
Datenende end of data, end of date
Datenendeinrichtung data terminal equipment
Datenendgerät data terminal, data terminal equipment
Datenerfassung data acquisition, data entry
Datenerfassungssystem data entry system
Datenfeld array, data field, data item, field, information field
Datenfeldbeschreibung data field description
Datenfernschaltgerät network termination unit
Datenfernübertragung data communication, long distance data transmission, telecommunications
Datenfernübertragungs-Schnittstelle remote terminal interface
Datenfernübertragungsstation remote communications terminal
Datenfernverarbeitung teleprocessing
Datenfernverarbeitungssystem remote data processing system

Datenfestnetz dedicated network
Datenfluß data flow, record stream
Daten-Flußdiagramm data flow diagram
Datenflußsteuerung data flow control
Datenforderungsliste data requirement list
Datenformat data format, data layout
Datenfortschreibung data update
Datenfreigabe data release
Datenfreigabetaste data release key
Datengewinnung data gathering
Datengruppe data group
Datenhaltung data retention
Datenintegration data integration
Datenkabel data cable, system cable
Datenkanal data channel
Datenkarte data card
Datenkategorie data category
Datenkommunikations-Schnittstelle data communication interface
Datenkommunikations-Transaktion data communication transaction
Datenkontrollwort data control word
Datenkonvertierung data conversion
Datenkonvertierungsvorschrift data conversion regulation
Datenkonzentrator data concentrator
Datenkonzept data concept
Datenlänge data length
Datenmanagement data management
Datenmanipulierungsprozessor data manipulation processor
Datenmanipulierungssprache data manipulation language
Datenmenge quantity of data
Datenmodell data model
Datenmodus data mode
Datenmultiplexer data multiplexer
Datennetz data network
Datennetzwartung network maintenance
Datenneuaufnahme data entry
Datenorganisation data organisation
Datenpaar im Wechselformat alternating data pair
Datenpaket data packet, packet
Datenpaketübermittlung packet mode operation
Datenparitätsbit data parity bit
Datenpfad data path
Datenpflege data administration
Datenpool data pool
Datenprüfung data validation
Datenpuffer data buffer
Datenquelle data source

Datenrate data rate
Datensätze sets of data
Datensätze pro Sektor records per sector
Datensätze pro Spur records per track
Datensammelkanal data bus line
Datensammelsystem data pooling system
Datensammlung data collection
Datensatz data record, data set, record
Datensatzbeschreibung data record description, record definition, record description
Datensatzbeschreibungsfeld record definition field
Datensatzdefinition data record definition, record definition
Datensatzlänge data record length, record length
Datensatzname data set name
Datensatznummer record number
Datensatzverwaltungsdienst record management service
Datensatzverwaltungssystem record management system
Datenschnittstelle data interface
Datenschutz data security
Datenschutz (für natürliche Personen) protection of data privacy
Datensenke data sink
Datensicherheit data integrity, data security
Datensicherung data back up, data protection
Datensicherungsband data back up tape
Datensicherungs- und Rückspeicherungsroutine disk dump restore utility
Datensichtgerät terminal
Datensichtstation remote site, terminal
Datensignal data signal
Datensignalkonzentrator data signal concentrator
Datensimulation data simulation
Datensortiergerät data sorter
Datensortierung data sorting
Datenspeicherplatz data storage position
Datenstapel data batch
Datenstation data station, remote device, remote terminal, terminal
Datenstation für Fernübertragung data communication station
Datenstation mit Tastatur keyboard data station
Datenstationsanschluß terminal connection
Datenstationsbenutzer remote user
Datenstationsjob dead end job
Datenstationsprozessor remote terminal processor

Datenstationstyp type of terminal
Datenstatuswort data status word
Datensteuerblock file control block
Datenstruktur data structure
datentechnisch data technical
Datenteil data division, data segment
Daten-Text-Endgerät data text terminal
Daten-/Textnetz data and text network
Daten-Text-Station data text station
Datenträger data carrier, data medium, medium, storage device, storage medium, volume
Datenträgeradresse data carrier address
Datenträgerarchiv data set archive
Datenträgeraufbau data carrier type
Datenträgeraustausch data medium exchange
Datenträgerband data tape
Datenträgerbeschreibungssprache device media control language
Datenträgerende data carrier end, end of volume
Datenträgerendekennsatz data medium end label
Datenträger für Software-Dokumentation release media
Datenträgerinhaltsverzeichnis data carrier content, volume table of contents
Datenträgerkennsatz volume header label, volume label
Datenträgerkennzeichen volume identifier
Datenträger mit Bootblock bootable medium
Datenträgername volume label, volume name
Datenträgernummer pack identification, volume serial number
Datenträgerüberprüfung pack verification
Datentransfer data transfer
Datentyp data type
Datenübergabeprogramm data delivery program
Datenübermittlung data communication
Datenübermittlungssystem data communication system
Datenübertragung communication, data communication, data communications, data transfer, data transmission
Datenübertragungsanlage data link
Datenübertragungsanschluß communication port, communications port
Datenübertragungsanschlußeinheit adapter equipment housing unit, communication adapter
Datenübertragungsanschlußkanal communications adapter channel

Datenübertragungsbenutzerprogramm communication user program
Datenübertragungsblock data transmission block, frame, transmission information block
Datenübertragungs-E/A-Programm remote transaction I/O
Datenübertragungseinrichtung data circuit terminating equipment, data communication equipment
Datenübertragungsgeschwindigkeit communication rate
Datenübertragungskanal communications intelligence channel
Datenübertragungskontrolleinheit transmission control unit
Datenübertragungslademodul communications load module
Datenübertragungsleitung communications line interface
Datenübertragungsnetzwerksteuerung communications network controller
Datenübertragungsschnittstelle communications line interface, communications port
Datenübertragungssteuerbereich communication control area
Datenübertragungssteuereinheit communication multiplexer controller, communication terminal module controller, general communication subsystem
Datenübertragungssteuerprogramm integrated communication access method
Datenübertragungssteuerteil communications line adapter, communications line terminal, microcoded line adapter
Datenübertragungssteuerungsverfahren communications protocol
Datenübertragungssteuerverfahren communication control procedure, data sets
Datenübertragungssystem telecommunications system
Datenübertragungstechnik über Lichtleiter optical data links
Datenübertragungsverfahren data transmission method
Datenübertragungsweg data bus
Datenübertragungsgeschwindigkeit bit rate
Datenumschaltsignal automatic changeover
Datenumsetzer data translator
Datenumwandlung data conversion
Datenunabhängigkeit data independence
Daten- und Steuerbus data and control bus
Datenveränderung data modification

Datenverarbeitung data handling, data processing
Datenverarbeitungsanlage data processing equipment
Datenverarbeitungsanlagenbetrieb data processor operation
Datenverarbeitungsanlagenbetriebszeit data processor operating time
Datenverarbeitungs-Dienstprogramm data processing utility
Datenverarbeitungsentwicklung data processing development
datenverarbeitungsgerecht compatible with data processing
Datenverarbeitungs-Hilfsprogramm data processing utility
Datenverarbeitungsprogramme data handling software
Datenverarbeitungsraum data processing area
Datenverarbeitungsschaltung data processing circuit
Datenverarbeitungsstelle processing station
Datenverarbeitungssystem data processing system
Datenverbindung data circuit, data connection, data path
Datenverdichtung data compression
Datenverkettung data chaining
Datenverknüpfung data merging
Datenverschiebung data movement, data shifting
Datenvervielfacher output multiplier
Datenverwaltung data administration
Datenverwaltungssystem data administration system
Datenverwaltungsytem data management system
Datenverzeichnis data dictionary
Daten von der Tastatur keyboard data
Datenwandler data convertor, data transducer
Datenwert data value
Datenwerte data figures
Datenwort data word
Datenzeile data line
Datenzentrum data center
Datenziel data target
Datenzugriffssicherheit data access security
Datenzugriffsverhalten mode of data access
Datex-L circuit switched service
Datex-P packet switched services
Datex-P-Netz German public data network, packet switching network in Germany
Datex-P-Netzwerk packet switching network

289

Datum data, data item, date
Datum der Sicherungsdiskette backup diskette date
Datumsänderung change of date
Datumsangabe date specified
Datumsobergrenze upper limit for date
Datumstrenner date separator
Datum Uhrzeit date time of day
Datum und Uhrzeit date and time
Datum Zeitangabe date time
Dauer duration
Dauerbeleg standing voucher
Dauerbestellung standing purchase order
Dauerbetrieb continuous operation
dauerbuchen make a standing entry
Dauerbuchung standing entry
Dauerbuchungsbeleg standing entry voucher
Dauerhaftigkeit durability
Dauerlauf continuous test
Dauermagnet permanent magnet
Dauerprüfung endurance test
Dauersignal continuous signal
Dauerspeicher permanent storage
Dauertaste repeat key
Dauerton continuous tone
Dauerumschaltung auf Großbuchstaben capitals lock, caps lock
Dauerverbindung full time circuit
Deadlockerkennung deadlock recognition
Deadlockfall instance of deadlock
Deadlocksituation deadlock situation
deaktivieren deactivate
Deaktivierung deactivation
Deaktivierungsaktivität deactivation process
Deaktivierungsbeleg deactivation voucher
Deaktivierungsdatum deactivation date
Deaktivierungsmöglichkeit deactivation option
Deaktivierungsvorgang deactivation process
debitorenabhängig customer based
Debitorenauswertungen accounts receivable analysis
Debitorenauszug statement
Debitorenbereich accounts receivable area
Debitorenbuchhaltung accounts receivable accounting
Debitorenhaben credit to accounts receivable
Debitorenkonto receivable account
Debitorennummer accounts receivable number
Debitorensoll debit to accounts receivable
Debitorenstamm accounts receivable master
Debitorenstammsatz accounts receivable master record
Debitorenteil accounts receivable section

Debitorenverrechnung reconciliation
Debitorenverzeichnis ledger
Debugger debugger
Debuggerausgabe debugger output
Deckblatt flyleaf
Deckel access cover, cover
Deckname alias, pseudocode
Deckung shortfall
dedizierter Rechner dedicated computer
DEE-gesteuert nicht bereit DTE controlled not ready
DEE-Restart-Anforderung DTE restart request
DEE-Rücksetzanforderung DTE reset request
DEE-Verbindungsanforderung DTE call request
Defaultkombination default combination
Defaultwert default value
defekt bad, corrupt, dead
defekter Sender dead transmitter
defekt geliefert dead on arrival
definierbar definable
definiere Konstante define constant
definieren define
definierte Datei defined file
Definition definition
Definitionsdatei definition file
Definitionskennsatz definition label
Definitionsmöglichkeit definition option
Definitionssatz definition record
Definitionssprache definition language
Definitionsteil definition section
Deformatierung deformatting
degenerieren degrade
degressiv degressive
Dehnung expansion
dekadische Zählröhre decatron
deklarieren declare
Dekoder decoder
dekodieren decode
Dekodierer decoder
Dekodierung decoding
dekrementieren decrement
delegieren delegate
Delimiter delimiter
Deltazeit delta time
dementsprechend correspondingly
Demo demo
Demodulator demodulator, detector
demonstrieren demonstrate
demontieren dismantle
Demultiplexen demultiplexing
Demultiplexer demultiplexer
demzufolge as a result

Depaketierer disassembly facility
Depositeinrichtung deposit tray
derzeitig actual, current
Deskriptor descriptor
Deskriptorabschnitt descriptor section
Deskriptorblock descriptor block
Deskriptorenliste descriptor list
Detail detail
Detailanzeige detail display
Detailanzeigemöglichkeit detail display option
Detailinformation detailed information
detailliert detailed, in detail
Detaillierungsgrad degree of detail
Detektorschaltung detector circuit
determinieren determine
deuten point
Deutsche Bundespost German Bundespost, federal post office
dezentral decentralized, remote
dezentrale Datenerfassung decentralized data entry, distributed data entry
dezentrale Datenverarbeitung distributed data processing
dezentrale numerische Maschinensteuerung distributed numeric control
dezentraler Arbeitsplatz remote workstation
dezentraler Druck remote print
dezentraler Drucker remote printer
dezentraler Montageplatten-Controller remote base controller
dezentrales System distributed system
dezentrale Station remote station
dezentralisierte Datenverarbeitung decentralized data processing
Dezibel decibel
dezimal decimal
Dezimalbereich decimal area
Dezimal-Binär-Umwandlung decimal to binary conversion
Dezimalbruchteil decimal fraction
Dezimalkomma decimal comma, decimal point
Dezimalkonstante decimal constant
Dezimalnull decimal zero
Dezimalpunkt decimal point, radix point
Dezimalstelle decimal digit, decimal place, decimal position
Dezimalsystem decimal system
Dezimaltabulator decimal tabulator
Dezimalzahl decimal number
Dezimalzeichen decimal symbol
Dezimalziffer decimal digit
DFÜ-Überwachungseinheit telecommunications monitor

Diablo Diablo
Diagnose diagnosis, diagnostic test, test
Diagnoseanzeige diagnostic display
Diagnosebereich diagnostic area
Diagnosediskette diagnostic diskette
Diagnoselauf diagnostic test, test
Diagnoselogeintrag diagnostic log entry
Diagnosemeldung diagnostic message
Diagnoseprogramm diagnostic program
Diagnoseroutine diagnostic routine, diagnostics
Diagnosesoftware diagnostic software
Diagnosezentrum diagnostic center
Diagnostik- und Wartungsprogramme online diagnostic and maintenance programs
diagnostizieren diagnose
Diagramm chart, diagram
Diagrammbeispiel sample chart, sample diagram
diakritisches Zeichen diacritical mark
Dialog dialog, interactive mode
Dialogablauf dialog sequence
Dialogantwort dialog answer, dialog response
Dialoganwendung conversational application
Dialoganwendungsprogramm dialog application program
Dialogbearbeitung conversational processing
Dialogbenutzer demand user, interactive user
Dialogbeschreibungssprache dialog specification language
Dialogbetrieb conversational mode, interactive mode, interactive processing
Dialogdatenstation interactive terminal
Dialogeingabe dialog input
Dialogeinheit interactive terminal
Dialogfall instance of dialog
Dialogfehler dialog error
Dialogfeld dialog field
Dialogkontrolle interaction management
dialogmäßig interactive
Dialog mit dem Bediener operator's communication process
Dialogmodus dialog mode, interactive mode
Dialognachricht interactive message
dialogorientierte Dienstleistungen interactive services
dialogorientierte Jobsteuerung interactive job control
Dialogprogramm interactive processor, interactive program
Dialogprogrammgenerator interactive program generator
Dialogprogrammschnittstelle dialog program interface

Dialogprotokolldatei audit file
Dialogprozessor dialog processor
Dialogregion interactive region
Dialogschritt interactive step
Dialogsegment dialog segment
Dialogseite dialog page
Dialogsitzung dialog session, interactive session
Dialogspeichergrenze dialog memory limit
Dialogstation demand site
Dialogsteuerung dialog control
Dialogsteuerungshinweis dialog control indication
Dialogsteuerungsprogramm dialog processor
Dialogstruktur dialog structure
Dialogstufe interactive level
Dialogsystem conversational time sharing, interactive system
Dialogtask interactive task
Dialogteil interactive segment
Dialogtesthilfe interactive debugging aid
dialogunterstützt dialog based
Dialogverarbeitungsfunktion dialog processing service
dicht retentive
dichter Bereich retentive area
Dichtlager seal bearing
Dichtung seal
Dichtungsmasse compound sealing
Dickschichtkondensator thick-film capacitor
Dickschichtschaltung thick-film circuit
Dickschichtwiderstand thick-film resistor
Diebstahlgefahr risk of theft
Dielektrikum dielectric material
dielektrisch dielectric
dienen serve
Dienst service
Dienstanbieter service provider
Dienstanforderung service request
Dienstaufsichtsbildschirmgerät monitor display
Dienstbenutzer service user
Dienstdateneinheit service data unit
Diensterbringer service provider
Dienstfähigkeit service capability
Dienstgüte quality of service, quality of services
Dienstgüteparameter quality parameter
Dienstkomponente utility component
Dienstleistung service
Dienstleistungsbetrieb services enterprise
Dienstleistungsrechenzentrum service computing center

Dienstprogramm utility program
Dienstprimitiv service primitive
Dienstprogramm service routine, utility, utility processor, utility program
Dienstprogrammdiskette utility diskette, utility program diskette
Dienstprogramm für das Zentralsystem host support facility
Dienstprogramm für Druckausgaben print utility
Dienstprogrammfunktion utility function
Dienstprogramm zum Aufteilen der Festplatte partition utility
Dienstprogramm zur Programmentwicklung development utility
Dienstsignal call progress signal
Dienst- und Serviceroutine utility and service routine
Dienstunterbrechungsdauer service off-time
Dienstzugangspunkt service access point
dieselelektrisches Kraftwerk diesel electric power station
Dieselgenerator diesel generator
Differentialanalysator differential analyser
Differentialrelais differential relay
Differentialverstärker differential amplifier
Differenz difference, discrepancy
Differenzbetrag difference
Differenzbuchen discrepancy posting
Differenzbuchung discrepancy posting
Differenzenbildung forming differences
Differenzierglied differentiating circuit
differenziert differentiated
Differenzmenge difference quantity
Differenzmitteilung discrepancy advice
Differenzwert difference
diffus diffuse
digital digital
Digital-Analog-Wandler digital analog converter, digital analog convertor, digital to analog converter
digitale Anzeigen digital readouts
digitaler Datenbus digital data bus
digitaler Radarextraktor digital radar extractor
digitaler Speicher mit sequentiellem Zugriff sequential access storage
digitaler Zielextraktor digital target extractor
digitales Datennetzwerk digital data network
digitales Filter digital filter
digitales Multimeter digital multimeter
digitales Querverbindungssystem digital cross-connect system
digitales Signal digital signal

Diskettensystem

digitales Vielfachmeßgerät digital multimeter
digitale Vermittlung digital branch exchange
Digitalisierer digitizer
Digitalisiergerät digitizer
Digitalisiertablett digitizer
Digitalisierung digitization
Digitalleitung digital line
Digitalrechner digital computer
Digitalschaltung digital circuit
Digitalvermittlung digital branch exchange
Digraph digraph
Diktatzeichen reference sign
DIL dual in line
Dimension dimension, dimensioning
Dimensionierung sizing
Diode diode
Diodenröhre thermionic valve
DIP dual inline pin
Dipol dipole
DIP Schalter DIP switch
direkt direct, immediate, straightforward
Direktabfrage direct enquiry, direct inquiry
Direktanschlußmodul data circuit module
Direktantrieb direct drive
Direktanwahl direct dialling
direkte Adressierung direct addressing
direkte BCD-Arithmetik direct bcd arithmetic
direkte Cursoradresse direct cursor address
direkte Datenerfassung direct data capture
direkter Gerätezugriff physical access
direkter Speicherzugriff direct memory access
direkter Zugriff physical access
direkte Schreibmarkenadresse direct cursor address
direkt geheizte Kathode directly heated cathode
direkt gesteuerter Roboter direct robotic control
Direktive directive
Direktmodus immediate mode
Direktoperand direct operand, immediate operand
Direktruf direct call
Direktrufnetz der DBP German PTT leased line service
Direktrufverfahren direct distance dialing
direktsequentielle Zugriffsmethode extended access method
Direktsteuerung direct drive
Direktverbindung direct connection
Direktwahl direct dialling, direct selection
Direktwahlkommando direct switching command

Direktwert direct value
Direktzugriff direct access, direkt access
Direktzugriffsdatei direct file
Direktzugriffsmethode direct access method
Direktzugriffsspeicher direct access storage, random access memory, random access store
Direktzugriffsverarbeitung random access processing
Disagio loan discount
Disjunktion disjunction
Diskarbeitsdatei disk work file
Diskbefehl disk instruction
Diskette disk, diskette, flexible disk, floppy disk
Diskette guter Qualität diskette of suitable quality
Diskette mit Anwendungsprogramm application program diskette
Diskette mit doppelter Schreibdichte double density diskette
Diskettenart diskette type
Diskettenaufkleber diskette label
Diskettenbearbeitung diskette maintenance
Diskettenbetriebssystem diskette operating system
Diskettenbox diskette box
Diskettencontroller floppy disk controller
Diskettendienste diskette services
Diskettenfehler disk error
Diskettenformatierer disk formatter
Diskettenformatierung disk formatting, diskette formatting program
Diskettenhülle diskette cover
Disketteninitialisierung diskette initialization
Diskettenkopierprogramm disk copy program, diskette copy program
Diskettenlaufwerk disk drive, diskette drive, floppy disk drive, removable disk drive
Diskettenlaufwerk aktiv diskette drive active, drive on
Diskettenlaufwerk verifizieren compare diskette drive, verify disk drive
Diskettennummer diskette number
Diskettenoperation disk operation
Diskettenseite disk side, diskette side
Diskettensicherungsmenü backup diskette menu
Diskettenstapelleser diskette stack reader
Diskettenstation disk station, floppy station
Diskettenstruktur verifizieren verify a diskette
Diskettensystem diskette based operating system, diskette system, flexible disk system, floppy disk system

293

Diskettenvorformatierung disk preformatting, diskette preparation
Diskontbuchung discount posting
diskontieren discount
Diskontierung discounting
Diskontobligo discount liabilities
Diskontsatz discount record
Diskontspesen discount expenses
Diskonttage discount days
diskret discrete
diskrete Adressierung discrete addressing
diskrete Bauteile discrete components
diskrete Daten discrete data
diskreter Speicher discrete memory
Diskriminator discriminator
Disparität mismatch
Displaydatei display file
Disponent planning manager, scheduler
Disponentengruppe logistics group
disponieren calculate, plan, schedule
Disposition plan
Dispositionsdaten scheduling data
Dispositionshilfe scheduling aid
Dispositionsmerkmal scheduling code
Dispositionsstelle scheduling office
Dispositionsstufe schedule level, scheduling step
disqualifizieren disqualify
Distanzadresse displacement, displacement address, offset, offset address
Distributor distributor
divers various
Division division
Division einer reellen Zahl real number division
DMA Grenzwertfehler DMA boundary error
DMA-Kanal direct memory access channel
DMA-Steuerbaustein direct memory access controller
DMA-Überlauffehler DMA overrun error
Dokument document
Dokumentation documentation
Dokumentationseintrag documentation entry
Dokumentationsprozessor documentation processor
Dokumentationsteil documentation paragraph, documentation section
Dokumentationstext documentation text
Dokumentationsübersicht documentation index, documentation map
Dokumentationsunterlagen documentation components
Dokumentdatei document file

Dokumentdiskette document diskette
Dokumentdiskette vorbereiten initializing diskettes
Dokumentenerstellung creation of documents
dokumentieren document
Dokumentnamen vergeben naming documents
Dokumentrückgewinnung document recovery
Dokumentübertragung document transfer mode
Dokumentverzeichnis index of documents
Dollarzeichen dollar sign
Domäne domain
Domänenspezifikation domain specification
dominieren dominate, take precedence
Doppel- double, dual, duplicate
Doppelbelegung double entry
Doppeldiskettenlaufwerk dual diskette drive
Doppelschlüssel duplicate key
Doppelstrom double current
doppelt double, dual, two fold
doppelte Dichte double density
doppelte Funktionseinheitengruppe dual cluster
doppelte Genauigkeit double precision
doppelte Schreibdichte double density
doppelte Zeichenbreite double width
doppelt genaue Ganzzahl double integer
Doppelverbindung double connection
Doppelvereinzelung dual single feed
Doppelwortgrenze double word limit
DOS Betriebssystem disk operating system
downline laden downline loading
Draht electric wire, thread, wire
Drahtwiderstand wirewound resistor
drehen turn
drehende elektrische Maschine rotating electric machine
drehender Generator rotating generator
Drehknopf control knob
Drehmomentmotor torque motor
Drehschalter rotary switch
Drehung im Uhrzeigersinn clockwise rotation
Drehverstärker rotating amplifier
Drehwartezeit rotational latency
Drehzahlverzerrung speed distortion
Dreiadressencode three address code
dreidimensional three dimensional
Dreifachnull triple zero
Dreiphasen-Anschluß three phase wiring
Dreiphasen-Gleichrichter three phase rectifier
Dreiphasenmotor three phase motor
Dreiphasen-Transformator three phase transformer

dreipoliger Schalter tri-pole circuit-breaker
dreistellig three character
Dreitasten-Bedienung three-key operation
Drei-Wort-Pipeline three-word pipeline
dreizeilig three line
Drei-Zustands-Ausgang three state output
dritte Normalform third normal form
Dropout drop out
Drosseltransformator constant current transformer
Druck print
Druckabschnitt print area, print section
Druckaufbereitung print editing, print preparation
Druckauftrag print job, print request
Druckausgabe print output
Druckausgabeformatsteuerung output printer spacing
Druckausgabezwischendatei intermediate output file
Druckauswahl print selection
Druckbereich extent print, print extent
Druckbereichsmodus extent mode
Druckdatei listing file, print file
Druckdateiname print file name
Druckdurchgang printing cycle
Druckeinheit print unit, printing unit
Druckeinstellung print setting
Druckeinstellungen einlesen retrieve stored print settings
Druckeinstellungen speichern store print settings
drucken print
Druckendeposition end of print position
Drucken des Bildschirminhaltes print screen
druckendes Terminal hardcopy terminal
Druckendezeichen print termination character
Drucken mit Doppelanschlag double strike print
Drucker computer printer, impact printer, printer
Druckeradapter printer adapter
Druckeranschluß printer connector, printer port
Druckeranschlußkabel printer communication cable
Druckeranweisungen printer control information
Druckerausgabe printer output
Druckerbahnbreite printer carriage width
Druckerbaudrate printer baud rate
Druckerbearbeitung printer handling
Druckerbefehl printer instruction

Druckregelung

Druckerbreite printer carriage width, printer width
Druckerdaten-Paritätsbit printer data parity bit
Druckerkabel printer cable
Druckerkennung printer identification
Druckerkette print chain
Druckerkonfiguration printer configuration
Druckermenü printer menu
Druckermerkmale printer characteristics
Druckernetzkabel printer power cord
Druckerpapier printer paper
Druckerschnittstelle printer interface
Druckersharing printer sharing
Druckerspooler für Einzelbenutzer single user print spooler
Druckerständer printer mount, printer stand
Druckerstation printer terminal
Druckersteuerung print controller, printer control
Druckertest printer test
Druckertyp printer type, type of printer
Druckerwarteschlange print queue
druckfertig ready to be printed
Druckfunktion print function
Druckfunktionen basic printing
Druckgerät list device
Druckgeschwindigkeit print speed, printer speed
druckgießen diecast
Druckkammer-Schaltkreis actuator circuitry (printer)
Druckkennzeichen print identifier
Druckknopf button, pushbutton
Druckknopfschalter pushbutton switch
Druckknopfsteuerung pushbutton control
Druckkontakt pressure switch
Druckkopf print head
Druckluftschalter air break switch
Druckluft-Stromkreisunterbrecher air blast circuit breaker
Druckmaskenaufbau printing mask format
Druckmenü print menu
Druckmenüauswahl print menu option
Druckname print name
Drucknummer print number
Druckparameter print parameter
Druckposition print position, printing position
Druckprogramm display program, print program
Druckpuffer print buffer
Druckqualität print density, print quality
Druckregelung pressure control

295

Druckschalter pressure switch, pushbutton switch
Druckstation printing station
Druckstelle print position
Drucksteuerkommando print control command
Drucksteuertaste printing key
Drucksteuerung printing control
Drucksteuerzeichen print control character
Druckstock print head
Druckstörung printing disturbance
Druckstopmenü stop printer menu
Drucksymbiont print symbiont
Drucktaste button
Drucktyp type of print
Druckverfahren print method
Druckvorgang printing cycle
Druckvorgang in Vorwärts- und Rückwärtsrichtung bidirectional printing
Druckvorschub-Steuerlochstreifen printer form control tape
Druckwagen carriage, print actuator carriage
Druckwalze platen
Druckwarteschlange print queue
Druckwerk printer mechanism, printing unit
Druckwerkart print unit type
Druckwerksart printing element type
Druckwerksparameter print unit parameter
Druckzeichendisparität printer mismatch
Druckzeichenungleichheit character mismatch
Druckzeile line of print
Druckzeilenbestimmung line counter specification
drücken press
DÜE-Störung DCE fault condition
DÜE und DEE-Daten DTE and DCE data
DÜE-Verbindung hergestellt DCE call connected
Dünnschichtgerät thin-film device
Dünnschichtschaltung thin-film circuit
dumpen dump
Dumpformat dump format
Dumpkennzeichen dump feature
dunkel dark, dim
Dunkellauf dry run
Dunkelschaltung CRT saver, screen saver
Dunkelsteuerimpuls blanking signal
Duplex duplex
Duplexbetrieb duplex mode, duplex operation
Duplexverkehr duplex communication
Duplikat copy
Duplikatausdruckdatei duplicate print file
Duplikatsatz duplicate record
Duplikatsteuerung duplicate control

duplizieren copy, duplicate
Duplizierfeld duplicate field
Duplizierfunktion copy function
Dupliziertaste duplicate key
durchblättern skip through
durch Cursor markierte Zeile cursor line
durchführen carry out, execute
Durchführung bushing, executing
Durchgang pass
durchkontaktierte Bohrung plated through hole
Durchlässigkeit porosity
Durchlauf iteration, pass
durchlaufen go through, pass, run through
durchlaufend continuous
Durchlaufnummer pass number
durchlesen read through
Durchsatz throughput, throughput ratio
Durchsatzklasse throughput class
Durchsatzleistung throughput performance
Durchschalten line switching
Durchschlag carbon copy, copy
Durchschlagformulare multicopy forms
Durchschnitt average, intersection
durchschnittlich average
durchschnittliche Bewertung evaluated according to average
Durchschnittliche Fehlergröße average magnitude of error
durchschnittliche Gesamtzeit average total time
durchschnittliche jährliche Wachstumsrate average annual growth rate
durchschnittliche Laufzeit average run time
durchschnittliche störungsfreie Zeit mean time between failure
durchschnittliche Zeit zur Befehlsabarbeitung average instruction execution time
durchschnittliche Zeit zwischen zwei Ausfällen mean time between failure
durchschnittsbewertet evaluated according to average
Durchschnittspreis average price
Durchschnittswertzeile average value line
durch Selbsttest festgestelltes Problem self-diagnosed problem
durchsichtig clear
durchsichtiger Plastikdeckel clear plastic cover
durchstarten initialize
durchstimmbarer Oszillator variable frequency oszillator
durchsuchen examine

DV-Anlage computer
DV-technisch dp technical
dynamisch dynamic
dynamisch aktivieren bring up dynamically
**dynamische Kompensation der Vor-/
   Nacheilung** lead lag dynamic compensation
dynamischer Prozeß dynamic process
dynamischer Speicher dynamic memory
dynamischer Zugriff dynamic access
dynamisches RAM dynamic RAM
Dynprodatei dynpro file
Dynpropflege dynpro maintenance
Dynpropuffer dynpro buffer
Dynprosprachenschlüssel dynpro language key

E

E/A-Auftrag   I/O order
E/A-Bedürfnis   I/O requirement
E/A-Befehlsprotokollierung   I/O trace
E/A-Code   I/O code
E/A-Einheitenadresse   I/O device address
E/A erzwingen   I/O forcing
E/A-Gerät   I/O device
E/A-Operation   I/O operation
E/A-Routinen des Supervisors   I/O facility
EA-Rückmeldung   late acknowledge condition
E/A-Wort   I/O word
EBCDIC-Code   extended binary coded decimal interchange code
Ebene   layer, level, plane
Ebenenverbund   compound layers, level network
Echo   echo, echo effect
Echofunktion   echo feature
Echtzeit   realtime
Echtzeitbibliothek   realtime library
Echtzeit Ein-/Ausgabe   realtime input/output
Echtzeitgerät   realtime device
Echtzeitsprache   realtime language
Echtzeitstatus   realtime status
Echtzeitsystem   realtime system
Echtzeituhr   realtime clock
Echtzeitverarbeitung   realtime processing
eckige Klammer   bracket, square bracket
EDEC-Speicher   EDEC memory
Edelmetall   precious metal
Editieren   editing
editieren   edit
Editieren im Nokeypad-Modus   nokeypad editing
Editieren im Überschreibemodus   overstrike editing
Editieren im Zeichenmodus   character editing
Editieren im Zeilenmodus   line editing
Editieren mit dem Computer   computer editing
Editiergerät   editing device
Editiermenü   edit menu, editor menu
Editiermodus   edit mode, editing mode
Editiermöglichkeit   editing possibility
Editierplatz   editing place
Editiersitzung   editing session
Editierstation   editing station
Editiertaste   editing key
Editiertastenblock   editing keypad
Editierverfahren   editing method
Editierzeichen   edit symbol
Editierzeile   edit line
Editmenü   edit menu
Editor   editor, general editor
Editzeichen   edit signal
effektiv   effective
effektive Adresse   effective address, real address
Effektivspannung   root mean square voltage
ehemals   previously
Ehrenrunde   lap of honour, round of honour
eichen   calibrate
Eichmaß   gauge
eigen   internal, own
Eigenbedarfseinspeisung   feeding for self-requirement
Eigenbestand   proper inventory
eigener Stromkreis   dedicated circuit
Eigenfertigung   internal production
Eigenfertigungsteil   self-manufactured part
eigengefertigt   internally produced
Eigenherstellung   internal production
Eigenkopie   local copy
eigens   especially
Eigenschaft der Schaltung   circuit property
eigenständig   independent
eigens zuordnen   dedicate
eigentlich   actual, actually, intrinsical
Eigentümer   owner
Eigentümervermerk   owner identification
Eigentum   ownership, property
Eigentumskennzeichen   property flag
Eignungsprüfung   performance test
Eilauftrag   urgent order
Einadreß-Befehl   single address instruction
Einadreß-Maschine   single address machine
Ein Aus   on off
Ein-/Ausgabe   in- or output, input/output
Ein-/Ausgabeadapter   input/output adapter
Ein-/Ausgabe-Anforderungsblock   input/output request block
Ein-/Ausgabeblock   input/output block
Ein-/Ausgabe-Bus   input/output bus
Ein-/Ausgabebus   input/output bus
Ein-/Ausgabeeinheit   device
Ein-/Ausgabegerät   input/output device
Ein-/Ausgabe-Gerät   input/output device
Ein-/Ausgabegeräte   input/output devices
Ein-/Ausgabeinterrupthandler   input/output interrupt handler
Ein-/Ausgabekanal   input/output channel

Ein-/Ausgabemikroprozessor input/output microprocessor
Ein-/Ausgabemodul input/output module
Ein-/Ausgabeprozessor input/output controller, input/output microprocessor, input/output processor, input/output unit
Ein-/Ausgabepuffer input/output buffer
Ein-/Ausgabequeue input/output queue
Ein-/Ausgaberegister input/output register
Ein-/Ausgabesteuereinheit input/output controller
Ein-/Ausgabesteuersystem input/output control system modules
Ein-/Ausgabesteuerung input/output control, input/output controller
Ein-/Ausgabesystem input/output system
Ein-/Ausgabeüberwachung input/output supervisor
Ein-/Ausgabe über Warteschlange queued input/output
Ein-/Ausgabeunterbrechung input/output trap
Ein-/Ausgabewarteschlange input/output queue
Ein-/Ausgang input/output
Ein-/Ausgangsprogramm input/output program
Ein- Ausrückhebel gear lever
Ein-/Ausschalttaste on off key
Einbau installation
einbauen incorporate
Einbaumodell rackmount model
Einbaumodem integrated modem
Einbaurahmen rack, rackmount, rackmount assembly
Einbauschrank cabinet
einbehalten deduct
einbinden merge
Ein-Bit-Fehler single bit error
Einbrennschutz CRT saver
einbringen yield
Einbruch failure
einbuchstabig one letter
Einchip-Mikrocomputer one-chip microcomputer
Eindeckungszeit availability time
eindeutig one-to-one, unique
eindeutiges Menükürzel unique menu keyword
eindimensional one dimensional
Eindrückung indentation
eine Art von a kind of
eine Million Gleitkommaoperationen pro Sekunde one million floating-point operations per second
Einerkomplement ones-complement
einfach plain, simple, simply, single

Einfachdatei single file
einfache Dichte single density
einfache Genauigkeit single precision
einfacher Übergang single transitition time
einfacher Wert single value
einfache Schreibdichte single density
einfädeln thread
einfarbig monochrome
Einfluß influence
einfrieren freeze
Einfügefunktion insert mode
Einfügemodus insert mode, insertion mode
einfügen include, insert, paste
Einfügen und Ersetzen inserting and replacing
Einfügen von Text text insertion
Einfügeoperation insert operation, paste operation
Einfügeprozedur insert procedure
Einfügestelle insert position, paste position
Einfügung insertion
Einfügungsbereich insertion area
Einfügungspuffer paste buffer
einführen thread into
Einführung getting started, introduction
Einführungs-Know-how introductory know-how
Einführungstülle bushing
Eingabe entry, input
Eingabeart entry type, input method
Eingabeaufforderung prompt, system prompt
Eingabeaufforderung des Systems system prompt
Eingabeaufruf input call
Eingabeauftrag input job
Eingabe aus einer Steuerdatei control file input
Eingabeband input tape
Eingabeberechtigung input authorization
Eingabebereich input area
eingabebereit ready for input
eingabebereit sein accept input
Eingabebibliothek input library
Eingabeblock input block
Eingabeblockgröße input block size
Eingabeblocklänge input block length
Eingabedatei enter file, input file
Eingabedateibestimmung input file destination
Eingabedaten input data
Eingabedatenfluß input job stream
Eingabedatum date of entry, input date
Eingabeeingang input gate
Eingabeende end of input
Eingabefach hopper

Eingabefehler

Eingabefehler input error
Eingabefeld input field
Eingabefeldbeschreibung input field description
Eingabefeld-Wiederholung repetition of input field
Eingabeformalismus entry syntax, input syntax
Eingabeformat entry format, input format, input specification
Eingabeformatierung input formatting
Eingabeformular entry form, input form
Eingabegerät input device
Eingabegeschwindigkeit input speed
Eingabekarte entry card, input card
Eingabekombination input combination
Eingabekontrolle input control
Eingabelänge entry length, input length
Eingabe löschen clear entry
Eingabelöschtaste clear entry key, clear input key
Eingabemodus entry mode, input mode
Eingabemöglichkeit input option
Eingabenachricht input message
Eingabe negativer Zahlen negative entry
Eingabeoperation input operation
Eingabeparameter input parameter
Eingabephase entry phase, input phase
Eingabeprogramm enter program, entry program, input program
Eingabeprozedur enter procedure, entry procedure
Eingabeprozeß enter process, entry process
Eingabepuffer input buffer, typeahead buffer
Eingabepufferregister input buffer register
Eingabepuffer voll input buffer full
Eingabequelle input source
Eingabesatz input record
Eingabeschablone input template
Eingabeschlitz input slot
Eingabesequenz input sequence
Eingabespeicher input buffer, input memory
Eingabestatement input statement
Eingabestatus input status
Eingabestrom control stream
Eingabesyntax input syntax
Eingabetag input date
Eingabetastatur input keyboard
Eingabetyp input type
Eingabeübersetzer input translator
Eingabe über Terminal terminal input
Eingabe-Verarbeitung-Ausgabe get-process-put
Eingabewert input value
Eingabezeichen entry symbol, input character

Eingabezeile entry line, input line
Eingang entry, input, port
Eingang 4-20mA 4-20mA input
Eingangsbedingung input condition
Eingangsformaloperand input formal operand
Eingangsfracht freight inwards
Eingangsimpedanz input impedance
Eingangs-LED input led
Eingangsleitung inbound line
Eingangsmenge quantity received
Eingangsmodul input module
Eingangsparameter entry parameter
Eingangspegel input level
Eingangspuffer voll input buffer full
Eingangspunkt entry point
Eingangsrechnung purchase invoice
Eingangssicherung input fuse
Eingangssignal input signal
Eingangsspannung input voltage
Eingangsvorschau preview
eingebaut built in
eingebauter Lautsprecher built in speaker, internal speaker
eingebauter Teil built in portion
eingebbar fit for input
eingeben enter, feed, input, type
Eingeben von Datum und Zeit set date and time
eingebettetes Rohr embedded conduit
eingebracht brought in
eingehen receive
eingehend come in, inbound, incoming
eingeholt caught up
eingerastet locked, locked in place
eingeschränkt captive
eingeschränkter Verteiler restricted distribution
eingeschränktes Benutzerkonto captive account
eingeteilt divided up
eingliedern incorporate
eingrenzen restrict
Eingrenzungsmöglichkeit restriction option
Eingriff intervention, operation
einhalten adhere
Einheit system, unit
Einheitenbasis unit basis
Einheitenregister unit register
Einheitensteuerblock unit control block
Einheitensteuerwort unit control word
Einheitenzähler unit counter
einheitlich uniform
Einheitsbewertung unit valuation

Einheitsbewertungsschlüssel unit valuation code
Einheitsschritt unit element
Einheitswert unit value
einig agreed
Einkäufer buyer
Einkauf buy, purchase, purchasing
einkaufen buy, purchase
Einkaufgruppenstamm purchase group master
Einkaufsabteilung purchasing department
Einkaufsangebot offer
Einkaufsbeleg purchase voucher
Einkaufsberechtigung purchase authorization
Einkaufsbereich purchase area
Einkaufsbestellung purchase order
Einkaufsbudget purchasing budget
Einkaufsdaten purchase data, purchasing data
Einkaufsdatum date of purchase, purchase date
Einkaufsfeld purchase field
Einkaufsgruppe purchasing group
Einkaufsgruppenschlüssel purchasing group code
Einkaufsgruppenstamm purchasing group master
Einkaufsgruppenstammsatz purchasing group master record
Einkaufsinformationen purchase information
Einkaufsinformationssatz purchase information record
Einkaufsinfosatz purchase info record
einkaufsintern internal to purchasing
Einkaufspreis purchase price
Einkaufspreiseinheit purchase price unit
Einkaufsstatistik purchasing statistics
Einkaufstransaktion purchase transaction
Einkaufsverhandlung purchasing negotiation
Einkerbung groove
Einkopflaufwerk single head running gear
Einkreis one shot
einlagern embed
einleiten initialize, initiate, open
Einleiterkabel single core cable
einlesen input in, read, read in, retrieve
Einleseoperation read in operation
Einlösungsfrist encashment period
Einloggen login, logon
einloggen login, logon
einmal once
einmalig unique
Einmaligkeit uniqueness
einmischen interfere
einphasen phase
Einphasenmotor single phase motor

Einphasenmotor mit Anlaßhilfsphase split phase motor
Einphasentransformator single phase transformer
einphasig single phase
einphasiger Stromanschluß single phase power
Einplanung planning for
Einplatinencomputer single board computer
Einplatinenrechner single board computer
Einplatz-System single user system
Einprozessorsystem unit processor
Einräumzeiger load pointer
einreichen enter
einreihen classify
einrichten allocate, configure, set up
Einrichtroutine adjustment routine
Einrichtung device, set up
Einrichtung zur Erstellung von Datenbankkopien mit anschließender Rückspeicherung dump and restore facility
Einrichtung zur Zeichenerkennung character recognition equipment
Einrückung tab
Einrückungsebene tab level
Einrückungsfaktor indentation level count, tab level count
Einsatz application, insert
Einsatzbeginnausfall initial failure
Einsatzfähigkeit useability
Einsatzgebiet field of application
Einsatzmittel resource
Einsatzmittelplanung resource allocation
Einsatzstoffe materials used
Einsatzvorbereitung application engineering
Einsatzvorbereitungsfunktion application engineering function
einschätzen estimate, rate
Einschaltart power-on mode
Einschalteinrichtung activate facility
Einschalten startup, switching on
einschalten enable, power-up, start, switch on, turn on
Einschalten der Übertragungsfunktion enable transmission, transmission enable
Einschalten der Uhr start clock
Einschalten des automatischen Answerback enable auto answerback
Einschalten des Grafikmodus enter graphics mode
Einschalten des Systems turning on the system
Einschalten des Unterbrechungszeichens enable disconnect character

Einschalten des Zeichens »Verbindung abbrechen«

Einschalten des Zeichens »Verbindung abbrechen« disconnect character enable
Einschalten des Zeilenendezeichens enable end of line
Einschalten und Überprüfen power-up and checkout procedure
Einschalttaste power on key
Einschaltverhalten switch-on reaction
Einschaltvorgang power up sequence, power-up
Einschaltzeichen caret letter
einschieben insert, paste
Einschnappklinke latch
einschränken degrade
Einschränkung restriction
Einschränkungsmöglichkeit qualifying option
Einschub insert, parenthetical remark, patch card, plug-in unit, plug-in-unit, slot
Einschub des Diskettenlaufwerks diskette drive slot
Einschubplatte skid plate
Einschwingverhalten transient response
Einseitenband single sideband
einseitig beschreibbar single sided
einseitige Datenübermittlung one way communication
einseitige Diskette single sided diskette
einsetzbar applicable, useable
einsetzen apply, mount, paste, use
Einspeicherung line-to-store transfer
Einspeicherungsfehler loading error
einspielen input, read in, run through
Einstandskosten acquisition costs
Einstandspreis acquisition price, cost price
Einstandswert acquisition value
Einsteck- plug-in
Einsteckmodul plug-in module
einsteigen enter
einstellbar adjustable, configurable
einstellbarer Alarm configurable alarm
einstellbare Rückkopplung feedback trim, adjustable feedback
einstellen adjust, employ, freeze, set, tune
Einstellen der Empfangsgeschwindigkeit receive speed feature
Einstellen des Übertragungsbeginns transmit execution feature
Einstellhebel control lever
einstellig single character
Einstellregler setting regulator
Einstellung adjustment, configuration, setting
Einstellung bei Fehlersuchbetrieb debugging setup

Einstellung der Kommunikationsparameter communications setting menu
Einstellung der Schreibränder setting margin
Einstellung der Tastatur keyboard setting
Einstellungen ändern adjust settings, change characteristics, set up
Einstellung im Zeilenlineal ruler setting
Einstieg entry
Einstiegsmodell entry level model, entry level system
Einstiegsmodelle entry level members
Einstiegspunkt point of entry
Einstellungsprogramm configuration program
einstreuen embed, intersperse
einstufig one level, single level
Eins-Zustand one state
Ein-Task-Betrieb one task operation
Eintastung keyboard entry
einteilen block, categorize, divide
Einteilung arrangement, classification
Eintrag entry
eintragen enter
Eintrag in der Partitionstabelle partition table entry
Eintrag in Stufensatz level header entry
Eintragslänge entry length
Eintragsname entry name
Eintragsnummer entry number
Eintragung entry
Eintragungsdatei entry file
eintreffen arrive
eintreten enter
Eintritt entry
eintrittsinvariante Routinen reentrant routines
einverstanden sein agree
Einweg-Betriebsmittel consumable resources
einweisen guide
einwiegen weigh in
einzeilig one line
einzel single
Einzelanforderung individual request
Einzelangabe single specification
Einzelanschlag single key stroke
Einzelanzeige individual display, single display
Einzelbedingungen individual terms
Einzelbeleg individual voucher, single document, single voucher
Einzelbelegposition individual voucher item
Einzelbenutzung single use
Einzelbereich single area
Einzelbewegung individual transaction
Einzelblatt sheet, single sheet

Einzelblatteinzug sheet feeder, sheet feeding, single sheet feeder
Einzelblattpapier single sheet paper
Einzelblattzufuhr single sheet feeding
Einzelblattzufuhreinheit sheet feeder, sheet feeding unit
Einzelblattzufuhrgerät sheet feeder, sheet feeding device
Einzelbrief single letter
Einzelbudget individual budget
Einzeldraht strand
Einzelfall individual case
Einzelfeld individual field
Einzelformular single sheet
Einzelformulareinzug single form chute
Einzelfunktion individual function
Einzelgang single cycle, single step mode
Einzelhändler retailer
Einzelhandel retail trade
Einzelimpuls single shot pulse
Einzeljob independent run
Einzelkonto individual account
Einzelmitteilung single message
einzeln individual, single
Einzelnachweis individual proof, single check
Einzelpartition single partition
Einzelposition single position
Einzelpositionsanzeige single item display
Einzelpositionserfassung registering single items
Einzelposten individual item
Einzelpostenanzeige displaying individual item
Einzelpostenausgabe detail output operation
Einzelpostenberechnung detail calculation operation
Einzelpostendatei detail file, single volume file
Einzelpostenjournal individual items daily ledger
Einzelpostenoperation detail operation
Einzelpostenvorschub single item ejection
Einzelpostenzeile detail line
Einzelpostenzeit detail time
Einzelpreis unit price
Einzelproblem one time job
Einzelprogramm individual program
Einzelprüfung individual checking
Einzelpufferung single buffering
Einzelpunktsteuerungssystem point to point positioning system
Einzelrechnung individual invoice
Einzelsatz individual record, single record
Einzelsatzanzeige displaying individual record
Einzelschritt single step
Einzelschrittverbuchung single step posting
Einzelschrittverfahren single step procedure
Einzelseite single page
einzelstehend stand alone
Einzeltabelle individual table
Einzeltastatur individual keyboard
Einzelverwaltung individual management
Einzelwert individual value
Einzelzeile individual line, single line
Einzelzulassung approval for specific use
einziehen draw in, retract
einzig only, solely
Einzug chute, direct debit, indentation
Einzugsart direct debit type
Einzugsbefehl draw in instruction, drawing in instruction
Einzugsdatum direct debit date
Einzugseinrichtung draw in facility
Einzugsermächtigung direct debit authorization
Einzugsliste direct debit list
Einzugsverfahren direct debit
Eisen iron
Eisenkern iron core
eisenkernloser Transformator air core transformer
Eisenkreis magnetic circuit
Eisenmetall ferrous metal
eklatant spectacular
Electronic Mail electronic mail
Electronic-Mail-System electronic mail system
Elektriker electrician, electricity worker
elektrisch electric, electrical
elektrische Behelfsinstallation temporary electrical installation
elektrische Box electric box
elektrische Bremsung electrical braking
elektrische Fassung electric socket
elektrische Hausinstallation domestic electrical installation
elektrische Innenraumanlage indoor electric equipment
elektrische Isoliermatte electrical insulation mat
elektrische Isolierung electrical insulation
elektrische Last electric ballast
elektrische Leistungssteuerung electric power control
elektrische Leitung electric wire
elektrische Maschine electric machine
elektrischer Anschluß electric connector
elektrischer Auslöser electric actuator

elektrischer Bürstenhalter electrical brush holder
elektrischer Durchschlag electrical breakdown
elektrischer Kontakt electric contact
elektrischer Kontaktschutz electric contact protection
elektrischer Läufer electric rotor
elektrischer Leiter electric conductor
elektrischer Regler electric regulator
elektrischer Schirm electric screen
elektrischer Schlag shock
elektrischer Wandler electric convertor
elektrischer Wert electrical value
elektrisches Bauteil electrical component
elektrisches Blockdiagramm electrical block diagram
elektrische Schleife electric lug
elektrische Schutzeinrichtung electrical protection equipment
elektrisches Filter electric filter
elektrisches Isoliermaterial electrical insulating material
elektrisches Isolierpapier electrical insulating paper
elektrisches Kabel electric cable
elektrisches Kraftwerk electric power station
elektrisches Netzwerk electrical network
elektrische Spule electric coil, electric reactor
elektrische Steuereinheit electric control equipment
elektrische Steuerung electrical variable control
elektrische Stromregelung electric current control
elektrische Synchronisation electric synchronisation
elektrische Unterverteilung electric substation
elektrische Verbundmaschine composite electric machine
elektrische Verkabelung electric cable system
elektrische Zelle electric cell
elektrisch isolierte Beilagscheibe electrically insulated bushing
elektrisch löschbarer Nur-Lese-Speicher electrically erasable read only memory
elektrisch löschbarer programmierbarer Nur-Lese-Speicher electrically erasable programmable ROM, electrically erasable programmable read only memory
elektrisch veränderbarer Nur-Lese-Speicher electrically alterable read only memory

elektrisch veränderbarer programmierbarer Nur-Lese-Speicher electrically alterable programmable read only memory
Elektrizität electricity
elektroakustisches Gerät acoustoelectric device, electroacoustic device
elektrochemisches Gerät electrochemical device
Elektrode electrode
Elektrodenabbrand electrode consumption
Elektrodenhalterung electrode holder
elektrodenlose Entladeröhre electrodeless discharge tube
Elektrodenwechsel electrode change
elektrofotografische Schreibeinheit electrophotographic recording unit
elektrofotografisches Papier electrophotographic paper
Elektrogenerator electric generator
Elektrogerät electrically operated device
Elektrogeräte electrical equipment
Elektroingenieur electrical engineer
Elektroinstallation electrical installation
Elektrolytgerät electrolytic device
Elektrolytgleichrichter electrolytic rectifier
elektrolytische Schreibeinheit electrolytic recording unit
elektrolytisches Papier electrolytic paper
Elektrolytkondensator electrolytic capacitor
Elektromagnet electromagnet
elektromagnetisch electromagnetic
elektromagnetische Beeinflussung electromagnetical interference
elektromagnetischer Impuls electromagnetic pulse
elektromechanisch electromechanical
elektromechanischer Speicher electromechanical storage
elektromechanisches Ausgabegerät electromechanical output device
elektromechanisches Filter electromechanical filter
elektromechanisches Gerät electromechanical device
Elektromotor electric motor
elektromotorische Kraft electromotive force
Elektronenrechner electronic calculator
Elektronenröhre electron tube
Elektronenstrahlröhre electron beam tube
Elektronenwellenröhre electron wave tube
elektronic Mail E-Mail
Elektronik electronic engineering, electronics
elektronische Ablage electronic file cabinet

elektronische Buchungsmaschine electronic accounting machine
elektronische Datenverarbeitung electronic data processing
elektronische Post E-Mail, electronic mail, mail
elektronische private Nebenstellenanlage electronic private branch exchange
elektronischer Briefkasten electronic mailbox
elektronischer Nachrichtenübermittlungsdienst electronic message service
elektronischer Speicher electronic storage
elektronischer Stift electronic pen
elektronisches Gerät electronic device, electronically operated device
elektronisches Nachrichtenübermittlungssystem electronic message system
elektronisches Netzteil electronic power supply
elektronisches Wählsystem electronic dialing system
Elektroschweißen electric welding
Elektroschweißgerät electric welding equipment
Elektroschweißung electric welding
elektrosensitive Aufzeichnungseinheit electrosensitive recording unit
elektrosensitives Papier electrosensitive paper
Elektrostarter electric starter
elektrostatischer Speicher electrostatic storage
elektrostatische Schreibeinheit electrostatic recording unit
elektrostatisches Gerät electrostatic device
Elektrotechnik electrical engineering, electro technology
Element element, item, module
Elementarprozessor element processor
Elementarumwandlung radix conversion
Element im Stromlaufplan ladder logic element
Elementverkettung element chaining
elementweise modular
Elementzeitgeber timing
eliminieren eliminate
Elite-Zeichenabstand elite pitch
Ellipsoid ellipsoid
E-Mail E-Mail, electronic mail
Emaillieren enameling, enamelling
E-Mail-System electronic mail system
Emitter emitter
emittergekoppelte Halbleiterschaltungen emitter coupled logic circuitry

Empfänger listener, receiver, recipient
empfängerabhängig receiver dependent
Empfängerkarte receiver card
Empfängerknoten destination node
Empfängersignal-Elementzeitgeber receiver signal element timing
Empfang receive
empfangen receive
empfangene Zeichen received characters
Empfangsabteilung recipient department
Empfangsadresse destination address
Empfangsadressregister destination address register
Empfangsaufruf selecting
Empfangsauftrag receive job
empfangsbereit ready to receive, receive ready
Empfangsbereitschaft ready to receive, receiver ready
Empfangsbestätigungsanzeige message confirmation indicator
Empfangsbetrieb receive mode
Empfangsblock receive block
Empfangsfolgenummer receive sequence number
Empfangsfolgezähler receive state variable
Empfangsgerät receiver
Empfangsgeschwindigkeit receive rate, receive speed
Empfangsgeschwindigkeit des Modems modem receive speed
Empfangskopie receive copy
Empfangsleitung received line
Empfangsliste receipt list
Empfangsparität receive parity
Empfangsprozessor receive processor
Empfangspuffer receive buffer
Empfangsschaltung receive circuit
Empfangsseite receiving end
Empfangssignalpegel carrier, receive parity
Empfangssignalumsetzer demodulator
Empfangsspielraum receiver margin
Empfangsstelle receiving point, reception point
Empfangsstörung radio frequency interference
Empfangszeittakt receive timing
empfehlen recommend
Emulation emulation
Emulator emulator
emulieren emulate
Endanweisung end statement
endausgeliefert finally delivered
endausliefern make the final delivery
Endauslieferung final delivery
Endbegrenzer terminator

305

Endbenutzer end user
Endbenutzer-Datenverarbeitung end-user computing
Endbenutzerpreis retail price
Endbestand final stock
Endbetrag total amount
Endbit stop bit
Enddruckposition final print position
Ende bottom, end
Endeanweisung end instruction
Endebehandlung end procedure
Ende Datei end of file
Endedatum end date
Ende der Nachricht end of message
Ende der Übertragung zur Steuereinheit control unit end
Ende des Dokuments bottom of document
Ende des Übertragungsblocks end of transmission block
Ende-Ende end to end
Endekennsatz ending label
Endekennzeichnung end indication
Endekriterium end criterion
Enderzeugnis end product
Endeseite end page
Endesprungbox end jump box
Endetaste end key
Endezeichen end character, termination character, terminator
Endezeit completion time
Endgerät terminal
endgültig final
Endisolator dead end insulator
Endkennzeichen end identifier
Endknoten end node
Endlauf end run
Endlieferkennzeichen final delivery flag
Endlieferung final delivery
Endlosformularsatz continuous fan-fold stock
Endlospapier continuous paper, continuous stationery, fanfold paper, pinfeed paper
Endlospapiereinrichtung continuous form device
Endmarke ending label
Endmarkierung ending label
Endnummer end number
Endposition final position
Endpunkt terminator point
Endsaldo final balance
Endsatz ending sentence
Endschalter end switch
Endsumme grand total
Endsystem end system

Endsystemadresse network address
Endsystemverbindung network connection
Endtermin completion date
Endung suffix
Endzeilennummer final line number
Energiedirektumwandlung direct energy conversion
Energieverbrauch power consumption
eng tight
Engpaß bottleneck
en gros bulk, mass
entbehrlich expendible
entblocken deblock, deblocking
entdecken detect, discover
Enterprozeß enter process
entfallen fall
entfernen remove
entfernt distant, remote
entfernte Prüfschleife remote loop
entfernter Benutzer remote user
entfernter Rechner remote computer
entfernte Station remote station
Entfernung distance, removal
Entflammbarkeit flammability
entgasen degasify
entgast degassed
Entgasung degassing
Entgeltbetrag amount of compensation
Entgeltbetrag-Maske compensation amount mask
entgeltpflichtig liable to pay
enthärtet decalcified
enthalten contain
Entität entity
Entity Relation entity relation
Entity-Relation-Modell entity relationship model
entkomprimieren decompress
Entkomprimierung decompression
entladen discharge, dump, unload
Entladezeit discharge time
Entladung discharge
Entlastung credit
Entlastungskonto credit account
entleert empty
Entleerung draining
Entnahmemenge quantity issued
Entnahmeschein stock requisition
entnehmen draw, take, take from
entpacken unpack
entrichten pay
Entriegelungshebel unlocking lever position
Entriegelungsklammer release tab

306

entscheiden decide
entscheidend decisive
Entscheidung decision
Entscheidungsbefehl decision instruction
Entscheidungselement decision element
Entscheidungsfähigkeit decision making ability
Entscheidungskästchen decision box
Entscheidungssymbol decision box
Entscheidungstabelle decision table
entschlüsseln decode
Entschlüssler decoder
entsperren release, unblock
entsprechen correspond
entsprechend according to, appropriate, corresponding
entstehen occur, result
Entstehung formation
Entstehungsdatum formation date
Entstörgerät suppressor
entwickeln develop
Entwicklung development, history
Entwicklungseinrichtung developing unit
Entwicklungsgeschichte history
Entwicklungsnummer development number
Entwicklungsperiode gestation period
Entwicklungsrechner host computer
Entwicklungssatz history record
Entwicklungssystem development system
Entwicklungsteil development part
Entwicklungs-Tool development tool
Entwicklungswerkzeug development tool
Entwicklungszeit development time
Entwicklungszyklus development cycle
Entwurf draft
Entwurfsingenieur design engineer
Entwurfsphilosophie design philosophy
Entwurfsrichtlinie design guideline
Entzerrer equalizer
entziehbare Betriebsmittel preemptible resources
EOF-Code end of file code
epitaxiale Schicht epitaxial layer
EPROM-Karte eprom card
EPROM-Programmiergerät eprom programmer
erbringen result
Erde ground
erden ground
Erdklemme ground terminal
Erdsammelschiene ground bus bar
Erdschlußreaktanz earthing reactor
Erdung ground
Erdungskabel ground wire

ereignisgesteuert event controlled
Ereignismarke event flag
Ereignismarkierung event flag
Ereignisschrittschaltwerk event drum
erfahren experience, skilled
Erfahrung experience, skill
Erfahrungswert based on experience
erfassen acquire, register
erfaßte Menge coverage, registered quantity
Erfassung acquisition, registration
Erfassungsabschnitt batch of data
Erfassungsabwicklung acquisition management
Erfassungsart type of acquisition
Erfassungsaufgabe acquisition task
Erfassungsaufwand acquisition effort, acquisition expense, registration effort
Erfassungsbeleg source document
Erfassungs-Bild acquisition screen
Erfassungsbild registration screen
Erfassungsblock acquisition block, registration block
Erfassungs-Feld acquisition field
Erfassungs-Form acquisition form
Erfassungsform registration form
Erfassungs-Format acquisition format
Erfassungsformular record form
Erfassungsliste acquisition list, source document
Erfassungs-Möglichkeit acquisition option
Erfassungs-Nachweis acquisition check
Erfassungsperiode registration period
Erfassungs-Programm acquisition program
Erfassungstechnik acquisition technique, registration technique
Erfassungsvorgang acquisition process, registering process
Erfassungsvorschrift input instruction
Erfassungszeitraum acquisition period, registration period
Erfolg success
erfolgen carry out, take place
erfolglos unsuccessful
Erfolgsmeldung success message
erforderlich necessary, required
erfordern require
erfragen inquire, question
erfrischen refresh
erfüllen fulfill, meet
Erfüllung fulfillment
Erfüllungsgrad degree of completion
ergänzen complete, supplement
Ergänzung completion, supplement
Ergänzungsfunktion supplementary function

Ergänzungsmodul supplementary module
Ergänzungsspeicher extended storage
Ergänzungswert remainder
ergeben result
Ergebnis result
Ergebnisbereich result area
Ergebnisbezugszahl resulting indicator
Ergebnis der Prüfung result of check
Ergebnis der Reparatur recovery result
Ergebnisdokument result document
Ergebnis größer results high
Ergebnis kleiner results low
Ergebnisnummer result number
Ergebnisnummerneingabe result number input
Ergebnisposition operating statement item, result statement item
Ergebnisrechnung operating statement, result statement version
Ergebnisrechnungsversion operating statement version
Ergebnisschlüssel result code
Ergebnisseite result page
Ergebniswert liefern return a value
Ergonomie ergonomics
ergonomischer Faktor human factor
ergonomische Tastenanordnung sculptured key array
erhalten obtain, receive
Erhaltungsladen trickle charge
erhöhen increase, increment
Erhöhung increase, increment
erinnern remind
Erinnerung reminder
Erinnerungssystem reminder system
Erinnerungswert reminder total
erkennen recognize
erkennen lassen suggest
Erkennung recognition
Erkennungsbit detection bit
erklärbar explicable
erklären explain, point out
erklärend explanatory
erklärende Meldung explanatory message
Erklärung assertion, entry, explanation
erkundigen enquire
erläutern explain
erläuternd explanatory
Erläuterung comment, explanation
Erläuterungsseite explanation page
erlangen attain
erlauben allow, permit
Erlaubnis allowance
erledigen complete, process

Erledigung completion
Erledigungskennzeichen completion flag
Erledigungsmerkmal completion flag
erleichtern facilitate, simplify
Erleichterung relief
Erlös proceeds
Erlösbuchung proceeds posting
erlöschen go out
ermäßigen reduce
ermitteln determine, evaluate
Ermittlung calculation, identification
Ermittlung des kritischen Weges critical path method
ermöglichen enable
Ermüden aging
ermutigen encourage
erneuern renew
Erneuerung renewal
erneut definieren redefine, restate
erneuter Start restart
erneute Übermittlung retransmission
erneut laden reboot, reload
erneut montieren remount
eröffnen initialize, open
eröffneter Job open run
Eröffnung opening
Eröffnungsart initialization type
Eröffnungsphase initialization phase
Eröffnungsstatus opening status
Eröffnungsbilanz opening balance
errechnen calculate
Errechnung calculation
Erreger exciter
erreichen achieve, attain, reach
errichten construct, set up
Errorcode error code
Ersatz backup, replacement, standby, substitute
Ersatzbatterie replacement battery, standby battery
Ersatzformular substitute form
Ersatzgerät replacement unit, standby unit
ersatzhalber as a backup, as a replacement, as a substitute
Ersatz-Hauptarbeitsplatz backup master workstation
Ersatzmasterplatz backup master workstation
Ersatzmaterial substitute material
Ersatzmaterialnummer substitute material number
Ersatzsektor alternate sector
Ersatzsektorentabelle alternate sector table
Ersatzspur alternate track

Ersatzspurverwaltung   alternate track administration
Ersatzteil   replacement part, spare, spare part
Ersatzzeichen   replacement character
Ersatzzeichenfolge   replacement string
erscheinen   appear
erscheinend   apparent
Erscheinung   appearance
erschöpft   exhausted
Erschütterungstest   jarring test
ersehen   gather, see
ersetzen   replace, substitute
Ersetzmodus   replace mode
Ersetzung   replacement
ersichtlich   evident
Erstanlegen   initial construction
Ersteingabe   primary input
Ersteintrag   primary entry
erstellen   build, build up, create, originate, produce
Erstellen eines Dokuments   creating a document
Erstellen eines Geschäftsberichtes   financial report generation
Erstellen von Text   creating text
Ersteller   author, creator
Erstellung   creation, production
Erstellungsdatum   creating date, creation date, date of creation
Erstellungsfunktion   create function
Erstellungshilfe für Anwendungen   application design tool
Erstellungskennzeichen   origin code
Erstellungsperiode   creation period
Erstellungsprogramm   build program, production program
Erstellungsprozeß   creation process
Erstellungsreport   creation report
Erstellungs- und Erweiterungsgröße des Speichers   cabinet size and extension
Erstellungszeit   creation time
erste Normalform   first normal form
erster Adreßbereich   first address range
erster Dateianfangskennsatz   head label
Ersterfassung   original acquisition
Ersterstellung   first creating
erstes Laufwerk   primary drive
erste Zeichenposition   leftmost character position
erstgenannt   first named
Erstimplementation   primary implementation
Erstinitialisieren   primary initialize
Erstinitialisierung   first time initialization

Erstinstallation   first installation
Erstladen   initial bootstrap, initial load
Erstlauf   initial run
erstmalig   first
erstmalige Geräteansteuerung   initial selection sequence
erstrecken   extend, stretch out
Erstübernahme   opening stock entry
erteilen   grant
Ertrag   income
erwägen   consider
erwarten   expect
erwartete Antwortzeit   expected time of response
erweisen   prove
Erweiterbarkeit   expandability
erweitern   expand, extend, upgrade
erweiterte Genauigkeit   extended precision
erweiterte Grafikkarte   enhanced graphics adapter
erweiterter Befehlssatz   extended instruction set
erweiterter Befehlsvorrat   micrologic expansion feature
erweiterter Dateiname   extended file name
erweiterte Resultatausgabe   extended result output
erweiterter Grafikadapter   enhanced graphics adapter
erweitertes Adreßregister   extended address register
erweitertes BASIC   advanced BASIC, extended BASIC
erweiterte Selbstdiagnose   extended selftest program
erweiterte serielle Schnittstelle   dual 8 bit interface
Erweiterung   expansion, extension, option, suffix
Erweiterungcode   extension code
Erweiterung des Stapelkommandos   batch command extension
Erweiterungsalternative   migration path
Erweiterungsbox   expansion box
Erweiterungseinheit   expansion unit
Erweiterungsfähigkeit   growth potential
Erweiterungsfunktion   extension function
Erweiterungskarte   extender card
Erweiterungsmodul   option module
Erweiterungspaket zur Grundsoftware   extended system software
Erweiterungsregister   expansion register
Erweiterungssteckplatz   expansion slot
erwünscht   desirable

309

erzeugen create, generate, produce
erzeugendes Programm generating program
Erzeugnis product
erzeugtes Produkt developed product
erzielen attain
erzwingen enforce
Erzwingen der Betriebsbereitschaft force attention interrupt
erzwungene Funktion forcing function
erzwungene Unterbrechung reverse interrupt
Escapesequenz escape sequence
Escape- und Steuersequenz escape and control sequence
Escapezeichen escape character
Ethernet Dateiübertragungsprotokoll ethernet file transfer protocol
Etikett label, tag
Etikettendruck label printing
etwaig possible
europäische Artikelnummer european article numbering
Eventualität eventuality
eventuell possibly
Exec-Schnittstelle für Papierperipherie-Gerätesteuerung arbitrary device handler
Executive-Modus executive mode
exemplarisch exemplary
existieren exist
Exitcode exit code
exklusiv exclusive
Exklusiv-ODER exclusive or
expandieren expand
Expandierung expansion
experimentieren experiment
explizit explicit
explosionsgeschützte Dichtung explosion proof seal
explosionsgeschützter Kanal explosion proof drain
explosionsgeschütztes Gehäuse explosion proof housing
Explosionszeichnung exploded view
Exponent exponent
Exponentenfaktor exponent modifier
exponentiell exponential
exponentielle Schreibweise exponential notation
exportieren export
extern external
externe Bezugszahl external indicator
externer Ausgang external output
externer Eingang external input
externer Rechner external computer

externer Sendetaktgeber external transmit clock
externer Speicher auxiliary storage, external storage
externes Kommando external command, transient command
externes Rücksetzen external reset
externe Subroutine external subroutine
externes Unterbrechungsstatuswort EI status word
externes Unterprogramm external subroutine
externe Tabelle external table
externe Takterzeugung external clocking
extrahieren extract
Extrakt excerpt, extract
Extraktband excerpt tape
Extraktsätze excerpt records

F

Fach drawer
Fachabteilung department, specialist department
Fachbereich specialist area
Fachnutzung specialist use
Fachwählertastenfeld classification keyboard
Fachwort technical term
Faden thread
fähig capable
Fähigkeit capability
fällig due
Fälligkeit due date
Fälligkeitsdatum due date, invoice due date
Fälligkeitsintervall maturity interval
Fälligkeitsvorschau preview of due dates
fällig werden accrue
Fahrbogen C-arm
fahren drive, move, run, travel
Fahrenheit Fahrenheit
Fahrgast passenger
Fahrgehäuse drive casing
Fahrkarte ticket
Fahrzeugsteuerung vehicle control
Fakt fact
Faktor factor
Faktorenaddition factor total
Faktura invoice
Fakturadatum invoice date
Fakturaindex invoice index
Fakturamenge quantity invoiced
Fakturanetto invoice net
Fakturaprogramm invoice program
Fakturatext invoice text
Fakturaverrechnung settlement of invoice
Fakturawährung invoice currency
Fakturazusammenführung combining invoices
fakturieren invoice
Fakturierung invoice function, invoicing
Fakturierungsdatum invoicing date
Fakturierungsmodul invoice module
Fakturierungsprogramm invoicing program
Fakturierungssatz invoicing record
Fakultätsdarstellung factorial notation
Fall case
fallen drop, fall
falsch erroneous, false, incorrect
falsche spitze Klammern unmatched angle brackets

Faltkarte zum Nachschlagen reference card
Farbauswahlregister color select register
Farbband cartridge, print ribbon, ribbon
Farbbandkassette print cartridge, ribbon cartridge
Farbbandtransport ribbon feed
Farbbildschirm color monitor
Farbcode color code
Farbe color
Farberkennungssignal color burst signal
Farbgrafik color graphics
Farbgrafik-Bildschirmadapter color graphics monitor adapter
Farbgrafikkarte color graphics adapter
farbhochauflösend high resolution color
Farbmischanzeige composite video
Farbmodus color mode
Farbsatz color set
Farbstofflaser dye laser
Farbstufenmodus color map mode
Farbtuchschutzleiste ribbon shield
fassen hold
Fassung electric socket, socket, version
Fassungsvermögen capacity, storage capacity
fatal fatal
Faustregel general rule
Fax fax, fax machine
Faxbox fax box
faxen fax
Fax Gruppe 2 fax group 2
Fax Gruppe 3 fax group 3
Fax Gruppe 4 fax group 4
Faxkarte fax card
Faxkompatibilität fax compatibility
Faxübertragung fax transmission
Federschalter snap switch
Fehlanpassung mismatch
Fehlantwort false drop
Fehlbestand shortfall
Fehleingabe incorrect input
fehlend missing
Fehler bug, error, failure, fault, mistake, trouble
Fehlerabfrage error inquiry
Fehlerabschätzung error estimation
Fehleradreßtabelle bad address table
Fehler am Terminal error from terminal
Fehleranalyse error analysis
Fehleranalyseprogramm failure analysis program
Fehleransteuerung error activation
Fehleranzeige error display, error indicator, fault indicator

Fehlerausgang error exit
Fehlerauswertung error evaluation
Fehlerbedingung error condition
fehlerbehaftet erroneous
Fehlerbehandlung error handling, treatment of errors
Fehlerbehandlungsprogramm error processing program, recovery program
Fehlerbehandlungsprogramm error handler
Fehlerbehandlungsroutine error handler, error processing routine
Fehlerbehandlungsunterprogramm error handling routine
Fehler beheben debug, trouble shoot
Fehlerbehebung debugging, elimination of errors, error detection, fault recovery path, trouble shooting
Fehler beim Herunterfahren shutdown error
Fehler beim Lesen read error
Fehler beim Lesen der Datei file data read error
Fehler beim Schließen einer Datei close error
Fehler beim Schreiben auf die Datei file data write error
Fehler beim Schreiben auf Diskette diskette write error
Fehler bei Neuaufteilung partition error
Fehlerbericht error report, trouble report
Fehlerbericht für Software software problem report
Fehlerbeseitigung debugging, elimination of errors, error correction
Fehlercode error code
Fehlercodeauswertung fail code diagnostic
Fehlercodeliste error code list
Fehlerdatei error file
Fehler des Programmierers programmer error
Fehlerdiagnose diagnosis, error diagnosis
Fehlereingangsstelle point where the error occurred
Fehlererkennung error correction, error detection and correction, error recognition
Fehlererkennungsbit error detection bit
Fehlererkennungscode error detecting code
Fehlererkennungshilfe debugging feature
Fehlererkennungshilfen debug mode
Fehlererkennungsmodus debug mode
Fehlerfall case of error
fehlerfrei error free, problem free, undamaged
Fehlerfreiheit accuracy
Fehlergrad severity
Fehlerhäufigkeit error rate
fehlerhaft bad, erroneous, in error, invalid

fehlerhafte Beendigung error off
fehlerhafter Block bad block
fehlerhafter Sektor bad sector
fehlerhaftes Bit failing bit
fehlerhafte Spur bad track
Fehlerhinweis error note
Fehler im Bereich error in partition
Fehler im Druckeranschluß printer port failure
Fehler im Steuermodul controller error
Fehler in der Hardware hardware error
Fehler in der Interrupt-Steuerung control interrupt failure
Fehler in der Systemuhr realtime clock failure
Fehler in der Tastaturschnittstelle keyboard interface failure
Fehlerinhaltsverzeichnis error listing
Fehlerkennzeichen error flag, invalid field
Fehlerkennzeichnungsbit flag bit
Fehlerkette chain of errors
Fehlerkonstellation error situation
Fehlerkontrolle error control
Fehlerkontrollzeichen error checking character
Fehlerkorrektur error correcting, error correcting code
Fehlerkorrekturcode error correcting code, error correction code
Fehlerkorrekturprogramm error correcting program
Fehlerliste error list, error listing, error report
Fehlerlogdatei error log file
Fehlerlokalisierung durch interpretatives Testen fault location by interpretive testing
Fehlermeldung error message, problem message
Fehlermeldungsunterprogramm error message subroutine
Fehlermöglichkeit possibility of error
Fehlernachricht error message
Fehlernummer error number
Fehlerortsuche trouble location
Fehlerprotokoll diagnostic log, error log
Fehlerprotokolldatei error listing file, error log file
Fehlerprotokollierung error logging
Fehlerprüfung bugcheck
Fehlerprüfung und Korrektur error checking and correction
Fehlerquelle source of error
Fehlerreport error report
Fehlerreportmaske error report mask
Fehlerschutzeinheit error control unit
Fehlerschutzgerät error correction device

Fehlerseite error page
Fehlerstatistikprogramm recoverable error edit
Fehlersuchcode error detecting code
Fehlersuche debugging, error search, fault finding, trouble shoot, trouble shooting
Fehler suchen debug, debugging
Fehler suchen und beheben debug
Fehlersuchprogramm debug program, diagnostic routine
Fehlersumme error amount
Fehlersymptom error indication
Fehlertext error text
Fehlertextnummer error text number
Fehlertextschlüssel key to error text
fehlertolerant fault tolerant
fehlertoleranter Computer fault tolerant computer
fehlertoleranter Rechner fault tolerant computer
Fehlertyp type of error
Fehler über mehrere Bits multiple bit error
Fehlerüberwachung error control procedure
Fehlerüberwachungseinheit error control unit
fehlerunempfindlich failsafe
Fehlerunterprogramm error handler, error subroutine
Fehlerursache source of error
Fehlerverteilung failure distribution
Fehlerverzeichnis error list, error listing
Fehlerverzweigung error clause
Fehlerwert error value
Fehlerzeile error line
Fehlerzustand contigency, error condition
Fehlerzustand dem Programm melden returning error
Fehlfunktion error, fault, malfunction
Fehlmenge shortfall
Fehlteileliste missing parts list
fein fine
Feinabstimmung fine tuning
Feinabstimmungsvariable fine tuning variable
Feinheit refinement
Feinstruktur fine structure
Feld array, cell, field
Feldadresse field address
Feldanfang begin field
Feldangabe field specification
Feldansteuerung field selection
Feldart field type
Feldattribut field attribute
Feldausrichtung field alignment
Feldauswahl field select, field selection
Feldbegrenzung field definition

Feldbeschreibung field description, field descriptor
Feldbeschreibungssatz field description record
Feldbeschreibungstabelle field description table
Feldbezeichnung field name
feldbezogen field related
Feldbezugszahl bei Null zero indicator
Feldcursor cell cursor, cell pointer
Felddaten field data
Felddefinition field definition
Felddefinitionskarte field description card
Felddimension field dimension
Feldeffekttransistor field effect transistor
Feldeigenschaft field characteristic
Feldende end of field
Feldendetaste end of field key
Feldendezeichenmodus field delimiter mode
Felderläuterung field declaration
Felderläuterungstabelle field declaration table
Feldformat field data format
Feldfunktion field function
Feldgröße field size
Feldgruppe array, field group
Feldgruppenauswahl field group selection
Feldgruppenauswahlmenü field group menu
Feldgruppenmaske field group mask
Feldgruppennummer field group number
Feldinhalt contents, field content
Feldkarte field card
Feldkonvertierung field conversion
Feldkonvertierungsbeschreibung field conversion description
Feldlänge field length
Feldname field name
Feldnamenbeschreibung description of field name
Feldnamentabelle field name table
Feldnummer field number
Feldpol field pole
Feldposition field location
Feldreferenz references to cell
Feldspezifikation field specification
Feldspezifikationszeichen field specification character
Feldsteuerung field control
Feldsteuerzeichen field control character
Feldtabelle field table
Feldtabellengenerator field table generator
Feldtrenner field separator
Feldtrennung field separation
Feldtyp field type
Feldversuch field test

Feldverweis references to cell
Feld von Zeigern pointer array
Feldweiser field
Feldwert field value
Feldzeiger cell cursor, cell pointer
Fenster window
Fenster löschen erase window
Fenstermenü pop-up menu
Fenster synchronisieren synchronize windows
Fern- long distance, remote
Fernanschluß remote port
Fernbetriebseinheit communication control unit
Ferndatenstation remote data station
Ferndiagnoseanschluß remote diagnostics link
Ferneinschaltung remote switching-on
Ferneinschaltversuch attempt to switch on remotely
ferne Prüfschleife remote loop
Ferngespräch long distance call
ferngesteuertes Fahrzeug remote controlled vehicle
Fernkopie facsimile, fax, long distance xerox
Fernkopierer facsimile equipment, fax machine
Fernkopiererkompatibilität facsimile communication equipment compatibility, fax compatibility
Fernladen downline loading
Fernleitungsbetrieb trunking
Fernmeldeamt local telecommunication authority
Fernmeldekabel communication cable
Fernmeldeleitung communication line
Fernmeldemietleitung leased common carrier
Fernmeldeverbindung communication link
Fernmeldeverdrahtung communication wiring
Fernprozeduraufruf remote procedure call
Fernprüfung remote testing
Fernrechner remote computer
Fernruf telephone call
Fernschaltgerät data circuit terminating equipment
Fernschreiber teletype, teletypewriter, telex, typewriter
Fernschreiberkonsole console typewriter
Fernschreibleitung telegraph line, teletype line
Fernschreibmaschine teletypewriter, telex machine
Fernschreibnachricht telegraph message, telex message
Fernschreibstandverbindung telegraph leased circuit

Fernschreib- und Datexdienst telex and datex service network
Fernschreibzeichen telegraph character
Fernsehen television
Fernseh-Videotext broadcast videotext
Fernsprechhauptanschluß direct dialling telephone
Fernsprechkanal voice channel
Fernsprechnetz public switched telephone network, telephone network
Fernsprechnummer telephone number
Fernsteuersystem remote control system
Fernsteuerung remote control, remote control unit
Fernsteuerungsanschluß remote control interface
Fernverarbeitung teleprocessing
Fernverarbeitungs-Symbiontenschnittstelle remote symbiont interface
Fernwartung remote technical assistance
ferroelektrisches Gerät ferroelectric device
fertigen construct, produce
Fertigerzeugnis finished product
Fertigfabrikat finished article
Fertigprodukt finished product
Fertigproduktlager finished article warehouse
Fertigstellung completion
Fertigung production
Fertigungsabschluß production completion
Fertigungsauftrag production order
Fertigungskontrolle manufacturing control, manufacturing inspection, production control
Fertigungslos production lot
Fertigungsorganisation production control
fest fixed, permanent, tight
feste Einsprungadresse fixed entry point, guaranteed entry point
feste elektrische Verbindung electrical bonding
fester Block fixed block
fester Isolator solid core insulator
fester Leiter solid conductor
fester Programmablauf fixed program flow
festes Blockformat fixed block format
festes Flugfernmeldenetzwerk aeronautical fixed telecommunications network
festes Format fixed format, fixed mode
festes Wagenrücklaufzeichen hard return
feste virtuelle Verbindung permanent virtual circuit
feste Wortlänge fixed word length
feste Zeilennummern fixed line numbers
feste Zeitspanne fixed time interval

festgefahren stuck
festgehalten laid down
festgeklemmt stuck
festgelegt fixed, laid down
festgeschaltete Punkt-zu-Punkt-Leitung leased point-to-point line
festhalten hold
Festkörperschaltung solid state circuit
Festkomma fixed point
Festkommaaddition fixed point addition
Festkommaarithmetik fixed point arithmetic
Festkommaautomatik fixed decimal
Festkommabetrieb fixed point operation
Festkommadarstellung fixed point representation
Festkommasystem fixed point system
Festkondensator fixed capacitor
festlegen define, lay down
Festlegung definition
Festname fixed identifier
Festplatte fixed disk, hard disk, hard disk option, winchester disk
Festplattencontroller hard disk controller, hard disk controller board
Festplattendatei file on the hard disk
Festplattenhilfsprogramm hard disk utility program
Festplattenlaufwerk disk drive, fixed disk drive, hard disk drive
Festplattenparameter hard disk parameter
Festplattenspeicher fixed disk, hard disk storage
Festplattenstatus hard disk status
Festplattensystem hard disk system
Festpunktschreibweise fixed point representation
Festspeicher nur zum Lesen read only memory
feststehend fixed
feststellen detect, determine, evaluate, locate
Feststellhebel cover release tab, release tab
Feststellhebel der Abdeckung cover release tab
Feststellmodus lock mode
Feststelltaste lock key
Feststofflaser solid laser
fest verdrahten hardwire
festverdrahtet hard wired
Festwert fixed value
Festwertspeicher permanent memory, read only memory
Festwiderstand fixed resistor
festziehen tighten

Festzins fixed interest
fest zugeordnet dedicated
fest zugeordnete Register dedicated register
fest zugeordneter Massenspeicher fixed mass storage
fest zugeordnetes Gerät dedicated device
fett bold
Fettdruck bold, bold print, bolding, emphasized print
Fettdruck geschützt bold protected
fettgedruckt bold
fettgedrucktes Zeichen bold face character
Feuchteregelung moisture control
Feuchtesteuerung humidity control
feuchtigkeitsbeständig moisture resistant
Feuchtigkeitsverhalten moisture resistance
Feuchtregelung humidity
FH-Trommel flying head magnet drum
FIFO-Speicher FIFO memory
File Server file server
Filiale branch
Filialkonto branch account
Film film
filmen film
Filmlochkarte aperture card
Filter electric filter
Filterschema filter scheme
Filtersicherungskarte fuse filter card
Finanz- financial
Finanzanlage financial asset
Finanzbuchhaltung financial accounting
Finanzen finances
finanziell financial
Finanzierungswechsel financing bill of exchange
Finanzmittel cash
Finanzplan budget
Finanzplankategorie budget category
finanzplankontiert budget posted
Finanzplankontierung budget accounting
Finanzplanperiode budget period
Finanzplanposition budget item
Finanzplanschlüssel budget code
Finanzplanstamm budget master
Finanzplanstammdatei budget master file
Finanzplanstammsätze budget master record
finanzplanwirksam budget-effective
finden discover, find
Findung calculation
Finite Elemente Modell finite element modeling
Firma company, factory, firm, plant
firmenabhängig company dependent

Firmenberechtigung company authorization
Firmenbezeichnung company name
firmenindividuell company specific
firmenintern in house
Firmenkennzeichen company marker
Firmenkonto company account
Firmenname company name, firm name
firmenspezifisch company specific
firmenübliches Netzteil standard plant power supply
firmenunabhängig company independent
firmenweit plant wide
Firmware firmware
Firmware-Kompatibilität firmware compatibility
fix fixed
Fixdefinition fix definition
Fixiereinrichtung fixing unit
Fixkontentabelle fixed accounts table
Fixkonto fixed account
Flachbandkabel flat cable, ribbon cable
Flachkupfer stripwound cut core
flackern flicker, flicker on
Flächendiode junction diode
Flächentransistor junction transistor
Flammbarkeitswert flammability rating
flammenverzögernd flame-retardant
Flammprobe flame test
Flanke edge, flank, slope
Flankenabfallzeit fall time
Flankenanstiegszeit rise time
Flankendetektor edge detector
Flankenerkennung edge detection
Flash flash
flexibel flexible
flexibler Leiter flexible conductor
flexibles Fertigungssystem flexible manufacturing system
Fließband manufacturing line
Fließkomma floating decimal, floating point
Fließkommabefehl floating point instruction
Fließkommaadapter floating point adapter
Fließkommadarstellung floating point representation
Fließkommaeinrichtung floating point availability
Fließkommamultiplikation floating point multiplication
Fließkommaoperation floating point operation
Fließkommarechnung floating point computation
Fließkommaschreibweise floating point representation

Fließkommawort floating point word
Fließkommazahl floating point number
Fließtext flow text
Fließtextverfahren adjust mode
Flip-Chip-Bauteil flip chip device
Flip-Flop bistable trigger unit, flip flop, scaling circuit
Floppy floppy disk
Floppy Disk flexible disk, floppy disk, floppy diskette
Floppy Disk-Laufwerk floppy disk drive
Floppy Disk-Speicher floppy disk storage
Floppy Disk-Steuerung floppy disk controller
flüchtiger Speicher volatile memory, volatile storage
flüssiger Starter liquid starter
flüssiges Isolationsmaterial liquid electrical insulating
Flüssigkeit liquid
Flüssigkeitsfilm liquid film
Flüssigkeitslaser liquid laser
Flüssigkeitsregulierung liquid controller
Flüssigkristallanzeige liquid crystal display
Fluggast passenger
Flugkurs-Kreuzung airway crossing
Fluglotse air traffic controller
Flugregelung flight control
Flugsicherungszentrale air traffic control center
Flugsimulator flight simulator
Flugzeug-Navigation aircraft navigation
Flugzielverfolgung über entfernte Radarstationen remote radar tracking
Fluidic-Steuergerät fluidic control equipment
Fluidic-Steuersystem fluidic control system
Fluoreszenzschirm fluorescent screen
Fluß flow
Flußdiagramm flow chart
Flußkontrolle flow control
Flußkontrolle bereit flow control ready
Flußplan flow chart
Flußregelung flow control
Flußsteuerung flow control
Flußwechsel pro Zoll flux changes per inch
Förderband conveyor belt
Folge sequence
Folgeabschnitt subsequent section
Folgeadresse sequence address
Folgeadresse anzeigen report address
Folgeanweisung sequence statement
Folgeaufruf subsequent call
Folgeband continuation tape
Folgebeleg continuation voucher

Folgebenutzer next user
Folgebild continuation screen, next screen
Folgebildschirm continuation screen, sequence screen
Folgeblatt continuation sheet, subsequent page
Folgedynpro subsequent dynpro
Folgeeingabe sequence input
Folgefehler sequence error
Folgekarte continuation card
folgen follow, succeed
folgend adjacent, following, next
Folgenummer continuation number, sequence number
Folgeprogramm subsequent program
Folgeprüfprogramm sequence checking routine
folgern conclude
Folgerolle following role
Folgesegment adjacent segment, subsegment
Folgeseite continuation page, following page
Folgesektor continuation sector
Folgestanzer gang punch
Folgestation secondary station
Folgesteuerkette servo controller
Folgesteuerung secondary, secondary control
Folgesteuerungsfunktion sequential control
Folgesteuerungssystem servosystem
Folgesuspendierung sequencing hold
Folgetransaktionscode sequence transaction code
Folgeverarbeitung subsequent processing
Folgezeile continuation line
fordern challenge, demand, require
Forderung claim
Forderungen accounts receivable
Forderungsart type of claim
Form aspect
formal formal
Formalfehler formal error, syntax error
Formalprüfung syntax check
Format form, format
Formatangabe form specification, format specification
Formatanweisung format instruction, format word
Formatart format type
Formatausgabe format output
Formatbehandlung form processing, format processing
Formatbehandlungsfunktion format processing function
Formatbehandlungssystem format handling system

Formatbeschreibung format notation
Formatbibliothek format library, forms library
Formatbibliothekseinsatzdatei format library application file
Formatbibliotheksname format library name
Formatbildeditierung format display editing
Formatdatei format file
Formatdateiname format file name
Format der einzelnen Felder individual format of cells
Formateingabe format input
Formateinsatz format application
Formateinsatzdatei format application file
Formaterstellung format creation, forms creation, forms generation
Formaterstellungsfunktion format creation function
Formaterzeugung format generation
Formatfeld format field
Formatfelderstellung format field creation
formatgebundener Netzwerkmodus network native mode
Formatgenerator form generator, format generator
Format-Handling-System format handling system
Formatieren formatting
formatieren format, initialize
Formatierer formatter
Formatierprogramm disk formatter
formatiert formatted
formatierte Diskette formatted diskette
Formatierung initialisation
Formatierungsschnittstelle formatting interface
Formatierungsseitenmodus formatting page mode
formatierungssteuernd formatting controlling
Formatierungssystem formatting system
Formatkennsatz format label
Formatkennzeichen format identifier
Formatkettung format chaining
Formatliste format list
Formatname format name
Formatprogramm für Lohn payroll format program
Formatschnittstelle format interface
Formatseite format page
Formatserviceseite format service page
Formatsteuerung data unit control, format control
Formatsteuerungsdaten format control data
Formatsteuerungssprache format control language

Formatsteuerzeichen format effector, format effector layout character, layout character
Formattyp type of format
Formatverwaltung format management
Formatvorschrift format rule
Formatwähler format selector
Formatwahl mode setting
Formatwechsel-Duplizierfeld chain duplicate field
Formbrief form letter
Form des Cursors cursor style
Formel formula
Formelauswertung formula evaluation
formell formal
Formelübersetzung formula translation
formen form
formlos informal
Formteil moulding
Formular form, mask
Formularart form type, type of form
Formularbeschreibung form description
Formularbeschreibungsmakro form description macro
Formularbeschreibungssprache forms description language
Formularbeschreibungstabelle form description table
Formulardatei form file
Formulardokument form document
Formulardruck form printing
Formulareingabe form input
Formulareingabesystem forms entry system
Formularende end of form, form overflow
Formularendeüberschreitung exceeding end of form
Formularfeld form field, form item
Formular für Druckanordnung printer format chart
formulargerecht according to form
Formularhalter copy holder, form holder, form rack
Formularhöhe height of the form
Formularjustierung form adjustment, form alignment
Formularkarte form card
Formularkennzeichen form designator
Formular-Nachdruckeinrichtung crash imprinter
Formularsatz multi copy form
Formularsteuerung form control
Formulartabelle form table
Formulartransport form transport
Formulartrenner form separator

Formularüberlaufbezugszahl overflow indicator
Formularüberlaufzeile overflow line
formularunabhängiges Format free from format
Formularwähler form selector, format selector
Formularwechselanzeige overflow control indicator
Formularzuführung form feed
Formularzuführungseinrichtung form feeding device
formulieren formulate
Formulierung formulation
Forschung und Entwicklung research and development
fortfahren continue
Fortführung continuation
fortgeschrittenes Arbeiten advanced procedures
fortlaufend continuous
fortlaufende Blöcke contiguous blocks
fortlaufendes Format contiguous format, stream
fortschreiben update
Fortschreibungsdatei updating file
Fortschreibungsversionsnummer update version number
Fortschreibungswert update value
Fortschritt progress
fortschrittliches Radarziel-Verfolgungssystem advanced radar traffic control system
fortsetzen continue
Fortsetzung continuation
Fortsetzungsaufforderung continuation call
Fortsetzungswert für die Datei file continuation value
Fortsetzungszeichen continuation character
Fotodiode photodiode
fotoelektrisches Relais photoelectric relay
Fotoelement photovoltaic cell
Fotokathode photocathode
fotoleitendes Gerät photoconductive device
Fotoröhre phototube
Fototransistor phototransistor
Fotozelle photoconductive cell, photoelectric cell
Fracht freight
Frachtabrechnung freight bill
Frachtanteil freight costs
Frachtbetrag freight amount
Frachtbuchung freight posting
Frachtelement freight element

Frachterfassung freight data input
Frachterledigung freight expediting
Frachtkasse freight collect fund
Frachtkassenkonto freight account
Frachtkennzeichen freight marker
Frachtkonditionen freight terms
Frachtkosten freight charges
Frachtkostenabrechnung settlement of freight charges
Frachtkostenverteilung apportionment of freight charges
Frachtlieferant carrier
Frachtlieferbedingungen freight terms
Frachtmuttersegment freight master segment
Frachtposition freight item
Frachtrechnung freight invoice
Frachtrechnungsprüfung freight invoice validation
Frachtroute freight route
Frachtrückstellung freight reversal
Frachttext freight details
Frachtvereinbarung freight agreement
Frachtverrechnungsmenge freight charge quantity accruing
Frachtverrechnungswert freight charges accrued
Frachtverteilung freight distribution
Frachtvorgang freight process
Frage enquiry, inquiry, query, question
Frageaktion query message
fragen ask, question
Fragestellung problem, question
Fragezeichen question mark
Fragmentierung segmenting
frei exposed, free, no connection
freie Abschnitte inclusive phase
freier Speicher free memory
freies Format free format
Freiformat free format
Freigabe enable, release
Freigabebedingung enable condition
Freigabedatum release date
Freigabe der Unterbrechungssperre release interrupt lockout
Freigabegrund reason for release
Freigabekennzeichen release identifier
Freigabemitteilung release notice
Freigabesperre release lock
Freigabetaste release key
freigeben deallocate, enable, release, unlock
freigegeben enabled
Freiheitsgrade degrees of freedom
freilassen leave blank

Freileitung overhead power line
Freiluft-Elektrogeräte outdoor electrical equipment
Freischalten (bei Leitungsvermittlung) clearing phase and quiescent states
Freispeicherliste free space list
frei wählbar freely selectable
Freizustand free line condition
fremd foreign, other
Fremdbenutzer remote user
Fremdbestellung bought in order
fremdbezogen bought in
Fremdbezug bought in
Fremdknotenkennummer remote identification, remote node indentification
Fremdpartition other partition, partition of unknown type
Fremdsystem other vendors' system
Fremdwährung foreign currency
Fremdwährungsbetrag foreign currency amount
Fremdwährungsbewertung foreign currency valuation
Fremdwährungsdisposition foreign currency schedule
Fremdwährungskurs foreign currency exchange rate
Fremdwährungsposition foreign currency item
Fremdwährungsschlüssel foreign currency code
Fremdwährungssumme foreign currency sum
Fremdwährungswert foreign currency value
Fremdwort foreign word
Frequenz frequency
Frequenzablage frequency departure
Frequenzantwort frequency response
Frequenzband band
Frequenzbereich frequency response
Frequenzfehler frequency instability
Frequenzfilter frequency selective filter
Frequenzhalbierschaltung frequency halver
Frequenzkennlinie frequency characteristic
Frequenzmodulation frequency modulation
Frequenzmodulationsaufzeichnung FM carrier recording
Frequenzmodulator frequency modulator
Frequenzmultiplex-Übertragungseinrichtung frequency division multiplex equipment
Frequenzregelung frequency control
Frequenzsteuerung frequency control
Frequenzvervielfacher frequency multiplier
Frequenzwandler frequency changer
Frist deadline

Frontpanelschalter

Frontpanelschalter front panel switch
Frontplatte bezel, face plate, front panel
Frontrechner front end processor
Frontschalter front panel switch, front switch
Frontverkleidung face plate
Frühlieferung early delivery
führen guide, lead
führend leading, leading
führende Flanke leading edge
führende Null leading zero
führende Nullen leading zeroes
führendes Minuszeichen leading minus sign
Führung alignment, form guide, guide, route
Führungsgröße control signal
Führungsplatte guide plate
Führungsrolle form guide roller, pulley
Führungsschiene guide
Führungssteg locating key
Füll- fill
Füllbyte filler byte
füllen fill
Füllsignal dummy
Füllungsgrad filling level
Füllzeichen fill character, filler, padding characters, record fill
Füllzeichenbehandlung filler processing
Füllzeichen zwischen Datenübertragungs-Blöcken interface time filler
Fünfergruppe pentad
für erschwerte Umweltbedingungen gebauter Computer ruggedized computer
für industriellen Einsatz factory hardened
für nicht betriebsbereit erklären down
für schwere Belastung heavy duty
Fuhrparkverwaltung vehicle management
fundiert sound
Funkensteuergerät arc control device
Funkfernsteuerung radio control
Funkfeuer beacon
Funkfrequenz radio frequency
Funkleitung radioguidance
Funknavigation radionavigation
Funkortung radiolocation
Funkpeilung radio direction finding
Funkstörung interface voltage
Funktion function, operation option, purpose, task, use
Funktion abgeschlossen function complete
funktional functional
funktionell ausgedrückt in functional terms
funktioneller Ausdruck functional term
funktionsabhängig function dependent
Funktionsablauf sequence of functions

Funktionsangabe given function
Funktionsangebot function offer
Funktionsanweisung function instruction
Funktionsaufruf function call, reference to function
Funktionsauswahl function selection
Funktionsbaugruppe functional module
Funktionsbaustein function block
Funktionsbeschreibung function description, function descriptor, functional description
funktionsbestimmend function defining
Funktionsbezeichnung action designator
funktionsbezogen function related
Funktionscode function code
Funktionscodeeingabe function code input
funktionscodiert function coded
Funktionsdetail function detail
Funktionseinheit component, functional unit
Funktionseinheitengruppe cluster
Funktionseintrag function entry
Funktionselement functional element
Funktionsergänzung enhancement
funktionsfähiger Bereich usable partition
Funktionsfeld function field
Funktionsgruppe function group
Funktionskarte function card
Funktionskennzeichen function identifier
Funktionsminderung deenhancement
Funktionsmodul function module
Funktionsnummer function code
funktionsorientiert function oriented
Funktionsparameter function parameter
Funktionsprüfung performance test
Funktionsschritt function step
Funktionssteuerblock function control block
Funktionsstreifen key strip, label strip, legend strip
Funktionssymbol functional symbol
Funktionstabelle function table
Funktionstaste function key
Funktionstastenblock alternate keypad, application keypad
Funktionstastenreihe function key row
Funktionstastenstreifen keyboard label strip
Funktionstest confidence test, functional test, operational test
Funktionstest starten invoke confidence test
Funktionstext function text
Funktionstrennung function separation
Funktionstyp function type
Funktionsübersicht functional overview
Funktionsumfang function extent
Funktionsunfähigkeitszeit inoperable time

Funktionsverzweigung branch function
Funktionsvorwahl function preselection
Funktionsweise function
Funktionswert function value
Funktionswort function word
Funktionswort für Peripherie external function word
Funktionszeichen function character
Funktion XON/ XOFF xon xoff feature
Funktion »Kombizeichen« compose character facility
Fuß feet, foot
Fußgänger pedestrian
fußgängergesteuertes System pedestrian-controlled system
Fußtext foot text, footer text
Fußzeile bottom line, footer

G

galvanisch galvanical
galvanisch isoliert galvanically insulated
Ganghebel gear lever
Ganzbrief complete letter, package letter
Ganzzahl integer
Ganzzahldivision integer division
ganzzahlig integer
Ganzzahlkonstante integer constant
Ganzzahllangwort longword integer
Ganzzahloperation integer operation
Ganzzahlvariable integer variable
Garantie warranty
Garantieablauf expiry of warranty
Gasentladungsröhre gas discharge tube
gasgefüllter Transformator gas filled transformer
Gaslaser gas laser
Gasschaltröhre gas filled switching tube
Gasstromschalter gas blast circuit breaker
Gasturbinen-Generator gas turbine generator
Gasturbinen-Kraftwerk gas turbine power station
Gateway gateway
Gateway-Anweisung gateway instruction
Gateway-bezogen gateway related
Gateway-Eingang gateway entry
Gateway-Menü gateway menu
Gateway-Nummer gateway number
Gateway-Wechsel gateway exchange
Gebäudeabschreibung depreciation of buildings
Geber input device
Gebiet area, realm
gebietsfremd extraneous, foreign
Gebinde bundle
Gebindeart special inventory type
Gebindebasis multiple package basis
Gebindebestand multiple package inventory
Gebindedatei special inventory file
Gebindekennzeichen multiple package marker, special inventory marker
Gebindenummer multiple package number
gebindepflichtig always bundled
Gebindesatz multiple package record, special inventory record
Gebindesatzkennzeichen multiple package record marker
Gebindesegment special inventory segment
Gebindestammsatz special inventory master record
Gebindevermerk special inventory remark
Gebläse fan
geblockt-ungeblockt blocked-unblocked
Gebrauchssteuer use tax
Gebühr charge, fee
Gebührenangabe indication of charges
Gebührenberechnung calculation of charges
Gebührenübernahme reverse charging acceptance
Gebührenzuschrift charging information
gebunden bound
Gedächtnisstütze mnemonic, reminder
Gedankenstrich hyphen
gedruckter Text printed text
gedruckte Leiterbahn printed wiring
gedruckte Leiterplatte printed circuit board
gedruckte Schaltung circuit card, printed circuit, printed circuit base, printed circuit board, printed wiring
gedruckte Seite printed page
gedrungen compact
geeignet eligible, suitable
gefährlich dangerous, hazardous
Gefahr danger
Gefahr einer Systemblockade danger of deadlock
Gefahr eines Schlages shock hazard
Gefahrenklassenmerkblatt hazard category sheet
geflochtener Leiter braided conductor
geflusht flushed
gegen- against, contra
Gegenbetrieb duplex transmission, full duplex
gegenbuchen contra post
Gegenbuchung contra posting, counter posting
gegen den Uhrzeigersinn counterclockwise
Gegen-EMK back EMF
Gegengewinde pipe thread
Gegenkonto contra account, counter account
Gegenkontobeschreibung description of counter account
gegenläufig moving in opposite directions
Gegenposition contra item
Gegenposten contra item
Gegenrichtung opposite direction
gegensätzlich conversely
Gegensatz contrast
Gegenstand object
Gegenstelle receiving station
gegenüber opposite
gegenübergestellt opposite

gegenüberstellen compare, oppose
Gegenüberstellung opposition
Gegenverkehr duplex communication
gegenwärtig at present, current
Gegenwart present
Gehäuse cabinet, cover enclosure, housing, package
Gehäuseabdeckung cover
Gehalt salary
Gehaltsliste payroll
geheimgehalten kept secret
geheimhalten keep secret
Geheimhaltung security
gehören belong
gehören zu belong to
gekapselter Transformator encapsuled transformer
gekettete Datei chained file
geladen resident
Geld cash
Geldausgabeautomat automated teller machine, automatic cash dispenser
Geldauszahlung cash dispensing
Geldautomat automated teller machine
Geldbewegung cash transaction
Geldfluß cash flow
Geldinstitut financial institute, financial institution
Geldkurs buying rate
Geldschein banknote
Geldscheinabzug banknote feed
Geldsortenliste list of money denominations
Geldvereinzeler cash sorter
Geldverkehr monetary transaction
Gelegenheit occasion
Gelenk joint
gelötete Verbindung soldered connector
gelten apply
geltend applicable
Geltungsbereich scope
gemacht done
gemäß according to
Gemeinde community
Gemeinkosten overhead
Gemeinkostenart overhead category
Gemeinkostenfaktor overhead factor
Gemeinkostenstelle overhead cost centre
Gemeinkostentabelle overhead table
Gemeinkostenzuschlag overhead surcharge
gemeinsam common
gemeinsam benutzbar common
gemeinsam benutzbares Coding shared code capability

gemeinsam benutzbares Feld common field
gemeinsame Bank für Prüfpunkt full checkpoint common bank
gemeinsame Bearbeitung common processing
gemeinsame Betriebsmittel shared resource
gemeinsame Datenschnittstelle common data interface
gemeinsamer Bereich common
gemeinsamer Kollektor common collector connection
gemeinsamer Prozeß common process
gemeinsamer Zugriff shared access
gemeinsamer Zugriff auf den Zeilendrucker shared line printer operation
gemeinsamer Zugriff auf eine Datei file sharing
gemeinsamer Zugriff auf ein Terminal shared terminal operation
gemeinsames Datenmanagement-Code-Element common code element
gemeinsames Datenverzeichnis common data dictionary
gemeinsame Spannung common voltage
gemeinsame Sperre common lock
gemeinsame Teilprüfpunktbank partial checkpoint common bank
gemeinsame Teilwiederanlaufbank partial restart common bank
gemeinsame Wiederanlaufbank full restart common bank
gemeinsam nutzbares Programm shareable image
gemessen appropriate
genau exact, precise
genauer more precise
Genauigkeit accuracy, precision
Genauigkeit des Zeitgebers timer accuracy
Genauigkeit von Dezimalstellen digits of accuracy
Genauigkeit von Kommastellen digits of accuracy
Generaladresse global address
Generation generation
Generator generator
Generator für zusammengesetztes Farbsignal composite color generator
Generator mit Permanentmagnet permanent magnet generator
Generatorprogramm generator program
generell general, in general
generieren generate, install
Generieren eines Emulators emulator generation

323

generierte Datei generation file
Generierungsfehler generation error
Generierungslauf generation, generation process
Generierungsschnittstelle generation interface
generisch generic
genügen suffice
geothermisches Kraftwerk geothermal electric power station
gepackte Zahl packed number
geplante Lieferzeit planned delivery time
gepuffertes System store and forward system
gerade even, just, straight, straightforward
Geradeninterpolation linear interpolation
gerade Parität even parity
gerade rechtzeitig just in time
gerader Stecker straight angle connector
geradzahlig even
Gerät appliance, device, equipment, machine
geräteabhängig device dependent, device specific, machine dependant
Geräteadresse device address
Geräteanschluß device connector
Geräteansteuerung device selection
Geräteansteuerungscode device selection code
Geräteattribut device attribute
Geräteausstattung device configuration
Gerätebefehl device instruction
Gerätebeschreibung device media control
Gerätebeschreibungssprache device media control language
gerätebezogen device related
Gerätedaten machine data
Gerätedisposition facility control
Gerätefunktion device function
Gerätekennung device identification, device identifier
Gerätemakro device macro
Gerätename device name
Gerätenummer device number
Gerätenummereingabe device number input
Gerätenummernstecker device number plug
Geräteoperation device operation
Gerätesperre device lock
gerätespezifisches Kommando device unique command
Gerätestatus facility status
Gerätestatusanzeige device status report
Gerätesteuerprogramm handler device
Gerätesteuerroutine device control routine
Gerätesteuerung device control, device controller

Gerätesteuerungsschnittstelle device control interface, direct data interface
Gerätesteuerzeichen component selection character
Gerätetreiber device driver, device handler
Gerätetreiberprozeß device driver process
Gerätewarteschlange device queue
Gerätezuordnungsfolge device assignment set
Gerätezustand device status
Gerät mit wahlfreiem Zugriff random access device
Gerät zur Personenidentifikation personal identification device
Geräusch noise, sound
Geräuschdämpfung silencing
geregelt regular
gerichteter Interrupt vectored interrupt
gerichtlich legal
gering minor, slight, small
Geringverdiener low income earner
geringwertig inferior, minor
Gerüst framework
gerufene Adresse called address
gerufene Station called station
gerundet rounded off
gesammelt schreiben gather write
gesamt overall
Gesamtabrechnungsdatei summary account file
Gesamtabzug total deduction
Gesamtanschaffungswert total acquisition value
Gesamtantwortverzug overall response delay
Gesamtanzahl absolute number, total, total number
Gesamtanzeige complete display
Gesamtaufbau total structure
Gesamtauftrag complete sales order
Gesamtauftragswert complete order value
Gesamtbasismenge complete base quantity
Gesamtbeleg complete voucher
Gesamtbestand complete inventory, total stocks
Gesamtdarstellung overall display
Gesamtdatei entire file
Gesamtdateigröße total file size
Gesamtergebnis end result
Gesamtfracht complete freight
Gesamtfrachtkosten total freight charges
Gesamtgewicht total weight
Gesamtgröße total volume
Gesamtkapazität total capacity
Gesamtkonfiguration total configuration

Gesamtkonzept overall concept, philosophy, strategy
Gesamtkonzeption philosophy
Gesamtlänge total length
Gesamtlauf complete run
Gesamtlieferschein complete delivery note
Gesamtmenge total quantity
Gesamtmenü total menu
Gesamtnachricht total message
Gesamtnettowert total net value
Gesamtobligo total liability
Gesamtprojekt overall project
Gesamtrabatt overall discount
Gesamtrabattkennzeichen overall discount flag
Gesamtrechnungsrabatt overall invoice discount
Gesamtsaldo total balance
Gesamtschema der Datenbank scheme
Gesamtschlüssel full key
Gesamtsimulationswert overall simulation value
Gesamtskonto total account
Gesamtspeicher total memory
Gesamtsumme grand total, total
Gesamtsystem overall system, total system
Gesamttext complete text
Gesamtübersicht total summary
Gesamtübertragungsrate total transfer rate
Gesamtumsatz total sales
Gesamtverbrauchswert total value consumed
Gesamtverstärkung system gain
Gesamtwert total value
Gesamtzahl absolute number, total, total number
Gesamtzeilenlänge total line length
Gesamtzuweisung total allocation
geschachtelte Sprunganweisung nesting jump instruction
geschachtelte Sprungfunktion nesting jump function
Geschäft business
geschäftlich business
Geschäfts- business, financial
Geschäftsbedingungen terms and conditions
Geschäftsbereich business division, division
Geschäftsbereichsaufteilung divisional organisation
Geschäftsbereichsebene business division level
Geschäftsbereichskennzeichen divisional code
Geschäftsbereichs-Konsolidierung consolidation of divisions
Geschäftsbereichskontierung divisional posting
Geschäftsbereichsumsätze divisional turnover
Geschäftsbericht financial report
Geschäftsgrafik business graphics
Geschäftsjahr financial year, fiscal year
geschäftsjahresabhängig dependent on financial year
Geschäftsjahresende end of financial year
Geschäftsjahreswechsel end of financial year
Geschäftskonto company account
Geschäftsmonat financial month
Geschäftspartner business partner
Geschäftsstelle local digital sales office, local office
Geschäftsvorfall business transaction
Geschick skill
geschickt skilful
geschlossene Benutzergruppe closed user group
geschlossene Teilnehmerbetriebsklasse closed user group
geschützt protected
geschützte elektrische Einrichtung protected electrical equipment
geschützter Motor protected motor
geschützte Unterstreichung underline protected
geschweifte Klammer brace, curly brace
Geschwindigkeit performance, rate, speed, velocity
Geschwindigkeitsklasse class of data signaling rates
Geschwindigkeitsmessung measuring of performance
Geschwindigkeitsregelung speed control, velocity control
Gesellschaft community, company, society
Gesellschafterkonto company account
Gesetz law
Gesetzgeber law
gesetzlich legal
gesetzlich geschützt proprietory
gesichert safe
gesichertes Übermittlungsverfahren safeguarded transmission mode
gesicherte Systemverbindung data link connection
Gesichtspunkt aspect, point
gesondert separate
gespeicherte Meldungen stored messages
gesperrt disabled
gesperrte Datei locked file
gesperrt-ungesperrt blocked-unblocked, locked-unlocked

gespiegelte Platte mirror disk
Gestalt aspect
gestatten allow
Gestell rack
Gestellrahmen rackmount
Gestellschrank cabinet
gesteuert controlled
gestreut lesen scatter read
gestrichelte Linie dashed line
geteilter Bildschirm split screen
getestetes System system under test
Getriebesäule gear column
Get-Unterprogramm get subroutine
gewähltes Laufwerk selected drive
gewählte Zeile chosen line, selected line
Gewähr guarantee, liability
gewähren grant
gewährleisten guarantee
Gewährleistung guarantee, liability
Gewährung allowance
Gewerbesteuer excise tax
Gewinn profit
Gewinnermittlung profit accounting
Gewinnkonto profit account
Gewinnrechnung profit calculation
Gewinn- und Verlustrechnung profit and loss
gewöhnlicher Verweis inclusive reference
Gezeitenkraftwerk tidal power station
gezielt aimed, deliberate
Gigabyte gigabyte
Giro-Buchungszeile giro posting line
Gitterableitwiderstand grid leak resistor
Gitterbasisschaltung grounded grid circuit
Gitterspannung grid voltage
Glättungsfaktor smoothing factor
Glasfaseroptik fibre optics
glasfaseroptisch fibre optique
gleich equal, equal to, same
gleichartig similar
gleichberechtigter Spontanbetrieb asynchronous balanced mode
gleichermaßen equally
Gleichheitszeichen equal sign
Gleichlaufzustand ganged condition, synchronous mode
gleichlautend identical
gleichmäßig even
Gleichpolgenerator homopolar generator
Gleichpolmaschine homopolar machine
Gleichpolmotor homopolar motor
Gleichrichter rectifier
Gleichrichterdiode rectifier diode
Gleichrichterröhre rectifier tube

Gleichrichterstation rectifier substation
Gleichrichter-Transformator rectifier transformer
gleichsetzen equate
Gleichstrom direct current
Gleichstromanteil DC component
Gleichstromgenerator direct current generator
Gleichstrom-Leistungsübetragung direct current power transmission
Gleichstrommaschine direct current machine
Gleichstrommotor direct current motor
Gleichstrom-Transformator direct current transformer
Gleichstromverstärker direct current amplifier
Gleichstromwiderstand direct current resistance
Gleichung equation
Gleichverbindung equijoin
gleichzeitig simultaneous
gleichzeitiger direkter Speicherzugriff shared direct memory access
gleiten float, glide, slide
Gleitkomma floating decimal, floating point
Gleitkommaadapter floating point adapter
Gleitkommaarithmetik floating point arithmetic
Gleitkommaautomatik floating decimal
Gleitkommabefehl floating point instruction
Gleitkommadarstellung floating point representation
Gleitkommaeinheit floating point unit
Gleitkommaeinrichtung floating point availability
Gleitkommamultiplikation floating point multiplication
Gleitkommaoperation floating point operation
Gleitkommaprozessor floating point processor
Gleitkommarechnung floating point computation
Gleitkommaroutine floating point routine
Gleitkommaschreibweise floating point representation
Gleitkommawort floating point word
Gleitkommazahl floating point number, floating print number
Gleitpunktarithmetik floating point arithmetic
Gleitpunktarithmetik mit doppelter Genauigkeit extended precision floating point
Gleitpunktdarstellung floating point representation
Glied element
Gliederung classification

Gliederungsprinzip classification principle
Gliederungspunkt classification point
Gliederungsschema classification scheme
Gliederungsschlüssel classifier
Glimmentladungsröhre glow discharge tube
Glimmer mica
Glimmerkondensator mica capacitor
Glimmodulationsröhre glow modulator tube
Glimmrelaisröhre trigger tube
global global
Globalanzeige global display
globaler Abschnitt global section
globale Servicefunktion global user service task
globales Suchen global search
globales Suchen und Ersetzen global search and replace
globales Symbol global symbol
globale Symboltabelle global symbol table
Globalformat global format
Glocke bell
Glockenisolator bell shaped insulator
Glossar glossary
Glühbirne light bulb
Glühkathode hot cathode
Glühkathodengleichrichter thermionic rectifier
Glühlampe incandescent lamp, light bulb
Grad degree
Grad der elektrischen Sicherheit degree of electrical protection
Grafik chart, graphics
Grafikanzeige graphic display
Grafikbetrieb graphic mode
Grafik-Betriebssystem graphics operating system
Grafikdrucker graphics printer
Grafikdruckverhältnis graphics aspect ratio
Grafikeditor graphic editor
Grafikfenster viewport
Grafikmodus graphics mode
Grafiksonderzeichen special graphics
Grafiksymbol graphic symbol, icon
Grafikzeichen graphic character, graphics character
grafisch graphic
grafische Anzeige graphic display
grafische Darstellung graphic rendition, graphic representation
grafische Darstellung wählen select graphic rendition
Graphik graph
Graphik-Arbeitsstation graphics workstation
Graphik-Workstation graphics workstation

gratis at no charge
Grauskala grey scale
Gravierung engraving
Gray-Code gray code
Grenzbereich frontier
Grenzbetrag limit amount, marginal amount
Grenze border, boundary, limit
Grenzfarbe border color
Grenzposition boundary position
Grenzprüfung marginal test
Grenzschalter limit switch
Grenzwert limit, threshold
Grenzwertfehler boundary error
griechischer Buchstabe greek character
Griff grip, handle
grob coarse
Grobeinsteller coarse control
Grobstruktur draft outline
Grobtakt raw clock
Größe scale, size
Größengeneration entity relation
Größenordnung magnitude, scale
größer als arithmetic greater than, greater than
größer oder gleich greater than or equal
größter gemeinsamer Teiler greatest common divisor
Größtintegration very large scale integration
Groß- bulk, mass
groß big, great, large
Großbestellung bulk order
Großbuchstabe capital letter, upper case letter
große Packungsdichte compact packaging
Großkernspeicher large core memory
Groß-/Kleinschreibung case
Groß-/Kleinschrift upper/lower case
Großmaschine large machine
Großmodul large scale module
Großrechenanlage large computer installation, mainframe, mainframe computer
Großrechner mainframe, mainframe computer
Großschreibung capitalization, upper case
Großschrift upper case
Groß- und Kleinschreibung upper and lower case, upper and lower case printing
großzügig generous
Grund reason
Grundbestandteil basic element
Grundbuch land register
Grundbucheintrag land register entry
Grunddaten basic data
Grunddatenverwaltung management of basic data
Grundeinheit basic unit

Grundfarbe basic colour
Grundfunktion basic function
Grundfunktionen basics
Grundgebühr basic charge
Grundgenerierung basic generation
Grundkosten basic costs
Grundlage basis
Grundlagen basics
grundlegend basic
grundlegender Programmschritt basic program step
grundlegendes Ein-/Ausgabesystem basic input/output system
Grundmodul basic module
Grundplatte base, base plate, chassis
Grundrahmen chassis
Grundregel basic rule
grundsätzlich as a basic principle, basic
Grundsoftware basic software
Grundstellung home position
Grundstellung Blattanfang home paper position
Grundstellungsschalter clear switch
Grundsteuertaste basic control key
Grundstück plot
Grundstücksdaten plot data
Grundsystem basic system
Grundtabelle basic table
Grundtransportfähigkeit basic transport capability
Grundübersicht basic listing
Grundversion basic version
Grundwert basic value
Gruppe bank, cluster, gang, group, set
Gruppe gemeinsamer Ereignismarkierung common event flag cluster
Gruppenadresse group address
Gruppenanfang beginning of group
Gruppen-Anfangsroutine group start routine
Gruppenangabe group specification
Gruppenanzeige group indicator
Gruppenbegriffsfeld control field
gruppenbezogen group related
gruppencodierte Datenaufzeichnung group coded recording
Gruppen-Ende-Routine group end routine
Gruppenfeld group field
Gruppenfeldbezeichnung group field description
Gruppenkarte group card
Gruppenkennung group identification, identification
Gruppenkontendatei group account file
Gruppenkontenliste group account list
Gruppenkonto group account
Gruppenleiter group leader
Gruppenmenü group menu
Gruppenmerkmal group identifier, qualifier
Gruppennummer group number
Gruppenschalter group selector
Gruppenschlüssel group key
Gruppenselektion group selection
Gruppenspezifikation group specification
Gruppenstufe control level, group level
Gruppenstufenbezugszahl control indicator, control level indicator
Gruppenstufenmerkmal level identifier
Gruppenstufenwechsel control break
Gruppensumme group total
Gruppentabelle group table
Gruppenverarbeitung group processing
Gruppenverwaltung group management
Gruppenwechsel control break, group control change
Gruppenwechselschrift group encoded recording
Gruppe von Ereignismarkierungen event flag cluster
gruppieren group
Grußabschnitt greeting paragraph
gültig valid
gültiger Zeitabschnitt valid time period
gültige Speicheradresse valid memory address
gültige Zeit valid time
Gültigkeit validity
Gültigkeitsbit validate bit
Gültigkeitsdatum date effective
Gültigkeitsdauer validity period
Gültigkeits-Kennzeichen validity feature
Gültigkeitsprüfung validation
Gültigkeitszeitraum validity period
Güte quality
Güter goods
gummiisoliert rubber insulated
Gummistecker rubber plug
Gunn-Diode gunn diode
Gutschrift credit note
Gutschriftsankündigung credit note advice
Gutschriftsart credit note type
Gutschriftsmenge credit note quantity
Gutschriftssumme credit note total
Gutschriftswert credit note value

H

Habenbuchung credit posting
Habenkennzeichen credit marker
Habenkonto credit account
Habenposten credit item
Habensaldo credit balance
Habensumme credit sum, credit total
Habenzeichen credit symbol
händisch manual
Händler distributor
Hängeisolator suspension insulator
häufig frequent
Häufigkeit frequency
Häufigkeitsdichte frequency density
Häufigkeitsverteilung frequency distribution
häufigst most frequent
haften adhere
Hafttabulator latch out tabulator
Haftung auf Schadensersatz liability for damages
halb half
Halbaddierer half adder
halbautomatisches System semiautomatic system
Halbbyte nibble
Halbduplex half duplex
Halbduplexbetrieb half duplex operation
halbgeschlossenes System semi-closed system
Halbglied half section
halbhell medium bright
halbieren bisect
halbjährlich half yearly
Halbleiter semiconductor
Halbleiterbauelement semiconductor device
Halbleiterdiode semiconductor diode
Halbleitergleichrichter semiconductor rectifier
Halbleiterkristall chip
Halbleitermodulator semiconductor modulator
Halbleiterrelais semiconductor relay, solid state relay
Halbleiterschalter semiconductor switch
Halbleiterspeicher semiconductor storage
Halbleitertechnologie semiconductor technology
Halbleiterverstärker semiconductor amplifier
Halbleiterwiderstand semiconductor resistor
Halbpunktzahlenverteiler half time digit emitter
Halbschrittaste half space key

Halbsubtrahierer half subtractor
Halbwort half word
Halbzeug semi-finished material
Halt grip, halt, stop
Haltbarkeit durability
Halteadresse stop address
Haltebügel retainer bracket
Haltemarkierung breakpoint
halten hold, keep, retain
Haltepunkt breakpoint
Haltering grip ring
Halterung holder
Halteschaltung holding circuit
Haltesperre holding interlock
Haltewarteschlange hold queue
Haltezeit holding time
Haltung attitude
Hamming-Abstand hamming distance, signal distance
Hamming Code hamming code
Handbuch documentation, handbook, manual
Handeingabegerät manual input device
Handeinstellsystem manual control system
Handel commerce, trade, trading
handeln trade
Handelsbezeichnung trade name
Handelsbilanz commercial balance sheet
Handelsrecht commercial law
handelsrechtlich commercial law
handelsübliche Qualität merchantability
Handelsware merchandise
Handelswaren commodities
Handgriff handle
handhaben handle, operate
Handhabung handling
Handler handler
handlich easy to use
Handsignal hand signal
Handsteuergerät manual positioning remote control
Handtaster handswitch, shock wave release handswitch
Handtaster für Stoßwellenauslösung shock wave release handswitch
Handvermittlungsnetz manual network
Hantierer handler
Hantierung manipulation
Hardcopy hardcopy
Hardware computer hardware, hardware, physical device
hardwareabhängig depending on hardware, hardware specific

Hardware-Betriebsbereitschaftsmeldung hardware confidence message
Hardwarefehler hardware error, hardware failure
Hardware-Fehlerbeseitigungssystem hardware error recovery system
Hardwarefehlermeldung hardware initiated error message
Hardware-Kompatibilität hardware compatibility
hardwaremäßige Verteilung der Daten externally specified index
hardwaremäßig nach Prioritäten gesteuerte Unterbrechung hardware priority interrupt
Hardwaremeldung hardware message
hardwarenaher Zugriff physical access
Hardware Service und Diagnose Handbuch hardware maintenance and service manual
Hardwareübersicht hardware overview
Hardwareumrüstung hardware conversion
hardwareunterstützt hardware supported
Hardwarewartung hardware maintenance
Hardwarezugriff physical access
Hardwarezusätze additional hardware
harmlos harmless
Harmonisierungsprotokoll enhancement protocol
hart formatieren hard format
hartgezogener Draht hardwire
hartlöten braze
hartsektoriert hard sectored
Hash-Bibliothek hash algorithm library
Haupt- main, master
Hauptaufgabe main task
Hauptauswahl main selection
Hauptbeleg main voucher
Hauptbelegkopf main voucher head
Hauptbelegposition main voucher item
Hauptbetriebsart basic mode
Hauptbibliothek main library
Hauptbild main screen
Hauptbuch general ledger
Hauptbuchhaltung general ledger accounting
Hauptbuchkontenbereich general ledger account area
Hauptbuchkontengruppe general ledger account group
Hauptbuchkontenschlüssel general ledger account code
Hauptbuchkonto general ledger account
Hauptbuchschreibung general ledger posting
Hauptbuchsonderkonto general ledger special account
Hauptbuchung general ledger posting
Hauptbuchverbindlichkeit general ledger liability
Hauptdatei main file, master file
Hauptdateikatalog master file directory
Hauptdateiverzeichnis master directory, master file directory
Haupteinfahrt gateway
Hauptfehlersuche und -behebung basic troubleshooting
Hauptfeld main field
Hauptfunktionseinheit major component
Hauptkanal forward channel
Hauptkarte master card
Hauptkomponente main component
Hauptkonsole main station
Hauptkontensystem master account system
Hauptkonto master account
Hauptkontonummer master account number
Hauptkostenstelle main cost centre
Hauptlager main warehouse
Hauptmenü main command menu, main menu, master menu
Hauptmodul main module
Hauptmodus main mode
Hauptnummer main number
Hauptoberbegriff main header
Hauptordnungsbegriff primary header, primary key
Hauptplatine main board
Hauptprogramm main program
Hauptprotokolldatei master log file, master long file
Hauptprozessor master processor
Hauptpuffer main buffer
Hauptrechner central processor
Hauptsatz master record
Hauptschalter master control
Hauptschlüssel main key, master key
Hauptspeicher central memory, core memory, main memory, main storage, main storage unit, main store, memory, primary storage
Hauptspeicheranforderung main memory request
Hauptspeicheranschlußeinheit main storage interface facility
Hauptspeicherauszug main memory extract, map, memory map
Hauptspeicherbank main storage unit bank
Hauptspeicherbereich main memory area
Hauptspeichereinheit mass storage unit

Hierarchieverdichtung

Hauptspeichererweiterung main memory extension
Hauptspeicherpartition main storage partition
Hauptspeicherregister main memory register
Hauptspeicherreorganisation main storage consolidation service
Hauptspeichertabelle main memory table
Hauptspeicherzugriffseinheit main storage processor
Hauptsprache host language
Hauptstation master station
Hauptsteuereinheit basic control unit
Hauptsteuerrelais master control relay
Hauptsteuerung master control
Haupttaktgeber master clock
Haupttastatur main keyboard, main keypad
Haupttastenblock main keyboard, main keypad
Hauptumsatzträger mainstay of sales
Haus house
hauseigen internal
hausintern in house
Hausnummer house number
Haussprache house language
HDDR-Verfahren high density digital magnetic recording
HDLC-Protokoll HDLC protocol
HDLC-Steuerung high level data link control
Heap-Überlauf heap overflow
Hebel lever
heben lift
hebräisches Zeichen Hebraic character
Heizstromversorgung filament power supply
Hektoschreiber hektowriter
helfen facilitate
hell bright, light
heller Bildschirm light screen
helles Kobaltblau light cyan
helleuchtend highlighted
hellgetastet unblanked
Helligkeit brightness
Helligkeitsanzeige brilliance
Helligkeitsgrad brightness
Helligkeitsregler brightness control
Helligkeitsregulierung brightness adjustment
Help help
Helpaufruf help call
Helpfunktion help function
heranziehen use
herausfallen drop out
herausfordern challenge
hereinführende Leitung inbound line, incoming line
hereinlesen read in
herkömmlich conventional
Herkunft origin
Herkunftsdatei from filename
Herkunftszertifikat certificate of origin
Herkunftszeugnis certificate of origin
hermetisch gekapselter Transformator hermetically sealed transformer
herstellen manufacture, produce
Hersteller manufacturer
Herstellersoftware manufacturer software
herstellerunabhängig manufacturer independent, producer independent, third party
Hersteller von Fremdfabrikaten original equipment manufacturer
Hersteller von steckerkompatiblen Geräten plug compatible manufacturer
Herstellkosten manufacturing costs
Herstellung production
Herstellung in Mehrschichttechnik multilayer fabrication, multilayer production
Herstellungsverfahren manufacturing method, manufacturing process
Hertz Hertz
Hertz'sche Linie Hertzian line
herunterfahren shutdown
herunterzählen count down, decrement
hervorgehobenes Zeichen bold face character
hervorheben emphasize, highlight, point out
Hervorheben von Text emphasizing text
hervorragend outstanding
hervorrufen cause
Herzkurve cardioid
Hexadezimal hexadecimal
hexadezimal hexadecimal
Hexadezimalcode hexadecimal code
Hexadezimaldarstellung hexadecimal representation
hexadezimales Zahlensystem hexadecimal number system
Hexadezimaltaste hexadecimal key
Hexadezimalverschlüsselung hexadecimal code
Hexadezimalzahl hexadecimal number
Hexadezimalzeichen hexadecimal character
Hexanzeige hex display
Hexverschlüsselung hexadecimal code
Hexzahl hexadecimal number
Hierarchie hierarchy
Hierarchieanzeige hierarchy display
Hierarchiebericht hierarchy report
Hierarchieebene hierarchy level
Hierarchienummer hierarchy number
Hierarchieverdichtung hierarchical compression

High hi
Hilfe aid, help
Hilfeaufruf help call
Hilfe bei schwerwiegenden Fehlern fatal error help
Hilfebibliothek help library
Hilfedatei help file
Hilfefunktion help function
Hilfemeldung help message
Hilfeseite help page
Hilfetext help frame, help text
Hilfezeile help line
Hilfs- auxiliary, temporary
Hilfsanzeige help screen
Hilfsausrüstung auxiliary equipment
Hilfsbeleg subsidiary voucher
Hilfsbildschirm slave monitor
Hilfsdatei auxiliary file
Hilfsduplizieren auxiliary duplication
Hilfselektromotor electric servomotor
Hilfsfeld auxiliary field
Hilfsfunktion auxiliary function
Hilfskanal backward channel, reverse channel
Hilfskontakt auxiliary contactor
Hilfsmerker auxiliary label
Hilfsmittel aid
Hilfsmotor servomotor
Hilfsprogramm auxiliary program, auxiliary routine, utility program
Hilfsregister auxiliary register, utility register
Hilfsspeicher auxiliary storage, auxiliary store
Hilfssteuerprozeß auxiliary control process
Hilfstext supplementary text
Hilfstoffe auxiliary supplies
Hilfszelle auxiliary cell
Hilfsziffer guard digit
hinaufziehen draw up
hinausgehen go out
hindern inhibit
hineinstellen put into
hinsichtlich concerning
Hinterbandkontrolle read after write
hintereinander consecutive
Hintereinanderschaltung daisy chain
hinterer rear
Hintergrund background
Hintergrund-Bildschirm background screen
Hintergrundfarbe background color
Hintergrundmodus anhalten halt background mode
Hintergrundtask batch slot
Hintergrundverarbeitung background processing

Hintergrundverarbeitungsabschnitt batch slot
hinwegziehen pull
Hinweis advice, clue, hint, information
Hinweisaktion informative message
hinweisen indicate, point
hinweisen auf point out
Hinweisgabe advice
Hinweisliste information list
Hinweismeldung reference message
Hinzufügemodus add mode
hinzufügen add, append, attach, insert
hinzutreten include
Histogrammrechner histogram computer
Historieauswertung history report
hoch high
hochauflösend high resolution
hochauflösende Farbgrafik high resolution color graphics
hochentwickelt sophisticated
hochfahren startup
Hochformat portrait, portrait format
Hochfrequenz high frequency
Hochfrequenztransformator high frequency transformer
Hochfrequenzverstärker high frequency amplifier, radiofrequency amplifier, radio-frequency signal amplifier
Hochgeschwindigkeit high speed
Hochgeschwindigkeitscode high speed code
Hochgeschwindigkeits-CPU ultra fast cpu
Hochgeschwindigkeitsmaschine high speed machine
Hochgeschwindigkeitspuffer high speed buffer
Hochgeschwindigkeits-Rechenwerk high speed arithmetic unit
Hochgeschwindigkeitsspeicher high speed memory
hochgestelltes Zeichen superscript
hochgradig highly
hochindizieren index
hochindiziert superscript
Hochintegrationstechnik large scale integration
hochintegriert large scale integration
Hochkomma apostrophe, single quote
Hochkommata quotation marks
Hochleistungs- high performance
Hochleistungsrechner high performance computer
hochohmig high impedance
Hochpassfilter high pass filter
hochrechnen extrapolate
Hochrechnung extrapolation
Hochspannungsgeräte high voltage equipment

Hochspannungsinstallation high voltage installation
Hochsprache high level language
Hochstellung superscript
Hochzahl superscript
Höchstbestand maximum stock
höchstwertig most significant
höchstwertige Bit most significant bit
höchstwertiges Bit most significant bit
Höhe height
höhere Programmiersprache high level language
höherwertiger more significant
Hörkapsel earphone
hohe Auflösung high resolution
hohe Aufzeichnungsdichte high density
hohe Dichte high density
hohe Rechengeschwindigkeit high speed computation
hohe Schreibdichte high density
holen fetch, get
Hollerithlängenfaktor Hollerith width
homogen homogeneous
Honorar fee
horizontaler Tabulator horizontal tab
horizontaler Titel horizontal title
horizontale Steuerung horizontal drive
horizontale und vertikale Position horizontal and vertical position
Horizontaltabulator horizontal tab
Horizontaltabulatoren horizontal tabulation set
Horizontaltabuliertaste horizontal tabulator key
Hostrechner host, host computer, remote system
hot back-up hot back-up
Hybridrechner hybrid computer
Hybridstation combined station
hydraulisches Steuergerät hydraulic control equipment
hydraulische Steuerung hydraulic control system
Hypothek mortgage
Hysteresemotor hysteresis motor

I

Idealfall ideal case
Idenfikation identifier
Identifikation id, identification
Identifikationsablauf identification process
Identifikationsblock identifier block
Identifikationsdatei identification file
Identifikationsdaten identification data
Identifikationsmeldung identification message
Identifikationsmerkmal identifier
Identifikationsnummer id number, identification number
Identifikationstabelle identification table
Identifikationsvorschlag identification proposal
identifizieren identify
identisch identical
if-then-else if-then-else
ignorieren ignore
Ikonozentrum iconocenter
illegal illegal
im Ablauf in progress
im Einzelschritt step by step
im Ganzteil einer Zahl in front of the decimal point
im Gegenuhrzeigersinn counterclockwise
im laufenden Betrieb during operation
im Nebenschluß anlegen shunt
im Onlinebetrieb online
Impact-Drucker impact printer
IMPATT Diode impatt diode
Impedanz impedance
Impedanzschalter impedance switch
Implementation implementation
Implementationshinweis implementation aid
Implementationsphase implementation phase
Implementationsunterstützung implementation support
implementieren implement
Implementierung implementation
implizit implicit
implizite Matrix implicit array
impliziter Jobstart implicit job startup
importieren import
Impressum imprint
Impuls pulse, step
Impulsantwort step response
Impulsbreite pulse with
Impulsebene signal level
Impulse pro Sekunde pulses per second
Impulsfolge pulse train
Impulsgenerator pulse generator
Impulsmodulationsröhre pulse modulator tube
Impulsperiode pulse period
Impulsregenerationsschaltung pulse regenerating circuit
Impulstransformator pulse transformer
Impulsverstärker pulse amplifier
Impulswahl pulse dialling, rotary
Impulswahlverfahren pulse dialling, rotary
im Realtimebetrieb benutzte gemeinsame Bank realtime common bank
im Regelfall as a rule
im Ruhezustand nonoperative
im Ruhezustand geöffnet normally open
im Ruhezustand geschlossen normally closed
im Uhrzeigersinn clockwise
inaktiv inactive
in Ausgangsstellung bringen master clear
in beide Richtungen betriebene optische Verbindung bi-directional optical link
Inbetriebnahme activation, line up
in Beziehung setzen set relation
in Bezug auf referencing, regarding
in Bezug stehen correlate
inclusiv inclusive
in den Ausgangsmodus zurücksetzen reset, reset to initial state
Index index, subscript
Indexart index type
Indexbaumbeschreibung index tree description
Indexblockkennung index block identifier
Indexdatei index file
indexdirekte Zugriffsmethode indexed random access method
Indexebene index level
Indexfaktor subscript modifier
Indexgröße subscript value
Indexklinke index pawl
Indexloch index hole
Indexmarke index marker
Indexmarkenzähler extraction counter
Indexmatrixvergleich index matrix compare
Indexöffnung index hole
Indexparameter index parameter
Indexregister index register
Indexregisterbefehl indexing instruction
Indexregisterstelle marker
Indexreihe index row
Indexreihenschlüssel index row key
Indexsatz index record
indexsequentiell index sequential, logical sequence

indexsequentielle Datei index sequential file
indexsequentielle Dateistruktur indexed file organisation
indexsequentielle Zugriffmethode indexed sequential access method
indexsequentielle Zugriffsdatei indexed sequential access file
Indexspur index track
Indextabelle index table
Indexteil index section
Index zur Rekonstruktion tracking index
Indikator indicator
indirekt indirect
indirekte Adressierung indirect addressing
indirekte Datei indirect file
indirekte Dateispezifikation indirect file
indirekte interne Programmfolgesteuerung delayed internal succession
indirekte Kommandodatei indirect command file
indirekt geheizte Kathode indirectly heated cathode
Individuallösung individual conception
Individualtext individual text
individuell individual
indizieren index
indiziert indexed, keyed
indizierte Datei indexed file, key-type file, keyfile
indizierte Direktzugriffsdatei indexed random access file
indizierte Variable subscripted variable
Induktionsgenerator induction generator, inductor generator
Induktionsmaschine induction machine, inductor machine
Induktionsmotor induction motor
Induktions-Spannungsregler induction voltage regulator
induktiver Näherungsschalter inductive proximity switch
Induktivität inductor
Industrie industry
Industriebetrieb industrial company
industrielle Steuerung industrial control, industrial control application
Industriesteuerung industrial control
Industriesteuerungsprotokoll manufacturing automation protocol
ineinandergreifen interact
in einer Richtung wirkend unidirectional
Infodatei info file
Information information

Informationsausgabe information output
Informationsanbieter information provider, information supplier
Informationsanbieterformat information supplier format
Informationsangebot information offer
Informationsanzeige information indication
Informationsanzeigeplaner information display planner
Informationsarbeitsdatei information work file
Informationsbasis information basis
Informationsbereich information area
Informationsbeziehung information relation
Informationscode information code
Informationsdarstellung data representation, information representation
Informationsdatei information file
Informationsdateienbenutzer information file user
Informationsdaten information data
Informationsdurchsatz throughput
Informationsebene information level
Informationserschließung information retrieval
Informationsfluß information flow
Informationsgehalt information content
Informationsgewinnung acquisition of information
Informationsgrundeinheit basic information unit
Informationshierarchie information hierarchy
Informationsinhalt information content
Informationslänge information length
Informationslücke information gap
Informations-Management-System information management system
Informationssatz information record
Informationsschwerpunkt concentration of information
Informationssegment information segment
Informationsseite information page
Informationsselektion information selection
Informationsspeicherung und -gewinnung information storage and retrieval
Informationsstrukturierung structuring of information
Informationssystem information system
Informationssystem für Agrikultur Ökologie und Geographie agricultural ecological and geographical information system
Informationstechnik information technology
Informationstechnologie information technology
Informationsumfang range of information

informationsverarbeitendes System information processing system
Informationsverbindung connection of information
Informationsverdichtung compression of information
Informationsverwaltungssystem information management software
Informationswert information value
Informationszeile information line
informativ informative
informieren inform
Infosatz info record
Infotext info text
infrarot infrared
Ingenieur engineer
in Gründung in formation
Inhalt contents
Inhalt einer Datei contents of file
Inhaltsverzeichnis contents, directory, table of contents
inhouse in house
Inhouse-System in house system
Inhouse-Tabelle in house table
initial initial
Initialfortsetzungswert für Datei initial file continuation value
Initialisation startup
initialisieren initialize, initiate
Initialisierung initialization, initializing
Initialisierungsdaten initialization data
Initialisierungsmodus initialization mode
Initialisierungsmuster initialization pattern
Initialisierungsphase initialization phase
Initialisierungsprozeß initialization process
Initialisierungsroutine initialization routine
Initialisierungsstart cold start
Initialisierungs- und Dienstprogramm initializer and utility
Initialisierungswert startup value
Initialsatz initial record layout
Initialsatzbett initial record layout
Initialschlüsselwort initial keyword
Initialwert initial value
Inkasso collection
Inkassogebühr collection fee
in Klassen einteilen categorize
inkompatibel incompatible
Inkrafttreten coming into force
Inkrement increment
Inkrementalkodierer incremental encoder
inkrementieren increment
Inlandsverbindung domestic connection

Inline-Transducer inline transducer
Innensechskantschraube Allen screw
innere Datenverarbeitung internal data processing
innerhalb geschlossener Räume indoor
in Reihe geschaltete Kontakte series contact
in sich definiert selfdefined
Inspektion inspection
Inspektionskennzeichen inspection marker
Installation electrical installation, installation, site
Installationsanweisung installation guide, installation instruction
Installationshandbuch installation guide, installation manual
Installationshandbuch der Festplatte hard disk installation guide
Installationshandbuch des Druckers printer installation manual
Installationsprozedur installation procedure
Installationsrohr electric conduit
Installationsvorgang installation procedure
installieren install
Installieren des Systems startup procedure
Installierung installation
Instandhaltung maintenance
Instanz entity
Institut institute
Instruktion instruction
intakt intact
integral integral
Integralmodem integral modem
Integrationsfähigkeit integration ability
Integrationsgrad degree of integration
Integrationsstufe integration level
integrierbar integrable
integrieren integrate
integrierte Analogschaltung analog integrated circuit
integrierte Datenübertragungsanschluß- einrichtung integrated communication adapter feater
integrierte Digitalschaltung digital integrated circuit
integrierte Gerätesteuerung integrated peripheral channel
integrierte Hybridschaltung hybrid integrated circuit
integrierte Linearschaltung linear integrated circuit
integrierte Logikschaltung integrated logic circuit

integrierter Mikrowellenbaustein microwave integrated circuit
integrierter Netzwerkprozessor integrated network processor
integrierter Refresh on board refresh
integrierter Schaltkreis integrated circuit
integrierte Schaltung integrated circuit
integriertes Datenübertragungsmodul integrated communication rack
integriertes Modem integrated modem
integrierte Speicherschaltung integrated memory circuit
integriertes Text- und Datennetz integrated text and data network
intelligente Kommunikationsschnittstelle intelligent communications interface
intelligenter Netzwerkprozessor intelligent network processor
intelligenter Sender intelligent transmitter
intelligente Speicherverwaltung intelligent memory manager
intelligentes Terminalsystem intelligent terminal system
intelligente Tastatur intelligent keyboard
Intelligenzebene intelligence layer
intensiv intensive
Intensivanzeige intensified display, intensive display
interaktiv conversational, interactive
interaktive Computergrafik interactive computer graphics
interaktive Dateiverarbeitung interactive file processing
interaktive Datenerfassung interactive data entry
interaktives Terminal interactive terminal
Intercomputer-Kommunikation computer computer communication
Interesse interest
Interessent interested customer, interested party, prospect
interessieren interest
Interface-Schaltung für Fernschreibanschluß teletype interface
Interimskonto suspense account
Interleaving interleaving
intermittierende Übermittlung start-stop transmission
intern internal
international international
internationale Norm international standard
Internationaler Normungsausschuß International Standardization Organization
internationaler Standard international standard
internationales Alphabet international alphabet
internationales Telegrafenalphabet international telegraph alphabet
internationale Tastatur international language keyboard
Internationalisierungswerkzeug multi language tool
interne Bezugszahl internal indicator
interne Bit-Tabelle master bit table
interne Datei internal file
interne logische Set-Ordnung set order
interner Arbeitssatz replay record
interner Ausgang internal output
interner Bus internal bus
interner Code internal code
interner Knoten internal node
interner Kommunikationsschalter internal communication switch
interner Test mit Rückkopplung internal loopback test
interner Wortausgang internal word output
interner Zinsfluß discounted cash flow field
interner Zwischenspeicher level storage
internes Durcharbeiten einer Datei batch relay option
internes Format internal format
internes Kommando internal command
internes Register internal register
internes Steuerbit internal control bit
internes Steuerwort internal control word
interne Tabelle internal table
Interpartitionsverschiebung interpartition-move
Interpreter interpreter
Interpreter-Verwaltungsbereich interpreter administration area, interpreter obsolence area
interpretieren interpret
Interpretierer interpreter
Interrupt interrupt
Interruptadreßregister interrupt address register
Interruptanforderung interrupt request
Interruptbestätigung interrupt acknowledge
Interrupthandler interrupt handler
Interruptmaske interrupt mask
Interruptregister interrupt register
Interruptroutine interrupt service routine
Interrupts Aus interrupts off
Interrupt Service Routine interrupt service routine

337

Interrupt-Stack interrupt stack
Intervall interval
Intervallzeitgeber interval timer
Inventar inventory
Inventarverzeichnis inventory register
Inventur inventory, stocktaking
Inventurabwicklung stocktaking procedure
Inventuraufnahmeprotokoll stocktaking returns
Inventurauswertung inventory analysis
Inventurbeleg stocktaking voucher
Inventurbelegsbuchung stocktaking voucher posting
Inventurbestand inventory result
Inventurbestandsliste inventory result list
Inventurbewertung inventory valuation
Inventurblatt stocktaking sheet
Inventurblattnummer stocktaking sheet number
Inventurdaten stocktaking data
Inventurdatum inventory date
Inventurdifferenz inventory difference, stocktaking discrepancy
Inventurdifferenzliste inventory difference list
Inventureingabedatei inventory entry file
Inventurerfassung stocktaking returns input
inventurmäßig inventorial
Inventurplan inventory schedule
Inventurprogramm inventory program
Inventurtransaktion stocktaking transaction
Inventurvorschlagsliste stocktaking proposal
Inventurzählkontrolle stocktaking
Inventurzählliste stocktaking list
Inventurzeile stocktaking line
invers dargestellt inverted
Inverter inverter
invertieren invert
invertierte Bilddarstellung reverse video
invertierter Bildschirm reverse screen
Investition investment
Investitionsabgabe investment costs
Investitionsanzahlung investment installment
Investitionsbestellung investment order
Investitionsjahr investment year
Investitionsplanung investment budgeting
Investitionszahlung investment payment
Investitionszulage investment premium
Investitionszulagenschlüssel investment premium key
IRAM-Datei iram file
irrtümlich erroneous
ISAM-Schlüssel isam key
ISDN-Fax fax group 4

isochron isochronous
Isochronverzerrungsgrad degree of isochronous distortion
Isolationsmaterial electrical insulation material
Isolator electrical insulation device
isolierend nonconducting
isolierendes Substrat insulating substrate
Isolierfilm insulating film
Isoliermaterial insulating material
Isoliermatte electrical insulation mat
Isolieröl insulating oil
Isolierpapier electrical insulation paper
Isolierscheibe electrically insulated bushing
Isolierschicht insulating coating
Isolierstoff electric insulator, insulating material
isolierte Durchführung grommet
isolierter Draht insulated wire
isoliertes Datenkabel shielded signal cable
isoliertes Gehäuse insulating enclosure
isoliertes Kabel insulated cable
Isoliertransformator isolating transformer, isolation transformer
Isolierung electric insulator, electrical insulation
ISO-Zeichen iso character
Ist-Bestand actual result, actual stock
Ist-Betrag actual amount
Ist-Daten actual data
Ist-Eindeckungszeit actual availability time
Ist-Koordinate actual coordinate
Ist-Lagerbestand actual stock on hand
Ist-Menge actual quantity
Ist-Saldo actual balance
Ist-Stand actual count
Ist-Wert actual value
Istwertvorgabe preset actual value
Ist-Zeile actual line
Iteration iteration
Iterationsindex iteration index
Iterationsschleife iteration loop
Iterationszähler iteration count

J

jährlich annual, annually
Jahr year
Jahresabgrenzung annual cut-off
Jahresabschluß year-end closing
Jahresabschlußkurs year-end closing rate
Jahresabschlußprogramm year-end closing program
Jahresabschreibung annual amortization, annual depreciation
Jahresangaben annual details
Jahresbescheinigung annual tax certificate
Jahresbestellwert annual purchase order value
Jahresende year-end
Jahresentwicklung annual development
Jahresergebnis year's result
Jahresergebniskonto year's result account
Jahresfeld year field
Jahreskontenschreibung annual account posting
Jahressaldo year's balance
Jahresstatistik annual statistics
Jahresumsatz annual turnover, year's turnover
Jahresverbrauchswert value consumed in the year
Jahresverkehrszahl year-to-date figure
Jahresverschiebung annual roll-over
Jahreswechsel change of year, year's end
Jahreswechselprogramm year-end program
Jahreszahl year
Jahr (jj) year (yy)
Ja-Nein-Code on off code
Ja-Nein-Kontrolle go-no-go test
je commercial at, per
jederzeit at all times
jedesmal every time
Jitter jitter
jjmmtt (Jahr Monat Tag) yymmdd (year month day)
jjmm (Jahr Monat) yymm (year month)
jj (Jahr) yy (year)
Job job, run
Jobablaufplanung job scheduler, scheduling
Jobabrechnungseinrichtung job accounting facility
Jobabrechungs-Protokollierungseinrichtung job accounting reporting facility
Jobbearbeitung job processing
Jobbereich job region
Jobbetriebsanweisung job control command, job control statement
Jobbetriebssprache job control language
Jobeingabestrom job control stream, job stream, runstream
Jobeinteilung job classification
Jobfernstart job remote initiation, remote job initiation
Job-Informationsvorspann Kopfzeile header
Jobkasten job box
Jobkennung run identification
Jobname job name, run identification
Jobnummer entry number
Jobschritt job step
Jobschrittsteuerung job step control, job step initializer
Jobsteuerungsdialog job control dialog
Jobtabellenplatz job slot
Jobtabellenplatznummer job slot number
Jobverarbeitungssteuerung job shop system control, run processing
Jobverteilungsprozessor job distribution facility, job distribution processor, job transfer facility
Josephson-Element josephson junction
Journal daily ledger
Journalart journal type
Journaldatei journal file
Journaldatum journal date, reference date
Journalfernschreiber journal teleprinter
journalisieren enter in the ledger
Joystick joystick
Joystickanschluß game control adapter
juristisch legal
Justiereinheit adjustment unit
Just-in-Time just in time
Just-in-Time Lieferung just in time delivery

K

Kabel cable, connecting cable
Kabelabdeckung cable shield
Kabelabschirmung cable shield
Kabelbinder cable tie, string tie, tie wrap
Kabelfernsehen cable television
Kabelführung cable guide
Kabelmantel cable cover
Kabel mit 50 Adern 50-conductor cable
Kabel mit Klinkenstecker jack plug cable
Kabelöse eyelet
Kabelschuh lug, tab connector
Kabelstecker cable connector
Kabeltext cable text
Kabelverbindung cable junction
Kabelverlauf path for cable
Kältespray coolant spray
Käufer buyer
Kalenderdatum calendar date
Kalendermonat calendar month, month
Kalendertag calendar date, day
Kalenderwoche calendar week
kalibrieren calibrate
Kalibrierstellung calibration position
Kalkulationsbasis basis for costing
Kalkulationsdaten imputed data
Kalkulationsmodell model
Kalkulationsprogramm spreadsheet program
kalkulatorisch imputed
kalt cold, cool
Kaltkathode cold cathode
Kaltkathodenröhre cold cathode tube
Kanal channel, conduit, duct
Kanalabstand channel spacing
Kanaladreßwort channel address word
Kanalaufteiler line splitter
Kanalauswahlregister channel select register
Kanalbefehlswort channel command word
Kanalbelegung channel loading
Kanalbeschreibungstabelle channel descriptor table
Kanalfernsteuerung remote channel controller
Kanalmodul channel module
Kanalnummer channel number
Kanalnummernraum channel numbering scheme
Kanalroutinenschnittstelle communications physical interface
Kanalschalter channel switch

Kanalstatuswort channel status word
Kanalsteuerroutine channel control routine
Kanalsteuerung direct memory access, remote input output control
Kanalteiler channel divider, channel splitter
Kanalverbindung channel connection
Kanal zu Kanal channel to channel
Kanalzustandswort channel status word
Kanneingabe optional entry
Kannfeld optional field
Kannvariable can variable, optional variable
Kansas-City-Standard Kansas City Standard
Kante edge
kantenperforiert edge sprocketed
Kapazität capacity, storage capacity
Kapazitätsberechnung capacity calculation
Kapazitätsparameter capacity parameter
Kapazitätsüberwachung overflow control
Kapitalbindung capital freeze
Kapitalwert present value
Kapitel chapter
Karte board, card, map
Kartenart card type
Kartenaufbau card pattern
Kartenausgabe card output
Kartenbehälter card cage
Kartenbild image, punch image
Kartendopplerroutine reproduce utility routine
Karteneingabe card input
Kartenformat card format
Kartenführung card support bracket
Kartenhalter card holder
Kartenleser card reader
Kartenlocher card punch
Kartenmagazin card cage, card case, hopper
Karten pro Minute cards per minute
Karten pro Sekunde cards per second
Kartensalat card jam
Kartensockel card edge socket
Kartenstanzer card punch
Kartenstapel talon
Kartenstapelende end of card deck, end of deck
Kartenstartadresse card start address
Kartenstau card jam
Kartenstecker card edge socket, edge connector
karthesisches Koordinatensystem cartesian coordinate system
Karton cardboard, carton
Kaskadenumformer motor convertor
Kaskadieren cascading
Kasse register

340

Kassenbeleg cash voucher
Kassensummen-Feld cash totals field
Kassenterminal point of sales terminal
Kassette cartridge, cassette
Kassettenlaufwerk cassette deck
Kassettenrecorder cassette tape recorder
kassettentypisch typical of cartridges
Kasten box
Kastenposition box position
Katalog catalog
Kataloganzeige catalog indicator
Katalogauswahl catalog selection
Katalogbearbeitungsprogramm catalog manipulation program, catalog manipulation utility
Katalogbearbeitungsroutine catalog manipulation routine
Katalogeintrag catalog entry
Kataloginhalt catalog content
katalogisieren catalog
katalogisierte Datei cataloged file
Katalogisierungsfunktion catalog facility
katalogwirksam catalog effective
Kategorie category
Kathode cathode
Kathodenstrahlröhre cathode ray tube
Kathodenverstärker cathode follower
Kauf buy, purchase
Kaufartikel purchase item
kaufen buy, purchase
Kaufpreis purchase price
Kaufsmengeneinheit purchase unit
Kaufteil part to be bought
kByte (Kilobyte) kbyte
Kegel shank
Kegel des Wellenstumpfs shank of the shaft drive pin
Keimzahl integer seed
keine Änderung an der Schnittstelle DTE DCE waiting
keine automatische Paritätsprüfung no forced parity
keine Parität no parity
Kellerspeicher last in - first out, push down storage, stack
Kennbuchstabe marker letter
Kenndaten characteristics
Kennlochung detection punch
Kennummer des Benutzerprozesses owner process identification
kennnzeichnen flag
Kennsatz header, label, volume label
Kennsatzdatei header file

Kennsatzdump header dump
Kennsatzeintrag header entry
Kennsatzfamilie label set
Kennsatzname label identifier, label name
Kennsatznummer label number
Kennsatz-Querverweistabelle label cross reference table
Kennsatzroutine label handling routine
Kennsatztabellen-Ausdruck label table listing
Kennsatztyp label type
Kenntnis knowledge
Kenntnisnahme perusal
Kennummer indicator
Kennung answerback, id, identification, identifier
Kennungsgeber answerback, answerback device
Kennwort password
Kennwortprüfung password test
Kennwortschutz password protection
Kennwort »nur Senden« send only password
Kennzahl code number, identifying number
Kennzeichen flag, marker, qualifier, tag
Kennzeichenbit flag bit
Kennzeichen für Grundformat general format identifier
Kennzeichensortierung tag sort
kennzeichnen designate, identify, mark
Kennzeichner label
Kennzeichnung indication, marking term
Kennzeichnungsbyte flag byte
Kennziffer code digit
Keramikkondensator ceramic capacitor
keramisch ceramic
Kern core, kernel
Kernel-Modus kernel mode
Kernspeicher core, core memory
Kernspeicherauslastung core memory work load
Kernspeicherauszug selective core memory dump
Kernspeicher-Seite core storage surface
Kernspeicherverwaltung organisation of core storage
Kettanker chain header
Kette chain
ketten chain, link
Kettenanfang beginning of a chain, start of chain
kettende Datei chaining file
Kettendrucker chain printer
Kettenmodus-Jobstart chain mode startup
Kettfehler chain error

Kettfeld chain field
Kettsatz member record
Kettsatzzähler component counter, member count
Kettungsanzeige chaining indicator
Kettungsbezugszahl chaining indicator
Kettungsfeld chaining field, link field
Kettungsfeld-Bezugszahl chaining field indicator
Kettungsfeldbezugszahl link field indicator
Kilobaud kilobaud
Kilobyte kilobyte
Kilogramm kilogram
Kilopaket kilopacket
Kilowort kiloword
Kippfenster hinged plastic window
Kippfuß tilt leg
Kippschaltung trigger circuit
Kippständer post
Kiste box, carton
klären clarify, clear
Klärung clarification
klaffen gape
Klammer bracket
Klammeraffe (@) at sign, commercial at
Klang sound
Klangdarstellung sound representation
Klangfarbe timbre
Klangmerkmal sound feature
Klangsystem sound system
Klappe door
Klappe des Diskettenlaufwerks disk drive door
Klappe des Kartenmagazins card cage door, card case door
klar clear, plain
klarmachen point out
Klarschrift plain text
Klarschriftleser character reader, optical character recognition
Klarschriftzeichen optical character
Klartext clear text, plain text
Klartextbezeichnung plain text designation
Klasse category, class
Klasseneinteilung categorization
Klassenkennzeichnung classification
Klassennummer category number
Klassentext category text
Klassifikation classification
Klassifikationsmerkmal classifier
klassifizieren classify
Klassifizierung classification
Klassifizierungsmerkmal classifier

Klassifizierungspunkt classification point
Klassifizierungsschema classifying scheme
klassisch classical
Klausel clause
klein micro, mini, small
Kleinbuchstabe lowercase letter
Kleincomputer small computer
kleiner minor
kleiner als less than
kleiner oder gleich less or equal
Kleinleistungstransformator small power transformer
Kleinlochkarte small punch card
Kleinrechner small computer system
Kleinstbaugruppe micromodule
Klemme clamp, electric terminal, terminal
Klemme des Hilfsmotors servo clamp
Klemmenblock terminal plate
Klemmenleiste terminal block
Klemmfeld patch area, patch panel
Klemmvorrichtung für nichtgelötete Drahtverbindungen solderless connector
Klick click
klicken click
klickendes Geräusch clicking sound
Klient customer
klingeln ring
Klingelzeichen bell
klingen sound
Klinkenbuchse jack plug
Klinkenstecker jack, subminiature phone plug
Klirrfaktor harmonic distortion
Klöppel striker
Klystron klystron
Knopf button
Knoten node
Knoteneinrichtung nodal equipment, node equipment
Knotennetz multipoint network
Knotenvermittlung nodal switching center
koaxial coaxial
Koaxialfilter coaxial filter
Koaxialkabel coaxial cable, coaxial line
Kodeprogrammierung coding programming
Kodierbeispiel coding example
Kodierdiagramm coding diagram
Kodieren encoding
kodieren encode
kodieren/dekodieren encode/decode
Kodierer encoder
Kodiererwelle encoder shaft
Kodierfehler coding error
Kodierformular coding sheet

Kodiermöglichkeit coding possibility
Kodiertabelle coding table
kodierte Darstellung coded representation
kodierter Stecker coded plug, key plug, keyed plug
kodierter Zeichensatz coded character set
Kodierung coding, keying
Kodierung der Funktionstasten keypad key codes
Kodierzeilen-Bearbeitung coding line handling
Kohle carbon
Kohlewiderstand carbon resistor
Koinzidenzprinzip coincident current selection
Koinzidenzspeicher coincident current memory
Kollektorfahne commutator riser
Kollektormotor commutator motor
Kollisionsschalter collosion switch
Kollisionsschutz collision protection
Kolonne column, field, gang
Kombination combination
Kombinationsschaltung combinational circuit
kombinatorische Logikschaltung combinational logic
kombinieren combine, compose
kombinierte Datei combined file
Kombizeichen compose character
Kombizeichensequenz compose sequence
Komfort convenience
Komma comma, decimal point
Kommaeinstellung point setting
Kommamarke decimal marker
Kommando command, instruction
Kommandoausführung command execution
Kommandobehandlung command processing
Kommandodatei command file
Kommandoebene command level
Kommandoebene des Betriebssystems operating system command level
Kommandoeingabe command input
Kommandoergänzung command complement, command modifier, command parameter
Kommandoerweiterung command extension
Kommandofeld command field
Kommandofolge command sequence
Kommando für lokale Sprachausgabe local speak command
Kommando für Sprachausgabe vom Host host speak command
Kommando für Stapelverarbeitung batch processing command
Kommandointerpreter command interpreter, command language interpreter

Kommandomodus command mode, immediate mode
Kommandooption command option
Kommandoprozedur command procedure
Kommandoprozessor command processor, parser
Kommandoqualifizierer command qualifier
Kommandorückweisung command reject
Kommandosatz command record
Kommandoschlüsselwort command keyword
Kommandosprache command language
Kommandosuchpfad command search path
Kommandotaste command key
Kommandowort command word, verb
Kommandozeile command line
Kommandozeilenform command line form
Kommandozusatz command option, command parameter, command tail
Kommastelle decimal place, digit
Kommentar annotation, comment, commentary, comments, note
Kommentarfeld comment field
Kommentarkarte comment card
Kommentarkennzeichnung comments
Kommentarsteuerkommando comment control command
Kommentarzeile comment line
kommentieren annotate, comment
kommentiert annotated, commented
kommerziell business
kommerzielle Datenverarbeitung business data processing
kommerzieller Befehlssatz commercial instruction set
kommerzielle Schriftart business print set
Kommissionierindex commissioned goods index
Kommissionierliste commissioned goods list
Kommissionierung commissioning
Kommissionierunterlagen commissioning documents
Kommunikation comm, communication
Kommunikationsabschnitt communication paragraph
Kommunikationsanschluß communication port, communications connector
Kommunikationsbereich communication area
Kommunikationsbeziehung communication relation
Kommunikationsfunktion communication function
Kommunikationsmittel means of communication

Kommunikationsmodus communication mode
Kommunikationspartner communication partner
Kommunikationsprotokoll communications protocol
Kommunikationsprozeß communication process
Kommunikationsrechner communication computer
Kommunikationsschnittstelle communications adapter
Kommunikationssoftware communication software
Kommunikationsstatus communication state
Kommunikationssteuerungsschicht session layer
Kommunikationsverbindung communication line
Kommunikationsverfahren communication procedure
Kommunikation zwischen Prozessen interprocess communication
kommunizieren communicate
kompakt compact, condensed
Kompaktbelegjournal abbreviated voucher journal
Kompaktkarteneinrichtung spread card feature
Kompaktkassette cassette
Komparator comparator
Kompaß compass
Kompaßeinstellung compass adjustment
kompatibel compatible
Kompatibilität compatibility
kompatible compatible
kompilieren compile
kompilieren des Quellcodes compiling the source code
Kompilierer compiler
Kompilierung compilation
Kompilierungsmodus compilation mode
Kompilierungszeittabelle compilation time table, compile time table
Komplement complement
Komplementbildung complementing
komplett complete
Komplex complex
komplex complex
kompliziert complicated
Komponente component
Komponentenerfassung component acquisition
Komponentensatz component record
komprimieren compress
Komprimierung compression

Kondensator capacitor
Kondensatorblock capacitor bank
Kondensatorladegerät capacitor charger
Kondensatorpapier capacitor paper
kondensieren condense
Kondition condition
konditionell conditional
Konditionen terms
Konditionensatz terms record
Konditionenschlüssel condition code
Konditionsartenkennzeichen terms marker
Konditionssatz terms record
Konditionsschlüssel condition code
konventionell conventional
Konfektionär original equipment manufacturer
Konferenzeinrichtung broadcast call equipment, conference call equipment
Konfiguration configuration
Konfiguration mit Produkten verschiedener Hersteller multivendor installation
konfigurationsabhängig configuration dependent
Konfigurationsanzeige configuration display
Konfigurationsblatt configuration worksheet
Konfigurationsdatei configuration file
Konfigurationshaupttabelle master configuration table
Konfigurationsmöglichkeit configuration option
konfigurationsorientiert configuration oriented
Konfigurationsprogramm configuration program
Konfigurationsprüfprogramm configuration verification program, installation verification program
Konfigurationsschablone configuration template
konfigurationsspezifisch configuration specific
konfigurierbar configurable
konfigurierbare Stapelverarbeitungsdatei configurable batch file
konfigurieren configure
Konfliktsituation conflict situation
Konfliktverhinderung conflict avoidance
Konjunktion conjunction
Konkrement concrement
konkret concrete
konkrete Syntax concrete syntax
Konkurrent competitor
Konkurrenz competition
Konkurrenzbetrieb contention mode
konkurrieren compete
Konponentensystem system of components

Konsequenz consequence
Konsignation consignment
Konsignations-Auffüllauftrag consignment replenishment order
Konsignationsauffüllung consignment filling
Konsignationsbestand consignment inventory, consignment stock
Konsignations-Bestellbestand consignment stock on order
Konsignationsbestellung consignment order
Konsignationsbewegung consignment movement
Konsignations-Bewertungspreis consignment valuation price
Konsignations-Entnahmeauftrag consignment withdrawal order
Konsignationskontrakt consignment contract
Konsignationslager consignment stores
Konsignations-Lagerbestand consignment stores inventory
Konsignationsmaterial consignment material
Konsignationssatz consignment record
Konsignationsware consignment goods
Konsistenzfehler consistency error
Konsolbetrieb console operation
Konsole console, console terminal, main station, panel
Konsolemulatorbetrieb console emulator mode
konsolidieren consolidate
Konsolidierunganweisung consolidation instruction
Konsolkassette console cartridge
Konsolkommando console command, system console command
Konsolnachricht system console message
Konsolprotokoll console sheet
Konsolschnittstelle console serial line
Konsolsubsystem console subsystem
Konsolterminal console, console terminal
konstant constant
Konstante constant
Konstanteneingabetaste constant data entry key, constant data input key
Konstanteninhalt contents of the constant
Konstantenlänge length of the constant
Konstantentyp constant type
konstantes Wachstum increment growth
Konstanthaltung automatic constant
Konstantspannungsquelle constant voltage source
Konstantstromquelle constant current source
Konstellation configuration
konstruieren construct, make up

Konstruktionsmerkmal construction detail
Kontakt contact, electric contact
Kontaktauflagedruck contact pressure
Kontaktbrücke jumper
Kontakt in der Fassung electric socket contact
Kontaktschutz electric contact protection
Kontaktzunge prong
kontaminieren contaminate
Kontenabstimmung reconciliation of accounts
Kontenabsummierung account totalling
Kontenanzeige accounts display
Kontenausgleich balancing of accounts
Kontenauswahl account selection
Kontenbearbeitung account processing
Kontenberechtigung account authorization
Kontenbestandsband account inventory tape
Kontenbezeichnung account name
Kontenbildung account formation
Kontenbuchung account posting
Kontenebene account level
Kontenfortschreibung updating of accounts
Kontenführung accounting method
Kontenklasse account category
Kontenniederschrift detailed account listing
Kontenpflege account maintenance, accounts maintenance
Kontenplan chart of accounts
Kontenrahmen system of accounts
Kontenschreibung accounts posting
Kontenschreibungsband accounts posting tape
kontenspezifisch account specific
Kontenstamm account master
Kontenstammsatz account master record, accounts master record
Kontenstand state of account
Kontensteuerung account control
Kontentabelle account table
Kontenverwaltung accounts management
Kontenverzeichnis account register
Kontenzuordnung account association
Kontenzusammenführung account consolidation
Kontenzusammenstellung account composition
kontieren post
Kontierungsblock posting block
Kontierungsdaten posting data
Kontierungsfeld posting field
kontierungspflichtig compulsory posting
Kontierungsvorschrift posting instruction
Kontierungszeile posting line
kontinuierlich continuous
kontinuierliches Abrollen pan scrolling
Konto account

Kontoanzeige account display
Kontoart account type
Kontoauflösung closing an account
Kontoauszug statement of account
Kontoauszugsdrucker statement printer
Kontoauszugstransport account withdrawal transport
Kontobeschreibungsdatei description file
Kontobezeichnung account designation
Kontoergänzung account supplement
Kontofindung account locating
Kontoführung account processing
Kontogliederung account classification
Kontogruppe account group
Kontoklartext account plain text
Kontoklassifikation account classification
Kontokorrent current account
Kontokorrentbuchung current account posting
Kontokorrentkonto current account
Kontokorrentobligo current account liability
Kontokorrentsaldo current account balance
Kontokorrentverwaltung current account management
Kontolaufzeit account duration
Kontonummer account number
Kontonummernaufbau account number setup
Kontonummernergänzung account number supplement
Kontonummernstelle account number position
Kontosaldo account balance
Kontoschlüssel account code
Kontotyp account type
Kontoüberschrift account header
Kontoverzeichnis accounts register
Kontrakt contract
Kontraktabrufe contract call offs
Kontraktabschlußdatum contract date
Kontraktabwicklung contract processing
Kontraktänderung contract change
Kontraktanfang start of contract
Kontraktanhang contract appendix
Kontraktart contract type
Kontraktbeleg contract voucher
Kontraktbelegnummer contract voucher number
Kontraktbuchungskreis contract accounting area
Kontraktdaten contract data
Kontraktdatum contract date
Kontraktende end of contract
Kontraktform contract form
Kontrakthauptbeleg main contract voucher
Kontraktkopf contract header

Kontraktlaufzeit contract duration
Kontraktmenge quantity contracted
Kontraktnummer contract number
Kontraktposition contract item
Kontraktpositionsbelegnummer contract item voucher number
Kontraktpositionsmenge contract item quantity
Kontraktpositionstyp contract item type
Kontrakttext contract text
Kontraktüberwachung contract monitoring
Kontraktwert contract value
Kontrast contrast
Kontrastentscheidung accentuated contrast
Kontrastregler contrast control
Kontrollabschnitt control paragraph
Kontrollampe active light
Kontrollampe RUN run indicator light
Kontrollanzeige control display
Kontrollbild control screen
Kontrollbildschirm auxiliary CRT for maintenance support
Kontrollblock control block
Kontrolle check
kontrollesen perform a read-after-write check
Kontrollfeld-Beschreibung control field description
Kontrollfeld-Inhalt control field contents
Kontrollfeld-Verarbeitung control field processing
Kontrollformat control format
kontrollieren check, control
kontrolliert abbrechen abort
Kontrollinformation control information
Kontrollintervall check interval
Kontrollintervallebene check interval level
Kontrolliste check list
Kontrollampe indicator light
Kontrollmodul check module
Kontrollmodus check mode
Kontrollprodukt control product
Kontrollpunktverfahren checkpointing
Kontrollrechner control computer
Kontrollstatusregister control status register
Kontrollstreifendrucker flight strip printer
Kontrollsumme checksum, control total
Kontrollsummenfehler checksum error, hash error
Kontrollsummenverwaltung checksum organization
Kontrolltabelle für Geräteverfügbarkeit hardware master bit table
Kontrollziffer check number
Kontrollzweck check purpose

Konvention convention
konventionelle Computersysteme commercial system
Konversationsnummer conversation number
konvertieren convert
Konvertierung conversion, data conversion
Konvertierungsbeschreibung conversion description
Konzentrationssteuerung density control
Konzentrator concentrator
konzentrieren concentrate
Konzept concept, design, philosophy
Konzeption philosophy
Konzern corporation, trust
Konzernbuchhaltung company accounting
Konzerngruppe corporation group
Konzerntochter subsidiary, subsidiary company
Konzessionsabgabe privilege tax
Konzessionsgebühr privilege tax
Kooperationsfaktor factor of cooperation
Kooperationsmodul index of cooperation
Koordinate coordinate
Koordinaten coordinates
Koordinaten des Grafikfensters viewport coordinates
Koordinatenlöser coordinate resolver
Koordination coordination
Koordinierungsauftrag control job
Kopf head, header
Kopfanfang start of header
Kopfbild header screen
Kopfdaten head data, header data
Kopfhörer earphones, headphones, headset
Kopfhörerbuchse headphone jack
Kopflandung head crash
Kopfnummer head number
Kopfrabatt header discount
Kopfrückzug return to header
Kopfsatz header record
Kopfsatzart header record type
Kopftext header text
Kopfträger carriage
Kopfzeile header line, heading
Kopfzeilenanweisung print page heading
Kopfzeilenoperation header operation, header time operation
Kopfzeilenzeit heading time
Kopf-Zylinder-Halbwort head and cylinder specification half word
Kopie copy, hardcopy
Kopiediskette destination diskette

Kopiendrucker communication output printer, console printer, hard copy printer, pagewrite printer
kopierbar copyable
kopieren copy, duplicate
Kopierfunktion copy function
Kopierlauf copy run
Kopierprogramm copy program
Kopierschutz copy protection
Kopiervorgang copy operation
Koppelbrief compound letter
Koppelmedium coupling medium
koppeln couple
Koppelung coupling
Korona corona
Korona-Entladungsröhre corona-discharge tube
korrekt correct
Korrektur correction, patch
Korrekturband lift off tape
Korrekturband für abdeckendes Löschen cover up tape
Korrekturbetrag revised amount
Korrekturbuchungen correction posting
Korrekturmaßnahme corrective action
Korrekturmitteilung correction message
Korrekturmodus correction mode
Korrekturmöglichkeit correction facility
Korrekturnummer correction number
Korrektursatz patch record
Korrekturstatus correction status
Korrektursystem correction system
Korrekturtaste delete key
Korrespondenz correspondence
Korrespondenzdrucker letter quality printer
korrigieren correct
Korrigiertaste correction key
korrosiv corrosive
Kosten cost
Kostenart cost category, cost type
Kostenbuchung posting of costs
Kostenermittlung cost calculation
Kostenfluß cost flow
Kostenfunktion cost function
Kostenkonto cost account, expense account
Kostenkontrolle cost control
kostenmäßig cost related
kostenoptimal at optimal costs
Kostenrechnung cost accounting
Kostenrechnungsverfahren cost accounting procedure
Kostenstelle cost centre

347

Kostenstellenauswertung cost accounting report
Kostenstellenrechnung cost centre accounting
Kostenstellenumlage cost centre number
Kostenträger cost objective
Kostenträgerrechnung cost objective accounting
Kostenüberwachung cost control
Kostenumlage cost centre allocation
Kostenverteilung cost allocation
Kostenvoranschlag quotation, quote
Kovarianzmatrix second order statistics
kräftig powerful
Kraft force, power
Kraftausgang force output
Kraftsteuerung force control
Kraftstromerzeugung electric power generation
Kraftstromfernleitung electric power distribution line, electric power transmission line
Kraftstromfernleitungsnetz electric power transmission line
Kraftstromnetz electric power network
Kraftstromübertragung electric power transmission
Kraftstromverteiler electric power distribution point
Kraftstromverteilung electric power distribution
Kragenisolator high collar insulator
Krankenhausverwaltungssystem interactive health care system
Krankenkasse health insurance company
Kredit credit
Kreditgrenze credit limit
Kreditkontrolle credit check
Kreditlaufzeit credit period
Kreditlimitprüfung credit limit check
Kreditorenanspruchnahme credit utilization
Kreditorenauswertung accounts payable analysis
Kreditorenauszüge payables account
Kreditorenbeleg accounts payable voucher
Kreditorenbereich accounts payable area
Kreditorenbild accounts payable screen
Kreditorenbuchhaltung accounts payable, accounts payable accounting
Kreditorenbuchung accounts payable posting
Kreditorenkonten accounts payable
Kreditorenkonto account payable
Kreditorenliste creditor list
Kreditorennummer accounts payable number
Kreditorenstamm accounts payable master

Kreditorenstammsatz accounts payable master record
Kreditorenteil accounts payable section
Kreditorenverrechnung accounts payable settlement
Kreditorenzahlung accounts payable payment
Kreditorenzeile accounts payable item
Kreditstatusbericht credit status report
Kreditüberwachung credit control
Kreis area, circle, range
Kreisausschnitt sector of a circle
Kreisdiagramm pie chart
Kreisebene area level
kreisförmig circular
Kreisinterpolation circular interpolation
Kreisverkettung cyclic concatenation
Kreuzschienenverteiler patch area, patch panel
Kreuzsteckfeld patch panel
Kriechstrom leakage current
Kriterien criteria
Kriterium criterion
Kritik criticism
kritisch critical
kritischer Abschnitt critical section
Kryostat cryostat
Kryotron cryotron
kühl cool
Kühlanlage cooling unit
kühlen cool
Kühlmittel coolant
Kühlmittelbehälter coolant reservoir
Kühlmittelpumpe coolant motor, coolant pump
Kühlmittelpumpe unter Druck coolant pump at pressure
Kühlmittelrücklauf coolant return
kümmern care
Kündigungszeitpunkt time of notice
Kürzel key word, option keyword
Kürzelsegment contraction segment
Kürzeltabelle contraction table, mnemonic table
kürzen cut, truncate
kürzester Abstand linear distance
Kugelschreiber ball point pen
Kulanztage period of grace
kumulativ cumulative
kumulieren accumulate, cumulate
kumuliertes Feld cumulated field
Kunde client, customer
Kundenadresse customer's address
Kundenauftrag customer order, sales order
Kundenauftragsnummer sales order number
Kundenauftragssatz sales order record

Kundenbeistellmaterial customer's processed-out material
Kundenbeistellung customer parts for processing
Kundenberechtigung customer authorization
Kundenbezirk customer area
kundenbezogen customer related, related to customers
Kundendatei customer file
Kundendaten customer data
Kundendiensttechniker customer engineer, service engineer, service technician
Kundenebene customer level
Kundenfach client slot
Kundengruppe customer group
Kundengruppierung customer grouping
kundenindividuell for the individual customer
Kundenkonsignation customer consignment
Kundenkontenauszug customer statement
Kundenkredit customer credit
Kundenkreditkontrolle customer credit check
Kundennummer customer number
Kundenorder customer order
kundenorientiert consumer oriented
Kundenpriorität customer priority
Kundensatz customer record
Kundenskonto debitor discount
kundenspezifisch customer specific, customized, for the individual customer
Kundenstamm customer master
Kundenstammfeld regular customer field
Kundenstammliste customer master list
Kundenstammsatz customer master record, regular customer record
Kundenumsätze customers' turnover
Kundenvermerk customer remark
Kundenwährung customer's currency
Kunststoff plastic
Kunststoffeinsteckrohr plug pipe plastic
Kunststoffgriff plastic handle
Kunststoffhülle diskette cover
Kunststoffolienkondensator plastic film capacitor
Kunststoffschaum foam, plastic foam
Kupfermantelkabel mineral insulated cable
Kupferwand copper wall
Kupplung coupler
Kurs exchange rate, rate
Kursdifferenz conversion discrepancy, exchange rate discrepancy
Kursdifferenzenbuchung currency conversion discrepancy posting
Kursivität currency

Kursschwankung exchange rate fluctuation
Kurstabelle exchange rate table
Kursumrechnung currency conversion
Kursverhältnis ratio of exchange rates
Kurswert exchange rate value
Kurve curve, graph
Kurvendifferenz curve difference
Kurvenleser curve follower
Kurvenschreiber graphic plotter, plotter
Kurz- short form, short format, shorthand
kurz brief, short, verbose
Kurzadressierung abbreviated addressing
Kurzadresse short form address
Kurzadressierung mnemonic addressing
Kurzaufruf abbreviated address call
Kurzbeschreibung brief description
Kurzbezeichnung mnemonic, short name
Kurzbrief short message
Kurzdialog short dialog
Kurzform short cut, short form
kurzfristig short term
Kurzinformation short information
Kurzinhalt brief content
Kurzinitialisierung brief initialization
Kurzliste brief list
Kurzlochkarte scored card
Kurzrufdokument abbreviation document
Kurzschlüssel short key
Kurzschluß short circuit
Kurzschlußläufermotor squirrel cage motor
Kurzschlußstecker short circuit plug
Kurzspeicher short time storage
Kurztext summary
Kurztextzeile summary line
Kurzwahl abbreviated address call
Kurzwahlzeichen abbreviated dial code
Kurzweg prime route
Kurzzeitarchivierung short term filing
Kurzzeitdatei activity file
kurzzeitiger Ausfall drop out
Kurzzeitüberwachung short term monitoring
Kuvertablage envelope stacker
Kuvertanlage envelope setting
Kuvertdurchlauf envelope run
Kuverteinzug envelope entry
Kuvertzuführung envelope feeding device

L

Label label
labial labial
Lackdraht enamelled wire
lackierter Draht enamelled wire
ladbare Feldgruppe executilon time array
ladbares Programm load module
Ladeanzeige load LED
Ladeausschlußfaktor load exclusion factor
Ladebereich loader area
ladefähiges Programm boot image
Ladegerät charger
Ladeliste load list
Lademodul load module
Lademodus load mode
laden boot, download, load, mount
Laden eines Satellitenrechners downline load
Laden eines transienten Steuerprogramms function loading
Ladepfad load path
Ladeprogramm boot program, load program, loader
Lader loader
Lader für verschiebbare Programme relocating loader
Lade-ROM boot ROM
Ladespannung load voltage
Ladesteuerprogramm starter supervisor
Ladeversorgungssektor loader input sector
Ladeverzeichnis load directory
Ladevorgang load operation
Ladezeit loading time
Ladezugriff loading access
Ladungsbild charge pattern
Länder countries
Länderbezeichnung country name
Ländername country name
Länderschlüssel country code, country key
Ländersummen totals according to country
Länge length
Länge des Feldes zur Angabe von Leistungsmerkmalen facility length
Länge des Ordnungsbegriffs length of defining argument
Länge des Signals break time, duration, signal time
Längenangabe length specification
Längenangaben-Bit length specification bit
Längenbyte length byte

Längenfeld length field
Längenparameter length parameter
Längenstatistik length statistics
Längensumme length sum
Längenverhältnis aspect ratio
Längssummenkontrolle summation check
Läufer armature, electric rotor
Läuferwicklung rotor winding
Lage lay, layer, location, position
Lager bushing, stores
Lagerabfrage stock query
Lagerabwicklung stock processing
Lagerausgabemenge stock quantity issued
Lagerausgabemengeneinheit stores issue unit
Lagerauskunft stores information
Lagerbasis stores basis
Lagerbedingungen storage terms
Lagerbestand inventory
Lagerbestandsdaten stock data
Lagerbestandsdatenbank stock data bank
Lagerbestandsführung inventory maintenance
Lagerbestandsführungsfunktion stock updating function
Lagerbestandsliste inventory listing
Lagerbestandsmenge inventory quantity
lagerbestandsneutral inventory neutral
Lagerbewegung stock movement
Lagerbewegungsliste stock movement report
Lagerbewegungsverarbeitung stock transaction processing
Lagerbewirtschaftungsmethode stock management
Lagerdichtung bearing seal
Lagerdisponent stock managing clerk
Lagereinstands-Durchschnittspreis average acquisition price
Lagereinstandspreis acquisition price
Lagerfähigkeit shelf life, storage life, storing properties
Lagergewicht stock weight
Lagerhüter slow and dead stock
Lagermaterial stock material
Lagermenge stock quantity
Lagermengeneinheit stores unit
lagern store
Lagerort stores, stores location
Lagerortbestand stores inventory
Lagerortebene stores level
Lagerortnummer stores number
Lagerortsatz stock location tariff
lagerortsbezogen stores-related
Lagerortsegment stores segment
lagerortspezifisch stores-specific

Lagerorttabelle stores location table
Lagerplatz storage space
Lagerplatzauskunft storage information
Lagerplatzbeschreibung stores description
Lagerpreis stores price
Lagersituation stock situation
Lagerstätte stores
Lagersteuerung stock control
Lagerübersicht stock survey
Lagerumschlagshäufigkeit stock turnover
Lagerverwaltung stock management
Lagerverwaltung mittels Computer computerized stock control
Lagerwert inventory value
Lagerwesen stock control
Lagerwirtschaftsparameter stock control parameter
Lagerzeit storage period
Lagerzugänge stores acquisitions
Lagerzugangsprogramm stock receipt program
Lampe bulb, lamp
Lampenfassung lampholder, socket
Landespaket country kit
Landessprache language of a country
Landesvorwahl country code
Landeswährung home currency
lang long
langfristig long term
langsam low speed, slow
Langsamerwerden deceleration
Langtext full text
Langtextnachrichten full text messages
Langtextzeilen full text lines
Langwort longword
Langzeitdaten long term data
Langzeitspeicher long term storage
Laser laser
Laserdrucker laser printer
Last electric ballast, load
Lastregelung load regulator
Lastschrift debit posting
Lastschriftsart debit type
Lastschriftsbeleg debit voucher
Lastschriftserfassung debit registration
Lastschriftshöhe debit amount
Lastschriftskopf debit header
Lastschriftsposition debit item
Lastschriftstext debit text
Lastschriftswert debit value
Latch latch
Latch-Schaltung latch circuit, latching circuit
lateinisches Zeichen Latin character
Latenz latency

Lauf run
Laufdatum current date
laufend current, perpetually
lauffähig executable
lauffähiges Programm executable program, image, task image
Laufkarte run card
Lauflänge run length
Laufnummerngeber sequence number generator
Laufwerk drive
Laufwerk aufheben remove a drive
Laufwerk belegt drive in use
Laufwerk nicht bereit drive not ready
Laufwerksbezeichnung drive ID
Laufwerksfehler drive error
Laufwerksgeschwindigkeit falsch drive speed out of range
Laufwerkskabel drive cable
Laufwerksklappe disk drive door, diskette drive door, drive door
Laufwerkskonfigurationsprogramm drive configurator
Laufwerksname drive ID
Laufwerksnummer drive ID, drive number, drive select number
Laufzeit period, runtime
Laufzeitbibliothek runtime library
Laufzeitfehler runtime error
Laufzeitgerät transit time device
Laufzeitpaket runtime package
Laufzeitprüfung runtime check
Laufzeitsystem runtime system
Laufzeit-Triftröhre velocity modulated tube
laut according to
Lautsprecher loudspeaker, speaker
Lautstärke volume
Lautstärkeregler volume control
Layout layout
Layoutdatei layout file
Layoutsatz layout record
Layoutsteuerung layout control
Leasing leasing
Leasingstatus leasing status
Lebensdauer endurance
Lebensversicherung life insurance
LED-Anzeige LED display, LED indicator
lediglich merely, solely
leer blank, empty, unused
Leerbit dummy bit
Leerblock dummy block
Leerdatei dummy file
Leereintrag blank entry

leeres Passwort null password
Leerfeld blank field
Leerformat blank format
Leergut empties
Leergutaußenstände empties outstanding
Leergutbeistellung empties submission
Leergutbewegung movement of empties
Leerguterfassung empties registration
Leergutmaterial empties
Leergutmenge empties quantity
Leergutrückgabedatum date for return of empties
Leerkarte blank card
Leerlauf idle
leerlaufen idle
Leerlaufzeit idle time
Leersatz dummy record
Leerschritterweiterungstaste space expand key
Leerseite blank page
Leerspaltensucher blank column detector
Leerstellen-Bezugszahl blank indictor
Leertaste dummy key, space bar
Leerwerte empties values
Leerzeichen blank, space
Leerzeichenkomprimierung space compression
Leerzeichenkomprimierungsmodus space compression mode
Leerzeichentaste space key
Leerzeile blank line
Leerzustand dummy condition
legen lay, place, put
Lehrprogramm tutor
Lehrzeugnis letter of apprenticeship
leichter lighter
leicht zu bedienen easy to use
leider unfortunately
leihen lend, loan
Leihpackung returnable packing
Leihverpackung returnable packaging
leisten achieve, perform
Leistung achievement, capabilities, performance, system performance
Leistung des Systems system performance
Leistungsabfall performance degradation
Leistungsaktivität performance activity
Leistungsaufnahme power consumption
Leistungsbestätigung confirmation of services
Leistungsbetrieb efficient operation
Leistungsdialog performance dialog
Leistungselektronik power electronics
leistungsfähig high performance, powerful
Leistungsfähigkeit performance
Leistungsfaktor power factor

Leistungsfluß power flow path
Leistungskondensator power capacitor
Leistungskontrolltabelle line control table
leistungsloses Schalten no load interruption
Leistungsmerkmal feature, user facility
Leistungsmerkmalanforderung facility request
Leistungsmerkmalaufruf facility request
Leistungsmerkmale der E/A-Einheit input/output features
Leistungsmerkmale des Zentralrechners central processor features
Leistungsmonitor performance screen
Leistungsoszillator power oscillator
Leistungsschalter power switch
Leistungssteuerung performance management, power control
Leistungstransformator power transformer
Leistungstransistor power transistor
Leistungsverbesserung improvement in performance, performance improvement
Leistungsverstärker power amplifier
Leistungsverteiler power divider
Leistungsverteilung performance management
Leistungswiderstand power resistor
leiten direct, guide, manage
Leiter conductor, electric conductor, manager
Leiterbündel bundled conductor
Leiter des Rechenzentrums facilities manager
Leiterholm ladder rung
Leiterplatte board, circuit board
Leitfaden guideline
Leitinformation routing information
Leitrechner system controller
Leitstation control station
Leitsteuerung primary, primary control
Leitsystem guidance system
Leitung electric wire, line, management, wire
Leitung anzapfen line tapping, tap a line
Leitungsabbau line clearing
Leitungsabschluß line terminator
Leitungsanschlußeinrichtung line connecting equipment
Leitungsausfall line fall-out, line outage
Leitungsbezeichnung line designation
Leitungsendgerät communications terminal module, line adapter, line terminal
Leitungsereignis line occurrence
Leitungskennzeichnung line designation
Leitungslaufzeit line propagation time
Leitungsnetz line network
Leitungsnummer line number
Leitungsprotokoll-Steuerprogramm line protocol handler

Leitungsrohr rigid conduit
Leitungsschalter circuit breaker
Leitungsschnittstelle line interface
Leitungsschnur cord
Leitungsschutzschalter circuit breaker
Leitungsspeisung line current feed
Leitungsstörung line interference
leitungsvermitteln line switching
leitungsvermitteltes Netz circuit switched network
Leitungsvermittlung circuit switched sevice, circuit switching, line switching
Leitungszusammenbruch open line
Leitweg route
Leitwegplanung routing
Leitwegsteuerung route control
Leitwerk computer control unit, control unit
Leitzahl code
Leporellonummer form tractor number
lesbar readable
Lesbarkeit legibility
Leseaufruf read call
Lesebereich read area
Lesefehler read error
Lesekopf read head
Lesemodus read mode
Lesen read
lesen read
Lesen-Drucken-Sortieren reading-printing-sorting
Lesen nach Schreiben direct read after write, read after write
Lesen-Sortieren reading-sorting
Leser reader
Leseroutine read routine
Lesestation read in unit, read unit
Leseversuch attempt to read, read attempt
Lesezugriff auf Speicher memory read
Lesezykluszeit read cycle time
letzte Eingabe last input
letzteingegeben last input
letztes eingegebenes Zeichen last character input, last character keyed
letzte Warnung final warning
letzte Zeile bottom line
letztgenannt last mentioned
Leuchtdiode light emitting diode
Leuchteinheit lighting device
leuchtend highlighted
Leuchtintensität illuminating intensity
Lexikon lexicon
Librarian librarian
Licht light

lichtelektrisches Gerät photoelectric device
Lichtgriffel light pen, lightpen
Lichtleiter optical channel cable, optical data link
Lichtleitertechnik optical fiber engineering
Lichtpunkt cursor
Lichtpunktspeicher flying spot store
Lichtsatzanlage phototypesetter
Lichtschreiber light pen
Lichtschutz light shielding
Lichtstift light pen
Lichtwellenleitersystem fiber optic system
Lieferanschrift shipping address
Lieferant supplier, vendor
Lieferantenangebot supplier's offer
Lieferantenanzahlung supplier's installment
Lieferantenauswahl selection of suppliers
Lieferantenberechtigung supplier authorization
lieferantenbezogen supplier-related
Lieferantendatei suppliers file
Lieferantenebene suppliers level
lieferantengebunden dependent on supplier
Lieferantennamen supplier's name
Lieferantennummer supplier number
Lieferantenrechnung supplier's invoice
Lieferantenspezifikation supplier specification
Lieferantenstamm suppliers master
Lieferantenstammdatei suppliers master file
Lieferantenstammsatz supplier master record
Lieferantenverzeichnis suppliers register
lieferbar deliverable, on stock
Lieferbedingung delivery terms
Lieferbeleg delivery voucher
Lieferbelegnummer delivery voucher number
Lieferbereitschaft stock availability
Lieferbeziehung source of supply
Lieferdatum delivery date
Liefereinteilung delivery arrangement
Liefererinnerung delivery reminder
Lieferkondition delivery terms
Liefermahnung delivery reminder
Liefermenge quantity delivered
Liefermoral delivery performance
liefern deliver, supply
Lieferpapiere delivery papers
Lieferplan delivery schedule
Lieferplananfangsdatum delivery schedule start date
Lieferplanart delivery schedule type
Lieferplandatum delivery schedule date
Lieferplaneinteilung delivery scheduling
Lieferplanendedatum delivery schedule end date

353

Lieferplanmenge delivery schedule quantity
Lieferplannummer delivery schedule number
Lieferplanposition delivery schedule item
Lieferplanschreibung delivery schedule printing
Lieferplanüberwachung delivery schedule monitoring
Lieferplanverwaltung delivery schedule management
Lieferschein delivery note
Lieferscheinänderung delivery note alteration
Lieferscheinart delivery note type
Lieferscheinbearbeitung delivery note processing
Lieferscheinbeleg delivery note voucher
Lieferscheinbelegsatz delivery note voucher record
Lieferscheindruck printing delivery notes
Lieferscheinerstellung creating the delivery note
Lieferscheinkopf delivery note header
Lieferscheinnotiz delivery note remark
Lieferscheinnummer delivery note number
Lieferscheinposition delivery note item
Lieferscheinpositionsgewicht delivery note item weight
Lieferscheinpositionsmengen delivery note item quantity
Lieferscheinschreibung printing delivery notes
Lieferscheintext delivery note text
Liefersperre delivery stop
Liefertermin delivery date
Lieferüberwachung delivery monitoring
Lieferumfang quantity for delivery
Lieferung delivery, supply
Lieferungsauftrag delivery order
Lieferverzug failure to deliver
Lieferwert delivery value, value delivered
Lieferwoche delivery week
Lieferzeit delivery time
Lieferzeitraum delivery period
Lieferzeitrechnung invoice accompanying delivery
Lieferzusage delivery commitment
liegen lie
Liegenbewegung patient table movement, patient table rotation
Lightpenabgleich lightpen adjustment
linear linear
lineare Gleichung linear equation
lineare Interpolation linear fit
lineare Mehrfachregression multiple linear regression

lineare Programmabtastung sequential program scan
lineare Programmierung linear programming
linearer Spannungsanstieg ramp voltage
Linearmotor linear motor
Linie line
Liniendiagramm line diagram, line graph
Liniereinrichtung line ruler
linkbar linkable
linken link
linke obere Bildschirmecke home, home position
Linker linker
linker Rand left hand margin, left margin
Linkfehler link error
Linklauf link run
Linkmakro link macro
Linkname link name
Linkoperand link operand
links left, left hand side
linksbündig ausrichten align at the left margin
linksbündig formatieren left justify
links oben upper left
Liste list, listing, report
Liste der für nicht betriebsbereit erklärt und reservierten Betriebsmittel down reserve list
listen list
listenabhängig list dependant
Listenabschnitt list section
Listenanzeige list display
Listenart list type
Listenaufbau list structure
Listenaufbereitung list editing
Listenausdruck list printout
Listenausgabe list output
Listenauswertung list analysis, list report
Listenbezeichnung list designation, list name
Listenbild list screen, printer layout
Listenbilddefinition list screen definition
Listendatei list file, listing file, report file
Listendefinition list definition
Listendokument list document
Listenentwurf list draft
Listenerstellungsprogramm list generation program
Listenform list form, list format
Listenfunktion list function
Listengenerator report writer
Listengruppe list group
Listeninhalt list contents
Listenkennung list flag
Listenkopf head of a list

Listenlänge list length
Listenname list name
Listennummer list number
Listenparameter list parameter
Listenposition list item
Listenprogramm list program, report program
Listenprogrammgenerator report program generator
Listenteil list section
Listentyp list type
Listenüberschrift list headline
Listenübersicht list summary
Listenverarbeitung list processing
Listenverarbeitungspaket list processing feature
Listenzeile list line
Listenzusammenfassung list summary
Listenzusammenstellung list composition
Literal literal
Literatur literature
Literaturmodul literature module
Lithium lithium
Lochbandvorschub feed tape carriage
lochen punch
Locher puncher
Lochkarte punch card, punched card
Lochkartenbefehl punch card instruction
Lochkartendatei card file, punch card file
Lochkartengerät punched card equipment
Lochkartenkopierer punched card reproducer
Lochkartenleser card reader, punched card reader
Lochkarten-Lochstreifen-Umsetzer punched card to punched tape
Lochkarten-Magnetband-Umsetzer punched card to magnetic tape
Lochkartenoperation punch card operation
Lochkartensortierer punched card sorter
Lochkartenstanzer card puncher
Lochschrift-übersetzung alphabetic interpreting, alphabetic translation
Lochspur punch track
Lochstreifen punch tape, punched tape
Lochstreifengerät punched tape equipment
Lochstreifenkopierer punched tape reproducer
Lochstreifenleser paper tape reader, punched tape reader
Lochstreifenlocher punched tape punch
Lochstreifen-Lochkarten-Umsetzer punched tape to punched card
Lochstreifen-Magnetband-Umsetzer punched tape to magnetic tape
Lochstreifenstanzer paper tape punch

Lochung sprocket hole
Locktabelle lock table
Löschanweisung delete instruction
löschbarer Speicher eraseable storage
Löschbarkeit eraseability
Löschbefehl clear instruction
löschen blank, cancel, clear, clear out, delete, destroy, erase, remove
Löschen auf dem Bildschirm erase in display
Löschen bestätigen get confirmation before deleting
Löschen bis Bildschirmende erase to end of screen
Löschen bis Zeilenende erase to end of line
Löschen des Speichers clear memory
Löschen eines Segments delete a segment
Löschen im Bildschirm erase in display
Löschen in Zeile erase in line
Löschen mit ultraviolettem Licht ultraviolet light erasing
Löschen ohne Speicher clear without memory
Löschfähigkeit deleteability
Löschfenster erase window
löschgeschützt delete protected
Löschkennmarke delete marker
Löschkennzeichen clear indicator, delete marker
Löschkriterium delete criterion
Löschliste deletion list
Löschmodus erase mode, erasure mode
Löschoperation delete operation
Löschoption delete option
Löschregister deletion record
Löschroutine cleanup routine
Lösch-Taste clear key
Löschtaste delete key
Löschüberwachung deletion monitoring
lösch- und programmierbarer Nur-Lese-Speicher erasable programmable read only memory
Löschung deletion, erasure
Löschungszeichen delete character
Löschvermerk deletion reservation
Löschvorgang delete procedure, deletion, erasure procedure
Löschvormerkung delete reservation
Löschvormerkungskennzeichen delete reservation marker
Löschvorschlag delete proposal
Löschvorschlagsliste delete proposal list
Löschvorschlagsprogramm delete proposal program
Löschzeichen delete flag, delete symbol

Lösungsmittel solvent
löten solder
Lötfahne lug, soldering lug
lötfreie Wickelverbindung solderless wrapped connector
Lötkolben soldering iron
Lötmaske solder mask
Lötzinn solder
Log log
Logband log tape
Logbandende end of log tape
Logdatei log file
Logik logic
Logikanalysator logic analyser
Logikbefehl logical instruction
Logikblock logical operation block
Logikdiagramm logic diagram
Logikgatter logic gate
Logikgerät logic device
Logikpegel logic level
Logikplatine logic board
Logikprogramm ladder logic, ladder logic program
Logikschaltung logic circuit
Logiksteuerkontakt logical control contact
Logiksteuerung logical control
Logiksyntax ladder logic syntax
Login login, logon
Loginformation log information
logisch logical
logisch abmelden dismount
logisch abschalten deselect
logisch anmelden mount
logische Addition logical add
logische Adresse data base key, logical address, logical construct
logische Bedingung logical condition
logische Beziehung logical relationship
logische Datensatzlänge logical record length
logische Entscheidung logical decision
logische Geräteadresse device mnemonic
logische Gerätenummer logical unit number
logische Masse logic ground
logischer Befehl logic instruction
logischer Block logical block
logischer Dateiname logical file definition
logischer Datensatz logical record
logischer Datensatzzugriff logical record access
logischer Kanal logical channel
logischer Name logical name
logischer Vergleich logical comparison
logischer Zustand logic level, logic state

logische Schaltung logical circuit
logische Schleifenfunktion logical looping capability
logisches Ein-/Ausgabe-Steuersystem logical input ouput control system
logische Seiten logic pages
logische Seitennummer logical page number
logisches Ende des Datenträgers logical end of media
logisches Gerät logical device
logisches »NICHT« logical not
logisches »ODER« logical or
logisches »UND« logical and
logische Unterteilung partition
logische Verknüpfung logic operation
logisch falsch false, logical false
logisch hoch high, logical high
logisch oder logical or, or
logisch und logical and
logisch voneinander unabhängig logically independent
logisch wahr logical true, true
Logistik logistics
Logon login, logon
Lohnauftragsbestellung processed-out purchase order
lohnend cost effective
Lohnverarbeitung outside processing
Lohnveredler subcontractor
Lohnveredlerbestände stock with sub-contractor
lokal local, offline
lokal angeschlossene Peripherie onsite peripheral equipment
lokal angeschlossenes Gerät onsite device
Lokalbetrieb local mode, offline operation
lokale Adresse local address
lokale Prüfschleife local loop, local loopback
lokaler Ablauffehler local procedure error
lokaler Anschluß local line
lokaler Knoten local node
lokales Editieren local editing
lokales Netzwerk local area network
lokales Symbol local symbol
lokale Syntax local syntax
lokales Zeichenecho local echo
lokale Terminalsteuereinheit local terminal controller
lokale virtuelle Adresse local virtual address
lokalisieren localize
Lokalisierungsmodus location mode
Losgröße lot size
Lotse tutor

lotsen tutor
Lotsenfunktion tutoring
Lücke gap
lückenlos continuous
Lüftungsöffnung ventilating opening
Lüftungsschlitz ventilation opening
Luftfeuchtigkeit humidity
Luftfeuchtigkeit im ausgeschalteten Zustand non operating humidity
Luftfeuchtigkeit während des Betriebs operating humidity
Luftlinie linear distance
Lufttransformator air core transformer
Luftspalt air gap, head gap
Luftspalt im Eisenkreis magnetic circuit air gap
Luftventil pneumatic valve

M

mächtig big, powerful
mäßig moderate
Magnet magnet
Magnetaufzeichnungsverfahren magnetic recording techniques
Magnetband magnetic tape, magtape, streamer tape
Magnetbandbegleitzettel magnetic tape form
Magnetbandeinheit magnetic tape unit
Magnetbandgerät magnetic tape device, magnetic tape equipment
Magnetbandkassette cassette magnetic tape, tape cartridge
Magnetbandlaufwerk tape drive
Magnetbandleser magnetic tape reader
Magnetbandnorm magnetic tape standard
Magnetbandspeicherung magnetic tape storage
Magnetbandsteuereinheit magnetic tape control unit, magnetic tape controller
Magnetbandtransport magnetic tape transport
Magnetbandtreiber magnetic tape handler
Magnetbandverarbeitung magnetic tape processing
Magnetblasenspeicher bubble memory, magnetic bubble memory
Magnetblasenspeicher-Steuerung bubble memory controller
Magnetfeldrechner magnetic computer
Magnetfilmspeicher magnetic film memory
magnetisch magnetic
magnetisch aufgezeichnete Daten magnetic recording data
magnetische Aufzeichnung magnetic recording
magnetische Mißweisung magnetic declination
magnetische Oberfläche magnetic surface
magnetischer Speicher magnetic memory
magnetischer Zeichensatz magnetic character set
magnetisches Dünnfilmgerät magnetic thin film device
magnetisches Gerät magnetic device
magnetische Speicherung magnetic storage
magnetische Steuerung magnetic variable control
magnetische Zeichenerkennung magnetic character recognition
Magnetisierungsschleife hysteresis loop
Magnetisierungszustand magnetic state

Magnetkarte magnetic card
Magnetkartenleser magnetic card reader
Magnetkern magnetic core
Magnetkernspeichermodule magnetic core stack modules
Magnetkompaß magnetic compass
Magnetkontokarte magnetic ledger card
Magnetkontokarteneinrichtung magnetic ledger card device
Magnetkontokartenzuführgerät magnetic ledger card dispenser
Magnetkopf magnetic head
Magnetkopfhalterung magnetic head mount
Magnetmotor reluctance motor
magnetohydrodynamische Umwandlung magnetohydrodynamic conversion
Magnetostriktion magnetostriction
magnetostriktives Gerät magnetostrictive device
Magnetplatte disk, magnetic disc
Magnetplatteneinheit magnetic disc unit
Magnetplattenlaufwerk magnetic disk drive
Magnetplattenspeicher magnetic disc storage, magnetic plate storage
Magnetron magnetron
Magnetschriftabtastung magnetic reading
Magnetspeicher magnetic store
Magnetspur magnetic track
Magnettrommel magnetic drum
Magnetventil solenoid operated valve
Magnetverstärker magnetic amplifier, saturable core reactor
Mahnablauf reminder procedure
Mahnadresse reminder address
Mahnanschrift reminder address
Mahnart reminding type
Mahndatum reminder date
mahnen remind
Mahngrenzbetrag minimum reminder amount
Mahnkriterium reminder criterion
Mahnliste reminder list
Mahnperiode reminder period
Mahnprogramm reminder program
Mahnrhythmus reminder frequency
Mahnschlüssel reminder code
Mahnstatistik reminder statistics
Mahnstatus reminder status
Mahnsteuerung reminder control
Mahnstufe reminder stage
Mahntext reminder text
Mahnung reminder
Mahnungsdruckdatei reminder print file

Mahnungsdruckprogramm reminder print program
Mahnverfahren reminder procedure
Mahnzähler reminder counter
Mailbox electronic mailbox, mailbox
Mailboxdienst mailbox service
Mailboxverwalter mailbox administrator, sysop
makeln conference
Makro macro
Makroassembler macroassembler
Makroassemblerprogramm macroassembly program
Makroaufruf macro call
Makrobefehl macro instruction, macro instruction
Makrobefehlsspeicher macroinstruction storage
Makrobibliothek macro library
Makrocodierung macro coding
Makrogenerierprogramm macrogenerating program
Makroprozessor macroprocessor
Makrosprache macro language
Malteserantrieb geneva drive
Malteserscheibe geneva disk
Management-Informationssystem management information system
Manager manager
Manchester-Code manchester encoding
Manchester-Kodierung manchester encoding
mandantenübergreifend for all corporations
Manipulation manipulation
Mannwoche man week
Manteltransformator shell type transformer
Mantisse mantissa
Manualbaum presentation plan
manuell manual
manuelle Antwort manual answer
manuelle Dateneingabe manual data input
manuelle Funktion manual function
manueller Anruf manual call
manuelles Schwenken frei manual swivelling enabled
manuelles Schwenken gesperrt manual swivelling locked
Mappe deck
Mappenidentifikation deck identification
Mappenkennung deck identification
Mappenname deck name
Mappennummer deck number
Mappenverzeichnis deck index
Marke flag, label
Markenartikelbereich proprietary item area
markieren flag, mark, select

Markierkanal mark channel
Markierung flag, label, tag
Markierzone marking zone
Marktanalyse market analysis
marktführende Anwendungen industry's leading applications
Maschennetz meshed network
Maschine machine
maschinell automatic
Maschinen machinery
Maschinenbefehl machine code
Maschinenbelastung machine capacity
Maschinencode machine code, object code
Maschinendaten machine data
Maschinendatum machine date
Maschinenfunktion machine function
Maschinengeschwindigkeit machine speed
maschinengestützte Erkennung machine aided cognition
Maschinengröße machine variable
Maschinenkopf machining head
maschinenlesbar machine readable
maschinenlesbares Material machine readable material
Maschinenprogramm machine program
Maschinenprogramm-Element absolute program element
Maschinenprogrammierung mit Crossassembler crossassembler machine programming
Maschinensprache low level language, machine language
Maschinensprachen-Debugger machine language debugger
Maschinensprachen-Programm machine language program
Maschinenstop drop dead halt
maschinenunabhängig machine independent, system independent
Maschinenwortlänge machine word length
Maschinenzyklus machine cycle
Maser maser
Maske display frame, mask
Maskenart type of mask
Maskenaufbereitung mask preparation
Maskenaufbereitungsprogramm screen format editor, screen format program
Maskenbeschreibung mask description
Maskendaten mask data
Maskendefinition mask definition
Maskenfeld mask field
Maskengenerator form management system, mask generator, screen format generator

Maskengenerierung generation of mask
Maskenkoordinator screen format coordinator
Maskenname mask name
Maskenpositionierung mask positioning
maskenprogrammierbare Festwertspeicher mask programmable read only memory
maskenprogrammierter Nur-Lese-Speicher mask programmed read only memory
Maskenregister mask register
Maskensatz mask set
Maskensatzname name of mask set
maskenspezifisches Dienstprogramm screen format service
Maskentext mask text
Maskenüberschrift frame heading, mask heading
Maskenverwaltungsprogramm screen format coordinator
Maskenzeichen mask symbol
maskierbarer Interrupt maskable interrupt
maskierbare Unterbrechung maskable interrupt
Maskieren masking
Masse earth, ground, mass
Masseelektrode earth electrode, ground
Maßeinheit unit, unit of measurement
Maßeinheit für biologische Strahlungsdosis roentgen equivalent man
Massekabel ground wire
Masseklemme earth terminal, ground terminal
Masseleiter bonding conductor, earth conductor
Masseleitung drain wire
Massen- bulk, mass
Massenbestellung bulk order
Massenerfassung bulk acquisition
Masseninitialisierung mass initialisation
Massenkopie mass copy
Massenspeicher mass memory, mass storage, mass storage system
Massenspeichereinheit mass storage subsystem
Massepunkt ground point
Masseschalter earthing switch
Masseschiene control ground bus bar
Masseverbinder connector ground
Massewiderstand composition resistor
maßgeschneidertes System dedicated system
massiver Leiter solid conductor
Maßnahme action, measure
Maßzahl yardstick
Master master
Masterplatz master workstation
Masterplatz-Protokollgerät master logging device

Masterplatzwechsel master console exchange
Masterterminal system console
Matchcode matchcode
Matchcode-Anzeige matchcode display
Matchcode-Erfassung matchcode acquisition
Matchcode-Suchbegriff matchcode search word
Material material
Materialabgang issues of materials
Materialart materials type
Materialartentabelle materials type table
Materialaufnahme materials entry
Materialausgabe issue of materials, issues of materials
Materialbedarf materials requirement
Materialbeistellung materials submitted
Materialbeleg materials voucher
Materialberechtigung materials authorization
Materialbereich materials area
Materialbereitstellung materials allocation
Materialbereitstellungsdatum date the materials are required
Materialbeschreibung description of the materials
Materialbestand inventory, materials inventory, stock in hand
Materialbestandsführung materials inventory update
Materialbestandskonto stock account
Materialbewegung stock movement
Materialbewertungskonto materials valuation account
Materialbezeichnung materials name
materialbezogen materials-related
Materialbuchung materials posting
Materialdaten materials data
Materialdatenbank materials database
Materialeinsatz materials utilization
Materialentnahme materials withdrawal
Materialentnahmeschein materials withdrawal note
Materialgruppe materials group
Materialinformation materials information
Materialkomponente component item number
Materialkontenklasse materials account class
Materialkurzbezeichnung materials brief designation
Materialkurztext materials summary
Materiallieferung materials delivery
Materialmenge quantity
Materialmonat materials month
Materialnummer materials number

Materialnummernvergabe materials number allocation
Materialpreis materials price
Materialpreisänderung materials price change
Materialreservierung materials reservation
Materialschlüssel materials code
Materialsegment materials segment
Materialstamm materials master
Materialstammdatei materials master file
Materialstammdaten materials master data
Materialstammdatenpflege materials master data update
Materialstammkennzeichen materials master marker
Materialstammsatz materials master record
Materialstammsegment materials master segment
Materialstammverwaltung materials master management
Materialstatus status
Materialsteuerbyte materials control code
Materialtext materials text
Materialunterdeckungsliste materials shortfall report
Materialverbrauch materials consumption
Materialverbrauchsliste materials consumption report
Materialverfügbarkeit materials availability
Materialverwaltungssatz materials management record
Materialverzeichnis materials register
Materialwert materials value
Materialwertkontrolle materials value monitoring
Materialwirtschaft materials management
Materialzugang materials acquisition
mathematisch mathematical
mathematische Funktion mathematical function
mathematische Operation mathematical operation
Matrix array, matrix
Matrix-Algebra matrix algebra
Matrixdruck matrix printer
Matrixdrucker matrix printer, mosaic printer
Matrixform matrix form
Matrixgröße matrix size
Matrixinversion matrix inversion
Matrixspeicher core storage
Matrix-Variable array variable
Matrixzeile matrix line
Matrix (Briefqualität) matrix (enhanced)
Matrix (Manuskriptqualität) matrix (normal)

Matrize array, matrix
Matrizengröße matrix size
Matrizenrechnung matrix algebra
Matrizenschreibweise matrix notation
maximal maximum
Maximalbelegung maximum occupancy state
maximaler Speicherbedarf maximum memory requirements
Maximalgrenze maximum limit
Maximalumfang maximum length
Maximalwert maximum value
Maximalzahl maximum number
Maximum maximum
MByte (Megabyte) MByte
Mechaniktest movement test
mechanischer Drucker impact printer
mechanisches Steuersystem mechanical control system
mechanische Steuerung mechanical control equipment, mechanical variable control
Mechanismus mechanism
Medium media, medium
Meeting meeting
Megabyte megabyte
Megawort megaword
Mehrachsentisch multi-axis table
mehradriges Kabel multicore cable
Mehrbenutzer multiuser
Mehrbenutzerbetrieb time sharing
Mehrdatenträgerdatei multivolume file
mehrdeutiges Kommando ambiguous command, ambiguous verb
mehrere Tastatursignale series of bell tones
Mehrfach- multi, multiple, multipoint
mehrfach multiple, multiplex, multipoint
Mehrfachablegung cross filing
Mehrfachanschluß multi access line, multi channel access line
Mehrfachausnutzung multiplex operation
Mehrfachbetätigung rollover
Mehrfachbus-Speicherdesign multibus memory design
Mehrfachdatei multiple file
mehrfache Genauigkeit multiple precision
mehrfach genutzte Leitung multiplex line
mehrfach indexdirekte Zugriffsmethode multiple indexed random access method
Mehrfachkommando multiple command
Mehrfachnutzung multiple use
mehrfach partionierte Datei multi partitioned file, multiple partitioned file
Mehrfachregelung multivariable control
Mehrfachschlüssel-Sortierung multi key sort

Mehrfachspeicherzugriffssteuerung multipoint feature, multiport feature
Mehr-Firmen-Verarbeitung multi firm processing
Mehrjobverarbeitung multijobbing
Mehrkanal- multiplex
Mehrkanalanschlußeinheit shared peripheral interface
Mehrkanalgerät multiplexing equipment
Mehrkanal-Übertragungseinrichtung multiplex equipment
Mehrlingssystem multiple system
mehrmals several times
Mehrphasenmotor polyphase motor
Mehrphasentransformator polyphase transformer
Mehrplatzsystem multiuser system
Mehrprogrammbetrieb multiprocessing, multiprogramming
Mehr-Prozeß-Betrieb multi task operation
Mehrprozessor multiprocessor
Mehrprozessorbetrieb multiprocessing
Mehrprozessorsystem multiprocessor system
Mehrpunktverbindung multidrop connection
Mehrpunkt-Verbindung multi-endpoint connection
Mehrpunktverbindung multipoint connection
Mehrrechnersystem multicomputer system
Mehrrollen-Datei multi roll file
Mehrschichtabschreibung multiple depreciation
Mehrschichtleiterplatte multilayer board
Mehrschrittgrößen multiple step sizes
Mehrspaltensucheinrichtung multiple column selection device
mehrspaltiges Drucken multicolumn printing
mehrsprachig multilingual
Mehrstationsadressierung multi destination routing
mehrstufig multi level, multi stage
mehrstufiges Zeitglied cascading timer
mehrteiliger Hängeisolator cap-and-pin insulator
Mehrwert value added
Mehrwertdienst value added service
Mehrwert-Netz value added network
Mehrwert-Netzwerkdienst value added network service
Mehrwertsteuer value added tax
Mehrwertsteuerart value added tax type
Mehrwertsteuerberechnung value added tax bill
Mehrwertsteuerbetrag value added tax amount
Mehrwertsteuerbuchung value added tax posting
Mehrwertsteuerkennung value added tax identification
Mehrwertsteuerkennzeichen value added tax code, value added tax marker
Mehrwertsteuerklasse value added tax category
Mehrwertsteuerkonto value added tax account
Mehrwertsteuerkorrektur value added tax correction
Mehrwertsteuersatz value added tax rate, value added tax record
Mehrwertsteuerschlüssel value added tax code
Mehrwertsteuer-Verrechnungskonto value added tax settlement account
Mehrzeichen-Sortierlauf multiple character sort
Mehrzeilenabfühlsteuerung multiple line read selection
Mehrzweckregister general register
melden report
Meldepunkt tracepoint
Meldung message
Meldung der Cursorposition cursor position report, position report
Meldung des Betriebssystems operating system message
Meldung des Gerätestatus device status report
Meldungsanzeige message display
Meldungsbeginnzeichen message beginning character
Meldungsentschlüsselungsroutine decoder
Meldungsformat message format
Meldungs-Statusanzeige message status display
Meldungszeile message line
Memorandum memo
Menge quantity, set
Mengenabweichung quantity discrepancy
Mengenänderung quantity alteration
Mengenangabe quantity given
Mengenbeziehung quantity reference
Mengenbuchung quantity posting
Mengenfeld quantity field
Mengengerüst application statistics
Mengengutschrift quantity credit note
Mengenkontrakt quantity contract
mengenmäßig quantitative
mengenorientiert quantity oriented
mengenproportional in proportion to quantity
Mengenprüfung quantity control
Mengensituation quantity situation
Mengenspalte quantity column

Mengensperrtabelle quantity lock table
Mengenstaffel quantity scale
Mengenüberprüfung quantity control
Mengenunterdeckung quantity shortfall
Mengenveränderung quantity amendment
Mengenverfügbarkeit availability
Mengenverfügbarkeitskontrolle availability check
menschlicher Faktor human factor
menschlich klingende Stimme human sounding voice
Mensch-Maschine man machine
Mensch-Maschine Dialog man machine conversation
Mensch-Maschinen-Modell man machine model
Mensch-Maschine-Schnittstelle human interface
Menu menu
Menü menu, menue, screen
Menüaktion menu item
Menüangebot menu offer
Menüanzeige menu display, menu indication
Menüauswahl menu selection
Menübaum menu tree
Menübaumanweisung menu tree instruction
Menübaumanweisungsfolge menu tree instruction sequence
Menübaumanweisungssprache menu tree instruction language
Menübaumdatei menu tree file
Menübaumdefinition menu tree definition
Menübaumgenerator menu tree generator
Menübaumschlüssel menu tree key
Menübaumstruktur menu tree structure
Menübaumstrukturliste menu tree structure list
Menübaumverfahren menu tree process
Menübaumzugriffsroutine menu tree access routine
Menübegriff menu term
Menübildschirm menu screen
Menüebene menu level
menügeführt menu driven
menügesteuert menu driven
Menükürzel menu keyword
Menüname menu name
Menüoption menu option
Menüorganisation menu organisation
Menüposition menu position
Menüpunkt menu item
Menüseite menu page
Menüstruktur menu structure

Menütechnik menu technology
Menü zur Auswahl der Sprache language selection menu
Merker label, marker
Merkerbyte marker byte
Merker-Halbwort indicator half-value
Merkerhalbwort marker half word
Merkerstellung indicator position
Merkmal feature, id, qualifier
Merkmale der Editiertasten edit key feature
Meßanordnung test setup
Meßaufbau test setup
Messe fair, trade fair
messen gauge, measure, meter
Messen im Stromversorgungsnetz electric power system measurement
Messenspeicher im Mehrfachzugriff shared mass storage
Meßgerät meter
Meßnetzwerk-Konzept distributed measurement network
Meßrelais measuring relay
Meßstation metering station
Meß- und Analysesystem measurement system
Messung measurement, measuring
Meßwandler instrument transformer
Metaassembler meta assembler
Metall metal
Metallasche metal tab
Metallmantelkabel metal clad cable
Metallrabatt metals discount
Metallschichtwiderstand metal film resistor
Metallzuschlag metals surcharge
Metasprache meta language
Metasyntax metasyntax
Methode method, principle, procedure
Microsoft Betriebssystem Microsoft disk operating system
Miete lease, rent
mieten lease, rent
Mietleitung leased circuit, leased line
Mietleitungsdienst leased line service
Mietleitungsnetz leased line network
Migration migration
migrieren migrate
Mikroassemblierung microassembling
Mikrobefehl microinstruction
Mikrocode microcode
Mikrocomputer microcomputer
Mikrocomputer-Anwendungen microcomputer application
Mikrocomputer-Software microcomputer software

363

Mikrofon microphone
Mikrometerantrieb micrometer drive
Mikrominiaturbaugruppe microminiature circuit
Mikroprogramm microcode, microprogram
Mikroprogrammierung microprogramming
Mikroprozessor microprocessor, microprozessor
Mikroprozessorarten microprocessor classification
Mikroprozessorbaustein microprocessor chip
Mikroprozessorbefehlssatz microprocessor instruction set
Mikroprozessorelemente microprocessor slices
Mikroprozessor-Entwicklungssystem microprocessor development system
Mikroschalter microswitch
Mikrowellen-Filter microwave filter
Mikrowellen-Mikroelektronik microwave microelectronic
Mikrowellenoszillator microwave oscillator
Mikrowellenröhre microwave tube
Mikrowellenschaltung microwave circuit
Mikrowellentransistor microwave transistor
Mikrowellenverstärker microwave amplifier
militärisch military
Milliarden Befehle pro Sekunde billions of instructions per second
Millionenbefehle pro Sekunde megainstructions per second
millionstel micro
mindern decrease
Minderung decrease
Mindest- minimum
Mindestanzahl minimum number
Mindestauftragsmenge minimum order quantity
Mindestbestand minimum stock, minimum stock level
Mindestbestandsmenge minimum stock quantity
Mindestbestellmenge minimum order quantity, minimum purchase order quantity
Mindestbestellung minimum order
Mindestbetrag minimum amount
Mindesteindeckungszeit minimum availability time
mindestens at least
Mindestfüllrand minimum contents level
Mindestlänge minimum length
Mindestmenge minimum quantity
Mini- mini, miniature

Miniatur-Leistungsschalter miniature circuit breaker
Miniaturrelais miniature relay
Minicomputer minicomputer
Minicomputer-Sichtgerät minicomputer display
minimal minimum
Minimalauswahl minimum selection
Minimalkonfiguration low end configuration, replicated system approach
Minimallaufkonfiguration minimum run configuration
Minimalwert minimum value
Minimalwertunterschreitung underflow
Minimum minimum
Minischalter switch
minus minus
Minuszeichen minus sign
Minute minute
mischen merge, mix
Mischen mit gleichzeitigem Trennen collate
Mischkreis mixer circuit
Mischlauf collation pass, merge run
Mischröhre mixer tube
Mischverarbeitung merge processing
Mist rein Mist raus garbage in garbage out
mit acht Karten 8-board
Mitarbeiter employee
Mitarbeitersuffix assistant suffix
Mitbenutzbarkeit shareability
Mitbenutzer co-user
Mitbenutzer-Bezeichnung co-user designation
Mitbenutzer-Verzeichnis co-user directory
Mitbuchkonto parallel-posted account
Mitbuchung parallel posting
Mitbuchungskennzeichen parallel posting marker
mit Byteversatz single byte interleaved
mit der Größe eines Bürorechners office-size package
miteinander together
mitgeführt kept in parallel
mitgepflegt maintained in parallel
mitgerechnet taken into account
Mitglied member
Mitgliederverzeichnis directory of members
Mitgliedsart member type
Mitgliedseintrag member entry
Mitnehmerstift drive pin
mitsetzen set as well
mit Sternchen versehen asterisked, starred
mitteilen inform
Mitteilung memo, memorandum, message

Mitteilungsart message type
Mitteilungsaustausch message exchange
Mitteilungsdatei communication file
Mitteilungskopf information header
Mitteilungsmenge quantity informed
Mitteilungsnummer message number
Mitteilungstext message text
Mitteilungs-Übermittlungsdienst message handling system
Mitteilungs-Übertragungszeit message transfer time
Mittel means
mittel medium
mittelbar indirect
mittelbarer Schaden consequential damages
mittelfristig medium term
Mittelkurs average exchange rate
Mittelpunkt focal point
Mittelpunkttransformator static balancer
mittels via
Mittelspannungs-Installation medium voltage installation
Mittelwert average, average value
Mittelwertspannungsmesser average voltmeter
Mittelwertvoltmeter average voltmeter
mittlere medium
mittlere Buchstabentastenreihe middle letter row
mittlere Einstellung midrange
mittlere fehlerfreie Rechenzeit mean time between failure
mittlere Instandsetzungszeit mean time to restore
mittlere Instandsetzungszeit mean time to repair
mittlere Integrationsdichte medium scale integration
mittlere Produktivzeit mean up-time
mittlere Reparaturzeit mean repair time, mean time to repair
mittlere Übertragungsgeschwindigkeit average transfer rate
mittlere Wartungszeit mean service time
mittlere Wiederherstellungszeit mean time to restore
mittlere Zeit bis zum Ausfall mean time to failure
mittlere Zeit zwischen Ausfällen mean time between failures
mittlere Zeit zwischen Fehlern mean time between errors
mittlere Zeit zwischen Wartungen mean time between maintenance

mitverwaltet also managed
mit Zeilensprung interlaced
Mix-Array mix array
Mix-Datei mix file
Mix-Daten mix data
mixen mix
Mix-Satz mix record
Mnemonic mnemonic
mnemonisch mnemonic
mnemonische Adresse mnemonic address
mnemonische Bezeichnung identifier
mnemonischer Code mnemonic code
Modell model
Modem data set, modem
Modem bereit data set ready
Modemdaten-Paritätsbit modem data parity bit
Modem-/Drucker-Taste modem printer select key
Modem nicht betriebsbereit data set ready off
Modemsteuerung modem control
Modemtestkarte modem evaluation board
Modifikation modification
Modifikationscode modification code
Modifikationsfehler modification error
Modifikationskonstante modification constant
Modifikationsteil modification section
modifizieren modify
Modifizierer modifier
modifizierte Frequenzmodulation modified frequency modulation
Modikon modicon
Modul module
modular modular
modularer Telefonstecker modular plug
modulare Telefonstecker telephone type modular connectors
Modularität granularity
Modulator modulator
Modulbestückung module population
Modulbibliothek module library
Module interleaved modules
Modulform module form
Modul für Bitmustergrafik extended bit map module
Modul für den oberen Bus upper bus module
Modul für den unteren Bus lower bus module
Modul für die Umwandlung von Buchstaben letter-to-sound module
Modulkomponente module component
Modulmenü module menu
Modulname module name
Modulo modulo

Modulo-n-Prüfung modulo n-check
Modulpool module pool
Modulstand module status
Modulsteckplatz option position
Modulteil module part
Modulzieher module puller
Modus mode
Modus auswählen set mode
Modus der Neuberechnung recalculation mode
Modusparameter mode parameter
Moduswechsel mode conversion
mögliche Belegung des numerischen Tastenblocks alternate keypad mode
mögliche Kommandoformen available command line forms
mögliche Ursache probable cause
Möglichkeit eventuality, feature, option
Möglichkeit zum Hervorheben von Text highlighting feature
Möglichkeit zur Mikroprogrammierung microprogrammability
Monat month
Monatsabgrenzung month's end
Monatsabschluß month end closing
Monatsbereich month area
Monatsfeld month field
Monatsmiete monthly rental charge
Monatsname name of the month
Monatssaldo month's balance, monthly balance
Monatsstatistik monthly statistics
Monatsultimo end of the month
Monatsverbrauch monthly consumption
Monatsverschiebeprogramm month end balance rollover program
Monatsverschiebung month end balance rollover
Monatswechsel end of the month
Monatswert month value
Monitor monitor
Monitor für erweiterten Speicher extended memory monitor
Monitorprogramm monitor image, monitor program
Monitorroutine monitor routine
Monitorsystem monitor system
Monitorunterbrechung monitor interrupt
monochrom monochrome
Monochrombildschirm monochrome display, monochrome monitor
Monokopfhörer monaural headphones
monolithisch monolithic

monolithisch integrierte Schaltung monolithic integrated circuit
monostabil one shot
monostabiler Multivibrator monostable trigger circuit
monostabile Schaltung one shot circuit
monostabiles Zeitglied single shot timer
Montageplatte base
Montageplattengehäuse base enclosure
Montageschiene rail
Montagesockel mounting socket
montieren assemble
morphem morpheme
MOS metal oxide silicon
Mosaikdrucker matrix printer
MOS-Technologien MOS-technologies
Motor engine, motor
Motorgenerator motor alternator
Motor mit Nennleistung unter 736 W fractional horsepower motor
Münzeinrichtung prepayment equipment
Muldex muldex
multinational multinational
multinationaler 8-Bit-Zeichensatz multinational 8-bit character set
multinationaler Zeichensatz multinational character set
multiplex multiplex
Multiplexbetrieb multiplex mode
multiplexen multiplexing
Multiplexer multiplexer
Multiplexer für Datenübertragung communications multiplexer subsystem
Multiplex-Fernschreibverfahren multiplex printing telegraphy
Multiplexkanalanschluß host adapter
Multiplexleitung multiplex line
Multiplikation multiplication
Multiplikator multiplier
Multiplizierer multiplying circuit
Multiprogramm-Priorität multiprogramming priority
Multiprozessor multiprocessor
Multitasking multitasking
Multivibrator multivibrator oszillator
Muß-Anweisung mandatory instruction
Mußeingabe mandatory entry
Muster model, pattern, sample, template
Musterangebot sample offer
Musterartikel sample item
Musterbeispiel example
Musterbeleg sample voucher
Musterdatensatz sample data record

Mustererkennung pattern recognition
Musterjob sample job
Mustersatz sample record
Musterstamm sample master
Musterstammsatz sample master record
Mustertabelle table of samples
mutmaßlich presumed
Muttergesellschaft mother company, parent company
Muttersegment master segment

N

nach after
Nachaktivierung reactivation
Nacharbeit maintenance
nach Auftragseingang after receipt of order
Nachbearbeitung finishing
Nachbelastung additional charge
Nachbelastungs-Auftrag additional charge order
Nachbildungsgerät simulation equipment
nachbuchen reenter
Nachbuchung update posting
nacheinander one after another
nacheinander drucken print subsequently
Nacherfassung post entry
Nacherfassungsbeleg reregistration document
nachfolgend adjacent, subsequent
nachfolgende Abbildung after image
nachfolgende Flanke trailing edge
nachfolgende Operation connected operation
nachfolgendes Feld adjacent cell
nachfolgendes Leerzeichen trailing space
Nachfolger successor
Nachfrageschwankung change of demand
Nachhaltedatei audit file
nachholen retrieve
nach Installation post installation
Nachkalkulation internal billing
Nachkommastelle post decimal position
nachlagern store
Nachlaufkarte trailer card
Nachlaufpotentiometer servo-driven potentiometer
Nachlaufregelsystem servo-controlled system
Nachlaufwerk servomechanism
Nachlaufzeit slowing-down time
nachlesen look up
Nachlieferung additional delivery
nach links verschieben shift left
nach oben rollen scroll up, shifting up
nachprüfen check
nach rechts verschieben shift right
Nachregler post regulator
Nachricht mail message, message
Nachrichtenanfang start of message
Nachrichtenart message type
Nachrichtenaufbereitung message editing
Nachrichtenausgabe message output
Nachrichtenaustausch interaction
Nachrichtenaustausch-Protokoll message interchange protocol
Nachrichtenbeginn start of message
Nachrichtenbereich message scope
Nachrichtenempfänger message recipient
Nachrichtenendesignal end of message signal
Nachrichtenformatierung message formatting
Nachrichtenkennung message identification
Nachrichtenkommunikation message communication
Nachrichtenkopfsender identification transmitter, identifier transmitter
Nachrichtenlänge message length
Nachrichtennummer message number
Nachrichten-Protokolldatei image journal file
Nachrichtenpufferung message staging
Nachrichtenschlußzeichen message ending character
Nachrichtenschnittstelle communication interface
Nachrichtenspeicherung information storage, message storage
Nachrichtensteuerprogramm message control program
Nachrichtensteuertabelle message control table
Nachrichtensteuerungsebene message control level
Nachrichtenübermittlung message switching
Nachrichtenwartezeit message waiting time
Nachsatz trailer
nachschlagen look up
Nachschlagewerk reference manual, reference work
Nachschlaginformationen reference information
nachsehen look up
Nachselektion additional selection
Nachsendeadresse forwarding address
Nachsilbe suffix
Nachspannseite trailer page
nachstehend following
nachstellen adjust
nachträglich later, subsequent
Nachtrag addition
Nachtragsbilanz additional balance
nach unten rollen scroll down, shifting down
Nachweis evidence
Nadel pin
Nadeldrucker needle printer, wire printer
Nadeldrucker-Druckkopf needle printer head
Nadelspitzen nibs
Nadelträgerriemen stylus belt
nächst next

nächstes Wort   advance one word
nächste Zeile   next line
nächstgrößer   next larger
nächsthöher   next higher
nächstniedrig   next lower
näher   more detailed
nähere Einzelheiten   further details
Näherungsschalter   proximity switch
Nahbereichsmodem   short range modem
nahe Prüfschleife   local loop
Nahtstelle   interface
Nahtstellenanordnung   interface equipment
Name   name, title
Name der Sicherungsdiskette   backup diskette name
Name der Standarddatei   default file name
Name des Diskettenlaufwerks   diskette device name
Name des Festplattenlaufwerks   hard disk drive name
Name des Standardgerätes   default device name
Namensangabe   name specified
Namensfeld   name field
Namensgleichheit   identity of names
Namensparameter   label parameter
Nasallaut   nasal
Nase   lug
national   national
Navigation   navigation
Navigationsmessung   navigational measurement
neben   adjacent, beside
Nebenabrede   special agreement
Nebenbestand   additional stock
Nebenbuchhaltung   subsidiary accounting
Nebenfunktion   secondary function
Nebeninduktivität   shunt reactor
Nebenkosten   additional expenses
Nebenrelation   subsidiary relation
Nebensaldo   subsidiary balance
Nebenschluß   shunt
Nebenschlußleitung   parallel circuit
Nebenstelle   extension
Nebenstellenanlage   private branch exchange
Nebenstellennummer   private branch number
Nebensteuereinheit   mini control unit
Nebenwiderstand   instrument shunt
negativ   negative, negative going
Negativbetrag   negative amount
negative Logik   negative logic
negativer Fehler   negative going error
negative Rückmeldung   negative acknowledgement

negative Zustandsmeldung   bad status
negativ-positiv   negative-positive
Negativwert   negation, negative value
negiertes UND   not AND
Neigungswinkel   viewing angle
Nenndrehzahl   rated speed
Nennfrequenz   rated frequency
Nennleistung   rated output, rating
Netto   net
Nettoauftragswert   sales order net value
Nettoausgleichsvolumen   net balance volume
Nettobedarfsermittlung   net requisition planning
Nettobedingung   net terms
Nettobestellpreis   net purchase order price
Nettobestellwert   purchase order net value
Nettobetrag   net amount
Nettobuchung   net posting
Nettodatum   net date
Nettofälligkeit   net due date
Nettokosten   net costs
Nettopreis   net price
Nettopreisermittlung   net price calculation
Nettosatzlänge   net record length
Nettoumsatz   net turnover
Nettowert   net value
Netz   net, network, network, power
Netzadresse   network address
Netzanalysator   network analyzer
Netzanschluß   power connection, power connector, power receptacle, socket
Netzanschlußwert   power requirement
Netzanzeige   power indicator
Netzausfall   AC dump, blackout, power failure, power source fault
Netzausfallmerker   power failure marker
netzausfallsicher   power failure protected
Netzbeschreibungssprache   network description language
Netzbetreiber   carrier
Netz ein   power on
Netzeingangsstrom   network bias current
Netze in Großstädten   metropolitan networks
Netzfrequenz   line frequency
Netzfrequenztoleranz   line frequency tolerance
Netzführung   network management
Netzgenerierung   network generation
Netzhauptknoten   network control node
Netzinformation   network information
Netzkabel   AC power cord, power cable, power cord
Netzkabelstecker   power cord plug
Netzkennung   network identification

Netzkontrolle network control
Netzkontrollzentrum network control center, network management center, node control center
Netzmanagement network management
Netzmanager network manager
Netz mit Leitungsvermittlung circuit switched network
Netz mit Mehrwertdiensten value added network, value added network service
Netzschalter on off switch, power switch
Netzschicht network layer
Netzsicherheitszentrum network security center
Netzspannung line voltage, power line voltage, voltage
Netzsteckdose electrical outlet, wall outlet
Netzsteuersystem network control system
Netzsteuerung network control
Netzsteuerungsmodul network control module
Netzsteuerungsprogramm network control program
Netzsteuerungsprozeß network control process
Netzsteuerungssprache network control language
Netzstrom power
netztaktgesteuerte Uhr frequency clock, line frequency clock
Netzteil electronic power supply, power supply, power supply module
Netzteilnehmer network user
Netzteiltyp power supply type
Netzüberlastung network congestion
Netzübertragungssystem network transmission system
Netzverbindung network connection
Netzverkabelung power wiring
Netzvermittlung network switching center
Netzwartung network maintenance
Netzwerk net, network
Netzwerkanalysator network analyzer
Netzwerkanalyse network analysis
Netzwerkberechner network analyser
Netzwerkbetreiber carrier
Netzwerkdateiübertragung network file transfer
Netzwerkdateizugriffsprotokoll network file access protocol
Netzwerkdateizugriffsverfahren network file access method
Netzwerkelement network resource
Netzwerkinformationsdienste network information services

Netzwerkknoten node
Netzwerkmanager network manager
Netzwerkparameter network parameter
Netzwerkpfad network path
Netzwerkschnittstellenprozeß network interface task
Netzwerksoftware network system software
Netzwerksteuerung network contol
Netzwerksteuerungsblock network control block
Netzwerksynthese network synthesis
Netzwerk-Topologie und Wegeauswahlverfahren network topology and routing, routing
Netzwerktuning network performance management, performance management
Netzwerkvorrechner front end network processor, front end processor, network front end
Netzwerkzugangsprotokoll network access protocol
Netzwerkzugangsrechner network access machine
Netzwerkzugangssteuereinheit network access contoller
Netzwerkzugangsverfahren network access method
neu fresh, new
Neuanlage initialization
neuanlegen initialize, recreate
neuanmelden logon again
Neuanmeldung logging on again
Neuaufbau new structure
neu aufbauen rebuild, reconstruct
Neuaufruf new call
Neuaufteilen der Festplatte repartitioning
Neuauswahl new selection, reselection
Neubeginn fresh start, restart
neu belegen redefine, remap
neubenennen rename
neu berechnen recalculate
Neuberechnung recalculation
neu definieren redefine
Neueingabe new entry, reenter
neu einrichten recreate
Neueinsprung reenter
Neueinstellung readjustment
neu errichten recreate
neu erstellen create anew, recreate
neue Seite new page
neue Zeile new line
neu formatieren reformat
Neuhinzufügung new addition
neu initialisieren reinitialize

Neuinitialisierung reinitialization
Neuinstallation new installation
Neukonfigurierung reconfiguration
neu laden reboot, reload
neu numerieren renumber, resequence
Neunumerierung repagination
neu ordnen rearrange
neurechnen recalculate
Neuselektion new selection
Neustart fresh start, new start, restart
neustarten reset, restart, start again
Neustart nach Stromausfall power fail restart
neustrukturieren restructure
Neuumbruch repagination
Neuzugang new acquisition
nicht angekommene Nachricht dead letter, dead mail
nicht angeschlossen disconnected, offline
nicht angeschlossene Leitung open line
nicht aufeinanderfolgend fragmented, non contiguous
nicht aufnehmen können overrun
nicht ausführbare Anweisung reserved instruction
nicht austauschbar non interchangeable
nicht betriebsbereit down
nicht bootfähig non bootable
nicht definiert undefined
nicht definierter Befehl undefined command
Nichteisen-Metall nonferrous metal
nicht empfangsbereit receiver not ready
nichtentflammbares Gehäuse flameproof enclosure
nicht erkannt negative acknowledge
nichtexistierendes Gerät nonstandard device
nichtflüchtiger Speicher non volatile memory
nichtfüchtig non volatile
nicht-funktionsbeteiligt nonfunctional
nicht intelligent non intelligent
nichtleitend dielectric, nonconducting
nichtleitendes Gerät dielectric device
nicht lesbar unreadable
nichtmaskierbarer Interrupt nonmaskable interrupt
nichtmaskierbare Unterbrechungsanforderung nonmaskable interrupt
nichtnumerierte Bestätigung unnumbered acknowledge
nicht programmiert unprogrammed
nicht reparierter Sektor unrecovered sector
nicht sichern discard
Nicht-Standardgerät arbitrary device
nicht stromführend dead

nicht verfügbar not available
nicht verkettet unconcatenated
nicht wahr false
nichtzerstörender Lesezugriff nondestructive read
nicht zulässig illegal
nicht zulässige Adresse illegal address
nicht zulässiger Wert illegal value
nicht zulässiges Zeichen illegal character
Nickel-Cadmium-Akku nicad
Nickel-Cadmium-Akkumulator nickel cadmium battery
Niederfrequenzsignal audiofrequency signal
Niederfrequenzverstärker low frequency amplifier
Niederlassungsauftrag branch order
Niederschrift statement
Niederspannungseinrichtungen low voltage equipment
Niederspannungsgerät low voltage equipment
Niederstbewertungsprinzip minimum valuation principle
niederwertig low order
niederwertige Ziffer low order digit
niedrige Programmiersprache low level language
niedriger Integrationsgrad small scale integration
niedrigstwertiges Bit least significant bit, low order bit
niedrigstwertige Stelle least significant digit
Niveau level
Niveaugeber level transducer
Niveaumeßgerät level measurement
Niveauregelung level control
Niveauschalter level switch
noch still
nochmals again
Nockenschalter cam switch
Nokeypad-Kommando nokeypad command
Nokeypad-Modus nokeypad mode
Norm standard
Normalbetriebsart native mode
normale Differentialgleichung ordinary differential equation
normaler Mehrwertsteuersatz standard value added tax
Normalform normal form
Normalmodus image mode, native mode
Normalpreis standard price
Normalvorschaltgerät reference ballast
Normalzustand standard state
normieren reset

Normkartengehäuse standard card enclosure
Normspule standard reactor
Normungsbüro standards office
Notabschaltung emergency shutdown
notfalls if necessary
Notfallziel emergency target
Notiz memorandum, note, notice
Notizblock scratch pad
Notizblock-Speicher scratchpad memory
Notlaufbuchung emergency run reservation
Notlaufbuchungszeile fail safe posting line
Notlaufeinschaltung emergency run activation
notlauffähig capable of an emergency run
Notlaufschlüssel emergency run code
Notlaufzustand fail safe state
Notstrominstallation emergency electrical installation
Notstromkreis emergency circuit
notwendig necessary, required
Notwendigkeit necessity
nützlich advantageous, useful
Null zero
Nulldurchgang intercept
Nulleintrag zero entry
Nulleiter common return, common wire, neutral conductor
nullen make zero
Nullenunterdrückung zero suppression
Nullfehler zero defect
Nullkennzeichen zero flag
Nullkontrolle zero balancing
Nullpotential zero potential
Nullpunktfehler zero error
Nullpunktverschiebung zero shift
Nullstelle zero
Nullstellenprüfung zero check
Nullstellungszustand reset condition
Nulltaste dead key
Nullunterdrückung beim Speichern von Daten zero compression
Nullzugriff zero access
Nullzustand zero state
Numeral numeral
numerisch numeric, numerical
numerische Maschinensteuerung computerized numerical control
numerischer Tastenblock keypad numeric mode
numerisches Tastenfeld keypad
numerische Steuerung numerical control
numerisch gesteuert numerical controlled
Nummer number
Nummernintervall range of numbers

Nummernkreis range of numbers
Nummernkreisangabe given range of numbers
Nummernobergrenze upper limit of numbers
Nummernschalterwahl dial selection
Nummernvergabe allocation of numbers
nur ankommende Verbindung outgoing call barred
nur Empfang receive only
Nur-Lese- read only
Nur-Lese-Datei read only file
Nur-Lese-Speicher read only memory, read-only memory
nutzbare Zeilenlänge usable line length
Nutzdaten information
Nutzen advantage
Nutzer user
Nutzungsausfall loss of use
Nutzungsdauer expected useful life, lifetime, lifetime period
nutzungsdauerbezogen useful life related
Nutzungshäufigkeit frequency of use
Nutzungsschaden loss of use
Nutzzeile listing line

O

oben above, top
obengenannt above mentioned, afore mentioned
obere Buchstabentastenreihe upper letter row
oberen und unteren Rand festlegen set top and bottom margin
oberer Rand top edge, top margin
oberer und unterer Rand top and bottom margin
oberes Halbwort upper half word
Oberfläche surface
oberflächenmontierbares Bauelement surface mounted device
Obergrenze upper bound, upper limit
oberirdische Leitung overhead line
oberirdisches Kabel overhead cable
oberste Tastenreihe top row of keys
Oberwellen mit höherer Ordnungszahl high order harmonics
Objectcode-Bibliothek object code library
Objekt entity, object
Objektbeziehung entity relationship
Objektbeziehungsmodell entity relationship model
objektbezogen object related
Objektcode object code
Objektdatei object file
Objektmodul object module
Objektmodul-Bibliothek object module library
Objektprogramm object program
Objektsprache object language
obligatorisch mandatory
Obligo liability
öffentlich public
öffentliche Dienste public services
öffentlicher Nachrichtenübermittler common carrier
öffentlicher Netzbetreiber common carrier
öffentlicher Schlüssel public key
öffentliches Datennetz public data network, public switched data network
öffentliches Fernsprechnetz public switched telephone network, public telephone network
öffentliches Netz public switched network
öffentliches Telefonnetz public switched telephone network, public telephone network
öffnen open
Öffnung opening

ölgekapselter Transformator oil-immersed transformer
Ölschalter oil circuit breaker, oil switch
örtliche Rufnummer local call number, local number
Öse eyelet
offen exposed, open
offene elektrische Einrichtung open electrical equipment
offene Leitung open line
offensichtlich obviously
Offerte offer
offline offline
Off-Line-Betrieb offline operation
offline editieren edit offline
Offline-Editierung offline editing
Offline-Editierverfahren offline edit method
offline erstellen create offline
Offline-Modus offline mode
Offline-Schritt offline step
Offline-Umschalten offline switching
Off-Line-Verarbeitung offline
Offset displacement, offset
Offsetadresse displacement address
Offset-Wert offset value
ohne Berechnung for free, no charge
ohne Rücksicht regardless
ohne Schreibschutz write enable
ohne System non bootable
ohne Zeilensprung non interlaced
Ohrhörer earplug
oktal octal
Oktaladresse octal address
Oktalcode octal code
Oktalsystem octal system
Oktalziffer octal digit, octal figure
On-Line online
online online
Online-Ablaufsteuerung online scenario controller
Online-Anzeige online indicator
Online-Betrieb online operation
Online-Diagnose online diagnostic
Online-Drucker online printer
Online-Fehlersuche online debugging technique
Online-Hilfstext online help
Online-Konteninformation online account information
Online-Modus online mode
Online-Programm online program
Online-Session online session
Online-System online system
on/off-line on/off-line

Opcode opcode
Open-Modus open mode
Operand factor, operand
Operandeingabe operand input
Operandenadresse operand address
Operandenfehler operand error
Operandenfehlercode operand error code
Operandenteil operand part, operand section
Operandenwert operand value
Operation operation
Operation nochmals ausführen retry operation
Operationscode operation code
Operationsname operation name
Operationsteil operation code, operation part
Operationsverstärker operational amplifier
Operationszyklus operation cycle
Operation zurücknehmen cancel, cancel the operation
Operator operator
Operatorconsole operator console
Operatoridentifikation operator identification
Operatorprotokolldatei operator log file
Optiksteuerung optical variable control
optimal optimum
Optimierung optimization
Optimierungsfall case of optimization
Optimierungskriterium optimization criterion
Option option
optional option, optional
optionaler Drucker optional printer
optionales Merkmal optional feature
Option im Hauptmenü main menu option
optisch visual
optisch abgeschirmt optically isolated
optische Abschirmung optical isolation
optische Anzeige visual indication
optische Datenübertragung optical data transmission
optische Einwegleitung optical isolator
optische Isolation optical isolation
optischer Markierungsleser optical mark reader
optisches Anzeigegerät annunciator
optische Schnittstelle optical interface
optisch isoliert optically isolated
optoelektronisches Gerät optoelectronic device
optogekoppelt opto-coupled
Optokoppler opto isolator
Ordermenge quantity ordered
ordnen order
Ordner file, folder
Ordnername file name, folder name
Ordnung order

Ordnungsbegriff sorting term
Ordnungsfolge index sequence, sequence string
ordnungsgemäß according to the rules, correct, proper
Ordnungsnummer ordinal number
Ordnungszahl ordinal number
Organisation organisation
Organisation eines Festwertspeichers ROM organization
Organisationsaufwand organisation expenditure
Organisationsbaustein organization block
Organisationsebene organisational level
Organisationsform organisation form
Organisationsmodul organisational module
Organisationsprogramm organisation program
Organisator supervisor
organisatorisch organisational
Organschaft subsidiary
orientieren orient
orientiertes Bit oriented bit
Orientierung orientation
Orientierungsanzeige orientation display
Orientierungshilfe orientation aid
originär original
Original master copy
Originalbeleg original voucher, source document
Originalbelegart original voucher type
Originaldaten original data
Originaldiskette source diskette
Originalsatz master set
Originalsoftwarepaket distribution kit
Originalspur primary track
Originalsystemdiskette master system diskette
Originalzustand original state
Ort location
Ortsgespräch local call
Ortskennzahl preselection number, preselection prefix
Ortung location
Ortungsarm locating arm
Ortungsarm-Transducer locating arm transducer
Ortungssystem locating system
Oszillator oscillator
Overhead overhead
Overheadfolie transparency
Overlay overlay operation
Overlaystufe overlay level
Overlay-Transaktion overlay transaction

P

Paar pair
Paarigkeitsbezugszahl matching record indicator
Paarigkeitsfeld matching field
Pacht lease
pachten lease
packen pack
Packung pack
Packungsdichte packing density
Packungsgröße package size
Packungssatz packing record
PAD packet assembler disassembler
PAD-Rechner-Protokoll PAD-Host protocol
Paging paging
Paginierstempel paginating stamp
Paginierung pagination
Paket package, packet
Paketebene packet level
Paketempfangslaufnummer packet receive sequence number
Paketierer packet assembly
Paketnetz packet switched network, packet switched services, packet switching network, packet switching services
paketorientiert packet mode
Paketreihung packet sequencing
Paketsendelaufnummer packet send sequence number
Pakettyp packet type
Paketübertragung packet switching
paketvermittelt packet switched, packet switching
paketvermittelter Dienst packet switched services, packet switching services
paketvermitteltes Datennetz packet switching data network
paketvermitteltes Netz packet switched network, packet switching network
paketvermitteltes Netzwerk packet switched network, packet switched services, packet switching network, packet switching services
Paketvermittlung packet switching
Paketvermittlungsdienst packet switching
Paketvermittlungsdienste packet switching services
Paketvermittlungsrechner packet switching processor
Paketvermittlungsstation packet assembler disassembler, packet assembly disassembly facility
Paketzähler packet count
Papier paper
Papierabdeckung paper cover
Papierableiter copy guide
Papierauflage paper support, paper table
Papierausdruck hardcopy
Papier ausrichten align paper
Papierauswerfeinrichtung paper ejection device
Papierauswurf paper ejection
Papierbefestigung paper clamp
Papierbremse paper brake
Papierdurchlaß paper feed aperture
Papierdurchlaßdicke paper capacity
Papierdurchlaßvorrichtung paper feed aperture
Papierdurchlauf paper runaway
Papiereinlegeautomat paper adjust routine
Papiereinzugsvorrichtung paper feed device, paper feed unit
Papierendeanzeiger end of paper indicator
Papierfenster paper window
Papierfreigabehebel paper release lever
Papierfühler paper sensor
Papierführung paper path
Papierhalter bail bar
Papierkondensator paper capacitor
Papierlängenanzeiger footage indicator
Papierlösehebel paper release lever
Papierlöser paper release
Papierperipheriegerät symbiont device
Papierrollenhalter paper cradle
Papierspanner paper clamping lever
Papierspannung paper holding tension
Papierstärke-Einstellhebel paper thickness lever
Papierstau paper jam
Papierstreifen paper tape
Papierstreifenablage paper stripe stacker
Papierstreifenauswurf paper stripe ejection
Papiertransporteinrichtung paper transport mechanism
Papiertransportgruppe paper transport group
Papiervorschub eject, form feed, paper feed
Papiervorschubtaste form feed key
Papierzufuhr paper insertion
Pappe cardboard
parallel concurrent, in parallel, parallel
Paralleldrucker parallel printer
parallele Ein-/Ausgabe parallel input/output

Parallelentwicklung concurrent development
parallele Übertragung parallel transmission
Parallelprozessor parallel processor
Parallelrechenwerk parallel arithmetic unit
Parallelresonanzkreis tank circuit
parallel schalten connect across, connect in parallel
Parallelschnittstelle auxiliary interface, peripheral interface
Parallelstromkreis parallel circuit
Parallelübergabe parallel transmission
Parallelübertragung parallel transmission
Parameter parameter
parameterabhängig parameter dependent
Parameterabruf parameter call
Parameterangabe given parameter, parameter indication
Parameterbeschreibung parameter description
Parameterblock parameter block, user control block
Parameterdaten parameter data
Parameterfeld parameter field
Parameterfolge parameter sequence
Parameterinhalt parameter contents
Parameterkarte parameter card
Parameterleiste parameter line
Parameterliste parameter list
Parameternummer parameter number
Parameterprüfprogramm parameter processor
Parametersatz parameter record
Parametersteuerung parameter control
Parametertestbetrieb parameter test mode
Parameterverwaltung parameter adminstration
Parameterwert parameter value
parametrieren parameterize
parametrischer Verstärker parametric amplifier
parametrisieren parameterize
Parität parity
Parität ignorieren ignore parity
Paritätsbit parity bit
Paritätseinstellung parity setting
Paritätsfehler parity error
Paritätsfehler im Speicher memory parity error
Paritätskontrolle parity check, parity control
Paritätsprüfung check parity, parity check, parity checking
Paritätsrückwandfehler parity rear panel error
Paritätszeichen parity character
parken deactivate, park
Parkstellung park position
Partie portion

partielle Startadresse partial starting address
Partition partition
Partitionsabbruch partition abort
Partitionsadresse partition control area
Partitionsaufbau partition structure
Partitionsbedarf partition requirement
Partitionsein-/ausgabe partition input/partition output
Partitionsende end of partition, partition end
Partitionsfehler error in partition
Partitionsgröße partition size
Partitionsmenü partition menu
Partitionsnummer partition number
Partitionsparametersatz partition parameter record
partitionsspezifisch partition specific
Partitionsstatus partition state
Partitionssteuerbereichs-Ergänzung expansion of partition control area, partition control block extension
Partitionstabelle partition table
partitionsunabhängig partition independent
Partitionsverbund partition network
Partitionsvergrößerung partition extension
Partitionsverwaltung partition administration
Partitionsverwaltungssegment partition administration segment
Partitionszuordnung partition assignment
Partnerprogramm partner program
Passagier passenger
Passagierliste passenger name record
passen fit
passend matching, suitable
passender Zeichensatz matching character set
Passiva liabilities
passives Filter passive filter
Passwort password
Passworteingabe password input
Passwortprüfung password check, password validation
Passwortschutz password protection
Passwortverarbeitung password processing
Patchbereich patch area
Patientendaten patient data
Patientenliege patient table
Patientenpositionierung patient positioning
Pausenphonem silence phoneme
PC personal computer
PCIOS-System processor common input output system
Peak peak
Pegelschalter level switch
Peiler direction finder

Pentode pentode
Performancegrund reason for performance
Periode period
Periodenfeld period field
periodengerecht appropriate to the period
Periodenrechnung periodical invoice
Periodensaldo year-to-date balance
Periodensummen totals to date
peripher peripheral
periphere Einheit peripheral equipment
peripherer Direktzugriffsspeicher mass storage subsystem
peripherer Schnittstellenadapter peripheral interface adapter
peripheres Gerät peripheral device
Peripherie peripheral device, periphery
Peripheriebehandlung peripheral handling
Peripheriegerät external device, peripheral device
Peripheriegerät-Steuerbereich peripheral unit control area
Peripheriegerät-Steuerblock peripheral control block
Peripheriekonfigurierungseinheit subsystem availability unit
Peripheriemerker peripheral marker
Peripheriesteuerung peripheral controller
Peripheriesystem peripheral system
permanent permanent
permanente Datei cataloged file
Permanentmagnet permanent magnet
Permanentspeicher permanent memory
persönliche Geheimnummer personal identification number
persönliche Kontonummer personal account number
persönlicher Rechnerzugriff personal computing
Person person
Personalcomputer personal computer
Personalinformation personnel information
Personalkostenanteil rate of personnel expenditure
Personalnummer personnel number
Personenerfassung person registering
Personenkonto private account
Personenkreis circle of people
Petersenspule arc suppression coil
Pfad path
Pfadangabe path specification
Pfadspezifikation path specification
Pfeil arrow
Pfeil nach links left arrow

Pfeil nach oben up arrow
Pfeil nach unten down arrow
Pfeiltaste arrow key, direction key
Pfeiltaste nach links left arrow key
Pfeiltaste nach oben up arrow key
Pfeiltaste nach unten down arrow key
Pfeiltastenblock set of arrow keys
Pfeiltaste vorwärts down arrow key
Pfeil vorwärts down arrow
Pflege maintenance, update
pflegen maintain, update
Pflegezustand maintenance condition
Pflicht duty
-pflichtig liable for
Pfund pound
Pfundzeichen pound sign
Phantomcursor phantom cursor
Phantomschreibmarke phantom cursor
Phase phase
Phase der Datenübertragung data transfer, transfer phase
Phasenabweichung phase deviation
Phasenbeziehung phase reference
Phasendemodulator phase detector
Phaseneigenschaft phase characteristic
Phasenfehler phase error
Phasenglied phase shifting unit
Phaseninvertierschaltung phase inverter circuit
Phasenkettenoszillator phase shift oscillator
Phasenmodulationsaufzeichnung phase modulation recording
Phasenname load name
Phasennamendatei phase name file
Phasenprogramm phase program
Phasenregelung phase control
Phasenschieber phase changer, phase shifter
Phasenschieberschaltung phase changing circuit
Phasenschiebertransformator phase shifting transformer
Phasenschieber-Transformator transformer phase shifter
Phasenumkehr phase reversal
Phasenvariable phase variable
Phasenverhalten phase characteristic
Phasenverschieber quadrature
Phasenverschieberausgang quadrature output
phasenverschobene Unterbrechung out-of-phase interruption
Phasenzittern jitter
Philosophie philosophy
Phonem phonem
Phonemcode phonemic code

Phonemik phonemics
Phoneminventar phonemic inventory
phonemischer Text phonemic text
phonemische Umschreibung phonemic transcription
Phonoausgangsbuchse audio output jack
Phrase phrase
pH-Wert-Steuerung ph control
physikalisch physical
physikalisch aufeinanderfolgend physical sequential
physikalische Blocknummer physical block number
physikalischer Zugriff physical access
physikalisches Ein-/Ausgabesteuersystem für Datenübertragung communications input/output control system
physikalisches Gerät physical device
physische Geräteadresse channel device identifier
Pica pica
Pica-Teilung pica pitch
Pieps beep
piepsen beep
piezoelektrisches Gerät piezoelectric device
Pin pin
Pipeline pipeline
Pixel dot, pixel
Plan budget, map, plan
Plananlagen budgeted assets
Planbetrag budgeted asset
Planbewegungen budget transaction
Planbilanz budget balance sheet
Planbuchungsbeleg budget posting voucher
Plandaten planning data
Plandatum budget date
planen budget, plan
plangesteuert plan controlled
Planjahr budget year
planmäßige Abfahrt scheduled time of departure
planmäßige Ankunft scheduled time of arrival
planmäßiger Start scheduled time of departure
planmäßige Wartung scheduled maintenance
Planmenge planned quantity
Planungssatz budget record
Plansatz budget record
Planspiele experimental gaming
Planungsart budget type, budgeting type
Planungsbetrag budgeted amount
Planungscharakter budget nature
Planungsebene planning level
Planungshorizont planning horizon

Planungsjahr budget year
Planungsmonat budget month
Planungsstadium planning phase
Planungsübersicht financial report
Planwert budget value
Plasma plasma
Plasmaanzeige gas plasma display, plasma display
Plasmabildschirm gas plasma display, plasma display, plasma display unit
Plasmadiode plasma diode
Plastik plastic
Plastikhülle protective cover
Platine board, circuit board, multichip carrier
Platte disk, plate
Platte auf Fehler prüfen surface scan
Platte mit Dateien in unzusammenhängenden Bereichen fragmented disk
Plattenadresse disk address
Plattenaufteilungsdaten disk partition data, disk partition data
Plattenauftrag disk order
Plattenbereich bucket, partition
Plattenbetriebssystem disk operating system
Plattendatei disk file
Plattendateiverwaltung disk file management
Platten-/Diskettendienste disk diskette services
Plattenfehler disk error
Plattengruppe volume set
Platteninhalt disk contents
Plattenkassette disk cartridge
Plattenkassetteneinheit cartridge disk unit
Plattenlaufwerk disk drive, disk drive unit
Plattenname disk label
Plattenquoten disk quota
plattenresidentes System disc resident system
plattenresidente Systemsteuerung disc resident system
Plattensatz volume set
Plattensektor disk sector
Plattenspeicher disk storage
Plattenspeicherdirektanschluß integrated disk adapter
Plattenspeicherkapazität disk storage capacity
Plattenspeicherprozessor disk processor
Plattenspeicherrechner cache disk processor
Plattenspeichersubsystem disk storage subsystem
plattenspezifisch disk specific
Plattenstapel disk deck, disk pack
Plattenstapelaufnahme disk pack well
Plattensteuereinheit disk control unit, disk controller

Plattensteuerung disk controller
Plattensteuerungsroutine disk handler
Plattentreiber disk driver, disk handler
Plattenwechsel disk change, disk exchange
Platten-Wiederherstellungsroutine disk dump restore
Plattenzugriffsmethode disk access method
Platz amount of space, room, space
Platzgründe space reasons
Platzgrund reason of space
Platzhalter ambiguous letter, wildcard
Platzschwierigkeit storage problem
Platzsoftware storage software
platzsparend space saving
plausibel plausible
Plausibilitätskontrolle plausibility check
Plazierungseinschnitt locating slot
plotten plot
Plotten von Ausschnitten window plotting
Plotter plotter
Plus plus
pneumatisch pneumatic
pneumatisches Steuersystem pneumatic control system
Pol pole
Polarisationsschwelle setting treshold
polarisiertes Relais polarized relay
Polarität polarity
Polarkoordinatenschreiber radial chart recorder
Pollaufruf poll call
pollen poll
Pollfrequenz poll frequency
polnische Notation polish notation
Polung polarity
Polynom polynom
polynom polynomial
Pool pool
Poolgröße pool size
Poolname pool name
Poolparameter pool parameter
Poolschlüssel pool key
Port interface, port
portieren port
Position item, location, position
positionieren position
Positionierfehler seek error
Positionierung positioning, positioning device
Positionierungsendestatus end of position status
Positionierungstaste distance key
Positionierzeit arm movement, seek time

positionsabhängiger Qualifizierer positional qualifier
Positionsangabe position indication
Positionsanzeige position display
Positionsart item type
Positionsbestimmung über Drehwinkel angular positioning
Positionsbetrag item amount
positionsbezogen item related
Positionsbild item screen
Positionsdaten item data
Positionsfracht item freight
Positionsgewicht item weight
Positionsmenge quantity
Positionsnummer item number, line number
Positionsqualifizierer positional qualifier
Positionsrabatt item discount
Positionsschalter position switch
Positionssteuerung position control
Positionstext item text
Positionstyp item type
Positionsübersicht item summary
Positionswert item value
positionswertabhängig dependent on item value
Positionszähler location counter
positiv good, positive
positive Logik positive logic
positiver Fehler positive going error
positive Zahl positive number
positive Zustandsmeldung good status
Post mail, post
postalisch postal
Postamt post office
Postanschrift mail address, mailing address, postal address
Postbox electronic mailbox
Posten item
Postenanzeige item display
Postenauswahl item selection
Postenbearbeitung item processing
Postenebene item level
Posteninformationen item information
Postenkennzeichen item marker
Postensatz item record
Postenselektion item selection
Postensortierung item sorting
Postensumme item total
Postenzeile item line
Postenzusammenführung consolidation of items
Postfach electronic mailbox, mailbox, postbox
Postkennzeichen postal marker

Postleitzahl

Postleitzahl postal code, postcode, zip code
Postmortem post mortem
Postmortemdump post mortem dump
Postscheck post office giro cheque
Postscheckamt post office
Postscheckkonto post office giro account
Postscheckkonto post office giro account
Postscheckküberweisung post office giro transfer
Postüberweisung postal transfer
Postverwaltung postal telephone and telegraph
Post-Wählverbindung public dial-up connection
Potentiometer potentiometer
Potenz exponential notation
Potenzierung exponentation
Prädialog predialog
Prädikat descriptor
Präferenz preference
Präferenzliste preference list
Präfix prefix
Präfixangabe prefix indication
Präfixdatei prefix file
präparieren prepare
Präposition preposition
Präsentation demo
präzise precise
Präzision precision
Präzisionsfaktor scale modifier
Präzisionswiderstand precision resistor
Preis cost, price
Preisabweichung price deviation
Preisänderung price change
Preisänderungsband price change tape
Preisanfrage price inquiry
Preisart price category
Preisauskunft price information
Preisauskunftsfunktion price information function
Preisdaten price data
Preisdifferenz price discrepancy
Preisdifferenzbuchung price discrepancy posting
Preisdifferenzkonto price discrepancy account
Preiseinheit price unit, pricing unit
Preisentwicklung price history
Preisentwicklungssatz price history record
Preisentwicklungsdatei price history file
Preisentwicklungselement price history element
Preisentwicklungsnummer price history number
Preisentwicklungszeitraum price history period

Preisfeld price field
Preisfindung selling price calculation
Preisgefüge price structure
Preisgruppe price group
Preisgültigkeit price validity
Preisgültigkeitsdatum price validity date
Preisgültigkeitszeitraum price validity period
Preiskonditionen price terms
Preiskonstellation price configuration
Preiskurve price curve
Preisliste price list
Preislistengruppe price list group
Preislistengutschrift price list credit note
Preislisteninhalt price list contents
Preislistennummer price list number
Preislistensatz price list record
Preislistenstaffel price list level
Preislistenstammsatz price list master record
Preislistentyp price list type, type of price list
Preismengeneinheit pricing quantity unit, pricing unit of measurement
Preismengenstaffel price quantity scale
Preissituation price situation
Preisstaffel price scale
Preisstellung quotation
Preissteuerung price code
Preissteuerungskennzeichen price code flag, price code marker
Preissteuerungsvariable price code variable
Preisteil price section
Preisüberwachungsliste price monitoring list
Preisvereinbarung price agreement
Preiswirksamkeitsdatum price validity date
Prellen bouncing
prellen bounce
pressen press
primär primary
Primärbatterie primary battery
Primärcomputersystem primary computer system
Primärdatei primary file
Primäreingabe primary input
Primärindex primary index
Primärprogramm source program
Primärspeicher primary memory
Primärstartprogramm primary start-up program
Primitivpuffer primitive buffer
Primitivtyp primitive type
Prinzip principle
prinzipiell always, as a matter of principle, basically
Priorität priority

Prioritätsebene level
Prioritätsnachricht priority message
Prioritätszuteilung priority grant
privat private
private Mietleitung leased private line, private leased line
private Paketvermittlung private packet exchange
private Telefongesellschaft private common carrier
Privileg privilege
privilegierter Prozeß privileged process
pro per
Probe sample, specimen
Probevereinzelung trial sort
Problem problem, trouble
Problemanalyse problem determination
Problemanalyseprozedur problem determination procedure
Problematik problem
Problemklasse problem category
Problemmodus problem mode
problemorientiert problem oriented
problemorientierte Programmiersprache problem oriented language
problemorientierte Sprache problem oriented language
Problemsprache problem language
Problemstellung issue
Produkt product
produktbezogen product-related
Produktgruppe product group
Produktion production
Produktionseinheit production unit
Produktionsjob production run
Produktionsmodus production mode
Produktionsplan production plan
Produktionsplanung und -steuerung production planning system
produktiv productive
Produktname product name
Produktplan product plan
Produktstamm products master
Produktstatus product status
produzieren produce
Prognose forecast, prognosis
prognostizieren forecast, prognosticate
Programm job, program, task
Programm abbrechen abort a program, cancel a program
Programmabbruch abort, program abort, program termination

Programmablauf program execution, program flow, program run
Programmablaufplan flow chart, program flow chart
Programmablaufsteuerung program flow control
Programmabschnitt program section
Programmabtastung program scan
Programmabtastzeit program scan time
Programmadresse program address
Programmadreßregister program address register
Programmanfang program start
Programmanlauf start of program
Programmanteil part of program
Programmanweisung program instruction
Programmaske setzen (Befehl) set program mask
Programmaufbau program layout, program logon, program structure
Programmaufruf program call
Programmausführung program execution
Programmband program tape
Programmbaustein module, program block
Programmbeendigung termination of the program
Programmbefehl program instruction
Programmbereich program area
Programmbeschreibung program description
Programmbezeichnung program name
Programmbezirksadresse program region address
Programmbezugszahl program indicator
Programmbibliothek program library
Programmbildformat reference format
Programmcode program code
Programmdatenpuffer program data buffer
Programm der Entwurfsrichtlinien design guideline program
Programmdiskette load disk
Programmeingabe program keyin
Programmende end of the program, program end
Programmende-Bezugszahl last record indicator
Programmentwicklungssystem program development system
Programmentwurf program design, program layout
Programmfehler bug, program error, program fault
Programmfluß program flow
Programmfolge program sequence

381

Programmfortschaltung

Programmfortschaltung program advance
Programmfortsetzung continuation, program continuation
Programmfunktion program function
Programmgenerator program generator, task builder
programmgesteuerter Interrupt program controlled interrupt, software interrupt
programmgesteuerte Unterbrechung program controlled interrupt, software interrupt
Programmgröße program size, size of program
Programmidentifikation program identification
Programmieranweisung programming instruction
Programmieraufwand programming effort
programmierbarer Lesespeicher programmable read only memory
programmierbarer Multiplexer programmable multiplexer
programmierbarer Taschenrechner personal programmable calculator
programmierbarer Vorrechner programmable front end processor
programmierbares Kassenterminal programmable point of sales terminal
programmierbare Taste user defined key
programmieren program
Programmierer programmer
Programmierfehler programming error
Programmierfehlerabbruch programming error abort
Programmiergerät programmer, programmer unit, programming device
Programmierhandbuch programmer manual, programmer reference manual, programmer's handbook
Programmierhinweis programming consideration, programming note
Programmierkenntnisse programming knowledge
Programmierrichtlinie programming rule
Programmiersprache programming language
Programmierstandard programming standard
Programmiersystem programming system
Programmiertechnik programming technique, software technique
programmierter Halt breakpoint, program stop
programmierter Jobstart forced job startup
programmiertes Lernen programmed learning
Programmierung programming
Programmierung in Maschinensprache machine language programming

Programminformationsblock program information block
Programm in Maschinensprache machine language program
programmintern inside the program
Programminterrupt program interrupt
Programmkomplex program body
Programmkonstante program constant
Programmkonstruktion program construction
Programmkopf program header
Programmkorrektur program correction
Programmkreis program circle
Programmlauf program run
Programmlogik program logic
Programmname program identification, program name
Programmnetzwerkplan program network chart
Programmnummer program number
Programmodul program module
Programmodus program mode
Programmorganisation program organization
Programmpaket program complex
Programmparameter program parameter
Programmplatte program disk
Programmproduktivzeit program production time
Programmprotokoll program listing
Programmprozessor program processor
Programmrahmen program frame
Programmregister program register
Programmroutine software routine
Programmschalter program switch, software switch
Programmschaltwerk microcontroller
Programmschleife loop
Programmschnittstelle program interface, software interface
Programmschritt program step
Programmschrittzähler sequence counter
Programmsegment module, program segment
Programmsegmentierung program segmentation
Programmspeicher program storage
Programmspezifikation program specification
programmspezifisch program specific
Programmsprung program skip
Programmstart start of program
Programmstatus program status
Programmstatus-Doppelwort program status doubleword
Programmstatus-Langwort program status longword

382

Programmstatuswort program status word
Programmsteuerblock program control block
Programmsteuerung program control
Programmsteuerungsblock program control block
Programmsteuerungstabelle program control table
Programmstop breakpoint, program stop
Programmstop-Feld breakfield
Programmstops entfernen clearing breakpoints
Programmstruktur program structure
Programmstufentaste program level key
Programmsystem program system
Programmteil part of program
Programmtesthilfe language system support
Programmtestzeit program test time
Programmträger distribution media, program carrier
Programmtyp program type
Programmüberprüfung program check, quality check
Programmübersicht program summary
Programmüberwachung monitor mode
Programmunabhängigkeit program independence
Programmunterbrechungs-Einrichtung interrupt facility
Programmvariable program variable
Programmverbund program group
Programmverknüpfung program linking
Programmversion program version
Programmverständigungsblock program communication block, software mailbox
Programmverteiler branching module, program selector
Programmverwaltung program management
Programmverzweigung program jump
Programmwahltaste program select key
Programmzähler program counter
Programm zur Ausgabe der Korrekturliste print patch history table utility
Programm zur Dateisteuerung file control program
Programm zur Dateiübertragung file transfer programm
Programm zur Fehleranalyse failure analysis program
Programm zur Steuerung von Datenübertragungsgeräten communication control record
Programmzustand-Doppelwort program status doubleword

Programmzustand-Langwort program status longword
Programmzustandswort program status word
Programmzyklus program cycle, scan
Projekt project
Projektberechtigung project authorization
projektbezogen project related
Projektbudget project budget
Projektdauer extent of the project
Projektebene project level
Projektgruppe project group
projektieren project
Projektkontierung project accounting
Projektkontrolle project control
Projektnummer project number
Projektplanung project scheduling
Projektsatz project record
Projektstamm project master
Projektstammdaten project master data
Projektstammsatz project master record
Projektsteuerung project control
Projekttext project text
Projektübersicht project summary
Projektüberwachung project control
Projektverlauf course of the project
Promille permill
Promilletaste permill key
Prompt prompt
proportional proportional
Proportionalband proportional band
Proportionaldruck proportional spacing
Proportionalschritt-Schalteinrichtung proportional spacing mechanism
Protected Mode protected mode
Protokoll handshake, log, proceedings, protocol
Protokollanweisung log statement
Protokoll aufnehmen record
Protokollausführung log utilities
Protokollband log tape
Protokollbyte log byte
Protokolldatei log file
Protokolldaten log data
Protokolldatenbank log database
Protokolldateneinheit protocol data unit
Protokolldokument log document
Protokollebene protocol layer
Protokoll für Maschinenvorgänge log sheet
Protokoll für Rechnernetzwerk computer network protocol
Protokollfunktion log function, protocol function
Protokollgerät log device
Protokollhandbuch protocol manual

383

Protokollheader log header, protocol control information
Protokollierdruckgerät log printout device
protokollieren log
Protokollieren der Daten nach einer Veränderung after looks
Protokollieren von Konsolnachrichten console logging
Protokolliergeräte-An-/Abwahl logging device selection/deselection
Protokollsatz log record
Protokollsatzart log record type
Protokollsteuerung protocol control
Protokollversion listing version
Protokollzähler log counter
Protokoll zur Dateiübertragung file transfer protocol
Prototypkarte prototype card
Provision commission
Provisionsabrechnung commission
Prozedur procedure
prozedurabhängig procedure dependent
Prozedurablauf procedure course
Prozeduranweisung procedure statement
Prozedurbeschreibung procedure description
Prozedurdefinitionsprozessor procedure definition processor
prozedurgemäß appropriate to the procedure
Prozedurname procedure name
Prozent percent
Prozentangabe given percentage, percentage figure
Prozentsatz percentage
Prozentschranke percentage limit
Prozentstaffel percentage scale
Prozenttaste percent key
prozentuale Auf- und Abschlagsrechnung direct percentage
Prozentzeichen percent sign, percentage sign
Prozeß process
Prozeßabbild process image
Prozeßautomatisierung process automation
Prozeßbeschreibungsblock process descriptor block
Prozeßdaten process data
Prozeßfunktion process function
Prozeßkennummer process identification
Prozeßkennzeichen process identification
Prozeßkommunikation process communication
Prozeßmakro process macro
Prozeßname process name
Prozessor central processing unit, processor

Prozessorbedienungsfeld processor control panel
Prozessoreinheit processing unit
Prozessorelement central processing element
Prozessor für Stapelfernverarbeitung remote batch processor
Prozessornummer processor number
Prozessorstatuswort processor status word
Prozessorunterbrechungsmöglichkeit processor interrupt facility
Prozessorzeitüberschreitung processor stall timer
Prozeßpriorität process priority
Prozeßschleife process loop
Prozeßsteuerblock process control block
Prozeßsteuersprache process control language
Prozeßsteuerung process control
Prozeßsteuerungsanwendung process control application
Prozeßsteuerungsblock process control block
Prozeßtabelle process table
Prozeßtyp process type
Prozeßwahl process selection
Prozeßzustand process state
Prüfanweisung test instruction
Prüfbereich routining scope
Prüfbit check bit, parity bit, test bit
Prüfdatei audit file, test file
Prüfdokument test document
prüfen check, examine, test, verify, view
Prüfen eines Programmes program testing
Prüfgerät exerciser, tester
Prüfkennzeichen test feature, verify indicator
Prüflesen read after write
Prüfling program under test, test sample
Prüflocher verifier
Prüfmodul check module, test module
Prüfmodus check mode, test mode, view mode
Prüfpartition partition of program under test
Prüfpfad audit trail
Prüfprogramm checking routine
Prüfprotokoll test log
Prüfpunkt checkpoint, historical record
Prüfpunktdatei checkpoint file
Prüfroutine check routine
Prüfschleife loopback
Prüfschleifenstecker loopback connector
Prüfschlüssel test code, test key
Prüfsumme check total, checksum
Prüfsummenbildung check total formation
Prüfsummenfehler check total error
Prüfsummenregister checksum register

Prüftabelle check off table
Prüftext check text
Prüfumfang amount of inspection
Prüfung check, test
Prüfung bei unterschiedlichen Umgebungstemperaturen variable ambient temperature test
Prüfung des elektrischen Durchgangs electrical continuity test
Prüfung durch Vergleich comparator check, comparison check
Prüfungsanweisung check instruction
Prüfungsergebnis test result
Prüfvorschrift checking rule, test provision
Prüfzeichen check digit, test character
Prüfzeugnis test certificate
Prüfziffer check digit, check number, modulo
pseudo dummy, pseudo
Pseudoanweisung pseudo statement
Pseudocode pseudocode
Pseudofeldgruppe dummy array
Pseudofloppy RAM disk, memory drive, silicon disk
Pseudoroutine pseudo routine
Publizieren am Arbeitsplatz desktop publishing
Puffer buffer, cache
Pufferanfangsadresse buffer start address
Pufferbelegung buffer occupancy
Pufferbereich buffer area, scratch pad area
Pufferbereichsgröße buffer pool size
Pufferdatei buffer file
Pufferendadresse end of buffer address
Pufferende buffer end, end of buffer
Puffergröße buffer size
Puffermodus buffer mode, cache mode, caching mode
puffern buffer, cache
Puffernummer buffer number
Pufferposition buffer position
Pufferspeicher buffer memory, buffer storage, buffer store, cache, cache memory
Puffersystem buffering system, store and forward system
Pufferüberlauf buffer overflow
Puffervorsatzfeld buffer offset field
Puffervorspann buffer offset
Pufferzeigerstand buffer pointer position
Puls-Amplitudenmodulation pulse amplitude modulation
Puls-Codemodulation puls code modulation
Pult desk
Pumpe pump
Punkt dot, full stop, item, period, pixel, point

Punkte pro Zoll dots per inch
Punktmatrixdrucker dot matrix printer, draft printer
Punktraster grid, raster
Punktüberwachung stock level monitoring
Punkt-zu-Punkt point to point
Punkt-zu-Punkt-Verbindung point to point connection
pysikalischer Datensatz physical record

Q

Quadrat square
quadratischer Stecker square plug
Quadratur quadrature
Quadratwurzel square root
Quadwort quadword
qualifizieren qualify
Qualifizierer qualifier
Qualität quality
Qualitätskontrollbestand stock in quality control
Qualitätskontrolle quality assurance, quality control
Qualitätsmängel quality faults
Qualitätsprüfung quality check
Qualitätssicherung quality assurance
Quantisierungsrauschen quantization noise
Quantisierungsstufe quantization level
Quarantäne quarantine
Quarantänedienst quarantine service
Quarantänezeit quarantine period
Quartal quarter
Quarz electronic crystal, quartz
Quarzfilter crystal filter
Quarzhalter crystal holder
Quarzkristall quartz crystal
Quarzoszillator quartz oscillator
Quasiausführung pseudo execution, quasi execution
Quasibefehl pseudo instruction, quasi instruction
Quasisonderabschreibung quasi special depreciation
Quecksilber mercury
Quecksilberdampf-Gleichrichter mercury arc rectifier
Quecksilberschalter mercury switch
Quelladresse calling DTE address, source address
Quelladreßregister source address register
Quellarchivnummer source archive number, source pack serial number
Quellbereich source area
Quellbibliothek source library
Quellbyte source byte
Quellcode source code, source text
Quellcodedatei source code file, source text file
Quellcodedatenträger source code data carrier
Quellcodeelement language processor source module, source code unit
Quelldatei source file
Quelldateiliste source file list
Quelldaten source data
Quelldeck source deck
Quelle source
Quellformatdatei source format file
Quellgerät source device
Quellgeräteart kind of source device
Quellgerätenummer source device number
Quellgerättyp type of source device
Quellimpedanz source impedance
Quellname source name
Quelloperand source operand
Quellplatte source disc
Quellposition source position
Quellprogramm source program
Quellprogrammbibliothek source program library
Quellpuffer source buffer
Quellsatz source record
Quellsegment source segment
Quellsprache source language
Quellstatement source statement
quer cross
Querformat landscape, landscape format
Querprüfung vertical redundancy check
Querrechnen crossfoot
Quersummenregister checksum register, crossfoot
Querverbindung cross connection
querverbunden cross connected
querverkettete Datei cross linked file
Querverweis cross reference
Querverweisprozessor cross reference listing processor
Querverweistabelle cross reference table
quetschen crimp
Quetschverbinder crimped connector
Queue queue
Queue-Kontrollblock queue control block
Queue voll queue full
quittieren acknowledge
Quittierung acknowledgement
Quittung acknowledge, acknowledgement, receipt
Quittungsbetrieb acknowledgement mode, handshaking
Quittungsdruck receipt printing
Quittungs-Maske acknowledgement mask
Quittungs-Meldung acknowledgement message
Quittungsnachricht reply message

Quittungstaste acknowledgement key
Quote quota

R

Rabatt discount
Rabattangaben discount information
Rabattbetrag discount amount
Rabattgefüge discount structure
Rabattgewährung discount
Rabattgrund reason for discount
Rabattgutschrift discount credit note
Rabatthöhe discount amount
Rabattkonditionen discount terms
Rabattmengeneinheit discount units
Rabattpreiseinheit discount price unit
Rabattrechnung discount calculation
Rabattrechnungsverfahren discount calculation
Rabattsatz discount rate
Rabattschlüssel discount code
Rabattstaffel discount scale
Rabattstufe discount
Rabattumrechnungsfaktor discount conversion factor
Radarantenne radar antenna, sensor
Radarantennenempfänger radar receiver, sensor receiver
Radarantennenempfänger und -prozessor sensor receiver and processor
Radarantennenprozessor sensor processor
Radardatenextraktor radar data extractor
Radardatenrückverfolgung target trail history
Radarsignalumsetzer scan converter
radieren blank, erase
Radix radix
Radixpunkt radix point
Radixschreibweise radix notation
Rändelschraube thumb screw
Räumdatum removal date
räumen clear out, remove
Räumkriterium removal criterion
Räumlogik clear out logic
Räumperiode clear out period
Rahmen chassis, frame, frame yoke, scope
Rahmenanfang frame start, start of frame
Rahmenauftrag skeleton sales order
Rahmenbitfehler framing error
Rahmendrehung rotating patient table frame
Rahmenfarbe border color
Rahmenfehler framing error
Rahmen pro Sekunde frames per second
Rahmenprüffolge frame check sequence

RAM-Auffrischoperation RAM refresh operation
RAM-Erweiterung expansion ram
RAM-Freigabe RAM enable
Rampe ramp
Rand boundary, edge, margin
Randanzeiger margin stop indicator
Randeinstellung margin setting
Randlösetaste margin release key
random random
randombearbeitet handled in a random manner
Randomspeicher random access memory
Randomverarbeitung random processing
Randsignal margin bell
Randsteller margin stop
Randstellerskala margin scale, margin stop scale
Randstelltaste margin stop setting key
Randwert boundary value
Randwertbedingung marginal condition
Randwertkontrolle marginal check
Randzonenbreite margin width
Rangierfeld plug board
Rangordnung hierarchy, order of precedence
rastbare Taste latch down key
rasten latch
Raster grid, schedule
Rasteranzeige resolution indicator
Rasterdatei schedule file
Rasterelektronenmikroskop scanning electronic microscope
Rasterfeinheit resolution
Rasterkennzeichen schedule code
Rasterparameter grid parameter
Rasterschalter resolution selector
Rasterung grid
Rasterzeile grid line
Rasttastenanzeige lock key indicator
Rasttastenauswurf lock key ejection
Rate rate
Rationalisierungseffekt rationalization effect
Rationalisierungsgesellschaft business consultancy
Rationalisierungspotential rationalization potential
Ratsche ratchet
Raum room, space
Raumbedingung space condition
raumladungsbegrenztes Gerät space-charge-limited device
Raumladungsröhre space-charge-controlled tube

Raumschiff-Navigation spacecraft navigation
Rauschen noise
Rauschfilter noise filter
Rauschgenerator noise generator
reagieren react
Reaktanzdiode varactor
Reaktion reaction
Reaktionszeit response time
reaktivieren reactivate
Reaktivierung reactivation
real real
Realisation implementing
realisieren implement
Realisierungsphase implementation phase
realistisch realistic
Realtime realtime
Realtimeverarbeitung realtime operation, realtime processing
Realtimeverarbeitungssystem realtime operating system
Realzeitbetrieb realtime operation
Realzeituhr realtime clock
Realzeitverarbeitungssystem realtime processing system
reassemblieren reassemble
Rechenanlage computer
Rechenanweisung computer statement
Rechenart calculation method
Rechenaufwand cost of computation
Rechenbaustein calculating module
Rechenbausteinverarbeitung calculating module processing
Rechenergebnis result of computation
Rechenfaktor calculation factor
Rechenfehler calculation error, computational error
Rechengenauigkeit computational accuracy
Rechengeschwindigkeit calculating speed, computing speed
Rechengröße figure, variable, value
Rechenleistung computing power
Rechenmaschine calculator
Rechenmethode computing method
Rechenmodul calculating module
Rechenmodulverarbeitung calculating module processing
Rechenoperation calculation
Rechenprozeß task
Rechenprozessor central processor module
Rechenschema computation plan
Rechenschieber slide rule
Rechensteuerbaustein-Kennung calculating control module-identification

Rechensystem data processing system
Rechenverfahren calculation procedure, computing procedure
Rechenvorgang arithmetic procedure
Rechenvorschrift calculation specification
Rechenwerk arithmetic logic unit, arithmetic logical function, arithmetic unit
Rechenwerksregister arithmetic register
Rechenzeit processing time
Rechenzentrum computer center, computing centre
Rechenzentrum der amerikanischen Luftwaffe air force data services center
rechnen calculate
Rechner calculator, computer, electronic calculator, personal computer
rechnerabhängig computer dependent
Rechneranwendung computer application
Rechner der Anzeigeeinheit display device computer
Rechner der Mittleren Datentechnik minicomputer
Rechnerfamilie computer family
rechnergekoppelt online
rechnergestützte Fertigung computer aided manufacturing
rechnergestützte Fertigungsplanung computer aided process planning
rechnergestützte Qualitätskontrolle computer aided quality control
rechnergestützter Entwurf computer aided design
rechnergestützter Maschinenbau computer aided engineering
rechnergestütztes Lernen computer based learning
rechnergestützte Verwaltung computer aided administration
Rechnerhierarchie computer hierarchy
Rechner im Time-Sharing-Betrieb time sharing computer
rechnerintegrierte Fertigung computer integrated manufacturing
Rechnerkompatibilität computer compatibility
Rechnernavigation computerized navigation
Rechnernetz computer network system
Rechnernetzwerk computer network, message network
rechnerorientiert computer oriented
Rechnerschaltung computer circuit
Rechnerschnittstelle computer interface
Rechnersteuerung computer control, computerized control

Rechnersystem computer system
Rechnertechnik computer technology
rechnerübergreifende Verarbeitung pass-thru processing
rechnerunabhängig offline
Rechnerverbund external data link
Rechnerverbundprotokoll computer network protocol
Rechnerverbundsystem computer network system
Rechnung bill, invoice
Rechnungeingangsverrechnungskonto invoice received settlement account
Rechnungsadresse invoice address
Rechnungsanzeige display invoice
Rechnungsausgang issue of invoice
Rechnungsbeleg invoice
Rechnungsbelegnummer invoice number
Rechnungsbetrag amount invoiced, invoice amount
Rechnungsdaten invoice data
Rechnungsdatum invoice date
Rechnungseingabe enter invoice
Rechnungseingang receipt of invoice
Rechnungseingangsbuchung posting of invoice received
Rechnungseingangsbuchungen postings of invoices received
Rechnungseingangsnummer invoice receipt number
Rechnungsempfänger invoice addressee
Rechnungsempfängernummer invoice addressee number
Rechnungslieferant invoicer
Rechnungsnettowert net invoice amount
Rechnungsposition invoice item
Rechnungspositionswert invoice item value
Rechnungsposten invoice item
Rechnungspreis invoice price
Rechnungsprüfer invoice controller
Rechnungsprüfung invoice validation
Rechnungsseite invoice sheet
Rechnungsstellung rendering of invoice
Rechnungsstorno invoice cancellation
Rechnungstermin invoice due date
Rechnungsverbuchung invoice posting
Rechnungswert invoice amount
Recht law
Rechteck rectangle
Rechteckgenerator square wave generator
rechteckig rectangular
rechter Rand right margin
rechtlich legal

Rechtmäßigkeit legal standard
rechts right, right hand side
Rechtsabteilung legal department
rechtsbündig right justified
rechtsbündig ausrichten align at the right margin
rechtsbündiger Rand right justified margin
rechtsbündiger Wiederholungstext right justified repeating label
rechtsbündig formatieren right justify
Rechtschreibung orthography
Rechtsshift right shift
redefinieren redefine
redundant redundant
Redundanz redundancy
Redundanzgruppe redundancy group
Redundanzprüfung redundancy check
Redundanzverminderung redundancy reduction
reduzieren decrease, reduce
reduzierte Helligkeit reduced intensity
Reedrelais reed relay
reell real
reelle Division real number division
reelle Konstante real constant
reelle Variable real variable
reelle Zahl real number
Referenz reference
Referenzanlage reference asset
Referenzattribut referencing attribute
Referenzauflistung reference listing
Referenzbeziehung reference relationship
Referenzbuchungskreis reference accounting area
Referenzhandbuch reference handbook, reference manual
Referenzkonto reference account
Referenzmaterial reference material
Referenzmodell reference model
Referenznummer reference number
Referenzstammsatz reference master record
Referenztext reference text
reformatieren reformat
Regel rule, standard
Regelabschreibung standard depreciation
Regelkreis loop
regelmäßig regular
Regelmäßigkeit regularity
regeln control
Regelplatine servo board
Regelteil ruling part
Regelung control, control system, regulation

Regelungscharakteristik control system characteristic
Regelungssystem feedback control system
Regelungstechnik control technology
Regelungstheorie control theory
Regelungs- und Computertechnik control and computer technology
Regelwiderstand rheostat
regenerierende Schnittstellenanpassungen regenerative interface converter
Regenerierung regeneration
Region region
regional regional
Register operating register, register
Register für Speicherzugriffssteuerung memory lockout register
Registerkonvention register convention
Registerrechner register computer
Registersicherung register safeguard
Registerstand register contents
Registerstelle register position
Registerstellenzahl register length
registrieren detect
Registrierkasse cash register
Registriernummer registration number
Regler control unit, controller, electric regulator
regulieren regulate
regulierter Dienst regulated service
Regulierungsdauer settlement period
Reibelaut fricative
reichen cover, extend, go, suffice
Reichweite coverage time
Reichweitenliste coverage list
Reihe bank, row, series
Reihenfolge order, order of precedence, sequence
Reihenfolge der Neuberechnung recalculation order
Reihen-Zykluszeit bank cycle time
rein clear, pure
Reinigungsmittel cleaner
Reißdehnung elongation at tear
Rejectfach reject drawer
Rejectseite reject page
Rekonfigurationsanzeige system application indicator
Rekonfigurierung reconfiguration
Rekonfigurierungsfehler reconfiguration error, reconfiguration fault
Rekonfigurierungs-Fehlererkennungseinheit reconfiguration error detection unit
Rekursion recursion

rekursiv recursive
Rekursivitätsprüfung recursive check
Relais gateway, relay
Relaisausgang output, relay output
Relaiseingang input
Relaiselement relay element
Relaisfunktion relay function
Relaiskontakt contact relay
Relaislogikprogramm relay ladder logic
Relaislogikprogrammierung relay ladder logic programming
Relaisschalter relay circuit breaker
Relaisspeicher relay storage
Relaissteuerung relay control function
relationale Datenbank relational data base
relativ relative, relative humidity
relative Adresse relative address
relative Adressierung relative addressing
relative Dateistruktur relative file organization
relative Datensatznummer relative record number
relative Luftfeuchtigkeit relative humidity
relativer Verweis relative reference
relative Satznummer relative record number
relatives Indexregister relative address register
relative virtuelle Adresse relative virtual address
relative Zugriffsmethode relative addressing method
Relativzeiger offset pointer
Releaseversion release version
relevant pertinent, relevant
Relevanz relevance
relozierbar position independent, relocatable
relozierbarer Code position independent code, relocatable code
Rennen race
rennen race
Rennzustand race condition
Rentabilität profitability
Reorganisation reorganization
Reorganisationslauf garbage collection, reorganization run
Reorganisationsprogramm reorganization program
reorganisieren reorganize
Reparatur corrective maintenance, repair
Reparaturauftrag repair order
Reparaturhinweis repair advice
Reparaturmaterial repair material
Reparaturprogramm recovery program
Reparaturteil spare part
reparieren repair, trouble shoot

reproduzierbar reproducible
reprogrammierbares ROM reprogrammable ROM
Reservebatterie standby battery
Reservekopie backup copy
reservieren allocate, reserve
reserviertes Wort reserved word
Reservierung allocation, reservation
Reservierungsblock reservation block
Reservierungsdatum reservation date
Reservierungskennzeichen reservation type
Reservierungsmenge quantity reserved
Reservierungsnummer reservation number
Reservierungssatz reservation record
Reservierungsstatus reservation status
Reservierungsübersicht reservation list
Reservierungsüberwachung reservation monitoring
Reservierungsverwaltung reservation management
Resetsignal reset pulse
resident resident
residenter Kompilierer resident compiler
residenter Makroassembler resident macroassembler
residenter Teil resident part
residentes Programm resident program
Residenz residency
Residenzprozentsatz residency percentage
Resonanzfrequenzen resonant frequencies
Ressource resource
Restanzahl remainder
Restartfehler restart error
Restartlogik restart logic
Restartvorkehrung restart arrangement
Restbetrag remaining amount
Restbuchwert net book value
Restbuchwertermittlung determining the net book value
Restfehlerwahrscheinlichkeit residual error probability
Restlaufzeit remaining time
Restpuffer residual buffer
Restrechnung final invoice
Restrechnungskennzeichen final billing flag
Restriktion restriction
Restspeicher residual memory
Resttilgung final repayment
Resultat result
Resultataddition sigma memory
resultieren result
retten save
Returncode return code

Returninformation return information
Returntaste carriage return key, enter key, return key
Rhythmus rhythm
richten direct
Richtfunkstrecke radio link
richtig correct, proper
Richtigkeit correctness
Richtlinie guideline, regulation
Richtung direction
Richtungsbetrieb simplex operation, simplex transmission
Richtungsmessung directional measurement
Richtungsschrift non return to zero
Richtungssteuerungsgerät steering control device
Richtungstaktschrift phase encoded
Richtungsverkehr simplex communication
Rille groove
Ring daisy chain, ring
Ringpuffer ring buffer
Ringschaltung daisy chain
Ringzähler ring counter
risikodeckend risk covering
Röhrenfassung electron tube holder, tube socket
Röhrenhalterung electron tube holder
Röhrenoszillator electron tube oscillator
Röhrentechnik electron tube technology, tube technology
Röhrenverstärker electron tube amplifier
Röhrenwicklung concentric winding
roh raw
Rohrleitung tube, tubing
Rohrtülle conduit, conduit bushing
Rohstoff raw material
Rollbereich roll area
Rolle roll
rollen roll
Rollgeld transport costs
Rollpuffer roll buffer
rotieren rotate
Rotor electric rotor
Route route
Routine procedure, routine
Routinearbeit routine task
routinemäßige Wartung preventive maintenance
Routine zum Ausdrucken des Jobabrechnungsprotokolls joblog report program
Routing routing
RS232-Schnittstelle RS232-Interface

RS-Flip-Flop RS flipflop
Rückänderung change back
Rückaktion return message
Rückantwort answer
rückblättern page backwards
rückbuchen back post
Rückbuchung back posting
Rückbuchungsmonat back posting month
Rückbuchungsperiode back posting period
Rückbuchungszeitraum back posting period
Rückfrage query, question, request
Rückfrageknopf request button
rückfragen query
Rückfragesignal request signal
Rückfragetaste request key
Rückführtaste return key
Rückgabedatum return date
Rückgabefeld return field
Rückgabemenge quantity returned
Rückgabewert return value
Rückgängigmachung cancellation
Rückgewinnung recovery
Rückkaufswert repurchase value
Rückkehr return
Rückkehrstatus returned status
Rückkehr-zu-Null-Verfahren dipole recording method, return to zero method
rückladen reload
Rücklauf-Regulierungsverfahren flyback regulation method
Rücklaufselbstdiagnose loopback self test
Rückleiter common return
Rücklieferung return
rückmelden answer
Rückmeldung answerback
Rücknahmekennzeichen cancellation flag
Rücknahmezeichen cancel symbol
Rückpositionieren reposition
rückschalten space back, switch back
Rückschaltzeit backspacing time
Rückscheck return cheque
Rückschein return ticket
Rückschritt backspace
Rückschrittaste backspace key
Rückschritteinrichtung backspace mechanism
Rückseite rear side, rear view
Rücksendedatum return date
Rücksendefunktion return function
Rücksendeprogramm return program
Rücksetzen reset, roll back
rücksetzen initialize, move backward, reset, reset
Rücksetzen der Druckdatei reprint

rücksetzendes Gerät resetting device
Rücksetzen des Verarbeitungsabschnitts run unit rollback
Rücksetzfunktion clear screen
Rücksicht consideration
Rücksprache consultation
Rücksprung jump back, return branch, return jump
Rücksprungadresse return address
Rücksprungadreßregister return address register
Rückspulen mit Sperre rewind with interlock
Rückspulfunktion tape rewind function
Rückspulmodus tape rewind mode
Rückspultaste rewind key
Rückstand arrears, backlog
Rückstandsbuchung backlog posting
Rückstandsverfolgung backlog investigation
Rückstauflußkontrolle back pressure flow control
rückstellen reset
Rückstelltaste reset key
Rückstellung restoration, reversal
Rückstrich backslash
Rücktaste backspace, backspace key
Rückübertrag end around carry
rücküberweisen transfer back
Rücküberweisung return transfer
Rückverweis backlink, backward link, backward linkage
rückwärts backward
rückwärtsblättern page backwards
Rückwärtskettung backward chaining
rückwärts neu positionieren reposition backward
Rückwärtspositionierung backspace positioning
Rückwärtsschritt backspace
Rückwärtssteuerung backward supervision
Rückwärtsverkettung backlink, backward link, backward linkage
Rückwärtswellen-Röhre backward wave tube
Rückwärtswellenröhre carcinotron
Rückwärtswiederherstellung shift recovery
Rückwirkung retroactive effect
Rüstkosten set up costs
Rüttler jogger
Ruf abgewiesen call not accepted, call rejected
Rufabweisung call not accepted, call rejection
Rufannahme call acceptance, call accepted
rufen call
rufende Adresse calling address
rufende Station calling station

Rufnummer call number
Rufzusammenstoß call collision
Ruhekontakt normally closed
ruhendes Programm inoperative program
Ruhespannung open circuit voltage
Ruhezeitglied dwell timer
Ruhezustand idle state
rund round
Rundablage circular file cabinet
Runde round
runde Klammer bracket, parenthesis
runden half adjust, round
Rundfunk broadcast, radio
Rundschreibnachricht multi address message
Rundsendebetrieb multiple destination routing
Rundsenden multi address calling
rundsenden broadcast
Rundspruch broadcast
Rundstahl steel rod
Rundungsfehler rounding error

S

Sachanlagenbestandsliste fixed assets listing
Sachbearbeiter operator
Sachbearbeiteridentifikationstabelle operator identification table
Sachbearbeiternummer operator number
Sachbearbeitertabelle operator table
Sachbuch general ledger
Sachbuchkonto general ledger account
sachdienlich pertinent
Sachgebiet area, subject
Sachkontenänderung general ledger alteration
Sachkontenauswertung general ledger report
Sachkontenberechtigung general ledger authorization
Sachkontenbereich general ledger area
Sachkontenbild general ledger screen
Sachkontenbuchung general ledger posting
Sachkontendatei general ledger file
Sachkontengruppe general ledger group
Sachkontenhaben general ledger credit
Sachkonteninhalt general ledger content
Sachkontenpuffer general ledger buffer
Sachkontensaldo general ledger balance
Sachkontenschreibung general ledger posting
Sachkontensoll general ledger debit
Sachkontenstamm general ledger master
Sachkontenstammdatei general ledger master file
Sachkontenstammsatz general ledger master record
Sachkontensumme general ledger total
Sachkontentabelle general ledger table
Sachkontenumsatz general ledger turnover
Sachkontenverzeichnis general ledger account register
Sachkontenzeile general ledger line
Sachkonto general ledger account
Sachkontonummer general ledger account number
Sachnummer article code
Sachzeichenfolge search string
Sackgasse dead end
sättigen saturate
Sättigung saturation
Sätze pro Sektor records per sector
Sätze pro Spur records per track
säubern clean up
saisonal seasonal
Saldenanzeige balance display
Saldenbestätigung balance confirmation
Saldenbilanz balance
Saldenliste list of balances
Saldenprüfung balance check
Saldenregister balance
Saldenübernahme balance transfer
Saldenverlauf balance process
Saldenvortrag balance carried forward
saldieren balance
Saldo balance
Saldomindestbetrag minimum balance
Saldoprüfung balance check
Saldovortrag balance carried forward
Saldovortragskorrektur correction of balance carried forward
Sammel- bulk
Sammelanlage compound asset
Sammelbegriff general comprehensive term
Sammelbeleg summary voucher
Sammelbestellung bulk order
Sammelbuchen collective posting
Sammelbuchung summary account posting
Sammeldatei pooling file
Sammelkonto summary account
sammeln accumulate, gather
Sammelnachweis summary advice
Sammelrechnung summary invoice
Sammelschiene bus bar
Sammelverwaltung summary management
Sammlung collection
Sample and Hold sample and hold
sandstrahlen sandblast
Satellit satellite
Satellitennetz satellite network
Satellitenrechner satellite computer, slave computer
Satellitenrechner laden downline loading
Satellitenstrecke satellite link
Satellitenverbindung satellite link
Satz block, kit, record
Satzadreßdatei record address file
Satzadresse block address
Satzadreßfeld record address field
Satzanalysesystem sentence parser
Satzanfang start of record
Satzart record type
Satzartbeschreibung record type description
Satzartenangabe record type specification
Satzaufbau record layout, record structure
Satzauswahlphrase record selection expression
Satzbeginn start of record

Satzbeschreibung record descriptor, record identification
Satzbeschreibungsarten associated record identification data
Satzbeschreibungswort record description word, record descriptor word
Satzbetonung emphatic stress
Satzbett record format
Satzbettwert record format value
Satzbezeichnung record designation
satzbezogen for the record
Satzbezugszahl record indicator
Satzbreite measure, record length, record width
Satzdefinition record definition
Satzende end of record
Satzendezeichen end of block character
Satzfeld record field
Satzfolge record sequence
Satzform record form
Satzformat record format
Satzglied clause
Satzgrenze record mark
Satzgruppe record group
Satzidentifikation record identification
Satzinhalt record contents
Satzlänge record length
Satzlängenfeld record length field
Satzlänge verändern changing record key length
Satznummer record number
Satzschlüssel record key
Satzsegment record segment
Satzteil clause, phrase
Satzteilgenerator phrase structure module
Satzteilmodul phrase structure module
Satztyp type of record
Satz von Bändern tape set, volume set
Satz von Platten disk pack, disk set, volume set
Satz von Sicherungsdisketten set of backup diskettes
Satzvorspann prefix
satzweise record by record
Satzzähler record counter
Satzzeichen punctuation mark
Satzzeile record cell
sauber clean, proper
Scanebene scan plane
Scanner scanner
Scannercomputer scanner computer
Schablone stencil, template
Schablonenpool template pool

Schachtel box, case
schachteln nest
Schachtelung nesting
Schachtnummer bin number, chute number
Schachtverschluß bin cover, chute cover
Schaden damage
Schadenersatzhaftung liability for damages
Schadensnummer damage number
schädlich harmful
Schärfe focus
Schärferegler focus control
schätzen estimate
Schätzung estimation
Schätzwert estimate, estimated value
schaffen generate, produce
Schaltalgebra boolean algebra
Schaltbild wiring diagram
schalten switch
Schalter flag, flag byte, interrupter, option, switch
Schalter an der Frontplatte front panel switch
Schalterstellung switch configuration, switch position
Schalter zum Ausschalten eines Ausgangs output off switch
Schaltfeld jack, patch panel, switch board
Schaltfunktion switching function
Schalthebel lever, switch tabs
Schalt-IC integrated switching circuit
Schaltkontakt contact, switching contact
Schaltkreis circuit
Schaltkreisplatine circuit board, logic printed circuit board
Schaltleistung breaking capacity
Schaltplan wiring diagram
Schaltröhre hot cathode gas-filled tube
Schalttafel switchboard
Schaltungsblock circuit block
Schaltungselement circuit element
Schaltungsnetzwerk circuit network
Schaltungstheorie circuit theory
Schaltungsverzweigung circuit branch
Schaltvorrichtung switchgear, switching device
Schaltwerk sequential circuit
Schaltzeit switching time
Schatten shade
Schattendruck shade print
Schaum foam
Scheck cheque
Scheckvorderseite cheque front side
Scheckzahlung cheque payment
Scheibe plate, slice, wafer
Scheinabzug banknote withdrawal

Scheingewinnermittlung apparent profit calculation
Scheinposition fictitious item
Scheinzusammenstellung banknote combination
Schelle clamp
Schema scheme
Schemasprache scheme language
schematische Darstellung schematic representation
Scheuerleiste skirting
Schicht layer, level
Schiebedaten shift data
Schiebefunktion data shift function
schieben shift
Schiebeoperation shift operation
Schieberegister shift register
Schiedsanalyse arbitrary analysis
Schiene rail
Schiffsnavigation marine navigation
Schild shield
Schlag key, shock, stroke
Schlagwort key word
Schlagwortauswahl selection of key words
Schlagwortkombination combination of key words
Schlagwortmenge set of key words
Schlagwortsuche search for catchwords
Schleife loop, recursion
Schleifenblock loop block
Schleifendurchlauf iteration
Schleifenstrom loop current
Schleifenverstärkung loop gain
Schleifring slip ring
Schleifringmotor slip ring motor
schließen close, terminate
schließlich eventually, finally
Schlüssel code, key
schlüsselabhängig key dependant
Schlüsselart key type
Schlüsselaufbereitung key editing
Schlüsselbegriff key term
Schlüsselcode key code
Schlüsseldaten key data
Schlüsseleintrag key entry
Schlüsselfeld key field
Schlüsselfeldanfang key field starting location
Schlüsselfeldposition key field location
schlüsselfertig ready for occupancy, turnkey
schlüsselfertiges System turnkey system
Schlüsselinformation key information
Schlüssellänge key length
Schlüssellänge verändern changing record key length
Schlüsseloption key option
Schlüsselparameter key argument
Schlüsselschalter key switch, keyswitch
Schlüsselverzeichnis key directory
Schlüsselwort key word, keyword
Schlüsselwortkennzeichen key word flag
Schlüsselwortklasse key word class
Schlüsselwortoperand key word operand
Schlüsselwortparameter key word parameter
Schlüsselworttabelle key word table
Schlüsselwortzeile key word line
Schlüsselzeichen key symbol
Schlupfgröße slack size
Schlußprogramm final program
Schlußseite final page
Schlußwindung end-to-end turn
Schlußzeile final line, last line
Schlußzeilensperre last line lock up
Schmalband narrow band
schmale Zeichenbreite compressed font
Schmelzeinsatz fuse link
Schmierzeichen scratch character
Schnappschalter snap switch
schneiden cut
schnell fast, rapid
Schnellabtastung high speed scan, high speed scanning
Schnellauslöser tripping mechanism
Schnelldrucker draft printer, draft quality printer, high speed printer, high volume timesharing system
schnelle Abtastfunktion high speed scan function
schnelle Abtastung high speed scan
schnelle Änderung rapid alteration
schnelle Antwort high speed response
schnelle Ausgabe draft outbot, rush draft
schnelle Dateisuchoperation fast file scan
schnelle Impulsfolge high speed pulse train
schneller Bilddurchlauf jump scroll
Schnellerfassung rapid input
Schnellerfassungsliste rapid input mask
schneller Hilfsspeicher fast auxiliary memory
schneller Steuerspeicher high performance control storage
schnelle Zugriffszeit auf Dateien speed in using files
Schnelligkeit speed
Schnellinformation quick information
Schnellrücklauf high speed rewind
Schnittpunkt intersection

Schnittstelle interface, port
Schnittstelle bilden zu interface to
Schnittstelle mit vier Anschlüssen four port interface
Schnittstellenbedingung interface condition
Schnittstellenbeschreibung interface description
Schnittstellenbewegung interface movement
Schnittstellenbus interface bus
Schnittstellendateneinheit interface data unit
Schnittstellenflußkontrolle interface flow control
Schnittstellenmodul interface module
Schnittstellenproblematik interface problems
Schnittstellenregister interface register
Schnittstellenschalter interface transfer switch
Schnittstellenstromkreis interchange circuit
Schnittstellentypen interface types
Schnittstellenvervielfacher port expansion unit
Schock shock
Schottky-Diode schottky-barrier diode
Schräglauf skew
Schrägstrich slash
Schrank cabinet
Schranke limit
Schraube screw
schrauben screw
Schraubenzieher screwdriver
Schraubklemme plug-on screw terminal
Schreibdichte character pitch, density, recording density
Schreiben letter
schreiben write
Schreiben eines Programmes program writing
Schreiben/Lesen/Ausführen read/write/execute
Schreiben und Lesen von Dateien file input output
Schreiber recorder
Schreibfehler write fault
Schreibkontrolle read after write
Schreibkopf recording head
Schreibkopfrücklauf carriage return
Schreib/Lese read/write
Schreib-/Lesefehler read write error
Schreib-/Lesekarte read write board
Schreib- Lesekopf head
Schreib-/Lesekopf read write head, recording head
Schreib-/Leseöffnung read write access slot, read write slot
Schreib-/Lesespeicher random access memory
Schreibmarke cursor
Schreibmarkenposition speichern save cursor
Schreibmarkentaste cursor control key
Schreibmaschine typewriter
Schreibmaschinentastatur typewriter keyboard
Schreibrand margin
Schreibschritteinrichtung letter spacing mechanism
Schreibschutz write protect
Schreibschutz für die Diskette removable disk write protect
Schreibschutz für die Festplatte fixed disk write protect
Schreibsperre print lock, write lock
Schreibstellenabstand column spacing
Schreibtaste printing key
Schreibtext record text
Schreibtisch desk
Schreibverfahren recording mode
Schreibversuch print attempt, write attempt
Schreibvorgang recording procedure
Schreibzeiger print pointer
Schreibzeile recording line
Schriftart font
Schriftenerkennung character recognition, optical character recognition
Schrifterkennung character recognition, optical character recognition
Schrifterkennung nach ANSI-Norm optical character recognition-ANSI standard
Schrifterkennung nach internationaler Norm optical character recognition-international standard
Schriftstück document
Schrifttyp typeface
Schriftverkehr correspondence
Schritt signal element, step
Schrittadresse step address
Schritttakt signal element timing
Schrittbaustein step block
Schrittfolge step sequence
Schrittgröße step size
Schrittmodus step mode
Schrittmotor stepping motor
Schrittschaltwerk drum
Schrittverzerrung digital signal distortion
schrittweise incremental
Schrittweite step extent
Schrott crap, scrap, trash
Schrottwert scrap value
Schubhebel vertical adjustment lock lever
schützen guard, protect
schützend protective
Schuld debt
Schulung training

Schulungsmodus training mode
Schulungszweck training purpose
Schuß shot
Schußauslösung shot release
Schußzahl number of shots
Schutz protection, protection, protective, protector
Schutzabdeckung access cover, protective cover
Schutzcode safety code
Schutz des Datenspeichers data storage protection
Schutz des Stromversorgungsnetzes electric power system protection
Schutzeinrichtung protector
Schutzgasrelais reed relay
Schutzgehäuse protective enclosure
Schutzhülle protective envelope
Schutz im Editiermodus protection in edit mode
Schutzkondensator protective capacitor
Schutzleiter grounding conductor
Schutzmantel protective cover
Schutzrohr conduit, protective conduit
Schutzspule protective coil
Schutzvorrichtung protective device
schwanken float
Schwankung in der Netzspannung brown out, power fluctuation
schwarzer Kasten black box
Schwelle threshold
Schwellwert threshold value
schwenken swivel
schwer heavy
schwerwiegend fatal
schwerwiegender Fehler fatal error
Schwestergesellschaft sister company
Schwierigkeit difficulty
schwimmen float, swim
Schwimmer floater
Schwingungsdauer periodic time
Scrollingfunktion scrolling function
Sedezimalsystem hexadecimal system
Segment segment
Segmentadreßregister segment address register
Segmentanfang segment beginning, segment start
Segmentart segment type
Segmentbeschreibung segment descriptor
Segmentbeschreibungsblock segment descriptor block
Segmentbeschreibungstabelle segment descriptor table

Segmentbibliothek segment library
Segmentdefinition segment definition
Segmente in der Meldungsdatei segments in message file
Segmentformat segment format
Segmentidentifikation segment type
segmentieren segment
segmentiertes Fenster cathedral window
Segmentkennung segment identification
Segmentkopf segment header
Segmentlänge segment length
Segmentpräfix segment prefix
Segmentpräfixtabelle segment prefix table
Segmentreihenfolge segment sequence
Segmentschlüssel segment key
Segmentsteuerbyte segment control byte
Segmentsteuerkennzeichen segment control flag
Segmentsteuerung segment control
Segmentstufe segment level
Segmenttabelle segment descriptor table
Segmenttext segment text
Segmenttyp segment category, segment type
Segmenttypprüfung check of the segment type
Segmentypenauswahl segment category selection
sehr hoch high high, hihi, hihigh, very high
sehr schneller Speicher high speed memory
sehr unterschiedlich very different
Seite page
Seite einer Unterteilung partition side
Seitenabruf demand paging
Seitenadreßfeld page address field
Seitenadressierung page addressing
Seitenadreßregister page address register
Seitenanfang beginning of the page
Seitenanforderung page request
Seitenanzeige page display
Seitenaufbereitung page editing
Seitenauswahl page selection
Seitenbasis page base
Seitenbereich page area, page range
Seitenende end of page
Seitenfehler page fault
Seitenfuß bottom margin, footer
Seitengröße page size
Seitenkopf header, page header
Seitenkopfinformation page header information
Seitenlänge form length, page length
Seitenlängenfeld page length field
Seitenlayout page layout
Seitenmarke page mark, page marker

Seitenmodus page mode
Seitenname page name
Seitennummer page number
Seitennummer der ersten Seite initial page number
Seitennummerdirektwahl page number direct choice
Seitennummerfeld page number field
Seitennummermaske page number mask
Seitennummernbereich page number range
Seitennummernvorgabe page number assignment
Seitenparameter page parameter
Seitenpreis page price
Seitenpuffer page buffer
seitenspezifisch page specific
Seitensteuerungsblock page control block
Seitensteuerungsregister page control register
Seitentabelle page table
Seitentrennzeichen page delimiter
Seitentyp page type
Seitenüberlauf page overflow
Seitenumbruch page makeup, pagination
Seitenumbruch im Druckmenü paginating from the print menu
Seitenverhältnis aspect ratio
Seitenverrechnung page accounting
Seitenvorschub form feed, page break, page feed
Seitenvorschubmodus form feed mode
Seitenvorschubsteuerung form feed control
Seitenwechselspeicher auxiliary memory, backing store
Seitenwechselverfahren paging
seitenweises Blättern page scrolling
Seitenzahlentext page number text
seit Jahresanfang year to date
seitlicher Spurabstand track pitch
seit Monatsanfang month to date
seit Wochenanfang week to date
Sektor sector
Sektorende end of sector, sector end
Sektoren pro Spur sectors per track
Sektorfolge sector sequence
Sektornummer sector number
Sektornummernregister sector number register
sekundär secondary
Sekundärdatei secondary file
Sekundäreingabe secondary input
Sekundärelektronenvervielfacher electron multiplier, photomultiplier
sekundäres Ladeprogramm secondary boot program

Sekundärhauptspeicher extended main storage
Sekundärindex secondary index
Sekundärradar beacon
Sekundär-Rundsichtradar secondary surveillance radar
Sekundärschlüssel alternate key
Sekundärspeicherbereich secondary storage area
Sekunde second
selbständig independent
Selbstanlauf auto restart, autorestart
Selbstbedienungszentrum self-service centre
Selbstdiagnose checkout procedure, selftest
Selbstdiagnose Datenrücklauf data loopback self test
Selbstdiagnose des Systems system's internal test
selbsteinstellendes System self-adjusting system
selbsterklärend self-describing
selbstgewählt auto dialled, self-chosen
selbstklebend adhesive
selbstkorrigierend self-correcting
Selbstladeblock boot block record
Selbstladeprogramm boot block record, bootstrap load program
Selbstprüfung self-checking
Selbststudienkurs self-paced instruction course
selbstsuchend self-searching
Selbsttest self-diagnostic, self-diagnostics
Selbsttest beim Einschalten power-on self-test, power-up self-test
Selektierbereich select range
selektieren choose, pick, select
Selektiermarke select mark
Selektion selection
Selektionsangabe selection statement
Selektionsanweisung selection instruction
Selektionsbedingung selection condition
Selektionsbegriff selection term
Selektionsbild selection screen
Selektionsbrief selection letter
Selektionsdatum selection date
Selektionseingabe selection input
Selektionsende selection end
Selektionsfeld selection field
Selektionsgrenze selection limit
Selektionsgruppe selection group
Selektionskarte selection card
Selektionskennzeichen selection flag
Selektionskriterium selection criterion
Selektionslauf selection run
Selektionsmerkmal selection feature

Selektionsmöglichkeit selection option
Selektionsprogramm selection program
Selektionsrestriktion selection restriction
selektiv selective
Selektorkarte selector control card
Semaphor semaphor
Sendeanforderung transmission request
Sendeaufforderung invitation to send
Sendeaufrufsignal idle probe
Sendeauftrag transmission job
sendebereit clear to send
Sendebereitschaft clear to send, ready for sending
Sendeblockgröße transmit block size
Sendedaten send data, transmission data, transmit data
Sendedatum transmission date
Sendeeinrichtung broadcast equipment
Sende-/Empfangs- send/receive
Sendefolgenummer send sequence number
Sendefolgezähler send state variable
senden send, transmit
Sendenachricht transmission message
Senden/Empfangen transmit and receive
Sendepuffer send buffer, transmit buffer
Sender sender, talker, transmitter, transreceiver
Sender an transmitter on
Sender aus transmitter off
Sender/Empfänger transceiver
Sendergehäuse transmitter housing
Senderidentifikation sender identification
Sendeschrittaktimpuls transmitter clock pulse
Sendesignalelement transmitter signal element
Sendesignalelementzeitgeber transmitter signal element timing
Sendesignalumsetzer modulator
Sendestation master station, master terminal
Sende- und Empfangsverstärker driver receiver
Sendewarteschlange transmission queue
Sendungsvermittlung message switching
Sendungsverzug message delay
Senior senior
senkrecht vertical
Sensor sensor
separat separate
separater Lautsprecher external speaker
separieren separate
sequentialisieren sequencing
sequentiell sequential
sequentielle Arbeitsweise sequential operation
sequentielle Datei sequential file

sequentielle Dateiorganisation sequential file organization
sequentielle Datentabelle sequential data table
sequentielle Logik sequential logic
sequentielle Logikschaltung sequential logic
sequentieller Speicher sequential storage
sequentieller Zugriff sequential access, sequential access method
sequentielles Schieberegister sequential shift register
sequentielle Zugriffsmethode sequential access method
Sequenz sequence
Sequenzdatei sequence file
Sequenzdateiname sequence file name
Sequenzname sequence name
Serialisierung serialization
Serialisierungsname serialization name
Serie series
seriell serial
Serielldrucker increment printer
serielle Daten serial data
serielle Druckerschnittstelle serial printer interface
serielle Ein-/Ausgabe serial input/output
serielle Leitungseinheit serial line unit
serieller Addierer serial adder
serieller Zugriff serial access
serielle Schnittstellensteuerung serial communication controller
serielles Zeichen serial character
serielle Übertragung serial transmission
serielle Verbindung serial line
Serienbrief serial letter
Serienbriefanforderung serial letter demand
Serienbriefauftrag serial letter command
Serienbrieferstellung serial letter creation
Seriendrucker serial printer
serienmäßig standard
serienmäßiger Speicher base memory
Seriennummer serial number
Serienstromkreis series circuit
Serienübergabe serial transmission
Serviceabkommen service contract
Servicefunktion service function
Serviceprogramm utility routine
servieren serve
Servospur last track
Servosteuerungs-Modul servo axis module
Sessionbeginn session begin
Sessionvariable session variable
Set-Beziehung set relation
setzen place, position, put, set

401

setzen auf set to
Setzen der Hauptspeicherschalter system board memory switch settings
Setzen des linken Schreibrandes left margin adjustment
Sherardisieren sherardizing
Shiftbefehl shift instruction
shiften shift
Shutdown-Fehler shutdown error
Shutdown-Fehlermeldung shutdown error message
Shutdown-Phase shutdown phase
sich beim System abmelden logout from, logout of
sich beim System anmelden login to
sicher certain, safe
Sicherheit safety, security
Sicherheitscode-Generator redundancy code generator
Sicherheitsgrad degree of safety
Sicherheitsmaßnahme safety measure
Sicherheitsprüfung security auditing
Sicherheitsüberprüfung clearance
Sicherheitsverantwortlicher safety officer
Sicherheitsvorkehrungen security measures
Sicherheitsvorrichtung security feature
sichern backup, keep, safekeeping, save, secure
sichernd protective
sicherstellen ensure, secure
Sicherstellungsbereich save area
Sicherung backup, fuse, save operation, stricker fuse
Sicherung der Energieversorgung durch Batterien battery backup
Sicherung Energieversorgung durch Batterien battery backup
Sicherungs- backup
Sicherungsaktion backup operation
Sicherungsautomat circuit breaker
Sicherungsbatterie battery backup
Sicherungsbit backup bit
Sicherungsdatei backup file
Sicherungs-Dateiverzeichnis backup directory
Sicherungsdiskette backup diskette
Sicherungsdiskettenset set of backup diskettes
Sicherungselement fuse element
Sicherungshalter fuse holder
Sicherungshalterung fuse retainer
Sicherungskappe fuse carrier
Sicherungskasten fuse box
Sicherungskennzeichen protection feature
Sicherungskopie backup copy

Sicherungskopie einer Diskette erstellen backup copy of diskette
Sicherungspatrone cartrige fuse-link
Sicherungsprogramm backup service
Sicherungsprozedur save procedure
Sicherungspunkt safeguarding point
Sicherungsring retainer ring
Sicherungsringaufnahme snap ring retainer
Sicherungsschicht data link layer
Sicherungsschnur restraining cable
Sicherungsschraube captive screw, retaining screw
Sicherungsset save set
Sicherungsvereinbarung security arrangements
Sicherungsverfahren backup procedure
Sicherungswert backup value
sich in einer Warteschleife befinden idle
Sicht sight, vision
sichtbar visibly
Sichtfenster sight
Sichtgerät display device, terminal
Sichtprüfung sight verification
Siebdruck silkscreen marking
sieben-bit kodierter Zeichensatz nach ISO iso seven-bit coded character set
siehe Abbildung see figure
siehe Abschnitt see section
siehe Anhang see appendix
siehe unten mentioned below
Signal signal
Signalablaufdiagramm interface signalling (sequence) diagram
Signal auf einem EA-Kanal output acknowledge
Signal ausgeben sounding the buzzer
Signaldiode signal diode
Signalempfänger signal receiver
Signalerde signal ground
Signalfunktion indicator function
Signalgeber für die Kopfposition head positioner flag
Signalgenerator signal generator
Signalgenerator mit Frequenzmodulation frequency modulated signal generator, frequency modulated signal generator
Signalisierungsinformation signaling information
Signalkabel signal cable
Signalleitung signal line
Signalleitung-Funktion control line function
Signallicht signal light
Signalmasse signal ground
Signalton bell, buzzer

Signalverstärker line driver
Signalverteilerplatte signal distribution board
signifikant significant
Signon-Angabe signon indication
Silbenkonsonant syllabic consonant
Silbentrenn-Modul syllabification module
Silbentrenn-Programm syllabification program
Silbentrennung syllabification
Silikagel silica gel
Siliziumplättchen silicon wafer, wafer
Siliziumtal Silicon Valley
simplex simplex
Simplexbetrieb half duplex operation, simplex mode
Simplexverkehr simplex communication
Simulation simulation
Simulationsbasiswert simulation base value
Simulationsdaten simulation data
Simulationsstatus simulation status
Simulationswert simulation value
Simulationszweck simulation purpose
Simulation von diskretem dynamischem System general purpose system simulator
Simulator simulator
simulieren simulate
simultan simultaneous
Simultanablauf simultaneous execution
Simultanbetrieb multitasking, simultaneous operation
Simultanlauf simultaneous run
Simultanverarbeitung multiprogramming
Simultanverarbeitungs-Programm multiprocessing program
Simultanverarbeitungs-System multiprocessing system
Simultanzeit simultaneous time
sinken drop, sink
Sinn sense
sinnlos pointless
sinnvoll sensible, useful
Sinusoszillator harmonic oscillator
Situation situation
Sitzung session
Sitzungsadresse session address
Sitzungsaufbau session structure
Sitzungsende end of session
Sitzungsfortsetzung session continuation
Sitzungsprotokoll session log
Sitzungsschicht session layer
Sitzungssteuerung session control
Sitzungsverbindung session connection
Skalar scalar
Skelett template

skizzieren sketch
Skonto discount
Skontoabzug discount deduction
Skontobasis discount base
Skontobasisbetrag discount base amount
Skontobetrag discount amount
Skontobuchung discount posting
Skontoertrag discount yield
skontofähig discountable
Skontofälligkeit discount due date
Skontoprozentsatz discount percentage
Skontorecht discount law
Skontosatz discount rate
Skontotage discount days
Skontoverlust discount loss
Skontoverrechnung discount settlement
Skontoverrechnungskonto discount settlement account
Sockel socket
Sofortwiederherstellung quick recovery
softsektoriert soft sectored
Software software
softwarebezogen software related
Softwareentwicklung software engineering
Software-Entwicklungssystem software development system
Software-Entwicklungsverfahren software development process
Softwareentwicklungswerkzeug toolkit
Softwarefehler software error
Softwarefehlerbericht software performance report
Softwarefunktion software function
softwaregesteuert software controlled
softwaregesteuerter Interrupt software interrupt
Software-Identifizierungsmerkmal software characteristic
softwarekompatibel software compatible
Softwarekomponente software component
Softwarekonfiguration software configuration
Softwaremeldung software message
Softwarepaket software package
Softwarepflegepaket software maintenance package
Softwareprodukt program product, software product
Softwareproduktbeschreibung software product description
Softwareschalter flag
Softwareseite software side
Software und Dokumentation media and documentation

403

Software- und Dokumentationspaket media and documentation box
Softwareversion software version
Softwarewerkzeug software tool
Sohn son
Solarzelle solar cell
solch such
Soll debit
Sollarchivnummer target serial number
Sollbestand planned stock, planned stocks
Sollbruchstelle supposed separation point
Sollbuchung debit entry
Solleindeckungszeit planned availability time
Sollieferzeit target delivery time
Sollkoordinate nominal coordinate
Sollmengen target quantity
Sollsaldo debit balance
Sollwert nominal value
Sollwertvorgabe preset nominal value
Sonar sonar
Sonder- special
Sonderabschreibung special depreciation
Sonderabschreibungsschlüssel special depreciation code
Sonderausschuß special interest committee
Sonderbehandlung special treatment
Sonderbehandlungsparameter special treatment parameter
Sonderbelegart special voucher type
Sonderbestand special inventory
Sonderbuchung special posting
Sonderbuchungsperiode special accounting period
Sonderfall special case
Sonderform special form
Sonderfunktion special function
Sonderfunktionstaste keyboard key with special use, special function key
Sonderhauptbuch special general ledger
Sonderhauptbuchfeld special general ledger field
Sonderhauptbuchkonto special general ledger account
Sonderhauptbuchsaldo special general ledger balance
Sonderhauptbuchumsatzfeld special general ledger turnover field
Sonderhauptbuchung special general ledger posting
Sonderkennzeichen special flag
Sonderkondition special condition, special term
Sonderkurs special rate

Sonderliste special list
Sondermaterial special material
Sonderprogramm special program
Sonderregelung special regulation
Sondersaldo special balance
Sonderschlüssel special code
Sonderstatus special status
Sonderstellung special position
Sondertaste special key
Sondertext special text
Sonderumsatz special turnover
Sonderzeichen compose character, special character
Sonderzeichenfunktion special character function
Sonderzeichentabelle special character table
Sonnenzelle photoelectric cell, solar cell
Sortieranweisung sort instruction
Sortierbegriff sort notion, sorting term
Sortierbruch sort break
Sortierdatei sort file
sortieren sort
Sortieren mit einem Schlüssel single key sort
Sortieren mit mehreren Schlüsseln multi key sort
Sortierfach sorting drawer
Sortierfehler sort error
Sortierfeld index field, key field, sort field
Sortierfolge collation sequence, sequence, sort sequence
Sortierinformation sort information
Sortierkriterium sort criterion
Sortierlauf sort run
Sortiermöglichkeit sort possibility
Sortierprogramm sort program
Sortierrichtung sort direction
Sortierschlüssel sort code
Sortierspezifikation sort specification
Sortiersteuersatz sort control record
Sortierung sort
Sortierung nach Sätzen full record sort
Sortiervorgang sort procedure
Sortierweiche sort program switch
Sortierzeit sorting time
Sortiment product range
Source source
Spalte column, gap
Spaltenanzeigeeinrichtung column indicating device
Spaltenaufteilung column splitting
Spaltenausschaltkontakt column cut out contact
Spaltenbreite column width

Spalteninhalt column content
Spaltenmodus column mode
Spaltennummer column number
Spalten pro Zoll columns per inch, rows per inch
Spaltenrand edge, edge of a column
Spaltenreihenfolge order of columns
Spaltenstand column width
Spaltenüberschrift column heading
Spaltenüberspringtaste column skip key
Spaltenwahl column selection
spaltenweise by row, columnwise
Spaltpolmotor shaded-pole motor
Spannung voltage, voltage setting
Spannungsabfall brownout
Spannungseinstellung voltage setting
spannungserniedrigend stepdown
spannungserniedrigende Einstellung stepdown configuration
Spannungsfernbedienung remote power controller
spannungsführende Leitung live line
spannungsgesteuerter Oszillator voltage controlled oscillator
spannungsgesteuertes Filter voltage controlled filter
spannungsgesteuerte Verstärkung voltage controlled gain
spannungslos dead
Spannungsregelung voltage control
Spannungsregler voltage regulator
Spannungsstabilisator power regulator
Spannungsstabilisierungsröhre voltage stabilizer tube
Spannungsteiler voltage divider
Spannungstoleranz voltage tolerance
Spannungsüberwachung voltage monitoring
Spannungsverstärker voltage amplifier
Spannungswahlschalter voltage selection switch, voltage selector switch, voltage switch
Spannungswandler potential transformer
Spannungswechsel voltage change
Spanplatte chipboard
Sparbuchauswurf passbook ejection
Sparbuchbewegung passbook motion
Sparbuchsaldo savings book balance
Sparbuchschacht passbook chute
Sparbuchung savings deposit
Sparbuchverarbeitung passbook processing
sparen economize, save
Spartrafo autotransformer
Spartransformator autotransformer
Spediteur carrier, delivery agent, forwarder

Spediteurnotiz carrier's note
Spediteurslieferantennummer carrier number
Spediteursrechnung carrier's invoice
Spedition carriage
Speicher bank, buffer, memory, reservoir, storage
Speicherabzug memory dump
Speicheradapter adapter memory
Speicheradreßerweiterung memory address extension
Speicheradresse storage address
Speicheradresse memory address, memory address, memory location
Speicheradressenroutine mapping routine
Speicheradressenzähler memory address counter
Speicheradreßregister memory address register, storage address register
Speicheranfang start of memory
Speicheranforderung storage request
Speicheransteuerung memory control
Speicher auffrischen refresh memory
Speicherauffüllung character fill
Speicherausdruck dump
Speicherauswahlregister memory select register, message select register
Speicherauszug dump
Speicherauszug bei Fehlern error analysis dump
Speicherauszugsdatei dump file
Speicherauszugsprozeß mapped memory process
Speicherauszugsroutine dump routine
Speicherbank bank, memory bank
Speicher-Basisregister memory base register
Speicherbedarf storage requirement
Speicherbefehl storage instruction
Speicherbelegung festhalten freeze memory
Speicherbelegung prüfen evaluate memory fit
Speicherbelegungsplan map, memory allocation map, memory map
Speicherbelegungsverdichtung memory consolidation
Speicherbereich bucket, memory area, storage area
Speicherbus memory bus
Speicherbussteuereinheit memory bus controller
Speicherdefekt memory failure, storage malfunction
Speicherdefinition memory definition
Speicher-Direktzugriffskanal direct memory access channel

Speichereinheit memory unit, storage device, storage unit
Speicherelement storage element
Speicherende end of memory
Speichererweiterung additional memory, expansion ram, memory expansion, memory expansion option
Speichererweiterungsmodul memory extension, memory extension option, optional memory board
Speichererweiterungsoption memory upgrade option
Speicherfehler memory failure, memory fault
Speicher für Terminalattribute feature memory
Speichergerät storage device
speichergeschützt memory protected
Speichergröße memory capacity, memory size
Speicherhierarchie layered storage
Speicherinitiierung memory initiation
Speicherkapazität amount of memory, capacity, file space, memory, memory capacity, memory size, storage capacity, storage space
Speicherkarte memory card, storage card
Speicher-Lesezugriff memory read
Speicherlimit storage limit
Speicherlöschtaste clear storage key
Speichermakro in Konfigurationsdatei storage space
Speichermangel lack of storage
Speicher mit hoher Packungsdichte high density date storage device
Speicher mit seriellem Speicherzugriff serial storage
Speicher mit wahlfreiem Zugriff random access storage
Speichermodul memory module
speichern file, save, store
speicherorientiertes System memory oriented system
Speicherplatine memory board
Speicherplatz location, memory space, space capacity
Speicherplatzanforderung memory requirement
Speicherplatz auf der Platte disk space
Speicherplatzverwaltung storage administration
Speicherplatzzuweisung memory allocation
Speicherproblem storage problem
speicherprogrammierbare Steuerung programmable controller

speicherprogrammierter Rechner stored program computer
Speicherregister memory data register
speicherresident memory resident
Speicherröhre storage tube
Speicherschablone template
Speicher-Schaltdiode change storage diode
Speicherschnittstelle memory interface
Speicherschnittstelle für Mehrfachzugriff multiport memory interface
Speicher-Schreibzugriff memory read
Speicherschutz memory protection
Speichersofortauszug panic dump
Speicherstelle storage point
Speichersteuereinheit memory control unit, memory controller
Speicherstruktur memory structure
Speichertabelle memory table
Speichertakt- und Steuermodul memory timing and control module
Speichertest memory test
Speicherung storage
Speicherung der letzten Zeile late line storage
Speicherungsform storage form
Speicherverarbeitungsgeschwindigkeit der Standard-Reihen-Zykluszeit basic bank cycle time
Speichervermittlung store and forward
Speichervermittlungssystem store and forward system
Speicherverwaltung memory management, store management
Speicherverwaltungsbaustein memory management unit
Speicherverwaltungchip memory management unit
Speicherverwaltungssystem memory management system
Speicherzelle memory cell
Speicherzugriff memory access
Speicherzugriffseinheit storage interface unit
Speicherzugriffskanal storage access channel
Speicherzugriffslogik memory access logic
Speicherzugriffsschaltkreis memory access logic
Speicherzugriffssteuereinheit memory access controller
Speicherzugriffssteuerung control memory access, memory access control, memory access unit, storage access control
Speicherzuordnungseinheit memory allocation unit, shared memory interface

Speicherzyklus memory cycle
Speicherzykluszeit storage cycle time
Speisestromkreis supply circuit
Sperranforderung lock request
Sperrbestand frozen stock
Sperrbestandsmenge quantity of frozen stock
Sperrbestellung freeze order
Sperrdatum freeze date
Sperre barrier, interlock, lock
Sperreingang inhibiting input
Sperreintrag freeze entry
sperren disable, drop, freeze, inhibit, interlock, lock
sperren/entsperren block/unblock
Sperrgrund reason for freezing
Sperrimpuls inhibit pulse
Sperrkennzeichen freeze flag
Sperrkondensator isolating capacitor
Sperrlager frozen stock stores
Sperrschichttemperatur junction temperature
Sperrschrifteinsteller character expand
Sperrschritt expand escapement
Sperrtabelle lock table
Sperrung freezing
Sperrvermerk blocking note
Sperrwirkung effect of freezing
Spesen expenses
Spesenbelastung expenses charged
Spesenbuchung expenses posting
Spesenkennzeichen expenses flag
Spezialsatz special record
Spezialtaste special key
speziell special
spezielle rückgekoppelte Schaltung bootstrap
spezielle Satzverwaltung defined record management
Spezifikation specification
spezifisch individual, specific
spezifizieren specify
Spezifizierung specification
Spiegel mirror
Spiegelfeld mirror field
Spiegelfrequenzverhalten image response
spielen play
Spielfunktion game function
Spielkonsole paddle
Spielpult joystick
Spielpultposition joystick position
Spielregler paddle
Spindel screw drive, spindle
Spindelöffnung spindle hole
Spirale coil
Spiralkabel coiled cord

Spitze peak
Spitzenspannung peak voltage
Spitzenspannungsmesser peak voltmeter
Spitze-zu-Spitze peak-to-peak
Spleiße splice
Spleißstelle splice
Spleißung splice
splitten split
Spontanbetrieb asynchronous response mode
spoolen spool
Spooler spooler
Spool-Fernverarbeitungsprogramm remote spoolout processor
Spoolkomponente spool component
Sprachanweisung language statement
Sprachausgabe spoken output, spoken response
Sprachauskunft voice advisary
Sprachauswahlmenu language selection menu
Sprachband voice band
Sprachbaustein frame of speech
Sprache language
Sprachebene level of language
Sprachelement language element
Sprachenauswahlmenge language selection quantity
Spracheneditor language editor
Sprachenpool language pool
Sprachenschlüssel language key
Sprachentabelle language table
Sprachenübersetzung language translation
Spracherkennung speech recognition
Sprache über Daten data under voice
Sprache zur Datenbankbeschreibung data base description language
Sprache zur Drucksteuerung print control language
Sprache zur Formatsteuerung format control language
Sprache zur Formularbeschreibung forms description language
Sprachkennzeichen language identifier, language key
Sprachklang speech sound
Sprachmodul speech module
Sprachprozessor language processor, speech processor
Sprach-ROM language ROM
Sprachsymbol language symbol
Sprachsynthese speech synthesis
Sprachsynthesizer speech synthesizer
Sprachübersetzer language processor

Sprachübersetzer für die Dialogbeschreibungssprache

Sprachübersetzer für die Dialogbeschreibungssprache dialog specification language translator
Sprachverarbeitung language processing
Sprachwellenform speech waveform
sprechen speak
Sprechmodus talk mode
Sprengung breakup
springen jump
Springer jumper
Sprossenteilung row pitch
Sprühwasserprüfung water spray test
Sprung jump
Sprungadresse branch address
Sprungadreßregister jump address register
Sprung aufgrund eines Busfehlers bus error trap
Sprungbefehl branching condition, jump instruction
Sprungfunktion skip function
Sprungprogramm jump routine
sprungsequentiell jump sequential
Sprungtaste skip key
Sprung-Zeitglied jumping around timer
Spule bobbin, coil, electric coil, electric reactor, reel
spulen spool
Spulenende end of reel
Spulenendmarkierung end of reel mark
Spulenisolator bobbin insulator
Spulennummer reel number
Spur track, track row
Spuradreßregister track address register
Spuranfangsadresse home address
Spurbreite track width
Spurende end of track
Spuren pro Zoll tracks per inch
Spurenwähler track selector
Spurnummer track number
Spurumschaltmerker continuation marker
Spurzustandstabelle track condition table
Stabilität durability
Stachel pin
Stacheltransporteinrichtung fin feed device
Stack Stack, stack
Stackbedarf stack requirement
Stackeintragung stack entry
Stackkontrollblock stack control block
Stack leer stack empty
Stackparameter stack parameter
Stackspitze top of stack
Stacküberlauf stack overflow
Stacküberschreitung stack overflow

Stack voll stack full
Stackzeiger stack pointer
Stackzugriffsblock stack access block
Ständer stator
Ständergehäuse stator frame
Ständerwicklung stator winding
ständig continuous, perpetually
Staffel scale
staffeln scale
Staffelnummer scale number
Staffelpreis price
Staffelwert scale value
Stahl steel
Stahlpanzerisolierrohr rigid conduit
Stahlpanzerrohr rigid conduit
Stamm master, root
Stammband master tape
Stammdatei master file
Stammdateiverzeichnis root directory
Stammdaten master data
Stammdatenänderung master data alteration, master file alteration
Stammdatenänderungsbeleg master file alteration voucher
Stammdatenaufbau master data structure
Stammdatenausdruck master data printout
Stammdatenbank master database
Stammdatenbereich master data area
Stammdatenlistenanzeige master data list display
Stammdatenorganisation master data organisation
Stammdatenübernahme master data transfer
Stammdatenverwaltung master data administration, master data management
stammen derive
Stammhausnummer main account number
Stammliste master list
Stammnummernkreise ranges of master record numbers
Stammsatz master record, owner record
Stammsatzänderung master record alteration
Stammsatzanlage master record asset
Stammsatzanzeige master record display
Stammsatzart master record type
Stammsatzberechtigung master record authorization
stammsatzbezogen for the master record
Stammsatzbild master record screen
Stammsatzdatenbild master record data screen
Stammsatzebene master record level
Stammsatzfeld master record field

Stammsatzinformationen master record information
Stammsatzpflege master record maintenance
Stammsatzwertfeld master record value field
Stammsystemplatte master disk
Stammverwaltung master administration
Stand booth, stage, stand, state
standalone standalone
Standalone-Anordnung standalone arrangement
Standalone-Operation standalone operation
Standalone-Programm standalone program
Standard default, standard, typical
Standardaktion für das Wiedereinlesen standard restore option
Standardaktion für die Sicherung standard backup option
Standardangabe default value
Standardanrede standard address
Standardaufteilung default partition
Standardausdruck default listing, standard listing
Standardauswahl default, default selection, standard selection
Standardauswertung standard report
Standardbelegung default mapping, standard mapping
Standardbibliothek default library
Standardbildsteuerformat standard display control format
Standardbrief standard letter
Standarddateiverzeichnis default directory
Standarddaten standard data
Standarddruckeinstellung default printer option
Standarddrucker default printer
Standarddump standard dump
Standardeditor default editor
Standardeingabe standard input
Standardeinstellung default, default setting, standard system setting
Standarderfassung standard acquisition
Standarderöffnungssegment initialization segment
Standarderweiterung default extension
Standardfehlerbehandlung standard error handling routine
Standardfehlermeldung standard error message
Standardfehlerroutine standard error routine
Standardformat standard format
Standardformat-Handlingsystem standard format handling system
Standardfortsetzung standard continuation

Standardisierung standardisation
Standardkondition standard condition
Standardlaufwerk default drive
standardmäßiges Begrenzungszeichen default import export terminator
standardmäßiges Zeilenlineal default ruler, standard ruler
Standardmehrwertsteuer standard value added tax
Standardmerkmale default characteristics
Standardordner default folder
Standardparameter default parameter, standard parameter
Standardplatte default disk
Standardposition standard position
Standardpreis standard price
Standardprogramm default program, standard program
Standardprozeduraufruf procedure calling standard
Standardregisterkonvention standard register convention
Standardroutine standard routine
Standardsatz standard record
Standardsatzlänge default record length, standard record length
Standardschnittstelle standard interface
Standardseitennummer standard page number
Standardspeicher default memory
Standardsprachenschlüssel default language key
Standardstempel standard stamp
Standardsteuerkommando default control command
Standardsystem default system, standard system
Standardtabelle default table, standard table
Standardtabulator default tabulator
Standardtaste default key, standard key
Standardtext standard text
Standardtextbaustein standard text module
Standardtextnummer standard text number
Standardtextverwaltung standard text management
Standardtextzeilen standard text size
Standardverarbeitung default processing, standard processing
Standardvorgabe default, default value, standard default
Standardwert default, default value
Standardzeichen standard character
Standardzeichensatz default character set
Standardzieldatei standard target file

Standardzugriffsmethode conventional access, standard access method
Standardzuordnung default assignment, standard assignment
Standardzustand default state, standard state
Standardzuweisung default allocation, standard allocation
Standfuß floor stand, optional floor stand
Standleitung dedicated line, direct cable connection, direct connection, private line
Standmodell floor stand model
Standortwechsel dislocation, relocation
Standverbindung dedicated connection, leased circuit
Standzeit downtime
Stanzabfall chad
Stanzabfallschacht chad chute
stanzen punch
Stanzer puncher
Stapel batch, stack
Stapelaufteilung batch splitting
Stapelbefehl batch command
Stapelbetrieb batch operating, batch processing
Stapelbuchen batch posting
Stapelbuchungskennzeichen batch posting flag
Stapeldatei batch file
Stapel-Datenstation batch terminal
Stapeleingabe batch input
Stapelende end of deck
Stapelerstellung batch generation
Stapelfernverarbeitung remote batch processing
Stapelfernverarbeitungsstation remote batch terminal
Stapelfernverarbeitungssymbiont remote symbiont
Stapeljob batch job
Stapelkommando batch command
Stapelkomponente batch component
Stapelmerkmal batch qualifier
Stapelmodus batch mode
stapelorientiert batch oriented
Stapelprogramm batch program
Stapelrahmen stack frame
Stapelspeicher stack
Stapelspeicher zurücksetzen unwind
Stapelteil batch part
Stapelüberspringkennzeichen batch bypass indicator
Stapel- u. Mehrprogrammverarbeitungseigenschaften batch multiprogramming
Stapelverarbeitung batch processing, pile processing

Stapelwarteschlange batch queue
Stapelzeiger stack pointer
Stapelzuführung stack feed
Stapelzuführungseinrichtung stack feeder
Starkstromleitung heavy duty power cable, power line
Starkstromleitungsfilter power line filter
starrer Leiter rigid conductor
starres Kabel rigid cable
Start activation, begin
Startanzeige home screen
Startbefehl start instruction
Startbit start element
Startdiskette load disk
starten activate, initialize, run, start
Startkommandoprozedur startup command file
Startladen initial program load, input program load
Startmaske starting mask
Startmeldung startup message
Startname initial name
Startprogramm startup program
Startprozedur starting procedure
Startpunkt offset
Startsprungbox start jump box
Start-/Stopbetrieb asynchronous operation
Start-Stop-Verzerrungsgrad degree of start-stop distortion
Startteilprogramm start partial program
Starttransaktionscode start transaction code
Startup-Modulname startup module name
Stationsadresse station address
Stationsaufforderung interrogation
Stationsgruppenkennung remote identifier, station group identification
Stationskennung station identification, station name
Stationsname station name
Stationsrechner cluster controller
Stationssteuerroutine remote device handler
Stationswähler media drive selector
statischer Prozeß static process
statischer Speicher static memory
statischer Umrichter static inverter
Statistik statistics
Statistikart type of statistics
Statistikbuchung statistical posting
statistikmäßig related to statistics
Statistikpaket für Sozialwissenschaften statistical package for social sciences
Statistiksammeldatei statistics pooling file
Statistiksatz statistics record

Statistikwert statistical value
statistischer Zeitmultiplexer statistical time division multiplexer
Status status
Status abfragen check state, probe
Statusänderung change of status, status change
Statusanzeige status display
Statusbezeichner status designator
Statusbyte status byte
Statuscode status code
Statusdaten status data
Statusfeld current item field, status field
Statuskennzeichen status code
Status-LED status led
Statusprotokoll status bulletin
Statusregister status register
Statusübertragung status transfer
Statuswortregister status word register
Statuszeile indicator, message line, status line
Stauung congestion
Steckbrücke jumper, jumper clip
Steckbuchse connector
Steckdose convenience outlet, electrical outlet, outlet, power receptacle, socket, wall outlet
steckenbleiben stuck
Stecker connector, electric connector, electric plug, male contact, male plus
Steckerhalterung connector fastener
Steckerhülse attachment-plug receptacle
Steckerkasten plug box
steckerkompatibler Großrechner plug compatible mainframe
steckerkompatibles Speichermodul plug compatible memory
Stecker mit Einsteckmarkierung key plug
Stecker mit quadratischem Kopf plug square head
Steckerstift pin
Steckerverriegelung cable connector latch
Steckfeld patch area, patch panel
Steckplatz slot
Steckrahmen backplane, frame
Steckstift electric pin
Stecktabulator plug-in tabulator
Steckverbindung connector
steigend ascending
steigende Flanke rising edge
steigern increase
Steigerung increase
Stelle, character, digit, location, place, position
stellen place, position, put
stellenrichtig in the correct position
Stellenverschiebung arithmetic shift
Stellenwertverschiebung cyclic shift
Stellglied actuator
Stellmotor servomotor
Stellung position
Stellungnahme perusal
Stellungsparameter position parameter
Stempel stamp
Stepmodus step mode
stereophonisch stereophonic
Sterilität sterility
Sternchen asterisk, star
Sternchenkonten asterisked accounts
Sternnetz star type network
Steuer tax
Steuerabschnitt control page, control section
Steueradreßerweiterung extended control address
Steueranweisung control statement, tax control statement
Steuerart tax type
Steueraufstellung tax listing
Steuerband control tape
Steuerbefehl control instruction
Steuerbereich control area
Steuerberichtigung tax rectification
Steuerbetrag tax amount
Steuerbilanz tax balance
Steuerbit control bit
Steuerblock control block
Steuerblockformat control block format
Steuerblockprozeß control block process
Steuerbuchung tax posting
Steuerbus control bus
Steuerbyte control byte
Steuercode control code
Steuerdatei control file
Steuerdiagramm scatter plot
Steuereinbehaltung tax deduction
Steuereinheit control unit, controller, master control unit
Steuereinheitenbezeichnung control unit name
Steuereinheitenname control unit name
Steuereinrichtung control equipment
Steuerempfänger control receiver
Steuerentrichtung payment of taxes
Steuererklärung tax declaration
Steuerfeld control field
Steuerfelderweiterung extended control field
Steuerfunktion control function
Steuergerät control device
Steuerinformation control information
Steuerkabel control cable, trailing cable
Steuerkarte control card, director card

Steuerkarte für Folgekontrolle check control card, sequence check control card
Steuerkartenübersicht control card listing
Steuerkategorie tax category
Steuerkennzeichen control identifier, tax flag, tax marker
Steuerknüppel joystick
Steuerkommando control command
Steuerkorrektur tax correction
Steuerleiste switch jump
Steuerleitung control cable, control line
Steuerlogik control steering logic
Steuermarkierung control flag
Steuermodul controller, controller module
steuern control, drive
steuerpflichtig taxable
Steuerplatine controller board
Steuerprogramm control program, handler
Steuerpult control panel
Steuerraum control room
Steuerrechner control computer
Steuerrecht tax law
steuerrechtlich according to tax law
Steuerregister control register, integrated control register
Steuerregister für Ein-/Ausgabekanal access control register
Steuerrelais master control relay
Steuerroutinen für Datenstationen remote device handler
Steuersatz control record, tax rate
Steuerschalter control switch, master control
Steuerschlüssel control code
Steuerschlüssel-Nummer control key number
Steuerschrank control cabinet
Steuerschütz contactor
Steuersegment control segment
Steuersender exciter
Steuersequenz control sequence
Steuersignal control signal
Steuerspeicher control memory
Steuerspeichercode control storage code
Steuerstatement control statement
Steuertaste control key
Steuerung control, controller, controller board, drive
Steuerung der Schreibmarke cursor addressing
Steuerung des Stromversorgungsnetzes electric power system control
Steuerung einer bestimmten Variable control of specific variable
Steuerung für Speicherzugriffe memory request controller
Steuerungsablauf control sequence
Steuerungsangaben control statement
Steuerungsdaten control data
Steuerungs-Echo-Test auf der Hostleitung host line control loopback test
Steuerungsfunktion control action, control function
Steuerungsinformation control info
Steuerungskennzeichen control flag
Steuerungsmechanismus control mechanism
Steuerungsparameter control parameter
Steuerungsschlüssel control code
Steuerungsstammdaten control master data
Steuerungstabelle control table
Steuerungsvariable control variable
Steuerverprobung tax assessment
Steuerverrechnung tax calculation
Steuerwarte control room
Steuerwerk control unit
Steuerwort control word
Steuerzeichen control character, control symbol
Steuerzeichenfolge control character sequence, control string
Stichtag base date
Stichtaginventur scheduled stocktaking
Stichtagsbestand base date inventory
Stichtagswert base date value
Stichwort keyword, topic
Stichwortdatei key word file
Stichworteingabe key word input
Stichwortgenerator key word generator
Stichwortliste key word list
Stichwortrecherche key word search
Stichwortsuche key word search
Stichwortverzeichnis index
Stickstoff nitrogen
Stickstoffüberwachung nitrogen flow-rate meter
Stiftbelegung pinout
Stiftisolator pin insulator
Stillstand deadlock
Stimmbänder vocal folds
Stimmeigenschaft voice quality
Stimmkreation design voice
stochastisch stochastic
Störblock noise block
Stördaten clutter
stören disturb
Störpegelabstand noise ratio
Störstelle place of malfunction

Störstrahlung interface field strength, interfering radiation
Störung disturbance, error, fault, malfunction
Störung im Stromversorgungsnetz electric power system disturbance
Störungsanzeige error indicator, malfunction indicator
Störungsbericht failure and malfunction report
Stoff material
Stop halt, stop
Stopadresse stop address
Stopanzeige stop indicator
Stopbezugszahl halt indicator
Stopbit stop bit
stoppen halt, stop
Stopplänge stop distance
Stopregister breakpoint register
Stoptaste break key, stop key
stornieren cancel
Storno cancellation
Stornobetrag amount cancelled
Stornomenge quantity cancelled
Stornorechnungsgutschrift cancellation credit note
Stoßbetrieb burst mode
Stoßkreis pulse circuit
Stoßwelle shock wave
Stoßwellenauslösetaste shock wave release switch
Stoßwellenauslösung shock wave release
Stoßwellenerzeugung shock wave generation
Stoßwellengenerator shock wave generator
Strahl beam
Straßenname street name
Streckenauftrag third party order, third party sales order
Streckenbestellung third party purchase order
Streckengeschäft third party business
Streckenlieferant third party supplier
Streckgitter expanded metal
Streuungsmaß scatter gram value
Strich dash, stroke
Strichcode bar code
Strichcodeleser optical Bar Code Reader
String string
Stringargument string argument
Stringkonstante string constant
Stringvariable string variable
Strom current, stream
Stromabnahmegerät current collecting equipment
Stromanstieg rush current
Stromanzeige power indicator
Stromausfallsicherung battery backup, uninterruptable power supply
stromführend current carrying, hot
Stromlaufplan ladder diagram, ladder logic, ladder logic circuit, ladder logic diagram, wiring diagram
Stromquelle power source
Stromrichter static convertor
Stromschleife current loop
Stromschleifen-Stromquelle current loop supply
Stromstoß surge current
Stromstoß-Löschschaltung surge quenching circuit
Stromstoßrelais latching relay
Stromverbrauch electricity consumption, power consumption
Stromversorgung power, power requirements, power supply, power supply module
Stromversorgungsmodul power supply module
Stromversorgungsnetz electric power system
Stromwandler current transformer
Stromwender commutator
Stromzuführung power lead
Struktur structure
Strukturanweisung structure instruction
Strukturanzeige structure display
Strukturbeschreibung structure description
Strukturbezeichnung structure designation
Strukturdarstellung structure representation
Strukturdaten structure data
strukturierte Programmierung structured programming
Strukturnummer structure number
Strukturregel structure rule
Strukturstückliste structure parts list
Strukturteileverwendung structure parts use
Strukturunabhängigkeit structure independence
Strukturverwaltung structure administration
Stück part
Stückliste bill of materials, part list, parts list
Stücklistenauflösung bill of materials dispersal
Stücklistenauflösungs-Kennzeichen bill of materials dispersal flag
Stücklistendatei parts list file
Stücklistenentnahme parts list withdrawal
Stücklistenkomponente component of a parts list
Stücklistenpflege part list maintenance
Stücklistenposition component sequence number
Stücklistenstamm parts list master

Stücklistenverwaltung parts list management
Stückpreis unit price
Stützisolator post insulator
Stützlager shaft support
Stützwert basic value
Stufe level
Stufenabschreibung stepped depreciation
Stufenkennzeichen level identification
stufenlos infinitely variable
Stufenvorsatz level header
stufenweise incremental
Stunde hour
Subpool subpool
Subroutine subroutine
substituieren replace, substitute
Substitut substitute
Substitutionsmaterial substitute material
Subsystem subsystem
Subtabelle subtable
Subtraktion subtraction
Suchargument search argument
Suchbaum search tree
Suchbaumverfahren search tree procedure
Suchbegriff search argument, search value, search word
Suchcode matchcode
Suche search
suchen locate, search
Suchfolge search string
Suchfrage search query
Suchlauf search run
Suchlogik search logic
suchlogisch search-logical
Suchmaske search mask
Suchoperation look up operation
Suchpfad für Kommandointerpreter command search path
Suchroutine search routine
Suchtabelle look up table
Suchzeit search time
Suffix suffix
Summationskriterium summation criterion
Summe sum, total
Summe mehrerer Spalten multicolumn total
Summenabzug total deduction
Summenanzeige totals display
Summenausgabe totals output
Summenbericht statement of totals
Summenblatt totals page
Summenblock totals block
Summenfeld accumulation field, total field
Summenfeld rücksetzen resetting total field
Summenliste totals list

Summenspalte totals column
Summenteil totals section
Summenübersicht totals summary
Summenverwaltung totals management
Summenzähler totals counter
Summenzeile total line
Summer buzzer
summieren sum, total
Summierschaltung summing circuit
Summierung summation
Superorthikon image orthicon
supraleitend superconducting
supraleitendes Gerät superconducting device
Supraleiter superconductor
suspendierter Prozeß suspended process
Symbiont symbiont
Symbiontendatei breakpointed file
Symbiontenladetechnik symbiont loader technique
Symbiontenname symbiont name
Symbol symbol
symbolisch symbolic
symbolische Adresse symbolic address
symbolischer Abschnittsname alias phase name
symbolischer Assembler symbolic assembler
symbolischer Code symbolic code
symbolischer Name mnemonic, symbolic name
symbolische Sprache symbolic language
symbolische Testhilfe symbolic debugger
Symbolquerverweistabelle symbol cross-reference table
Symbolsubstitution symbol substitution
Symboltabelle symbol table
Symboltabellenausdruck symbol table listing
Symboltaste symbol key
Symptom symptom
Symptommenü symptom menu
synchron synchronous
Synchronadapter separate clock unit
synchrone Datenverbindungskontrolle synchronous data link control
synchrone Übertragung synchronous transmission
Synchrongenerator synchronous generator
Synchronisation synchronization
Synchronisationsfehler synchronization error
Synchronisationspunkt synchronization point
Synchronisationszeichen sync character, synchronisation character
Synchronisiereinheit timing generator
Synchronisierer synchronizer
Synchronisierung synchronisation, timing

Systemmerkmal

Synchronisierung der Fenster aufheben unsynchronize windows
Synchronmodul synchronous line module
Synchronmotor synchronous induction motor, synchronous motor
syntaktische Leseanweisung syntactic marker
syntaktischer Fehler syntax error
Syntax syntax
Syntaxfehler bad syntax, syntax error
Syntaxschreibweise syntax notation
Syntaxüberprüfung syntax check
Syntaxvorschrift syntax requirement
System system
Systemabbruch system termination
Systemablage system cabinet
Systemablauf system run
Systemabsturz crash, system crash
Systemabsturzfall case of system crash
Systemanalytiker system analyst, systems analyst
System anhalten shutting down, stopping the system
System-Anlaufschlüssel code for system start-up
Systemanwendungsdiskette system application diskette
Systematik systematic
systematisch systematic
Systemattribut system attribute
Systemausfall system crash
Systemausgaberoutine output writer
systembedingt system dependent
Systembefehl system command
Systembenutzer system user
Systemberater system consultant
Systembeschreibung system description
Systembetreuer system attendant, system operator
Systembetrieb system operation
systembezogen system-related
Systemblockade deadlock
Systemblockdiagramm system block diagram
Systemdatei system file
Systemdateiverzeichnis system directory
Systemdaten system data
Systemdatenbank system data base
Systemdienst system service
Systemdienstdiskette services diskette
Systemdiskette load disk, operating system diskette, release diskette, system diskette, system floppy
Systemdrucker line printer, system printer
systemeigen native

System eines Drittanbieters other vendors' system
Systemeingabedatei system input file
Systemeingaberoutine input reader
Systemeinheit system box, system unit
Systemeinheitstest system unit test
Systemeinstellung system setup
Systemende absolute shutdown
Systementlastung relieving the load on the system
Systementwicklung system development, system engineering
Systementwurf system design
Systemeröffnung initialization
Systemerweiterung system extension
Systemfehler internal error, system error
Systemfehlerdaten system error data
Systemfehlermeldung system error message
Systemfirmware system firmware
systemfremd foreign
Systemfunktion system function
Systemgenerierung generating a system, system generation
Systemgeschwindigkeit system performance
Systemgröße system size
Systemgrundeinstellung system setup
Systemhandbuch owner's manual, systems manual
Systemhauptmenü main system menu
System herunterfahren stopping the system
System im Einsatz field system
Systeminitialisierungsprogramm system startup program
systemintern system internal
Systemjoblaufbibliotheksdatei run library
Systemkenntnis knowledge about the system
Systemkern kernel, system nucleus
Systemkomponente external item
Systemkonfiguration system configuration
Systemkonfigurierungseinheit availability control unit
Systemkonfigurierungsprogramm partitioning program
Systemkonsole console workstation, system console
Systemkonstante system constant
Systemkontrollzentrum system control center
Systemkorrekturroutine system patch routine
Systemleseroutine reader
Systemlogik system logic
Systemmanager system manager
Systemmeldung prompt, system message
Systemmerkmal system feature, system setup

415

System mit verteilter Intelligenz distributed intelligence system
System mit Zwischenspeicherung store and forward system
Systemmodul system module
Systemnetzschalter system unit power switch
System neu laden reboot, reload, reload the system
System nicht vollständig geladen system load incomplete
systemnotwendig required by the system
Systempaket system kit
Systemparameter system parameter
Systempartition system partition
Systemplaner system scheduler
Systemplanung system design
Systemplatine system board
Systemplatte system disk
Systemprogramm system image, system program
Systemprogrammbibliothek processor library, system program library
Systemprogrammfunktion system program function
Systemprozeß system process
Systemreaktion system reaction
Systemrechner system computer
Systemresource system resource
Systemschlüssel system code
systemseitig system internal
Systemsoftware operational software, system software
Systemsoftwarediskette system software diskette
Systemsoftwarekomponente system software component
Systemspeicherauszugsdatei system dump file
Systemspezialist system manager
Systemsprache system language
Systemsprachenübersetzer system language translator
Systemstart startup procedure, system initialization, system startup
System starten start the system
Systemstatus system status
Systemsteuerabschnitt system control section
Systemsteuerprogramm mini operating system
Systemsteuerung exec, executive, executive system, system control
Systemtabelle system table
Systemtest system test
Systemträger system residence pack
Systemträgerart type of system residence pack

Systemträgerwechsel system carrier change
Systemtransaktion system transaction
Systemüberlastung system overload
Systemüberprüfung system checkout, system inspection
Systemübersicht system outline, system overview
Systemübertragung system transfer
Systemüberwachungsstation system monitoring station
Systemumgebung system environment
systemunterstützt system based
Systemvariable system variable
Systemvariablenfeld system variable field
Systemverbund system network
Systemverwalter administrator, system administrator, system supervisor
Systemverwalter-Handbuch system manager's manual
Systemverwaltung systems management
Systemverwaltungsdatei systems management file
Systemverzeichnis system directory
Systemvorschlag system proposal
Systemwarnung system warning
Systemwartungsdiskette system maintenance diskette
Systemzeitgeber virtual memory timer
System zur Fertigungssteuerung production control system
System zur Informationsverarbeitung information processing system
System zur Installation und Wartung von Software automated installation and diagnostic service
System zur Quellcodeverwaltung source code control system
Systemzustandsbericht system status report

T

Tabelle array, list, table
Tabelle der Dateizuweisungen file allocation table
Tabelle der lokalen Symbole local symbol table
Tabelle der nichtbelegten Sektoren free sector list
Tabelle der Plattenbereiche partition table
Tabelle der transienten Steuerfunktionen function loader table
Tabelle der verfügbaren Geräte facility pool
tabellenabhängig table dependent
Tabellenänderung table alteration
Tabellenanfang table beginning
Tabellenanzeige table display
Tabellenargument table argument
Tabellenaufbau table composition
Tabellenbenutzung table use
Tabellenbezeichnung table designation
Tabellenbuch table book
Tabellendatei table file
Tabellendefinition table definition
Tabelleneintrag table entry
Tabellenelement table element
Tabellenende end of the table
Tabellenfehler table error
Tabellenformat display format, list format
Tabellenfunktion table function
Tabellengenerierung table generation
tabellengesteuert parameter driven, tabel driven
Tabellengruppe table group
Tabellenhandbuch table manual
Tabelleninhalt table contents
Tabellenkalkulation spreadsheet, spreadsheet program
Tabellenkompilierer table compiler
Tabellenlesen table read
Tabellenliste table list
Tabellenmodifikation table modification
Tabellenname table name
Tabellennummer table number
Tabellenpflege table maintenance
Tabellenplatz place in the table
Tabellenpuffer table buffer
Tabellensatz table record
Tabellensuche look up table, table look-up
Tabellentechnik tabular technology

Tabellentransport table transfer
Tabellenüberlauf table overflow
Tabellenverknüpfungsfeld table linkage field
Tabellenverwaltungssystem table management system
Tabellenverzeichnis table index
Tabellenvormerkung table reservation
Tabellenwert classification table, list value
Tabellenzugriff table access
Tabelle zur Adreßübersetzung address translation table
Tabelle zur Fehlerbestimmung problem isolation chart
Tabellierzeile ruler line
Tab-Ende tab end
Tabulator horizontal tab, tab, tab position, tabulator
Tabulatoränderung ruler change
Tabulatoreinstellung tab setting
Tabulatoren tab stops
Tabulatorfeld tab field
Tabulator-Gesamtlöschtaste clear key
Tabulator löschen clear tab
Tabulatormarke tab mark
Tabulatorsetztaste tabulator set key
Tabulatorstop tabulator stop
Tabulatortaste tab key
Tabulatorweite tab size
Tabulatorwert tabulator value
Tabulatorzeile line ruler
täglich daily
tägliche Benutzung day to day operation
tätig active
Tätigkeit activity
Tätigkeitsbericht proceedings
Tätigkeitswort verb
Tagesabschluß daily closing
Tagesarbeit daytime work
Tagesauswertung daily report
Tagesdatum current date, today's date
Tageslicht daylight
Tageswert day's value
Tageszeit time of day
Taggrenze due date
taghell daylight
Takt clock, clock rate, cycle, strobe
Taktfrequenz clock frequency, frequency
Taktgeber clock
Taktgeberrate clock rate
Taktgenauigkeit clock accuracy
Taktgenerator clock generator
Taktimpuls timing pulse
Talon talon

Tandemgerät tandem device
Tangens tangent
Tanknummer tank number
Tantalkondensator tantalum capacitor
Taschenrechner calculator, electronic calculator
Taschenterminal hand held terminal
Task task
Taskbereich task area
Taskbetrieb task operation
Taskende task end
taskspezifisch task specific
Tasksteuerblock task control block
Tasksteuerung task control
Tasktyp task type
Taskverarbeitungspriorität task switching priority
Taskverwaltung task management
Tastatur keyboard
Tastaturanpassung keyboard driver
Tastaturanzeige keyboard indicator
Tastaturaufgabe keyboard task
Tastaturauswahl keyboard selection
Tastaturauswahlmenü keyboard selection menu
Tastaturbearbeitung keyboard process
Tastaturbedienung keyboard handling
Tastaturbefehl keyboard instruction
Tastaturbereich keypad area
Tastaturcodierer keyboard encoder
Tastaturdatei keyboard file
Tastaturdaten keyboard data
Tastatureingabe keyboard entry
Tastaturfreigabe keyboard release
Tastatur für industriellen Einsatz factory hardened keyboard
Tastaturfunktionsmodus keyboard action mode
Tastaturfuß keyboard feet
Tastatur gesperrt keyboard locked
Tastaturkabel keyboard cable
Tastaturkommando keyboard command
Tastaturmerkmal keyboard feature
Tastaturmodus keyboard mode
Tastaturmonitor keyboard monitor
Tastatur nicht funktionsfähig actual keyboard failure
Tastaturschlüssel keyboard access code
Tastatursignal beep, bell tone, keyboard beep, keyboard bell
Tastatursprache keyboard language
Tastatursteuerung keyboard control
Tastaturteil keyboard section
Tastaturtest keyboard test

Tastaturtreiber keyboard driver
Tastaturumkodierung keyboard mapping
Tastaturzeichenpuffer keyboard transmit buffer
Taste button, key, keyboard key
Taste Ausgangsposition home key
Tastenanschlag key stroke
Tastenbetätigung key stroke
Tastenbetätigungskrafteinsteller key touch selector
Tastenblock keypad
Tastendefinition key assignment
Tastendefinitionen der Arbeitsplatzstation system-wide keyboard definitions
Tasteneingabe key input
Tastenfunktion key function
Tastenkappe keycap
Tastenkennzeichnung function identifier
Tastenklick keyclick
Tastenposition button position
Tastenreihe key row
Tastensperre key lock
Tastenwahl push button selection
Tastenwechselbetätigung alternate key stroke
Tastenwiederholung key repeat, typamatic key stroke
Taste zum Bewegen des Cursors cursor movement key
Taste zum Hervorheben von Text highlighting key
Taste »Zeichen rückwärts« character backspace key
Taste »Zeichen vorwärts« character advance key
Tastfläche keytop touch area
Tatsache fact
tatsächlich actual, actually, in fact
tatsächlicher Bestand actual stock
tauschen exchange, swap
Tausenderpunkt thousand position indicator
tausendstel milli
Technik technique
Technik der integrierten Schaltung integrated circuit technology
Technik des kreativen Denkens area thinking
Techniker engineer, technician
technisch technical
technische Daten specification
technischer Ausschuß technical committee
technischer Kundendienst field service
technischer Leiter operations manager
technisches Dokumentationspaket technical documentation kit

technisches Handbuch technical manual, technical reference manual
Teil component, element, item, part
Teilabgang partial decrease, partial issue
Teilabschnitt subsection
Teilauszug partial statement
teilbeliefern make a partial delivery
Teilbereich part area, subarea
Teilbestände distributed inventory
Teilcharge partial lot
Teil eines Leistungsschalters circuit breaker component
teilen divide, part, share
Teilenummer part number
Teilerfassung subacquisition
Teiler-Speicher für Bandgenerator band generator divisor latch
Teileverwendung use of parts
Teileverwendungsnachweis evidence of use
Teileverwendungsstamm use of parts master
Teilfeld partial field
Teilformat partial format
Teilformatierung partial formatting
Teilformatname partial format name
Teilfunktion subfunction
Teilhaberbetrieb online transaction processing
Teillieferung partial delivery
Teillieferungskennzeichen partial delivery flag
Teilliste sublist
Teilmenge part quantity, subset
Teilnachricht part message, partial message
teilnehmen participate
Teilnehmer participant, subscriber, user
Teilnehmeradresse transport address
Teilnehmeranforderung user request
Teilnehmerberechtigung user authorization
Teilnehmerbetrieb demand processing, time sharing, user operation
Teilnehmerbetriebsklasse closed user group
Teilnehmerdatei join file, user file
Teilnehmerdialogbetrieb demand processing
Teilnehmereinrichtung user equipment
Teilnehmerkennung subscriber identification
Teilnehmerleitung local loop
Teilnehmernetz transport network
Teilnehmersitzung user session
teilnehmerspezifisch user specific
Teilnehmerstation demand site
Teilnehmersteuerbereichsliste list of user control blocks
Teilnehmersteuerungsbereich subscriber control area
Teilnehmersystem user system

Teilnehmertabelle join table
Teilnehmerverbindung transport connection
Teilnehmerverhältnis user relation
Teilnehmerverhalten user behaviour
Teilnetz subnetwork
Teilproblem partial problem
Teilprojekt partial project
Teilprüfpunkt partial checkpoint
Teilschema subschema
Teilschicht sublayer
Teilschlüssel partial key
Teilstreckenverfahren store and forward technique
Teilstring substring
Teilstromausfall brownout
Teilstrukturen parts structure
teilweise partial
Teilwert fractional value
Teilwertabschreibung fractional depreciation
Teilwertermittlung fractional valuation
Teilwort partial word
Teilzeichenfolge substring
Telefax faksimile, fax, long distance xerox, telefax
Telefaxdienst telefax service
Telefaxgerät facsimile equipment
Telefon phone, telephone
Telefonanschlußdose telephone wall jack
Telefonat phone call, phone conversation, telephone call
Telefonauskunft directory service
Telefondienst telephone service
Telefonnummer phone number, telephone number
Telefonschalter common carrier switch, phone switch
Telefonstecker modular plug, modular plug on telephone, phone plug
Telefonwahl dialling, telephone dialling
Telefonzentrale automatic switching center
Telekommunikationsanlage telecommunications installation
Telekommunikationsordnung telecommunications law
Telekommunikationssystem telecommunications system
Telemetrie telemetry
Teletextdienst teletext service
Teletextgerät teletext machine, teletext terminal
Teletextsystem teletext
Telex teletypewriter exchange, telex
Telexdienst telex service
Telexgerät telex machine

Telexleitung

Telexleitung teletype line
Telexnetz telex network
Temexdienst temex service
Temperatur temperature
Temperaturbedingung temperature condition
Temperaturmessung temperature measurement
Temperaturregelung temperature control
Temperaturregler temperature controller
temporär temporary
temporäre Datei scratch file, temporary file
Term term
Termin date
Terminabgrenzung due date
Terminänderung change of date
Terminal terminal
Terminalanschluß terminal interface
Terminaldatei terminal file
Terminaldrucker terminal printer
Terminaleingang terminal entry
Terminalemulation terminal emulation
Terminalinterface terminal interface
Terminaljob dead end job, terminal job
Terminalmodus terminal mode
Terminalnachricht terminal message
Terminalname terminal name
Terminalnummer terminal number
Terminalschnittstelle terminal interface
terminalspezifisch terminal specific
Terminalstatusblock terminal status block
Terminalsteuereinheit terminal access controller
Terminalsteuerplatine terminal controller board
Terminaltyp terminal type
terminieren schedule
Terminkontrolle date monitoring
Terminplan schedule
Terminposition due date entry, due date item
Terminstapeljob deadline run
Terminüberwachung date monitoring
Test check, diagnostic test, test
Testablauf test run
Testabschnitt test section
Testaktivität test activity
Testbericht test report
Testberichtsdefiniton test report definition
Testbit test bit
Testbrief test letter
Testbrieferstellung test letter production
Testbuchungskreis test accounting area
Testdatei dummy file
Test-Ein-/Ausgabe test input/output
Testen debugging

testen check, debug, test
Testen des Systems system testing
Testhilfe debug, debug monitor, debugger, debugging aid, test aid
Testhilfe generieren generate debug code
Testkit test kit
Testlauf subtest, test
Testlaufeinrichtung selftest device
Testlauftaste test button
Testmodus test mode
Testphase test phase
Testprogramm test program
Testprotokoll test log
Testpunkt test point
Testsatz test record
Testschalter test button
Testschleife loop test, test loop
Teststand test state
Testsystempartition test system partition
Testvorlage test chart
Testzweck test purpose
Tetrade tetrad
Tetrode tetrode
Texid-Steuerblock texid control block
Text label, text
Textabschnitt text paragraph
Textanfang beginning of text, start of text
Textanzeige character indication
Textart text type
Textartkennzeichen type of text identifier
Textaufbereitung text editing
Textaufkommen text quantity
Textaufzeichnung text recording
Textautomat automatic text processing machine
Textbaustein text module
Textbearbeitung text processing, word processing
Textbeginn beginning of the text
Textbeleg text voucher
Textbereich text area
Textbeschreibung text descriptor
Textbild text screen
Textblock text block
Textbrief text letter
Textdatei text file
Textdokument text document
Texteditor text editor
Text einfügen inserting text
Texteingabe text entry, text input
Textende end of text
Texterfassung text registration
Textfeld information field, text field
Textgenerierung text generation

Textgruppe text group
Texthandbuch text manual
Texthervorhebungsfunktion highlighting feature
Textkatalog text catalog
Textkennzeichen text identifier
Textkonserve text preservation
Textkonstante text constant
Textkorrespondenz text correspondence
Textleerzeile text blank line
Text löschen delete text, erasing text
Textmanipulator data processor, text processor
Textmenge text quantity
Textnetz text network
Textnummer text number
Textnummernkreis text number range
Textposition text position
Text prüfen viewing text
Textpuffer text buffer
Textsatz text record
Textschlüssel text code
Textsteuerzeichen text control character
Textsystem text system
Texttabelle text table
Textteil portion of text
Textvariable text variable
Textvariablenbezeichnung text variable designation
Textvariablenname text variable name
Textverarbeitung document processing, text processing, word processing, word processing system, word processor
Textverarbeitungsfunktion text processing function
Textverarbeitungsmarkt text processing market
Textverarbeitungsprogramm editor, text processor, word processor
Textverarbeitungssystem text processing system
Textverwalter text manager
Textverwaltung text maintenance
Textvolumen text volume
Textzeile text line
Textzeilennummer text line number
Thema issue, topic
theoretisch theoretically
Therapiedaten therapy data
Therapieeinheit therapy unit
Therapiekopf therapy head
Therapiemode therapy mode
thermionische Umwandlung thermionic conversion

thermische Steuerung thermal variable control
Thermistor thermistor
Thermodrucker thermal printer
thermoelektrisches Gerät thermoelectric device
thermoelektrische Umwandlung thermoelectric conversion
Thermokette thermopile
thermoplastischer Kunststoff thermoplastic
Thermostat thermostat
Thyristor thyristor
Tiefe depth
tiefgestelltes Zeichen subscript, subscript character
Tiefpaßfilter low pass filter
tiefstellen lowering
Tiefstellung subscript
Tieftemperaturlagerung cryogenic storage
Tilgung repayment
Tilgungsplan repayment plan
Tilgungsrechnung repayment invoice
Timeout timeout
Timesharing time share
Timesharing-Modus time sharing mode
Timesharing-Programm time sharing program
Timesharing-Service time sharing service
Timesharing-Steuerung time sharing control
Timesharing-System time sharing system
Timesharing-Zyklus time sharing cycle
Tintenstrahldrucker ink jet printer
tippen type
Tisch desk
Tischcomputer desktop computer
Tischmodell tabletop model
Tischrechner calculator, desk calculator, electronic calculator
Tischrechnermodus desktop calculator mode
Titel title
Titulierung title
Tochterfirma subsidiary
Tochtergesellschaft daughter company, subsidiary company
Tochterstation slave station
Toleranz tolerance
Toleranzgrenze tolerance limit
Toleranztag tolerance day
Ton sound
Tonbandgerät tape recorder
Tonhöhe pitch
Tonsignal bell
Tool tool
Top-Down top-down
Top-Down-Entwicklung top down development

Tortendiagramm

Tortendiagramm pie chart
Totalexport total export
Totalstop master hold
toter Sektor dead sector
Tottaste dead key
Tottastenausgleicher dead key override
Totzeit dead time, deadtime, downtime, time delay
Totzeitkompensation deadtime compensation
Tour round, route
Tourennummer route number
Trabantenstation tributary station
Tracefunktion trace function
Tracemöglichkeit trace possibility
träge slo blo
Träger carrier
Trägersignal carrier
Trägheitsnavigation inertial navigation
tragbares Terminal hand held terminal
Tragearm boom
Tragegriff carrying handle
tragen bear
Traktor tractor
Traktorvorschub tractor feed
Transaktion transaction
transaktionsabhängig transaction dependent
Transaktionsablauf transaction procedure
Transaktionsarbeitsbereich transaction work area
Transaktionsart transaction type
Transaktionsaufruf transaction call
Transaktionsauftrag transaction request
Transaktionsauswahl transaction selection
transaktionsberechtigt legitimately transacted
Transaktionsberechtigung transaction authorization
Transaktionsbeschreibung transaction descriptor
Transaktionsbetrieb transaction processing
Transaktionsbezeichnung transaction name
Transaktionscode transaction code
Transaktionsdatei transaction file
Transaktionsdokument transaction document
Transaktionsende end of transaction
Transaktionsfolge transaction sequence
Transaktionsfolgenummer transaction sequence number
Transaktionsfunktion transaction function
Transaktionsmonitor transaction monitor
Transaktionsprogramm transaction program
Transaktionsschritt transaction step
transaktionsspezifisch transaction specific
Transaktionsstatus transaction status
Transaktionssteuerung transaction control
Transaktionsstufe transaction stage
Transaktionstabelle transaction table
Transaktionstext transaction text
Transaktionsverarbeitung transaction processing
Transaktionverarbeitung transaction processing
Transfer transfer
Transfereinheit data transfer unit
Transfersyntax transfer syntax
Transferzeit transfer time
Transformator current transformer
Transformator des Netzteils power supply transformer
Transformator mit Luftkühlung dry type transformer
Transformatorstation transformer substation
transistorbestücktes Gerät solid state device
Transitsystem intermediate system
Transparenz transparency
Transparenzmodus transparency mode
Transport feed, transfer, transport
Transportbefehl feed instruction
Transportdatum transport date
Transporteinheit transport unit
Transportloch sprocket hole
Transportlochung transport perforation
Transportmedium transport medium
Transportnetz transport network, transport network
Transportquittung transport acknowledgement
Transportrahmen shipping block
Transportschicht transport layer
Transportsicherung card, cardboard, cardboard retainer
Transportsicherungskarte carriage restraint card
Transportsicherungskarton cardboard slip case
Transportstachel fin
Transportsystem transport system
Transportunternehmen delivery agent
Transportverbindung feed connection
Trapatt-Diode trapatt
Treffen meeting
treffen meet
Treffer hit
Trefferquote hit ratio
Trefferwahrscheinlichkeit hit probability
Trefferzähler hit counter
Treiber driver, handler
Treiberprozeß driver process

trendbeeinflußt influenced by tendency
Trenncode separation code
Trennen disconnection, separation
trennen disconnect, part, separate
Trennerdefinition separation character definition
Trenngenauigkeit separation accuracy
Trennkondensator isolating capacitor
Trennschalter isolator switch
Trennschiene parting bar
Trennsicherung switch fuse
Trennstrich breaking hyphen
Trenntransformator safety isolating transformer
Trennung separation
Trennzeichen delimiter, hyphen, information separator, separator
Trennzeichen f. Tausendereinheiten thousands separator
Tresorschalter safe throwover switch
Triadenmarkierung punctuation
Trigger trigger
Trimmer des Taktgenerators clock chip trimmer
Trimmkondensator trimmer capacitor
trocken dry
Trockeneinrichtung drying unit
Trockenklebeband adhesive tape, pressure sensitive adhesive, tape
Trocknungsmittel dehumidifier
Trommel drum
tropfen drop
Tür door
Türtransportfehler door opening error
tun make
Tunneldiode tunnel diode
Turbogenerator turbo generator
Turingmaschine turing machine
turnusmäßig in turn
Typ model, type
Typangabe type specification
Typennummer type number
Typenrad daisy wheel, print wheel, type wheel
Typenraddrucker daisy wheel printer
typisch characteristic, typical, typically

U

überblättern   page over
Überblick   summary
Überdeskriptor   over descriptor
überdies   moreover
übereinander drucken   overprinting
übereinstimmen   agree, correspond, match
Übereinstimmung   correspondence, match
überfällig   overdue
Überfälligkeit   days overdue
überflüssig   superfluous, unnecessary
Übergabe   handover, transfer
Übergabebereich   continuity data area
Übergabeschnittstelle   transfer interface
Übergabeseite   transfer page
Übergabeseitenbearbeitung   transfer page processing
Übergabeseitenformat   transfer page format
Übergabeseitennummer   transfer page number
Übergabeseitensatz   transfer page record
Übergabestelle   interchange point
Übergang   transition
Übergangsdatum   changeover date
Übergangsfunktion   transfer function
Übergangsstelle   connector
übergeben   pass across, submit
übergehen   bypass, skip
übergeordnet   higher level, superior
übergeordneter Stop   master hold
übergeordnetes Datenverzeichnis   parent directory
übergeordnete Station   master station
Überhang   overflow, overhead
überhaupt   at all
überholen   overtake
Überkompensation   overcompensation
überladen   overload
überlagern   overlay
Überlagerung   overlay
Überlagerungsbereich   overlay area
Überlagerungsprogramm   transient program
Überlagerungssegment   overlay segment
Überlagerungsursprung   overlay origin
Überlandleitung   rural electric power network
überlappen   overlapping
Überlappung   overlap
überlassen   leave, left
Überlastanzeiger   overload indicator
Überlastschutz   overload protection

Überlauf   excess, overflow, overrun
Überlaufdaten   excessive data
Überlauf des Eingabepuffers   input buffer overflow
überlaufen   excess, overrun
Überlauffehler   overrun error
Überlaufkopf   overflow heading record group
Überleitung   link
überlesen   read over
Überlieferung   excessive quantity, over delivery
Überlochzeichen   overpunch, overpunch sign
übermäßig   excessive
Übermittlungsabschnitt   data link
Übermittlungsabschnitt mit gleichberechtigter Steuerung   balanced data link
Übermittlungsprotokoll   link protocol
Übermittlungsvorschrift   link protocol
Übernahme   buyout, takeover
Übernahmejahr   takeover year
Übernahmeprogramm   transfer program
Übernahmezeit   time of transfer
Übernahme (von Betriebssoftware in eigenes System)   integration
übernehmen   import, include, integrate, take over
überprüfen   check, inspect, test
Überprüfen von Variablen   examining variables, testing variables
Überprüfung   check, checkout, test
Überprüfungstechnik   review technique
Überrechnung   excess billing
überschneiden   overlap
Überschneidung   overlapping
überschreiben   override, overtype, overwrite, restore over
überschreiben mit x   clear to x
Überschreibsperre   overprint lock
überschreiten   exceed
Überschrift   heading
Überschriftspalte   column heading
Überschriftszeile   headline
Überschußbeteiligung   surplus participation
übersehen   overlook
übersetzen   compile
Übersetzer   compiler
Übersetzer für höhere Programmiersprachen   high level compiler
Übersetzung   compilation
Übersetzungsablauf   translation procedure
Übersetzungsanweisung   compiler directing statement
Übersetzungsprogramm   compiling program, translator program

424

Übersetzungstabelle translation table
Übersicht overview, summary
Übersichtsanzeige overview display
Übersichtsbild summary screen
Übersichtsdatei summary file
Übersichtskarte reference card
Übersichtsseite summary page
Überspannungsschutz overvoltage protection
überspielen overplay
Überspringbefehl skip instruction
überspringen bypass, jump, override, skip
Überspulen overspool
übersteigen exceed
Überstrombegrenzer overcurrent limiter, surge limiter
Überstromschalter overcurrent circuit-breaker
Überstromschutz overcurrent protection, surge protection, surge suppressor
Überstromsensor overcurrent detector, surge detector
Übertischposition above-table position
Übertrag amount carried forward, borrow, carry
übertragen download, move, port, transfer, transmit
Übertragen von ganzen Seiten full page transmit
Übertragen von geschütztem Abschnitt guarded area transfer
Übertragen von Teilseiten partial page transmit
Übertragsbit carry bit
Übertragsregister carry register
Übertragssteuerung transfer control
Übertragsvorschub overflow ejection
Übertragung message transmission, transfer, transmission
Übertragung abbrechen abort transfer, bye, cancel transmission
Übertragungsablauf-Steuerung communication controller, communications control
Übertragungsadapterkabel communications adapter cable
Übertragungsanfang start of transmission
Übertragungsbereitschaft readiness for data transmission, ready for data
Übertragungseinrichtung data communication equipment
Übertragungs-/Empfangsmodus send receive mode
Übertragungsende end of transmission, end of transmission

Übertragungsendemodus transfer termination mode
Übertragungsendezeichen transmit termination character
Übertragungsereignis transmission occurence
Übertragungsgerät transceiver, transmission device
Übertragungsgerät transmission equipment
Übertragungsgeschwindigkeit baud rate, communication line speed, data signalling rate, data transfer rate, line speed, transfer rate, transmission speed, transmit speed
Übertragungsgeschwindigkeit des Modems modem transmit speed
Übertragungsgeschwindigkeit zum Drucker printer baud rate
Übertragungskabel transceiver cable
Übertragungskanal channel, transmission channel
Übertragungskanalzustand data link channel state
Übertragungsleitung line, transmission line
Übertragungsmodus transmit mode
Übertragungsmöglichkeit transmission possibility
Übertragungsprozedur transmitting procedure
Übertragungspuffer transmit buffer
Übertragungsrate baud rate, bit rate, line speed, transmission rate, transmission speed
Übertragungsselektor transaction control selector
Übertragungssicherungs-Verfahren communication control, data link control, protocol
Übertragungsstatus einstellen set transmit state
Übertragungssteuerung data link control, transmission control, transmission control
Übertragungssteuerungsverfahren data link control procedure, link control procedure
Übertragungs-Steuerzeichen transmission control character
Übertragungssteuerzeichenfolge control message, information message
Übertragungsstrecke communication link, data link, link
Übertragungstaste transfer key
Übertragungsvorlage document, document to be transmitted
Übertragungsweg transmission path
Übertragungswelle transmitter shaft
Übertragungszeichenfolge information message
Übertragungszeit duration, line time, transfer time, transmission time, transmit time

Übertragung von geschützten Feldern protect field transmission
Übertragung von Zeichen character transmission, transmitting characters
Übertragungsbereitschaft ready to transmit
übertreffen outperform
überwachen control, monitor, screen
Überwachung der Integrität des Systems system integrity verification
Überwachungsfunktion monitor function
Überwachungsliste control list
Überwachungsprogramm monitor program, supervisory and executive program
Überwachungssteuerung supervisory control
Überwachungszeit monitoring period, monitoring period, monitoring time
Überweisung transfer
überzählige Zeichen excess characters
Überziehungskredit overdraft
Überzugstage overdraft period
üblich normal, usually
UHF-Röhre ultra high frequency tube
UHF-Verstärker ultra high frequency amplifier
Uhr clock
Uhr-Interrupt timer interrupt
Uhr-Partition timer partition
Uhr und Kalender clock calendar
Uhrzeit current time, time of day
Uhrzeit der Sicherungsdiskette backup diskette time
Uhrzeiteindruck time stamp
Ultimo last day of the month
Ultraschall ultrasonic location
Ultraschallspeicher ultrasonic storage cell
umbelegen redefine, remap
umbenennen rename
Umbewertung revaluation
Umbewertungsbeleg revaluation voucher
Umbewertungsdifferenz revaluation discrepancy
Umbewertungskonto revaluation account
umblättern page
umbrechen format, paginate
Umbruch page makeup
Umbruchbreite paging width
umbuchen transfer
Umbuchung transfer posting
Umbuchungsbeleg transfer voucher
Umbuchungsbetrag amount transferred
Umbuchungsliste transfer list
Umbuchungssumme transfer total
umdefinieren redefine, remap
umdrehen invert

Umdrehungswartezeit rotational delay time
Umfang extent
umfangreich big, extensive
umfassen comprise, contain
umfassend extensive
umformen convert, reformat, repaginate, transform
Umformer electric convertor
Umformergruppe motor generator set
Umgebung environment
umgebungsbedingte Ausfallzeit environmental lost time, external loss time
Umgebungsbedingung ambient condition, environmental condition, environmental requirements
Umgebungstemperatur ambient temperature, environmental temperature
Umgebungstemperatur im ausgeschalteten Zustand non operating temperature
umgehen avoid, circumvent
umgekehrte polnische Notation reverse polish notation
umgekehrter Schrägstrich backslash
umgeschaltete Belegung einer Taste shifted character
umgestalten reformat
Umkehr reversal
Umkehranzeige reverse video
Umkehrbetrieb conversation operation
umkehren invert, revert
Umkehrzeichen turnaround character
umlagern relocate
Umlagerschlüssel stock relocation code
Umlagerung stock relocation
Umlagerungsbestand relocated stock
Umlaufspeicher circulating memory
Umlaut-Punkt umlaut dot
Umlautverschlüsselung encoding of mutated vowels, encoding of umlauts, umlaut encoding
Umleitung bypass
ummantelte Klemme shielded terminal
ummantelter Leiter sheathed conductor
ummanteltes Kabel sheathed cable
Umrechenmöglichkeit conversion option
umrechnen convert
Umrechnung conversion, converting
Umrechnungsfaktor conversion factor
Umrechnungskurs conversion rate
Umrichter rotary convertor
Umsatz sale, turnover
Umsatzanzeige turnover display
Umsatzart turnover type
umsatzbezogen turnover-related

Umsatzfeld turnover field
Umsatzfortschreibung turnover update
Umsatzkennzeichen turnover marker
Umsatzsegment turnover segment
Umsatzsteuer sales tax, turnover tax
Umsatzsteuervoranmeldung advance filing of turnover tax
umsatzwirksam influencing turnover
Umsatzzahl turnover figure
Umschaltebene keyboard shift level
Umschalteinheit transfer switch
umschalten switch
Umschalter commutator
Umschaltfeststeller shift lock
Umschaltfeststelltaste shift lock
Umschaltmodus shift mode
Umschalttaste shift key
umschlagen roll
Umschlagsablage envelope stacker
Umschlagsanlage envelope setting
Umschlagsdauer turnover
Umschlagsdurchlauf envelope run
Umschlagseinzug envelope entry
Umschlagszuführung envelope feeding device
umschlüsseln recode
umseitig overleaf
umsetzen convert, transform, transpose
Umsetzer converter
Umsetzer für virtuelle Adressen virtual address translator
Umsetzmodus transposition mode
Umsetzprogramm transposition program
Umsetztabelle transformation table
Umsetzung conversion, mapping
Umsetzungsregister translation register
umsortieren rearrange
Umspielroutine play back routine
umsponnener Draht textile-covered wire
umstellen change, invert
Umstellung changeover
Umstellungsdatum changeover date
Umstellungsjahr changeover year
umstülpen invert
umverdrahten connect to
Umverteilung redistribution
umwandeln compile, convert, transform
umwandeln in Ganzzahl cast into integer, integerize
Umwandlung conversion, transformation
Umwandlungsliste transformation list
Umwandlungstabelle conversion list, conversion table

Umwandlung von Buchstaben in Phoneme letter to phoneme conversion
Umweg bypass, roundabout route
Umwegsteuerung alternate routing
umwerten revalue
unabdingbar indispensable
unabhängig independent, independently, standalone
unabhängiger Betrieb standalone operation
unabhängiger Programmlauf detached program operation
unabhängiger Prozeß detached process
unabhängiger Wartezustand asynchronous disconnected mode
unabhängiges Programm standalone program
unaufgefordert unsolicited
unbar cashless
unbeabsichtigt unintentional
unbearbeitet raw, unprocessed
unbedeutend insignificant, meaningless
unbedingt absolute, unconditional
unbedingter Sprung unconditional jump
unbedingtes Ende unconditional end
unbedingte Übertragung unconditional transfer
unbelegt free, unoccupied
unbenutzt unused
unberechtigt illegal, unauthorized
unbestimmt indefinite
unbewertet unvalued
undefinierbar indefinable
undefiniert undefined
UND-Gatter AND gate
UND-Schaltung AND circuit, coincidence circuit
und umgekehrt vice versa
unendlich infinitely
unerfüllbar unfulfillable
unerheblich insignificant
unerlaubt illegal
unerledigt incomplete
unerregt deenergized
unerwartet unexpected
unformatiert unformatted
ungeeignet unfit
ungefähr approximately
ungeklärt undefined
ungeneriert ungenerated
ungenügend insufficient
ungeplant unplanned
ungeprüft unchecked
ungerade odd
ungerade Parität odd parity, parity odd
ungeschützt exposed

ungeschütztes Feld unlocked cell
ungesicherte Systemverbindung physical connection
ungleich not equal, unequal
ungleiches Vergleichsergebnis comparison disagreement
ungültig bad, illegal, invalid
ungültig definiertes Symbol improperly defined symbol
ungültige Adresse illegal address, invalid address
ungültige Daten bad data, illegal data, invalid data
ungültiger Block illegal frame, invalid frame
ungültiger Blockaufbau illegal frame structure, invalid frame
ungültiger Dateiname illegal file name
ungültiger Empfang invalid reception
ungültiger Verbindungsaufbau illegal call, invalid call
ungültiger Wert illegal value
ungültiges Argument illegal argument, invalid argument
ungültiges Trennzeichen illegal separator, invalid separator
ungültiges Zeichen illegal character, invalid character
Unipolar-Tastung unipolar modulation
Universalität flexibility
Universalmotor universal motor
Universalprogrammiergerät general purpose programmer, universal programmer
Universalrechner general purpose processor
universelle Ein-/Ausgabe universal input/output
universelle Peripheriesteuereinheit universal peripheral controller
universelle Programmiereinheit universal programmer unit
universeller asynchroner Schnittstellenbaustein universal asynchronous receiver/transmitter
universeller Programmierer universal programmer
universeller synchroner/asynchroner Schnittstellenbaustein universal synchronous/asynchronous receiver/transmitter
universeller Zeichensatz general purpose character set, universal character set
universelle Schnittstelle versatile interface adapter
unlesbar garbled, unreadable
unlogisch illogical
unmittelbar immediate

unmittelbare Adressierung immediate addressing
unnötig unnecessary
Unnumbered Acknowledge unnumbered acknowledge
unpaarige spitze Klammern unmatched angle brackets
unplausibel implausible
unrealistisch unrealistic
unschädlich harmless
unscharf diffuse
unsichtbar invisible
unsichtbares Trennzeichen invisible hyphen
unsinniges Computerergebnis garbage
Unsinn rein Unsinn raus garbage in garbage out
untengenannt mentioned below
Unterabschnitt subsection
Unterausschuß subcommittee
Unterbeleg subvoucher
Unterbelegkopf subvoucher header
unterbrechen break, interrupt, stop
Unterbrechen von Programmen stopping programs
Unterbrecher circuit breaker, interrupter
Unterbrechung break, exception, interrupt, interrupt
Unterbrechung durch periphere Einheit external interrupt
Unterbrechungsadreßregister interrupt address register
Unterbrechungsanforderung interrupt request
Unterbrechungsantwort bus interrupt acknowledge signal, interrupt acknowledgement
Unterbrechungsbehandlungsroutine des Benutzers user interrupt code subroutine, user interrupt service routine
Unterbrechungsbestätigung interrupt acknowledge, interrupt confirmation
Unterbrechungscode break scan code
unterbrechungsfreie Stromversorgung uninterruptable computer power, uninterruptable power supply, uninterruptable power system
unterbrechungsgesteuert interrupt driven
Unterbrechungskriterium interrupt criterion
Unterbrechungsmaske exception mask, interrupt mask
Unterbrechungsprotokoll interrupt protocol
Unterbrechungspunkt breakpoint, breakpoint register
Unterbrechungsregister interrupt register

Unterbrechungsroutine interrupt service routine
Unterbrechungssignal break signal
Unterbrechungssperre interrupt lockout
Unterbrechungsstatus exception state, interrupt state
Unterbrechungsstelle breakpoint, point of interruption
Unterbrechungszeichen break character
unterbrochen interrupted
Unterdeckung shortfall, understocking
Unterdeckungsmenge shortfall quantity, understocking quantity
Unterdeckungssatz shortfall record
unterdrücken suppress
Unterdrückung suppression
untere Buchstabentastenreihe lower letter row
unterer Adreßbereich des Speichers low order storage, lower address range
unterer Adressenhinweis bottom address pointer
unterer Rand bottom margin
Unterfunktionsanwahl subfunction selection
untergliedern subdivided
Untergrenze lower bound, lower limit, lower margin, lower threshold
unterirdisches Kabel underground cable
unterirdische Starkstromleitung underground power line
unterirdische Stromverteilung underground cable
Unterkennung subaccount
Unterkommando subcommand
Unterkonto subaccount
unter Kontrolle under control
Unterlage document
Unterlager subwarehouse
Unterlauf underflow
Unterlegscheibe flat washer
unterlegtes Symbol shaded symbol
Unterlieferung under delivery
Untermenge subquantity
Untermenü submenu
Unternehmen enterprise
unternehmen carry out
Unternehmensgruppe entrepreneurial group
Unternehmer entrepreneur
Unternehmung enterprise
Unternummer subnumber
Unter-/Ober- upper/lower
unterordnen subordinate
Unterprogramm subprogram, subroutine
Unterprogrammaufruf subroutine call

Unterprogrammfunktion subroutine function
Unterprogrammrücksprung subroutine branch
Unterprogrammsteuerung subroutine control
Unterprogrammstufe subroutine level
Unterprogrammverzweigung branch and link
Unterprozeß subprocess
unterscheiden differ, distinguish
Unterscheidung distinction
Unterscheidungsmerkmal distinguisher
Unterschicht sublayer
Unterschied delta
unterschiedlich differently, unequal
unterschreiten fall short
Unterschreitung falling short
Unterseekabel submarine cable
Untersee-Starkstromkabel submarine power line
Untersegmentnummer subsegment number
unter Spannung stehendes Teil live part
unterstellen assume, imply
unterste Zeile bottom line
unterstreichen underline
Unterstreichung underline
Unterstreichungszeichen underscore
Unterstruktur substructure
unterstützen support
Unterstufe lower level
untersuchen examine, inspect
Untersuchung examination, inspection
Untersystem slave system, subsystem
Untersystem für die Datenübertragung communications subsystem
unterteilen block, divide
Unterteilung segmentation
Unterthema subtopic
Untertischposition below-table position
Unterverzeichnis subdirectory
Unterwassernavigation underwater navigation
Unterweisungsmodus guide mode
unübersehbar indeterminable
unumgänglich inevitable
ununterbrochen uninterrupted
unverändert unchanged
unverbucht unposted
unverdichtet uncompressed
unverträglich incompatible
Unverträglichkeit incompatibility
unverwechselbar non interchangeable
unverzüglich immediate
unvollständig incomplete
unvorbereiteter Datenträger unformatted media, virgin media
unwirksam ineffective

429

unzulässig inadmissible, invalid, unallowed
unzulässige Adresse illegal address, invalid address
unzulässige Operation illegal operation, invalid operation, operation exception
unzulässiger Dateiname illegal file name
unzulässiger Wert illegal value
unzusammenhängend fragmented
unzusammenhängende Sektoren fragmented sectors
unzustellbar undeliverable
Update update
Update-Lauf update run
Update-Programm update program
Update-Prozedur update procedure
Urabschnitt root phase
Urbeleg source document, source voucher
urladbarer Datenträger bootable medium
Urladeblock boot block
Urladekommandoprozedur bootstrap command procedure
Urlademenü boot menu
urladen boot, bootstrap, bootstrap loading
Urlader bootstrap, bootstrap loader, initial program loader
Urladerbereich bootstrap area
Ursache cause, reason
ursprünglich original
Ursprung origin
Ursprungsbeleg original voucher
Ursprungswert original value
Urwert original value
UV-Licht UV light
UV-löschbares PROM ultraviolet erasable PROM

V

Vakuumkondensator vacuum capacitor
Vakuumröhre vacuum tube
Vakuum-Stromkreisunterbrecher vacuum circuit breaker
Valuta validity
Valutadatum currency date
Valutatage value days
Varec-Norm varec gauge
variabel variable
Variable variable
Variablenanzahl amount of variables
Variablenart type of variable
Variablenbezeichnung designation of variables
Variableneingabe entry of variables
Variablenermittlung determination of variables
variable Netzwerkstruktur distributed network architecture
Variablenfeld field of variables, variable data field
Variablenfeld mit Ein- und Ausgaberichtung bidirectional field
Variablenidentifikation identification of variables
Variableninhalt variable content
Variablenkennzeichen variable identification
Variablenlänge length of variables
Variablenname variable name
Variablenselektion selection of variables
Variablenspeicher variable memory
Variablensteuerung control of variables
Variablentabelle table of variables
Variablenwert value of variable
Variablenzeichen variable label
Variablenzuordnung variable assignment
variabler Kondensator variable capacitor
variable Satzlänge variable block format
variables Blockformat variable block format
Variante variant, version
Variantenliste list of variants
Variation option
variieren vary
Vater father
Vaterversion father version
Vektor vector
Vektoradresse vector address
Vektordatenpuffer vector data buffer
Vektorgenerator vector generator
Vektorlänge vector length
Vektorprozessor vector processor
Vektorschalter vector switch
Ventilkühlanlage valve cooling unit
Verabredungsdaten arranged data
Verabredungstext appointment text
veränderlicher Widerstand variable resistor
verändern change, edit, manipulate, modify
Verändern von Sätzen in Datei updating file records
Veränderung change, manipulation, modification
Veränderungscode modification code
Veränderungsschlüssel modification code
Veränderungsstatus modification status
veranlassen cause, instigate
Veranlassung instigation, reason
veranschaulichen illustrate
Veranstaltung proceedings
verantwortlich responsible
Verantwortung responsibility
verarbeiten manipulate, process
Verarbeitung process
Verarbeitungsablauf processing run
Verarbeitungsabschnitt run unit
Verarbeitungsart computer operation, type of processing
Verarbeitungsbereich process area
Verarbeitungscomputer processing computer
Verarbeitungsdatei processing file
Verarbeitungsfehler processing error
Verarbeitungsform mode of processing, processing form
Verarbeitungsgang processing run
Verarbeitungsgeschwindigkeit speed of operation
Verarbeitungskennzeichen processing marker
Verarbeitungsleistung processing output
Verarbeitungsmodul processing module
Verarbeitungsmodus mode of processing, process mode
Verarbeitungspfad processing path
Verarbeitungsprozedur processing procedure
Verarbeitungsprozessor central processor
Verarbeitungsschicht application layer
Verarbeitungsschritt processing step
Verarbeitungsstruktur processing structure
Verarbeitungsstufe processing level
Verarbeitungsweise manner of processing
Verarbeitungszeiger processing indicator
Verb verb
verbal verbal
Verbalphrase verb phrase
verbergen conceal

431

verbessern enhance, improve
Verbesserung correction, enhancement, improvement
verbieten forbid
verbinden connect, join
verbindlich obligatory
Verbindlichkeit liability
Verbindlichkeiten accounts payable
Verbindlichkeiten aus Lieferungen und Leistungen accounts payable
Verbindung connection, interface, joint, pin
Verbindungsabbau call clearing, connection clearing, linkage removal
Verbindungsanlage connected arrangement
Verbindungsaufbau call set up, connection establishment, linkage set-up
Verbindungsdauer call duration
Verbindungsdraht jumper
Verbindungskabel connecting cable
Verbindungskennung connection identifier
Verbindungsleitung junction line
verbindungslos connectionless
Verbindungsmodul linking module
Verbindungsnetz connection network, network
verbindungsorientiert connection oriented
Verbindungssteuerungsverfahren call control procedure
Verbindungsversuch call attempt
Verbindung trennen disconnect
Verbindung zum Hostrechner host line
Verblassen der Anzeige aging, fade out
verbleiben remain
Verbrauch consumption
Verbraucherstation consumer substation
Verbrauchsart mode of consumption
Verbrauchsbuchung consumption posting
Verbrauchsdaten consumption data
Verbrauchsentwicklung development of consumption
Verbrauchsfeld consumption field
Verbrauchskennzeichen consumption marker
Verbrauchskonto consumption account
Verbrauchsliste consumption list
Verbrauchsmaterial consumables
Verbrauchsmenge quantity consumed
verbrauchsorientiert consumer oriented
Verbrauchssteuer excise tax
Verbrauchswert value consumed
verbraucht consumed
verbuchen nach post
Verbuchungsanforderung request for posting
Verbuchungsbeginn start of posting
Verbuchungsbereich posting area

Verbuchungsmeldung posting message
Verbuchungsmodul posting module
Verbuchungsprogramm posting program
Verbuchungsseite posting page
Verbuchungssteuerung posting control
Verbuchungstransaktion posting transaction
Verbuchungsvorgang posting process
Verbuchungszähler posting counter
Verbund compound, hybrid
Verbunden-Signal call-connected signal
Verbundkennzeichen integration marker
Verbundoperation gang operation
Verbundrechner cluster computer, satellite computer
Verbundschaltung coupled circuit
Verbundsoftware integrated software
Verbundtest integrated test
Verdacht suspect, suspicion
verdeutlichen clarify, point out
verdichten compress, consolidate, pack
Verdichtung/Entzerrung compression/expansion
Verdichtungsgruppe compression group
Verdichtungsschlüssel compression code
verdienen earn
Verdrahtung electric cable system, electric wiring system, electrical wiring
Verdrahtung des Grenzschalters limit switch wiring
Verdrahtung vor Ort field wiring
verdrillte Doppelleitung twisted pair cable, twisted wire pair
verdunkeln darken
vereinbar compatible
vereinbaren agree upon
vereinbart agreed
Vereinbarung agreement, declaration
vereinfachen simplify
Vereinfachung simplification
Vereinfachungsregel simplification rule
vereinigen reassembling, unite
Vereinigung union
Vereinigung der amerikanischen Elektroindustrie Electrical Industries of America
vereinnahmt taken in
Vereinzeler single feeder
Vereinzelungsauftrag single feed job
Vereinzelungsband single feed tape
Vereinzelungsbefehl single feed instruction
Vereinzelungsfunktion single feed function
Vereinzelungsmotor single feed motor
Vereinzelungsvorgang single feed process
Verfahrbereich travel range

Verfahren method, principle, procedure, process
verfahren move, process, travel
Verfahrensauswahl procedure selection
Verfahrenserläuterung procedure documentation
Verfahren zur Steuerung der Datenübertragung data transmission
Verfall expiration, expiry
Verfallsdatum date of expiry, expiration date
verfallen expire
verfassen draft
Verfasser author
Verfeinerung refinement
verfilmen film
verfolgen monitor, trace
verfügbar available, disposable
Verfügbarkeit availability, uptime
Verfügbarkeitsanzeige availability display
Verfügbarkeitsdatum availability date
Verfügbarkeitskontrolle availability check
Verfügbarkeitsrechnung availability calculation
Verfügbarkeitsspeicher availability store
Verfügbarkeitsübersicht availability summary
Verfügbarkeitszeit availability time
verfügen possess
verfügen über feature, include
vergangen gone, passed, past
vergangene Zeit elapsed time
Vergangenheit past
Vergangenheitsfeld past field
vergebbar allocatable
vergeben allocate
vergehen elapse, pass
vergessen forget
Vergleich relation condition
vergleichen compare, match
Vergleicher comparator
Vergleichsbefehl compare instruction
Vergleichscode matchcode
Vergleichsdatensatzdatei matching record file
Vergleichsdezimalfeld relational decimal array
Vergleichsergebnis result of comparison
Vergleichsfeld matching field
Vergleichsfunktion compare function
Vergleichsfunktion auf Satzbasis matching record function
vergleichsgesteuerte Verarbeitung matching
Vergleichsgröße comparison value
Vergleichsjahr comparison year
Vergleichskriterium comparison criterion
Vergleichsmonat comparison month

Vergleichsoperator comparison operator, relation operator
Vergleichsoperator gleich comparison equal
Vergleichsoperator größer als comparison greater than
Vergleichsoperator größer oder gleich comparison greater than or equal
Vergleichsoperator kleiner als comparison less than
Vergleichsoperator kleiner oder gleich comparison less than or equal
Vergleichsoperator ungleich comparison not equal
Vergleichspaare matching pairs
Vergleichsperiode comparison period
Vergleichssaldo comparison balance
Vergleichssatz matching record
Vergleichssatztechnik matching record technique
Vergleichstyp comparison type
Vergleichswert comparand, comparison value
Vergleichswerte comparison figures
Vergleichszeitraum comparison period
Vergleich: Compiler-Assembler compiler-assembler
vergrößern expand, extend, increase
Vergrößerung enlargement
vergüten reimburse
Vergütung reimbursement
Verhältnis ratio, relation
Verhältnisregelung ratio control
Verhalten behavior
verhindern avoid, prevent
Verhinderung prevention
Verifikation verification
verifizieren check, make sure, verify
Verkabelung electric cable system
Verkäufer seller
Verkauf sale
verkaufen sell
Verkaufsabrechnung sales accounting
Verkaufsabteilung sales department
Verkaufsartikel sales product
Verkaufsbeleg sales voucher
Verkaufsbezirk sales area
Verkaufsdaten sales data
Verkaufsfeld sales field
Verkaufsgespräch sales talk
Verkaufsgruppe sales group
Verkaufsgruppensatz sales group record
Verkaufsgruppenschlüssel sales group code
Verkaufsinfo sales info
Verkaufsinformationen sales information

Verkaufsinformationssatz sales information record
Verkaufsmenge quantity sold
Verkaufsmengeneinheit sales unit
Verkaufsort point of sale
Verkaufspreis retail price, selling price
Verkaufspreiseinheit selling price unit
Verkaufspreisliste sales price list
Verkaufsprodukt sales product
verkaufsspezifisch sales specific
Verkaufstabelle sales table
Verkaufstext sales text
Verkaufstransaktion sales transaction
Verkaufsverhandlung sales negotiation
Verkaufsvermerk sales remark
Verkaufswert sales value
Verkehr traffic
verkehren communicate
Verkehrsabteilung transport department
Verkehrsbelastung volume of traffic
Verkehrssignal traffic signal
Verkehrszahl transaction figure
Verkehrszahlenfeld transaction count field
verketten chaining, concatenate
verkettete Daten chain data
Verkettung chaining, concatenation, daisy chain
Verkettungs-Adresse chaining address
Verkettungsadreßwort chain pointer word
Verkettungsfehler chaining error
Verkettungsoperator concatenation operator
Verklagter respondent
verknüpfbar linkable
verknüpfen connect, gate, link
verknüpfte Bedingung compound condition
Verknüpfung connection, link
Verknüpfungsassembler map assembler
Verknüpfungsausgabeliste linker map
Verknüpfungsglied logic element, logical element
Verknüpfungsprogramm builder segment, linkage editor, linker, memory allocation processor
Verknüpfungsprotokoll link edit map
Verknüpfungspunkt mode point
Verknüpfungsregister linkage register
verkürzt verbose
Verladeliste bill of lading
verlängern extend, prolong
Verlängerungskabel extension cable
Verlag publisher, publishing company
Verlangsamung deceleration
verlassen leave

Verlauf behavior, run
verleast leased out
verleihen lend
verletzen damage
Verletzung violation
verloren lost
Verlust dissipation, loss
Verlustkonto loss account
Verlustrechnung loss accounting
Verlustzeit lost time
vermeiden avoid
Vermerk memorandum, remark
vermieten let
vermindern decrease, reduce
vermindertes Leistungspotential degraded mode
Verminderung decrease, decrement
Vermittlung exchange, switchboard, switching unit
Vermittlungseinrichtung switching equipment
Vermittlungsknoten exchange, switching center, switching exchange, switching node
Vermittlungsrechner switching computer
Vermittlungsschicht network layer
Vermittlungssimulation simulation of the public switching center
Vermittlungsstelle switching center
Vermittlungssteuerung switching control
Vermögensermittlung net asset calculation
vermögenssteuerpflichtig liable for wealth tax
Vermögenssteuerwertermittlung assessment of wealth tax
Vermögenswert net assets
vermuten estimate, presume, suppose
vermutlich presumably
verneinen negate
vernetzte Datenverarbeitung distributed data processing
vernünftig sensible, sound
Verordnung decree
verpachten lease
verpacken pack, package
Verpackungsanleitung packing procedure
Verpackungskonditionen packing terms
Verpackungslieferbedingungen packing delivery terms
Verpackungsmaterial packing material
Verpackungsmittel packaging
Verpackungsvereinbarung packing agreement
Verpackungsmaterialnummer packing materials number
verpflichten oblige
Verpflichtung obligation

verrechnen bill, settle
Verrechnung offsetting, settlement
Verrechnungskennzeichen settlement marker
Verrechnungskonto clearing account
Verrechnungspositionen clearing items
Verrechnungspreis sliding average price
Verrechnungsverfahren settlement
Verrechnungswert adjusted amount
verrichten perform
Verriegelung interlock
Verriegelungsroutine interlock routine
Verringerung decrease
verrollen scroll
Versand dispatch, shipment
Versandabteilung dispatch department
Versandadresse address for dispatch
Versandanstoß dispatch release
Versandart dispatch type
Versanddaten dispatch data
Versanddatum dispatch date
Versandfälligkeit dispatch due
Versandhinweis dispatch advice, dispatch information
Versandindex dispatch register
Versandkarton shipping box
Versandkennzeichen shipment label
Versandmenge quantity dispatched
Versandpapiere dispatch documents
Versandpunktüberwachung dispatch control
Versandvorlaufzeit dispatch lead time
Versandvorschrift forwarding instruction
Versandzeitraum dispatch period
Versatz displacement, interleave, offset
Versatzfaktor lace factor
verschachteln nest
verschachteltes Programm nested program
Verschachtelung interlacing, nesting
Verschachtelungsebene nesting level
Verschachtelungszuordnung interlaced storage assignment
verschiebbar relocatable
Verschiebebefehl move statement
Verschiebedatensätze relocatable data
Verschieben relocation, scrolling
verschieben advance, move, scroll, shift
Verschieben nach links left shift, shift left
Verschieben nach rechts right shift, shift right
Verschieben von Text moving text
Verschiebeprogramm roll over program
verschlüsseln code, encode
verschlüsseln/entschlüsseln encode/decode
Verschlüsselung coding, encoding

Verschlüsselungsalgorithmus mit öffentlichem Schlüssel public key algorithm
Verschlüsselungsmuster data encryption standard
Verschlüssler encoder
verschränkt organisierter Satz interleaved set
verschrotten scrap
verschütten spill
verschwinden disappear
versehen provide
verseilter Leiter stranded conductor
versenden dispatch, send, ship
versetzen interleave, move, offset
versichern insure
Versicherung insurance
Versicherungsabschluß conclusion of an insurance
Versicherungsbasiswert insurance base value
Versicherungsbeitrag insurance premium
Versicherungsgesellschaft insurance company
Versicherungsindex insurance index
Versicherungskonditionen insurance terms
Versicherungswert insured value
Versicherungswertermittlung calculation of insurance value
Version level, release, version
Versionsbegrenzung version limit
Versionshinweise release notes
Versionsnummer version number
versorgen supply
Versorgung supply
Verständigungsbereich communications region
Verständigungsgebiet communications area
Verständigungsprozedur handshake procedure
verstärken amplify, boost
Verstärker amplifier, booster, driver
verstärkter Druck emphasized print
Verstärkungsregelung gain control
versteckte Systemdatei hidden system file
Verstellhebel adjusting lever
verstoßen contravene
verstreichen elapse, expire
verstrichene Zeit elapsed time
verstümmelt garbled
Verstümmelung corruption
Versuch attempt
versuchen attempt, try
Versuchsteil probe, specimen, trial part
verteilen distribute
Verteiler distributor
Verteilerkanal distribution channel
Verteilerkasten distribution box
Verteilerkreis distribution circuit

Verteilerliste distribution list
Verteilerplatte distribution panel
Verteilerplatteneinheit distribution panel assembly
Verteilerroutine dispatcher
Verteilerschaltung switching circuit
Verteilerstelle distributing center
Verteilertransformator distribution transformer
Verteilerverzeichnis switch directory
Verteilstation switching substation
verteilt distributed
verteilte Datenverarbeitung distributed data processing
verteiltes Endsystemrelais distributed end system gateway
verteilte Station remote station
Verteilung distribution
Verteilungsbasis distribution basis
Verteilungsintervall pickup interval
Verteilungsprozeß distribution process
Verteilungssummen distribution totals
Verteilung von Rechenzeit control processor dispatching, dispatching
Vertiefung indentation
vertikal vertical
vertikaler Titel vertical title
vertikale Steuerung vertical drive
Vertikalpositionierung vertical positioning
Vertikaltabulator vertical tab
Vertikaltabuliertaste vertical tabulator key
vertippen mistype
verträglich compatible
Verträglichkeit compatibility
Vertrag agreement, contract
Vertragsende end of contract
Vertragsstrafe contractual penalty
Vertragswert contract value
Vertreiber von schlüsselfertigen Systemen turnkey system vendor
vertreten represent
Vertreter representative, sales representative, salesperson
Vertreterbesuch representative's visit
Vertreternummer representative number
Vertrieb marketing
Vertriebsabteilung marketing department
Vertriebsbeauftragter representative, sales representative, salesperson
Vertriebsdaten marketing data
Vertriebssystem marketing system
Vertriebsunterstützung sales support
verunreinigen contaminate, pollute
Verunreinigung contamination, pollution

verursachen cause, initiate
vervielfältigen duplicate
vervollständigen complete
verwalten administer, manage
Verwalter administrator, manager
Verwaltung administration, housekeeping, management
Verwaltung der Systemeinrichtungen facilities management
Verwaltungsaufwand administration effort
Verwaltungsbereich management area
Verwaltungsdatei management file
Verwaltungskennzeichen management identifier
Verwaltungsmodul management module
Verwaltungsmöglichkeit management option
Verwaltungsprogramm management program
Verwaltungssatz management record
Verwaltungsspur housekeeping track
Verwaltungssystem management system
verwechseln mess up, mistake, mix up
verweigern refuse
Verweildauer period spent
verweilen remain
Verweilzeit dwell time, time spent
Verweilzeitprüfung dwell time check
Verweis reference
Verweise references
verweisen refer
Verweisfeld function item
Verweisstruktur chaining structure
verwendbar usable
verwenden use
Verwendungsart type of use
verwendungsfähig usable
Verwendungskennzeichen bill of materials marker
Verwendungsnachweis evidence of use
Verwendungszweck purpose
verwertbar realisable, useable
verzahnen interleave, interlink
verzeichnen catalog, register
verzeichnete Datei cataloged file
Verzeichnis catalog, directory, index, register, table of contents
Verzeichnisanzeige catalog indicator, index display
Verzeichnisauswahl catalog selection, directory choice, directory selection, index selection
Verzeichnisbearbeitungsprogramm catalog manipulation program
Verzeichnisbearbeitungsroutine catalog manipulation routine

Verzeichnis der Dateinamen filename directory, files catalog
Verzeichniseintrag catalog entry, directory entry
Verzeichnisfunktion catalog facility
Verzeichnisinhalt catalog content, directory content
Verzeichnispfad directory path
verzeichniswirksam catalog effective
Verzerrung distortion
Verzerrungsgrad distortion degree
verzichten omit, renounce
Verzinsung interest accrual
Verzinsungsart interest type
verzögern delay
verzögert deferred, delayed, lagged
verzögertes Kommando deferred command
Verzögerung delay, lag, time delay
Verzögerungsleitung delay line
Verzögerungsrelais time delay relay
Verzögerungsschaltung delay circuit
Verzögerungszeitglied on delay timer
Verzollungskondition customs term
Verzug delay
Verzugstage delay days
Verzugszinsen default interest
verzweigen branch
Verzweigung branch, branching, decision
Verzweigungssymbol branch symbol
Verzweigungsvorhersage branch prediction
Verzweigungsziel branch destination
V-Format V format
Vibrationsregelung vibration control
Video video
Videoausgang video output, video output connector
Videocontroller video display controller
Videogenerator video display generator
Videokommunikationsanlage video communications system
Videokommunikationssystem video communications system
Videosichtgerät video display unit
Videosignalkabel video signal cable
Videoverbundsignal composite video
vielfach multiple
Vielfach-Einfügeoperation multiple insertion operation
Vielfachleitung bus
vielfältige Konfigurations- und Verarbeitungsmöglichkeiten multi environment processing
Vielfalt variety
vielseitig feature rich

Vielzahl multiplicity
Vieradressenbefehl four address instruction
Vierdraht 4-wire, four wire
Vierfachkarte quad height module
Vierkanalbinärcode four line binary code
Vierpol black box
vierstellig four character, four digit
Viertel quarter
Viertelwortverarbeitung quarter word mode
vierte Normalform fourth normal form
Vierundzwanzig-Stundenmodus twenty-four hour clock
vier Zeichen lang four digit
violett magenta
virtuell virtual
virtuelle Adresse virtual address
virtuelle Daten virtual data
virtuelle Matrix virtual array
virtuelle Platte memory drive, silicon disk
virtueller Overlay virtual overlay
virtueller Prozessor virtual processor
virtueller Rechner virtual computer
virtueller Speicher virtual memory
virtuelles Diskettenlaufwerk virtual disk
virtuelle Seitennummer virtual page number
virtuelles Laufwerk memory drive, silicon disk
virtuelle Speicherung virtual storage
virtuelle Verbindung virtual call, virtual connection
virtuelle Wählverbindung virtual call
visuell visual
Vocoder vocoder
voll complete, full
Vollabgang total loss
voll abgeschrieben totally depreciated
Vollabschreibung total depreciation
Volladdierer full adder
Vollauslieferung full delivery
Volldraht solid wire
Vollduplex both way communication, full duplex
Vollduplexkommunikation full duplex communication
Volleiter solid conductor
Vollieferung full delivery
Vollieferungsauftrag full delivery order
vollintegriert fully integrated
vollständig complete, entire
vollständige Dateikennung qualifier filename
vollständige Operation complete operation
vollständiger Lese-/Schreibzyklus complete read/write cycle

Vollständigkeitsfeld completeness field
Vollständigkeitsprüfung check for completeness
Vollstorno total cancellation
vollziehen carry out
Vollzugsmeldung completion notice
Volt volt
Voltampere volt ampere
Volt Wechselspannung volt alternating current
Volumen volume
Volumengebühr volume charge
vom Benutzer definierbarer Kommentar user definable comment
vom Benutzer festgelegt user defined, user specified
vom Benutzer installiert customer set up, user installed, user set up
vom Benutzer programmiert user programmed
vom Hersteller eingestellt extract factory setting, factory preset, factory setting
vom Programm gesteuert program controlled, software controlled, under program control
von Hand manual
von links nach rechts left to right
Vor- front end
Vorablieferschein temporary delivery note
vorangegangen previous
vorangestellt preceding
Voranmeldung advance notification
voransetzen place before, put in front
vorarbeiten preprocess
voraus advance
Vorausanordnung preorder
Vorausschau forecast
Voraussetzung condition, prerequisite
voraussichtlich presumed
voraussichtliche Ankunft estimated time of arrival
vorauswählen preselect
vorbelegen preallocate
Vorbelegung preemption
vorbereiten prepare
Vorbereitung preparation
Vorbereitungsarbeit preprocessing work
Vorbereitungsliste preparation list
Vorbereitungsphase initialization mode
vorbesetzen preoccupy
vorbeugende Wartung preventive maintenance
vorbringen suggest
vordatieren predate
Vordatierungstabelle predating table
vordefinieren predefine

vor dem Dezimalpunkt in front of the decimal point
Vordergrundanzeige foreground display
Vordergrundbit foreground bit
Vordergrund/Hintergrund foreground/background
Vordergrund-/Hintergrundbetrieb foreground/background operation
Vordergrund-/Hintergrundmonitor FB monitor
Vordergrundprogramm foreground program
Vordergrund-Stapelverarbeitung batch job foreground
voreingestellter Zählerstand preset count value
voreingestelltes Laufwerk default drive
voreinstellen preset
Voreinstellung default setting
Voreinstellungstaste default key
Voreinstellung vom Hersteller factory preset, factory setting
vorfertigen preproduce
Vorformatieren prepping (disk)
vorformatieren disk prep, hard format, low level format, preformat
Vorführung demo
Vorgaben für das Setzen der Bezugszahlen indicator initialization
Vorgabewert default value, preset value
Vorgabezeichen preset symbol
Vorgänger predecessor
Vorgängerband preceding tape
Vorgang act, procedure
vorgangsabhängig process dependent
Vorgangsart procedure type
Vorgangsautomatisierung transaction automation
Vorgangsbearbeitung transaction processing
Vorgangsbeginn start of process
vorgangsbezogen process-related
Vorgangsdaten process data
Vorgangsebene process level
Vorgangsende end of process
vorgangsorientiert process-oriented
Vorgangsschluß procedure code
vorgangsspezifisch process-specific
Vorgangsverarbeitung process proceeding
Vorgangszeile transaction process line
Vorgang wiederholen try another
vorgeben default, give, preset
vorgegebenes Laufwerk default drive
vorgehen proceed
Vorgehensweise methodology
vorgemerkt earmarked, preselected, reserved

Vorgeschäftsjahr previous financial year
vorgesehen provided for
vorgesehener Platz allocated space
Vorgriffsfeld look ahead field
Vorgriffssatz look ahead record
vorhaben intend
Vorhaltekarte control card
vorhanden available, existing, present
vorhandener Ordner active folder
vorhandenes Segment available segment
Vorhandensein presence
vorhanden sein exist
vorher beforehand
vorherbestimmen predefine
vorhergehen preceeding
vorhergehend previously
vorhergehende Abbildung before image
vorherig previous
Vorhersageschlüssel forecast code
vorig former
Vorjahr previous year
Vorjahresbewegung previous year's transaction
vorjahresindiziert previous year indexed
Vorkaufsrecht purchase option
Vorkommastelle integer digit
vorkommen occur
Vorladeprogramm preboot program
Vorlage submission
Vorlagedatum submission date
Vorlagezeit submission period
Vorlauf lead, leader
Vorlaufband leader tape, tape leader
Vorlaufdatei leader file
Vorlaufinformation header information
Vorlaufkarte control card, header card
Vorlaufkartenaufbau control card format, header card format
Vorlaufkartenbeispiel example of control cards, example of header cards
Vorlaufkartenbeschreibung control card description, header card description
Vorlaufkartendatei header card file
vorlaufkartengesteuert card controlled
Vorlaufkartenkennung control card identification, header card identification
Vorlaufkartenprüfung control card check, header card check
Vorlaufsatz leader record
Vorlaufzeit lead time
vorlegen submit
vorletzter last but one
vorliegen be present
Vormerkbestand reserved stock

Vormerkdatum reservation date
vormerken reserve
Vormerkfeld reservation field
Vormerkkette reservation chain
Vormerkmenge reservation quantity
Vormerktermin appointed date
Vormerkung reservation
Vormonat previous month
Vormonatsfeld previous month field
Vor-/Nacheilung lead lag
vornehmen carry out
Vornull leading zero
Vornullenunterdrückung preceding zero suppression
vor Ort austauschbare Einheit field replaceable unit
Vorperiode previous period
Vorrang precedence
Vorrangdaten expedited data
Vorrangreihenfolge precedence sequence
Vorrat repertoire, stock
Vorratsanlegung stockpiling
Vorrat schaffen stockpiling
Vorratsschaffung stockpiling
Vorrechner front end computer, front end processor
Vorrechner- und Steuerfunktionen front end capabilities
Vorrichtung appliance, device
Vorsatz header record, prefix
Vorschaltdrossel series reactor
vorschalten insert
Vorschaltrechner front end processor
Vorschau preview
Vorschlag suggestion
vorschlagen suggest
Vorschlagsliste proposal
Vorschlagsprogramm proposal program
Vorschlagswert proposed value, suggested value
vorschreiben specify, stipulat
Vorschrift regulation
Vorschub drill advance, eject, feed
Vorschubaggregat feed unit
Vorschubeinrichtung feed feature
Vorschubsteuerlochstreifen vertical format unit tape
Vorschubsteuermechanismus vertical format unit
Vorschubsteuerung carriage control, line feed control
Vorschubsteuerungspuffer vertical format buffer

439

Vorschub-Zeichen alignment mark
Vorschuß advance payment
vorselektieren preselect
vorsetzen move forward
Vorsetzen der Druck/Stanzdatei advance print/punch
vorsortieren presort
Vorsortierungsgrad degree of presorting
Vorspann header, leader
Vorspannband leader tape
Vorspann einer Nachricht message header prefix
Vorsprung protrusion
Vorstandsvorsitzender chief executive officer
Vorsteckeinrichtung front feed device
Vortabelle pretable
Vorteil advantage
Vorteile der Mikroprogrammierung microprogramming advantages
Vorteile von Kompilierern compiler advantages
vorteilhaft advantageous
vortragen carry forward
Vortragsbuchung carry forward posting
Vortragskonto carry forward account
Vortragsmonat carry forward month
vorübergehend temporary
Vorverstärker preamplifier
Vorvertrag letter of intent, letter of understanding, pre-contract
Vorvorgeschäftsjahr financial year before last
Vorvorjahr year before last
vorwärts forward
vorwärtsblättern page forward
Vorwärtsdeklaration forward declaration
Vorwärtskettung forward chaining
vorwärts neu positionieren reposition forward
Vorwärtspositionierung forward positioning
Vorwärts/Rückwärtszähler up down counter
Vorwärtssteuerung forward supervision
Vorwärtsverkettung forward linkage, forward linking
Vorwärtsverweis forward reference
Vorwärtswiederherstellung long recovery
Vorwahl area code, dialling code
vorwegnehmen anticipate
Vorzeichen sign
vorzeichenabhängig dependent on sign
Vorzeichenbearbeitung sign handling
Vorzeichenbit sign bit
vorzeichengerecht related to polarity symbol
Vorzeichensymbol sign
Vorzeichenwechsel change sign

vorzeitige Beendigung abnormal termination
Vulkanfiber vulcanized fiber

W

Wählbetrieb circuit switching, switching
Wähleinrichtung dial up equipment, dialling equipment
wählen choose, dial, select
Wählende end of selection
Wählereinrichtung selector facility
Wählleitung switched line
Wählmodus dialler mode
Wählnetz für Telekommunikation switched telecommunications network
Wählnetzwerk switched network
Wählnummer dial up number, dialling number
Wählscheibe rotary
Wählton dial tone
Wählverbindung dial connection
Wählversuch dialling attempt
Wählzeichen selection signal
Wählzeichenfolge selecting signals, selection signal sequence
Wählziffernpuffer dial digit buffer
während der Laufzeit at run time
Währung currency
Währungsabweichung currency deviation
Währungsbetrag currency amount
Währungsdifferenz currency discrepancy
Währungseinheit currency
Währungsforderung currency requirement
Währungsformat currency format
Währungskurs currency exchange rate, exchange rate
Währungskurstabelle exchange rate table
Währungsposten currency item
Währungssaldo monetary balance
Währungsschlüssel currency code
Währungsschutz currency conversion
Währungssymbol currency symbol
Währungstabelle currency table
Währungsverhältnisse currency ratios
Währungszeichen currency sign
Wärmeabgabe heat dissipation
Wärmekraftwerk thermal electric power station
Wagenlöser carriage release lever
Wagenrücklauf carriage return
Wagenrücklaufkommando carriage return command
Wagenrücklauftaste carriage return key, return key

Wahl choice, selection
Wahlangabe optional specification
Wahlaufforderung proceed to select, selection instruction
Wahlaufforderungszeichen proceed to select signal
Wahl der Funktion choosing the function
Wahl des Aufstellungsortes site consideration
Wahleingabe optional input
Wahlendezeichen end of selection signal
wahlfrei random
wahlfreier Zugriff random access, random seek
Wahlmöglichkeit option
Wahlschalter selector switch
wahlweiser Halt optional stop
Wahrheitstabelle truth table
Wahrheitstafel truth table
wahrnehmen notice
wahrscheinlich probably
Wahrscheinlichkeit chance, probability
Walze platen
Walzendrehknopf platen knob
Walzenknopf platen knob
wandeln transform
Wanderwellenröhre travelling wave tube
Wandler converter
Wandsteckdose outlet
Waren goods
Warenannahme goods received
Warenausgabebeleg goods issued voucher
Warenausgang goods dispatch
Warenausgangsbeleg goods dispatched voucher
Warenausgangsbuchung goods dispatched posting
Warenausgangsdatum date of goods dispatch
Warenbestandskonten goods inventory accounts
Warenbewegung stock movement
Wareneingang goods received
Wareneingangsabwicklung goods received processing
Wareneingangsbeleg goods received voucher
Wareneingangsbewertung goods received valuation
Wareneingangsbuchung goods received posting
Wareneingangsfunktion incoming goods function
Wareneingangskennzeichen goods received marker
Wareneingangskontrolle incoming inspection
Wareneingangsmenge quantity received

441

Wareneingangsnummer goods received number
Wareneingangsposition goods received item
Wareneingangsschein goods received note
Wareneingangsstorno goods received reversal
Wareneingangsverrechnungskonto goods received clearance account
Wareneingangswert goods received figure, value received
Warenempfänger recipient
Warenempfängeradresse customer address
Warenempfängerort customer home town
Warenempfängerpostleitzahl customer postcode
Warenentnahme goods withdrawal
Warengruppe stock category
Warenlieferant goods supplier
Warenlieferung goods delivery
Warenmenge quantity
Warennummer goods number
Warenschuld goods liability
Warenversand goods dispatch
Warenverzeichnis goods directory
Warenwechsel trade draft
Warenzeichen trade mark
Warenzugang acquisition
Warnaufkleber caution label, voltage caution label, warning label
Warnton acoustic warning, alert, beep, warning beep
Warnung caution, warning
Wartbarkeit maintainability
warten maintain, pause, wait
wartendes Programm waiting program
Warteschlange preexecution time table, queue
Warteschlange für Hauptspeicherbelegung core chain
Warteschlangendatei queue file
Warteschlangeneintrag queue entry
Warteschlangen-Kontrollblock queue control block
Warteschlangenspeicherung auf Platte disk queuing facility
Warteschlangenverwalter queue manager
Warteschlange voll queue full
Wartestation passive station, ready station
Wartezeit latency, waiting period
Wartezustand disconnected mode, hold
Wartezustand anfordern yield request
Wartezustand im Augenblick der Arbeitsablauferöffnung initial facility hold
Wartung maintenance operation, maintenance, service

wartungsbedingtes Abschalten maintenance shutdown
Wartungsdiskette diagnostic diskette
Wartungseintrag maintenance entry
Wartungsfeld control indicator panel
Wartungskalender maintenance schedule
Wartungskanal maintenance access channel
Wartungskontrolleinheit maintenance control unit
Wartungsplan maintenance schedule
Wartungsprotokoll maintenance log
Wartungsprozessor maintenance controller
Wartungsschnittstelle maintenance interface
Wartungstechniker technical specialist
Wartungsvertrag servicing contract
Wartung zur Beseitigung von Störungen corrective maintenance
Wasserkissen water cushion
Wasserkraftwerk hydroelectric power station
Wasserkreislaufsteuergerät water circulation control unit
Watchdog Timer watch dog timer
Watt watt
Wattleistung wattage
Wechsel bill of exchange, exchange
Wechselabrechnung settlement of a bill
Wechselanforderung bill of exchange request
Wechselbetrieb half duplex transmission
Wechselbuchung bill of exchange posting
Wechseldaten bill of exchange data
Wechseldiskont bill of exchange discount
Wechselfälligkeit bill of exchange due date
Wechselforderung bills due
Wechselforderungsbuchung bills due posting
Wechselklemme changeover terminal
Wechsellaufzeit bill of exchange period
wechseln change, exchange
Wechselobligo bills payable
Wechselplattenlaufwerk removable disk drive
Wechselpuffer interactive buffer
wechselseitige Datenübermittlung either way communication
Wechselspesen exchange costs
Wechselspesenkennzeichen bills of exchange charges marker
Wechselsteuer bill of exchange duty
Wechselstrom AC power, alternating current
Wechselstromanteil AC component
Wechselstromgenerator alternating current generator
Wechselstrommaschine alternating current machine
Wechselstrommotor alternating current motor

Wechselstromtransformator alternating current transformer
Wechselstromübertragung AC power transmission
Wechselverbindlichkeit bill of exchange liability
Wechselzahlung bill of exchange payment
Weg path, route, way
wegblenden blank out
Wegewahl routing
weglassen omit
wegwerfbar disposable
weiblich female
weicher Bilddurchlauf smooth scroll
weicher Bildlauf smooth scroll
Weichheit smoothness
Weit- long distance
weiterarbeiten continue, continue to work, proceed
weiterbearbeiten process further
weiterbenutzen retain
weitere Anwendungen additional applications
weitere Benutzerdaten advanced user data
Weiterentwicklung further development
weiterer Name alias
weitere Sicherungsaktionen advanced user backup options
weiterführende Hilfe additional help
weiterführende Unterstützung additional help
weitergeben pass on, pass through, transfer
weiterhin furthermore
weiterkommen get ahead
Weiterlauf continuation
weiterleiten forward, relay
weitermachen continue
weiterschalten pass on, proceed
weiterschreiben continue to write
weitersuchen nach gleichen Zeichenfolgen continue search
weiterverarbeiten continue to process
Weiterverarbeitung continued processing
Weiterverwendung further use
weitgehend extensive
Wellendrehung shaft rotation
Wellenkupplung shaft coupler
Wellenlager shaft support
weltweites Netz global network
wenden turn
wenn if
wenn-dann-sonst if-then-else
Werk factory, plant
Werksabnahmetest factory acceptance test
Werksangabe factory information

Werksberechtigung factory authorization
Werksbestand factory inventory
Werksebene factory level
Werkseinstellung factory preset, factory setting
Werksnummer factory number
Werkssätze factory records
Werksschlüssel factory code
Werkssegment factory segment
Werkstabelle factory table
Werkstoff material
Werkzeug tool
Werkzeugmaschine machine tool
Werkzeugmaschinensteuerung machine tool control
Wert amount, value
Wertansatz estimated value
Wertanteil proportional value
Wertberichtigung value adjustment
Wertberichtigungsbuchung value adjustment posting
Wertberichtigungskonto adjustment account
Wertbeziehung value relationship
Wertbildung accumulation of value
Wert der Eingangssicherung input fuse rating
Wert des Strings string value
Wert einer Zeichenfolge string value
Wert eines Ausdrucks ermitteln evaluate an expression
Werterfassung value registration
Wertermittlung valuation
Wertesperrtabelle value lock table
Werte übertragen transferring numbers
Wertfeld value field
Wertfeldfortschreibung value field update
Wertfeststellung ascertaining the value
Wertfortschreibung value updated
Wertgröße value
Wertgutschrift value credit note
werthöchste Ziffer most significant digit
Werthöhe value
wertig significant
Wertigkeit valency
Wertkontrakt value contract
wertmäßig in terms of value
wertniedrigstes Bit least significant bit
wertniedrigste Ziffer least significant digit
Wertpapiere securities
Wertstellungsdatum valid date, value base date
Wertsteuer value tax
Wertübertragung value transfer
Wertung valuation
Wertungslauf valuation run
Wertungsschlüssel valuation code

443

Wertveränderung additions and improvements
Wertvortrag value carried forward
Wertzuweisung value allocation
wesentlich essential
Wickelwiderstand wirewound resistor
Widerruf cancellation
widersprechen contradict
Widerspruch contradiction
Widerspruchssatz contradiction sentence
widmen dedicate
wiederanfangen recommence, restart
Wiederanlauf restart
Wiederanlauf im Fehlerfall error recovery
Wiederanlaufsequenz im Fehlerfall error recovery sequence
Wiederanlaufsoftware recovery software
wiederauffinden refind
Wiederauffindung relocation, retrieval
Wiederaufnahme restart
Wiederaufruf recall
wiederaufrufen recall
wiederaufsetzen reposition
Wiederaufsetzpunkt breakpoint register
wiederbeleben reactivate
Wiederbelebung reactivation
Wiederbeschaffungskosten replacement costs
Wiederbeschaffungsstückkosten replacement costs per article
Wiederbeschaffungsvorschlag replacement proposition
Wiederbeschaffungswert replacement cost
Wiederbeschaffungszeit replacement time
Wiedereingabe reentry
wiedereinlesen restore
Wiedereinlesen von Dateien restoring files
wiedereinschalten reactivate
Wiedereintritt reentry
wiederfinden find again, regain
wiederherstellen recover, restore
Wiederherstellung restoration
Wiederherstellungsladen recovery bootstrap
Wiederherstellungsstart hot start
Wiederherstellungsvorgang recovery procedure
wiederholen echo, repeat, retry
Wiederholfunktion repetitive funktion
Wiederholung repeat, repetition, retry
Wiederholung nach Aufforderung automatic repeat request
Wiederholungsanforderung repeat request
Wiederholungsaufforderung DTE repeat
Wiederholungsfaktor repeat count
Wiederholungsfall instance of repetition
Wiederholungsversuch rollback attempt

Wiederholungszeichen für Bezugszahlen asterisk indicator
Wiederholungszeit rerun time
wiederkehrend repetitive
Wiederkehrspannung recovery voltage
wieder montieren remount
wieder mounten remount
wiederprüfen recheck
Wiederverwendung reuse
Wiedervorlage resubmitting
Wiedervorlagetag resubmission day
Wiedervorlagezeit resubmission period
willkürlich arbitrary, random
Winchester-Platte winchester disk
Winkel angle
Winkelabstand angular distance
Winkelgeber angle selector
Winkelstecker right angle connector
Wippschalter momentary toggle switch
wire wrap wire wrap
wirken cause
wirksam effective
wirksame Adresse effective address
Wirksamkeit effectiveness
Wirksamkeitsdatum effective date
Wirkung effect
Wirkungsweise method of operation
Wirtschaft economy
wirtschaftlich economical
Wirtschafts- financial
Wirtschaftsgüter assets
Wirtschaftsjahr financial year
Wirtschaftsverkehr financial transactions
Wissenschaft science
wissenschaftliche Darstellung scientific notation
wissenschaftliche Kalkulationsmodelle scientific modeling
wissenschaftliche Zahlendarstellung scientific notation
Wörterbuch dictionary
Wörterbuchverwaltungssystem dictionary manager
Wohnort home town
Workstation-Host workstation host
Wort word
Wortbetonung lexical stress
Wortende end of word
Worte pro Minute words per minute
Wortlänge word length
Wortlöschpuffer delete word buffer
Wort verschieben shift word
Wortwert word value

wünschen desire, request, want
wünschenswert desirable
Wunsch desire, request
Wunschlieferdatum requested delivery date
Wurzel root
Wurzelelement root element

X

XOFF Übertragung aus xoff transmit off
XON Übertragung ein xon transmit on
XON/XOFF xon xoff
XY-Schreiber xy recorder

Z

Zählbeleg count voucher
Zählbestand stock count
Zähldifferenz count discrepancy
zählen count
Zähler count, counter
Zählergebnis result of the count
Zählerstand counter reading
Zählervariable counter variable
Zählfehler counting error
Zählkontrolle counting check
Zählmenge quantity counted
Zählrohr counter tube, counting tube
Zählschaltung counting circuit
Zählstörung metering failure
Zählung count
Zählwert count value
Zahl amount, figure, number
Zahl als Mantisse und Potenz darstellen exponential notation
Zahldatum payment date
zahlen pay
Zahlenbereich range of numbers
Zahlendarstellung number representation
Zahlender payer
Zahlenreihe column of numbers
Zahlensystem number system
Zahlenverwaltungsprogramm spreadsheet program
Zahlenwert value of the number
Zahlung payment
Zahlungsart method of payment, payment type
Zahlungsaufforderung demand for payment
Zahlungsauftrag payment order
Zahlungsausgang payment
Zahlungsausgleich clearing payment
Zahlungsbedingung payment term
Zahlungsbedingungsschlüssel payment terms code
Zahlungsbeleg payment voucher
Zahlungsbetrag amount for payment, payment amount
Zahlungsbuchung payment posting
Zahlungsdatum payment date
Zahlungseingang payment received, receipt of payment
Zahlungseingangsvorschau preview of payments received
Zahlungsempfänger payee
Zahlungserinnerung payment reminder
Zahlungsfrist payment deadline
Zahlungsfristenbasis payment deadline base
Zahlungsfristenbasisdatum base date for payment deadlines
Zahlungsgepflogenheit payment record
Zahlungsgewohnheiten payment habits
Zahlungskondition payment condition, payment term
Zahlungskonditionsschlüssel payment terms code
Zahlungslauf payment run
Zahlungsliste payment list
Zahlungsmitteilung payment advice
Zahlungsmittelarten means of payment type
Zahlungsmittelkonto payment account
Zahlungsmittelterminierung means of payment scheduling
Zahlungsmodus method of payment, mode of payment
Zahlungsprogramm payment program
Zahlungsschlüssel payment code
Zahlungssperre stoppage of payment
Zahlungsstatus payment status
Zahlungssteuerung payment control
Zahlungstermin payment date
Zahlungsträger payment voucher
Zahlungsträgerdatei payment voucher file
Zahlungsträgerprogramm payment voucher program
Zahlungsverhalten payment history
Zahlungsverhaltensanalyse payment history analysis
Zahlungsverkehr payment transaction
Zahlungsvorgang payment
Zahlungsvorschlag payment proposal
Zahlungsvorschlagsliste payment proposal list
Zahlungsweg payment method
Zahlungsweise method of payment
Zahlungswesen payment
Zahnrad sprocket
Zahnscheibe star washer
z.B. e.g.
Zeichen character, symbol
Zeichenabstand character pitch, pitch
Zeichenattribut character attribute
Zeichenattributbyte character attribute byte
Zeichenausgabe character output
Zeichenausgabefeld character output field
Zeichenausrichtung character alignment
Zeichenaustausch dualing
Zeichenaustauschcode character dualing code
Zeichen austauschen transporting characters

Zeichenbereich range of characters
Zeichenbit character bit
Zeichencode character code
Zeichendarstellung character representation, representation of character
Zeichendaten plot data
Zeichendauer character duration
Zeichendrucker character printer
Zeichenecho echo, line echo
Zeichen einfügen insert character
Zeichenende end of character
Zeichenerkennung character recognition, optical character recognition
Zeichenfehlerratentester character error rate tester
Zeichenfeld character field
Zeichenfolge character sequence, character string, portion of the text, string, string of symbols
Zeichenfolgeargument string argument
Zeichenfolgekonstante string constant
Zeichenfolgevariable string variable
Zeichenformat character feature
Zeichengenerator character generator
Zeichengerät plotter
Zeichengeschwindigkeit character rate
Zeichengröße character size
Zeichen in der niederwertigen Position low order digit
Zeichenkette character string
Zeichenkombinationen composite characters
Zeichenlöschpuffer delete character buffer
Zeichenlöschtaste delete character key
Zeichenmodus change mode, character mode
zeichenorientiert character based, character mode, chararcter oriented
Zeichenpaket packet of characters
zeichenparallel parallel by character
Zeichenposition character position
Zeichen pro Sekunde characters per second
Zeichen pro Stunde characters per hour
Zeichen pro Zeile characters per line
Zeichen pro Zoll characters per inch
Zeichenpuffer character buffer
Zeichenreihen character lines
Zeichensatz character code, character set
Zeichensatz auswählen select character set
Zeichensatzdienstdiskette character set utilities diskette
Zeichenschablone character template
Zeichenschutz protect feature, protection
Zeichenschutz für blinkende Zeichen blink protect
Zeichenschutz für fettgedruckte Zeichen bold protect
Zeichenschutz für invertierte Zeichen reverse protect
Zeichenschutz für unterstrichene Zeichen underline protect
Zeichensignal character signal
Zeichenspalte character row
Zeichenspeicher character memory
Zeichenstoptaste character stop key
Zeichentaste printing key
Zeichenübertragung character transfer mode
Zeichenumfang character scope
Zeichen umschalten shift lock
Zeichenunterdrückung blanking
Zeichenuntergruppe character subset
Zeichenverschlüsselung character coding
Zeichenvorrat character repertoire, character set
Zeichenwechsel change of sign
zeichenweise character by character
Zeichenwert character value
Zeichenzeilen character lines
Zeichen zum Beenden einer Datenübertragung data line escape character
Zeichen zur Codeerweiterung code extension character
Zeichen zur Umschaltung der Datenübertragung data link escape character
Zeichen »Verbindung abbrechen« disconnect character
zeichnen draw, sketch
Zeichnung drawing
Zeichnungsart drawing type
Zeichnungsnummer drawing number
Zeichnungsversion drawing version
zeigen point, show
zeigen auf point to
Zeiger cursor, pointer
Zeigerbereich pointer array
Zeigermatrix pointer array
Zeigerreferenz pointer reference
Zeigerstand pointer state
Zeile line, row
Zeile einfügen insert line, line insert
Zeile löschen cancel line, delete line
Zeile mit doppelt breiten Zeichen double width line
Zeile mit doppelt hohen Zeichen double height line
Zeile mit einfach breiten Zeichen single width line
Zeilenabstand line distance, line spacing

Zeilenabstandeinsteller line space selector
Zeilenabtastfrequenz scanning line frequency
Zeilenabtastzeit scanning line period
Zeilenanfang beginning of line, line beginning, start of line
Zeilenangabe given line, line indication
Zeilenart line type
Zeilenattribut line attribute
Zeilenaufbau line structure
Zeilenauswahl line selection
Zeilenbereich line range, range of lines
Zeilenbezeichnung line designation
Zeilendichte print density, scanning density
Zeilendrucker line printer
Zeilendruckerspooler line printer spooler program
Zeileneditor line editor
Zeilenende end of line, line end
Zeilenendezeichen end of line character, line terminator
Zeilenendsignal end of line signal, line end signal
Zeilenendsperre line end lock
Zeilenendsteuertaste line end control key
Zeilenkennbuchstaben line identification letter
Zeilenlineal ruler
Zeilenlineal löschen remove a ruler
Zeilenlöschpuffer delete line buffer, line buffer
Zeilenmodus line mode
Zeilennummer line number, row number
Zeilennummersequenz line number sequence
zeilenorientiertes Protokoll line oriented protocol
Zeilenposition line position
Zeilen pro Minute lines per minute
Zeilen pro Sekunde lines per second
Zeilen pro Zoll lines per inch
Zeilenpuffer line buffer
Zeilenrand line margin
Zeilenrest line remainder
Zeilenschalttaste line space key
Zeilenschaltung line feed, vertical spacing
Zeilensprung line skip
Zeilenstoptaste line key
Zeilenteilung scanning pitch
Zeilentransport line skip
Zeilentyp line type
Zeilenumbruch line makeup, line wrap
Zeilenvoreinsteller line space preset key
Zeilenvorschub line feed
Zeilenvorschubgeschwindigkeit line feed speed
Zeilenvorschub neue Zeile line feed new line
Zeilenvorschub rückwärts reverse line feed

Zeilenvorschubtaste line feed key
zeilenweise line by line, row wise order
zeilenweises Abrollen roll scrolling
zeilenweises Übertragen line transmit
Zeilenzähler line counter
Zeit time
Zeitablauf time out
Zeitabschnitt period
Zeitabstand interval
zeitanteilig time-proportional
Zeitdiagramm timing chart
Zeiteinheit time unit
Zeitgatter time gate
Zeitgeber clock, time base, timer, timing circuit
Zeitgeberfunktion timer function
Zeitgeberwarteschlange timer queue
Zeitgeberwert time base value
Zeitgeberzähler timer counter
Zeitgebühr duration charge, time charge
zeitgesteuerte Bearbeitung timer processing
zeitgleich chronological
Zeitimpuls time pulse
Zeitintervall time interval
Zeitkreis timing circuit
zeitkritisch time critical
zeitlich chronological
Zeitmarke time stamp
Zeitmessung timing
Zeitmultiplexer time division multiplexer
Zeitprüfung time check
Zeitpunkt point in time, time
Zeitraum period
Zeitrechnung time calculation
Zeitschalter time switch
Zeitscheibe time slice
Zeitscheibenanteil time slice period
Zeitscheibendauer time slice duration
Zeitscheibenrest time slice remainder
zeitscheibenweise in time slices
Zeitschiene time track
Zeitspanne zwischen Ausfällen interfault interval
Zeitspanne zwischen Fehlern interfault interval
Zeitstempel time stamp
Zeit überschreiten time out
Zeitüberschreitung exceeding the time, time out, time out error, timeout
Zeitüberschreitungsfehler runaway check, time out error
Zeitüberwachung time control, time out
Zeitüberwachungsprozessor daylock interrupt processor

zeitunkritische Servicefunktion deferred user service task
Zeitursprung time origin
Zeitverhalten time performance
zeitverzahnt overlapping in terms of time
Zelle cell
Zellencursor cell cursor, cell pointer
Zenerdiode voltage reference diode
zentral central
Zentrale head office
Zentraleinheit central processing unit, data processing unit
zentraler Computerkomplex central computer complex
zentraler Reparaturdienst central repair service
zentraler Reparaturstützpunkt central repair facility
zentraler Telefonservice help line, international help line, telephone support
zentrales Computersystem host data processing system
zentrales Datenmanagement consolidated data management
zentralisierte Datenverarbeitung centralized data processing
Zentralkomplex central group
Zentralkonto main account
Zentralkontrakt central contract
Zentralperipherie central peripheral
Zentralprozessor central processor
Zentralrechner host, host computer, host processor, host system, mainframe
Zentralrechnersoftware host software, mainframe software
Zentralschrank central cabinet, concentrator
Zentralspeicher common storage
Zentralsteuerung centralized control
Zentralsystem central processing system, central site, host, host system
zentrieren center
Zentriermarke centering mark
Zentrum center
Zerbrechlichkeit fragility
Zerhacker chopper
Zerhackerschaltung chopper circuit
Zerlegungsdatei segmentation file
Zeropoint zeropoint
Zeropoint-Offset zeropoint offset
zerstören clobber, corrupt, destroy
zerstörendes Lesen destructive readout
Zerstörung corruption

zerstörungsfreies Lesen non destructive readout
zerstückelt fragmented
Zerstückelung segmentation
ziehen draw, pull
Ziel destination, scope, target
Zieladresse destination address
Zieladreßregister destination address register
Zielangabe target, target indication
Zielarchivnummer target archive number
Zielbereich destination area, target area
Zielbibliothek target library
Zielcodeelement language processor output module
Zielcodeliste code edit listing
Zieldatei destination file, target file
Zieldatenextraktor radar data extractor
Zieldiskette destination diskette
Zieldiskettenlaufwerk destination diskette drive
Zielformat destination format, target format
Zielgerät destination device, target device
Zielgerätenummer target device number
Zielgerätetype target device type
Zielgruppe destination group, target group
Zielinformation destination information, target information
Zielknoten destination node, target node
Ziellaufwerk destination drive
Zielort destination
Zielpositionierung target positioning
Zielprogrammelement relocatable element
Zielsprache target language
Zieltage settlement period
Zielzeile target line
Ziffer digit
Ziffer mit höchstem Stellenwert most significant digit
Ziffer mit niedrigstem Stellenwert least significant digit
Ziffernstelle digit position
Zifferntaste figures key
Ziffernteil digit position
Zimmer room
Zins interest
Zinsforderung interest due
Zinsprozentsatz interest rate
Zinssatz interest rate
Zinswert interest value
Zinszahlung interest payment
zitieren cite, quote
zittern judder
Zoll customs, inch

Zuordnung aufheben

Zollnummer customs number
Zoll pro Sekunde inch per second, inches per second
Zollsatz rate of duty
Zolltarif customs tariff
Zollvereinbarung customs agreement
Zone zone
Zonenendetaste end of zone key
Zubehör accessories, supplies
Zubehörteil accessory
Zubuchung posting to
Zündspule ignition transformer
Zündtransformator ignition transformer
zufällig by chance, coincidental
Zufall chance, coincidence
Zufallsfunktion random function
Zufallsgenerator random number generator
Zufallsschlüssel random code
Zufallswert random value
Zufallszahl random number
Zuführfach feeder
Zuführungsfehler feed error
zugängliches Register accessible register
Zugang access, acquisition
Zugangsart access method, access mode
Zugangsberechtigung access authorization
Zugangsberechtigungs-Prüfung access authorization check
Zugangsbuchung acquisition posting
Zugangsdatum acquisition date
Zugangsgebühr access charge
Zugangsinformation access information
Zugangskennzeichen acquisition marker
Zugangslagerort receiving warehouse
Zugangsliste acquisition list
Zugangsmenge quantity acquired
Zugangsprüfung access check
Zugangssteuerung access control
Zugangswert acquisition value
zugeben admit
zugeführt conveyed
zugehen approach
zugehörig associate
zugehörige Operation associated operation, connected operation
Zugentlastung strain relief
Zugentlastungsklammer strain relief clip
zugreifen access, make access, retrieve
Zugriff access, retrieval
Zugriff auf indexsequentielle Dateien access to index sequential files
Zugriffsart access method
zugriffsberechtigt access authorized

Zugriffsberechtigung access authorization
Zugriffseinheit access unit
Zugriffsfehler seek error
Zugriffshilfe access aid
Zugriffskanal-Schaltmodule access channel circuit modules
Zugriffskontrolle access control
Zugriffskontrolliste access control list
Zugriffsmakro access macro
Zugriffsmatrix access matrix
Zugriffsmethode access method
Zugriffsmethoden-Name access method name
Zugriffsmodul access module
Zugriffsmodus access mode
Zugriffsoperationscode access operation code
Zugriffsprogramm access program
Zugriffsroutine access routine
Zugriffsschlüssel access key
Zugriffsschutz access protection
Zugriffssteuerwort access control word
Zugriffsteuerliste access control list
Zugriffsweg means of access
Zugriffszeit access time
Zugriff über Schlüssel keyed access
Zugspannung tension
zugunsten in favor of
zu irgendeiner Zeit at any one time
zu jeder Zeit at any time
zukunftsweisend trend setting
zulässig permissable, valid
zulässige Stromstärke ampacity, current carrying capacity
Zulässigkeit permissibility
Zulage extra pay
zulassen admit, allow, enable, homologate, permit
Zulassung acceptance, approval, homologation
Zulassungsantrag application for approval
Zulassungsbedingungen homologation regulation
Zulassungsprüfung acceptance test
zulesen read on
Zulieferer supplier
zum Prozessor führende Leitung inbound line
zunächst at first
zunehmen increase
zu niedrig too low
zuordnen allocate, assign, associate, attach
zuordnen von Systemresourcen allocate system resources
Zuordnen von Zeitscheiben time slicing
Zuordnung assignment
Zuordnung aufheben deassign

451

Zuordnungsanweisung

Zuordnungsanweisung assignment statement
Zuordnungsbegriff association term
Zuordnungsdaten allocation data
zuordnungsfähig allocatable
Zuordnungsfehler allocation error
Zuordnungsliste allocation map
Zuordnungsmethode allocation method
Zuordnungsnummer association number
Zuordnungsnummernbildung forming association numbers
Zuordnungsnummerntabelle association number table
Zuordnungssektor des Dateiverzeichnisses directory allocation sector
Zuordnungstabelle allocation table
zurechnen add, include
zur Peripherie führende Leitung outbound line
zur Startzeit at start time
zurück back
zurückblättern page back, page backwards
zurückbleiben remain
zurückbuchen back post
Zurückbuchung back posting
Zurückbuchungsmonat back posting month
Zurückbuchungsperiode back posting period
Zurückbuchungszeitraum back posting period
zurückführen attribute, trace back
zurückhalten keep back, retain
zurückkehren return
zurückkopieren retransfer
zurückladen reconstruct, reload, restore
zurücklesen read backwards
zurückliefern return the delivery
zurückliegend past
zurückmelden echo
Zurücknahme-Modus cancel mode
zurücknehmen abort, cancel
zurückrollen roll back
zurückrufen recall
zurücksetzen reset
zurückspeichern roll in
zurückspringen branch back
zurückspulen rewind
zurückstellen pend
Zurück-Taste backspace key
zurückübergeben transfer back
zurückverfolgen retrace, trace back
Zurückverfolgen der Subroutine subroutine traceback
zurückweisen reject
zur Verfügung stellen provide

zusätzlich additional, alternate, in addition
zusätzliche auxiliary
zusätzliche Aktion additional option
zusätzliche Hilfe additional help
zusätzliche Option additional option
zusätzlicher auxiliary
zusätzlicher Grafikzeichensatz supplementary graphic set
zusätzlicher Kommunikationsanschluß optional communications port
zusätzlicher Name alias
zusätzliche ROM-Zeichensätze alternate ROM character sets
zusätzliches auxiliary
zusätzliche Software layered product
zusätzliche Zeichen padding characters
zusätzlich installierte Festplatte hard disk upgrade
zusammen together
zusammenarbeitend interworking
zusammenbauen build, build up
zusammenbrechen collapse, crash
Zusammenbruch crash
zusammenfallen coincide
Zusammenfassen von Bewegungsdaten zu Stapeln batching
Zusammenfassung summary
zusammenführen consolidate
Zusammenführung junction
zusammengehören belong together, correlate
zusammengesetzter Bereich compound range
zusammengesetztes Zeichen compose character
zusammenhängende Blöcke blocks of contiguous space, contiguous blocks
zusammenhängende Dateien contiguous files
Zusammenhang conjunction, context
zusammenkoppeln intercouple
zusammenlaufen combine
zusammenpassen mit mate with
Zusammenschaltung interconnection
zusammensetzen build, build up, compose
Zusammenspiel combination
Zusammenstellung composition
Zusammenstoß von Verbindungswünschen call collision
zusammenzählen add up
Zusatz- addition, auxiliary, overhead
Zusatzadresse additional address
Zusatzangaben additional information
Zusatzbetrag additional amount

Zusatzeinrichtung additional device, auxiliary device
Zusatzfunktion additional option
Zusatzfunktionstasten additional options key
Zusatzgerät option
Zusatzinformationen additional information
Zusatzkontierung additional posting
Zusatzkontierungsverprobung additional posting check
Zusatzlautsprecher auxiliary speaker
Zusatzname additional name
Zusatzregister extension register, extention register
Zusatzschlüssel supplementary code
Zusatzsegment additional segment
Zusatzsegmentbearbeitung additional segment processing
Zusatzspeicher adapter memory
Zusatzsuche additional search
Zusatzsumme additional total
Zusatztext additional text
Zusatztexteingabe additional text entry
Zusatztextmaske additional text mask
Zusatztitel additional title
Zusatztransformator booster transformer
Zusatzvereinbarung additional agreement
Zuschlag surcharge
zuschlagen surcharge
Zuschlagmengeneinheit surcharge unit
zuschneiden adapt
zuschreiben charge
zuständig responsible
Zustand condition, state, status
Zustandsbericht status report
Zustandsbit status bit
Zustandsbyte sense byte, status byte
Zustandsdaten sense data, status data
Zustandsdiagramm zum Verbindungsaufbau-Steuerverfahren interface signalling state diagram
Zustandsmeldung report
Zustandsregister status register
Zustandswort status word
zuteilen allocate
zutreffen apply
zutreffend applicable, matching
zuverlässig reliable
Zuverlässigkeitsangaben reliability data
zuweisen assign, direct
Zuweisung assignment
Zuweisung der Ersatzsektoren alternate sector assignment
Zuweisungskommando assignment statement

Zwang obligation
zwangsbeenden forcibly terminate
zwangsläufig forcibly, unavoidably
zwangsweise compulsory
Zweck purpose
Zwei-Adreßbefehl two address instruction
Zwei-Adreßmaschine two address machine
Zwei-Byte-Versatz double byte interleaved
zweidimensional two dimensional
Zweidraht 2-wire, two wire
Zweidrahtschnittstelle two wire direct interface
Zweierkomplement two's complement
zweifach dual
Zweifachkarte dual height module
Zweifachzugriff dual access, dual channel access
Zweig branch, path
zweigeteilt divided into two parts
Zweiginformationssystem branch information system
Zweikanalbetrieb dual channel
zweimal twice
Zweiphasenmotor two phase motor
Zweiphasen-Servomotor two phase servomotor
Zweipol dipole
Zweirichtungszähler reversible counter
zweiseitig double side
zweiseitige Diskette double sided diskette
zweiseitige Floppy double sided floppy
zweiseitiges Laufwerk double head drive assembly
zweistellig two character, two digit
zweistufig two stage, two tier
Zweitanbieter second source
zweite second
zweite Ladestufe secondary boot program
zweite Normalform second normal form
zweites Ausgabefach alternate stacker, second stacker
zweite Sendebereitschaft secondary clear to send
Zweitkanal auxiliary channel, co-channel
Zweitname alias
zweizeilig two line
Zwillingstastatur dual keyboard
Zwillingstastaturanschluß dual keyboard connection
zwingen force
zwingend compulsory, mandatory
zwischen between
Zwischendatei buffer file
Zwischendokument temporary document
Zwischenfeld intermediate field

453

Zwischenfrequenzverstärker intermediate frequency amplifier
zwischengespeicherte Druckdatei line counter file
zwischengespeicherte Jobeingabeströme saved job control modules
Zwischenknoten subnode
Zwischenkonvertierung intermediate conversion
Zwischenlösung interim measure
Zwischenpuffer paste buffer, temporary buffer
Zwischenraum space
Zwischenraum zwischen zwei Blöcken interblock gap
zwischenschalten insert
zwischen Schlagworten between key words
Zwischenspeicher buffer, clipboard, latch, paste area, temporary storage
Zwischenspeicherbereich buffer area, holding area, intermediate storage area
Zwischenspeicherdatei intermediate file
zwischenspeichern buffer, cut, save, store and forward
Zwischenstufe intermediate level
Zwischensumme intermediate total, subtotal
Zwischensumme aufaddieren sum subtotal
Zwischenzeile interlace
Zyklen pro Sekunde cycles per second
zyklisch circular, cyclic
zyklisch durchlaufen cycle
zyklische Bearbeitung cyclic processing
zyklische Blockprüfung cyclic redundancy check
zyklischer Code cyclic code
zyklische Redundanzprüfung cyclic redundancy check
Zyklus cycle
Zyklus-Ablaufplan cycle flowchart
Zykluszeit cycle time, scan time
Zylinder cylinder
Zylinderüberlaufbereich cylinder overflow area
Zylinderwicklung concentric winding

Computer-Wissen wird immer wichtiger.

**1990. 384 Seiten. Geb.
ISBN 3-88322-267-4
DM 88,-**

Superprogramming — Mehr Erfolg im EDV-Beruf

Superprogramming ist ein geistiger Hochleistungsprozeß, der ungenutzte Kräfte des Gehirns befreien und dadurch die Produktivität des Programmierers verzehnfachen kann. Gerade beim Programmieren sind oft ungeteilte Konzentration und scharfes Kombinieren gefragt. Die konsequente Umsetzung von Kenntnissen der modernen Gehirnforschung in die Praxis verhilft zu höherer Leistung und Kreativität bei weniger Streß.

Superprogramming bedeutet aber nicht nur hohe Geschwindigkeit, sondern auch hohe Effizienz in allen Bereichen. Dieses Buch zeigt deshalb, wie man z.B. mit strategischem Denken mehr erreichen oder mittels Zeitmanagement sein wichtigstes Kapital in den Griff bekommen kann. Die Effizienz zu erhöhen heißt aber auch, sich um die Gesunderhaltung zu kümmern: Augen- und Atemübungen, Ernährung und positives Denken gehören ebenso dazu wie die Bemühung um ein streßfreieres Leben oder ausgeklügelte Arbeitsmethoden, um mit weniger Aufwand mehr Wirkung zu erzielen.

Superprogramming faßt sämtliche Erfolgsmethoden zusammen, die sich in der Praxis bewährt haben. Deshalb ist dieses Buch ein Muß für jeden, der mit EDV zu tun hat.

Aktenzeichen Computer

Dieses Buch gibt einen umfassenden Einblick in den weiten Bereich der Computerkriminalität. In zunehmendem Maße wird die moderne Technik für die unterschiedlichsten Straftaten genutzt. Die Gesetzgebung und der Sicherheitsschutz hinken gerade hier immer der Realität hinterher.

Das Buch wurde von zwei Fachleuten geschrieben, die sich auf dem Gebiet besonders gut auskennen: einem Computerprofi und einem Mitarbeiter des Referates für Datenverarbeitung der Stuttgarter Polizeidirektion. Sie beschreiben die neuesten Gesetze und kommentieren sie mit anschaulichen Beispielen. Aus dem geltenden Straf- und Zivilrecht ziehen sie mögliche Folgerungen für das sich rasant ausbreitende Neuland der Computerkriminalität.

Aktuelle Fälle von Urheberrechtsverletzungen und Raubkopien, Datenspionage, Sabotage, Manipulation und Computerviren werden geschildert und ausführlich erläutert.

Das sehr informative Buch wird ergänzt durch viele nützliche Ratschläge (z.B. werden erprobte Maßnahmen zur Datensicherung und zum Datenschutz empfohlen), die so aus dem Buch auch einen wertvollen Ratgeber machen.

**1990. 218 Seiten. Geb.
ISBN 3-88322-251-8
DM 58,-**

Großes Lexikon der Computerfachbegriffe

Einen Überblick über die komplexe und schnell anwachsende EDV-Terminologie bietet dieses Nachschlagewerk. Dabei liegt der Schwerpunkt des Buchs auf dem PC-Sektor. Man findet unter anderem alle DOS-Befehle, Hardwarekonfigurationen, Softwarehäuser, BASIC-Kommandos, kurz alles, was mit EDV, insbesondere mit der PC-Welt zu tun hat.
1990. 632 Seiten. Geb.
ISBN 3-88322-257-7
DM 78,-

Kleines Lexikon der Computerfachbegriffe

Computer sind heute aus der Schule nicht mehr wegzudenken. Unter diesem Aspekt erläutert das Lexikon Begriffe, Abläufe und Kommandos, bezogen auf die speziellen Anforderungen des Bildungssektors. Tabellarische Übersichten ermöglichen einen gezielten Wissenserwerb und die Kontrolle des Gelernten.
1989. 280 Seiten. Kart.
ISBN 3-88322-258-5
DM 38,-

Wörterbuch der Computerei

Wer hat nicht bereits verzweifelt versucht, das „Computerenglisch" zu verstehen? Hier hilft das Wörterbuch der Computerei mit seinen über tausend Begriffen. Außerdem sind die wichtigsten Begriffe erklärt. Ein handliches Nachschlagewerk für jeden, der sich mit Computerei beschäftigt.
1989. 8. Aufl. 128 Seiten.
Kart.
ISBN 3-88322-026-4
DM 38,-

Immer zur Hand: Das richtige Wort.

Man braucht nicht alles zu wissen, wenn man weiß, wo man alles findet: Die IWT - Wörterbücher und Lexika zum Thema Computer, EDV, Datenverarbeitung oder Mikroelektronik sind die richtige Informationsquelle und die Nachschlagewerke für alle, die immer das richtige Wort zur Hand haben müssen.

Großes Iwt-Wörterbuch: Datenverarbeitung und Programmiertechnik

Dieses Fachwörterbuch umfaßt ca. 20.000 Stichwörter aus den Bereichen der Programmierung, Textverarbeitung, Datenbanken, Datenfernübertragung, Betriebssysteme, Speichertechniken und vieles andere mehr. Und orientiert sich an der in der Praxis tatsächlich gebräuchlichen Sprache. Es richtet sich z.B. an technische Autoren, Übersetzer, Techniker, Informatiker und an Technik interessierte Laien.
1989. 704 Seiten. Geb.
ISBN 3-88322-235-6
DM 78,-

Großes Iwt-Wörterbuch: Elektronik und Mikroelektronik

Dieses Fachwörterbuch mit ca. 20.000 Stichwörtern umfaßt den neuesten Stand der Technologie. Es richtet sich z.B. an techn. Autoren, Übersetzer, Techniker, Informatiker und an Technik interessierte Laien. Die Zusammenstellung der Begriffe orientiert sich an der in der Praxis tatsächlich gebräuchlichen Sprache.
1989. 664 Seiten. Geb.
ISBN 3-88322-218-6
DM 78,-

Großes Iwt-Wörterbuch der Computer-Technik und der Wirtschafts-Informatik

Im Zeitalter der Informationstechnologie stammt der überwiegende Teil der Fachsprache aus dem Englischen oder Amerikanischen. Mit diesem Wörterbuch (über 20 000 Begriffe) haben Sie Zugriff auf die moderne Terminologie von heute.
1988. 2. Aufl. 568 Seiten.
Geb.
ISBN 3-88322-140-6
DM 78,-